This text was created to provide you with a high-quality educational resource. As a publisher specializing in college texts for business and economics, our goal is to provide you with learning materials that will serve you well during your college studies and throughout your career.

The educational process involves learning, retention, and the application of concepts and principles. You can accelerate your learning efforts utilizing the supplement accompanying this text:

Workbook for use with BUSINESS COMMUNICATION:
A STRATEGIC APPROACH by Douglas M. Catron

This learning aid is designed to improve your performance in the course by highlighting key points in the text and providing you with assistance in mastering basic concepts.

Check your local bookstore or ask the manager to place an order for you today.

We at Irwin sincerely hope this text package will assist you in reaching your goals both now and in the future.

BUSINESS COMMUNICATION

A STRATEGIC APPROACH

BUSINESS COMMUNICATION

A STRATEGIC APPROACH

John J. Stallard
Western Kentucky University

E. Ray Smith
Western Illinois University

Sandra F. Price
Oakwood College

1989

Homewood, Illinois 60430

Sponsoring editor: *William R. Bayer*
Developmental editor: *Kristen E. Rabe*
Project editor: *Jane Lightell*
Production manager: *Carma W. Fazio*
Designer: *Michael Warrell*
Artist: *Rolin Graphics*
Compositor: *Better Graphics, Inc.*
Typeface: *10/12 ITC Garamond Light*
Printer: *R. R. Donnelley & Sons Company*

Library of Congress Cataloging-in-Publication Data

Stallard, John J.
Business communication : a strategic approach / John J. Stallard, E. Ray Smith, Sandra F. Price.
p. cm.
Includes index.
ISBN 0-256-03169-X
1. Business communication. I. Smith, E. Ray. II. Price, Sandra. III. Title.
HF5718.S68 1989
808′.066651—dc19 88-10295

Printed in the United States of America
1 2 3 4 5 6 7 8 9 0 DO 5 4 3 2 1 0 9 8

PREFACE

Time after time, one hears the statement "the ability to communicate is the most critical skill needed in the business world." The literature is replete with studies that show communication at or near the top of requisite skills essential to success in business.

Writing and speaking are at the center of thousands of business activities that are transacted every single day. The uses of these communication tools are infinite.

Business Communication: A Strategic Approach is a composite of principles, concepts, and activities designed to assist students with the development and refinement of their communication skills. The authors cannot overestimate the importance of our students' mastery of these skills, which are so essential for career advancement in any field. The problem-solving (process) approach employed in this textbook will provide students with enduring lifelong skills to enhance their competitiveness in the business world.

ORGANIZATION OF THE TEXT

Part I: Foundations for Communicating in Business (Chapters 1-5) introduces a perspective of business communication, the effect of technology on the communication process, the role of international communication, and the various concepts associated with style in writing. The last chapter in this section presents the *strategy for communicating,* which becomes the major focus for the remaining chapters.

Part II: A Process for Communicating Letters and Memos (Chapters 6-10) introduces techniques, concepts, and guidelines for writing business letters and memos integrating the strategy for communicating. Distinguishing features between letters and memos are covered in this section. Principles regarding editing, appearance, persuasive writing, and maintaining goodwill are also discussed. This section presents an abundance of examples pertaining to all types of request letters, positive letters, negative letters, and other types of business messages.

Part III: A Process for Communicating Business Reports (Chapters 11-17) introduces techniques, concepts, and guidelines for writing business reports. This section presents characteristics about informational and analytical reports and applies the strategy for communicating to both. The significance of forms for data is also emphasized. Techniques for gathering primary and secondary data and methods for presenting the data are discussed. A unique part of this section is that students are taught not only the appropriate use of graphics, but also how to write accompanying narrative to interpret the graphics. The last chapter of this section presents the distinguishing feature of writing indicative and informative abstracts applying the strategy for communicating.

Part IV: A Process for Communicating Other Special Applications (Chapters 18–22) presents a discussion of all the necessary elements associated with the employment process. Beginning with a self-analysis, the student is led through all phases of the job search including follow-up once the job offer is received. In this section, the student is introduced to the value of oral communication for a business environment. Listening skills and large and small group meetings are also emphasized. Two distinguishing features of this section include the writing of policy and procedure statements and the writing of case analyses. The strategy for communicating is applied throughout this section.

The Appendixes serve as an English and style reference source. The coverage includes punctuation, forms of address, capitalization, use of numbers, commonly misspelled words, confusing words, letter styles, and two-letter state abbreviations.

TEXT FEATURES

The text has a number of distinguishing features that will prove valuable to both students and teachers. The text employs a process that guides the student through the planning, drafting, editing, and revising stages of communicating in business. One of the strongest features is the use of the strategy for communicating as a part of the planning stage. The strategy embraces five components—Problem, Objectives, Reader/Audience, Order, and Format. Students are provided actual business settings from which to determine these components. The strategy for communicating employs a problem-solving (process) approach to communication. The student will like the "pull"—the feeling that as readers they experience the process of going through interesting, explanatory, and relevant information in an organized manner. From the settings and the abundance of examples, students will develop their communication skills by applying this strategic approach.

Here are other distinguishing features:

- *Legal/Ethical Issues* relate to specific concepts covered in each of the chapters. These issues will promote lively discussion as a means of introducing the content for each chapter.
- *Letters from Chief Executive Officers* present their perceptions on the importance of communication in business.
- *The Special Communication Strategy Form* provides a framework for analyzing all types of communication.
- *Modern Technology,* which has changed business communication considerably in the past 10 years, is explained lucidly throughout the text.
- *Multiple Drafts of Sample Documents* provide the student opportunities to analyze, discuss, and revise communications. This approach offers an important first step in making students more critical and self-conscious as they reflect on their communication objectives.

- *Abstracting, Writing Policy and Procedures, Writing Case Analyses, and Oral Presentations,* topics now pervasive in business, add new dimensions to the business communications course.

Here are additional features:

- *A Global Perspective to Business Communication* emphasizes the need for developing cross-cultural communication skills.
- *Learning Objectives* include a diversity of cognitive, affective, and psychomotor competencies.
- *Marginal Notations* guide the student's reading and call attention to major concepts presented.
- *Model Examples* for numerous types of communications, based on the strategy, enhance students' understanding of effective communication.
- *Discussion Questions* provide students with material that embraces cognitive learning at all levels as well as some abstract thinking.
- *End-of-Chapter Activities* link examples to body of chapter content. Activities demand preparation, evaluation, and editing which are highly productive in sharpening students' skills as business communicators. Abundant activities support the text's goals.
- *The Appendixes* serve as a ready reference for students needing help in English Mechanics (punctuation, forms of address, capitalization, use of numbers, commonly misspelled words, words frequently misused), Letter Styles, and Two-Letter State Abbreviations.

SUPPLEMENTARY MATERIALS

The *Instructional Resource System* for our book consists of the following materials:

- *Course Planning Resource.* The Instructor's Resource Manual includes syllabi, suggestions for evaluation, and suggestions for teaching at community colleges and four-year colleges. This supplement provides chapter-by-chapter resources. Included are chapter outlines, learning objectives, key concepts coded to applicable transparencies, teaching suggestions, answers and comments to end-of-chapter discussion questions, and suggestions for completing end-of-chapter exercises.
- *Test Bank Resource.* A chapter-by-chapter examination system includes over 1,400 evaluation items. The items are divided into completion, true/false, matching, multiple choice, and essay/case types. The extensive test bank allows for flexibility in administering daily quizzes, chapter tests, or comprehensive exams.
- *Computerized Test Resources.* These test items are available in

printed as well as in COMPUTEST II format which provides the opportunity to generate an exam using a personal computer. COMPUTEST II also permits instructors an avenue for adding their own test items.

- *Visual Resource.* Color transparencies based on key concepts are presented for each chapter. Additional transparency masters depicting concepts, terms, models, and figures are also a part of the visual resource system. All transparencies are coded to indicate their use in each of the respective chapters.
- *Software Resource.* An analyzer for evaluating students' writing is available.

Student Guide Resource. Developed by Dr. Doug Catron, the Study Guide contains chapter-by-chapter summaries and concise discussions of the principles of business communication. It also includes numerous exercises and cases for applying these principles. These exercises are designed to build the student's confidence in drafting and polishing business documents as well as in identifying elements of the strategy for communicating.

ACKNOWLEDGMENTS

A project of this magnitude becomes reality only when the collective efforts involve many people. We express our appreciation to the reviewers whose comments and suggestions were invaluable in the development of the manuscript.

Mary Ellen Adams, *Indiana State University*
Michael W. Bartos, *Harper College*
Edward Byrne, *Valparaiso University*
Douglas M. Catron, *Iowa State University*
Robert D. Gieselman, *University of Illinois*
Robert Gresock, *College of DuPage*
Maxine B. Hart, *Baylor University*
Betty S. Johnson, *Stephen F. Austin State University*
Judith R. Levine, *University of Kentucky*
Patricia Mantabe, *Santa Monica City College*
Robert T. Newcomb, *Broome Community College*
Zane K. Quible, *Oklahoma State University—Stillwater*
Diana C. Reep, *The University of Akron*
L. Marilyn Stinson, *St. Cloud State University*
Max Waters, *Brigham Young University*
Roberta Whitney, *University of Nevada-Las Vegas*
Gloria N. Wilson, *Arizona State University*

This text incorporates suggestions from over 250 business communication professors who responded to a comprehensive survey conducted by Richard D. Irwin, Inc. The authors are thankful for the contributions of those professors.

We express our appreciation to all the companies, agencies, and corporations who supplied examples and ideas for this text. In particular, we would like to mention those companies and agencies who contributed actual letters, reports, forms, and case material:

American Express—Travel Related Services, Inc.—*New York, New York*

AT&T—*Kansas City, Missouri*

Athens Insurance Center—*Athens, Georgia*

Chevron Travel Club—*Louisville, Kentucky*

Chrysler Corporation—*Detroit, Michigan*

Coca-Cola Company—*Atlanta, Georgia*

Dalton Communications, Inc.—*New York, New York*

Deloitte Haskins & Sells—*Atlanta, Georgia*

Exxon Education Foundation—*New York, New York*

Georgia Power Company—*Atlanta, Georgia*

Harrington Insurance Agency—*Knoxville, Tennessee*

Harvard Business Review—*Boston, Massachusetts*

HearthStone Company, *Dandridge, Tennessee*

Heilig-Meyers Furniture Company—*Richmond, Virginia*

Modern Office Technology—*Cleveland, Ohio*

Bobby L. Meyers Insurance Agency—*Huntsville, Alabama*

Nabisco Brands, Inc.—*East Hanover, New Jersey*

Price Real Estate Company—*Huntsville, Alabama*

Rightsoft, Inc. (RightWriter)—*Sarasota, Florida*

Rockwell Corporation—*El Segundo, California*

Lynn Sheeley Company—*Knoxville, Tennessee*

Sperry Rand Corporation—*Huntsville, Alabama*

South Central Bell—*Nashville, Tennessee*

Teachers Insurance & Annuity Association, College Retirement Equities Fund—*New York, New York*

United Space Boosters International (USBI) A Division of United Technologies, Inc.—*Huntsville, Alabama*

U.S. Army Ballistics Missile Agency—*Huntsville, Alabama*

U.S. Department of Labor—*Washington, D.C.*

U.S. Senate—*Washington, D.C.*

Wyle Laboratories—*Huntsville, Alabama*

The professional staff at Irwin deserves special recognition. We are especially grateful to Kristen Rabe, Developmental Editor. Her thoughtful, timely comments, positive dialogue, and in-depth perceptions concerning business communication make the product stronger. We also extend a thank you to other Irwin professionals who contributed to this project, especially those with whom we had frequent contact: William Bayer, Editor, Management and Communication; Cristopher Will, Editorial Assistant; Bevan O'Callaghan, Executive Director, Marketing and Sales; Diane Hilgers, Atlanta Marketing Representative.

Additional appreciation is expressed to Ed Nelson, Brigham Young University, for his direction in the use of the strategy approach to communication.

Finally, we are deeply indebted to our colleagues, close friends, and family members who continue to "believe" in us and who continue to support our professional work. Without them, projects of this scope would never be fulfilled.

John J. Stallard
E. Ray Smith
Sandra F. Price

CONTENTS

PART ONE FOUNDATIONS FOR COMMUNICATING IN BUSINESS 3

Chapter 1
Business Communication in Perspective 5

Importance of Communication in Business, 6 What Is Business Communication? 9 Qualifications of Business Communicators, 16

Chapter 2
Electronic Technology and Communication 19

Advantages of Using Electronic Technology, 20 Expansion of Technology, 33 Person-To-Machine Dictation, 36 Technology and the Communication Process, 38

Chapter 3
International Communication 45

The Importance of International Communication, 46 A Process for Communicating Internationally, 47 Distinguishing Cultural Characteristics, 50 Barriers to International Communication, 57 Common Traits of Successful International Firms, 58

Chapter 4
Strategy for Communicating 64

The Problem, 65 The Objective, 66 The Reader/Audience, 68 The Order, 74 The Format, 79 A Review—The Strategy, 86

Chapter 5
Style in Writing 96

Choosing Words, 97 Writing Sentences, 107 Developing Paragraphs, 113 Writing Analysis, 123

PART TWO A PROCESS FOR COMMUNICATING BUSINESS LETTERS AND MEMOS 135

Chapter 6
Introduction to Letters and Memos 137

Contrasts Between Letters and Memos, 139 Principles of Effective Letters and Memos, 139 Good Writing Achieves a Dual Goal, 145 Appearance, 146

Chapter 7
Writing Request Letters 157

Strategy: Request for Action Letter, 158 Strategy: Request for Information Letters, 162 Strategy: Request for Adjustment Letter, 167 Strategy: Letters of Invitation, 169 Contrasts Between Direct and Indirect Approaches, 171 Request for Payment Letters, 174 Strategy: Early Stage of Collection, 175 Strategy: Intermediate Stage of Collection, 180 Strategy: Final Stage of Collection, 184

Chapter 8
Writing Positive Letters 198

Strategy: The Acceptance Letter, 199 Letters of Recommendation, 201 Strategy: Writing a Recommendation, 202 Letters of Acknowledgment, 205 Strategy: Acknowledging an Order, 206 Letters Answering Inquiries, 208 Strategy: Answering an Inquiry, 211 Letters Granting Adjustments, 220 Strategy: Positive Response to an Adjustment, 222

Chapter 9
Writing Negative Letters 233

Letters About the Incomplete Order, 235 Strategy: Reporting Missing Information, 235 Letters About the Order Substitute, 238 Strategy: Suggesting an Order Substitute, 238 Letters Refusing a Request, 243 Strategy: Refusing a Contribution Request, 243 Letters Refusing Adjustment, 246 Strategy: Refusing to Replace an Item, 246 Strategy: Refusing to Repair an Item, 252 Letters Refusing Credit, 254 Strategy: Refusing a Credit Card Application, 254

Chapter 10
Writing Other Types of Messages 263

Letters of Introduction, 264 Strategy: Introducing a New Employee, 264 Special Request Letters, 268 Strategy: Explaining a Change in Procedure, 268 Messages About Changes, 270 Strategy: Announcing a Price Change, 272 Strategy: Transmittal Memo on Procedure Change, 274 Follow-Up Letters, 277 Strategy: Follow-Up for Group Conference, 277 Order Messages, 280 Strategy: Requesting an Order Letter, 281 Unsolicited Sales Message, 283 Strategy: Direct-Mail Sales, 283 Letters That Transmit, 287 Strategy: A Form Transmittal Letter, 288 Messages That

Congratulate, 289 Strategy: Writing Congratulations, 292 Sympathy Messages, 293 Strategy: Handwritten Sympathy Message, 294

PART THREE A PROCESS FOR COMMUNICATING BUSINESS REPORTS 309

Chapter 11
Introduction to Reports 311

Nature and Definition of Business Reports, 312 Classification of Reports, 315 Formality and Length Characteristics, 316 Announcement Reports, 317 Strategy: Announcing a Change in Management, 317 Status Report, 320 Strategy: Sales Status Report, 321 Proposal Reports, 323 Strategy: A Bid Proposal, 324 Forms for Reporting Data, 330

Chapter 12
Sources of Data 342

Secondary and Primary Sources of Data, 345 Sampling, 359 Appendix A: Selected References for Industry Directories, 369 Appendix B: Bibliography Entries, 371

Chapter 13
Presentation of Data and Graphics 375

Quantitative Representation, 376 Frequency, 377 Percent, 377 Central Tendency, 377 Dispersion, 380 Correlation, 383 Graphics, 384 Tables, 385 Pie Charts, 394 Bar Charts, 395 Line Charts, 398 Other Graphics, 400

Chapter 14
Writing Informational Reports 411

Periodic Report, 412 Strategy: Monthly Production Report, 412 Progress Report, 415 Strategy: Monthly Progress Report, 416 Sample Informational Reports, 419 Recommendation for Future Action Report, 420 Biweekly Comparative Summary Report, 420 Quarterly Transactional Report, 421

Chapter 15
Introduction to the Analytical Report 434

Organization of the Analytical Report, 435 Preliminary Section, 436 Initial Section, 437 Middle Section, 447 Final Section, 448 Supplementary Section, 452

Chapter 16
Writing the Analytical Report 463

Know the Setting, 464 Strategy: The World's Fair Report, 464 Writing the Initial Section, 466 Middle Section of Analytical Report, 471 Final Section of Analytical Report, 480

Chapter 17
Abstracting 495

An Indicative Abstract, 497 Informative Abstracts, 498 Strategy: A Book Abstract, 499 Writing an Abstract of a Journal Article, 502 Strategy: Abstract of Current Literature, 503 Writing An Executive Summary, 508 Strategy: An Executive Summary of Recommendations, 510

PART FOUR A PROCESS FOR COMMUNICATING OTHER SPECIAL APPLICATIONS 519

Chapter 18
Understanding the Employment Process 521

Knowing Yourself, 522 Looking for a Job, 528 Knowing Your Employer, 528 Preparing Your Resume, 531 Strategy: The Basic Résumé, 540 Writing Your Letter of Application/Cover Letter, 544 Strategy: The Letter of Application, 545 Letters of Recommendation, 548

Chapter 19
Preparing for the Interview 557

Preparing for the Interview, 558 Managing Yourself in the Interview, 563 Following up, 566

Chapter 20
Speaking in Business 574

The Oral Presentation, 575 The PMM Concept, 579 Strategy: The Oral Presentation, 589 Formal and Informal Speaking, 591 Conducting Meetings, 594 Strategy: Conducting an Informal Meeting, 595 The Listening Process, 596

Chapter 21
Writing Policy and Procedure Statements 602

Policy Statements, 603 Strategy: A Policy Statement, 604 Procedure Statements, 606 Strategy: Procedure Memo, 608 Strategy: Writing

Step-By-Step Instructions, 611 Strategy: Informative Guidelines, 615 Strategy: Flow Chart Procedures, 620 Strategy: Directions for Completing a Form, 625

Chapter 22
Writing Case Analyses 633

Background Information, 634 The Case Method Approach, 635 Methods of Case Analyses, 637 Strategy: Case Analysis, 639 Additional Comments on the Case Method, 651 Appendix: Case Study 1: *The Fry Cook Who Was Late,* 653 Case Study 2: *Competition in the Toothpaste Industry,* 654 Case Study 3: *A Simple Problem of Communication,* 655

Appendix A
English Mechanics 659

Appendix B
Letter Styles 683

Appendix C
Two-Letter State Abbreviations 691

Bibliography 693

Index 699

PART ONE

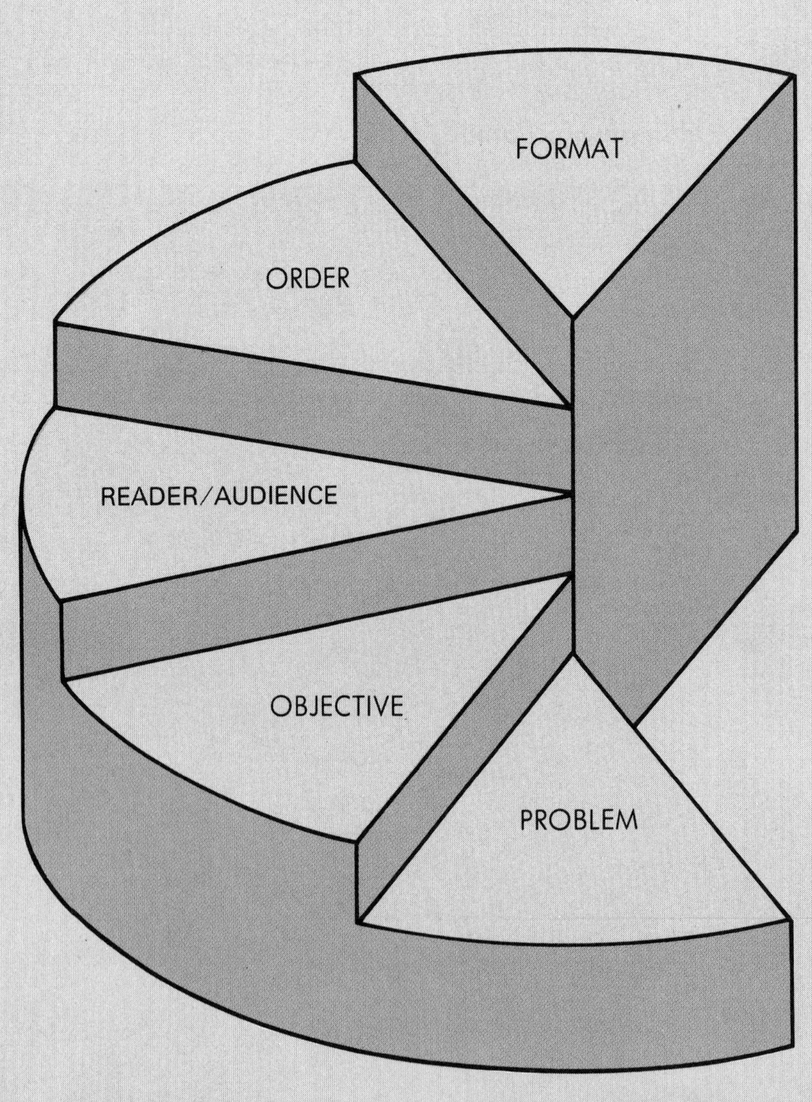

FOUNDATIONS FOR COMMUNICATING IN BUSINESS

1. BUSINESS COMMUNICATION IN PERSPECTIVE
2. ELECTRONIC TECHNOLOGY AND COMMUNICATION
3. INTERNATIONAL COMMUNICATION
4. STRATEGY FOR COMMUNICATING
5. STYLE IN WRITING

CHAPTER 1

BUSINESS COMMUNICATION IN PERSPECTIVE

Learning Objectives

After studying this chapter, you will be able to:

- ☐ Identify a process of communication.
- ☐ Recognize types of communication.
- ☐ Support the importance of business communication.
- ☐ Recognize the importance of developing good communication skills for career advancement.
- ☐ Define communication from a business perspective.
- ☐ State the competencies needed to become an effective communicator.

Can you imagine a world without communication?

Our society and our existence are dependent upon the process of communication. From the simplest to the most complex tasks, the process of communication plays a major role in our daily lives and in our activities. When you plan a picnic, you check the weather forecast. If you decide to invite friends, you call them on the telephone. If the picnic is on a holiday and you need money to buy gas, you can drive by the bank, insert a plastic card in a slot, press a few numbers, and you have instant cash. On the way to the picnic spot, road signs direct you to the destination, and billboards inform you of other activities. The car radio provides music, news, and other information. Even an activity as simple as a picnic involves many types of communication.

Types of communication

The picnic illustrates only a few of the many examples of how we communicate. Other ways we communicate include TV, magazines, newspapers, books, business reports and letters, gestures, and meetings. The means of communication are almost infinite: in our society, communication is inescapable. We are a part of a world that routinely employs the spoken word (oral communication), electronic communication (both oral and written), nonverbal communication, and the printed form. Since communication touches so much of your daily life, it is important that you learn how to communicate effectively.

IMPORTANCE OF COMMUNICATION IN BUSINESS

The need for effective communication is not new. Actually, letter writing and business administration were introduced as formal courses at the university in Renaissance Florence in the early 15th century.[1] This fact shows that the need for skill in communication has been recognized for centuries. Written and oral communication skills are still important, and evidence suggests that these skills will continue to be important. Let's review some of the facts which support this statement.

The American Management Association conducted a study of corporate executives to determine what characteristics are needed for moving up the corporate ladder. The executives cited *communication,* human resource management, and strategic planning as the skills needed for success.[2] Communication is the key concept here, because both the management of people and the development of strategic plans require good communication skills.

Jack N. Behrman and Richard I. Levin make clear the importance of business communication in an article in the *Harvard Business Review:* "Provision must be made for significantly greater development of written and oral communication skills, including advocacy, elocution, formal report prepara-

---

[1] James Burke, *The Day The Universe Changed* (Boston: Little, Brown, 1985), p. 69.

[2] "U.S. Business—Trends That Shape the Future," *U.S. News & World Report* 97, no. 9, August 27, 1984, p. 54.

tion, extemporaneous speaking, oral response under pressure, and group leading."[3] This statement embraces all facets of communication.

Harry J. Gray, chairman and chief executive officer of United Technologies Corporation, emphasizes the need for developing good communication skills:

Technology and communication interface

> As technology transforms society, communication skills will be fundamental to success. Everyone—regardless of field of study—will have to master the ability to read, write, listen and speak effectively. As the information age evolves, knowledge skills will grow in importance. The ability to think, to listen and understand, to organize, analyze, and synthesize information will be essential. These abilities will be increasingly valued in our burgeoning information based economy.[4]

Even though written and oral communication skills are important in today's society, some critics think that because we live in the age of telephone and television, young workers need not know how to write well. John C. Quinn, editor of *USA Today,* disputes this statement when he writes, "An inability to write will haunt students all their lives. More than 60 percent of the USA's 110 million workers write regularly as part of their work."[5]

Extent of writing at work

Are you convinced that good communication is important in business? Let's explore this issue further.

Businesses spend millions of dollars each year to train people to communicate. Still, meetings drag on unproductively, memos are ignored or misread, and personal discussions end in confusion and conflict. We are doubly frustrated because we communicate with the best of intentions. We are genuinely surprised and disappointed when others don't understand us.

Most of us recognize the importance of communication skills to our success at work, but we spend little time consciously developing the art. We think of communication as an innate ability. Some people are naturals, others are not, we believe. People who have made a profession of observing great communicators know that they possess common skills that can be learned and practiced.

Strengths of effective communicators

In general, great communicators work at it. Their strengths are knowing what they want to communicate, learning how to communicate to different people in different circumstances, and having a system for measuring their progress and developing the flexibility to change strategies when they need to.[6]

---

[3] Jack N. Behrman and Richard I. Levin, "Are Business Schools Doing Their Job?" *Harvard Business Review* 62, no. 1 (January-February 1984), p. 144.

[4] Harry J. Gray, "The Changing Technological Times," *Business Week's Guide to Careers* 3, no. 2 (March-April, 1985), p. 9.

[5] John C. Quinn, "Kids Need to Write If They're to Succeed," *USA Today,* December 9, 1986, p. 12A.

[6] Virginia M. Hall and Joyce A. Wessel, "Communication Skills Are Basic to Good Results on the Job," *Atlanta Journal,* October 12, 1986, p. 71L.

LEGAL / ETHICAL ISSUE

> Where law ends, there tyranny begins.
>
> *William Pitt*

> Do not be too moral. You may cheat yourself out of much life so. Aim above morality. Be not simply good; be good for something.
>
> *Henry David Thoreau*

The law (what is legal) and ethics (what is morally right or what is good and bad) are steeped in controversy in today's corporate world. The misuse and abuse of the law and ethics are commonplace. Almost daily, there are incidents of businesses breaking legal and ethical principles of conduct. Examples include fraud and deception, piracy, price-fixing, patent infringements, and overcharging, to name a few. You have probably heard that "honesty is the best policy and that the good of the people is the supreme law."

On the surface, it appears that some people can rationalize almost any behavior, even if it is illegal and unethical. What you say, what you do, and to an extent, what you don't say or do affect the communication process. Should you as a student and prospective businessperson be concerned with the law and moral responsibility? What consideration should you give to the law and ethics in relation to business?

In the past, many schools have emphasized the cosmetics of writing—spelling and usage, for instance—and have ignored the *thinking* that's central to the writing process. When you graduate from college and enter the work force, no doubt you will want to move up the corporate ladder. Your communication competencies must go beyond the ability to spell, punctuate, and use correct grammar. What communication skills do you think you will need to advance in the corporate environment? Consider what these authors have to say.

In a special issue devoted to communication skills in *USA Today,* a guest columnist voiced this opinion:

> During the next two or three generations, young people will need a personal inventory of solid, basic skills and a good command of critical-thinking skills. In order to enjoy a decent life, he or she must be able to read, understand, and communicate well orally and in writing, possess a body of general knowledge common to our culture, and be able to apply higher-order thinking skills to ever-changing situations. Technology and a competitive world economy are daily demonstrating society's needs for these competencies.[7]

---

[7] Archie Lapointe, "If We Demand More, We Can Expect to Get It," *USA Today,* December 9, 1986, p. 12A.

Martin Manzer, marketing vice president of Ashton-Tate, incorporated the world of software and technology in a statement on communication in business:

> People work with many kinds of data, many kinds of ideas . . . authors blend notes, sentences and paragraphs, numerical data, and graphic information, and need to be able to work with all those elements at once. We don't think in a linear way—we think in bits and pieces, add ideas here and there, move from one project to another . . . this is the way most of the 25 million information workers in analytic and creative positions in America actually think.[8]

Another study merits mention. In-depth interviews were conducted with 15 insurance marketing representatives to determine the kinds of writing they do and what they believe schools should be teaching about business communication.[9] The respondents divided their writing tasks into formal and informal communication and identified the following categories where good communication skills are needed:

Explanation.
Analysis.
Problem solving.
Tactful refusal.
Persuasion.
Tactful criticism.

The skills are implemented through four communication principles:

- ☐ Write clearly.
- ☐ Write concisely.
- ☐ Write coherently.
- ☐ Write correctly.

What importance do people who represent American corporations place on communication skills? Read these letters (Figures 1.1, 1.2, 1.3, and 1.4) for the perceptions of these CEOs or former CEOs.

Your future success in business will be largely dependent upon how well you communicate—both orally and in writing.

WHAT IS BUSINESS COMMUNICATION?

Communication defined

Since studies show that you will spend approximately 75 percent of your work time communicating, you need to know what is involved in communication. Webster defines the term *communication* as follows: an act or instance of transmitting; a verbal or written message; an exchange of informa-

---

[8] Daniel Burstein, "The Year of Software," *United Airlines Magazine* 19, no. 10 (October 1984), p. 90.

[9] *CPCU Journal* 39, no. 3 (September 1986), pp. 174-79.

Figure 1.1
Illustration of corporate communication

R. Anderson
Chairman of the Board and
Chief Executive Officer

Rockwell International Corporation

Rockwell
International

February 24, 1986

Professor John J. Stallard and
Professor E. Ray Smith
Office Systems Management
College of Business Administration
The University of Tennessee
Knoxville, TN 37996-0565

Dear Professors Stallard and Smith:

Thank you for your letter of January 14 asking me to comment on the importance of oral and written communications in business.

They are very important, but before getting to that, I'd like to discuss two other factors that occurred to me while reading your letter.

I understand that, as students of business, your primary interest lies with business communications. But the ability to communicate effectively across professional and occupational boundaries is equally important.

Lawyers can communicate with lawyers, but frequently non-lawyers have difficulty understanding legal documents.

Doctors use very precise medical terms readily understood by their peers but virtually meaningless to most others.

So, point one is: we should all be able to communicate with one another. Students of any discipline -- law, medicine, engineering, business, and others -- should be trained to communicate effectively to those not of their specialty.

Corporate Offices
600 Grant Street, Pittsburgh, Pennsylvania 15219
2230 East Imperial Highway, El Segundo, California 90245

Figure 1.1 (concluded)

Professors Stallard and Smith
February 24, 1986
Page Two

Point two is: in business, as in other organizations, communication can be enhanced by proper structure and organization.

At Rockwell we have streamlined our organization, eliminated many reports and other types of paperwork and pushed much responsibility and decision-making down closer to the levels where the actual selling, engineering and manufacturing activities are carried out.

These factors alone improve communications, because more information is passed through shorter pipelines to people who have a better understanding of the subject matter.

Finally, addressing your primary question: good written and oral communications skills are very necessary to the smooth functioning of a business organization.

Such fundamentals should be a part of the skills and knowledge students bring to their freshman year. However, if they are not, it seems to me that colleges and universities have a responsibility to make sure that students obtain communications skills before they are presented to industry as well-rounded and competent job candidates.

Sincerely,

RA:ss

Figure 1.2
Illustration of corporate communication

P.O. 1931
East Hanover
New Jersey 07936-1931
(201) 884-4500

Chairman of the Board

January 31, 19__

John J. Stallard & E. Ray Smith
Professors
The University of Tennessee
College of Business Administration
Knoxville, Tenn. 37961

Dear Professors Stallard & Smith:

Thank you for your letter of January 14, in which you asked for my views on the importance in the business world of the ability to communicate effectively.

While I can't speak for everyone in business, I personally am convinced that the ability to communicate well is a key attribute of the successful business executive.

This is more true today - in this era of rapid and substantial changes in the marketplace - than ever before. An executive must be able to express his views quickly, clearly and compellingly, and he must be just as adept at comprehending the views expressed by others.

For this reason, I would urge all students of business to acquire a thorough knowledge of English. A mastery of our language is the first essential step toward success in any field, for in the final analysis, we think in words.

I also subscribe to brevity, thus close this letter commending your effort to increase awareness of excellent communication.

Sincerely,

R. M. Schaeberle
/Q

Figure 1.3
Illustration of corporate communication

CHRYSLER
CORPORATION

LEE A. IACOCCA
CHAIRMAN OF THE BOARD
CHIEF EXECUTIVE OFFICER

December 11, 19__

Mr. John J. Stallard
Mr. E. Ray Smith
Office of Systems Management
College of Business Administration
The University of Tennessee
Knoxville, TN 37996-0565

Dear Messrs. Stallard and Smith:

Thank you for your letter and for your interest in my opinion of the importance of communication in the business environment.

Simply put, communication competency in the business world is essential. Without the efficient exchange of information within a corporation many vital ideas and decisions could be adversely affected, or even lost altogether.

I hope your students realize the great value of communication competency in the working world and take the proper courses to enhance these skills.

Best wishes.

Sincerely,

Lee Iacocca

DETROIT, MICHIGAN 48288

Figure 1.4
Illustration of corporate communication

The Coca-Cola Company
ATLANTA, GEORGIA

DONALD R. KEOUGH
PRESIDENT
AND
CHIEF OPERATING OFFICER

ADDRESS REPLY TO
P. O. DRAWER 1734
ATLANTA, GA. 30301
404 676-2371

April 3, 1987

Mr. John J. Stallard
Associate Professor
The University of Georgia
Department of Business Education
Athens, Georgia 30602

Dear Professor Stallard:

In response to your letter, let me share with you the following thoughts on communication.

Effective communication is vital to the success of The Coca-Cola Company, as it is to the success of any business. We follow a few simple guidelines.

Good communication is clear. A good communicator does not try to display intelligence through jargon or unnecessarily long words. Clear, precise language insures that all will know what you mean and not be confused by what author Charles Morton called, "The elongated yellow fruit school of writing." (Those are bananas to you and me.)

Good communication is concise. It gets to the point. Which are you more likely to read? A letter that states its premise quickly, or one that rambles on from page to meaningless page? The KISS method keeps it short and simple.

Good communication is thoughtful. A noted author once apologized to a friend, "I would have written a shorter letter, but I did not have the time." If you take the time to think through what you want to say, you will be able to say it clearly and concisely.

Figure 1.4 (concluded)

Page 2
Mr. John J. Stallard
April 3, 1987

Finally, good communication is memorable. It need not be long. The Preamble to the Constitution has 52 words. The Lord's Prayer: 71 words. The Gettysburg Address: only 271.

Advertising, for example, distills everything down to one phrase. "The Pause That Refreshes." "I Like Ike." "Where's the Beef?"

There is no place (or success) in the business world for someone who is unable to express himself or herself clearly, concisely and thoughtfully. Given those qualities, the communication and the communicator will be memorable.

It is as short and simple as that.

Sincerely,

Donald R. Keough

DRK:fa

tion; a system (as of telephone) for communicating; and a process by which meanings are exchanged between individuals through a common system of symbols.[10]

Business communication encompasses all the definitions provided by Webster. Letters, memos, and reports are the primary forms for transmitting business communications.

QUALIFICATIONS OF BUSINESS COMMUNICATORS

Building competencies for effective communication

What are some of the competencies you need to become an effective business communicator? Here are some of the more basic ones:

Ability to express yourself.

Ability to use analytical (conceptual) skills.

Ability to exercise some creativity in writing and speaking.

Ability to use a personal computer.

Ability to empathize with the reader.

Ability to use good English skills.

A look ahead

You have already mastered some of these skills. The major objective of this textbook is to assist you in refining your present skills and in developing additional expertise in writing and speaking. The focus is on business-related applications. Concepts, strategies, guidelines, and principles for further development of your communication skills are presented throughout. Mastery of the content of this textbook will provide invaluable assets for your upward mobility in the corporate world.

SUMMARY

Our society is dependent upon the process of communication. The means of communication are the spoken word (oral communication); electronic communication (both oral and written); nonverbal communication; and the printed form.

The need for communication has been recognized for centuries. Contemporary studies cite the need for those who work in business to gain expertise in such areas as strategic planning, human resource management, written and oral communication skills, formal report writing, extemporaneous speaking, and the ability to use technology. The importance of these skills is confirmed from a quote from one of the letters from CEOs, "Simply put, communication competency in the business world is essential."

This chapter placed some emphasis on the need to go beyond spelling and usage in communication to that of developing critical thinking or higher-

---

[10] *Webster's Third International Dictionary of the English Language* (Springfield, Mass.: G & C. Merriam, 1981), p. 460.

order thinking skills. Ability to use technology and software are important skills to master.

Letters, memos, and reports are the primary forms of transmitting business communication. Your future success in business is dependent upon these basic competencies: ability to express yourself; ability to use analytical (conceptual) skills; ability to exercise creativity in writing and speaking; ability to use a personal computer; ability to empathize with the reader; and ability to use good English skills.

END-OF-CHAPTER ACTIVITIES

DISCUSSION

1. Define business communication.
2. What do you think is meant by the process of communication?
3. State five reasons why good communication is important to business.
4. What are the major qualifications of business communicators? In which of these skills do you think you need more work?
5. Distinguish between the cosmetics of writing and the thinking that is central to the writing process.
6. In the Rockwell Corporation CEO letter, this statement is made: "In business, as in other organizations, communication can be enhanced by proper structure and organization." Explain this statement.
7. The Coca-Cola Company CEO offers these thoughts concerning communication:

   - ☐ Good communication is concise.
   - ☐ Good communication is clear.
   - ☐ Good communication is thoughtful.
   - ☐ Good communication is memorable.

   What is meant by each of these statements?
8. Give your interpretation of the quotation from Behrman and Levin (*Harvard Business Review*) cited in footnote 3.

ACTIVITIES

9. Joseph Sitton, a college sophomore majoring in finance, has been advised by his counselor to take a course in written business communication as an elective. He is contemplating the advice and isn't sure if he should take such a course. He thinks, "I already know how to write term papers. Perhaps another course would be better for me."

Assuming that Joseph came to you and asked your advice, what recommendation would you make? What information would you use to support your recommendation?

10. Carolyn McClain, a researcher in communication systems, develops and submits a research proposal to a funding agency. As she developed her proposal, Carolyn carefully followed the guidelines published by the funding agency. The guidelines indicated that notification of funding or nonfunding action would be received within 60 days, after all proposals were reviewed by five readers. After 30 days, Carolyn received the following letter:

Dear Ms. McClain:

The research proposal entitled "The Effects of Automation on Executives" you recently submitted to us has been reviewed. We have given it a careful review and have concluded that we are not in a position to provide funds for your project.

As you probably know, we receive a large number of research proposals, and unfortunately, we are able to approve only a limited number. Our decision does not reflect any lack of interest in your proposal idea but rather our inability to stretch our resources to cover all worthwhile requests.

I am sorry we cannot be of assistance to you and hope you will be able to find financial support from another source.

Sincerely,

From the viewpoint of Carolyn McClain, the receiver, use a 3-point scale (1 = poor; 2 = average; 3 = excellent), and rate the *effectiveness* of the letter. Be sure to consider how well the message helped Carolyn solve her problem.

CHAPTER 2

ELECTRONIC TECHNOLOGY AND COMMUNICATION

Learning Objectives

After studying this chapter, you will be able to:

- ☐ Understand how the computer affects the communication process.
- ☐ Analyze the expansion of technology for communicating in the future.
- ☐ Cite advantages of using electronic technology.
- ☐ Define key electronic communication terms.
- ☐ Assess the impact of technology for communicating on the job at all levels.
- ☐ Analyze how to adapt to change in relation to future technologies for communication.
- ☐ Understand how machine dictation improves productivity in creating written communication.
- ☐ Understand the theory of communication using electronic technology for creating, transmitting, and receiving messages.
- ☐ Understand how storage and distribution technologies speed the communication process.

Technology changes our way of life

In 1946, the world's first all-electronic computer was unveiled. And from that moment forward there has been no stopping the computer invasion. In fact, you probably have become so accustomed to microchip technology that you take many of its wonders for granted. Stop for just a moment and consider the ways technology affects your life! Every time you watch TV, record a program on your VCR, glance at your digital watch, or pop a potato in the microwave oven, you are using one of the century's greatest discoveries.

Indeed, the computer has opened up a whole array of products and services. New products and new adaptations of old products appear on the scene every month. The impetus for this innovation is the office, where computers provide a better, faster, and more efficient way of doing business.

Old communication system

In times past, if you wanted to send a written message to another person, you would compose the message; write it in longhand or dictate it to a secretary or to a machine; distribute it either by mail or in person; and then store a copy—usually in a file cabinet. If you later wanted to use that message, you would go to the storage area and spend time finding it among the hundreds of other stored documents. Then you would need to follow a procedure or checkout system to take the document back to your office.

New communication system

Today, significant changes are occurring in the business office in the ways messages are originated, produced, distributed, reproduced, stored, and later retrieved. Through the use of the computer—linked to a total communication network system—ideas and information can be transmitted almost instantaneously to and from people close by or far away, all without leaving the desk.

ADVANTAGES OF USING ELECTRONIC TECHNOLOGY

Information overload defined

Information now doubles every six years, causing managers to spend an increasing amount of time receiving, absorbing, creating, and distributing information. This abundance of information is called *information overload.* Information overload is forcing managers to look for ways to reduce the amount of paperwork. They realize that information is an extremely valuable resource only if received in a timely, concise, and accurate manner. Hence, control becomes a key factor in the management of information. In this context, using electronic technology is highly recommended because of the advantages it offers:

Advantages of technology

- ☐ The elimination of monotonous routine tasks.
- ☐ A savings in time.
- ☐ Cost effectiveness.
- ☐ Timeliness and greater accessibility of data/information.
- ☐ The accuracy and quality of output.
- ☐ The ability to forecast outcomes.

LEGAL / ETHICAL ISSUE

The use of computers is invading our privacy! At least so say critics of computer networks. They point out that various governmental and business entities collect and store huge quantities of facts about people. Critics are concerned that the interconnection of these computer data bases can result in a Big Brother who will monitor and conceivably control the lives of individuals. The IRS has vast stores of data about each worker, such as social security number, salary for each year, dependents, and permanent address. Credit-card companies have financial information about each cardholder, such as salary, history of payment, permanent address, and credit limit. The telephone company and local credit bureau also collect data about each person. Computerized information systems now provide an economic edge for those companies using them. The computerized information system is recognized as a competitive tool.

Various members of the U.S. Congress are now trying to enact legislation concerning privacy of information. This reflects a national concern for an individual's privacy.

How can businesses use the competitive tools of computers and data bases without endangering the privacy of individuals? Will national legislation keep Big Brother from invading our privacy?

The Elimination of Monotonous Tasks

> There is a new ideal about work emerging in America today. For the first time, there is a widespread expectation that work should be fulfilling—and that work should be fun. . . . Though appalling to traditionalists, this new value is remarkably suited to the needs of the information society.[1]

Routine tasks eliminated with technology

People are interested in work that is satisfying and enjoyable—not mundane and monotonous. Such routine tasks as formatting, proofreading, editing, filing, retrieving, copying, calculating, and mailing mean drudgery to many people. With a word processor or a personal microcomputer, most of these tasks can be handled electronically. By pressing one or more special keys, you can accomplish these chores easily, converting drafts into finished texts, printing them immediately at high speed or storing them electronically for later use.

Rework eliminated

Boredom also results because of the need to redo unsatisfactory work. Many times work labeled unsatisfactory actually contains a bulk of satisfactory

---

[1] John Naisbitt and Patricia Aburdene, *Re-inventing the Corporation* (New York: Warner Books, 1985), pp. 79-80.

work, but has small portions which need to be redone. Since electronic equipment has built-in intelligence, you can edit work by adding or deleting only the needed changes. In this context, technology virtually eliminates rework.

Technology—A Time Saver

Productivity defined

Because of the worldwide competition in industrial production, accompanied by inflation and economic instability, corporations are searching for ways to increase productivity. All businesses are interested in ways to help employees accomplish more output in less time. Unlike other resources, time cannot be amassed; time, if underutilized, cannot be regained.

Communication time savers

The greatest amount of time can be saved through the integration of technologies. In an integrated office system, computers, word processors, telephones, facsimile devices (transmitters of pictures and data to distant sites), micrographics equipment (microfilm technology), optical character readers (scanners), and printer/copiers linked together accomplish numerous tasks in a semi- or fully automated fashion.

In such an environment, executives can feed information into the system or check an electronic mailbox for messages via a phone line or terminal, whether in or out of the office. All office workers become facilitators; they can take previously stored information and create new documents or messages with little or no additional keyboarding. Thus, form letter design takes on new meaning.

Advantages of form letters

Form letters, which previously seemed impersonal, can be individualized. A stored message can be merged with a data file of names, addresses, and other specified information to produce an original or customized look.

To illustrate how this technology works, examine the form letter and data file shown in Figure 2.1. Notice that the form letter has a number of code commands embedded in its contents. These codes will not be printed. They are merely directions to the computer system. These codes tell the computer:

A form letter matrix

.OP	To omit the page number of this document.
.MT 13	To leave a margin of 13 lines at the beginning of the document.
.DF Roster	That Roster is the name of the data file where the list of names and addresses for this form letter is stored.
.RV a, b, c, d	The variables you want read from the data file. (The names—a, b, c, and d—are chosen at will.)
&A& etc.	The spots where the variable information goes. Note that each variable must have been identified by the .RV code at the beginning of the document.

The computer will merge the information from the form letter matrix with the variables contained in the data file. The data file called Roster contains hundreds of names and addresses. By merging the two files, you need only

Figure 2.1
Form letter matrix and data file

```
.OP
.MT 13
.DF roster
.RV a, b, c, d

April 16, 19



&A&
&B&
&C&

Dear &D&:

Professional Secretaries International has notified us that you will be
taking the CPS Exam at Oakwood College on May 1 and 2. We want to
welcome you to our campus and to give you some information that
might be helpful.

Enclosed is a small map for your convenience in finding our campus
on Oakwood Road. The CPS Exam will be administered in Green Hall,
Room 101.

Be sure to check the times and dates on your Admission Card for each
of the six parts. The test will be administered at these exact times.

Should you require overnight accommodations, there are a number of
motels located within two miles of the campus on University Drive. A
listing of the motels, addresses, phone numbers and rates is enclosed.

If you have any questions or if I can help you in any way, please call
me at (205) 837-1630, Ext. 311.

Cordially,



Michelle Ramey

Enclosure
```

```
Mrs. Lavonne Smith, 1876 Spring Street, "Huntsville, AL 35810", Lavonne
Ms. Lucy Smith, 502 Spring Street, "Knoxville, TN 37916", Lucy
Mrs. Kate Stenson, 2589 Ensley Drive, "Nashville, TN 37203", Kate
Mr. Bobby Garret, 345 Main Street, "Huntsville, AL 35806", Bobby
Mrs. Joyce Kenny, 3715 Beechmont Drive, "Huntsville, AL 35811", Joyce
Mrs. Edna Craig, 3617 Corning Road, "Nashville, TN 37203", Edna
Mr. Curt Sealy, 2815 Woodridge Drive, "Birmingham, AL 35294", Curt
Ms. JoAnn Masters, 649 Coventry Road, "Montgomery, AL 36109", JoAnn
Mrs. Kristen Duncan, 5010 Maple Street, "Knoxville, TN 37916", Kristen
Ms. Sharon Herman, 34 West 17th Street, "Birmingham, AL 35294", Sharon
```

Figure 2.2
First file of merged activity

OAKWOOD COLLEGE HUNTSVILLE, ALABAMA 35896 (205) 837-1630

April 16, 19__

Mrs. Lavonne Smith
1876 Spring Street
Huntsville, AL 35810

Dear Lavonne:

Professional Secretaries International has notified us that you will be taking the CPS Exam at Oakwood College on May 1 and 2. We want to welcome you to our campus and to give you some information that might be helpful.

Enclosed is a small map for your convenience in finding our campus on Oakwood Road. The CPS Exam will be administered in Green Hall, Room 101.

Be sure to check the times and dates on your Admission Card for each of the six parts. The test will be administered at these exact times.

Should you require overnight accommodations, there are a number of motels located within two miles of the campus on University Drive. A listing of the motels, addresses, phone numbers, and rates is enclosed.

If you have any questions or if I can help you in any way, please call me at (205) 837-1630, Ext. 311.

Cordially,

Michelle Ramey

Enclosure

Data file defined

one letter and one list of names and addresses. (See Figure 2.2 for the first letter from this merged activity.)

Data files can contain stored paragraphs, figures, names, addresses, or any other information which is likely to be needed on a repetitive basis. For instance, a bank of coded paragraphs can be retrieved in any desired order to meet specific situations. What makes this technology so exciting is that hundreds of thousands of original messages can be sent from information that was entered into the computer memory only one time. Collection reminders, mass mailings, reports to stockholders, and the like make good use of this technology.

Time-saving features

Another time saver for business communicators is the automatic formatting of written documents using word processors. Such functions as underscoring, centering, setting italic or boldface, and line justifying (right and left margins aligned) can be performed at the touch of a key.

Technology also reduces waiting times. Such steps as paper and envelope feeding, addressing, processing, and dating are performed automatically.

When a fixed category of variable data/information is required, business forms can be a real time saver to an organization. However, too many forms hinder productivity—not to mention the high cost due to its creation, printing, handling, and storage.

Advantages of forms

In a business environment, a good computer-based management system can facilitate the forms design and control functions. Such a system allows you to produce requisitions, purchase orders, invoices, inventory records, or any similar form with ease. Additionally, you can easily update these forms when needed.

This system also facilitates accuracy in filling out forms by preventing the entry of wrong information. For instance, if the form asked for your social security number and you entered your name, the computer would reject the information since it recognizes only numerical data for that entry.

A good forms control program prevents the proliferation of forms. Such a program eliminates unnecessary forms, consolidates forms requesting duplicate information, aids in forms design, etc.

Cost Effectiveness

Paul Strassmann, retired vice president of Xerox, indicates in his book *Information Payoff* that "almost half of the U.S. information workers are . . . in executive, managerial, administrative, and professional positions."[2] He further states that "managers and professionals spend more than half of their time in communicating with each other."[3]

Controlling personnel costs

In other words, people are a corporation's most expensive resource. For a typical office, over 90 percent of the operating budget is for salaries, benefits, and overhead. With this investment, is it any wonder that managers are focusing more and more attention on employee productivity? They realize that the paper jungle cannot be tamed simply by hiring more people. To receive a return on their investment, wise corporate executive officers are recognizing what industrialists and agriculturists learned long ago—efficient tools are essential for increased productivity.

Technology—a cost-effective tool

A direct relationship exists between efficient flow of information/data and the quality and speed of the output or the end product. For those companies using technology, the per document cost of information processing is only a fraction of what it was a few years ago. The decreasing cost of computers and

---

[2] Paul A. Strassmann, *Information Payoff: The Transformation of Work in the Electronic Age* (New York: Free Press, 1985), p. 43.

[3] Ibid., p. 43.

peripherals (equipment tied to the computer) will continue to make technology a cost-effective tool in the future.

An example of this type of savings is illustrated in the case of the Western Division of General Telephone and Electronics Company (GTE). By making a one-time investment of $10 million to automate its facilities, management estimates an annual saving of $8.5 million for the company. This savings is realized mainly through the elimination of support people once needed for proposal projects. Through a telecommunications network that supports 150 computer terminals with good graphics capabilities, the engineers who conceptualize the projects are now direct participants. They use the graphics capabilities of the computer rather than rely on drafters to prepare drawings; they enter their own text rather than employ typists; and they use the network to track project progress rather than conduct meetings.[4]

Timeliness and Greater Accessibility of Data/Information

Databases provide information

To make sound decisions, relevant information must be available when needed. Information sharing is one of the most effective tools of today's information society. Large databases (stockpiles of information categorized by subject and type) make tens of millions of pieces of information available within minutes. Table 2.1 shows a partial listing of the 180 databases available from the DIALOG search service.

DIALOG is just one of many database services to which a person or organization can subscribe. To subscribe, you pay a monthly fee for an access code. All that is needed is an intelligent computer terminal linked to a phone system. Once you enter your code, you access the database which will appear on your TV-like screen. You can broaden or narrow your search for relevant information by specifying one or more categories or key words.

Using a job search database

For example, if you are interested in finding a job opening in the Southeast, you would access a *job search* database and key in the category *Southeast.* To narrow the search further, you could specify the *city, type of job, special skills, or any other specifics* necessary to obtain the data desired. Such a service is available in the state of Missouri, where its sophisticated computer network system matches people to jobs through the Division of Employment Security. From September 1983 to October 1985, this system located 200,000 jobs for workers who took advantage of this service. More than 25 percent of the state's labor force is included in the database.[5] The *I*nsurance *E*xecutive *R*egistry (IER) is another example of a job match database. This particular database is devoted exclusively to the insurance industry. Registrants include

---

[4] John J. Connell, "Return on Investment in Information Technology," *Information Center* 11, no. 10 (October 1986), p. 51.

[5] Eds., "On-Line Jobs," *Training* 23, no. 5 (May 1986), p. 93.

Table 2.1
Partial listing of DIALOG© databases*

Database (Supplier)	On-line charge: $/hour	Off-line printing charge: $/record	Number of records in database†
CIS (Congressional Information Service)	$ 90	$0.25	140,000
FOUNDATION GRANTS INDEX (Foundation Ctr.)	60	0.30	90,000
PAIS INTERNAT'L (Public Affairs Info. Serv.)	60	0.15	113,000
SSIE CURRENT RESEARCH (Smithsonian)	78	0.20	144,000
AGRICOLA	35	0.10	1,140,000
BIOSIS (Bioscience Information Service)	58	0.15	1,260,000
CA SEARCH (Chemical Abstracts Service)	64	0.20	5,102,000
EXCERPTA MEDICA (Excerpts Medica)	70	0.20	1,200,000
HEALTH PLANNING (US Natl. Library of Medicine)	35	0.15	185,000
MEDLINE (US National Library of Medicine)	35	0.15	3,300,000
CLAIMS/US PATENTS ABSTRACTS (IFI/Plenum)	95	0.15	1,782,000
ERIC (Educational Resources Info. Center)	25	0.10	383,000
PSYCINFO (Amer. Psychological Association)	65	0.10	325,000
SOCIAL SCISEARCH (ISI)	110	0.20	910,000
ADTRACK (Corporate Intelligence, Inc.)	95	0.25	150,000
PTS U.S. FORECASTS (Predicasts, Inc.)	90	0.20	196,000
PTS INTERNAT'L FORECASTS (Predicasts, Inc.)	90	0.20	230,000

* Daniel Abelow and Edwin J. Hilpert, *Communications in the Modern Corporate Environment*, © 1986, p. 202. Reprinted by permission of Prentice-Hall, Inc., Englewood Cliffs, New Jersey.

† Some data bases are made of multiple data bases that cover various categories. For example, CA SEARCH includes File 2 (1967–71: 1,314,000 records), File 3 (1972–76: 1,772,000 records), File 104 (1977–79: 1,267,000 records), and File 4 (1980-present: 749,000 records).

middle or upper management professionals employed in any positions requiring insurance expertise.[6]

Consider how databases improve the quality and timeliness of proposals and reports. The survival of most companies in the Information Age depends on securing needed information quickly. To meet bid deadlines and obtain contracts, this information becomes critical.

[6] Thomas M. Maher, "Job Search DataBase Set," *National Underwriters*, March 30, 1987, pp. 65-69.

Information broker defined

A new professional who should prove helpful to business communicators is the *information broker*. Rather than selling stocks, bonds, or real estate, this broker is an expert, trained to guide users through the maze of commercial databases. To receive information, the broker can set up an automated search choosing from over 3,000 commercial databases available. These databases are periodically updated, making the information timely and relevant.[7]

Accuracy and Quality in Written Documents

Technology enhances accuracy

To ensure accuracy of information/data, computers can be programmed to perform a number of important functions. Some of the options especially relevant to business communicators include spell dictionaries, calculators, analyzers of statistics or raw data, grammar checkers, programs to generate forms, maintain calendars, and produce schedules. These programs (software packages) are extremely beneficial and can be purchased rather inexpensively. Such programs not only benefit the communicator in terms of providing accurate data but also save the communicator time by eliminating the need for verifying some types of data, especially figure totals, percentages, discounts, balances, and similar calculations.

Technology improves quality

A new generation of inexpensive laser printers is making documents appear as though they were typeset. Using a variety of fonts (different type styles) in creating documents also enhances the appearance and quality of communications. Appearance is important. The first impression a receiver has of you and your company is made on the basis of appearance.

Forecasting

Managers plan future strategies

The ability to take past data and chart future business operations on the basis of trends and conditions is essential in today's ever-changing economic environment. Goals are important for success. Because of this, most companies develop short-range as well as long-range goals. By taking data generated in recent weeks, months, and sometimes even years, managers plan budgets, produce schedules, control inventories, determine pricing, and plan for the best use of their resources. With computerized operations, data/information that once took weeks or months to obtain can now be available in a matter of hours.

To better understand how these technologies can aid both oral and written communications, consider the following short cases:

---

[7] Nicholas Basta, "Computer Update: Where We Are, Where We're Going," *Business Week Careers* 5, no. 2 (March-April 1987), pp. 51, 52.

CASE 1: A PERSONAL COMPUTER

Technology changes the way people communicate

Jill Greer uses a stand-alone computer. Jill is a design engineer in a company involved with the design and manufacture of control units for high-tech equipment. In her work, she writes specifications for various components that are then incorporated into a bid proposal submitted to a prospective buyer of the control unit. With the use of her personal computer, Jill enters the specifications via a keyboard.

A company investment in personal computers often increases the productivity of each employee.

Courtesy: Apple Computers.

Drawing on information from previous proposals stored on disks, she is able to produce a set of specifications within a short period of time. Jill gives the floppy disk containing the new specifications to a specialist who "polishes" the technical content then returns the polished version to Jill for checking and possible revisions. This process is repeated until the specifications are complete. After final approval, the specialist combines Jill's specifications with sections created by several other people to produce the bid proposal.

Old method

Before she learned to use the personal computer, Jill used a pencil and yellow pad to create a set of specifications. She spent many hours writing in longhand, rereading, crossing out, and revising to complete the document. She gave this longhand version to a technical typist to prepare a draft for her approval. Each time a change was made, the entire draft was retyped for another reading-revision cycle until the specifications were completed. This process took several days—sometimes weeks—since Jill had to wait for the drafts to come back from the typist.

The personal computer has speeded up the processes, both of original creation and of the revision cycles. More time is now available for creative thinking. Instead of taking several weeks to prepare a proposal, Jill can now complete her portion within a few hours. For the company, the timeliness of the proposal is critical in securing additional contracts—and thus the survival of the company. The company investment in personal computers has increased the productivity of each employee and provided a rapid turnaround for bid proposals.

New method

For Jill, the use of a personal computer meant that she had to learn to keyboard and to compose her messages at the terminal. She learned these skills in a relatively short time, even though she was not a proficient typist. The "spell-check" feature of her word-processing software made correct spelling of those highly technical terms a breeze. Jill did, however, still need to proofread the message for meaning since the spell-check feature does not check meaning—*to* for *two,* for example. The use of the computer also made her more valuable since she was able to produce more specifications in less time. The addition of personal computers with word processing enhances the productivity of employees and makes the work more enjoyable.

Personal computer—a tool for communication

CASE 2: ELECTRONIC MAIL

Mark Elliot, an attorney in a 12-member law firm, is certainly glad he has a personal computer with word-processing and communications capability.

A personal computer with word-processing capability can be used to send electronic mail.

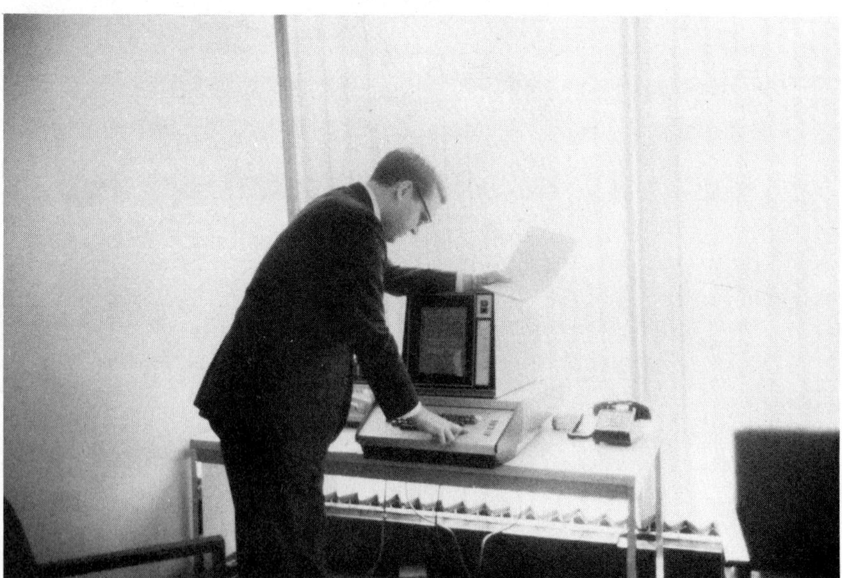

Courtesy: First National Bank of Chicago.

To contact another attorney, he composes a message at his computer terminal and sends it to that person's electronic mailbox. When Mark returns to the office, the first thing he checks is his electronic mailbox. Thus he is able to complete his out-of-the-

Figure 2.3
Example of electronic mail

Electronic Mail Service

From: OC314
Subject: Invoice No. 3489
Date: April 6, 1987
To: OC789

The charges on Invoice No. 3489 are different from the bid prices submitted by your representative, Mr. Wayne Hallock.

Please check with Mr. Hallock for details on this bid.

office activities and at the same time keep up with the events within the office. Telephone tag (calling back and forth) is kept to a minimum.

Communication among attorneys has improved through the use of electronic technology and people's willingness to change. The attorneys have expanded their base for background information by using on-line databases. Case material can be prepared faster than with manual systems. Mark now spends more time on creative and professional activities and is, therefore, more productive. (See Figure 2.3 for an example of a message by electronic mail.)

CASE 3: TELECONFERENCING

Donald Rhodes, manager of regional sales offices for a modular phone system, effectively manages three geographically separated offices through the aid of his teleconferencing system.

Teleconferencing is an alternative to face-to-face meetings.

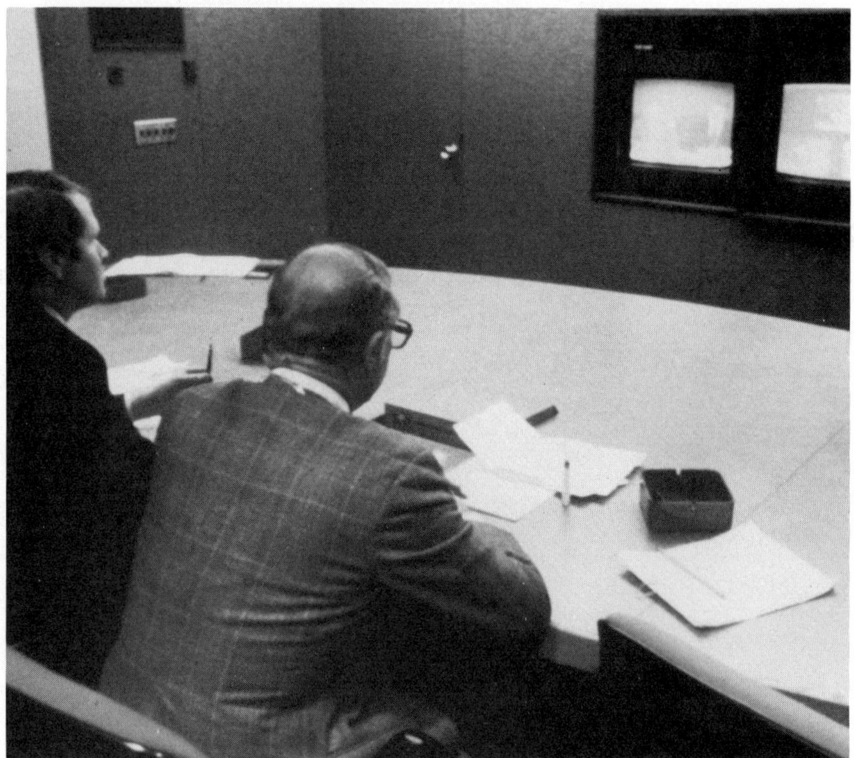

Courtesy: Illinois Bell.

A telephone/video system for staff conferences is located at each office. Each Monday he conducts a meeting with his entire sales staff from one of the three offices. Each person is provided with an agenda and is able to contribute valuable information to the others at the sales meeting. The teleconferencing system eliminates staff travel to attend a sales meeting.

After using the teleconferencing system for a year, Donald feels that communication among the three offices is better. He certainly likes the reduction in travel costs. Donald schedules periodic trips to the three offices, varying the site where the conference is initiated. Donald believes that the interaction of all sales people has boosted morale and increased productivity.

CASE 4: PORTABLE COMPUTER

Advantages of a portable computer

Eric McCormick, an information manager for a large, Eastern metropolitan bank, is pleased with his portable personal computer. The small lap-size computer makes it possible for him to complete paperwork while away from the office. Recently, Eric attended a conference in Texas. While there, he received messages, composed responses, and transmitted them electronically back to the home office. Even in flight he was able to create and store several reports and notes.

Using a portable computer, an employee can complete and transmit paperwork while away from the office.

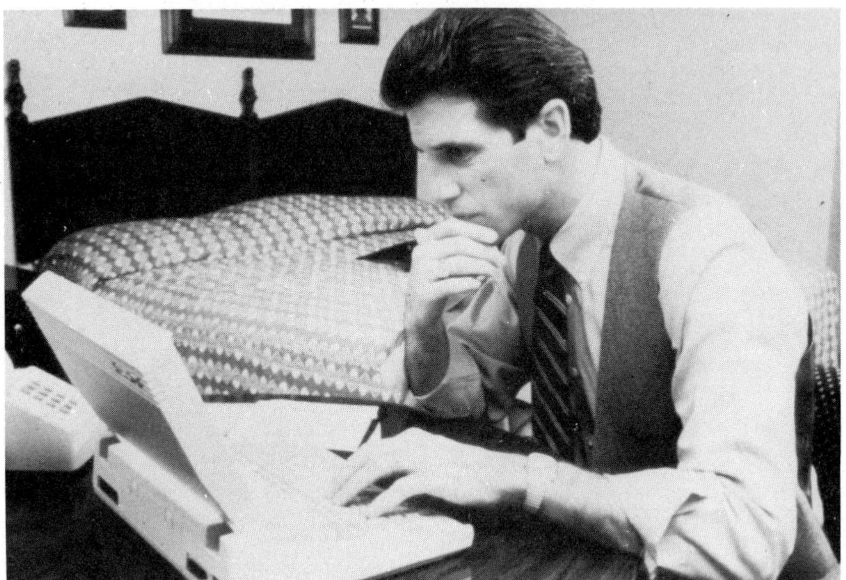

Courtesy: Hewlett Packard.

Eric certainly appreciates a working environment that provides electronic devices making his communication with the home office almost as effective as though he were there. Instead of finding large stacks of paper waiting for him, he now returns from a trip with most paperwork up to date; and he keeps current on the important happenings within the office. Electronic tools expedite the communication between people at different locations.

EXPANSION OF TECHNOLOGY

Key concepts for future communicators

As the Information Age continues, more sophisticated means of communication in business are inherent. Key concepts in business communication include sophisticated multifunction workstations, communication networks, and flexibility.

These three concepts go hand in hand. By creating a single networking system for such office functions as word processing, data processing, records management, micrographics, etc., information is easily transmitted among the components. The system is then capable of performing many kinds of tasks within the company as well as outside the company. In this context, information can be transmitted to any area in the world.

Survival depends on change

As technology expands, change will continue to pervade the workplace. Flexibility will be the key to survival—in how we work, where we work, whom we work with, and what tools we will use to perform our work. Technology opens up a whole new range of options for processing information in the future.

Telecommuting

Flexible work schedule

More and more companies allow some employees to do their work at home. With a computer terminal at home connected to a phone system, communicators can send or receive dictation, prepare and send written documents, or use the electronic mail system. This substitution of computer communication for travel is called *telecommuting*. Employees who telecommute go into the main office only occasionally as the need arises.

Speech Compressors

In the future, communication receivers will be able to play back recorded messages at rates of up to 500 words per minute without increasing the pitch. Busy executives will then be able to listen to messages of recorded meetings

In the electronic office of the future, flexibility will be the key to success.

Courtesy: Texas Instruments.

or conferences in half the time required to attend those sessions. The Donald Duck-like sounds once common to fast-playing recordings will be eliminated.[8]

Teleconferencing

Forms of teleconferencing

Teleconferencing allows people in different locations to hold conversations through a communication link connecting one or more sites. These meetings can take one of three forms or combination thereof: audio (voice transmission only), audio-video (voice plus television images), and graphics (transmission of materials using special imaging or printing equipment). According to Westinghouse Electric, teleconferencing can reduce per meeting costs by 75 percent.[9]

Desktop Publishing

Technology replaces typesetting

Electronic technology now gives you the ability to write, layout, and print quality-looking documents without using expensive typesetting and printing machinery. The advent of laser printers at a modest cost (less than $3,000) enables the computer to use software especially designed for publishing functions. This means that anyone can print professional-looking documents in small or large quantities at costs far below yesterday's typesetting costs.[10] With this technology, you can prepare graphs, brochures, pamphlets, newsletters, bulletins, etc. at your desk.

Optical Disk Reader Recorders

Tomorrow's information center

In the near future, you will be able to store up to 4,000 pages of text or 50,000 pictures on a 14-inch optical disk, making your home into a comprehensive information center. This disk uses a special plastic into which small holes are cut and then read by a laser beam.

This disk is so dense that it stores the equivalent of 1,500 floppy disks' worth of information. With this revolutionary technology, you will be able to have the equivalent of a university-sized library stored on a handful of disks sitting on your shelf.

In addition, this optical disk can also record movies and TV programs, making your system an entertainment as well as an information center.[11]

---

[8] Marvin Kornbluh, "The Electronic Office—How It Will Change the Way We Work," *Career Tomorrow: The Outlook for Work in a Changing World* (Bethesda, Md.: World Future Society, 1983), p. 63.

[9] Harold T. Smith, *The Office Revolution* (Willow Grove, Pa.: Administrative Management Society Foundation, 1983), p. 34.

[10] Basta, "Computer Update," p. 50.

[11] Ibid., p. 58.

Voice Communications

Dictating messages to a computer

Another technology available in limited form is the ability of the computer to recognize, synthesize, store, and play back human speech. Because of the complexity of this technology, it will probably be a few years before it is perfected and becomes commonplace. When refined, it will allow the computer to accept voice dictation, display the message on a terminal screen for proofing, and then either transmit the message electronically or print out a copy for distribution.

Until voice technology becomes state of the art, you need to understand person-to-person dictation using present technology.

PERSON-TO-MACHINE DICTATION

Advantages of person-to-machine dictation

Dictation is a one-to-one communication process. This can be either face to face with a stenographer or person to machine. For many years research has shown the latter method to be more productive and less costly for several reasons:

- ☐ Only one person's time is involved.
- ☐ Dictation can be done at any time and on any day.
- ☐ Turn around time is faster since output can be generated by the next available transcriber/editor or sent immediately if an electronic mail system is available.
- ☐ Dictation can take place at any location through telephone hookups. This allows people who travel to get their messages encoded and sent without delay.

How messages are encoded

Unfortunately, most people do not use either method but continue to write messages out in longhand to submit them to a transcriptionist or word processor for completion. This is the least effective means of encoding any written communication. As technological advances continue, managers will be forced to discard this slow method and use sophisticated electronic equipment which speeds up the communication process.

Encoding messages in the future

For instance, as voice recognition/voice response technology becomes the state of the art, transcribers per se will no longer be needed. In their place will be editors skilled in proofreading, sentence construction, punctuation, and grammar. A number of firms, both large and small, are already using this type of equipment. Managers in these companies can dictate directly to the computer center where voice patterns are stored digitally and later recalled in the dictator's own voice. To use present and future technology, managers must become more adept at person-to-machine dictation.

When to dictate

The first step in developing this practice is to set aside time each day when interruptions are least likely to occur. This can be first thing in the morning or late in the afternoon. Many people prefer early mornings when the mind is alert and the transcriber has time to prepare the documents for that day's mail. Other people prefer late afternoons when more quiet time is available for thinking. Also, there are fewer interruptions in the late afternoon. Scheduled meetings, appointments, and most telephone calls are morning activities. You may divide dictation into a three-step process, regardless of the time schedule you select. This art for dictating includes

A three-step process for dictation

The Pre-dictation Stage

The Dictation Stage

The Post-dictation Stage

The Pre-dictation Stage

Pre-dictation stage defined

Before beginning the dictation, determine which correspondence really needs a written response. In some cases a telephone call will accomplish your objective. In other cases, a note of response at the bottom of an incoming letter or memo might be all that is necessary. This practice is becoming more acceptable as a means of cutting down on paper handling and filing, especially with internal communications. But if you decide you really need that written response, prior to dictation complete the following:

Guidelines for pre-dictation

- ☐ Arrange the dictation documents in order of importance. Answer/initiate the most urgent correspondence first.
- ☐ Plan your strategy for communicating for each message (see Chapter 4).
- ☐ Use a planning sheet for each message. Based on your planned strategy, jot down any notes pertinent to encoding the message. Once you become experienced, a planning sheet may not be necessary for each document. For short, routine correspondence, a few notes in the margin of the supporting materials may be sufficient. However, for important and difficult letters, the planning sheet is a must.
- ☐ Assemble all supporting materials and have them ready to give to the transcriber with the recorded dictation. Be sure to verify all facts and figures. "Supporting materials" include any materials that would aid the reader/transcriber—invoices, incoming letters, shipping receipts, etc.
- ☐ Write down any special instructions on the planning sheet. This includes copies needed; type of mail service, if special; format of document, if unusual; special spelling, etc.
- ☐ Be competent in the use of the equipment. If the equipment is highly sophisticated, a training session would be worth the time invested. A training course helps the user to fully utilize all the capabilities of the equipment.
- ☐ Practice dictating using the playback or retrieval mechanism, until you achieve satisfactory results.

Having completed the pre-dictation step, you are now ready to begin dictating.

The Dictation Stage

Techniques for the dictation stage

Relax! With the microphone or telephone approximately six inches from the mouth, begin by checking your planning sheet and dictating any special instructions.

Now pause and get a clear picture of the person you are addressing. Determine what you want to say, speak slowly, and enunciate your words carefully and distinctly. Be sure to speak naturally. If a transcriber or word processor is employed, group your words together in thought patterns so the employee will have an indication of how to punctuate the message. Some writers dictate commas, periods, and semicolons. However, if you employ a good transcriber, this is not necessary. You need specify only special punctuation.

Continue to use your planning sheet to make sure that you include all important points. Concentrate on the message so that clear, concise, and courteous documents—free from repetition—are the result. The guidelines contained in Figure 2.4 will serve as a checklist for correct dictation practices.

When the dictation is complete, submit all supporting documents to the transcriber along with the recorded tapes.

The Post-dictation Stage

Consideration for post-dictation stage

After the transcriber processes all documents, have them returned to you again for final editing and your signature. Proofread carefully! The responsibility for an error-free message rests with you. Once you are satisfied that the materials are exactly as you want them, sign each document, then follow company procedure in making sure that they are transmitted properly.

Do not sign any documents containing errors. Edit to indicate needed changes and return them to the transcriber/editor for corrections. Then again proofread carefully the corrected documents before signing. Any errors which appear on the document reflect on the person who signed it. Even if dictation seems difficult or awkward at first, keep practicing and you will soon develop good techniques.

TECHNOLOGY AND THE COMMUNICATION PROCESS

To understand how the technologies discussed in this chapter operate in a communications environment, examine the model in Figure 2.5. This model includes the four basic components of the communication process: the communicator (creator of the message), the channel (means of transmission), the receiver (reader/audience receiving the message), and the feedback (response based on receiver's reaction).

Figure 2.4
Guidelines for dictation

1. Identify yourself—name, department, phone number, correspondence symbol, etc. (This applies only when you are dictating into a machine . . . your secretary already knows you!)
2. State what you are dictating—letter, memo, report, rough draft, or finished product; double-spaced or single spaced; margin size.
3. Identify the priority—when dictating more than one item, give them in priority order. If your company has a word-processing center, notify the center of high-priority items before dictating. (Otherwise, how will the typist know that your third letter should have been typed first?)
4. Indicate what paper should be used—company letterhead? If more than one type of paper, which types? Interoffice memo? Personal stationery? How many copies? What type (e.g., office copier or offset)? Must envelopes be addressed?
5. Describe the distribution and identify each receiver—spell out names and addresses. Use phonetic alphabet for initials. Spell out numbers that might be confusing (e.g., 50 and 15, 60 and 16, etc.)
6. Load brain before firing mouth—decide objectives first; select your points and sequence them so as to meet these objectives; organize ideas into paragraphs; break up long sequences into paragraphs; make notes on scrap paper or in margins of letter you are answering; indicate approximate length of letter (number of paragraphs) in advance and during dictation; indicate each paragraph with ". . . period. New paragraph."
7. Spell out any words that might give trouble.
   a. Homonyms—accept, except . . . council, counsel . . . elicit, illicit . . . forward, foreword . . . incidence, incidents.
   b. Uncommon—holocaust, impugn, enigma, renege, surfeit, ensconced.
   c. Foreign—tête-à-tête, coup, gestalt, viscount, risqué, kaput.
   d. Slang—megillah, "no-no," guesstimate, satisficing, kitsch, razzmatazz, chutzpah, schmaltz.
   e. Technical—phenol, emulsified, tensile, viscous, ductile, catalytic, electrolytic, pneumatic.
   f. Words that might be misunderstood—fiscal, physical . . . erratic, erotic . . . formally, formerly . . . abeyance, obeyance . . . error . . . monetary, monitory.
8. Dictate all punctuation—commas and parentheses, colons and semicolons, quotes, apostrophes, hyphens, and final punctuation.
9. Spell out all mechanical instructions—paragraphs to be indented beyond the regular margins, quotes to be given special margin treatment, columns of figures, entries to be numbered and typed under one another, titles to be underlined, space to be left for a hand-drawn table or illustration, etc.
10. Maintain voice control.
    a. Relaxed, normal conversational tone.
    b. Not too fast (especially on material that's familiar).
    c. Avoid mumbling, smoking, chewing pencil or gum, fumbling with instrument.
    d. Use appropriate inflections and pauses.
    e. Signal instructions to typist (e.g., change tone, give beeps, use her/his name).

Courtesy: Dictaphone Corporation, Rye, N.Y.

Figure 2.5 Technology and the communication process model

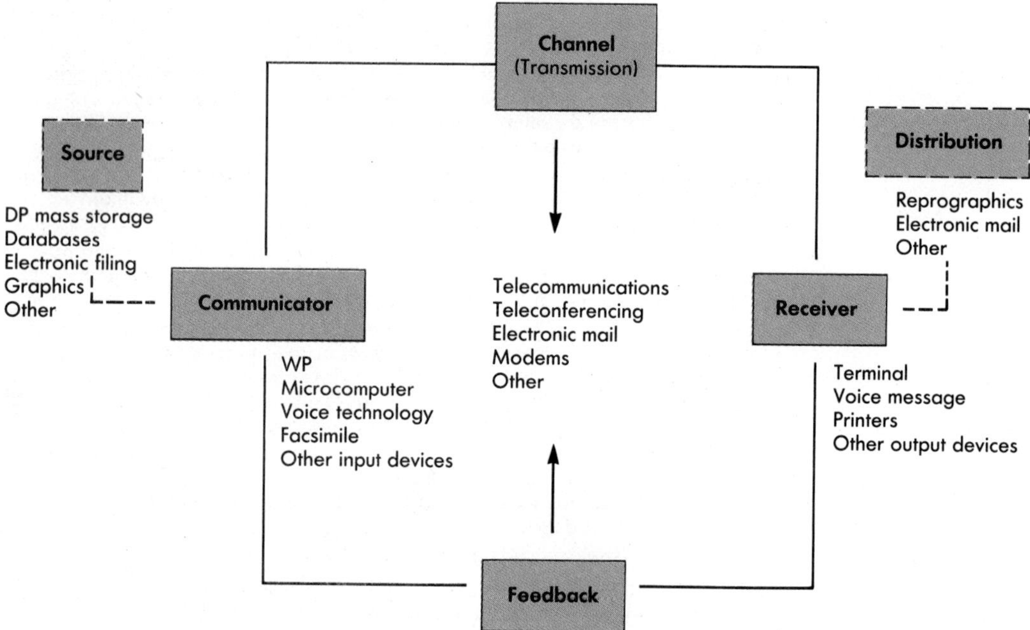

In an automated environment, the communicator may use a word processor, a microcomputer, a voice recognition system, facsimile technology, or any other input device available for capturing her/his thoughts and ideas for transmission. At times, the communicator may want to merge his/her thoughts and ideas with other information already documented. In these instances, source documents can be accessed through such technologies as data processing, databases, electronic files, micrographics, or other stored data/information. For an additional explanation of terminologies, see Figure 2.6.

You could compare this merging ability to a manual cut-and-paste procedure where pieces of data/information have been cut and pasted together, then placed on a copy machine to produce an original-looking document. With integrated technologies, the cut and pasting is done electronically.

Once the communicator decides what he/she wants the message to convey, the next step is the transmission of that message. Rather than using the regular mail service, which is slow and unpredictable, telecommunications, teleconferencing, electronic mail, and modems are examples of options available for transmission. These technologies transmit the message almost instantaneously.

The receiver also has a number of options available for receiving the message, depending on the technology used. Examples include a printed document similar to a typed copy, a terminal readout similar to words on a TV

Figure 2.6
Electronic communication terms

Computer-based management system—assists all levels of management in a decision-making process; presents data in a form that has meaning for the decision maker.

Database—a collection of data/information files compiled by subject and stored in the computer; for example, a database in a university that contains student information can be used by different programs to print class enrollments, grades, transcripts, etc.

Electronic files—a computer filing system where files are handled electronically in a centralized system; a nonpaper storage system.

Electronic mail (E-Mail)—one form of telecommunications involving the transfer of written messages from one computer to another instead of using the post office.

Facsimile (FAX)—device for transferring documents over telephone lines; especially equipped for transmitting pictures, graphs, photos, and figures to distant sites.

Floppy disk—magnetic-coated, record-shaped disk used to store information/programs for the microcomputer; the computer has the ability to read information from as well as store information onto the disk.

Graphics—representation of data, ideas, or concepts in picture form.

Hardware—the physical equipment and components of a computer system.

Integrated office system—a variety of electronic technologies connected together to form a complete office system; allows the sharing of information from a central location.

Lap-size computer—a portable computer about the size of a briefcase.

Microchip—a small device (about one-fourth inch square) made from silicon used in today's computers; the chip contains thousands of transistors and other components in miniaturized form.

Microcomputer—a device with electronically activated chips that performs input, output, and other functions; also referred to as desktop computer and personal computer; has built-in intelligence to handle word processing, data processing, budgeting, games, etc.

Micrographics—the process of photographing to a sheet of microfilm hundreds of documents in greatly reduced form.

Microprocessor—the brains of the computer.

Modems—a device placed between a communicating machine and a telephone line to permit the transmission of digital pulses to and from distant sites.

Network—a cabling system that interconnects a variety of information-related devices such as microcomputers and printers; provides a means of sharing information and computer hardware/software.

On-line database—a computer directly connected to a database source through cabling, telephone hookup, or satellite; example: the university library linked to a database system such as ERIC (Educational Resources Information Center) in California.

Optical character recognition (OCR)—device that scans typewritten pages and digitizes the scanned characters so that the information can be stored in the computer or sent to other locations through a telecommunications system; can also be used for sorting; example: post office uses OCR to read and sort by ZIP code.

Peripherals—any device used for input/output operations with the computer; for example, a tape drive, disk, terminal, printer, etc.

Personal computer—a relatively low-cost microcomputer with built-in intelligence; useful for such applications as word processing, budget maintenance, data file maintenance, etc.

Figure 2.6 (concluded)

Portable computer—small microcomputer that can be transported; usually housed in one unit; may contain a battery pack.

Reprographics—the total process of data/information reproduction and duplication.

Stand-alone computer—see personal computer.

Telecommunications—ability to send and receive data to and from various sites through a cabling, satellite, or modem system

Teleconferencing—meetings over communications links connecting two or more sites; may include simultaneous transmission of voice, data, and/or video.

Terminal—a device through which data can exit from or be entered into a computer; example: travel agencies or airline reservation stations use terminals connected to a central data/information center.

Word processing—system of translating messages onto magnetic media.

Word processor—a device that records typing onto a medium or into computer memory for later use.

screen, a facsimile printout, a voice system, or other output format available to the receiver. After reading or listening to the message, the receiver can transmit feedback to the original communicator, copy and distribute the message to others in or out of the organization, or store the message for future use.

In the case of feedback, the same transmission technologies available to the communicator would apply to the respondent. If storage is preferred, the data/information is then stored as a source document. For distribution, such technologies as reprographics and electronic mail are options for speeding the dispersement of the message at a fraction of the time required by a manual method.

This model merely presents an overview of how technology affects the communication processes. As innovations continue to push back horizons, many more opportunities for enhancing business communications will be uncovered.

You will find numerous references for using electronic technologies and the process of communication throughout this textbook; many of the activities have been designed for use with this technology in mind.

SUMMARY

Electronic technology affects the way we live. While the computer invasion has thrust us into an Information Age where information now doubles every six years, it also helps us manage information in a timely, concise, and accurate manner.

Some of the benefits electronic technology provides are the elimination of monotonous routine tasks, a savings in time, cost effectiveness, timeliness and greater accessibility of data/information, accuracy and quality of output, and the ability to forecast outcomes.

The greatest benefits come in an environment where electronic technologies are integrated through a communications network. This network allows information once generated and stored to be accessed and used over and over again. In this context, form letters, formatting, forms design and control, graphics, data verification, calendaring, data analysis, forecasting, word processing, data processing, electronic filing, electronic mail, and a host of other functions can be handled automatically or semiautomatically.

For creating documents, person-to-machine dictation is the most efficient. Therefore, business professionals must become adept at person-to-machine dictation which speeds up communication. Dictation requires a three-step process—preparing for dictation, dictating to a machine, and following through until the document is edited, signed, and transmitted.

Business communicators need to take advantage of state-of-the-art technologies for creating, transmitting, receiving, responding, storing, and distributing information in both oral and written form. Effective use of these technologies will not only improve the quality of the message but will also increase productivity of data/information handling at all levels.

END-OF-CHAPTER ACTIVITIES

DISCUSSION

1. Discuss some of the ways technology is affecting communication processes in your personal life.
2. With information doubling every six years, discuss the impact of technology on the problem of information overload. Does it solve or compound the problem?
3. With databases making information virtually unlimited:
   a. What impact will databases have on the user?
   b. Do you think databases enhance or hinder a user in writing effective messages?
   c. What skills do you think the communicator will need in the future?
4. Discuss how technology ensures accuracy of data. How can mistakes be eliminated?
5. Analyze each situation in Chapter Cases 1, 2, 3, and 4 by identifying:
   a. The problem/s of the old system if any existed.
   b. The types of technology used to enhance communication.
   c. The benefits derived from changing to an electronic system.
   d. Other types of technology that would be beneficial if used.
6. Based on readings of current literature, discuss the impact of technology on the job performance of the manager/executive; clerk/secretary; other business professionals.

7. What future technologies do you foresee as having an impact on the way people will communicate? Discuss.
8. Discuss some of the social and ethical issues that result from communicating electronically.
9. Interpret and discuss what is meant by the formula: "Better machine performance + Quality human performance = Greater cost savings."
10. Interpret and discuss the statement: "To survive in the future, flexibility will be important—flexibility in how we work; whom we work with, and what tools we will use to perform our work."

ACTIVITIES

11. Interview a manager at a local firm and determine:
    a. What technologies are employed for enhancing productivity.
    b. The impact technology is having on communication processes. On people. On environment.
    c. What problems, if any, the company is encountering as a result of installing electronic equipment.
    d. What technologies are being considered for the future. Why?
12. View a national TV news program. What communication technologies do you feel were employed in making the broadcast?
13. Make a collection of form letters. Discuss:
    a. How you think the messages could be personalized.
    b. How you think technology affected the message.
    c. What features could be used to make the message look original?
    d. What impact you think the message had on the receiver. On productivity. On achieving its goal.
14. Check current periodicals on electronic mail and determine what impact this technology is having on the message format. On the content.
15. Visit some technology stores in your locality and make a comparison chart of a minimum of three types of equipment capable of performing word processing functions; then answer the following questions:
    a. What features do you feel are the most helpful in creating written messages?
    b. Which equipment would you consider a best buy?
    c. What is the difference between a dedicated word processor and a microcomputer that performs word-processing functions?
    d. Which equipment would you buy? Why?

CHAPTER 3

INTERNATIONAL COMMUNICATION

Learning Objectives

After studying this chapter, you will be able to:

- □ Understand the complexity of international communication.
- □ Comprehend the importance of international communication skills for competing in an expanding global market.
- □ Analyze the components required for processing a communication in an international environment.
- □ Define culture as it relates to the values, thoughts, and feelings of people in a group.
- □ Cite cultural characteristics that affect international communication.
- □ Identify communication barriers that lead to misinterpretation in cross-cultural communication.
- □ Compare traits that are common to successful international firms.
- □ Identify human skills essential for effective international communication.

> Globalization of business has set loose thousands of newcomers upon the international scene, many of them badly prepared for the challenges and stresses they will face. Men and women scouting for new markets, living out of hotels, struggling with phrasebooks—they are the first wave of new internationals.[1]

Importance of communication in a global environment

The growth of international business is reflected by the hundreds of multinational companies around the world. These organizations are looking for a special breed of manager—one who possesses the skills and sensitivity to "orchestrate the productive intermingling of culturally distinct individuals and to function effectively when working in different cultures."[2]

Leadership requires communication skills

Because many U.S. companies have assumed a leadership role in the world marketplace, businesspeople today vitally need excellent communication skills, particularly in the international community. Should U.S. owned companies fail in this new and challenging business environment, another world power would assume this position of leadership. According to former AMS International President Jack W. Mynett, "We no longer have all the answers to management problems and we better learn to listen to all parts of the world—we're not the center of the universe."[3]

The complexity of international communication

In the best of circumstances, communication is not a simple process; but in an international environment, it becomes even more complex. Understanding such elements as ethnicity, race, history, territory, religion, language, and other distinguishing cultural characteristics is necessary for effective communication in the international marketplace.

This chapter addresses the importance of international communication in today's global society; it presents a process for communicating in this environment; it identifies distinguishing cultural characteristics; it reviews several barriers to effective communication; and it illustrates the common communication strategies of successful international firms.

THE IMPORTANCE OF INTERNATIONAL COMMUNICATION

The ability to compete requires communication skills

The trade deficit for 1986 rose to an all-time high of $180 billion. To ward off a recession, America is fiercely trying to compete in the international market. U.S. companies are expanding their operations abroad where the cost of labor is lower. The managers of these companies know that growth overseas will be faster than at home. One type of industry certain to receive top billing in future trade talks is the service industry. Providing quality service in any environment, whether foreign or domestic, requires effective use of all forms

---

[1] Prabhu Guptara, "Searching the Organization for the Cross-Cultural Operators," *International Management* 41, no. 8 (August 1986), p. 40.

[2] Germaine Shames, "Training for the Multicultural Workplace," *Cornell Quarterly* 26, no. 4 (February 1986), p. 25.

[3] "AMS Officer Reaches Out to Japan, Hong Kong." Quoted in *Management World* 13, no. 3 (March 1984), p. 42.

of communication. Many business people are not yet ready to enter into this international market. To compete, they must be able to speak, listen, read, and write in the host language, particularly when transactions are handled face to face.

Advantage of other countries

From this standpoint, people from other countries have an advantage. They understand us better than we understand them. In most major countries, English is required as a second language. In Japan, for example, students must complete six years of English study before high school graduation.[4] By comparison, foreign language study is not required in the U.S. educational system.

Service industry trend requires face-to-face communication

In the past, we could afford to sit back and let the world come to us; but today, such a provincial attitude has serious consequences. Between 1974 and 1984, some 20 million jobs were created as a result of the structural shift toward service employment, including the expansion of service industries overseas. According to some observers, this shift will accelerate as a result of the invasion of new technologies and the battle for international markets. One company, the China National Machinery I/E Corporation, located in the People's Republic of China, understands the communication limitations that U.S. companies face. The advertisement in Figure 3.1 that appeared in U.S. business publications shows how ready such companies are to provide their consulting services.

Communication skills overcome barriers

While investors from other countries have little difficulty setting up shop in the United States, the same is not true for U.S. investors overseas. Many barriers must be overcome.

Studies confirm the need for students entering the business world to have a better understanding of other cultures and the ability to communicate effectively in international environments. As multinational companies continue to expand, the ability to communicate effectively with people of other countries and cultures will be even more important.

A PROCESS FOR COMMUNICATING INTERNATIONALLY

Importance of planning

In planning a communication process for an international audience, you must analyze each component to cut through the barriers or noise that would hinder desired results. Like defensive drivers, writers and speakers must be alert to all environmental elements and must use a mix of communication techniques to achieve success.

A process for communicating internationally

The components to be analyzed for processing a communication in an international environment are the same as those in a domestic one—the *why* of the message, the *what* of the message, the *who,* the *how,* and the *type.* How you apply the components, however, can produce very different results,

---

[4] John W. Gould, "For Doing Business Abroad, How Much Foreign Language Proficiency is Enough?" *Bulletin of the Association of Business Communication* 49, no. 3 (September 1986), p. 26.

Figure 3.1
Example of ad in domestic periodicals

China National Machinery I/E Corp., Consultancy and Information Services Division

China National Machinery Import & Export Corporation Consultancy and Information Services Division offers excellent services for friends from industrial and trade circles all over the world who want to enquire and import Chinese mechanical and/or electrical products with spare parts and semi-finished products, to make contacts for business in processing with supplied materials, processing to supplied drawings, assembling with supplied parts, joint ventures or cooperative production to introduce their products to Chinese endusers, to distribute their catalogues, promotional materials and to advertise in Chinese newspapers. For domestic industrial enterprises, open cities and foreign firms in China, we offer services in dissemination of market information and I/E business consultancy, import enquiry, export recommendation, international advertising and printing catalogues.

We have more than 30 years of experience in import and export of mechanical and/or electrical products. We have now more than 30 branches in all parts of China and many organizations in overseas countries. Over the years, we have established extensive business contacts and have many trade partners all over the world. With a host of experts on our staff, our services are professional, efficient and reliable.

Courtesy: China National Machinery Import and Export Corporation.

depending on the type of communication and the audience addressed. To determine just how elements will change, you must consider each component separately and concentrate on the special needs of your international readers or listeners.

The Why of the Message

Understand why the communication is needed

The first step in a communication process is to understand the situation which prompts the communication. Every communication addresses a need. This is the why of the message. For example, suppose your company manufactures a product that is highly competitive in the domestic market. Profits are low. Therefore, you wish to expand your sales to an international market where a scarcity of your product exists. The why of your communication emanates from anticipated profits. Since the sender of the message determines the desired outcome of the message, the process of determining the why of international correspondence is identical to that for domestic correspondence.

The What of the Message

Establish the purpose of the communication

Every communication has an objective. This is the what of the message and should be the answer to why the message is needed. In other words, if the why of the message is that the home market is highly competitive with larger profits anticipated abroad, then the what of the message would be to convince the reader to market your products by pointing out the benefits to both reader and customer. The differences between an international and domestic audience have little effect on the what of a message. It is in the process of carrying out the purpose that vast differences emerge.

The Who of the Message

Focus on the reader

The who of the message focuses on the person receiving the message. You must predict how the reader will interpret your message and structure the content for a positive response. To do this you must try to understand the thinking processes of the reader. When you communicate with persons of other countries and cultures, you must consider how these thinking processes are uniquely different.

You cannot rely on your own feelings and attitudes, as you do when you address domestic readers. Instead, you must extend yourself imaginatively, anticipating the response of your international readers, relying on their values, behavior patterns, and cultural attitudes. Many international communicators fail to do this.

Making wrong assumptions

An easy assumption is that because all people are biologically the same, they have the same needs and values. Such a view in an international environment can result in failure. Consider this illustration:

A U.S. design engineer working with his local affiliated office in Asia called for a general meeting of his professional staff. Wanting to be helpful and give credit for the progress made on a project, he singled out for praise a particular individual. The person showed little if any emotion and did not seem pleased to be receiving the praise. The American later learned that this event caused considerable embarrassment to the individual since, in that country, collective effort is valued over individual effort and competition.[5]

Each group has its own value system

In this example, the design engineer made assumptions on the basis of his own values and behavior patterns. In the United States, most employees would consider it a great honor to be singled out and praised at a professional staff meeting. When doing business overseas, however, you must keep in mind that people are guided by their own culture and value system. Remember, too, that behavior patterns vary from culture to culture. Therefore, the way you communicate should vary accordingly.

The How of the Message

Structure the message for a favorable response

The structure or how of your message is based on the expected reaction of your reader or listener. Typically, in conducting business in the United States, if you expect a favorable response, you will probably use a direct approach (get right to the point.) If you anticipate an unfavorable response, you'll choose an indirect approach (gently lead into the bad news.) In international

[5] James A. McCaffrey and Craig R. Hafner, "When Two Cultures Collide: Doing Business Overseas," *Training and Development Journal,* 39, no. 10 (October 1985), p. 26. Copyright 1985, *Training & Development Journal,* American Society for Training and Development. Reprinted by permission. All rights reserved.

Vary the structure based on culture

communication, the approach can vary, however. Depending on your reader or listener, you may need to be more wordy. While U.S. citizens are aggressive and want to get to the point, other cultures might consider such tactics rude and objectionable. In Asia, for example, courtesy is extremely important. To Asians, a blunt message to an older professional would indicate disrespect.

Obstacles leading to miscommunication

Leave nothing to chance. Take special measures to avoid jargon or figurative expressions. Such expressions as "The project was temporarily placed on the back burner," or "We have beefed up our product line," are sure to be obstacles for many international readers. Avoid these obstacles by writing clear messages that are easy to interpret.

Important considerations

Although letter styles used in other countries differ slightly from the U.S. style in the placement of dateline, salutation, and close, you should not expect a negative reaction simply because you use a structure and style typical of U.S. business correspondence. Openness, acceptance, diplomacy, and courtesy are more important than letter style.

Type preferences for international communication

A study by Kilpatrick cited in Figure 3.2, identifies some of the more common characteristics of letter styles used in other countries. Since cultural differences are responsible for some of the major problems arising in international communication, this information will help you understand the viewpoint of your reader or listener.

The Type of Communication

The type of communication depends on the circumstances. As with domestic communication, the type of international communication can be either oral (staff meetings, formal gatherings, phone conversations, or teleconferencing) or written (letter, memo, report, or computer mail); formal (letters, written reports, staff meetings, formal gatherings, etc.) or informal (phone conversations, luncheon discussions, informal gatherings, etc.) But realize that at least in some cultures, formal communication is preferred over informal; and oral communication is preferred over any other format.

DISTINGUISHING CULTURAL CHARACTERISTICS

Characteristics that pinpoint culture

In considering cultural characteristics, it is not feasible to discuss every possible variable. Nor is it reasonable to expect communicators to know much about every type of culture to which they might be exposed. A more practical approach is to examine some of the most common elements that might affect communication in an international environment. Understanding these elements will make you more effective in communicating with people in other countries. These common elements include cultural history, language, religion, attitude toward time, human behavior, and style as they relate to communication.

Figure 3.2
Common characteristics of international correspondence

- ☐ A modified block style with indented paragraphs.
- ☐ A Continental dateline style (day/month/year).
- ☐ A salutation of "Dear (Title/Surname)" or "Dear Sir/Madam."
- ☐ A closed punctuation style (punctuation at the end of each line).
- ☐ A complimentary closing of "Sincerely" or "Sincerely yours" ("Faithfully" or "Faithfully yours" is also popular).
- ☐ A formal and impersonal writing style.
- ☐ A writing style that uses exaggerated courtesies (superlatives, "esteemed," "great pleasure," etc.).

Retha H. Kilpatrick, "International Business Communication Practices," *Journal of Business Communication,* 21, no. 2 (Fall 1984), pp. 33–44.

Cultural History

Culture defined

Webster defines culture as "the integrated pattern of human behavior that includes thought, speech, action, and artifacts and depends upon man's capacity for learning and transmitting knowledge to succeeding generations." These patterns of human behavior are what give a racial, religious, or social group its identity and shape the values, thoughts, and feelings of every person in the group.

Because this identity varies with different groups or societies, how you communicate will depend on your understanding of the culture. In other words, what might be *positive* in one culture could be *scandalous* in another. Notice the different viewpoints in this example:

Contrasting cultures

On a sea voyage, you are traveling with your wife, your child, and your mother. The ship develops problems and starts to sink. Of your family, you are the only one who can swim and you can only save one other individual. Who would you save?

This question was posed to a group of men in Asia and the U.S. In the U.S., more than 60 percent of those responding said they would save the child, 40 percent would choose to save the wife, and none would have saved the mother. In the Eastern or Asian countries, 100 percent said they would save the mother. Their rationale? You can always remarry and have more children—but you cannot have another mother.[6]

The value systems of the two groups represented in this example are quite different. Both groups are family-oriented but from a different perspective. Americans place a high value on the present family unit, whereas Asians place a high value on their ancestry.

Cultural identity

Value systems based on cultural history are part of the thinking process of the group they represent. For many Americans, one such value system is the Protestant work ethic—part of the philosophy which formed our country.

[6] McCaffrey and Hafner, pp. 27-29. Copyright 1985, *Training & Development Journal,* American Society for Training & Development. Reprinted by permission. All rights reserved.

Because of this philosophy we place great value on individual effort. What a person accomplishes is more important than his or her ancestry. Such proverbs as "A penny saved is a penny earned," "The idle mind is the devil's workshop," and "He who does not work does not eat," reflect how much we value material things, efficiency, and hard work.

Language

English—the international language

English is considered the business, scientific, and diplomatic language for communicating internationally. To illustrate how universal the English language is, Michael Skapinker states that "when Saudi Arabia's Sheikh Yamani speaks to the oil minister of Norway, or when Israel's Shimon Peres speaks to Egypt's Hosni Mubarak, they speak in English. When Carlo de Benedetti of Olivetti speaks to Bjorn Svedberg of Ericsson, or Akio Morita of Sony speaks to Corvan der Klugt of Phillips, they speak in English."[7]

With the increase in international trade, English is more important than ever (see Figure 3.3). In 1983, approximately 100 million Chinese viewed the BBC television series on learning English. Recent estimates indicate that in China more people are learning English than make up the entire population of the United States.[8] Other countries are also stepping up English proficiency.

Because learning English is considered more important than ever, you may feel that your command of the English language is adequate for communicating anywhere—both internationally and at home. This is probably true for most circumstances. However, for more and more companies, even domestic ones, English alone may not be enough.

Examine the following situations in which you might need to communicate in a language other than English:

Importance of a second language

- ☐ As an expatriate manager (an employee of a U.S. multinational company who works overseas).
- ☐ As a marketing representative interested in selling goods or services overseas.
- ☐ As a supervisor or manager of a domestic firm located in the United States and employing immigrant workers.
- ☐ As an employee of a non-U.S.-owned firm located in this country.

Disadvantage of using an interpreter

Since most managers don't have the time to learn a second language, many hire bilingual nationals to carry out needed operations or employ interpreters to translate messages. Either solution can cause enormous problems: bilingual nationals lack training in U.S. management techniques, and great misunderstandings can arise through inaccurate translations.

---

[7] Michael Skapinker, "Why Speaking English Is No Longer Enough," *International Management,* 41, no. 11 (November 1986), p. 39.

[8] Skapinker, p. 49.

Figure 3.3
English-speaking statistics

- □ Over 300 million people use English as their primary language.
- □ Six hundred and fifty million people use English as a second language.
- □ English is spoken, written, and broadcast on every continent.
- □ English is an official language in 29 countries.
- □ About three-fourths of the world's letters are written in English.
- □ One-half of the world's newspapers are printed in English.
- □ English is the language of three-fifths of the world's radio stations.
- □ English is the most widely studied language in the countries in which it is not native.

Vern Terpstra and Kenneth David, *The Cultural Environment of International Business*, 2nd ed. (Cincinnati, Ohio: South-Western Publishing, 1985), p. 32.

Stories about embarrassing situations caused by faulty translation are commonplace. Consider the following:

Translation blunder

When a Chinese delegation visited North America as guests of an influential newspaper recently, the newspaper organized a banquet in the delegation's honor . . . The interpreter . . . was a young Chinese woman who had graduated in English language studies. . . .

[After] the meal, the leader of the Chinese delegation made a warm speech in which he said he greatly appreciated the hospitality of the newspaper, which he described as one of the most influential, not only in North America, but in the world. The interpreter hastily came up with an English translation: "Thank you for lunch, and we hope your newspaper will be successful one day."[9]

Use a local language to establish rapport

Such embarrassing blunders convince many managers of a need to learn a second language. Even if face-to-face communication is not required, an understanding of the local language is a plus. Language is more than just words or phrases. Language reflects the way people think and what they value.

A language philosophy

Another point to consider when communicating internationally is that some internationals may resent conducting business in any language other than their own. This is true in France as well as French-speaking Canada. French is the second most widely used language for international business. The French are proud of their language, and business executives in that country insist on doing business in their mother tongue. Understandably, their philosophy is "While in Rome, do as the Romans do." Our own attitudes are not so different; we expect others to learn our language, usually within a two-year period.

Importance of oral communication in an international environment

The need for a second language is especially critical if you are marketing goods or services to buyers in other countries where face-to-face communication is necessary. When people are *buying*, they prefer to do business in their

[9] Skapinker, p. 40. Reprinted from November 1986 issue of *Business Week* by special permission © 1986 by McGraw-Hill Inc.

own language. A company with representatives who speak the buyer's language has a competitive edge when communicating customer needs. From this standpoint, fluency in the local language becomes essential.

Language inadequacies

In discussing language, you must consider other factors. For instance, words in one language may have no counterparts in other languages. Because of the culture, certain words receive greater emphasis. In Arabic, for instance, there are more than 6,000 different words for a camel, its parts, and its equipment. The English language would be greatly limited in describing camels, yet rich in describing automotive transport, industry, and commerce—resources greatly valued in this country.[10]

Religion

The U.S. Constitution separates matters of church and state and guarantees religious freedom for all its citizens. Thus, in this country business policies and procedures are established with little or no consideration of religious beliefs.

Religion sometimes dictates culture

In other countries, however, the whole society's religious, economic, and political organization may be one and the same. When communicating with readers from other countries, you should take note of the impact of religious beliefs on business activities. For example, in Islamic countries you wouldn't want to serve alcoholic beverages to native citizens since alcohol is forbidden by religious law.

Recognizing religious holidays facilitates communication

Holy days and special religious observances should be considered when communicating internationally. Schedule your communications so they don't conflict with these events. Being aware of the religious beliefs of your readers will open doors for better communication.

One refrigerator company made the mistake of advertising its product in the Middle East with a picture that displayed a ham inside the refrigerator. Since Moslems do not eat ham, this ad was considered insensitive and unappealing.[11]

Time

Americans are extremely time-conscious. "Time is money" is part of our cultural belief. The many seminars and training sessions on time management attest to the value placed on this resource. In fact, Americans are willing to set aside tact and diplomacy and will even tolerate outrageous behavior in business dealings in order to meet deadlines and schedules.

Time viewed from different perspectives

In an international environment, such attitudes about time can backfire. Although Americans like to get to the point, professionals in other countries

---

[10] Terpstra and David, p. 18.

[11] David A. Ricks, *Big Business Blunders* (Homewood, Ill.: Dow Jones-Irwin, 1983), p. 66.

LEGAL / ETHICAL ISSUE

Judy Kramer is a sophomore engineering student at a major university in Florida. She and a number of the other students are concerned about their upcoming grades in Calculus 202. At a get-together in the snack bar of the student center, Judy and her classmates discuss the concerns for their grades. Some of them contend they have difficulty understanding their foreign instructor. They feel the instructor's inability to communicate effectively is responsible for their inability to perform well. The conversation becomes lively, capturing the attention of students from surrounding tables. A diversity of opinions surface concerning this issue. The students made these major points:

- □ Every student at a major university has had or will have a foreign teaching assistant or professor during her/his college years.
- □ If you can't understand the professor, then there is no need to go to class.
- □ The language barrier is just another way of rationalizing a bad grade.
- □ The blame on foreign instructors for bad grades is just another way of sugarcoating bigotry.

A 1983 Florida law requires university instructors to be proficient in the English language. If a problem is perceived, instructors are required to take oral and written communication tests to prove their fluency.

Since we are living in a global society and conducting business on an international level, shouldn't students expect to have a number of foreign instructors during their college days? Since the university administration hired the foreign professor knowing her/his language background, do they now have a right to come back and impose a test like that required by the state of Florida? Should all states have a law similar to Florida's? What are the legal and ethical issues involved?

are usually more sensitive to protocol and the social amenities. Many place a higher value on formalities than on time. Thus, Americans are sometimes regarded as pushy and rude; Americans are unsettled by what they consider unnecessary formalities.

One U.S. company insulted the Greeks by imposing time limits on contract negotiation meetings. The Greeks considered the Americans' forthright and outspoken behavior as well as their time consciousness to be in poor taste.[12]

[12] Ibid., p. 8.

Human Behavior

Nonverbal considerations

In this country, our attitudes toward one another are shaped by human behavior. The same is true in other cultures, only more so. Nonverbal behavior can profoundly influence business decisions. Inappropriate gestures and negative body language can spoil our best efforts and cause misunderstanding. Even something as simple as the use of color, numbers, or exposure of body parts must be considered when communicating internationally. Here are some examples of blunders that resulted when these nonverbal elements were not considered.

Color as a nonverbal consideration

The Singer Company made a potential blunder when it began a promotional campaign in which the outdoor ad was prepared using blue as the background color. This color represented death to the local people. Luckily, Singer discovered the error just prior to its introduction. In other countries, death is represented by different colors—black (United States and other European countries); white (Japan); purple (Latin America); dark red (Ivory Coast); and so forth.[13] Inappropriate color can cause communication misinterpretations.

Numbers as a nonverbal consideration

Failure to consider numbers can also cause communication embarrassments. In the United States, the number 7 is considered lucky; 13 unlucky. Each country has similar lucky and unlucky numbers. In Japan, the number four is considered undesirable because *four* in Japanese sounds like the Japanese word for *death*. A U.S. golf ball company made a blunder when it tried to sell golf balls in Japan packaged in groups of four. Similarly, a soft-drink company offended an Arab nation when it used a six-pointed star as a decoration on its label. This was interpreted as being pro-Israeli.[14]

Gestures as a nonverbal consideration

You can avoid embarrassments by studying the meanings of nonverbal motions and signs common to a particular culture before attempting to communicate. For instance, the OK sign (finger and thumb touching in a circle) used in the United States signifies a zero in France, money in Japan, and a vulgar gesture in South America. One company made the blunder of using an OK stamp on each page of its printed catalog. This mistake proved costly, necessitating a six-month delay while catalogs were reprinted.[15]

Body parts as a nonverbal consideration

Another U.S. company in the business of manufacturing shoes failed to consider culture when it used promotional photos that depicted bare feet. Exposure of the foot in Southeast Asia is considered an insult.[16]

Each culture is different. A nod or wave of the hand in one country can mean something totally different in another. When communicating, be sensitive to cultural differences.

---

[13] Ibid., p. 5.

[14] Ibid., p. 32.

[15] Ibid., p. 17.

[16] Ibid., p. 63.

Style

Culture dictates writing styles

Many countries emulate the American style of writing, partly because of the widespread use of American textbooks in overseas universities and also because U.S. business practices are highly respected throughout the world. Yet the writing style in each country still retains unique qualities. When communicating with persons from other countries, let their culture determine the style and tone of the communication.

BARRIERS TO INTERNATIONAL COMMUNICATION

Communication barriers occur when people misinterpret the intended meaning of the message. The purpose of studying cross-cultural communication is to reduce the gaps which cause these misinterpretations. Since meanings lie in people, not in words, identifying the factors that lead to misinterpretations is the first step in achieving better international communication.

Although no comprehensive list exists, the following broad areas are most often responsible for breakdowns in cross-cultural communication:

Barriers to effective communication

- □ *Language misunderstanding*—an inability to interpret accurately the message. This barrier is often cited as the number one basis for miscommunication. Errors in translation, vocabulary, punctuation, pronunciation, nonverbal gestures, plus an inability to communicate in the local language emphasize cross-cultural differences.
- □ *Weak listening skills*—a lack of concentration to listen critically. This often results in misunderstanding. People using English as a second language usually speak with an accent, and we tend to ignore what we don't catch.
- □ *Culture shock*—the inability to understand or accept people with different values, standards, and lifestyles. Implicit here is a lack of awareness of what other people consider important.
- □ *Ethnocentrism*—the belief that your culture is superior to any other. This barrier exists when written or oral communication conveys an attitude of superiority. People do not like to be talked down to or to feel their ideas are interesting, but wrong.
- □ *Insensitivity*—a lack of concern for other people's needs and feelings. To many readers, writers appear insensitive when their communication is abrupt and displays an aggressive or self-centered attitude.
- □ *Lack of openness*—a feeling that exists when the climate is formal and people don't feel at ease to express their opinions. This type of environment breeds distrust. People may even feel that information is being withheld. To avoid this barrier, you must

promote a feeling of mutual acceptance by providing a relaxed environment for intercultural exchange.

How to reduce misinterpretations

You can greatly reduce communication barriers by participating in awareness and cross-cultural training programs. Some successful international corporations require their managers to receive such training prior to departing for an overseas assignment. Even on the homefront, some companies require this training since many managers work in multicultural environments.

Where to go for training

If you will be working in another country for any length of time, you should know that more and more companies are investing in intense employee training. Some of the largest training centers include the Business Council for International Understanding (BCIU) in Washington, D.C.; The American University in Washington, D.C.; the Key Man Course at the Thunderbird School in Phoenix, Arizona; and the Monterey Institute of International Studies in Monterey, California.[17]

Additional information on other countries is available through The Industry and Trade Division of the Department of Commerce in Washington, D.C., upon request. You can also contact a member of a foreign consulate who is usually happy to furnish information on her/his country. As a starting point, ask the consulate to address the areas listed in Figure 3.4. This list contains basic information that you need prior to embarking on a business trip overseas.

COMMON TRAITS OF SUCCESSFUL INTERNATIONAL FIRMS

Research as an aid to international communication

By observing and comparing traits of successful international firms headquartered in different countries, we have a better understanding of the needs, values, standards, and expectations of one another's cultures. The Administrative Management Association in collaboration with Management Centre Europe—a comparable management development organization in Europe—conducted such a study comparing business in the United States and Europe. They found a number of characteristics common to successful firms in both cultures.[18] These include:

Common traits of successful international firms

- ☐ A high-energy level—a driving force for both individual and corporate achievement.
- ☐ A visible and strongly felt personality of culture—a feeling of belonging to the organization which portrayed a clear sense of direction. This trait came about with good management practices.

---

[17] Letitia Baldridge, *Letitia Baldridge's Complete Guide to Executive Manners* (New York: Rawson Associates, 1985), p. 160.

[18] Frederick Harmon and Garry Jacobs, "Survey: Looking Beyond Profitability: Where U.S. and European Cultures Meet," *International Management* 41, no. 7 (July 1986), pp. 54-56.

Figure 3.4
What to Know Before Conducting Business Abroad

Before going on a business trip to another country, you should:

- ☐ *Learn a few key phrases in the country's language,* including "Good morning," "Good evening," "Thank you," "It's a pleasure meeting you," and "Excuse me."
- ☐ *Become familiar with the code of dress in that country,* so that you pack the proper clothes.
- ☐ *Familiarize yourself with any religious taboos* that are important.
- ☐ *Know basic information about the country,* such as who is the head of state, the name of the political party that person represents, and the name of the U.S. ambassador to that post.
- ☐ *Know how to greet someone properly,* whether that means shaking hands and giving your name or immediately offering your card or whatever is the usual protocol in that country.
- ☐ *Know what kind of gift is appropriately given to whom and when.* For example, should you bring or send flowers to your dinner host? What kind?
- ☐ *Learn about punctuality in keeping both business and social engagements.* Should you be on time, slightly late, or quite late? When you are the guest of honor at dinner, should you leave first, and if not, who should? At what time should you leave?
- ☐ *Know the way people refer to their own country.* For example, the Soviets want you to say "the Soviet Union," not "Russia." East Germans want you to use "the German Democratic Republic," not "East Germany."
- ☐ *Be cognizant of the names of the major newspapers and magazines* and their political stance.

Letitia Baldridge, *Letitia Baldridge's Complete Guide to Executive Manners* (New York: Rawson Associates, 1985), p. 160. Reprinted with the permission of Rawson Associates, an imprint of Macmillan Publishing Company.

- ☐ A commitment to basic values—a pledge to such values as quality, customer satisfaction, administrative efficiency, teamwork, and profit.
- ☐ A specialized organization structure—an implementation process for translating corporate values into reality.

Additional studies identify other traits as essential for effective international communication:

Human skills essential for effective communication

- ☐ *Perception*—the ability to read inherent values and logic in other cultures, that is, to "see through other people's eyes."
- ☐ *Sensitivity*—the ability to tailor a message to the values, attitudes, and needs of the reader/audience.
- ☐ *Adaptability*—the ability to adjust to a different climate or culture.
- ☐ *Flexibility*—the ability to shift gears or modify plans on the basis of reader/audience response.
- ☐ *Receptiveness*—the ability to relate and build relationships with people of other cultures.
- ☐ *Awareness*—the ability to recognize strengths, weaknesses, limitations, and assumptions both in yourself and in others.

To be effective in international communication, you need to develop greater cultural awareness and intercultural skills. You can develop these skills by studying human behavior. Rather than focusing on a list of do's and don'ts, be open to how other people think and what they value.

Our globe is shrinking. People from every corner of the world face us every day—in the office, in the classroom, in the factory, and in the neighborhood. America is a society of immigrants. By learning to communicate in your own multinational environment, you are preparing yourself for tomorrow's global opportunities.

SUMMARY

Globalization of business requires professionals to function effectively in different cultures. They must learn to communicate with people from other countries in languages other than English. Communication in this context is very complex because of the intermingling of distinguishing cultural characteristics.

Effective communication in any environment is extremely important because of the fierce competition among investing companies. International communication takes on even greater significance, since much of the business expansion is now taking place overseas where labor costs are lower. From this standpoint, U.S. companies are at a disadvantage because of communication breakdowns. Foreign language skills are not required in the U.S. educational system. In contrast, most of the major countries outside the United States require extensive training in English as a second language.

To overcome language and other barriers, you must plan your communication process by analyzing each element and use a mix of communication techniques to achieve success. The elements to be analyzed include the why of the message, the what, the who, the how, and the type. The focus of the analysis is on the interpretation of the message. For some elements, the analysis for domestic and international readers may be the same; for others, the analysis may be very different, depending on the background and culture of the person receiving the message.

An understanding of the way other people think and what they value will promote effective communication. When communicating internationally, you can usually determine this by studying such variables as cultural history, language, religion, attitude toward time, human behavior, and style. This information along with an understanding of communication barriers—such as language misunderstanding, weak listening skills, cultural shock, ethnocentrism, insensitivity, and lack of openness—will help to avoid breakdowns in cross-cultural communication.

Another avenue for improving international communication is to identify common traits found in successful global firms. In a collaborative study, these traits have been identified as a high-energy level, a visible and strongly felt personality of culture, a commitment to basic values, and a specialized organization structure.

Other traits essential for effective international communication include perception, sensitivity, adaptability, flexibility, receptiveness, and awareness. To develop these traits, begin by learning to communicate in your own multinational environment.

END-OF-CHAPTER ACTIVITIES

DISCUSSION

1. What makes international communication complex?
2. Why is the market shifting to a foreign environment? Discuss current news items that impact on this issue.
3. On the basis of current news releases, discuss future trends in the foreign market. How will communication affect that market?
4. Why are communication barriers greater for Americans?
5. What assumptions, if any, can you make when communicating internationally?
6. What communication formats do people from other countries prefer? Why?
7. What gives a group identity?
8. What are some of the ways you can break down communication barriers in your own multinational environment?
9. What is meant by the statement that our "globe is shrinking"? Discuss some of the evidence.

ACTIVITIES

10. Assume the position of a foreign manager. Describe your feelings concerning English as the international language. Identify situations which produce both positive and negative reactions.
11. Interview a person in your community who is of a different nationality, race, or ethnic group. Determine common and unique cultural characteristics. Which American cultural traits does the individual most admire; which does she/he disapprove of?
12. Study Figures 3.5 and 3.6 and identify the characteristics that are indicative of a non-American culture. How well could you communicate if you were applying for admission to a university in Africa or China?
13. Before the next class period, observe those with whom you associ-

Figure 3.5

Oct. 14, 1985

Mrs. Vivian A. Dennison
Office of Admissions
Oakwood College
Huntsville, Alabama 35896

Dear Mrs. Dennison:
I thank you for your letter and all materials necessary, and now I send instructions that I have filled.

I will refund processing fee at the time of registration, because Chinese People's Currency cannot be changed into dollar in my country, and I have not any person pay the fee in U.S.A.

I have been studying English for already ten years. My command of English, both spoken and written, is above average. Now I am studying at Fu Dan University majoring in law and I gets higher scores on courses. I think I would be a promising student and you would be fully satisfied with me.
I wish I be offered a place at your college.

Yours sincerely
Hua Liu-Sha
457 An Yuan Road
Shanghai, The People's Republic of China.

ate—family/friends. What nonverbal elements can you identify that are uniquely American? Describe gestures and give meanings.

14. Before the next class period, observe people who are obviously of a different culture. What nonverbal elements can you identify that are uniquely non-American? Discuss.
15. Have class members who have traveled abroad present to the class some of the communication barriers that were the most frustrating.

Figure 3.6
Yapa College of Technology, Yapa, Lagos

Our Ref: SEC/V/70 2nd July

P.O. Box 135
Apapa
Lagos

Dear Sir/Madam,

ADMISSION FOR 1984/85 SESSION: INVITATION TO TEST/INTERVIEW

I refer to your application for admission to this College for a three-year part-time (evening) Certificate Course in Secretarial Studies for the 1984/85 Session beginning in September, 1984.

As the number of prima facie qualified candidates far exceeds the available places for the course, it has been found necessary to set an Entrance/Aptitude test and/or interview for all the qualified candidates with a view to selecting the best for the limited places.

I have pleasure therefore to invite you for a written test/interview in this College on Thursday, 2nd August, 1984 at 8.00 a.m. YOUR EXAMINATION NUMBER, which is SSC 464 should be written boldly on all your answer papers. On arrival at the College, you should report to the Director, School of Management and Business Studies who will direct you to the venue for the Test/Interview.

The College takes no responsibility for the receipt or nonreceipt of this letter which is being dispatched by post long enough for you to receive it before the date of the examination/interview.

You are required to bring along with you your original Certificates, Diplomas or Statement of Results as well as your pen, pencil, rubber, a mathematical set (where appropriate) and in case of Art Course, examples of your work.

Please note that sleeping accommodation and/or meals are not provided for candidates for the examination. Transport is not provided either.

Only successful candidates will be informed of the results.

Yours faithfully,

Director, School of
Management and Business Studies

CHAPTER 4

STRATEGY FOR COMMUNICATING

Learning Objectives

After studying this chapter, you will be able to:

- ☐ Define strategies for communicating.
- ☐ Understand how to identify a problem (the why) of the communication process.
- ☐ Determine how to identify objectives (the what) of the communication process.
- ☐ Assess the importance of the reader/audience (the who) of the communication process.
- ☐ Distinguish among several classifications of the reader/audience.
- ☐ Understand how order (the how) and its relevant parts contribute to effective communication.
- ☐ Differentiate the meanings of direct and indirect order and their relationship to the communication process.
- ☐ Determine the appropriate format or type of presentation for various communications.
- ☐ State specific characteristics of memos, letters, reports, oral presentations, and handwritten notes.
- ☐ Understand the conceptual relationship of the components which make up the strategies for communicating.

Strategy defined

Effective communication requires planning. A strategy helps you develop a workable plan to achieve a specific goal or objective. Simply stated, strategy is the art of devising or employing a plan toward a goal. In business a strategy determines "what entrepreneurial, competitive and functional area approaches and actions will be taken to put the organization into the desired position. A strategic plan is a . . . detailed road map of the direction and course the organization presently intends to follow in conducting its activities."[1] Just as you need a road map when you travel unfamiliar territory by car, you also need a strategy to communicate effectively.

Developing your strategy

The strategy approach to business communication implies several things. Before you start to create your message, you need to assess all the possibilities needed to achieve a specific objective. A strategy for communication is similar to outlining. A useful strategy should include some sort of framework for all the goals and options of a particular occasion for writing. You will be successful only to the extent that you make a valid assessment of all the variables involved.

You are the author of your strategy. Since others might evaluate and assess the variables or components differently, they would prepare their messages differently. The extent to which your decisions and choices are correct can be measured only by the extent to which your communication accomplishes your objective (s).

The basic components of a strategy for business communication include:

Strategy components

- ☐ The Problem.
- ☐ The Objective.
- ☐ The Reader/Audience.
- ☐ The Order.
- ☐ The Format.

These five components are discussed in detail in this chapter.

THE PROBLEM

Identifying the problem (the why)

The first component of your strategy should be to identify the problem by analyzing the setting or situation. All business communication emanates from a particular setting or background.

Some communications may require an evaluation of the *internal* strengths and weaknesses of the various functional areas of business—marketing, finance, accounting, and management. These factors help determine where the company is right now. Other communications may require an evaluation of such *external* factors as competition, customer attitudes, labor supply, or social, economic, and technological conditions. Before making decisions on where a company's future should be, managers must consider opportunities

[1] Arthur A. Thompson, Jr., and A. J. Strickland III, *Strategic Management: Concepts and Cases* (Plano, Tex.: Business Publications, 1987), p. 18.

and threats from the external environment. These are examples of the types of internal and external factors that make up the setting.

To identify the problem, then, you need to look at the work setting and assess the specific circumstances that require you to communicate. The problem generally centers on the lack of something. Identifying the problem helps you address the question "Why am I communicating?"

Study the following short case and from the situation identify the problem(s).

STOKELY ENTERPRISES, INC.

A new phone system was installed in Stokely Enterprises, Inc., on January 20, 19-, to provide a more efficient phone system and to reduce costs. The phone service was purchased from a reputable company that provides satisfactory service to other companies. Among the features of the new phone system are Call Forward, Call Waiting, Call Hold, and identification of calls by individual persons for end-of-month control. A memo, sent to all employees three months ago, explained the use of the new system. However, employees still feel frustrated and complain that the new phone system is difficult to use. Customers have complained that they have been unable to reach the correct person, that they have been transferred to the wrong persons, and that they have been disconnected frequently. In fact, some customers have even gone to competitors with their orders.

As the setting above indicates, the circumstances here have led to employee frustrations, customer complaints, and loss of customers with possible loss of income to the company. Both internal and external factors are involved. The initial problem is: *The employees do not know how to operate the new telephone system.* At this point, the answer to your first question "Why am I communicating?" is "Because the employees do not know how to operate the new telephone system."

Your first task in developing the strategy is to review the setting and identify the problem. (See Figure 4.1).

THE OBJECTIVE

Identifying the objective (the what)

The objective for communicating is the second component of the strategy. Objectives, or goals, provide direction and meaning. Andrews emphasizes that an objective helps us keep "moving in a deliberately chosen direction and prevents [our] . . . drifting in undesirable directions."[2] If you don't have a plan or objective, your communication will be confusing and disorganized.

---

[2] Kenneth R. Andrews, *The Concepts of Corporate Strategy* (Homewood, Ill.: Dow Jones-Irwin, 1987), p. 23.

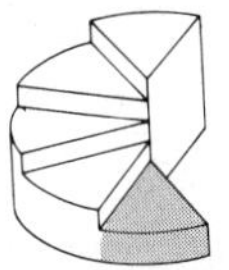

Figure 4.1
Strategy diagram:
The Problem

Problem
Internal
and external
factors

The Why

When you write or speak, first establish the general objective of your writing or your speech and then define the specific objectives or details which *must* be included in the message. By doing this, you answer the question "*What* am I communicating?"

General Objective

Developing the general objective

The general objective of your communication should indicate the overall reason for the communication. It may be to notify, to persuade, to inform, to teach, to obtain approval, to obtain information, etc. As you begin a communication, identify the general objective and make it a conscious theme of your message. Knowing your objective or purpose is critical to the success of your communication.

Effective business communicators usually include only one major objective for each piece of writing or oral presentation. Whenever there is more than one general objective, careful attention to order is needed so that the objectives are clearly identified for the reader. If the objectives aren't clearly identified, the results are:

- ☐ Scrambled messages.
- ☐ Long and involved explanations.
- ☐ Emphasis on one objective at the expense of the other objectives.
- ☐ Ineffective communication.
- ☐ Misinterpretation.

Specific Objectives

Specific objectives are the details you need to include in the communication. What is important is to list all of the essential details. Don't worry initially about the order. *How you say things and in what order you present them are not important at this point.*

If you are writing a policy statement concerning the correction of payroll

Developing the specific objectives (details of the communication)

check errors, you need to make sure that all specific details are included: "what to do," "how to," "when to," and "where to." For example:

What to do	Fill out form 234B, include social security number.
How to	Have supervisor's signature to verify hours worked.
When to	Make application within five days after you receive the check with the error.
Where to	Take to payroll office.

The absence of important details can result in:

- ☐ Additional or unnecessary work.
- ☐ Additional communication to clarify message.
- ☐ Unnecessary errors.

The objective component of the strategy can now be applied to the Stokely Enterprises, Inc. case.

General Objective. The objective of the communication is to resolve the problem you have identified: *Inform the employees about the new system and how to use it.*

Specific Objectives. The details you must include are:

How to handle incoming calls.
How to transfer calls.
How to place a call (local and long distance).
How to use special features of the system.
How to report problems.
How to make conference calls.

Now you should understand the first two components in developing your strategy for communicating—determining the Problem and defining the Objective. (See Figure 4.2).

THE READER/AUDIENCE

Assessing the reader/audience (the who)

Importance of knowing the reader

The third component in developing the strategy for communicating is the Reader, or Reader/Audience. The person who receives your communication is one of your primary concerns. The importance of the reader is emphasized in the following statements: "The first rule of effective writing is to help the reader. . . . Failure to do so will result in your losing money for your business and the opportunity to promote good will. When writing letters, reports, or memos, it is critical that you first determine specifically who the reader is and then decide how to meet that reader's need."[3] Selzer stresses

[3] Charles T. Brusaw, Gerald J. Alred, and Walter E. Oliu, *The Business Writer's Handbook* (New York: St. Martin's Press, 1987), p. 471.

Figure 4.2
Strategy diagram:
The Objective

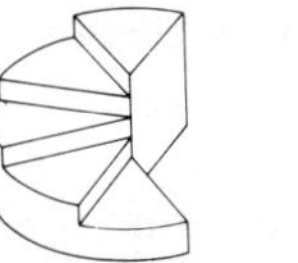
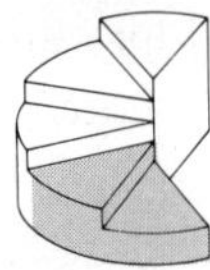

Problem	**Objective**	
	General	*Specific*
Internal and external factors	To persuade to inform, etc.	How to, when, where, what, etc.
The Why	**The What**	

that "a writer should be sensitive to audience needs since good writing nearly always engages its readers."[4]

Busy executives and professionals appreciate clear, unambiguous writing; they dislike letters and reports that require much time to decipher. As a writer, you should have some regard for the reader's time. In oral communication, "a good audience analysis will yield time savings for the participants. When you know your audience, you tailor the presentation for that audience. This vital element results in a perception of respect on the part of the audience and significantly contributes to a successful communication."[5]

Written and oral communications are prepared for someone else—not for yourself. For most communications, you may assume that the reader is intelligent but uninformed. Therefore, you need to understand, as much as possible, the characteristics of the audience and their reactions to the communication. By doing such analysis, you answer the question "*With whom* am I communicating?"

Characteristics

Readers can be classified in a number of ways. It is probably impossible to develop a generic system that would include every conceivable individual who may receive your communication. No one system covers everyone. However, a general understanding of some of the various types of classifications will help you.

Classifications of readers

Initially, you should establish whether your reader is inside or outside the organization. Even inside an organization, according to William Paxson, the

[4] Jack Selzer, "Some Differences between Journalism and Business Writing," *ABCA Bulletin* 46, no. 3 (September 1983), pp. 8-9.

[5] Thomas Leech, *How to Prepare, Stage, and Deliver Winning Presentations* (New York: American Management Association, AMACOM, 1982), p. 47.

reader can be divided into three general classes—public, expert/layperson, or decision maker.[6]

General public

General Public. When you write to the general public, you need to realize that reading levels have steadily declined in the past 10 years. Some people may have reading problems; others may not be native English users. Publishers who provide magazines for the general public try for reading levels near the seventh grade.

Expert/layperson

Expert/Layperson. As an expert, you usually make a livelihood from expertise in a selected field. When you read outside that field, you become a layperson. If you communicate with an individual in your field, you are one expert writing to another expert. In this case, you use the specialized vocabulary that each of you understands. If you are writing a message that will be read by people outside your field, then you are writing for lay readers. You will need to use a common vocabulary or provide definitions of special terms. For example, if you used the acronym BDOS, you need to help your reader with the meaning. The layperson might not know BDOS is a term from computer science which means "basic disk operating system."

Decision maker

Decision Maker. Perhaps your most important reader will be a decision maker—another manager. Decision makers want clear and concise messages that save them time. You must select and arrange the ideas in your communication to make them easy to read and understand.

Primary/secondary audience

In addition to Paxson's classification of general public, expert/layperson, or decision maker, you may also classify your audience as either *primary* or *secondary*. Each audience may consist of one or many persons. A primary audience includes those who make decisions or take specific actions on the basis of content. A secondary audience consists of those who are affected by the decisions or actions contained in a communication. Consider this example:

The Board of Directors of Phillips Petroleum has voted to decrease personnel by 10 percent in the Information Center at corporate headquarters in Bartlesville, Oklahoma. A written report with supporting rationale, prepared by the Board, will be sent to the president of the company, the vice president of personnel, and the manager of the Information Center.

In this brief scenario, the primary audience is composed of the:

- □ President of Phillips Petroleum.
- □ Vice president of personnel, Phillips Petroleum.
- □ Manager of Information Center, Phillips Petroleum.

---

[6] William C. Paxson, *The Business Writing Handbook* (New York: Bantam Books, 1981), pp. 3-4.

LEGAL / ETHICAL ISSUE

Corporations, states, and local governments are tightening ethics codes and accountability laws as a result of so many corruption scandals. Businesses and governmental agencies are now requiring that a code of ethics become a part of their overall mission statement or strategic plan. The importance of such concepts as honesty, integrity, fairness in all dealings, duty, and responsibility are becoming standard in codes of ethics with an emphasis on stressing social responsibility. Consider these examples:

- ☐ A major city requires its higher paid city employees to disclose the amount and source of outside income.
- ☐ A particular state prohibits elected officials and employees from accepting compensation for services that result in a contract.

Some say that one cannot survive in business or government if one is ethical, and others say that there is "no such thing as business ethics." If one means by business ethics honesty, fair play, and law-abidingness, is there an obligation to practice these principles?

Should businesses impose, as a part of their written strategic plan, a standard of conduct on their employees? If so, how can these standards be imposed? Are employees legally bound to abide by a company's code of ethics?

The secondary audience in this situation includes those employees who work in the corporate headquarters. Ten percent of the personnel will lose their jobs. Perhaps other divisions that use their services may also be affected.

An analysis of both primary and secondary audiences should be done before you complete your written or oral communication. Do not neglect this important factor when planning your communication. You may have several primary and secondary audiences for your communication. Consider this example:

You have written a proposal of possible funding by the U. S. Office of Education (USOE) for a $50,000 grant to complete a study of "The Impact of Automation on the Report Writing Ability of 100 College Freshmen."

The primary audience in this example includes the person(s) within USOE responsible for making decisions about funding such a proposal. In all probability, the several people who will review the proposal to determine its merit and future value will become part of the secondary audience. These reviewers will make comments to officials at USOE, after which you will be notified of the decision to fund or not to fund the project. You, as the writer of the proposal, must consider both the primary and secondary audiences. Since you probably know neither the primary audience (USOE officials) nor the

Figure 4.3
Example of communication network

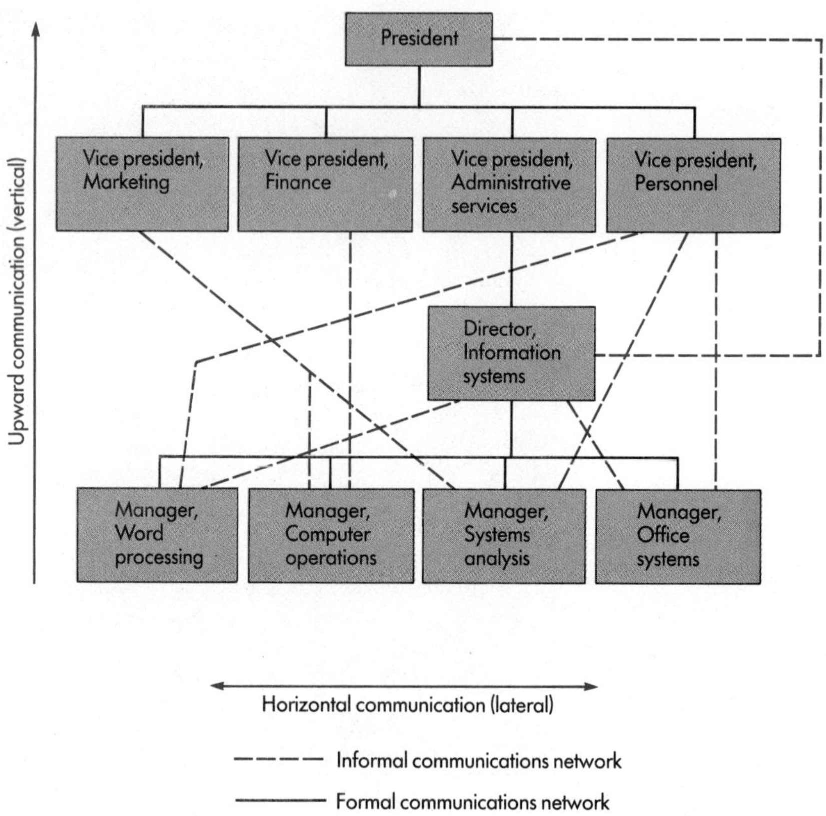

secondary audience (external reviewers), your writing approach will be somewhat formal. The relationship that the communicator has with the readers always has a bearing on the content of the message.

Organizational chart

Still another view of the reader may be gained by studying a basic organizational chart for a company (Figure 4.3). Review the structure and the respective departments. The solid lines show the formal communication channels. The individuals who hold administrative positions within such a company may at times be classified as either primary or secondary readers. The situation for a communication determines which is appropriate.

Vertical communication

Communication may be upward or downward (vertical) within a firm. The president communicates downward to the vice presidents, the director or information systems, or the managers. Likewise, the vice presidents, the director of information systems, or the managers communicate upward to the president. Each level of principals within the company communicates upward or downward to the next level.

Horizontal communication

Principals within an organization may also communicate horizontally within the firm. The vice president for marketing, who works and talks daily with the vice president for finance and is indeed on the same administrative level, would probably use a slightly different style and tone when writing to this colleague than when writing to subordinates.

Informal communication

The dotted lines in Figure 4.3 show how communications occur informally within the firm. This is especially true for oral communications. Informal networks (sometimes referred to as the grapevine) are powerful mechanisms within any organization. Informal groups emerge naturally and can have a major influence on the decisions made by managers. Informal groups may form among principals (or administrative personnel) within a company; informal groups may also be made up of administrative and nonadministrative personnel.

Assessing the audience

The more you know about your reader before you communicate, the better. You can then adapt your communication to that person or that group. Job and employment information are useful. What job does the reader hold? Is this job a supervisory position? What level? How long has the reader been in the position?

Personal information about the reader can also help. Does the person have an outgoing personality? Is the person people-oriented? Difficult to get along with? Detail-minded? A sports enthusiast? Does the person know you well? What formal education does the person have?

In addition, it is important to know how much the reader knows about your subject. Does the person have preformed opinions about your subject? All these questions reinforce the three classes of reader/audience—public, expert/layperson, or decision maker.

Reaction

Anticipation of reader reaction

You should anticipate how your reader will react to your message. Will the reaction be a positive feeling (pleasure, enjoyment)? A negative response (displeasure, disgust)? Or perhaps a neutral one (disinterest)? If you anticipate the reader's reaction accurately, you can write or speak to lessen the unpleasant reaction or to emphasize the pleasant.

You are probably wondering how you can know or find out all these detailed things about an audience. You will probably write to some of your readers only once, or you may speak to them in a group and not even know their names. Other important details vie for your attention, and you cannot afford the luxury of investigating and developing individual data on everyone with whom you communicate.

It is important to reemphasize that the better you know someone the easier it is to write effectively to her/him. If you do not know the characteristics of your reader, you are the most logical source for obtaining the information needed. You react to a communication the same way other people do—negatively or positively. You probably like recognition and agreement just as others do. You have feelings and reactions similar to those that your readers will have. So you should be able to anticipate some of your reader's characteristics simply because you are quite similar. Put yourself in the reader's role and consider how you would react to the content of the message.

The Reader component of the strategy can now be applied to the Stokely Enterprises, Inc. case. (See Figure 4.4.)

Figure 4.4
Strategy diagram:
The Reader/Audience

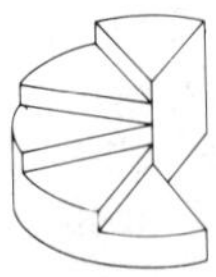

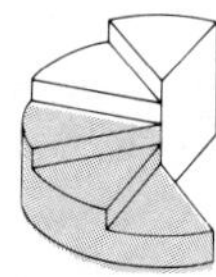

Problem	**Objective**		**Reader / Audience**	
Internal and external factors	*General*	*Specific*	*Characteristics*	*Reaction*
	To persuade to inform, etc.	How to, when, where, what, etc.	Inside / outside primary / secondary expert / layperson etc.	Pleasure Disgust Neutral
The Why	**The What**		**The Who**	

Reader Characteristics

Employees inside the organization.

Employees who understand the system very well (experts).

Employees who are fairly familiar with the system.

Employees who are in management positions (decision makers).

Employees who are in nonmanagement positions.

Audiences who are both primary (people in the company who will use the telephone) and secondary (visitors).

Reaction

1. Some will be pleased.
2. Some will resist the new technology.
3. Some will be neutral about the change.

Now you should understand the first three components in developing your strategy for communicating—the Problem, the Objective, and the Reader.

THE ORDER

Order defined (the how)

Once the Problem, Objective, and Reader have been identified, you are ready for the fourth component in developing your strategy—the *Order* of presentation. Order is simply the arrangement of selected data and information to achieve an identified purpose. Business executives reported on the importance of order in a survey of business communication.[7] When asked what communication characteristics they considered most important, the executives ranked clarity, conciseness, and organization as the top three. They also

[7] Donna Stine and Donald Skarzenski, "Priorities for the Business Communication Classroom: A Survey of Business and Academe," *Journal of Business Communication* 16, no. 3 (Spring 1979), pp. 16-26.

listed the shortcomings (related to order) they saw in communications crossing their desks: wordiness, awkward sentence structure, lack of precision, illogical organization, poor word choice, lack of coherence, faulty paragraph structure, and lack of unity. By striving to improve order, clarity, and precision, you can improve the overall effectiveness of your message.

The arrangement of data and information can be approached at three levels: the overall message, the paragraph, and the sentence. By considering arrangement specifically, you answer the question "*How* will I communicate?" When planning the order of your communication, you need to keep in mind the other components of the strategy.

Overall Message

Types of arrangement

When deciding on the order of the overall message, you can select from two basic arrangements—*direct* and *indirect.* Basically, the direct arrangement presents the most important idea(s) at the beginning of the message. This arrangement helps the reader immediately recognize the objective of the message. In an example of *direct* order (Figure 4.5) notice that the objective of the communication can easily be identified in the first sentence of the letter.

Direct arrangement

If you choose to use the *indirect* arrangement for your message, the objective or intent will be placed at or near the end. The revised version of the letter to Maxim is shown in Figure 4.6—this time in indirect order.

Indirect arrangement

When you communicate, assess the situation and carefully select either the direct or indirect arrangement to achieve your desired objective. The decision to use the direct or indirect arrangement is based on the type of message, objective, and previous relationship with the reader rather than on some "recipe" approach. According to most recipes, you should "use the direct arrangement for all positive messages and an indirect arrangement for negative messages." Depending on the circumstances, however, sometimes it may be best to place the objective at the beginning of a negative message. Sometimes the reader expects to receive some negative responses. When you sent out a dozen applications to various schools, didn't you expect some negative responses? So will most readers. Consider the job applicant who sends out many letters of application to a broad range of companies. Wouldn't it be reasonable to expect that a few will say no? As an effective communicator, you need to assess the situation and select the appropriate arrangement to achieve your desired objective.

Determining appropriate arrangement

Paragraphs

Developing paragraphs

A paragraph is composed of several sentences that relate to a similar topic. Just as you can order the overall message, you can also arrange the sentences within a paragraph to emphasize a particular point or direct the reader's attention to an especially important fact. Actually, there are few hard-and-fast rules which govern paragraphing. The main point to remember is that an

Figure 4.5
Direct order

an association for management success

333 Perth Way
Colorado Springs, CO 80901

February 1, 19__

Mr. Harry P. Maxim
First Security Bank
887 Ninth Street
Colorado Springs, CO 80900

Dear Mr. Maxim:

Objective

Would you present a 20-minute talk on "Time Management" at the April 14, 19__ meeting of the Administrative Management Society? Since your article about your time management program appeared in the October issue of the MANAGEMENT JOURNAL, several people in our society have suggested that we invite you to speak to us about your program. Perhaps a brief question-and-answer session could follow.

The meeting will be held at the Alexander's Restaurant, 605 State Street, on April 14. Please join us at 6:30 p.m. for dinner; please extend an invitation to your wife to be our guest also. After dinner, you will present your talk to approximately 40 men and women from this area who want to improve their managerial skills.

So that advance publicity can be given, please let me know by February 20 whether you can accept. Your comments about your experience in directing a time management program will certainly be of great benefit to our members. We are looking forward to your presentation.

Sincerely,

Kermit Evans
Program Chairman

ms

effective paragraph has a controlling idea, or topic sentence. The sentences we combine to make up a paragraph must be related.

A paragraph should be *coherent* (with the organization following a definite plan); it should be *developed* (with its sentences adequately explaining or qualifying the main point); and it should be *unified* (with all its sentences relevant to the main point).[8]

[8] John C. Hodges and Mary E. Whitten, *Harbrace College Handbook,* 10th ed. (New York: Harcourt Brace Jovanovich, 1986), p. 346.

Figure 4.6
Indirect order

ams *an association for management success*

333 Perth Way
Colorado Springs, CO 80901

February 1, 19__

Mr. Harry P. Maxim
First Security Bank
887 Ninth Street
Colorado Springs, CO 80900

Dear Mr. Maxim:

Your article in the October issue of the MANAGEMENT JOURNAL about your time management program is excellent! Many members of the Administrative Management Society, a group of men and women interested in improving their skills, have suggested you as a speaker for one of our monthly meetings.

Our regular monthly meetings are held the second Thursday of each month at Alexander's Restaurant, 605 State Street. Dinner is at 6:30 p.m.; and the program starts at 7:30 p.m. About 40 men and women from this area attend the meetings.

Objective

Would you present a 20-minute talk on "Time Management" at our April 14 meeting? A brief question-and-answer session could follow. So that advance publicity can be given, please let me know whether you can accept our invitation by February 20, 19__. Comments about your experience in time management will be timely and of great benefit to our members. Please join us for dinner as our guest at Alexander's Restaurant; please extend an invitation to your wife to be our guest also.

Sincerely,

Kermit Evans
Program Chairman

ms

The following paragraph about the human element in office automation is written twice to show how placement of the topic sentences (the underscored portions) subtly changes the order of ideas:

Topic sentence

There must be regard for the human element in office automation. It is not simply a matter of optimizing machine operating hours or minimizing processing time. The human equation must be given prime consideration. Vital are the people's belief in, training for, and adaptation to the automated system.[9]

[9] John J. Stallard, E. Ray Smith, and Donald Reese, *The Electronic Office: A Guide for Managers* (Homewood, Ill.: Dow Jones-Irwin, 1983), p. 142.

Topic sentence

Office automation is not simply a matter of optimizing operating hours or minimizing processing time. The people's belief in, training for, and adaptation to the automated system need to be recognized. It is vital that the human element be given consideration in office automation.

Sentences

Developing sentences

The sentence is a basic unit of any message. The words within the sentence can also be ordered to achieve emphasis and direct the reader's attention to specific details. Notice in the following sentences how the *secretarial function* is emphasized because of its placement at the beginning of the sentence:

The secretarial function will also become more specialized.

Now, by placing the words at the end of the sentence, you can change the emphasis:

Specialization will become a part of the secretarial function.

The word *specialization* is now emphasized more than the *secretarial function.*

Your sentence construction should contribute to ease of reading and clarity. It is a constant challenge to maintain relatively short sentences and yet avoid monotony in sentence structure.

To create an effective message, vary your sentence structure. Generally, use more simple sentences than compound and complex ones. Use compound sentences when you want related ideas expressed as a unit and complex sentences to show a relationship.

In addition to ordering the overall message, paragraphs, and sentences, you need to sequence, or order, those items identified as specific objectives in the strategy. Your ideas can be arranged according to various standard patterns, such as:

Determining sequence

Least important to most important.
Most important to least important.
Familiar to unfamiliar.
Unfamiliar to familiar.
Time sequence (chronological).
Cause and effect.
Simple to complex.

The *Order* component of the strategy can now be applied to the Stokely Enterprises, Inc. case (see Figure 4.7):

Order

1. *Overall Message:* Indirect (to temper the negative impact of the technological change and provide a mind set to encourage the reader to learn the new instructions).

Figure 4.7 Strategy diagram: The Order

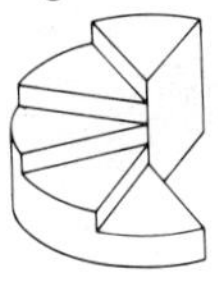 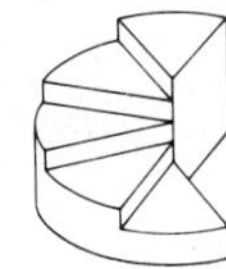 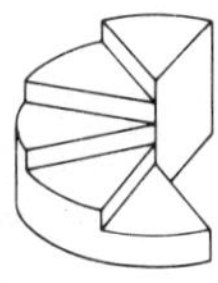 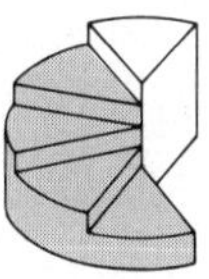

Problem	**Objective**		**Reader/Audience**		**Order**
	General	*Specific*	*Characteristics*	*Reaction*	
Internal and external factors	To persuade to inform, etc.	How to, when, where, what, etc.	Inside/outside primary/secondary expert/layperson etc.	Pleasure Disgust Neutral	Arrangement of selected information
The Why	**The What**		**The Who**		**The How**

2. *Paragraph and Sentences:* Techniques for creating effective sentences and paragraphs are presented in Chapter 5.
3. *Specific Objectives:* These items *may be* ordered from "most often used" to "least often used." The decision to order them in this way makes good sense because, if the things done most often are done correctly, most of the problems will be eliminated.

Now you should understand the first four components in developing your strategy for communicating—the Problem, the Objective, the Reader Audience, and the Order.

THE FORMAT

Format defined (the type)

Format, the fifth component of the strategy, refers to the manner or type of presentation you select as appropriate for your communication. There are several choices you can consider—memo, letter, report, oral presentation, or handwritten notes. Determining an appropriate format helps you answer the question "What *type* of communication will I use?"

Memos (memorandums)

Characteristics of memos

Memos are probably the preferred way of presenting written material in business, especially within the company. Memos are usually no more than two pages, and the message is written in an informal style. The memo contains two different parts—heading and message. The heading of a memo contains:

The date.

The name of the person to whom the correspondence is going.

The name of the person who wrote it.

The topic of the communication.

Figures 4.8 and 4.9 show two different arrangements of the heading material. You may be able to choose your own format in some organizations, but more

Figure 4.8
Memo

January 5, 19—

TO: Gilbert Word, Marketing Director

FROM: Joseph Miller, Personnel Coordinator

SUBJECT: Applicants for Marketing Position

Attached are the résumés of five applicants who have applied for your department position:

Jessica Elbers
Ronald Hogan
Kevin Kiljoy
Elizabeth Matthews
Amanda Rogers

Please evaluate these and then recommend the people you want to interview. As soon as I have the names, I will make arrangements for the interviews.

Figure 4.9
Memo with alternate form

TO:	Gilbert Word Marketing Director	DATE:	January 5, 19—
FROM:	Joseph Miller Personnel Coordinator	SUBJECT:	Applicants for Marketing Position

Attached are the résumés of five applicants who have applied for your department position.

Jessica Elbers
Ronald Hogan
Kevin Kiljoy
Elizabeth Matthews
Amanda Rogers

Please evaluate these and then recommend the people you want to interview. As soon as I have the names, I will make arrangements for the interviews.

than likely the company you join will already have an established format for memos. Many companies create their own printed memo forms, making it very easy to identify sender, receiver, and topic.

Letters

Letters defined

Letters are generally used to correspond with people outside the company—clients, customers, community officials, etc. A letter differs from a memo primarily in terms of its layout; the writing style can be formal or informal.

Figure 4.10
Letter—Block style

Heading	**ROCKWELL MANUFACTURING, INC.** 4200 WEST CLAIBORNE DRIVE KNOXVILLE, TN 37906 PHONE (615) 292-6610
Date	October 17, 19___
Inside address	Mr. Gene Glass, Manager ABC Consultants 320 Cedar Bluff Road Knoxville, TN 37923
Salutation	Dear Gene
Body	Thanks for a very informative one-day seminar on Techno-Stress for our employees. Both managerial and support staff commented on the superb job you did with the seminar. Our managerial staff is now incorporating some of your ideas into the corporate strategy for handling Techno-Stress within the company. Perhaps you will be available later for some consulting activities. Gene, thanks for a job well done! I shall be in touch with you later.
Close	Cordially
Signature Title	E. Ray Smith Seminar Coordinator
Reference initials	dwc

Letter parts

Traditionally, a letter includes the date, inside address, salutation, body, close, signature line, and reference initials. Today, letters can be written without the salutation and the complimentary close.

Letter styles

When you write letters, you may choose from three popular arrangements or styles, shown in Figures 4.10 to 4.12. The block and modified styles are popular, but the simplified style is also frequently used.

In block style, all parts of the letter start at the left margin. As shown in Figure 4.10, the date line, inside address, salutation, all paragraphs, closing signature line, and reference initials all begin at the left margin and give a blocked appearance. The differences between the block and modified styles

Figure 4.11
Letter—Modified style

Heading	**The Georgia Educational Center** 802 Hathaway Lane, Athens, GA 30604, Phone 404-546-0051
Date	October 17, 19__
Inside address	Mrs. Nathan Goodfellow Vendor and Associates 43794 Oklahoma Avenue Charlotte, NC 28200
Salutation	Dear Mrs. Goodfellow:
Body	By answering some questions, you will help us decide whether to install a staff lounge on the sixth floor of our building. We want our 100 employees to use the lounge on a staggered basis for morning and afternoon breaks. 1. What type appliances would you recommend for coffee and hot water? Cost of each? 2. What type of refrigerator would you recommend? Cost? 3. What other items should be included? Is our space adequate? 4. What are your suggestions for operating the lounge? 5. Could you install the lounge by May 1? Since the Executive Board will decide on this project at its April 2 meeting, I would appreciate receiving your reply by March 25.
Close	Sincerely,
Signature Title	George A. Huber Facilities Coordinator
Reference initials	rt

are in the placement of the date line, the close, and signature lines. Notice in the modified style of Figure 4.11 that the date line, close, and signature lines all begin in the center of the page. In addition, the paragraphs may or may not be indented.

When including these two parts, however, you have the option of choosing between open or mixed punctuation. Open punctuation differs from mixed by omitting the colon in the salutation and the comma in the complimentary close. See Figure 4.10.

For some time, many writers have dropped the salutation and closing lines because they have little purpose beyond satisfying a tradition. Instead of the

Figure 4.12
Letter—Simplified style

WGS

WGS Inc. 37 East 38th Street
New York, New York 10019
(212) 755-2396

Date	May 3, 19__
Inside address	Mr. or Ms. W. T. Bailey 1701 White Avenue Waco, TX 76700
Subject line	SUBJECT: Career in Television
Body	Enclosed are an application, a pamphlet entitled "Television Career Opportunties," and a pre-addressed envelope as you requested in your April 26 letter. If you are interested in a career in TV, complete and return the enclosed application. As soon as your application has been reviewed, you will get a call from Marilyn N. Morrison, our agent. Thanks for your interest.
Signature Title	Larry A. Estep Personnel Director
Reference Initials	rn
Enclosure	Enclosures: Application Pamphlet - "Television Career Opportunities" Envelope

salutation, a subject line is substituted. The subject line helps the reader quickly identify the objective of the letter. The simplified style shown in Figure 4.12 is a block arrangement in which the salutation and close have been eliminated. Note also the courtesy title Mr. or Ms., which may be omitted if desired, since the sex of the reader is not known. Note also the listing of enclosures.

Figure 4.13 presents a common style for a personal letter with the use of personal stationery. Note that the return address is at the bottom.

Deciding on a letter style is frequently a matter of personal choice; however, a preferred style may be dictated by company policy. All of the

Figure 4.13
Letter—Personal stationery

Alex Stovall

Date

April 8, 19___

Inside address

Mr. Carl Campbell
Director of Sales
Jockey International, Inc.
Kenosha, WI 53410

Salutation

Dear Mr. Campbell:

Body

One year ago while visiting Denver, I purchased six pairs of your Slim Guy Briefs in a print design. I have looked for these print design briefs in my area but have not found them. All I can find are plain colors. Do you still make the Slim Guy Briefs in the print design? If so, how can I get them? If not, would you consider making them again?

I have been a Jockey user for over 25 years and like the innovative styling and designs you use. I shall look forward to your reply.

Close

Sincerely,

Signature

Alex Stovall

Return address

111 State Street
Louisville, KY 40200

styles above are used in business today. See Appendix B for other options in letter styles.

Reports

Report defined

Although reports are often presented in memo or letter form, they can be prepared in the format of a formal report. The techniques for writing reports and explanations of the various parts of formal and informal reports are discussed in Chapters 11 through 17. If you select a report format in your strategy, specific stylistic decisions are influenced by your objective and the characteristics of your reader.

Characteristics of reports

A report is a presentation of facts or data to a specific audience for a particular purpose. Generally, reports inform the reader about the subject, procedures, and findings and conclusions of investigations or research. Therefore, the style of writing is more formal. Facts are emphasized. Visuals in the form of tables, graphs, or pictures are typically used to present the findings of the report. The "meat" of the report is frequently presented in condensed form, sometimes called an *executive summary,* to a person or group of people for decision making. The findings from the study, then, are gathered to solve some problem. Given the supporting data, an executive or management group can decide on a course of action on the basis of hard evidence rather then guesswork.

Oral Presentation

Planning an oral format

The techniques for organizing and making oral presentations in business are discussed in Chapter 20. As you plan your strategy, you may consider it best to present your communication orally rather than in writing. If you need immediate feedback and personal interaction to accomplish your objective(s), you will select the oral method of communication. For a group presentation, you need to use visual aids to present a clear picture to your audience, particularly to present data.

You should also decide on the type of oral presentation you think would meet your audiences' needs. Will your group be large or small? How formal will your presentation be? What time constraints do you have?

Handwritten Notes

Planning the handwritten format

Often it is appropriate and acceptable to reply to a request or inquiry by simply jotting your response on the original letter or memo and returning it to the original author. You should make a copy of this original letter with your handwritten reply if you want a file copy. This method of communicating is becoming more common in business. It reinforces the philosophy that business communication should facilitate and assist employees in doing their job efficiently and effectively. Figure 4.14 is an example of a handwritten response.

The Format, which is the last component of the strategy, can now be applied to the Stokely Enterprises, Inc. case. (See Figure 4.15.)

Format. The memo format was chosen because:

1. The reader needs the details for immediate and repeated reference.
2. The memo was selected since the reader is within the organization and the information is brief (two pages or less). Because of the large number of employees and their need for repeated reference to the instructions, an oral presentation did not seem appropriate as an effective means of communicating the instructions.

Figure 4.14
Handwritten note reply

DATE: May 10, 19__
TO: Walter Henderson
FROM: Albert G. Foner
SUBJECT: Request for approval to purchase an executive desk, Administrative Division, Nyack

Re: Requisition 82093466; copy attached

Administration Division, Nyack, requests the purchase as specified in the attached requisition form.

May we have approval to proceed with the purchase?

AGF:WAG

Enclosure: Requisition from Administrative Division

cc: Jerry Maxwell

OK to purchase—
I have signed requisition
W Henderson

Another point you may want to consider when deciding on the format is that there may be times when a combination written/oral communication is desirable. Cost of the format used should be assessed. The amount of resources devoted to the action should be proportional to the problem—a $200 report to address a $50 problem is a waste.

A REVIEW—THE STRATEGY

Reviewing the strategy

As you plan your business communication, study the following diagram which summarizes all of the components you should consider in developing a strategy that will help you communicate effectively.

Figure 4.15 Strategy diagram: The Format

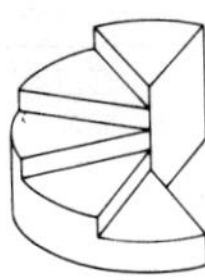
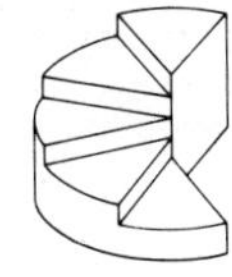
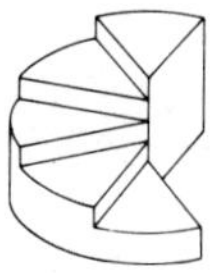

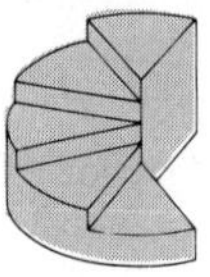

Problem	**Objective**		**Reader/Audience**		**Order**	**Format**
	General	*Specific*	*Characteristics*	*Reaction*		
Internal and external factors	To persuade to inform, etc.	How to, when, where, what, etc.	Inside/outside primary/secondary expert/layperson etc.	Pleasure Disgust Neutral	Arrangement of selected information	Memo, Letter, Report, Oral, Handwritten note
The Why	**The What**		**The Who**		**The How**	**The Type**

The strategy discussed in this chapter provides you with a framework for planning your communication. Remember, the strategy is a means for helping you develop the major components of your communication. The strategy is not intended, however, to be a rigid plan for a written document or an oral presentation.

Whenever you write or speak, you must assess the situation, the objective(s), and the audience. Knowing in advance the content and order for your message will help you draft your communication; style, tone, and format become more important at the postdrafting stage. Since writing or composing is most often a recursive process, your strategy for communicating should remain flexible. If you need to tinker with organization during revisions or consider changes in content during the predrafting or even polishing stages, you must be free to do so.

The form shown in Figure 4.16 may be used when planning your written and oral communication. The parts of the form serve as an aid to ***outlining*** your communication rather than using the standard outline format. The form provides space for detailing the Problem, the general and specific Objectives, the Reader/Audience, the Order, and the Format. You may simply highlight the major points for each component of the strategy ranging from one-word statements to short phrases or sentences. The form will assist your seeing the whole picture of your planned communication; and the outline synopsis will increase your development of effective oral and written communication.

SUMMARY

A strategy is your plan to achieve a specific goal or objective; preparing your strategy for a communication requires both mental and preceptive abilities. Before creating a message, you should identify all needs, components, and options. Each person will evaluate these variables differently; therefore, each communication will reflect the writer's perceptions.

The basic components of a strategy for communicating include the *Problem, Objectives, Reader/Audience, Order,* and *Format.* Since all business

Figure 4.16
Communication strategy form

Problem
Objective General: Specific:
Reader/Audience Characteristics: Reaction:
Order Overall Message: Specific Objectives:
Format

communications emanate from a particular setting, look at the internal and external factors in the work setting to identify the problem.

The Problem component addresses the question "*Why* am I communicating?" From the business setting, assess the specific situations that require you to communicate.

The Objective component addresses the question "*What* am I communicating?" It provides direction and meaning to accomplishment. The general objective indicates the overall reason for communicating—to inform, to notify, to teach, to obtain information, etc.—while specific objectives provide the details that must be included. The specific details include: "what to do," "how to," "when to," and "where to." Not identifying the general and specific objectives can lead to ineffective communication.

The Reader/Audience component addresses the question "To *whom* am I communicating?" Recognizing the characteristics and possible reactions of the reader/audience aids in tailoring the message to achieve your objectives. Written and oral communications are prepared for someone else—not for yourself.

The Order component addresses the question "*How* will I communicate?" For the overall message, you can select from two basic arrangements—direct and indirect. The direct arrangement presents the most important idea at the beginning of the message; the indirect, at or near the end. Specific objectives are also sequenced at this stage. The actual message consists of carefully selecting words and arranging them in grammatically correct sentences. Sentences about one topic are sequenced to form a paragraph.

The Format component addresses the question "*What* type of communication will I use?" Choices include memo, letter, oral presentation, handwritten note, etc. Each carries its own criteria for structure.

END-OF-CHAPTER ACTIVITIES

DISCUSSION

1. What is meant by a strategy as a means of communication?
2. What is involved in identifying the problem, the first component of the strategy for communicating?
3. How do you distinguish between the general objective of a communication and the specific objectives?
4. How does one go about assessing the reader/audience?
5. Describe the three classes of reader/audience as they relate to business communication—general public, expert/layperson, decision maker.
6. Distinguish between a primary and secondary audience.
7. Describe what is involved in the fourth component of the strategy for communicating—order.
8. Define format as it relates to business communication.
9. What are the characteristics of each of these types of letters—block style, modified block style, and simplified style.
10. You have been asked to write a letter to a customer who is three months behind in account payments. As you develop your strategy for your message, what details might be included in your specific objectives?

ACTIVITIES

11. Rewrite the following sentences so that you reorder the words to change the emphasis.
    a. The production schedule needs to include a consideration of projected holidays and employee turnover.
    b. The two companies make things and then distribute them to local farmers.
    c. The Finance Department makes sure that operating funds are available.
    d. Competitive information is usually provided by the sales force.
    e. Management has chosen Anderson City as the location for our new plant.
    f. Many techniques are available to provide the manager with the information needed to make decisions.
12. Write a paragraph for each of the following topic sentences. Place the emphasis of the topic at the beginning of the paragraphs. Then, rewrite the paragraphs to put the emphasis at the end of the paragraph.
    a. Sales during the past quarter have dropped 10 percent.
    b. Automation has increased the effectiveness of the office staff.
    c. Increased productivity should not be achieved at the expense of quality control.

d. New employee profiles need to be established soon if we are to get funds for a training program.

13. You are the manager of the shoe department in a large retail outlet. You have 15 salespersons in your department, and there are 10 other department managers in the store. You suspect that shoplifting is the cause of your increased inventory losses. You are required to notify the Security Office immediately in writing. Analyze this situation, and prepare the Reader/Audience component of your strategy.
14. Mark Charleston is 24 years old and a systems analyst with Kennington Insurance Company. He recently completed a study of the information network and work flow at Kennington's office in Ririe, Kansas. The office has always been late in submitting its reports to the main office in Chicago. Customers enjoy the personal attention they receive from the agents and staff at Ririe; but these same customers complain about delays in receiving policies and correspondence from the main office. These delays are not the fault of the main office; rather, they seem to stem from the outdated office procedures at the Ririe office. Most of the employees at Ririe have worked for the company for at least 15 years. They consider each other "family." Mark had a difficult time collecting the data he needed to complete his study because the other employees seemed to resent his expertise and enthusiasm for his work. Imagine that you are Mark and need to advise the Ririe personnel, as well as the appropriate personnel at the main office in Chicago, of the results of your study. Using the strategy approach discussed in this chapter, plan your communication. Use the form shown in Figure 4.16 to plan your strategy for communicating.
15. Using the strategy for communicating, analyze each of the letters shown in Figures 4.17 through 4.21.
    a. What are the strengths of each of the letters?
    b. What are the weaknesses of each of the letters?
    c. Do you believe that the authors of each of the letters used a strategy for communicating? If not, how could the strategy serve as a means for improving the communications?

Figure 4.17

Lynn Sheeley Co.
EST 1908

Allen ORGANS

Steinway - Sohmer - Everett - Currier-Kincaid PIANOS

February 16, 19__

John J. Stallard
U.T., P.O. Box 8412
Knoxville, TN 37916

Dear Mr. Stallard:

May I extend to you, a customer of Lynn Sheeley Company, my personal "Thank You" for your confidence, loyalty, good will and patronage. Without your faithful support our 72 years would not have been a success.

We keep the interest of our customers foremost in mind and maintaining their friendship is very important to us. We pledge to continue to measure up to the high standards that the Lynn Sheeley Company has set for the past 72 years.

In 19__ our sales surpassed previous years and our store continues to grow. This we attribute to you and your help. We know that satisfied customers are happy people who become our best salesmen. I know of no products other than our Steinway, Sohmer, Everett, Kincaid and Currier pianos and our Allen organs that maintain such tremendous stability, long life, and beautiful tone. Our famous brand names are endowed with quality, built-in dependability, the finest engineering and authentic designing.

We see that trained service personnel are efficient, competent and thorough. Their skills assure our customers a life-time of enjoyment from the new or used piano or organ they purchased from Lynn Sheeley Company.

I consider it a pleasure and privilege to have you in our large family of customers. Lynn Sheeley Company will be honored to serve your future musical needs.

Sincerely,

Lynn Sheeley, Jr.

LSJr:dhr
Enclosure: Paid Contract

Phone 523-6104 – 2358 Magnolia Avenue – Knoxville, Tennessee 37917

Figure 4.18

Harrington Insurance Agency

603 NORTH BROADWAY P. O. BOX 3388 KNOXVILLE, TENNESSEE 37927-3388 TELEPHONE 615/525-5147

Oct. 17, 19__

Mark Smithson
8612 Wimbledon Dr.
Knoxville, TN 37923

RE: E 52 29 21

Dear Mark;

In February of 19__ you were added as a driver to your parents' Safeco Insurance Company auto policy, and our records indicate that you have not had an accident during that 2½ years. Please accept our congratulations for your excellent driving record which we appreciate very much. We did not check about traffic violations, but we feel sure that you have had none.

Keeping your driving record clean helps to keep your insurance costs down, and it sets a good example for other young persons. We urge you to continue driving defensively, lawfully and carefully. A copy of this letter is being sent to Safeco Insurance Company to be placed with your records there.

Thank you for allowing us to serve you, and whenever we may be of assistance let us know. Lastly, congratulations on those excellent grades. We are real proud of you.

Sincerely,

Tom R. Harrington III

Tom R. Harrington III

cc: Safeco Insurance Co.
Stone Mountain, GA.
Doug Hutcherson

Figure 4.19

P.O. Box 418176
Kansas City, Missouri 64141-0176

YOUR MONTHLY LONG DISTANCE COSTS DON'T HAVE TO BE A SURPRISE... WITH AT&T'S REACH OUT℠ AMERICA PLAN! NOW AVAILABLE AT ITS LOWEST PRICES EVER.

Dear AT&T Customer:

Surprises can be fun...but not in your monthly bills.

However, AT&T has a way you can be sure your monthly long distance bill will never give you an unpleasant surprise: our "Reach Out" America plan.

It gives you the opportunity to know -- in advance -- what your long distance costs will be. That's because you pay by the hour, not by the mile.

For just $8.95 a month, you get an hour of AT&T Calls to any other state -- including Alaska and Hawaii. You can even call as far as Puerto Rico and the U.S. Virgin Islands.

And if you'd like to talk for more than an hour, relax. Each additional hour is even less than the first--just $7.80 each. Better yet, you only pay for the minutes you use.

Just dial the calls yourself during our weekend and night calling period. That way, you won't have to worry about different long distance prices whenever you pick up the phone. Because your calls all across the country will cost the same!

To find out if "Reach Out" America is for you, please read the enclosed brochure. It could give you the peace of mind you're looking for. Because you'll never have to expect the unexpected in your monthly long distance bills!

Sincerely,

Judy Dunlop

Judy Dunlop
Program Manager
AT&T "Reach Out" Services

P.S. Take advantage of our new lower prices! To enroll in AT&T's "Reach Out" America plan, just fill out the enclosed order form, or if you prefer, call toll free: 1 800 CALL ATT, ext 424. (1 800 225-5288, ext. 424)

Figure 4.20

Aldo Papone
President and
Chief Operating Officer

May 4, 19__

Dear Mr. Stallard:

I'm pleased to let you know we are about to initiate a significant new service for selected Cardmembers.

In fact, you will be among the first to know all the details.

Your personal invitation will arrive in about two weeks, signaled by the name, Optima.

This invitation will reflect the regard we have for you, for the personal equity you have established with us. Not every Cardmember will receive one.

I'm writing in advance, simply because it's all too easy to overlook something amid the variety of the day's mail. I don't believe you'll want to miss this news.

In the meantime, thank you for being an American Express® Cardmember. We value our association with you.

Sincerely,

Aldo Papone

American Express Travel Related Services Company, Inc., American Express Tower, World Financial Center, New York, NY 10285-3490. 1-800-528-4800

Figure 4.21

EXXON EDUCATION FOUNDATION

111 WEST 49th STREET, NEW YORK, NEW YORK 10020

WALTER KENWORTHY
Vice-President

November 4, 19__

Dr. E. Ray Smith
Office Systems Management
University of Tennessee
608 Stokely Management Center
Knoxville, TN 37996-0565

Dear Dr. Smith:

RE: A Computer Storage and Retrieval System

This brief note is to let you know that the proposal you submitted has been received.

If in our review process we find that we need additional information, we shall contact you before making a final judgment on the project. Consequently, you need not call us to verify that your material is in the appropriate form for consideration.

Under normal circumstances you may anticipate a decision within three months from this date, although it is possible that we shall be able to notify you earlier.

Thank you very much for you interest in the Foundation's programs.

Sincerely yours,

Walter Kenworthy

WJK:bas

CHAPTER 5

STYLE IN WRITING

Learning Objectives

After studying this chapter, you will be able to:

- □ Define writing style.
- □ Adjust the writing style to the situation.
- □ Apply a strategy for writing and speaking through word selection, sentence construction, and paragraph development.
- □ Distinguish between the use of denotations and connotations when choosing words.
- □ Assess the appropriateness of using positive and negative words when communicating.
- □ Apply the use of concrete and abstract words, short and long words, timesaving words, familiar words, and unbiased words.
- □ Apply the principles for writing simple, compound, complex, and compound-complex sentences.
- □ Apply the principles for writing paragraphs to include the topic sentence, unity, substance, position, order, continuity, and emphasis.
- □ Understand the capabilities of microcomputer software as an editing tool for writing.

Writing style defined

Writing style is often described as a person's ability to use correct grammar and writing principles to accomplish an objective. This definition, while appropriate, doesn't seem to capture the uniqueness of each person's writing style. And although writing style is enhanced by good language skills, it still remains unique to the author (writer).

Adjust the writing style for the situation

Effective business writing is concise, to the point, yet complete. The reader extracts the meaning intended by the sender. How you use your language skills will determine how well you accomplish your objective. This book emphasizes a basic concept: you can adjust your writing style to meet the various situations that require you to write. You evaluate the circumstances, or reasons for writing, and plan a strategy; then write a message that your reader can easily understand.

Planning a strategy, then, implies that you can adjust your style of writing, too. By carefully combining the appropriate words, sentence structures, and paragraph orders, you can create a powerful message designed for a specific audience. This chapter explains *why* writing style needs to change occasionally and *how* you can change it to fit the reader's needs. You can still retain your unique writing style by your choice of words, phrases, and organization. Check your writing for these characteristics of weak writing: poor language usage, incorrect word choice, unclear purpose, and illogical thinking. Correct these weaknesses and let your personality show through.

Evaluate writing style

Those who have learned to adjust their writing style to meet various situations enjoy the challenge of planning their writing to meet certain objectives. The real test of whether you have used appropriate styles in your writing comes when you evaluate whether you accomplished what you wanted to with your writing: Did you secure all of the data you needed to prepare your report? Did you persuade the budget committee to increase the funds for your project? Did you get the interview? Did you meet your reader's needs?

Plan a strategy for writing/speaking

This text emphasizes the use of a strategy for planning your writing and speaking. The use of a strategy implies a choice: a choice in word selection, sentence construction, and paragraph development. In this chapter, you will review how to choose your words carefully, how to use correct words, how to create sentences that contain appropriate words in the right positions, and how to develop paragraphs that are coherent and easy to follow.

CHOOSING WORDS

Factors affecting word choice

Each person possesses a unique writing style. This uniqueness begins to develop even in early childhood as a result of the environment in which learning takes place. Depending on your background, experiences, and education, you developed a vocabulary first out of necessity, then later for social and business reasons.

You soon learn that the words you choose can affect what people think about you; select words with care so your reader will interpret the message as you intended.

This may sound easier than it really is, since words mean different things to different people. If each word in our vocabulary had only one meaning, few misunderstandings would occur. Since there are well over one million words to choose from—each with various meanings—effective communication cannot be left to chance.

Denotation versus Connotation

Understanding potential word meanings

A word by itself has little meaning. It is better to say that words have *potential* meaning. Their actual meanings come from the context in which you use them, your intention and knowledge, and the understanding and attitude of the receiver.

Denotation defined

Every word has two categories of meanings: denotation and connotation. *Denotation* refers to the factual definition of an object, act, situation, quality, or idea. Words can also have more than one denotative meaning.

Connotation defined

Connotation refers to how a person feels about a word, based on past experiences. Sometimes it is difficult to project a person's reaction to a word within the context of a message.

Attitudes/feelings affect word connotations

To illustrate these two categories of meanings, examine the following: *ignorant*, *dumb*, *unintelligent*, *unaware*, *uninformed*, *illiterate*, *unlettered*, *untutored*, *unlearned*. The denotative meaning is the same—"a lack of knowledge or the absence of knowledge." But attitudes and feelings associated with these words vary. Sometimes unfavorable or even antagonistic connotations are given to one or maybe even all of these.

Nevertheless, even connotations can change based on social acceptance. For instance, most people would object to being described as *ignorant* because of negative connotations. In some situations, such as in a legal dispute, the word *ignorant* could have positive connotations. Consider this example: "My client was totally *ignorant* of any fraud or misuse of funds." The denotative meaning is "a lack of knowledge"; the connotative meaning is, "My client is blameless."

Check for correct denotations

In choosing words, consider the denotations as well as the connotations so that your reader will have a clear picture of the message. For the correct denotation, you have two very good sources you can rely on—a dictionary and a thesaurus. As you work to improve your writing or speaking, keep these two resources nearby so that you can refer to them often.

The dictionary gives you standardized meanings of words. A good dictionary will also provide usage, pronunciation, spelling, syllabication, antonyms, synonyms, parts of speech, inflected forms, abbreviations, capitalization, and cross-references.

The thesaurus gives you additional words that have the same general denotative meaning as the word you are using. Avoid using the same word in your writing—unless you are using it purposely to provide emphasis, or unless the word you are repeating is technically the most exact word for your purpose. Variety in usage increases reader interest in the communication. The only impression the reader may have of you is what the written docu-

LEGAL / ETHICAL ISSUES

Litigation has become an American way of life for solving problems. Recent estimates state that approximately two-thirds of America's 500 largest corporations have been involved in some form of illegal behavior over the past 10 years.

- ☐ An entertainment figure sues a publication for defamation of character and wins handsomely. The publication had reported so-called facts that were proven to be untrue.
- ☐ A giant American firm conceals information on one of its products where evidence was available to show the product caused a fatal disease. The courts took the company to task when they found it guilty of unethical behavior in misrepresenting its product and in concealing vital information.
- ☐ Employees are becoming increasingly concerned over individual rights, and more than 70 pieces of legislation designed to protect individual employee rights are pending in 29 states, according to the Research Institute of America, New York. Areas of concern include: Does the company have a right to monitor the productivity of word-processor operators? Does the company have a right to tap employee telephone calls?
- ☐ Employees are annoyed with managers who monitor their performance and then send written messages informing them of the number of words typed per minute with implications that productivity needs improving. Employees are also annoyed with employers who listen in on their conversations. The employers feel that employees should not have unrealistic expectations of privacy when at work.

What legal and/or ethical implications do these cases have for business communicators? How do these cases relate to word choice? Sentence structure? Paragraph structure? Message tone?

ment reveals. A few misused words may cause the reader to discard your message entirely.

Positive versus Negative Words

Word choice affects message tone

Just as words can convey various denotative and connotative meanings, these same words and combinations of words can also convey positive, neutral, or negative impressions. These impressions create the *tone* of the message. Your objective for the communication and your relationship to the reader will help you determine the most appropriate words to use.

Sometimes writers associate negative words such as *difficult*, *criticism*, *no*, *cannot*, or *unable* with negative communication. But consider these sentences:

He completed the difficult task in record time.

Mary takes criticism well.

No other person could fill his shoes.

We cannot say enough good about the athletic program at your school.

We are unable to identify a single weakness in the system.

Although negative words appear in each of these sentences, the tone for each is positive. A good rule to follow, then, is to select words that express a positive tone. Note in Figure 5.1 how effectively the editor of the *Harvard Business Review* conveys positive thoughts using negative words.

Word choice for negative ideas

Another alternative to consider is the replacement of negative words with positive statements. This is not always easy, because sometimes you will have to write messages that convey bad news. Sometimes you will want to be direct and say no with a negative word. Thus you will need to select carefully which words you choose to express negative ideas. Compare these examples:

Negative	**Positive**
No refunds are made after 30 days.	Merchandise is fully refundable for the first 30 days.
Your credit application is refused on the basis of gross income.	When your gross income exceeds $20,000, credit will be granted.
You failed to mention the date of arrival.	Please mark the enclosed card to indicate your date of arrival.

Figure 5.2 presents guidelines for developing positive impressions in your writing.

Concrete versus Abstract Words

Concrete words—direct, precise

When possible, use *concrete* words that denote tangible persons, objects, places, or events. Concrete words such as *tree, house, football, smile, parade,* and *rose petals* are direct and precise. The reader is unlikely to misunderstand these words because they are so specific in nature.

Abstract words—concepts, ideas, or virtues

You cannot always use concrete words, however, and still express what you mean. What if you want to discuss concepts, ideas, or virtues? *Abstract* words such as *family, honesty, deception, truth, professionalism, friendliness,* and *quality control* are all a part of the everyday vocabulary of the business world; yet their meanings are a little more difficult to pinpoint than the concrete examples listed above.

Connotations of abstract words

Abstract words have varied connotations that carry the reader beyond the literal and the precise to underlying feelings, qualities, and/or beliefs. To communicate clearly when using abstract words, you may need to define or illustrate them so your reader will know what you mean. For example, if you

Figure 5.1
Harvard Business Review letter

Harvard Business Review
Soldiers Field Road
Boston, Mass. 02163

WELCOME TO HBR

We are delighted that you are now an HBR subscriber.

In becoming affiliated with us, you will be in good company. Of our 240,000 subscribers, nearly all are in management ranks. Half are corporate officers, principals, or senior managers. Further, our subscribers represent every major industry in the world and live in over 150 countries.

Although we try to represent advanced management thinking and practice in all fields of management, we do not claim to be omniscient. Any time you feel strongly that some subject should be covered which has not been analyzed in HBR, I hope you will write me on the subject. I can promise you that every letter that comes in will receive my personal attention.

Once again, we are pleased you have joined us and hope that you will find HBR rewarding for a long time to come.

Yours sincerely,

Theodore Levitt

TL/gzd

Reprinted by permission of the *Harvard Business Review.*

use the word *family,* the reader may interpret it in several ways: your immediate family; your extended family; or a much broader definition that includes others, such as a company family.

Use abstract words cautiously

Some abstract words leave the interpretation to the reader. Vague words such as *several, few, most,* and *majority* fall in this class. Say what you mean! At times it is expedient to use abstract words, but use them with caution since meanings vary from person to person.

In these examples, notice how the clarity of the message is improved by replacing the abstract words with others that are more concrete:

Figure 5.2
Guidelines for Developing Positive Impressions

Use

1. Words that express: sincerity.
   courtesy.
   consideration.
2. A style that is conversational.
3. A "you" attitude—one of helpfulness.
4. Words that have positive connotations.
5. Words that put you in step with the reader.
6. Words that express an attitude of service.
7. Words that build goodwill.

Avoid

1. A selfish point of view.
2. Exaggerating: bragging.
   gushiness.
   making promises you cannot keep.
3. Irritation, doubt, or indifference.
4. Criticizing or arguing with the reader.
5. Talking down to the reader.
6. Pompous or stuffy writing.
7. Words that have negative connotations.

Concrete writing improves clarity

Abstract	**Concrete**
The auditorium is quite large.	The auditorium will seat 2,000 people.
She lives close to the beach.	She lives about 10 miles from the beach.
Are family rates available?	What are the rates for a family of four?
We are several dollars short of our goal.	We are $300 short of our goal.

Short versus Long Words

Have you ever thought about how profound and vivid short, simple words are? Most readers appreciate short words that are simple and to the point. Did you know that 77 percent of Lincoln's "Gettysburg Address" consists of words of five or fewer letters?

Business communication usually involves writing that is short and simple. Advertising specialists recognize the importance of simple words and use them to reach the general public. In fact, you are bombarded every day by advertisements for products or services that use simple words. Observe these powerful, clear slogans:

Short, action-oriented words make powerful sentences

We do it all for you!—McDonald's
M'm! M'm! Good!—Campbell's Soup
When it rains, it pours.—Morton Salt

Don't leave home without it.—American Express
Delta gets you there with care.—Delta Airlines

For *most* of your writing, choose simple words to convey your message. However, the use of short, simple words does not always guarantee clear communication. In Figure 5.3 most of the words are simple, yet the letter is ineffective.

What is the writer attempting to communicate? What makes the letter ineffective? The key to effective communication is to consider the reader/audience and then determine the level of writing.

Overused words/phrases lack power

Sometimes even simple short words can be overused to the point they lose their power. These overused words are like stagnant water—there is no life left in them. Use words that form an image in the reader's mind. Choose vivid, lively words that give your message impact. The English language is so versatile that you don't need to confine yourself to just a few words or phrases. Contrast these examples of overused/outdated words and phrases with the improved versions.

Overused/outdated	Improved
If we can be of further service, please do not hesitate to call.	Let us serve you again; just call 883-1943.
In reference to your letter of May 24, . . .	You mention in your May 24 letter . . .
Enclosed is a self-addressed envelope for your convenience.	Just slip your reply in the enclosed, preaddressed envelope.
Pursuant to your request, we are enclosing herewith a copy of our financial report.	Here is the financial report you requested.

Timesaving Words

Timesaving words improve readability

Research shows that wordy communication is costly—costly to write and costly to interpret. Managers and people in general have come to appreciate and expect quick results. We like instant coffee, instant cameras, instant playbacks on TV, drive-in food service, and microwave ovens. And we also like to receive communications that are concise and easy to read. You can simplify your writing by eliminating unnecessary words. Wordy phrases can usually be expressed in one or two words.

Phrase	Substitute
At the present time	Now
Due to the fact that	Because
For the purpose of	For
In the event that	If
In the near future	Soon
In very few instances	Rarely
In view of the fact that	Since, because

Figure 5.3 Ineffective Letter Using Simple Words

Supplemental Security Income Notice of Revised Determination

579

From: Department of Health and Human Services
Social Security Adminstration

Dear Mrs. Neel:

We will stop your payment as shown above, beginning December 19___.

This action is in step with the law and is based on information supplied by you or in our records--

You have monthly income which must be considered in figuring your eligibility as follows--

Your Social Security benefits--before any deductions for Medicare medical insurance premiums —— of $175.22 for December 19___ on.

Your special one-time payment of rents, interest, dividends, or royalties received December 19___, of $550.75.

Because of your income, you are not eligible to receive extra income payments for December 19___ on.

This decision refers only to your claim for extra income payments.

If at any time in the future you think you qualify for extra income, please contact us at once. If you are not eligible to receive payment during a month before December 19___, you will have to file a new request to receive payment. Since we cannot make payment for a month before the month in which a request is filed, a delayed request will result in a loss of payment for any months in which you are otherwise eligible.

Although we plan to take the action shown above, you may have your current payment continued if you request an appeal within 10 days of receiving this notice.

Cordially yours,

Important: See other side for an explanation of your appeal rights and other information.▶

Form **SSA-L8100-C1** (6-82)
Use prior editions until supply is exhausted

In the vicinity of	Near
Is of the opinion that	Thinks
Is equipped with	Has
Make a decision	Decide
Subsequent to	After
Until such time as	Until
Was in communication with	Talked with
With the exception of	Except

Familiar Words

Note the technical jargon in this paragraph:

These processes apply to the choice of compositional parameters—pitch, for example. You can characterize each process by its power-density spectrum, the variation of the random sequence's energy versus its frequency. The spectral characterization applies only to the random variable's sequence of values; it says nothing about the acoustical spectra of the actual sounds.

Jargon defined

Unless you know the technical terms, this paragraph is difficult to understand. *Jargon* is defined as *a hybrid vocabulary unique to a special group of people.* Suppose you wrote a memo to someone with a technical background similar to yours. In this instance, you could appropriately use technical terms. When you do decide to use them, however, you should be certain your reader will understand them. Otherwise, you run the risk of being misinterpreted or misunderstood. And even if your reader understands your message, technical reading is more difficult and, for some readers, boring.

Avoid jargon

For most business communication, avoid jargon and choose familiar words appropriate for a general audience. This same principle holds true for the use of acronyms—letters that stand for such words as TV (television), ACM (Association for Computing Machinery), MICR (magnetic ink character recognition), or CBIS (computer-based information system). Select your words and terms to fit your audience.

Avoid slang expressions in business communications. Slang expressions inappropriate for business communication include:

Avoid slang expressions

Cotton pickin'	Y'all
Top dog	Fly-by-night outfit
Driving everyone bananas	Screwed up
Throw in the towel	It's real cool
Jolly good time	It sounds hip

Unbiased Words

Sex-role stereotypes are widespread

Although women now comprise over 50 percent of the work force, they still have a long way to go to break the invisible barriers of sex-role stereotypes. A study conducted by the *Harvard Business Review* in 1985 found sex-role stereotypes widespread. Sex discrimination lawsuits and deregulation have helped women make inroads into the once male-dominated corporate world, but progress is slow.

Effects of sex-role stereotypes

Studies are currently being conducted to determine whether the effects of low salaries and prestige are a result of sex-biased language. There is reason to believe this is the case since other studies give clear evidence that sex-role stereotypes as well as sex-characteristic stereotypes influence individuals' perceptions of women in leadership roles.[1]

Eliminate sex discrimination

In this context, the selection of words takes on new meaning. When communicating, choose words carefully to avoid sex discrimination both in the selection process and by assigning a person—or group—to a leading or subordinate role.

□ Eliminate these stereotype contrasts.[2]

Worried family man	versus	Harried housewife
Man who protests	versus	Woman who complains
Man as breadwinner	versus	Woman as extra income earner
Man's career	versus	Woman's job
Authoritative man	versus	Domineering female

□ Eliminate unnecessary gender pronouns.[3]

Change from:	**To:**
If *his* position	If *the* position
Provided the person can prove that he or she suffered a loss. . . .	Provided the person can prove a loss was suffered. . . .

□ Avoid using words denoting gender:

Incorrect	**Correct**
Anchorman	News anchor
Businessman	Business executive
Congressman	Member of Congress
Craftsman	Artisan
Forefathers	Ancestors
Foreman	Supervisor
Mailman	Letter carrier

[1] Leann K. Ellis, Wallace V. Schmidt, and Virginia Eman Wheeless, "An Empirical Study of Sex-Characteristic Stereotypes versus Sex-Role Stereotypes Affecting Women in Management," *Proceedings of the Association for Business Communication, Southwest Division* (1985), p. 83.

[2] *Irwin-Dorsey Guidelines for Use of Nonsexist Language* (Homewood, Ill.: Richard D. Irwin, 1981).

[3] Ibid.

Mankind	People
Manpower	Work force
Policeman	Police officer
Salesman	Salesclerk
Workmen's compensation.	Workers' compensation.

Choose unbiased words

Sex-related stereotypes are just one of the areas to consider when choosing unbiased words. Our society is now aware of the importance of avoiding discrimination because of age, race, or national origin. This awareness has made us more sensitive to people's feelings. In developing good language skills, select words that express this sensitivity.

□ Avoid using words that demean a person because of age:

Incorrect	**Correct**
Young, upstart intern	Newly hired intern
For our elderly employees	For experienced employees

□ Avoid words that show racial and ethnic bias:

Incorrect	**Correct**
Blacks who are less fortunate	Individuals who are less fortunate
Mary, the Jewish secretary who was. . . .	Mary, the secretary who was. . . .

WRITING SENTENCES

Composing grammatically correct sentences

So far, you have examined word choices and discussed some of the cautions in selecting words. But words are like automobile parts; they are interesting but do very little until combined with other parts. The way Ford and Jaguar design and assemble their automobile parts gives each car its class, style, and distinctiveness. So it is with words. The way they are put together, first in sentences and then in paragraphs, is what determines your writing style. You select the words and then arrange them into grammatically correct sentences to form paragraphs. With the selection of appropriate words and careful arrangement of them, you can make a positive impact on your reader.

You have attended English classes throughout most of your school years. By now, you have a basic knowledge of English grammar. Your use of correct grammar is important since most people associate poor grammar with the uneducated or the illiterate. This negative attitude will prejudice your reader against accepting your thoughts, regardless of how valid or important they are.

This section reviews some basic characteristics for developing sentences.

Types of Sentences

A sentence defined

A *sentence* is a *group of words expressing a complete thought.* Sentences can be classified into one of four groups: simple, compound, complex, and compound-complex.

Types of sentences

Simple sentence

A simple sentence must have at least two parts, a *subject* (noun or pronoun) and a *verb.* In these simple sentences subjects are underlined once and verbs underlined twice:

> Margaret danced.
>
> The attentive listener noticed the quiver in the speaker's voice.
>
> The faculty and administration met and talked in a closed session.

In each of these examples, only one thought is expressed. Note, however, that the third example has a compound subject and compound verb.

Compound sentence

A second type, the compound sentence, is actually two simple sentences connected with a coordinating conjunction and a comma (*and, but, or, for, nor*) or a semicolon. This type of sentence expresses two separate thoughts of equal rank.

> People are an organization's most valuable resource, and highly successful companies realize this.
>
> He shouted again, but no one heard him.
>
> Bob caught on quickly; he became the liberated bookkeeper.

Complex sentence

A third type, the complex sentence, contains at least two clauses—one independent clause and one or more dependent clauses. An independent clause, like a simple sentence, must contain a subject, a verb, and express a complete thought. A dependent clause contains a subject and verb but cannot stand alone; it needs help from the independent clause to complete the thought. The dependent clauses are underlined in these examples.

> After they left the classroom, the students discussed the lecture.
>
> Significant changes, which challenge our world today, affect our values as well as our technologies.
>
> We manage crises and learn to resolve conflicts, which this course teaches.

Compound-complex sentence

The fourth type of sentence, the compound-complex, contains two or more independent clauses plus one or more dependent clauses. Use this type sparingly in business writing since it is more difficult for the reader to understand. Again, the dependent clauses are underlined.

> The problem, which has been described in many ways, is still present; and we see no solution in sight.
>
> Because the people were feeling intimidated by the computer, we tried a new approach; and the report contains the results.

Use a mix of a sentence types

Effective business communication usually contains a mix of these four sentence types. Variety, the spice of life, could help keep your readers interested. Nevertheless, variety, like any writing tool, should be used with purpose. When you wish to call attention to a specific idea, you might choose to emphasize the point by using a sentence structure different from those around it. Using a different sentence pattern for each sentence in a paragraph would surely make the paragraph more difficult to read. In addition to simply avoiding an endless string of similar sentences, variety can help you accentuate an idea, emphasize a particular point, orchestrate ideas, or demonstrate their relationships. Variety is more than just spice: it can be a powerful structural tool as well. Now let's review another sentence characteristic—active and passive voice.

Active versus Passive Sentences

Active voice/ passive voice

In addition to sentence types, you have another choice to consider—whether to write in the active or passive voice. In active voice, the subject of the sentence does the acting. In contrast, the subject is acted upon in passive voice. *The active voice is the stronger of the two; and most writers prefer the active form.* Why? When writers use the active voice, messages come alive, are vivid, are more personable, require fewer words, and are easier to follow. Contrast these versions:

Active	Passive
You always say the right things.	Saying the right things is a talent of yours.
Bob developed and presented the plan.	The plan was developed and presented by Bob.
We all celebrated the victory.	The victory was celebrated by all.

Active voice and strong, action-oriented verbs add strength to your writing.

At times, however, the passive voice is preferred. This voice can soften the impact of negative news, for example. What if the objective of the message is to establish blame or to refuse a request? In these instances, the use of the passive voice is helpful. The passive voice is also appropriate to place emphasis on action already taken: "Your order was shipped on August 10, 19__." Examine the differences in tone for these examples:

Active	Passive
You made several errors in the ads.	Several errors were made in the ads.
You broke the video when you dropped it.	The video was broken when it fell.
I cannot give you any copies of classified materials.	Copies of classified materials are not allowed.

Sentences That Succeed

In constructing sentences that are sure to succeed, professional writers follow these simple guidelines:

Guidelines for effective sentences

Keep Your Sentences Short. When listening to someone talk, have you thought, "I could say that in five minutes"? Such speakers soon lose their audience. The same holds true for readers of business communication. Readers simply won't take time to wade through a lot of rhetoric. If they read the message at all, they will probably skim it, pick out the highlights, and disregard the rest. Careless writers chance having pertinent information overlooked. Long sentences are hard to follow and are usually dull. However, don't make your sentences so short that they sound blunt and choppy or fail to show the logical connections between ideas you wish the reader to see. Eliminate unnecessary details. The average sentence length is 16 words. In your writing, strive to achieve a balance. Contrast this example and its revision:

Short sentences

Example: The 150 employees from our company who attended our recent workshop on communications and then filled out the questionnaire about the workshop responded positively to it.

Rewrite: The computer questionnaires indicate a positive response from those who attended the July 17 communication workshop.

Consider the reader

Show Consideration for the Reader. Everyone likes to feel important. By viewing things from the reader's standpoint, you show respect and consideration for that person. This is called the *you viewpoint.* The you viewpoint builds personal relationships, business relationships, and goodwill. By assuming the reader's viewpoint, you establish a climate of helpfulness. Compare these "we" and "you" viewpoints:

"We" Viewpoint

We feel you should be commended on your accomplishments.
Our shipping department mailed the order on March 15.
I am a responsible person.
We will be happy to serve you again.

"You" Viewpoint

Congratulations on your accomplishments!
Your order was mailed on March 15.
You can count on me to be responsible.
Please let us serve you again soon.

In these examples, note the use of both the first person (I, my, me, we, us, our) and second person (you) in the same sentences. How do you know which sentences are "you focused"? You determine this by examining the overall attitude or tone of the message. If your message benefits the reader, comes across as sincere, is courteous and considerate, you are on the right track. No such rule says, "Never use *I, me, my, we, our,* or *us*"; nor is there one that says, "Always use the second person (you)." You need a balance in your messages. Messages that "overdo" are messages that need to be "done over."

Let Your Sentences Say What You Mean. Misplaced words or phrases can produce a totally different meaning from the one intended. Read this sentence:

Correct sentence meanings

Miss Brown only responded to the request.

This says that Miss Brown didn't do anything else but respond. Connotations of this message might be:

She didn't make any recommendations—only responded.
She didn't fully perform other functions that were pertinent to the request.
She does only minimal work.
She was the only one who took time to answer.

The sentence needs to be revised to say, "Only Miss Brown responded to the request." This message is totally different from the first one. The connotations here might be:

Miss Brown is a totally responsible person.
She is a helpful person.
She is not a procrastinator.

Make sure your sentences say what you mean. You make fewer mistakes in this area if you:

1. Place modifiers next to the words they describe.
2. Check to see that you correctly position phrases beginning with "which, that, who, or whom."

Compare these samples.

Incorrect	**Correct**
We located the gentleman looking through the lobby. (Who is looking through the lobby? We? The gentleman?)	While looking through the lobby, we located the gentleman.
Each employee was asked to contribute, but Miss Miller only has given $1.95. (Is Miss Miller a cheapskate, or is she the only person contributing?)	Each employee was asked to contribute, but only Miss Miller has given $1.95.

The letter to our employees in the attached envelope was sent on June 10. (Are the employees in the envelope, or is it the letter?)	The letter in the attached envelope was sent to our employees on June 10.

Unintentional repetition

Don't Be Unintentionally Repetitive. Needless repetition of words detracts from the message. Why would you need to say "new innovations" or "join together"? Edit your writing and delete such redundancies as:

above and beyond
angry, irate boss
modern, up-to-date
newly created
past history
repeat again
true facts
very unique
most rare

These redundancies add nothing to the communication. At times, however, you may want to repeat words or phrases for emphasis. This type of repetition does add to the communication. Some of the most powerful speeches in history contain repetitive phrases. Many speakers and writers know how to use this technique effectively. Martin Luther King, Jr., used it. In his famous speech "I Have a Dream," King used the phrase "I have a dream" *eight* times.

Thoughtful repetition can achieve impact and emphasis, as shown in some excerpts from persuasive letters.

We can meet the deadline!
We can save you money!
We can give you quality!
You have many, many friends in the industry.

Parallel construction

Be Consistent in Expressing Parallel Ideas. To achieve harmony and rhythm in your writing, present similar ideas in a similar manner. For example, in a series you would use "developing, writing, and editing" rather than "developed, writing, and to edit." The first three words end in "-ing"—they are parallel in form. In contrast, the next three words are not parallel ("-ed," "-ing," "to" + a verb). Parallel construction improves clarity and readability. Some incorrect and correct expressions of ideas are shown.

Incorrect	**Correct**
For relaxation, Mary likes to read, to sew, and watches TV, especially in the evenings.	For relaxation, Mary likes to read, to sew, and to watch TV, especially in the evenings.

Common characteristics of successful people are: a. They are goal-oriented. b. They understand the importance of human relations. c. Willing to work hard.	Successful people are goal oriented, understand the importance of human relations, and are willing to work hard.

Fact-supported statements

Don't Overstate Your Facts. Have you ever received this type of message? "This rug cleaner is being offered at the lowest price ever—just $8.95?" You look at the price and realize that you bought this same cleaner two months ago at the same store for $6.95. This company loses its credibility with you. You no longer have confidence in what the company says.

Try to avoid comparative words such as *best, least, worst, most, lowest, highest* (called superlatives) unless you can furnish evidence to support your claim(s). Use them with care.

Incorrect	**Correct**
These tires are the best on the market.	According to Consumer Reports, XYZ tires are the best on the market.
Mary never seems to get here on time.	Mary has been late every day this week.

In summary, follow these suggestions to create effective sentences:

Sentence principles summarized

- ☐ Use correct grammar.
- ☐ Use a mix of sentence types for variety; stress the use of simple sentences.
- ☐ Generally, write in active voice with action verbs.
- ☐ Avoid sexist and other discriminatory words.
- ☐ Be precise in word choice and word/phrase placement.
- ☐ Use repetition purposefully.

DEVELOPING PARAGRAPHS

You have just reviewed how important word selection and sentence construction are for conveying your exact meaning. Some of the same characteristics that apply to writing sentences also apply to the development of paragraphs.

Paragraph defined

A *paragraph* is *a group of related statements that form a unit.* You develop strong paragraphs by first selecting a central idea and then adding other parts in an organized manner to complete your unit of thought. Careful planning and thinking are required. Paragraphing aids your reader in understanding the message by highlighting the separate units of thought and their relationships. Here is a chance for you to use your creativity and to demonstrate your unique style.

Keep in mind that a paragraph is a part of a whole piece of writing—just as words are a part of a sentence. Paragraphs offer a chance for the eyes to rest and an opportunity to collect thoughts. You could write a one-page message in one paragraph, but your reader would probably react negatively. In contrast, many one- and two-sentence paragraphs are so choppy that the communication would be hard to read. Use judgment in building each paragraph.

Consider audience and objective

Before you start to write, think about your audience and your overall objective. You are writing so that the reader will understand your thoughts. Therefore, visualize the reader and anticipate possible reactions. The basic characteristics to consider in developing effective paragraphs include the topic sentence, unity, substance, position, order, continuity, and emphasis. These basic concepts are interrelated and sometimes overlap.

Topic Sentence

Topic sentence defined

The *topic sentence* contains *the central idea or theme of the paragraph.* Use the other sentences in the paragraph to give substance to your main thought or to add details. As you develop the paragraph, use the central idea as your gauge to avoid introducing irrelevant material. Revise or eliminate unrelated material.

Topic sentence suggestions

Ordinarily, the topic sentence appears first in a paragraph. You can, however, add variety to your writing with these three suggestions:

Vary position

- □ Vary the position of the topic sentence within the paragraph—at the beginning; at the end; in the middle.

Imply topic

- □ Imply the topic—a well-constructed paragraph will lead the reader to sum up the central thought of the paragraph.

Change form

- □ Express the topic in a different form—instead of a declarative sentence, use an interrogative (question) or other type of sentence.

Placement of topic sentence

When presenting the topic idea, give priority to the audience and to the objective of your written message. Careful placement of the topic sentence and use of an expressed or implied form of the topic idea help you build strong paragraphs. Which of the following versions do you prefer? Why?

Topic Sentence at Beginning of Paragraph

Beginning

<u>Please write your social security number on the tear-off portion of this notice, sign on the line indicated, and mail it back to us at once.</u> Since you receive interest on your insurance contract, a revised Federal Income Tax law requires that you send us your correct taxpayer identification number. If we don't have your correct taxpayer number, we will withhold tax at a 20 percent rate. In addition, a $50 penalty may be imposed by the Internal Revenue Service.

Topic Sentence at End of Paragraph

End

Since you receive interest on your insurance contract, a revised Federal Income Tax law now requires you to furnish us with your correct taxpayer identification number. Your social security number is your taxpayer identification number. If you do not send us your correct taxpayer number, we will withhold tax at a 20 percent rate. In addition, you may be subject to a $50 penalty imposed by the Internal Revenue Service. Therefore, please write your social security number on the tear-off portion of this notice, sign on the line indicated, and mail it back to us at once.

Topic Sentence in Middle of Paragraph

Middle

Since you receive interest on your insurance contract, a revised Federal Income Tax law now requires you to furnish us with your correct taxpayer identification number. Therefore, please write your social security number (your taxpayer identification number) on the tear-off portion of this notice, sign on the line indicated and mail it back to us at once. If you do not send us your correct taxpayer number, we will withhold tax at a 20 percent rate. In addition, you may be subject to a $50 penalty that the Internal Revenue Service may impose.

Topic Idea Implied: "You Aren't Being Admitted."

Implied

Thank you for applying for admission to State University. Each year more than 1,000 out-of-state residents apply to State University. Because of the high demand and limited spaces, we place a cut-off score of 30 on the ACT as an entrance requirement. Your ACT score was 27. You are to be congratulated on your ACT score, which indicates your potential success in college.

Topic Idea in Beginning

Question

Have you mailed your first-quarter Sales Tax Return for 19__? We have not received your return. If you have not paid your sales tax, please pay immediately, using the enclosed envelope. If you have paid, please send copies of your canceled check and the Sales Tax return form.

Unity

Unity defined

Paragraph *unity* refers to *the singleness of thought, purpose, or mood.* Each sentence in a paragraph must relate to the central idea, or it is irrelevant. Irrelevant material confuses or irritates the reader. Test each paragraph for unity by reading and asking yourself: "Does each idea refer to the topic thought?"

Read and determine why this following paragraph lacks unity (the sentences have been numbered for convenience):

Weak example lacking unity

(1) As you probably know, new requirements, including preadmission certification, will go into effect for your Blue Cross/Blue Shield group insurance cover-

age on October 1. (2) The preadmission certification program also requires that you obtain a second opinion for the surgical procedures listed in Special Report No. 441-86. (3) The areas listed elsewhere are reviewed for location of services and the timing of the services to be provided. (4) Exceptions to the hospital admission requirements are emergencies, maternity, psychiatric, alcoholism or drug abuse care, and out-of-the-country hospital stays. (5) Preadmission certification requires that hospital admission be approved or certified by Blue Cross/Blue Shield before the patient enters the hospital. (6) Emergency admissions must be certified within 24 hours following the admission or within one working day.

Now compare your reasons with these comments about the lack of unity in the above paragraph. Note the action that could be taken for each sentence:

Sentence analysis

Sentence No. 1: (topic sentence)	Introductory clause "As you probably know," has no substance—eliminate. Phrase "on October 1" misplaced; place after "go into effect." Place "group insurance coverage" after "requirements."
ACTION:	Revise sentence.
Sentence No. 2:	Sentence does not refer to topic idea but introduces another topic, second opinion. Word *also* indicates that something else has to precede the sentence.
ACTION:	Transfer to another paragraph.
Sentence No. 3:	Sentence is a lead-in for a listing. Sentence is confusing.
ACTION:	Transfer to another paragraph and revise for clarity.
Sentence No. 4:	Sentence is out of sequence.
ACTION:	Modify and place after Sentence No. 5.
Sentence No. 5:	Defines "preadmission certification." Word *patient* seems distant; passive voice—"be approved."
ACTION:	Replace *patient* with *you* or *your dependent.* Place after Sentence No. 1. Change to active voice.
Sentence No. 6:	Idea is OK for last sentence in paragraph.
ACTION:	Add transitional word *and.* Place after modified Sentence No. 4.

With these revisions, the modified paragraph possesses unity.

Good example with unity

New requirements for your Blue Cross/Blue Shield group insurance coverage, including preadmission certification, will go into effect on October 1. Preadmission certification requires that Blue Cross/Blue Shield approve or certify hospital admission before you or your dependent enters the hospital except for emergencies, maternity, psychiatric, alcoholism or drug abuse care, and out-of-the-country hospital stays. Emergency admissions must be certified within 24 hours following admission.

Each sentence now contributes to the central thought and belongs in the paragraph. Check each sentence in your paragraphs for unity.

Substance

Methods for paragraph development

Once you decide on your topic thought, you need to present the related facts to communicate your ideas. Six frequently used methods for developing your central idea are *definition, illustration/explication, reasoning, analogy, comparison/contrast, and reiteration.*

By definition

When you develop an idea by *definition,* you include details and examples to help your reader understand various words/phrases. You anticipate the reader's reaction: "What do you mean by this?"

By illustration/explication

Development by *illustration/explication* uses evidence/proof through examples or instances. Examples that are familiar to your reader will be more potent than unfamiliar ones. Think of your reader; then select illustrations that present clear and concrete ideas.

By reasoning

Development by *reasoning* presents evidence to convince or persuade a reader to accept your point of view. This method is especially useful in sales and goodwill messages and may require more length, depending on the situation.

By analogy

Development by *analogy* is a process that leads the reader from something known (the static electricity that builds up in a sweater, for instance) to something unknown (a similar kind of static electricity in lightning). Analogies help readers use what they already know to discover something they don't know.

By comparison/contrast

Development by *comparison/contrast* involves opposing or contrasting ideas to communicate your meanings. Advantages and disadvantages are sometimes helpful.

By reiteration

Development by *reiteration* uses repetition of an idea, word, or phrase—a company name, for example. Planned repetition gives emphasis and can create a favorable image. Any one or a combination of the six methods can help you develop effective paragraphs. First, consider your purpose and your reader; then select appropriate techniques to achieve your objective. Practice using each of these methods so that you can write effectively no matter what the situation. These samples show how substance can be developed.

Definition

The following typing rate standards are based on a recent Keyboard Productivity Research Project in our offices. Expect speeds of 188 to 204 net lines per hour (LPH) on origination (first-time) typing of narrative material. The term "net lines" refers to the total number of lines typed minus a deduction of one line for each line containing an error. Therefore, consider a speed of 188 LPH the minimum acceptable typing speed for narrative material.

Illustration

Compare the turnaround time for work tasks with the real needs of the organization rather than with personal preference. If turnaround time is a problem, examine the scope of the problem to identify potential solutions. For example, if turnaround time is acceptable for 90 percent of the work, the problem is within the remaining 10 percent. The problem may be due simply to the lack of a system for identifying and handling priority work. Instituting procedures for assigning priorities to the work tasks could resolve this problem.

Reasoning (Ex. 1)

Now you don't have to change the way you dial your phone calls to get lower rates on long distance. MCI—one of the fastest growing long-distance companies in the U.S.—now offers you a vastly improved long-distance phone service. MCI handles more than four million long-distance calls each day for satisfied customers. And we are doing this with the cooperation of your local phone company.

Reasoning (Ex. 2)

To start your savings, simply sign and return the enclosed Authorization Card instructing your local phone company to connect you to MCI's Long Distance Service. You can then enjoy calling long distance to any other phone in the Continental United States, 24 hours a day, 7 days a week—and save from 5 percent to 35 percent over your present cost. And you can even qualify for quantity discounts.

Analogy

Computer scientists now realize the way to more number-crunching power is to clump lots of tiny computer chips into one big system. Attempts to do this, though, often fall short because of the soldier-teller syndrome. When the processors act too much like soldiers, they unite easily to attack common problems but aren't good at independent thinking. Like bank clerks, teller chips can do separate tasks simultaneously but stumble when they need to work together.[4]

Comparison contrast

A financial forecast is the expected financial position, results of operations, and change in financial position of the company. It's what management expects to happen. Different from a financial forecast is a financial projection, which includes one or more hypothetical situations and is the company's expectations of results given an assumption that may not occur. The distinction between these two types of forecasts is fairly important since one, the forecast, denotes management's expected financial results and the other, the projection, denotes management's financial results only if some unexpected event or decision occurs. In effect, a financial projection is a "what if?" type of situation and is not expected to occur.[5]

Reiteration

Here's some good news for the new year! You've been approved for a MasterCard with a $2,500 credit line from Central Bank. You can use your MasterCard to consolidate your holiday bills or take it shopping for those great January bargains. Either way, your Central MasterCard with its outstanding benefits is yours for the asking.

---

[4] "Transputer Chips: Linchpins of a Mighty Supercomputer," *Business Week,* no. 2942, April 21, 1986, p. 47.

[5] Alex B. Cameron, "CPA Savvy," *Management World* 14, no. 7 (July/August 1985), pp. 40–41.

Position

Emphasize ideas through placement

Position of your ideas plays an important part in writing effective paragraphs. Place your major idea first or last to achieve emphasis. First and last impressions are important. Use the middle sections to develop or support your main idea(s) or to deemphasize them.

Purpose of opening paragraph

Paragraphs have different purposes depending on their location within a piece of writing—opening, closing, or middle. The opening paragraph performs a dual purpose—to get the subject under way and get the interest of the reader. The nature of the communication determines the attention-getting technique. Look at this *weak excerpt* from a publisher's sales letter:

Remember the promise you made to yourself years ago?
You remember, don't you?

This example does get the interest of the reader but fails to get the subject under way. What promise?

Questions are used sometimes to get the reader's interest. This rewrite is better since it fulfills the dual purpose.

Weak example

Remember the promise you made to yourself to lose weight? You remember, don't you?

Here is a second example that also fulfills the dual purpose.

Good example

Good news for the New Year! You have a VISA credit card with a $3,000 credit line reserved for you at the State Bank. That's $3,000 to use any way you want—and at the time you need it most.

Purpose of closing paragraph

The closing paragraph performs two functions—brings the message to an end and gives a final emphasis. This paragraph should give your reader a sense of having reached the end. As you complete your message, answer this question: "What final thought do I want the reader to have?" Does this closing paragraph (from the State Bank letter above) accomplish these two objectives?

Act now! Sign the enclosed Acceptance Certificate and start the New Year with a $500 cash reserve.

Since this letter was sent at the beginning of a new year, the opening reference to the new year provides consistency. Now contrast the action-oriented paragraph about the Visa Card with this weak example from a letter answering a request for information about a product:

Weak example

I hope this answers your questions. If I can be of any further assistance, please feel free to contact me at any time.

You probably stopped reading in the middle of the first sentence since you knew what the rest of the paragraph said. This closing paragraph falls into the trap of showing doubt (I hope) and closes with an insincere, conventional sentence—words that have little or no meaning.

Purpose of middle paragraph

Middle paragraphs perform various functions. They may state a condition, provide an illustration, or provide a transition from one part to another.

Order

Order defined

Very closely related to position is the characteristic of *order*. In business writing, order refers to the *sequencing of the ideas/sentences to give reading a forward movement*. Each part of the paragraph should help move the reader from beginning to end. Four common arrangements include:

Types of order

- ☐ Chronological.
- ☐ Geographical/spatial.
- ☐ Logical.
- ☐ Psychological.

Chronological order

Chronological order arranges the ideas in terms of time—from beginning to end. This arrangement is especially good for narratives, descriptions, and procedures.

Geographical/spatial

Geographical/spatial order presents the ideas in relation to some geographical point or space relationship. It may be from here to there or there to here, from left to right or front to back, or some other useful arrangement suggested by the data.

Logical

Direct approach

Indirect approach

Logical order refers to the arrangement of items from whole to parts or parts to whole. The whole-to-parts order is called direct; and the parts-to-whole, indirect. The specific-to-general or general-to-specific is a variation of this order. In the *direct* approach, state a generalization first; then offer statements with supporting details. With the *indirect* approach, give the details first; then finish with a generalization.

In a list of items, you can use an alphabetical or numerical sequence, or other logical arrangement. For instance, if you report the scores of the baseball teams for the American League, you might arrange the lead-in sentence and listing as follows:

```
The scores for the American League baseball teams for April 20 were:

    Chicago 6, Cleveland 2
    Detroit 5, Baltimore 3
    New York 15, Boston 2
    Oakland 5, Minnesota 1
    Seattle 7, Milwaukee 0
    Texas 6, California 3
    Toronto 8, Kansas City 5
```

Note that the winning team is placed first in each row; winning teams are arranged alphabetically as you move down the list. This is the arrangement you see in the newspaper. If you were to view the same scores on TV, you probably would see the information presented in the following manner:

```
New York 15          Kansas City 5
Boston    2          Toronto     8

Baltimore 3          California  3
Detroit   5          Texas       6

Cleveland 2          Minnesota   1
Chicago   6          Oakland     5

Seattle   7
Milwaukee 0
```

Why the different arrangement? Is the order numerical? Alphabetical? Typically, scores are reported on TV with the home team listed first. Also, there isn't an alphabetical sequence as you move down the listing. Usually, the lists are already prepared—perhaps in the order of the game time; then the scores are inserted later. So you can see that paragraphs and ideas can be arranged to achieve a specific goal. Just be sure that your reader/listener understands your arrangement.

Psychological

The *psychological* order uses an arrangement that is especially appropriate when you want to convince your reader. When you use a cause-effect approach or the known-to-unknown approach, you are using the psychological order. You develop your ideas and then present the main conclusion or point of view. In this sense, this order is similar to the indirect approach. In the psychological approach, however, you decide on the order that best achieves your purpose. The psychological order is especially helpful when you expect the reader may react negatively to the message. Giving reasons for the action can soften the negative impact. This arrangement is also useful in persuasive writing.

Order examples

Effective arrangement of your ideas demonstrates to your readers that you are logical and concerned for them. Logical structures help to lead your reader through the material. Consider these examples of order:

Chronological

Current employment indicates a continued concern for our economic status. In February, the unemployment rate jumped six-tenths of a percentage point to 7.2 percent; in March it fell to 7.1 percent. However, this leaves the jobless rate higher than it was last November and December.

Geographical

The 1986 regional unit sales for the Exhilor Corporation are New England, 105,000; Middle Atlantic, 208,000; South, 135,000; Southwest, 50,000; Midwest 150,000; Rocky Mountains, 45,000; and the Far West, 75,000.

Indirect/logical

The February employment losses in the oil and gas industries brought overall mining employment to its lowest figure in the past five years. Even though these types of jobs account for less than 1 percent of total nonfarm employment, jobs in the oil and gas sectors fell by 24,000 in February; this was in addition to a 17,800 drop in January.

Direct/logical

Job losses in the oil and gas industries fell by 17,800 in January and 24,000 in February. Even though these type jobs account for less than 1 percent of total nonfarm employment, these job losses have been a significant drain on February employment. This continued downward trend has brought overall mining employment to its lowest figure in the past five years.

Psychological

Have you ever wondered, as I have, what makes the difference in people's lives? It isn't a native intelligence or talent or dedication. It isn't that one person wants success and others don't. The difference lies in what each person knows and how she or he makes use of that knowledge. You can gain that difference over others by reading the *Executive Digest*. That is the whole purpose of the *Digest*: to give you essential knowledge that you can use in business.

Continuity

Continuity defined

Continuity refers to the natural progression of ideas from start to finish. Tie ideas together in a logical manner. Continuity can be achieved by two general ways:

- ☐ Use of transitional expressions.
- ☐ Repetition of words/ideas or structure.

Using transitional words or phrases

Transitional words or phrases are useful in leading the reader smoothly from one idea to the next. They can also provide connections between paragraphs. A partial list of transitional words and phrases includes:

however	in addition to
therefore	on the other hand
thus	for example
moreover	reasons one . . . two . . . three
because	as a result
second	in contrast

Effective writing through repetition

Repetition of words/ideas or structure refers to repeating selected words/ideas consciously for an effect. A repeated phrase, sentence, or paragraph structure can also help move the reader through your message. Note in this example the effective use of repetition in both words and structure.

Dear Customer:

Example

Here is something FREE from your Bell Company. FREE connections for Custom Calling Services so you can enjoy your telephone like never before! You'll get

Caps

Repeated structure

NEW CONVENIENCE. . . by dialing urgent calls just by touching one number on your phone. We call that Speed Calling, and you can have it connected FREE.

Indentions

NEW EFFICIENCY. . . by getting a call from a friend while you're on the phone with someone else. We call that Call Waiting, and you can have it connected FREE.

NEW COMMUNICATIONS. . . by transferring all calls to a friend's house when you're visiting. We call that Call Forwarding, and you can have it connected FREE.

Emphasis

Emphasis defined

Emphasis is achieved by using techniques for stressing selected ideas. If you are speaking, for example, you may pause, use gestures, or increase your voice volume to create emphasis. In your writing, you need to use such mechanical aids as position, underscoring, caps, paragraphing, or italics. Refer to the "Dear Customer" letter for these techniques. Emphasize important facts or ideas so that the reader can get the intended meaning of your message.

WRITING ANALYSIS

Analyzing writing using a microcomputer

To strengthen your writing, you can now analyze your messages with the aid of microcomputer software. One such software is RightWriter ™ (registered trademark of Decisionware Corporation). After storing your message on a microcomputer disk, you can analyze the contents for areas of improvement. With RightWriter, you get a message printout with comments inserted about grammar, style, usage, and punctuation. Look at Figure 5.4.

In addition to the message printout with comments, a summary report provides overall message analyses/recommendations including a:

Types of analyses:

- □ Readability index (reading grade level).
- □ Strength index (suggestions for improving message).
- □ Descriptive index (use of adjectives and adverbs).
- □ Jargon index (jargon and buzz words).
- □ Sentence structure analysis (recommendation for change).
- □ Uncommon word list (list of slang, uncommon, and misspelled words).
- □ Word frequency list (alphabetical list of all words and frequency of each).

Look at Figure 5.5 which shows the summary for the entire message.

This method is a vast improvement over manual means of determining readability of text material used in the past. In addition to readability, this easy-to-use tool provides a detailed analysis of the message content. *One word of caution*: use judgment when making changes in your writing. If everything is changed according to the analysis, your writing can become too structured, making the reading dull, rote, and uninteresting.

Figure 5.4
Sample of RightWriter analysis of one page of a communication

```
Welcome to The Hideaway! At The Hideaway, you and your
family
                  ^<<* 6. COLLOQUIAL: Hideaway *>>
       <<* 6. COLLOQUIAL: Hideaway *>>^
will be able to ski over well-groomed slopes and then sit
in front of a crackling hot fire in your own private
townhome. As
                  <<* 17. LONG SENTENCE: 31 WORDS *>>^
                        <<* 31. COMPLEX SENTENCE *>>^
you requested, here are answers to your questions about
The Hideaway--one of the area's newest and most lux-
urious WINTER
     ^<<* 6. COLLOQUIAL: Hideaway *>>
resorts.
     ^<<* 31. COMPLEX SENTENCE *>>

After the opening date of November 1, 19__, you can se-
lect from a townhome (2 or 3 bedrooms) or a Tower unit
(studio; 1 or 2 bedrooms). See the enclosed brochures for
each type with
   ^<<* 17. LONG SENTENCE: 27 WORDS *>>
   ^<<* 27. SEMICOLONS SEPARATE INDEPENDENT CLAUSES *>>
accompanying prices and the fees for ski passes. In addi-
tion, you can enjoy the luxurious sauna or continue your
exercising program in the Bill Weider Exercise room.
Then, perhaps you might like to take a refreshing dip in
the heated outdoor pool; or if you prefer, in the Olympic
indoor pool.
       <<* 17. LONG SENTENCE: 24 WORDS *>>^

While at The Hideaway, you will be able to ramble through
the
            ^<<* 6. COLLOQUIAL: Hideaway *>>
nearby 1800s mining town with its narrow streets lined
with soft gas lamps. Or you can browse through the quaint
boutiques and
```

Figure 5.4 *(concluded)*

```
        ^<<* 17. LONG SENTENCE: 25 WORDS *>>
century-old stores filled with antiques. Or eat a fes-
tival of foods at one of the many sidewalk cafes and
restaurants.

A special bus will pick you up at the Denver airport and
deliver you right to the door of The Hideaway. The mini-
mum length of
     <<* 6. COLLOQUIAL: Hideaway *>>^
stay is one week with a $100 per person deposit made
within 30 days of verbal confirmation. All major credit
cards are accepted.
         ^<<* 21. PASSIVE VOICE: are accepted *>>

Call 800_532-2346 (our toll-free number) today to make
your reservations for an exciting Winter Vacation you
won't forget.
<<* 4. NEGATIVE. CONSIDER REPHRASING won't forget *>>^
                            <<* 31. COMPLEX SENTENCE *>>^

In addition to skiing and sightseeing, you can ice skate,
snowmobile, and sleigh ride as shown in the enclosed bro-
chures. Whatever your pleasure, you'll find the
excitement and relaxation you've been looking for at The
Hideaway. Call today!
       <<* 6. COLLOQUIAL: Hideaway *>>^

Sincerely
```

Figure 5.5
Sample of RightWriter analysis of an entire document

```
                    <<** SUMMARY **>>
  OVERALL CRITIQUE FOR: B:ABC.ASC
  READABILITY INDEX: 8.25
Readers need an 8th grade level of education to under-
stand.

    Total Number of Words in Document: 304
    Total Number of Words within Sentences: 303
    Total Number of Sentences: 17
    Total Number of Syllables: 454

  STRENGTH INDEX: 0.20
The writing can be made more direct by using:
          - the active voice
          - shorter sentences
          - more common words
          - less slang

  DESCRIPTIVE INDEX: 0.48
The use of adjectives and adverbs is in the normal range.

  JARGON INDEX: 0.25

SENTENCE STRUCTURE RECOMMENDATIONS:
    1. Most sentences contain multiple clauses.
       Try to use more simple sentences.
   12. Many exclamations are used.
       Review the use of exclamation points.
   14. Consider using more predicate verbs.
                  << WORDS TO REVIEW >>
Review the following list for negative words (N), collo-
quial words (C), jargon (J), misspellings (?), misused
words (?), or words which your reader may not understand
(?).
    1800S(?)   1                  BOUTIQUES(?)   1
   BROWSE(?)   1               CONFIRMATION(J)   1
CRACKLING(?)   1                   FESTIVAL(J)   1
 HIDEAWAY(C)   6                  LUXURIOUS(J)   2
  OLYMPIC(?)   1                     QUAINT(?)   1
   RAMBLE(N)   1                 RELAXATION(J)   1
    SAUNA(?)   1                SIGHTSEEING(?)   1
   SLEIGH(?)   1                 SNOWMOBILE(?)   1
 TOWNHOME(?)   2                   VACATION(J)   1
   WEIDER(?)   1
            << END OF WORDS TO REVIEW LIST >>
```

SUMMARY

Every individual possesses a unique writing style based on good language skills. This style can be adjusted through the use of a planned strategy. By combining appropriate words, sentence structures, and paragraph orders, you can write a powerful message designed for a specific audience.

You can adjust your writing style by eliminating such characteristics of weak writing as poor language, incorrect word choice, unclear purpose, and illogical thinking. By correcting these weaknesses, your personality emerges.

However, the real test of your writing and speaking ability is determined by the response of the reader/audience.

How do you learn to write and speak effectively? You begin by recognizing that, on the basis of context, words have both denotation and connotation meanings which affect people in different ways. Therefore, choose words from the reader's viewpoint to gain positive acceptance.

Each message also conveys a positive, neutral, or negative impression—tone. Other important principles to consider when choosing words include: positive versus negative, concrete versus abstract, short versus long, time-saving words, familiar words, and unbiased words.

Words do very little until combined with other parts. The way you put words together, first in sentences and then in paragraphs, is what determines the writing style. Arrange your ideas into grammatically correct sentences to form paragraphs. Vary the sentence types to maintain reader interest. Sentence types to choose from include: simple, compound, complex, and compound-complex.

Generally, write in the active voice using action verbs. Eliminate sexist language and other discriminatory practices. Be precise in word choice and word phrase placement, and use repetition purposefully.

Keep in mind the important concepts related to paragraph development—topic sentences, unity, substance, position, order, continuity, and emphasis.

An excellent tool for analyzing your writing style is the use of microcomputer software such as RightWriter™.

END-OF-CHAPTER ACTIVITIES

DISCUSSION

1. Define writing style.
2. Discuss how you can adjust your writing style to various situations.
3. How can you incorporate effective principles of communication and still maintain your own unique writing style? Discuss.
4. Discuss how you can employ negative words and yet produce a positive tone.
5. Discuss the characteristics of each of these types of words: concrete/abstract, short/long, time-saving, familiar, unbiased.
6. Discuss how sex-biased language or ethnic-biased language influences corporate world perceptions.
7. In your business writing, when would you use simple, compound, complex, compound/complex sentences?
8. What are the meanings of the terms *unity, substance, position, order, continuity,* and *emphasis* as they relate to writing paragraphs?

9. What are the advantages and disadvantages of using microcomputer software as an editing tool for writing?
10. What is the relationship between the strategy for communicating in business and writing style?

ACTIVITIES

11. Which of the following words are high in denotative meaning? Which have strong connotative meaning?

happy	gasoline	widespread
staircase	heartthrob	shallow
party	wretched	portrait
city slicker	highway	apartment
astronaut	burden	sex appeal

12. In the following sentences change the vague abstract words or phrases to achieve a more concrete statement:
    a. Mark received a high score on the exam.
    b. The senator was reelected by a wide margin.
    c. In the last month, the typewriter has been serviced a number of times.
    d. Gloria was several minutes late.
    e. The building is located on a large piece of land.
    f. Our representative will call on you soon.
    g. A substantial discount is given to those who pay by the 10th of the month.
    h. Everyone needs to prepare for a career.
13. Replace the following long words with short, simple ones.

dominate	passageway	underneath
ferocious	enumerate	estrangement
remuneration	innumerable	notwithstanding

14. Rewrite the following sentences to eliminate overused/outdated words and phrases:
    a. Let me take this opportunity of expressing my appreciation.
    b. I hope that the above meets with your approval.
    c. As of this date, we have not heard from you.
    d. In accordance with your request, we are herewith forwarding all documents to you.
    e. I wish to take the liberty of expressing my thanks for a job well done.
    f. Please be advised that the goods were sent via parcel post.
    g. Let us hear from you again in the near future.
    h. Please contact us if we can be of any further service.

i. Due to the fact that Monday is a holiday, we are postponing the meeting until further notice.

j. Thanking you in advance, I remain

15. Indicate the sentence construction type—(*a*) simple (*b*) compound (*c*) complex or (*d*) compound-complex—for each of the sentences listed below.

a. The government will sharply expand efforts to collect bad debts; warnings will be mailed.

b. Mary and John both had high production rates for the month of December.

c. As the strike entered the fifth day, managers became very nervous.

d. May sales were up and unemployment was down.

e. With 30 percent of today's teenagers not finishing high school, new methods are being studied to reach these young people.

f. After placing an ad in the journal, 4 million readers responded immediately; and letters are still coming in.

g. Future cashiers will be able to check customer credit faster than ever.

16. Identify the weaknesses in each of these sentences:

a. Once the project is underway, we will hire additional staff, diversifying our product line, produce greater profits, and make a greater appeal to the public.

b. Our policy forbids you to return merchandise purchased on sale.

c. In the event that you would like us to return the merchandise, just indicate your preference on the enclosed, self-addressed envelope.

d. We probably don't stand a ghost of a chance on getting the bid.

e. Each and every time the situation occurs, a record should be made and kept on file.

f. We checked with PAC and found they were willing to support us.

g. Today's company executive is less conservative than he was 10 years ago.

h. The figures were somewhat overstated in the report.

i. This is the fastest sports car on the road today.

j. The company president emphasized the importance of secretaries speaking at a management meeting.

k. We would like to have you write us and let us know when we are to begin remodeling the kitchen.

l. In the majority of instances, we will be available.

m. I was very happy to bring the matter to the attention of Mr. Charles Bendall for his input on the matter.

n. Our secretaries are willing to demonstrate their ability to produce typed documents in record time by providing the reports to you by the deadline.

17. Find three articles. Select the topic sentences from several paragraphs.
18. From some source, find a paragraph that you consider "good" which has no topic sentence stated. State the implied topic idea.
19. Write a paragraph based on the following topic sentence: Smoking should be banned from the corporate work place.
20. Use the topic sentence from No. 3 above and rewrite the paragraph using different forms and in different positions.
21. Identify why the following paragraphs do *not* possess unity:
    a. We are enclosing with this letter a copy of our booklet. It is entitled "How to Learn Netting." Your letter of inquiry was received today. I hope you will find it interesting and useful as we have. We thank you for your interest in our products.
    b. I will go into detail as to my routine chores in setting up a client's file. To set up a file is probably one of my least favorite things to do. After the new client is interviewed, I get the file, which reminds me that another thing I do is set up blank files, which means making sure that everyone of our forms to fill out or be signed by the client is in a file folder so an initial interview can be performed. This is thirty odd forms, along with brochures, etc. which are also kept in my office. Anyway, I'll get a new file and it has to be sorted into four or five odd files, these labels typed up and put on new file folders which have to be stamped with our firm name and address, holes have to be punched and fasteners put in and the correspondence put in order to make up a medical file.
22. For each example above, select the topic sentence; rewrite to achieve unity.
23. Select a topic sentence related to your major and develop a paragraph using one or more of the methods mentioned in this chapter.
24. Select a business article and identify each of the methods used to develop the topic sentences.
25. From your reading of business periodicals, select paragraphs that illustrate each of the methods of developing substance as presented in this chapter. Find an example that uses a combination of these methods.
26. Write a paragraph on the topic sentence "Equal work should bring equal pay."
    a. Use the opening for the topic sentence.
    b. Rewrite the paragraph using the topic sentence at the end of the paragraph.
    c. Rewrite the paragraph again placing the topic sentence in the middle.

27. Rearrange these sentences to form a coherent piece of writing: Description of a Lead Pencil

    a. Typically, a wooden lead pencil is about 0.8 cm in diameter and about 19 cm long.

    b. The shape of a wooden lead pencil resembles that of a piece of dowel, or the shaft of an arrow, with the exception that many pencils are hexagonal, rather than round, in cross section, and that occasionally still other cross-sectional shapes are found.

    c. The purpose of the wooden case is to make the pencil comfortable to hold and to provide rigidity.

    d. The case is composed of two parts; that is, it is divided lengthwise into identical halves.

    e. A wooden lead pencil is a device for drawing or writing on a suitable medium with a piece of graphite permanently encased in a slender wooden shaft or holder.

    f. Before it can be used, a wooden lead pencil must be sharpened: wood must be shaved off the end opposite the eraser end, and the graphite itself must be shaved down to a point.

    g. The purpose of the eraser is to remove unwanted marks from the medium being written upon.

    h. Each half of the case contains a semicircular groove centered along the length of the flat side, to receive the graphite, and each has a slightly diminished cross-sectional area at one end over which to slip the metal ferrule.

    i. In appearance, the ferrule is a simple piece of metal tubing about 1.5 cm long, and 0.8 cm in diameter, often painted to harmonize with the case and the eraser.

    j. When assembled, the two halves of the case are glued together, with the graphite held in the hole created by the matching semicircular grooves.

    k. It is usually in the form of a cylinder about 0.3 cm in diameter and is the same length as the case.

    l. As the graphite wears away in use, the pencil must be resharpened.

    m. This diminished cross-sectional area is usually round, regardless of the shape of the rest of the case.

    n. It is typically a rubber cylinder about 1.5 cm in length which will fit tightly inside the ferrule; and it is often made of colored rubber.

    o. It is made up of four parts: the graphite, the wooden case, an eraser, and a ferrule by which the eraser is attached.

    p. The purpose of the ferrule is to attach the eraser to the case.

    q. The eraser and the case are inserted into opposite ends of the ferrule; they are secured in place by indentions which have been stamped into the ferrule after assembly.

r. The case is normally painted.

s. For pencils having a novel cross section, the graphite may be molded in some form other than that of a cylinder.

t. The purpose of the graphite is, of course, to make marks on the paper or other medium.[6]

28. Write a paragraph on a topic sentence related to business and use chronological order; circle all transitional words.

29. Assume that you are a visitor at a prominent university. You have just entered the elevator of a six-story College of Business Administration building and want to see someone in the Marketing Department. The directory inside the elevator looks like this:

	DIRECTORY
P Plaza	Plaza Exit Level Stairways to Auditorium Exit for 1st Floor, Classroom Building Exit for Student Center
M Mezzanine	Computer Center Exit for Broadway and 2nd Floor, Classroom Building
2 Second Floor	Computer Center Staff Offices Duplicating Center
3 Third Floor	Department of Marketing Department of Management Information Systems Department of Transportation
4 Fourth Floor	Department of Statistics Department of Industrial Relations Systems Computing Services
5 Fifth Floor	Small Business Assistance Center Department of Economics Student-Faculty Lounge Department of Finance
6 Sixth Floor	College of Business Administration Office of the Dean and the Associate Dean Department of Accounting Graduate Programs Office Executive Development Programs

Was this directory arranged for instant communication? Explain. How would you suggest revising the directory? Rewrite the directory.

[6] Gordon H. Mills and John A. Walter, *Technical Writing*, 4th ed. (New York: Henry Holt, 1978), pp. 122-23. Used with permission.

30. Write a paragraph on a business topic which contains repetition of words and structure to achieve emphasis.
31. Find three examples of business writing that use repetition of words and structure to achieve emphasis. Explain how the writer achieved emphasis.
32. The following paragraph lacks unity, order, and proper transitional aids. Rewrite the paragraph for more effectiveness.

    In 1985, the average corporate chief in the U.S. took home a hefty $1.2 million. The top five highest-paid executives were as follows. Victor Posner was ranked first with $12,739,000. He is chairman of DWG. Ranking fifth was Robert L. Mitchell. As chairman of Celanese, he earned $4,756,000. The next highest-paid executive to him was chairman of Chrysler with an income of $11,426,000. The chairman's name was Lee A. Iacocca who has been responsible for the bailout of Chrysler and who has served as chairman of the foundation for the restoration of the Statue of Liberty. And the person coming in next was T. Boone Pickens, Jr. Can you believe an income of $8,431,000? He works for Mesa. He is also the chairman of Mesa. Rounding out the list of the top five highest-paid executives in fourth place is the chairman of Warner Amex—Drew Lewis. His salary comes to $6,000,000.[7]

33. Select the topic sentence; then arrange the other sentences to form an effective paragraph:
    a. Laser printers have fallen in price dramatically since their introduction in the mid-1970s.
    b. The cost effectiveness of today's laser printer becomes obvious as the need to stockpile forms and documents is eliminated, and the outside professional print shop becomes almost obsolete.
    c. If you've contemplated purchasing a laser printer for your office but were put off by the price tag, it may be time to shop again.
    d. In addition to their ability to combine graphics and a variety of font styles and type sizes simultaneously on a page, most have the capacity to store, alter, and print documents upon command.[8]

---

[7] *Business Week,* no. 2945, May 5, 1986, facts taken from cover page.

[8] Clifford Meth, "Write with Light!" *Administrative Management* 47, no. 3 (March 1986), pp. 39–43.

PART TWO

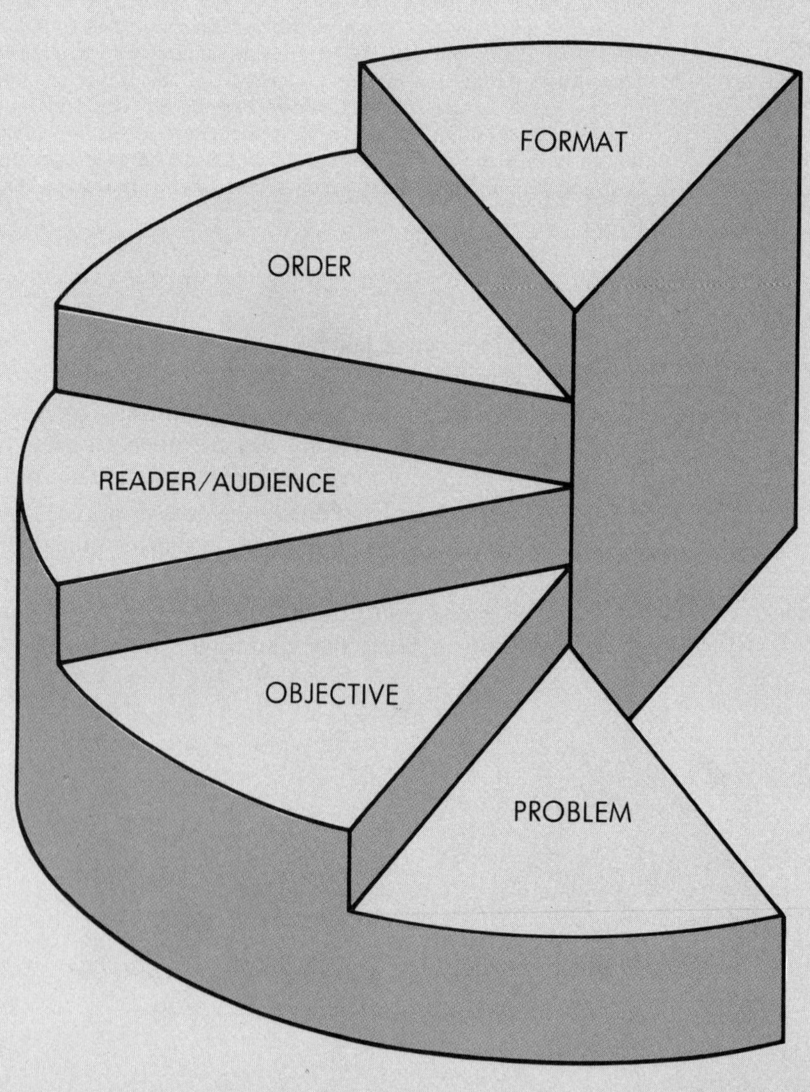

A PROCESS FOR COMMUNICATING BUSINESS LETTERS AND MEMOS

6. INTRODUCTION TO LETTERS AND MEMOS
7. WRITING REQUEST LETTERS
8. WRITING POSITIVE LETTERS
9. WRITING NEGATIVE LETTERS
10. WRITING OTHER TYPES OF MESSAGES

CHAPTER 6

INTRODUCTION TO LETTERS AND MEMOS

Learning Objectives

After studying this chapter, you will be able to:

- □ Understand the importance of letters and memos in business.
- □ Recognize the importance of effective writing to your career advancement.
- □ Distinguish the major characteristics of letters and memos.
- □ Appreciate the necessity of editing drafts to attain effective messages.
- □ Identify the principles that contribute to an effective communication.
- □ Understand the relationships between persuasive writing and goodwill.
- □ Select the appropriate techniques for sales writing.
- □ Understand how an attractive appearance contributes to the communication.

Reasons for developing writing competencies

How important are effective letters and memos to businesses? Why should you concern yourself about developing business writing competencies? Although not exhaustive, four comments highlight the major reasons:

Job requirements

- □ Businesses use letters and memos to carry on the day-to-day activities of the organization. Therefore, you have a 100 percent probability of writing letters and memos on the job. In numerous studies, scholars have asked business people to rank the importance of on-the-job activities. Writing ability always appears in the top three activities. Businesses value effective communicators.

Poor writing is expensive

- □ Letters and memos represent a major expense (investment) to businesses and should not be wasted. The Gibbs Consulting Group estimated that American offices generated about 76 million letters a day—approximately 20 billion letters for the year.[1] Using the $7.60 average cost of a business letter reported by the Dartnell Institute, the estimated annual cost for letters alone has passed $152 billion.[2] By 1986, the cost of the letter increased to $9.33. If this trend continues, the total cost for letters alone in 1989 could be an astounding $700 billion. Effective letters cost no more than weak ones—usually less. A poorly written letter can result in additional communications that add to the overall cost of solving a particular problem. Today, businesses consider information a major resource of the firm.

Builds goodwill

- □ Well-written letters create positive feelings on the part of the reader (called *goodwill*) and result in repeat business. Even though such feelings of goodwill may be subjective, trying to create a positive attitude is critical to the success of your messages. The need for continued goodwill perhaps distinguishes business messages from general writing. If the reader is a customer, goodwill can mean future sales. Thus, administrators value employees who can foster favorable attitudes through their letters and memos.

Enhances professional advancement

- □ Being an effective writer can enhance your professional career since employers highly value effective writing. Each message you create serves as your ambassador—it becomes a historical record of your effectiveness. People in other parts of the organization get to know you through your writing. Good communicators get the attention of superiors. Your image as an effective or ineffective communicator can determine your advancement.

In these four chapters, you will study how to evaluate different business situations and how to construct effective letters and memos.

---

[1] Timothy R. V. Foster and Alfred Glossbrenner, *Word Processing for Executives and Professionals* (New York: Van Nostrand Reinhold, 1983), p. 1.

[2] Frank Greenwood and Mary M. Greenwood, *Office Technology: Principles of Automation* (Reston, Va.: Reston Publishing, 1985), p. 101.

Figure 6.1
Strategy for communicating letters and memos

Strategy component	Letter	Memo
Problem	Outside-related	Inside-related
Objective		
Overall	Persuade/inform/request	Inform/request/persuade
Specific content	Longer than memo More formal than memo Personal	Shorter than letter Less formal than letter Personal
Reader/Audience	External	Internal
Order		
General	Same	Same
Specific	Same	Same
Format	Seven basic parts Letterhead	Five basic parts Special form

CONTRASTS BETWEEN LETTERS AND MEMOS

Comparison of letters and memos

The letter is the most common format for transmitting information outside the firm; the memo is the most common form used within the firm. The overall approach in constructing each type of message is similar, however. Figure 6.1 contrasts the strategy for communicating letters and memos.

PRINCIPLES OF EFFECTIVE LETTERS AND MEMOS

Principles of good letters/memos

As was pointed out in Chapter 5, you need to choose your words carefully, arrange the words into powerful sentences, and join the sentences in a way that conveys your thoughts to the reader. In addition, effective writing needs to be easy to understand, oriented to your reader, concerned with the goodwill objective as well as the general objective, and attractive in appearance.

Easy to Understand

Principles of good writing

No written message is effective unless your reader understands what you mean. Because of the volume of paper they receive daily, people in business often read hastily; readers also scan materials and sometimes miss key elements if they are improperly placed. To make your writing easy to understand, be sure that your letters and memos are *clear, concise, complete, forceful,* and *well organized.*

Clarity

To be *clear,* the meaning of your message should be apparent on a first reading. A busy reader shouldn't have to reread your message to understand it. Can you understand the following letter after a single reading?

Dear ________

With reference to my letter (attached) as well as your order (a copy of that is attached also), I am happy to enclose herewith our check No. 3789 dated February 10 for $2.00 as reimbursement of prepayment on an out-of-print publication.

Sincerely,

The ideas are contained in the letter, but the style wastes the reader's time. The reader must first identify the facts and then rearrange them for meaning. Imagine that the following sentences were spoken over the phone. Which example is clearer? Why?

Our meeting on Friday at 11 a.m. has been cancelled. We will meet at 1 p.m.

Our meeting on Friday has been changed to 1 p.m.

As people often do, the listener might have stopped *hearing* the message after the word *cancelled* in the first example. Obviously, the speaker, then, would have failed to transmit the message accurately. By contrast, the key word in the second example is *changed,* not *cancelled.*

Conciseness

To be *concise,* you need to say what you have to say in the fewest possible words— yet still be complete and courteous. Lincoln's "Gettysburg Address" has been acclaimed as a masterpiece of conciseness. As you edit your writing, eliminate words as long as you don't adversely affect completeness and courtesy. Which of the following examples are concise?

We want to take this opportunity to say thank you for your March 22 order.

OR

Thank you for your March 22 order.

Is the signature on the enclosed contract yours?

OR

I surely would appreciate it very much if you would check the signature on the enclosed contract and let me know if possible if it is your signature.

Be careful that you don't confuse *conciseness* with *brevity.* When you eliminate words and sacrifice completeness and courtesy, you are being too brief. Reread your messages to make sure that you have included all essential elements.

Completeness

To be *complete,* your letters and memos need to include an appropriate mix of *who, what, when, where, why,* and *how.* Examine this from a memo about a planned meeting:

Please plan to meet on Tuesday in Room 7-C to review the qualifications of the four candidates for the Office Systems Analyst position.

LEGAL / ETHICAL ISSUE

Attorney Bill Mason handles consumer collection accounts for a number of major retail firms in the Houston, Texas, area. He has an excellent reputation for collecting consumer debts incurred through default on credit card, installment, and mortgage loans.

About five years ago, Attorney Mason expanded his services to include debt collection. He uses such techniques as collection letters, phone calls, and even lawsuits to obtain results.

While building his practice, he assured the managers of the firms employing his services that their companies were protected against counterclaims based on unfair collection practices. Since lawyers were exempted from the 1978 Fair Debt Collection Practices Act, Attorney Mason was free to use tough debt-collection practices, even threatening legal action if the consumer didn't pay up. He could be very persuasive.

However, in July 1986, the law was amended to restrict lawyers in their debt-collection practices. Among the new restrictions are:

- ☐ Lawyers can't call debtors before 8:00 a.m. in the morning or after 9:00 p.m. in the evening.
- ☐ Lawyers must send a written notice within five days of initial contact detailing the specifics of the debt and repayment.
- ☐ Lawyers may not accept checks postdated over five days unless they send a written notice to the debtor stating intention to deposit the check.

How does this law impact communication practices for (*a*) the lawyer collecting the debt, (*b*) the firm holding the debt, and (*c*) the debtor? What implications does this case have for writing all types of letters and/or notices?

Two important facts are omitted—the time and date of the meeting. Customers often omit style, size, or other characteristics about items when they order from mail-order companies. Omission of important details causes delays and additional communications. Before sending out a memo or letter, give it a final check for completeness.

Forcefulness

To be *forceful,* blend the use of specific words and action-oriented writing. Look at this sentence:

It is our policy to give a substantial discount to all those who pay promptly.

How would you rewrite it to focus on the benefits the reader can receive if payments are made promptly? The words *substantial* and *promptly* are vague. The revised version provides a more forceful image:

By paying within 15 days of the invoice date, you can earn a 10 percent savings on each of your orders.

Contrast these two examples. Which is more forceful?

Your remittance is expected by return mail.

Please send your $50.25 check by June 13.

Well-organized

In addition to being clear, concise, complete, and forceful, your letters and memos need to be well organized—the Order component of the strategy for communicating. Putting your ideas in the right sequence helps you convey to your reader the exact meaning you intend, thus achieving your overall communication objective. Which of the following letters is better organized?

Dear Mr. Goodfellow:

Because our floor is located quite a distance from the staff lounge, we are considering installing a staff lounge for our floor. I have been asked to head up the project.

Your company has been recommended to me by several people in other companies and I am therefore writing this letter to you.

We plan to locate the staff lounge in a central place for convenience of our employees. Will you, therefore, send me all the information you have concerning the needed items and costs for this projected staff lounge?

Sincerely,

Dear Mr. Goodfellow:

By answering some questions, you will help us decide whether to install a 12-foot by 12-foot staff lounge on the sixth floor of our building. We want our 100 employees to use the lounge on a staggered basis for morning and afternoon breaks.

1. What type appliances would you recommend for coffee and hot water? Cost of each?
2. What type refrigerator would you recommend? Cost?
3. What other items should be included? Is the space adequate?
4. Will someone have to be in charge of the lounge? What are your suggestions for operating the lounge?
5. Could you install the lounge by November 30?

Since the Executive Board will decide on this project at their October 30 meeting, I would appreciate receiving your reply by October 20.

Sincerely,

Reader-Oriented

On a scale of 1-10, rate the effectiveness of this message:

Dear Ms. Ivanhoe:

Your order for one pair of Nike tennis shoes was received yesterday. The order clerk sent your letter to me since you failed to give the size of tennis shoes in the

November 15 order letter. Of course, we are unable to mail the tennis shoes until we know the size you want. We can't read your mind. This seems to be a common omission with you consumers.

You must send us the size (sizes 5 to 10 available plus half sizes) tennis shoes you want immediately. We are pleased you ordered from us.

Sincerely yours,

Characteristics of reader-oriented messages

This letter is easy enough to understand, and it has the virtues of clarity, conciseness, completeness, forcefulness, and appropriate organization. Yet it is ineffective. The letter isn't reader-oriented. It fails in three important categories: *tone, viewpoint,* and *sales content.* The tone would be insulting to most readers. The Ivanhoe letter fails because it:

Stresses the "I" viewpoint—it is writer-centered.

Dwells on the negative—"failed," "unable," "omission."

Demands rather than requests—"must."

Belittles the reader—"We can't read your mind" and "This seems to be a common omission with you consumers."

Ends with an insincere courtesy statement that doesn't fit with the tone of the letter.

Tone

Tone is that intangible ingredient that produces a feeling on the part of your reader—either positive, negative, or neutral. Your goal is to create a positive attitude. Use of positive and negative words determine the tone of your message. Remember, the "you" attitude is not achieved simply by scattering second person pronouns throughout your letters and memos. Rather, to achieve an effective "you" viewpoint, you must keep your reader's needs in mind as you write. What does my reader want? Expect? Need?

Being natural, friendly, courteous, and personal helps create good tone. Avoid:

Bluntness.

Negative words or meaning.

Evasiveness.

Finger pointing; blaming.

Pompous words.

Demanding words such as *must.*

Exclusive "I" viewpoint.

Viewpoint

Viewpoint refers to the focus of the message—either the reader (you), the writer (I), or something else (it, they, he/she, etc.). In the Ivanhoe letter, the focus should be on what the reader has to do and the action to be taken to get the shoes. Note the many references to I-we-us. The letter is not reader-centered. Contrast the revised version with the original. Describe the differences in overall effectiveness. What specifically contributes to the change in tone?

Dear Ms. Ivanhoe:

Thank you for your November 14 order for one pair of innovative Nike tennis shoes. As soon as you send us the size you want, the popular Nike tennis shoes will be rushed to you. Just check the desired size on the attached card and return it today.

Shortly, you will be joining thousands of others who enjoy hours of recreational activities in Nike Comfort.

Sincerely,

Sales

This version presents a more appropriate viewpoint and tone for a letter to a customer. Note the use of adjectives (*innovative* and *popular*) before the name of the shoe and the addition of a *sales*-oriented sentence at the end. Don't neglect the potential for sales as you write your letters to customers. Effective *sales writing* develops or enhances the reader's favorable attitude toward you or your company's products or services. This can also be referred to as persuasive writing. In reality, though, all effective writing is persuasive. The reader must be persuaded to believe the information presented.

Persuasive/sales writing defined

Since each person has self-interests and emotional needs, persuasive or sales writing focuses on the use of logical and emotional appeals. These appeals must satisfy the reader's self-interests and emotional needs and thereby justify an action. The last statement in the second Ivanhoe letter assures the reader that the Nike tennis shoe is a good buy since "thousands" of other people use Nikes. The use of the words *comfort, popular,* and *innovative* also help convince the reader that she's made a good choice.

In every letter or memo, you will need to persuade others either to do or accept something. The degree of persuasion needed will depend on the situation. In the highly specialized sales letter, you will need to achieve the same goals of an effective advertisement: get attention, arouse interest, create desire, and request action.

Techniques of persuasive/sales writing

When you write, use a mixture of these techniques to create sales messages:

- ☐ Adjectives.
- ☐ Underlining, capital letters, or other mechanical features.
- ☐ Color, bold, or italic print.
- ☐ "You" viewpoint; reader benefits.
- ☐ Positive tone.
- ☐ Action verbs (picture words).
- ☐ Endorsement by a well-known person.
- ☐ Repetition of key words.
- ☐ Promptness.

Be careful to balance these techniques; otherwise, your message can fail because of the overkill effect. Now contrast the following examples. Which is more effective? Why?

Your order for camera supplies has been received.

OR

Your March 10, 19__, order for the ever-popular AMERICAN CAMERA supplies is being shipped to you by Transport, Inc., on March 10, 19__.

Whether you are traveling by plane or in your car, you can carry your compact Tony Portable (only 12 inches long, 8 inches wide, and 3 inches high) to keep up to date on your dictation.

OR

The machine measures 12 inches long, 8 inches wide, and 3 inches high.

Good tone, appropriate viewpoint, and the right degree of persuasion can create action and goodwill—a feeling of confidence and a readiness to deal with you again.

From time to time, you will write persuasive memos to people within your company. Notice how this memo appeals to pride and civic responsibility in persuading the reader to contribute.

Your assistance is needed. We have a challenge to meet the 100 percent contribution goal to United Way again this year. Last year the United Way was able to give significant assistance to 15 local agencies in carrying out worthwhile activities.

Your contribution to United Way benefits the youth of our community through Girl Scouts, Boy Scouts, the YMCA, the YWCA, and Boy's Club. You no doubt have seen the benefits of these fine youth organizations. Our local social agencies also assist with one of the community's most pressing problems—that of the homeless and indigent people.

To make your contribution to United Way, fill out the attached pledge card and return to me in the enclosed envelope. You may choose a payment plan that fits your needs—contribution by check with your completed card or a weekly/monthly payroll deduction plan. Complete, sign, and return the pledge card today. You can take great pride in attaining another 100 percent contribution goal. Although you may not see it, many people will thank you throughout the year for your generous contribution to the United Way.

The tone in the memo is more personal than letters; appeal to pride of "our" organization stimulates the reader to respond. The message encourages the reader to respond to meet the 100 percent goal.

GOOD WRITING ACHIEVES A DUAL GOAL

Dual goal of communication

An effective letter or memo is one that communicates ideas clearly and accomplishes its general objective plus the all-important objective of goodwill. Unless your messages build or retain goodwill, they haven't accomplished your public relations responsibilities.

Accomplishes objective

Promotes goodwill

If you're writing a letter requesting information about a product or service, the success of that letter can be measured by one simple question: "Did you get the information you wanted?" For a persuasive request to employees about contributing to United Way, the question is similar: "Did the employees contribute?"

To measure the success of a letter to a turned-off customer, the critical question is "Did the customer place another order?" If you're writing an application to a college or perhaps a letter of application for a job, the question is "Did you get a positive response?"

A balance of persuasive techniques and clear writing provides the basis for creating effective communications. A message that accomplishes both objectives reflects the writer's understanding of human nature.

APPEARANCE

Importance of first impression

Professional correspondence should be attractive. Word-processing software can help you improve the appearance of your messages. Be sure, however, for professional letters to use a letter-quality printer rather than a dot matrix. Appendix B presents the various forms that are appropriate for letters and memos. Remember that the first impression the reader has of your message (and of *you*) is important—be sure to proofread to eliminate misspelled words as well as grammatical and other errors. A well-developed letter with the reader's name misspelled or one with errors is perhaps worse than no letter at all. Certainly, such a letter can damage the whole communication. Before sending out a letter or memo, check it for first impressions.

Study the following form letter in which the addressee's name is inserted in an effort to make it more personal. Even though such results can easily be achieved with current word-processing packages, these attempts sometimes fail.

Dear Edgar Smith:

I saw your name on a list of computer professionals who should be receiving COMPUTERS. But our subscriber data files don't show Edgar Smith!

So, Ed, we offer you the opportunity to subscribe to COMPUTERS at a special rate: just 85 cents an issue. And we'll give you a solar desk top calculator free with your paid subscription, Ed.

How does this letter fail? The recipient's name is Edgar Ray Smith, but his friends call him Ray. The sender of the above message used the first name in an effort to make the letter personal—even the use of Ed. The entire letter is ineffective because of the inappropriateness of the name. If you use computer-generated messages, be sure the names are appropriately used and correctly spelled.

SUMMARY

Businesses use letters and memos to carry on the activities of the organization. These two forms represent a major expense (investment) and should not be wasted. Effective letters cost no more than weak ones, usually less. Well-written letters can create goodwill and result in repeat business.

The letter is the most common format for transmitting information outside the firm; the memo, the most common format within the firm. Although the overall approach is similar, letters and memos differ in some aspects.

No written message is successful unless the reader understands what you mean. To make the writing easy to understand, be sure that your letters and memos are clear, concise, complete, forceful, and well organized.

To orient your writing to the reader, pay attention to the tone, viewpoint, and sales appeal. Tone is that intangible ingredient that produces a feeling—positive, negative, or neutral. Being natural, friendly, courteous, and personal help create good tone. Viewpoint refers to the focus of the message—on the reader (you), the writer (I), or something else (it, they, she/he, etc.). Sales writing refers to the appropriate tone and viewpoint plus techniques of persuasive writing that build goodwill.

An attractive appearance is also important for letters and memos. The reader's first impression can contribute to the success of the message. Be sure that no words are misspelled and that each word contributes to the communication; make a final check of the correctness of the form.

END-OF-CHAPTER ACTIVITIES

DISCUSSION

1. Discuss the importance of letters and memos to business.
2. In what ways are letters and memos similar? Different?
3. Define these terms as they relate to letters and memos: clearness, conciseness, completeness, forcefulness.
4. Can a letter possess clearness, conciseness, and completeness, and still be ineffective? Explain.
5. Define tone and its significance in written business communication.
6. Discuss the relationship between tone and viewpoint.
7. From a company perspective, what is meant by persuasive writing?
8. What does appearance have to do with the effectiveness of a letter or memo?

ACTIVITIES

9. Evaluate the following sentences for clarity, conciseness, completeness, courtesy, tone, and viewpoint. Rewrite them to achieve greater effectiveness.
   a. You should use the order forms that are found at the back of our catalog, which we are mailing to you along with our latest price lists that you indicated you wanted us to send. Don't use a letter in the future as you just did; be sure to use the convenient order forms for all future orders.
   b. We are very glad to tell you that all deliveries will now be made on the first day of each week.

c. We are unable to get your order to your store by January 15; in fact, it will be February 15 before you will even get the order. We can't deliver if we don't have it in stock.

d. The results of a user survey reveal that there is considerable dissatisfaction among some of our customers with the software.

e. It has been our experience that during the months of December and January most of our customers' electrical bills are higher than in other months. Therefore, your complaint is unjustified.

10. Evaluate the following statements used in a questionnaire designed for high school students; rewrite the statements for clarity:

a. Alcohol use among friends is:

(1) no problem. (3) a moderate problem.
(2) a mild problem. (4) a serious problem.

b. Marijuana use among friends is:

(1) no problem. (3) a moderate problem.
(2) a mild problem. (4) a serious problem.

c. Do the parents of your friends set the same rules and limitations for their children as your parents do for you?

(1) Usually. (4) Seldom.
(2) Often. (5) Never.
(3) Sometimes.

11. Using the form in Figure 6.2, evaluate the letters and memos in figures 6.3 to 6.9 in terms of how well they achieve these characteristics:

Figure 6.2
Evaluation form for memos and letters

	Good	**Average**	**Weak**
Easy to understand			
Clarity			
Conciseness			
Completeness			
Forcefulness			
Organization			
Reader-oriented:			
Tone			
Viewpoint			
Persuasiveness			
Objectives:			
General			
Goodwill			
Appearance:			
Attractive			
Correct form			

Figure 6.3

MEMO

FOR	All Department Heads	DATE 10-5-19__
FROM	Dean Parsons W12B24	PHONE 2110

ADMINISTRATIVE LEAVE TO VOTE

It has been determined that Administrative Leave to vote is not authorized for employees who are enrolled in afterhours classes. Our regulations state that time off is given only when the employee's work schedule will not allow him or her to vote.

Please distribute this information to supervisors as soon as possible.

Figure 6.4
Response from one employee

MEMO		DATE
FOR	Marion Stroud, Director E4A22	7/10/___ PHONE
FROM	Dale Buchanan W22B10	3044

SUBJECT: MEMO FROM DEAN PARSONS

FIRST, I AM NOT A STUDENT; THEREFORE, THIS MEMO DOES NOT DIRECTLY AFFECT ME. HOWEVER, I HAVE FRIENDS WHO ARE STUDENTS AND ARE DIRECTLY AFFECTED. SINCE OUR COMPANY ACTIVELY ENCOURAGES ITS EMPLOYEES TO ATTEND AFTERHOURS CLASSES, THE ATTACHED MEMO SEEMS COUNTER PRODUCTIVE. TO PUT IT BLUNTLY, IT SEEMS THOSE ATTENDING THE CLASSES BY MAKING AN ARBITRARY INTERPRETATION OF THE ADMINISTRATIVE PROCEDURES. FUTHERMORE, JUST WHO IS DEAN PARSONS TO INTERPRET THAT IN THIS MATTER? THERE ARE NO INSTRUCTIONS, EITHER EXPLICIT OR IMPLICIT, WHICH GIVES HIM ANY AUTHORITY TO ISSUE MEMOS ON THIS MATTER!

Figure 6.5
Message in memo

I found this pronuclear propaganda and policy views of Charles Elliott that I disagree with dominating the display outside out energy R & D office. There was nothing on solar energy.

I'm not opposed to nuclear power, but you should know by now that this material does not represent my views. Please take immediate action to bring our publications up to date and stop handing out material that you know I can't stomach.

Figure 6.6
Letter from a lawyer

W.E. Young and Associates
ROWAN COUNTY PLAZA SUITE 2
MOREHEAD, KY 40351
PHONE (606) 784-1905

April 10, 19___

Re: Central Wholesale
Vs: State Construction Company

Ms. Donna Irwin:

This letter is to advise you as to the status of the above styled matters. The defendant has answered our Request for Admissions and Interrogatories and has indicated to his attorney that he will be making an offer of settlement on these cases prior to our May term of Court. However, this debtor has a history of procrastination and I think that the creditor should prepare itself for trial of these matters during our May term of court. These cases will be set for the trial docket beginning May 15, 19___, and on May 5, 19___, I will advise you as to the exact date of each setting. Creditor must provide the credit manager as a witness who will be competent to testify as to the books and records of the plaintiff and the fact that the account has not been paid together with the correct amount owed. I will be talking with credit directly concerning the production of competent witnesses. Please advance your file to May 10, 19___, by which time you should receive your next report.

Yours truly,

W. E. Young
Attorney at Law

WEY/rs

Figure 6.7
Sales letter

Chevron Travel Club
P.O. Box 1189, Louisville, Ky. 40201

R.J. LaVaun
Vice President
and General Manager

Dear Travel Card holder ...

Now, your Chevron National Travel Card has become even more valuable than it was before!

Because now that same little plastic card that helps provide so handsomely for your car's needs <u>also</u> entitles you to membership in a most unusual club!

It's a special club - the Chevron Travel Club - and it already has over 100,000 members in other parts of the country.

<u>Now we are happy to announce that for the first time Club membership is available in your area.</u>

The Chevron Travel Club offers you and your family five valuable benefits that you won't find all together anywhere else in the world!

I'll tell you more about these later. But first I want to talk about this valuable benefit:

> This benefit is accidental loss of life insurance. Member coverage is $15,000, plus an additional amount equal to ten times the total of all charges (up to a maximum additional payment of $10,000) billed to the member's Travel Card account during the twelve months immediately preceding the loss.

If you know anything about insurance costs you're probably wondering: "Only $2.50 a month membership fee for up to $25,000 coverage? How can they do it?"

The answer is that we can't do it for anyone except a bona fide member of the Chevron Travel Club. The Chevron Travel Club, you see, is an insurable "group." All members are automatically covered under Group Policy Number GA 5144-A issued by Insurance Company of North America.

As you know, group insurance is almost always less expensive than comparable individual coverage. That's because everything is simplified. The group (in this case Chevron Travel Club) presents the insuring company with large numbers of insureds in easily processed "groups." Since coverage is automatic for our members, applications are extremely simple and can be checked

-2-

through at minimum cost. (There are no health questions asked, <u>no</u> age restrictions and <u>no</u> medical examinations required of Chevron Travel Club members!)

This insurance made available to me as a Chevron Travel Club member is the "best buy" in my own insurance portfolio and, I'm sure, in thousands of other families' insurance programs, too. It provides big coverage at remarkably low monthly dues. What's more, its benefits focus directly on the situation many families, especially young and growing ones, are not equipped to cope with: sudden unexpected accidental loss of life. (What would happen to your <u>family</u> if you or your spouse or both suffer a fatal accident <u>tomorrow</u>?)

Chevron Travel Club membership protects your family in the event of a travel accident or any of thousands of other kinds of accidents that might befall you! It covers you in trains, planes (as a passenger), buses, car -- when you're hunting, fishing, golfing, swimming -- at home, in the office, in the factory, on vacation.

> You're protected around the clock, 24 hours a day, 365 days a year, anywhere in the world!

It covers any accidental loss of life occuring within one hundred (100) days of an accident, except loss resulting from intentionally self-inflicted injuries or suicide, acts of war, while serving as pilot or crew member of an aircraft or while flying in an aircraft being used for test purposes or a military aircraft other than MAC. There are no health questions or medical examinations.

And, because we recognize that every family has its own special character and needs, you have the opportunity to tailor your membership to fit your particular situation by selecting from four different plans:

Plan 1 covers Member only for up to $25,000 for $2.50 monthly dues.

Plan 2 covers Member and spouse. Member's benefit is up to $25,000, plus $2,400 in monthly payments; spouse's is $9,900. $2.75 monthly dues.

Plan 3 covers Member and eligible children. Eligible children are unmarried child or children (including stepchildren, legally adopted and foster children) less than twenty-one (21) years of age. Member's benefit is up to $25,000, plus $2,400 in monthly payments; children's are $3,500 each. $3.00 monthly dues.

Plan 4 covers Member, spouse and eligible children. Member's benefit is up to $25,000, plus $2,400 monthly payments; spouse's $9,900, children's $3,500 each. $3.50 monthly dues.

Figure 6.7
(continued)

-3-

The worst catastrophe of all would be for Member and spouse to die in a common accident. In this event, Plan 4 pays a single benefit of up to $37,300, plus $100 a month to each eligible child until the child's death or twenty-first birthday, whichever occurs first.

Chevron Travel Club insurance is underwritten by one of the country's most respected companies: Insurance Company of North America. Since our inception, over $5,000,000 in benefits have been paid to Chevron Travel Club members or their beneficiaries. A Certificate of Insurance containing a complete schedule of benefits and exceptions will be issued to you as a member.

But wait! I hope I haven't given you the impression that the Chevron Travel Club is just insurance, because that isn't so. Our Club offers four other wonderful benefits, too!

First, there's a subscription to "Chevron USA"--

The 48-page Chevron USA magazine was designed with your family in mind. It's leisure oriented, featuring activities close to home, including arts and crafts plus armchair adventures.

This beautiful magazine is sent to you four times a year... The magazine is packed with colorful pictures and lively reading for the entire family. Future issues will include features on family crafts, gardening, outdoor recreation, sports, plus outstanding pictorials portraying the beauty of America's scenery and wildlife.

Second, there's the registered "Come-Home" Key Ring --

As soon as your Membership Application is processed, we assign you your own personal "Come-Home" number and stamp it on the medallion of a handsome and sturdy key ring. When and if you lose your keys, the medallion tells the finder to drop them in any mail box. When the keys arrive at our headquarters, we mail them back to you promptly.

Third, there's the Chevron Road Atlas and Scenic Guide --

These days, when much of our traveling may be simply "armchair trips," this indispensable 84-page atlas will give pleasure to every member of the family. Great for quick review or long range planning, this handy guide can always be at your fingertips. It's also a welcome book to your library and especially to children for easy reference in studying geography.

Bright and colorful, this big, comprehensive highway encyclopedia is crammed with maps (all 50 states, Canada and Mexico, special maps on principal cities and mileage charts that accurately denote the distances between major cities).

-4-

Specially designed to fold down and fit into your glove compartment, the durable plastic binder is made to open instantly and conveniently the moment you want to use it.

Fourth, there's the Mileage-saving Chevron Routing Service --

Our trip planning service is a specially important benefit at this time when it is necessary to conserve energy. Not only will our clearly marked maps point out the shortest and fastest routes (a great help when all of us are trying to conserve fuel), they will also indicate the best roads to take in order to avoid construction and detours. It makes more sense than ever before to have this wonderful convenience.

As a Club member, you can use this service as often as you like, always without cost. Tell us where you're planning to go by mailing in a Trip Request Form. Our travel experts will promptly send you maps with your trip routed out to the last detail using the most direct and economical route.

Our experts will include tips on points of interest along the way. And don't be too surprised when you also receive such useful items as a trip expense record, a first aid kit - even a supply of wash and dry towels. This is the kind of hospitality that helps make our members feel at home anywhere.

Would you, too, like to enjoy all these benefits, including that all-important family insurance coverage? It's easy!

Just complete the Application Form enclosed and mail it in the postpaid envelope. No need to send any money. Simply check off the Plan you prefer and sign. You don't even have to write in your address. It's already on the Application!

Remember: the sooner you get your Application in the mail, the sooner your family will be protected against the unexpected, by Chevron Travel Club insurance. And the sooner you'll start receiving those other valuable benefits.

I look forward to welcoming you to our Club.

Sincerely,

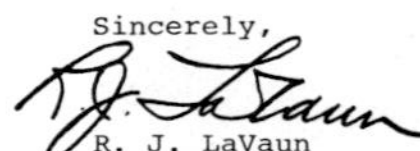

R. J. LaVaun

P. S. The Garment Bag pictured on the enclosed insert is colorfully trimmed in red and blue and made to give your clothes protection...both in your travels and for storage at home, and it's yours when you become a member of the Chevron Travel Club.

Why not join now while you have everything conveniently in front of you?

Figure 6.8
Acknowledgment

TELECOMMUNICATION SYSTEMS, INC.
301 NORTH MICHIGAN AVENUE
CHICAGO, IL 60610
PHONE (312) 209-5208

Dear Mr. Standard:

We are sending you under separate cover our pamphlet ILLINOIS MOVES FORWARD, which is a summary report of the installation of integrated paperwork controls in Illinois.

If we can be of further service to you, please do not hesitate to call upon us.

Sincerely,

Figure 6.9
Acknowledgment

DEPARTMENT OF HOUSING AND URBAN DEVELOPMENT
FEDERAL HOUSING ADMINISTRATION
MEMPHIS INSURING OFFICE
100 NORTH MAIN STREET—28TH. FLOOR
MEMPHIS, TENNESSEE 38103
May 12, 19__

Mr. Ben B. McDonald
Vice President
DRG Financial Corporation
1195 North Omni International
Atlanta, Georgia 30303

Dear Ben:

Thank you for your letter of May 3, 19__. I apologize for the unnecessary delays that were encountered as a result of our requesting information prematurely. I regret that I have not personally had time to involve myself in the details of processing this case. Also, you are aware that our office has had very little experience in processing cases under the 223(f) program.

Your letter certainly indicates a comprehensive and thorough knowledge of the program and quite frankly has been very helpful to me. We have now forwarded the Winchester Square case to our Washington Office for their review. I hope this will be completed at an early date.

It is certainly a pleasure doing business with such a professional firm as yours and again I apologize for the delay and error on our part.

Sincerely,

Director
Housing Development Division

CHAPTER 7

WRITING REQUEST LETTERS

Learning Objectives

After studying this chapter, you will be able to:

- □ Identify situations that call for request letters.
- □ Assess your relationship to the reader.
- □ Identify the importance of writing from the reader's perspective.
- □ Understand the necessity for rewriting and editing.
- □ Understand the persuasive aspect of request letters.
- □ Determine the degree of persuasiveness to use in writing request letters.
- □ Evaluate a situation and plan an appropriate strategy for request messages.
- □ Compose effective request letters.
- □ Demonstrate the use of correct format.

In business, the two most common reasons why you will communicate are:

Reasons for communicating

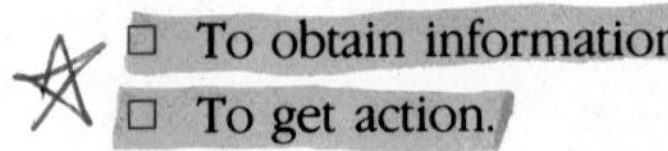

- ☐ To obtain information.
- ☐ To get action.

As the writer, you initiate the communication requesting information about credit, merchandise, service, money, routine action, a catalog or related information, hotel reservations, a former employee recommendation, an adjustment, or some other specific situation. These situations are all related to external communication. Ordinarily, memos are written for internal use within the company; letters are for external communication. The principles for writing letters and memos are similar—the distinguishing feature is the format. Some examples of internal communication include requesting a time for a vacation, the use of physical facilities for a meeting, a person to serve on a project team, or an authorization to purchase equipment. Once you join the business world, you will very likely write many such request letters or memos.

Roles in the communication process

You need to be aware of the role you and the receiver play in the communication process. You may be an individual at home writing to a retailer; a retailer writing to a wholesale supplier or vice versa; a wholesaler writing to another wholesaler; a manager writing to another manager within the company; or any combination of these. A retailer who is writing to a wholesaler has an advantage in that both are accustomed to business practices. An individual at home, on the other hand, may not be familiar with the day-to-day procedures of business transactions. The content and structure of your message will be affected by the circumstances and the relationship betwen you and your reader.

Request letters

Most request letters are short and to the point. This approach saves the reader time and eliminates errors. In this chapter you will see how the strategy for communicating is applied to various situations that result in the following kinds of requests:

- ☐ Membership cancellation.
- ☐ Recommendation request about former employee.
- ☐ Adjustment request—incomplete order shipment.
- ☐ Invitation to speak.
- ☐ Request for payment of overdue account.

In addition, models of effective messages are presented for each.

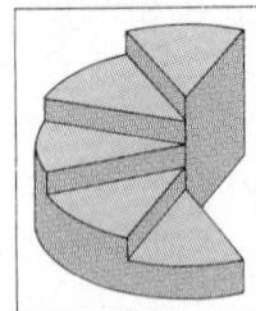

STRATEGY: REQUEST FOR ACTION LETTER

Follow Marilyn Stallard (a consumer at home) as she writes to cancel her membership in a record/tape club. Two years ago on June 10, 19__, Marilyn Stallard joined the Columbia Record/Tape Club (P. O. Box 1130, Terre Haute, Indiana 47811) by completing and mailing a form that appeared in a national magazine. She also included her check. The form gave the following as a condition of the special offer: "You simply agree to buy eight more tapes or records at regular club prices within the next three years—and may cancel membership anytime after doing so."

Now, Marilyn wishes to discontinue her membership in the club at once since she has obtained a good music library. Her membership number is A34-47921; and her account is up to date—she owes no money. She wants to send the cancellation request along with her check for her twelfth purchase ($9.95 plus $2.00 handling charges).

Marilyn's first attempt at writing the request to cancel her membership is shown in Figure 7.1.

Marilyn obviously did not use the strategy in writing her initial request letter—she did not consider her reader/audience. Obvious weaknesses of the letter include the following:

- ☐ The specific request for cancellation is implied, not stated: the clause "Now I want to stop buying any more" and the sentence "Will you please take care of this matter for me?" would probably lead the reader to the conclusion that Marilyn wanted the membership cancelled. A specific request placed at the opening would help the reader grasp the purpose of Marilyn's letter.
- ☐ Information is too general: the use of "several years ago" and "bought several tapes" doesn't give the reader specific information. How many years ago? When? How many tapes? Providing specific facts will assist the person at Columbia to comply with her request to cancel the membership.
- ☐ Facts are omitted. Stating the membership number and date of membership helps the individual at Columbia locate the appropriate information and take positive action in processing the request. Some mention of the enclosed check ($11.95) for the twelfth purchase is also needed.
- ☐ The author uses vague or confusing phrases: the use of the words "this matter" in the request "Will you pleasc take care of this matter for me?" poses the question: What is meant by this matter? Does it mean to assist in the storage of tapes? To cancel the membership? Specifically stating the request in the beginning alerts the reader to the objective of the message.
- ☐ Extraneous information is included: the reader only needs to know that this is a request for cancellation of membership. Marilyn's membership number and the length of time she's been a member are supporting facts. The words "since I have so many and really don't want to have any more for the small space I have to store them," and "I appreciate this. Thanks." don't help the reader to make a decision about the cancellation. Include only the necessary information for the reader to take action.

Figure 7.1 Marilyn's initial request letter

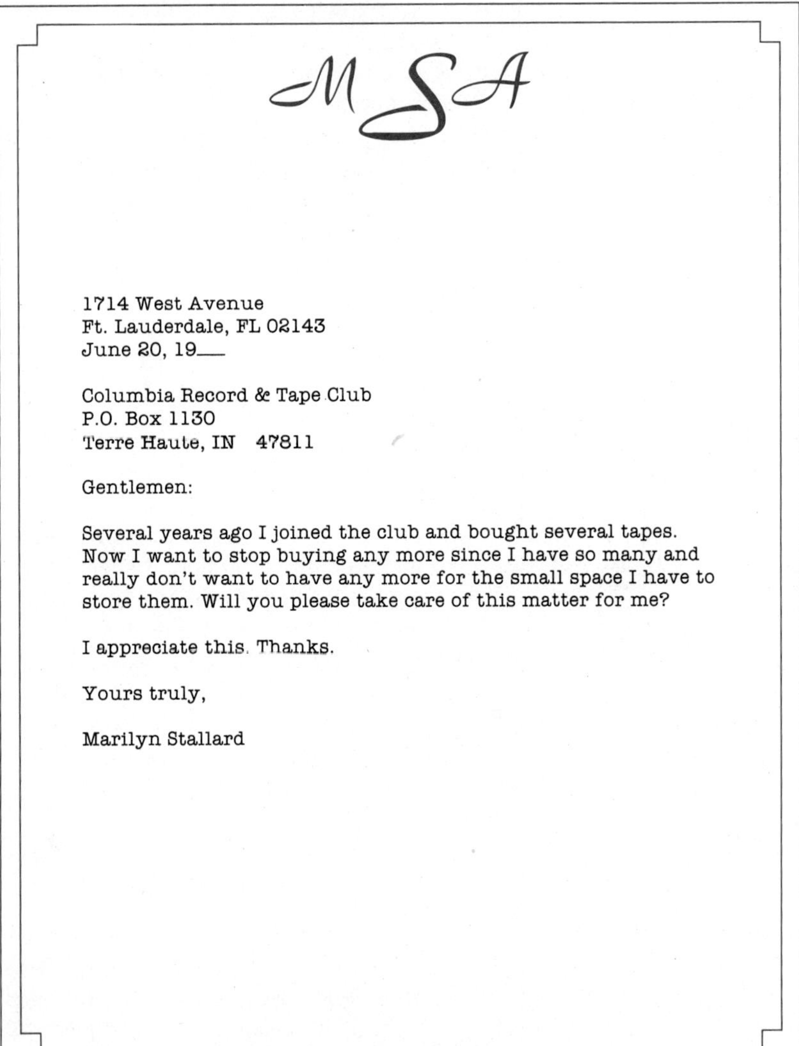

MSA

1714 West Avenue
Ft. Lauderdale, FL 02143
June 20, 19__

Columbia Record & Tape Club
P.O. Box 1130
Terre Haute, IN 47811

Gentlemen:

Several years ago I joined the club and bought several tapes. Now I want to stop buying any more since I have so many and really don't want to have any more for the small space I have to store them. Will you please take care of this matter for me?

I appreciate this. Thanks.

Yours truly,

Marilyn Stallard

Now let's apply the strategy to the setting to show how Marilyn can improve this communication.

PROBLEM
Marilyn doesn't want any more tapes.

OBJECTIVES

General: To request action from Columbia.
Specific: To cancel membership in the Record/Tape Club.
To provide facts about membership.

To enclose check for 12th purchase.

To be courteous.

As an individual at home writing to a company, Marilyn assesses her reader/audience as follows:

READER/AUDIENCE

Characteristics:	Person at Columbia responsible for member records.
	Accustomed to granting routine requests like this one.
Reactions:	Probably positive, since conditions of agreement have been met.
	May try to convince her to retain membership.

ORDER

OVERALL MESSAGE: DIRECT

Probably several thousand persons are enrolled in this record/tape club. Since Marilyn has completed the contract agreement, hers is an everyday, routine request from the club's perspective. The reader at Columbia would no doubt appreciate a short, direct request letter that will save the reader time and eliminate errors.

SPECIFIC OBJECTIVES

1. To cancel membership (include number) in the Record/Tape Club.
2. To enclose check for 12th purchase.
3. To provide facts about membership: number of records purchased; agreement; date.
4. To be courteous.

FORMAT

LETTER

As a consumer at home writing to a business, Marilyn can use the *letter* to request that her membership be cancelled. A letter serves as an appropriate cover for the check she's enclosed for the 12th and final payment. She will not use a letterhead, of course.

Given this strategy for the situation, Marilyn's revised letter requesting membership cancellation appears as Figure 7.2. Note that the normal salutation and complimentary close have been omitted; also note the placement of her return address at the bottom of the letter after her name. The last paragraph of the revised letter could be omitted without loss of

Figure 7.2 Marilyn's revised request letter

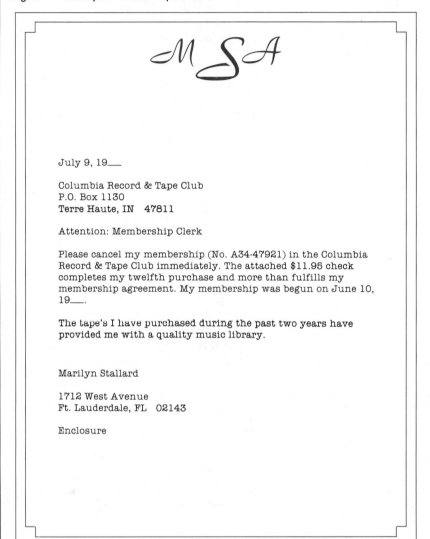

MSA

July 9, 19___

Columbia Record & Tape Club
P.O. Box 1130
Terre Haute, IN 47811

Attention: Membership Clerk

Please cancel my membership (No. A34-47921) in the Columbia Record & Tape Club immediately. The attached $11.95 check completes my twelfth purchase and more than fulfills my membership agreement. My membership was begun on June 10, 19___.

The tape's I have purchased during the past two years have provided me with a quality music library.

Marilyn Stallard

1712 West Avenue
Ft. Lauderdale, FL 02143

Enclosure

pertinent information; however, it does provide a courtesy statement and rounds out the letter.

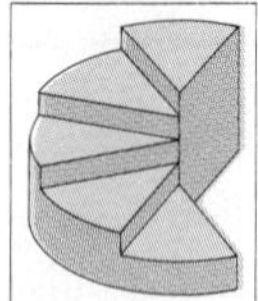

STRATEGY: REQUEST FOR INFORMATION LETTERS

In this situation, a professional writes to another professional requesting information about a former employee. Look at this setting for the conditions and decisions to be requested in the communication.

Ann Rowland, a lawyer in Denver, Colorado, interviewed Jonathan Kelley for a position as legal assistant in her law firm. Jonathan Kelley made a fine impression during the interview and listed Steve Wilkins (One Broadway Plaza, Atlanta, Georgia 30325), also a lawyer, as a reference. Kelley said that he had been a legal secretary for three years in Wilkins's law firm and had learned much about the legal profession; he also indicated that he had worked with a legal assistant. Kelley felt certain he was qualified to assume the position as legal assistant.

Ann decides, therefore, to write Kelley's former employer for his assessment. Since Kelley would be working with other legal assistants and several lawyers, Ann wants to know how he works with others. She also needs to know about the following points: his attention to details and desire to learn; his knowledge of law practice; his experience with automated retrieval records systems as well as other computer-related systems; his ability to organize his work and produce quality documents; and his attitude toward work. The law office sometimes becomes rushed, so Ann wants to find out how dependable Kelley is in times of crisis. Since the interview itself was positive, Ann anticipates that she will offer the position to Kelley if she receives a favorable reaction from Wilkins.

PROBLEM

Vacant legal assistant position—needs a competent person to fill the vacancy.

Ann is interested in obtaining the best person available. Work in the law firm will go more smoothly once she has hired a competent person. She is eager to fill this opening so she can spend more time on her own work. She thinks, "I hope Kelley is the person for the job."

OBJECTIVES

General: To obtain information from Kelley's former employer (Wilkins).

Specific: To request the recommendation.

To discover:

- How Kelley works with others.
- His ability to organize his work; produce quality documents.
- His dependability during pressure times.
- His knowledge of law practice/terminology.
- His desire to learn.
- His experience with automated systems—records retrieval, other systems.

To provide background information on Kelley.

To provide reason for request.

To obtain overall assessment of Kelley for legal assistant position.

To request reply by July 10.

There are several specific areas Ann wants Wilkins to comment on; his response will help her decide whether to hire Kelley for the legal assistant position.

READER/AUDIENCE

Characteristics:	Wilkins—listed on reference sheet.
	Fellow lawyer.
	Outside the firm; almost 2,000 miles from Denver.
	Does not know Ann.
Reaction:	Will send a reply with answer to questions.
	Will give an honest assessment.

Even though Wilkins will be the major contributor to the response letter, he will very likely ask others in the firm for comments. Ann realizes the confidential nature of the response letter. She has written many such letters in the past, and not all have been positive. Since Wilkins is listed as a reference and is a lawyer, Ann can assume he is authorized to write the letter of recommendation.

ORDER

OVERALL MESSAGE: DIRECT

Ann anticipates that Wilkins will want to respond to her request right away. She knows that people in business routinely write letters of recommendation. She also recognizes that this is a courtesy to her and wants to save Wilkins time by getting right to the point. Thus, she selects the ***direct approach*** and determines the following *order.*

SPECIFIC OBJECTIVES:

1. To provide reason for request.
2. To request the recommendation.
3. To obtain the following information about Kelley:
   a. Work relationship with others.
   b. Knowledge of law practice/terminology.
   c. Ability to organize his work and produce quality documents.
   d. Desire to learn.
   e. Dependability during pressure times.
   f. Experience with automated systems—records retrieval, other systems.
4. To obtain overall assessment of Kelley for legal assistant position.
5. To request reply by July 10.

Listing the specific questions will make them stand out and will make it easier for Wilkins to respond. A special request in the close of the letter will motivate Wilkins to respond quickly. Ann anticipates a good-news response.

FORMAT

LETTER

Ann's first impulse is to telephone Wilkins and ask him about Kelley. However, a written statement is required by company policy; she decides to send a *letter*. The letter is shown in Figure 7-3.

Note the following characteristics of Ann's request letter:

- □ *Letter Style.* Ann selected the simplified style: full block; salutation and complimentary close are omitted.
- □ *Subject Line.* The subject line identifies the major objective of the request message for Wilkins; Wilkins's secretary can attach Kelley's folder to the request letter for Wilkins. When Wilkins reads the letter, he can readily see the subject and prepare his response.
- □ *Opening.* The first sentence identifies the former employee's name, informs the reader of the position for which he is applying, and why she is writing to Wilkins—Kelley gave him as a reference. The second sentence provides information obtained from the interview and gives Wilkins an opportunity to verify the years of experience. Also, Wilkins can assess whether Kelley is qualified as a legal assistant.
- □ *Middle.* The specific objectives are listed in order of importance to Ann. Each is numbered and treated as a separate item. This makes it easy for Wilkins to gather information and then write his response. Contrast the list format with this paragraph version:

  How well did he work with others? From your experience, what degree of knowledge does he have about law practice? Does he have a grasp of the terminology? How would you rate him on his ability to organize? his desire to learn? the quality of the documents he produces? How well does he perform during pressure times? How experienced is he with automated office systems such as records retrieval systems? Would you hire him as a legal assistant in your office?

If you were answering the questions, which would be easier for you?

- □ *Questions.* When writing questions, avoid ones that can be answered with a "yes" or "no" response. If question 1 stated, "Does Kelley work well with others?" it could be answered

Figure 7.3 Ann's request for recommendation

ROWLAND AND SON LAW FIRM
1703 North Broadway Lexington, KY 40508 Phone (606) 299-4844

June 25, 19__

Mr. Steve Wilkins
Attorney at Law
One Broadway Plaza
Atlanta, GA 30325

SUBJECT: RECOMMENDATION FOR JONATHAN KELLEY

Jonathan Kelley, a former employee of yours, has interviewed for a position as a legal assistant with my firm and has given you as a reference. During the interview, Jonathan indicated that he had worked as a legal secretary in your office for three years and had gained sufficient background to qualify as a Legal Assistant. Will you please answer the following questions about Jonathan Kelley:

1. How well did he work with others?
2. From your experience, what degree of knowledge does he have about law practice? Does he have a grasp of the terminology?
3. How would you rate his ability to organize his work? his desire to learn? the quality of the documents he produces?
4. How well does he perform during pressure times?
5. How experienced is he with automated office systems such as records retrieval systems?
6. Would you hire him as a legal assistant in your office?

So that I can make the decision shortly, will you please respond by July 10, 19__. Your answers to these questions will assist me greatly in deciding whether to hire Jonathan.

Ann Rowland
Attorney at Law

AR;js

with a simple "yes" or "no" response. Ann wants more information than this. In some instances, a person may answer the questions in the margin on the original—especially when the answers are short. In Wilkins's case, however, he will need to write a response letter since the answers are more extensive. Notice how related questions are grouped in questions 2 and 3.

- *Close.* The special request for a reply by July 10 tends to motivate Wilkins to reply quickly. The last sentence is a goodwill gesture indicating that Wilkins's time and effort in responding are important to Ann; his response will help her make a decision about Kelley.

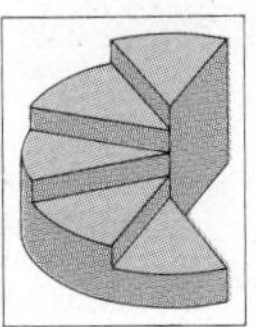

STRATEGY: REQUEST FOR ADJUSTMENT LETTER

If you received a service or purchased a product and something was wrong, you would probably request an adjustment of some type. This type of request usually involves some effort to persuade the reader that the adjustment is warranted. Read the following setting for such an adjustment request:

Thomas Kirkpatrick, owner and president of Kirkpatrick & Associates, had his office equipment and furniture moved from 200 Morningside Lane, Raleigh, North Carolina 27609, to 214 East 53rd Avenue, Boise, Idaho 83712, by the Pittman Transfer Co. (114 East Terrace Street, Raleigh, North Carolina 27611). Arrangements were made for the move on March 19, 19__ (Contract No. 341-271-22); items were picked up on May 10—Kirkpatrick did the packing. After the items were delivered on May 25, 19__, Kirkpatrick discovered the following discrepancies: one bookcase was missing—purchase price, $450; one carton of books was missing—estimated value, $150; one couch was soiled and had to be cleaned—cost $75.50; and three items (a small lamp, a small book rack, and a framed picture) were evidently lost—value estimate, $150. The movers marked the bookcase as missing on the delivery form. Kirkpatrick paid the total amount before the move, as agreed.

Kirkpatrick called Pittman and was instructed to make the claim in written form. He needs to write to Pittman requesting a reimbursement for these items. He first plans his strategy.

PROBLEM

Pittman (the mover) has lost/soiled items.

Kirkpatrick feels that Pittman is responsible for the lost and damaged items and should reimburse him.

OBJECTIVES

General: To convince Pittman of its liability.

Specific: To request a reimbursement of $825.50.
To identify the lost/damaged articles and cost figures.
To provide background information.

Kirkpatrick realizes that he will need to be firm in his message to Pittman and provide all the needed details.

READER/AUDIENCE

Characteristics: Person at Pittman who will respond to the adjustment request is unknown.
Person designated to process all adjustments.
Person experienced with this type of request.

Reaction: Will react favorably to reasonable request.
May be constrained by various company policies.

Figure 7.4 Adjustment request using indirect approach

Thomas and Mary Kirkpatrick

309 Ward Oates Drive
Boise, Idaho 83703
Phone (208) 761-8092

June 1, 19___

Pittman Transfer Co., Inc.
114 East Terrace Street
Raleigh, NC 27611

Attention: Adjustment Manager

Gentlemen:

On March 19, 19___, I made arrangements for your company to move my office equipment and furniture from Raleigh, North Carolina, to Boise, Idaho, during the first part of May. After we had completed the packing, your movers came on May 10 and picked up all of the items. The items were delivered to my new address in Boise, Idaho, on May 25.

When we unpacked, the following items were missing:

1. One bookcase, value $450;
2. One carton of books, value $150;
3. Three small items (lamp, book rack, and framed picture), value $150.

In addition, one couch was soiled and had to be cleaned at a cost of $75.50. The movers marked the bookcase as missing on the delivery form; we found the other items missing or soiled after your movers left.

Please send me a check for $825.50 to cover the cost of these items.

Sincerely,

Thomas Kirkpatrick
President

ot

Since the primary reader of the message is unknown, Kirkpatrick must use an attention line in his letter.

ORDER

OVERALL MESSAGE: INDIRECT

Kirkpatrick could ask for a reimbursement before stating the facts. However, this could put the reader on the defensive and complicate the situation. An *indirect approach* is more likely to convince Pittman of its liability.

SPECIFIC OBJECTIVES

1. To provide background information.
2. To identify the lost/damaged articles and cost figures.
3. To request a reimbursement of $825.50.

FORMAT

LETTER

Kirkpatrick's request for reimbursement is shown in Figure 7.4.

Kirkpatrick makes his specific request for reimbursement in the closing paragraph of the letter after he presents the facts. The tone of the request is not demanding; Kirkpatrick assumes that someone at Pittman will review the request and then make a decision on the basis of the circumstances. Kirkpatrick, of course, wants full reimbursement for each of the items listed.

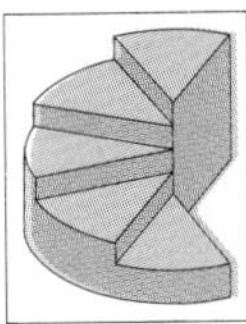

STRATEGY: LETTERS OF INVITATION

Several kinds of requests call for an element of persuasion—especially if someone is going to do a favor for you with little or no money involved. When you write a letter inviting someone to speak, for instance, you will need to use some persuasion. Complimentary statements or other honest statements will help set the stage for a positive response from the receiver. Sincere statements rather than superficial ones are important in creating a satisfactory tone for this type of message. The following setting describes such a request.

Kendra Smith, program chairperson for the Nashville Chapter of the National Association of Accountants (P. O. Box 1223, Nashville, Tennessee 37202) wants to invite Professor Don Reese of the Management Department, The University of Tennessee, Knoxville, Tennessee 37996-0565, coauthor of *The Electronic Office,* to speak at the May banquet meeting. The May meeting is a special event each year since that is the last of the regular September-May monthly meetings.

Since businesspeople are feeling the impact of technology, several members have suggested Reese (a well-known speaker on computer technology) and the topic "Office Automation" for this special event. It is now October 5, 19--, and Kendra wants to write a message asking Reese to be the speaker at the May 20, 19--, meeting. The May meeting will be held at the Marriott Hotel (Interstate 40, West) in Nashville; the banquet will start at 7 P.M. followed by a short business meeting and then the speaker—about 40 minutes is sufficient for the speech and a short question-and-answer session. Overnight hotel reservations will be made at the Marriott (2200 Briley Parkway). In addition to the cost of hotel accommodations, the association will pay $50 toward other travel expenses—limited funds make it impossible to pay an honorarium. Approximately 75 members are expected to attend.

Kendra Smith begins her task by completing the strategy.

PROBLEM
Speaker needed for May meeting.

OBJECTIVES

General: To convince Dr. Reese to speak at the May meeting.
Specific: To invite Reese to speak.
To compliment Reese on his book and speeches.
To provide facts about the May meeting.
To request a reply by a definite date.

Kendra realizes that she needs to make Reese sense that the group really wants *him* to speak—not just any speaker. She needs to make him feel special. The tone is important in this message.

READER/AUDIENCE

Characteristics: Well recognized.
Has given speeches many times.
Busy person.
Reaction: Probably will respond favorably.
Probably would like to have an honorarium.

Kendra visualizes Reese as someone who is personable and who will, given the right approach, accept the invitation. The fact that the group recognizes his contributions is a plus. In this setting, Kendra is only concerned with persuading Reese to accept.

ORDER

OVERALL MESSAGE: DIRECT
Since Reese is coauthor of a book, he probably would accept the no-fee invitation. He will probably consider this an excellent opportunity for consulting contacts. Because of the anticipated reaction, the *direct approach* is chosen.

SPECIFIC OBJECTIVES

1. To invite Reese to speak.
2. To compliment Reese on his book and speeches.

Figure 7.5 Invitation to speak—Direct approach

NAA

Nashville Chapter, National Association of Accountants
720 Gallatin Road Nashville, TN 37206-2392
Phone (615) 329-4107

October 5, 19__

Dr. Don Reese
Department of Management
The University of Tennessee
Knoxville, TN 37996-0565

Dear Dr. Reese

The Nashville Chapter of the National Association of Accountants invites you to be guest speaker at our end-of-the-year dinner meeting. Several members have heard you speak about corporate technology and have suggested you as an excellent speaker for this event. These people were very complimentary concerning the practical suggestions in your book, THE ELECTRONIC OFFICE, about the emerging technological environment. Since most businesses now have some degree of automation within their operation, each of our members could benefit from your comments.

The special meeting will start at 7 p.m. on Tuesday, May 20, 19__, at the Marriott Hotel, 2200 Briley Parkway, Nashville. Approximately 75 members regularly attend this special event. After the meal and brief business session, plan on approximately 40 minutes for your speech and a short question-and-answer session. May we suggest a topic related to issues involved with technology in the corporate world. Because of limited funds, the Association will pay for your overnight hotel expenses and provide $50 to help defray your travel expenses; I will make the hotel reservations for you as soon as you send me your acceptance.

May we have your reply by October 29, 19__, so that final arrangements can be made. The members who have heard you praise you highly, and we are excited about the prospect of your coming.

Sincerely

(Ms.) Kendra Smith
Program Chairperson
Nashville Chapter

3. To provide facts about the May meeting.
4. To request a reply by a definite date.

FORMAT

LETTER

Since the invitation is going out of the office, Kendra selects the *letter* as the appropriate format. Kendra's letter using the direct approach is shown in Figure 7.5.

CONTRASTS BETWEEN DIRECT AND INDIRECT APPROACHES

Analyzing the writing approaches

To help you review the direct and indirect approaches to writing, study Figure 7.6, which presents the same letter but in the indirect style. Kendra could have analyzed this situation differently and then decided on the indirect approach. She might have concluded that Reese was a much sought-after speaker who usually commands a hefty fee. Under these circumstances, Kendra would want to persuade Reese of the benefits this speaking engagement would bring him. An *indirect approach* gives Kendra an opportunity to describe the conference in more detail before asking Reese to speak.

Rationale

Contrast versions

Note that the direct version (Figure 7.5) starts with the request to speak while the indirect version (Figure 7.6) delays the request until the midsection of the letter. Contrast the opening paragraphs of the two versions. The middle portion giving the facts about the meeting for Reese (What? Who? When? Where?) are similar in both versions. The closing paragraphs are the same for both letters. The special request for a reply by October 29, 19--, motivates him to respond promptly. Kendra will also know by this date whether Reese will or will not speak; if he doesn't, she has time to locate another speaker. The complimentary and positive statements at the end provide a final persuasive comment. Note how the indirect version (Figure 7.6) uses more compliments and identifies reasons for and benefits of being the dinner speaker. The situation calls for a higher degree of persuasion.

When you write a request letter of this type, be sure that the statements you use to motivate the reader are sincere. The statements given in the opening and closing paragraphs appear to be sincere on the basis of the reports of persons who have heard Reese speak. That he has been recommended as "an excellent speaker" should be taken as a compliment and will help to develop a positive attitude on the part of Reese. Everyone likes to feel appreciated.

Content

In both versions, note that the middle portion presents the money limitation in as positive a manner as possible. Since the professional association has limited funds, only a small amount ($50) in addition to the hotel bill is available for payment. The writer of the message assumes that Reese will be willing to travel to Nashville for the speech even though a fee isn't involved. Such an assumption should be justified, of course. The writer does not want to appear to be taking advantage of Reese. Since Reese is coauthor of *The Electronic Office,* he probably will accept the no-fee invitation, hoping that contacts can be made with members of the organization on future consulting opportunities. This potential could help motivate Reese to take positive action. Mentioning the "approximately 75 members" helps Reese assess the potential for consulting and also plan for handout materials for the session.

Contrast the opening paragraphs in Figures 7.5 and 7.6 with the following weak paragraph characteristic of some found in invitation letters:

Weak example

I have heard about your outstanding book, The Electronic Office, and hope you will not be too busy to accept an invitation to speak to our association. I am sure you could help each of us with your brilliant knowledge about office automation.

Figure 7.6 Invitation to speak—Indirect approach

NAA

Nashville Chapter, National Association of Accountants
720 Gallatin Road Nashville, TN 37206-2392
Phone (615) 329-4107

October 5, 19__

Dr. Don Reese
Department of Management
The University of Tennessee
Knoxville, TN 37996-0565

Dear Dr. Reese

Would you like the opportunity of making contact with approximately 75 business professionals, some of whom may need your consulting services? These professionals are aware of the competitive advantage that comes with automation. They are looking for direction from someone like yourself with insight into strategic planning for technology in business.

Many of our chapter members of the National Association of Accountants know of your expertise; several have heard you speak on corporate technology. They value the suggestions you make in your book, THE ELECTRONIC OFFICE.

A special dinner meeting for members of this organization will be held on Tuesday, May 20, 19__, at the Marriott Hotel, 2200 Briley Parkway, Nashville. We sincerely hope that you will consent to speak on issues involved with technology in the corporate world. Because of limited funds, the Association will pay for your overnight hotel accommodations and provide $50 to help defray your travel expenses. I will personally make your hotel reservations as soon as you send me your acceptance.

After the dinner and brief business session, which start at 7 p.m., approximately 40 minutes are planned for your speech and a short question-and-answer session. Dr. Reese, I can assure you that in these 40 minutes you will be making contact with some of Nashville's leading accountants.

May we have your reply by October 29, 19__, so that final arrangements can be made. The members who have heard you praise you highly, and we are excited about the prospect of your coming.

Sincerely

(Ms.) Kendra Smith
Program Chairperson
Nashville Chapter

LEGAL / ETHICAL ISSUE

In some states higher education is funded on the basis of the number of students enrolled in credit-generating classes during the fifth week of the Fall quarter or semester. These enrollment statistics are reported to the State Board for Higher Education in mid-November each year. The budget for the next fiscal year is based on these data.

Ted Burchett, a new faculty member at a major university in the Northeast, has just become aware of the way in which university programs are funded. Ted's dean has requested in writing that he pad enrollment figures by 10 percent in each of his three sections of Business Communication. The request letter from the dean also indicated that Ted should not withdraw any student who had left his classes until November 20. This request would allow the dean to report only minimal withdrawals from all courses taught in the college.

Ted is perplexed concerning the request from the dean. He is a new, nontenured business faculty member whose sense of personal ethics is at odds with the college's administration.

Should Ted comply with the dean's request? Since the dean's request is in writing, would that eliminate the legal issue? The ethical issue? Why or why not?

Analysis

This weak version shows that the writer isn't really familiar with Reese's accomplishments and is therefore insincere. Such a bold attempt at flattery will not motivate him to react positively. Since the opening phrase "I have heard about" indicates only a vague reference to the author and his book, the words "outstanding book" appear insincere. The words "hope you will not be too busy to accept" reveal doubts and a negative approach instead of a positive one. The clause "I am sure you could help each of us" is wordy and doesn't add anything specific to motivate Reese to respond positively. The term "brilliant knowledge" is overdone and inappropriate. When you want to persuade, be sure to use words and sentences that show sincerity and integrity. Tone is important in any persuasive message.

Kendra prefers the direct aproach. Which do you prefer? Why?

REQUEST FOR PAYMENT LETTERS

Continuing collection request

A request for payment of an overdue account is a specialized type of business message that involves a persuasive approach. This type of business writing may involve a series of messages—from the first, which merely indicates that the client may have "overlooked a payment," to the final one, which might state that "the account is being turned over to a collection agency" or some other legal action is being taken. These collection requests are presented

Collection stages

below under three stages—early, intermediate, and final. A number of messages can be sent at each stage, depending on the writer and the circumstances.

Because of legal requirements in collection letters, some companies prefer to use form letters that have been approved by their legal staff. The Fair Debt Collection Practice Act (1978) protects an individual from unreasonable means of collection—unreasonable means can be considered an invasion of privacy. You can't falsely imply that a lawsuit has been filed to get a person to pay—your company would violate the act. Check your state statutes for specifics. Using form letters is a safeguard and also aids productivity of written documents.

If you write this type of communication, you will need to decide on the appropriate number of messages to send at each stage. Generally, a well-written message will obtain a positive response without the need for additional letters. Since some customers are slow to pay, however, a series is appropriate. An account 30 days overdue is more likely to be collected than one 90 days overdue. The older the account becomes, the less likely you will collect it. Thus it is important to take steps early in collecting overdue accounts.

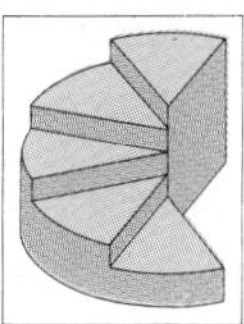

STRATEGY: EARLY STAGE OF COLLECTION

Modern Supply, a wholesale heating and air conditioning firm, in Hutchinson, Kansas, sells over 2,000 items to retail stores and building contractors. Their inventory includes a variety of sizes of heating and/or air conditioning units as well as wiring, repair parts, and other electrical parts. Jerry Austin, a co-owner, is in charge of accounts for Modern Supply. He periodically reviews all accounts with the aid of his personal computer and an efficient decision-support software system.

On his last report of overdue accounts, the following appeared on the listing:

Name	Amount	Days overdue
Joe Ellis, contractor	$ 2,205	15
Jaynes Heating & Air Conditioning Co.	5,020	90
Elliot Contractors & Associates	15,024	120

Jerry wants to establish a collection letter series to use in encouraging customers to keep their accounts current. He knows he must consider various factors since each customer is unique. Modern Supply has built its successful business on a philosophy of personal service and quality products. Jerry also wants to maintain this philosophy as he prepares a series of collection letters to use with all overdue accounts. He plans to start with the three accounts given above, and then adapt the contents of the letters for other situations. He knows that some modification will be necessary for each letter that he writes.

Jerry is surprised to see the name of Joe Ellis with $2,205 on his account, now 15 days overdue. Jerry queries his database system for an account profile. He learns that during the last 10 years Ellis has paid 90 percent of his previous purchases within the discount period and the other 10 percent within the regular period. He must now decide what action to take to collect the $2,205 that is overdue.

Jerry begins his task by completing the strategy.

PROBLEM

Past-due account of Ellis.

Jerry realizes that if he doesn't collect on his accounts, then his business will be in trouble, too. It is important to collect money when due to maintain his planned cash flow.

OBJECTIVES

General: To convince Ellis to pay his overdue account.
To retain Ellis as a regular customer.

The main objective is to convince Ellis to pay; however, a secondary objective is to write the message in such a way that Ellis still believes that he is a valued customer. This dual objective makes the letter more complex.

Specific: To remind Ellis about the $2,205 that is now 15 days overdue.

Jerry wants to keep Ellis as a customer. Because Ellis has been an excellent customer for the past 10 years, Jerry assumes that he has just overlooked the last statement.

READER/AUDIENCE

Characteristics: Contracter.
Regular customer for 10 years.
Excellent credit rating.
Probably has overlooked last statement.

Reaction: May be embarrassed at having overlooked the payment.
Will respond to request with payment.
Will want to retain his excellent credit rating.

ORDER

OVERALL MESSAGE: DIRECT

Because of the philosophy at Modern Supply, and because he assumes that Ellis has overlooked or misplaced the July statement, Jerry is certain Ellis will send in his payment as soon as he gets the notice of the overdue amount. Perhaps a short message in the *direct approach* will motivate Ellis to send in his payment.

SPECIFIC OBJECTIVE

To remind Ellis that the $2,205 is now 15 days overdue.

FORMAT

Since Jerry has decided to send a reminder, he thinks of the various formats it might take:

A copy of the July statement.

A copy of the July statement with a handwritten reminder or preprinted label.

A reminder letter with statement attached.

Jerry decides to send Ellis a duplicate of the July 10, 19__ statement with a handwritten comment.

To retain the goodwill of this excellent customer, Jerry plans to include a short, courteous note with the July statement. Ideas to include in the message are:

```
Your account for $2,205 is now 15 days past due.
Send your check or $2,205 at once.
```

Here's Jerry's first draft:

```
Your account is now past due. Send your check at once!
```

How does it compare to the following revised note?

```
Reminder. Please send your $2,205 check to keep your account current.
```

This message, written in longhand on a duplicate copy of the last statement, has a personal touch and should get Ellis to pay his past-due account.

Assume that another 30 days have elapsed and in the computer printout Joe Ellis's name appears again, but now 45 days past-due. Under these circumstances, Jerry decides to write a letter and attach another copy of the July statement. A review of the account provides these facts: customer for 10 years; "Excellent Customer" rating (90 percent of payments within discount period); increased credit limit last year at his request; peak purchasing season just ahead.

In examining the strategy above, he perceives that the problem and the general objectives remain the same. Jerry still wants to retain Ellis as a regular customer but must now assume that some condition makes it difficult for Ellis to pay his account. The *specific objectives* can now be listed as:

To emphasize past relationships.

To request payment of $2,205 that is now 45 days overdue.

To motivate Ellis to send his check.

To encourage action.

In the reader/audience component above, the characteristic "probably overlooked this statement" is no longer accepted. Ellis's overdue account is getting more serious. Jerry decides to use the letter as the *format* with a copy of the July statement enclosed.

The order for the second communication to collect the overdue account changes to the *indirect approach.* To begin this message with the statement of the problem would be a slap in the face. Jerry reasons that the positive relationship with Ellis over the past 10 years is a good starting point.

He then sequences his specific objectives in the following way:

1. To emphasize past relationships.
2. To request payment of the $2,205 that is now 45 days overdue.
3. To motivate Ellis to send his check (reasons).
4. To encourage action.

As an alternative, Jerry wants Ellis to call him if he cannot send his check. In this way, they can work out a method for Ellis to bring his account up to date. Knowing that he will eventually get the money is better than taking a chance of losing the entire amount.

Using the revised strategy, Jerry drafts this opening paragraph:

We sent you a statement for $2,205 on July 10, 19__ (copy enclosed). The amount was due on August 10, but we did not receive your check. On August 11, we sent you a copy of our July statement; we wrote a note asking you to send us your check. We didn't receive your check nor a response this time, either.

After reading the opening paragraph, Jerry realizes that something is wrong with the way the message reads. He checks the paragraph against the strategy and determines these flaws:

1. Not indirect approach.
2. Inappropriate subjects: statement, amount, your check, copy, note, response.

Figure 7.7 Jerry's collection letter, early stage

MODERN SUPPLY
34 NORTH WILSON AVENUE, TOPEKA, KANSAS 66619-1558, PHONE (913) 656-9001

September 25, 19___ INDIRECT

Mr. Joe Ellis, Contractor
223 Gate Lane
Topeka, KS 66608

Dear Joe:

During the past ten years, we have enjoyed a business relationship with your firm that has been built on respect, dependability, and trust. Your prompt payments have earned you the "Excellent Customer" rating. We value you as a long-standing business friend and want to continue supplying you with quality products.

When you asked to increase your limit of credit last year, we gladly complied. What are friends for but to be available when you need them? Well, Joe, we now need you to do something for us--take a moment and send your check for $2,205 today; or call me at 614/273-0011 to discuss a payment plan for your 45-day past-due account (statement enclosed). With the heightened building season ahead, you will want to make additional purchases.

Your prompt action will let you retain your "Excellent Customer" rating with Modern Supply. May we hear from you today?

Cordially yours,

Jerry Austin, Manager
Customer Services

wb

Jerry then takes a different approach and drafts this opening paragraph:

3. Choppy reading: short sentences; the same construction makes for hard-to-read message.
4. Lacks benefits/reasoning.
5. Creates negative feeling (tone): weak wording—"but we did not receive your check" in the second sentence; "your check nor a response" in the last sentence.
6. Too I/we/us/our-oriented.

During the past ten years, we have enjoyed a business relationship with your firm that has been built on respect, dependability, and trust. Your prompt payments have earned you the "Excellent Customer" rating. We value you as a long-standing business friend and want to continue supplying you with quality products.

He concludes that this is the right approach and tone, then continues with the middle portion:

When you asked to increase your limit of credit last year, we gladly complied. What are friends for but to be available when you need them? We now need you to do something for us—take a moment and send your check for $2,205 today; or call me at 614/273-0011 to discuss a payment plan for your 45-day past-due account (statement enclosed). With the heightened building season ahead, you will want to make additional purchases.

"Now this is what I wanted!" Jerry thinks. "It has the right tone but it's strong enough for the situation to motivate Joe to respond. Now all I need do is write a short paragraph to round out the message." Here's the final paragraph:

Your prompt action will let you maintain your "Excellent Customer" rating with Modern Supply. May we hear from you today?

The final version of the request-for-payment letter is shown in Figure 7.7.

Consider the reminder and the request letter as appropriate communications in the early stage of the collection series. If Ellis doesn't respond, Jerry could send an additional letter before starting the intermediate stage.

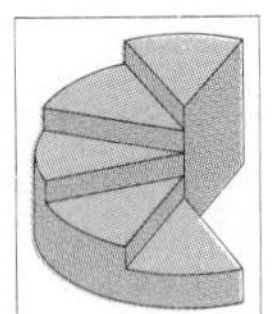

STRATEGY: INTERMEDIATE STAGE OF COLLECTION

Jerry now goes back to his past-due client list and focuses on the second customer, the Jaynes Heating & Air Conditioning Co., Fred Jaynes, owner.

The computer printout shows that the Jaynes Heating & Air Conditioning account is now 90 days in arrears in the amount of $5,020. Since Jerry earlier contacted this company on three separate occasions, a stronger letter to request payment is now needed.

The intermediate stage, like the early stage, may consist of several letters. In the intermediate stage, a strong appeal is made to the customer to maintain the credit rating by paying the past-due amount. Of course, such letters review the previous attempts at collection and stress the benefits of continued credit purchasing. Each letter in this stage gets stronger in its request for payment or action.

Before writing the collection request, Jerry Austin first checks his personal computer system for additional background information. He obtains the following:

1. Jaynes is a local company which has purchased periodically during the past five years.
2. Payments have usually been made within the regular 30-day credit time; two payments were made after phone calls.
3. Jaynes has recently faced competition from a new, progressive business.
4. Early attempts to collect included: phone calls shortly after due date—indicated payment shortly; three early stage letters sent—no payment or response to arrange payment.

Jerry's intermediate-stage letter, using a more forceful approach, is designed to convince Jaynes either to pay or make arrangements for the amount due. Jerry is getting concerned that Jaynes's competition may be having a permanent effect on his economic situation.

In light of these facts, Jerry designs his strategy.

PROBLEM

Possible loss of accounts receivable.

OBJECTIVES

General: To collect past-due account.

Specific: To convince Jaynes either to make payment or make arrangements to pay.
To be direct but courteous.
To retain Jaynes as a customer.

READER/AUDIENCE

Characteristics: Local company.
Facing progressive competition.
Customer for past five years.
Regular—pay in past.

Reaction: Negative.
Will try to avoid contact.
Might want to make arrangements.

ORDER

OVERALL MESSAGE: DIRECT

SPECIFIC OBJECTIVES

1. Request payment or response.
2. Include facts about amount past due, date due, invoice number.
3. Importance of credit—appeal for paying.
4. Review of past credit history with Modern Supply.

5. Courteous but direct statements; future purchasing on account jeopardized.

Note that the order for the intermediate stage is *direct* as compared with the indirect approach used in the initial stage. The matter has become more serious; now Jerry's major concern is to collect the outstanding liability.

FORMAT

LETTER

Using the strategy components and background information, Jerry begins the letter with the following ideas:

1. Statement about amount due and number of days past due.
2. Request for $5,020.
3. Review of previous attempts: phone calls; Jaynes promised check within 10 days; three request letters—no response.
4. Five years of regular payment.
5. Question: What has gone wrong?

From these ideas, Jerry constructs the following opening paragraph:

Please send a check for $5,020 to bring your account up to date; the balance is now 90 days past due. Shortly after the account was due, you indicated by phone you would send a check within 10 days. Now, after the phone call and three request letters, we still do not have a check nor an explanation from you. Over the past five years, you have paid your account regularly. What has happened?

Notice how the *you* and *we* are balanced in the letter. In the first sentence, the implied *you* is used to begin the letter: rather than "your check," "a check" is used; rather than "your balance is now 90 days past due," "the balance" is used to make the tone more palatable to the reader.

Jerry still wants to keep Jaynes as a customer. In the second sentence, Jerry merely reviews the actions that have been taken, using the "you" viewpoint. Notice in the next sentence how the emphasis shifts to *our* not having received the check or an explanation. This sentence construction is potentially irritating to the reader. It could destroy goodwill. The question at the end of the paragraph is to motivate Jaynes to act—either to send a check or provide an explanation.

In the second paragraph, Jerry decides to focus on the importance of keeping the credit rating to be able to continue purchasing on account. In addition, he decides to emphasize the advantages of purchasing from Modern Supply.

Having considered the opening and second paragraphs, Jerry considers his ending for the intermediate stage request letter. Since there is a special discount promotion being offered in September by one of Jerry's suppliers, Jerry can use this idea in the closing paragraph. This may motivate

Figure 7.8 **Collection letter—Intermediate stage**

MODERN SUPPLY

34 NORTH WILSON AVENUE, TOPEKA, KANSAS 66619-1558, PHONE (913) 656-9001

September 26, 19__

Mr. Fred Jaynes
Jaynes Heating & Air Conditioning Co.
203 State Street
Hutchinson, KS 67501

Dear Mr. Jaynes:

Please send a check for $5,020 to bring your account up to date; the balance is now 90 days past due. Shortly after the account was due, you indicated by phone you would send a check within ten days. Now, after the phone call and three request letters, we still do not have a check nor an explanation from you. Over the past five years, you have paid your account regularly. What has happened?

Buying on account has offered you a convenient way to phone in your orders in the past; and you have been able to offer your customers the latest in energy efficient heating and air conditioning systems and supplies which have helped build your business. We are sure that you will want to maintain your regular-pay status and continue purchasing on account from Modern Supply. Without a good credit rating, Jaynes Heating and Air Conditioning Co. will find it more difficult to conduct business.

So that you can take advantage of the special discount promotion being offered in September, send us a check for $5,020 today! Or call me personally (614/273-0011) to work out satisfactory arrangements for bringing your account up to date.

Protect your valuable credit rating by acting at once.

Sincerely yours,

Jerry Austin, Manager
Customer Services

wb

Jaynes to pay and to continue to purchase from Modern Supply. Only one final statement needs to be added now—one that stresses the importance of the credit rating:

Protect your valuable credit rating by acting at once.

Figure 7.8 illustrates Jerry's collection letter for the intermediate stage. Perhaps this request will bring a check for $5,020 or a response. If it does not, Jerry may decide to write one or two more before taking final action on the account. The number of letters to use in this intermediate stage will depend upon the writer and the conditions at the time.

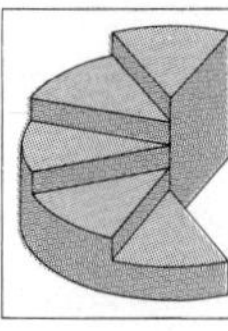

STRATEGY: FINAL STAGE OF COLLECTION

Jerry returns once more to his computer printout of past-due accounts. He is ready to deal with the last name on the list. Elliot Contractors & Associates (owner, T. L. Elliot) is so far behind in payment that there is little hope of collection. The Elliot account calls for a last resort letter—either turning the account over to a collection agency or requiring other serious action. Before writing a last resort letter, the writer has already tried all possible means to obtain the money owed (phone calls, various statements and letters requesting payment or an explanation, etc.). Now it is time to take the final step to collect the amount—Jerry can assume that this final action will also result in a loss of any further business from Elliot Contractors & Associates.

In the final stage letter, you should review the attempts to collect the past-due account, strongly suggest that credit rating will be affected, and tell the reader what action is being taken.

Here is what Jerry's computer system reveals about Elliot:

1. Has been purchasing from Modern Supply for one year.
2. Has been slow in paying previous statements.
3. Early attempts to collect: phone calls; four requests.
4. 120 days past due.
5. Amount, $15,024.

Jerry identifies the components of the strategy for this case.

PROBLEM
Loss of account and customer.

OBJECTIVES

General: To collect a bad debt.

Specific: To notify Elliot of action being taken (account being turned over to collection agency).

To persuade Elliot to send in payment or make arrangements before a definite date for action.

READER/AUDIENCE

Characteristics: Customer for one year.
Slow paying.
Local firm.

Reaction: Negative.
Probably will ignore request.

Figure 7.9 Collection letter: final stage

MODERN SUPPLY

34 NORTH WILSON AVENUE, TOPEKA, KANSAS 66619-1558, PHONE (913) 656-9001

September 28, 19__

Mr. T. L. Elliot, Owner
Elliot Contractors & Associates
204 Pennsylvania Road
Lawrence, KS 66044

Dear Mr. Elliot:

Account No. 234A, Final Notice

Your account for $15,024, which is 120 days past due, will be turned over to the Monroe Collection Agency on October 13, (15 days from today) if a check has not been received or satisfactory arrangements have not been made to pay the amount. As you know, maintaining a good credit rating is important to any business.

When your Account No. 234A was ten days past due, we called and asked if something were wrong but were assured that payment would be received shortly. Since then, four letters (January 10, 19__; January 25, 19__; February 15, 19__; and February 29, 19__) have been sent to you asking for payment or a response.

No payment or response has been received to date; therefore, your account is being turned over for collection to the Monroe Collection Agency. You may avoid this process either by sending a check for $15,024; or by calling 614/273-0011 and making satisfactory arrangements for payment before October 13.

Sincerely yours,

Jerry Austin, Manager
Customer Services

wb

ORDER

OVERALL MESSAGE: DIRECT

SPECIFIC OBJECTIVES

1. To notify Elliot of action being taken.
2. To persuade Elliot to send in payment or make arrangements before a definite date for action.

FORMAT

LETTER

Study Jerry's letter for this situation (Figure 7.9). Note that the first paragraph presents the action to be taken, the exact amount owed ($15,024), and the number of days past due (120 days). In addition, Jerry makes one last effort to convince Elliot Contractors & Associates to avoid this process by paying or making satisfactory arrangements before the designated date. The last statement in the first paragraph reemphasizes the importance of credit and implies that Elliot's credit rating probably will affect his business.

The second paragraph reviews previous attempts to collect the overdue account. The last paragraph notes that there has been no response from Elliot Contractors & Associates and restates that the account will be turned over to a collection agency to provide emphasis. The last statement is one final attempt to persuade Elliot to make payment or arrangements.

The overall tone of the letter is direct and to the point. Observe the professional way in which Jerry informs Elliot of the action that will be taken if he does not respond. In this model of the final-stage collection letter, the writer doesn't make threats. After sending this letter, Jerry will then proceed with the indicated action if Elliot Contractors does not respond. This type of letter ends the collection series.

SUMMARY

The two most common reasons for communicating in business are: (*a*) to obtain information, and (*b*) to get action. Requests are made about credit, merchandise, services, money, routine action, needed information (catalog), a hotel reservation, a recommendation, an adjustment, and other similar situations.

Recognize your role in the communication process—consumer at home writing to a retailer; retailer writing to a wholesaler; wholesaler writing to a manufacturer; or other situation. The circumstances and the relationship between you and the reader affect the content, structure, and format of the communication. Ordinarily, use memos for internal communication; use letters for external communication.

The principles for writing letters and memos are similar—the distinguishing feature is the format. Most request letters are short and to the point. This saves reader time and eliminates errors. Some requests require persuasive writing.

Emphasis is given to applying the principles of writing request letters using a strategy for communicating. Situations include routine requests (for action and information) and persuasive requests (an invitation to speak and a payment of an overdue account). For routine requests, state the specific request, provide sufficient background and rationale, add special request if needed, and use courtesy.

Situations of a nonroutine nature require persuasion. In a request for adjustment, use a moderate degree of persuasion. Establish the reader's responsibility for making the adjustment, establish the reasonableness of the request, provide needed background/facts, and use a nondemanding, positive tone.

Requests for overdue accounts usually include a series of messages—early stage, a reminder; intermediate stage, a review of previous contacts and request for payment; final stage, a notification of legal action. Use caution in writing requests for payment messages. The Fair Debt Collection Practice Act (1978) protects an individual from unreasonable means of collection. Using a previously prepared form letter is a safeguard and also aids productivity of written documents. Each stage becomes more serious and more direct in tone. Benefits of maintaining credit standing and a review of previous attempts may help persuade the reader to respond. The older the account becomes, the less likely it is that you will collect it.

END-OF-CHAPTER ACTIVITIES

DISCUSSION

1. What are the two basic reasons for writing?
2. How does the strategy for communicating apply to the writing of letters and memos?
3. Discuss the significance of editing as a principle of effective business writing.
4. Why is the direct approach generally appropriate for a request letter?
5. What purpose does a subject line achieve?
6. How does the tone in an adjustment letter differ from the tone in an information-request letter?
7. If you were responsible for writing a series of collection letters, explain what you would include in the series. Give a rationale for your suggestions.
8. How are ideas ordered when using the direct approach? The indirect approach?

ACTIVITIES

9. Pat Summers (605 Stokely Road, Norman, Oklahoma 73060), was reading a magazine and found an advertisement for a book entitled *Improving Managerial Productivity* in the December 19__ issue of *World Management.* She filled out the handy order card attached and mailed it to get a copy for the office. Several days later, she received

Figure 7.10
Request Letter

WORLD MANAGEMENT PUBLICATIONS

67832 WEST PARK AVENUE • NEW YORK, NEW YORK 10017-3112 • PHONE (212) 318-4800

December 15, 19___

605 Stokely Road
Attn: Pat Summers
Norman, Oklahoma 73060

Dear Customer:

Thank you for returning the attached order card. We are asking you to confirm this order by signing this letter and completing the missing information. Please return this request with the original order card so we can mail your order just as soon as possible.

Your cooperation is greatly appreciated in this matter.

Full Company Name ______________________

Your Full Name ______________________

Your Signature ______________________

Street (other than P.O. Box) ______________________

If this is a home address, check here ______________________

Check here ______________________ If this is a personal order.

Telephone ______________________

Cordially Yours,

Williams Parsons
Credit Department

Enclosure

P.S. If a purchase order is required by your company, please attach it to this letter. Thank you.

the letter shown above. Use the strategy to critique the request message in Figure 7.10.

10. Read and critique each of the following form collection letters representing different stages of collection. Use the strategy components and suggest ways for improving the requests.

Letter A

(Date)

Re: Acct. of ____________

Amount Due: $__________

Dear Sir:

Have you overlooked the recent statements we mailed you concerning the balance due on your account?

We know you are willing and able to pay. Please bring $_______ to our Business Office within the next five days. If you would prefer, a check or a money order will be all right.

No further action will be taken until this time.

Sincerely,

Collection Manager

Letter B

(Date)

Regarding Account of: ______________

Balance due: $___________

Dear Mr. ___________:

This letter is to remind you that your account has run well past the time usually extended to our patients. We feel that we have been more than patient, yet you have shown very little willingness to cooperate.

We will expect you to pay this account within the next five days; otherwise, we shall seek professional assistance in liquidating your account.

We trust this measure will not be necessary and that payment in full will be forthcoming by return mail.

Sincerely,

David Perry, Collection Manager

Letter C

(Date)

Re: Acct. of: ____________

Amount Due: $__________

Dear Sir:

Because you have not replied to our many requests for payment of your drastically delinquent account, you leave us no choice but to proceed with further unpleasant action.

Payment within five days will save you this embarrassment.

Sincerely,

Collection Manager

11. Collect sample request messages (routine and persuasive situations) from local businesses. Compare your samples with your classmates. How do the samples differ from guidelines presented in this chapter?
12. Survey local businesses for practices in collecting overdue accounts. How do businesses comply with federal legislation?
13. In the following situation, you will assume the role of the dean of the College of Business Administration at your school. Read the following background first:

    During the summer of 19--, the AACSB (American Assembly of Collegiate Schools of Business) will be conducting an Advanced Information Systems Faculty Development Institute at Indiana University, Bloomington, Indiana, on July 7-29, 19--. The announcement booklet states that each applicant must provide the following:

    a. A current curriculum vitae.
    b. A statement explaining why attendance at the institute is desired.
    c. A list of any MIS classes taught during the last three years—syllabi should be included, if possible.
    d. A description of all prior computer and information systems experience (including any relevant research experience).
    e. A list of the MIS classes the applicant plans to teach in the next two academic years.
    f. A letter from the business school dean to include:
        (*1*) A recommendation on why it would be desirable that the applicant be accepted at the institute.
        (*2*) A list of the specific courses the applicant will be expected to teach in 19--.
        (*3*) The applicant's role in MIS curriculum development and a list of all other MIS faculty at the school.
        (*4*) An indication of the share of tuition and travel costs provided by the applicant's institution.

    As dean, you have just appointed a task force of five faculty members to develop a new curriculum in MIS (Management Information Systems). Two of the five faculty members want to attend the upcoming summer institute and you are eager to have them attend. You want to use the current faculty in upgrading the curriculum and believe the best way is to offer financial support and encouragement for the development of faculty in this area. You have secured the necessary funds for the travel costs and the $3,400 fee tuition, computer use charges, text materials, basic supplies, dormitory room, three meals a day, and refreshment breaks. After a brief discussion with the faculty who are interested in attending the institute, you ask both of them to submit a copy of their curricula vitae. You are now faced with the task of writing a letter of recommendation (item no. *f* above in the application requirements) for each since you would like for both to attend. You decide to write one letter and then adapt it for the other person. The following represent the facts you have gathered for writing the recommendation letter for one applicant:

a. *Why desirable to attend.* Alexander Ober currently serves on a task force for developing an MIS curriculum; has served on other major curriculum committees related to computers in the College; currently teaches Introduction to Information Systems.

b. *Specific courses taught in past two years.* Information Systems Analysis; Introduction to Information Systems; Office Automation; Computers in Business.

c. *Applicant's role in MIS:* See (*a*) above.

d. *List of other MIS faculty.* Grant Rhodes, Eleanor Perkins, Donald Sutton, Perry Allison.

e. *Share of tuition/travel.* Total $3,400 fee and transportation paid by College of Business.

The dean thinks to himself: "I am really supportive of this program; this is a way of developing our own faculty to move into this important area. I have known Ober for the past 15 years; he has done a fine job, and his teaching and research are outstanding; I am glad he is undertaking this additional education to help us develop this fast-growing area. I am glad to write this letter of recommendation and hope that Ober will be accepted since there are only a limited number of spaces for the summer institute."

With these notes, develop the strategy for writing this message as the dean of the College of Business. Then write the message.

DUE FRIDAY

14. Joe and Rebecca Rowland of Nashville, Tennessee 37224 (340 Broom Road), have been collecting bonus coupons from the frequent flying trips their jobs demand and have decided to take their three children on a one-week skiing expedition during the Christmas holidays. A friend suggested Park City, Utah, as a good place for such an event for the whole family. Therefore, Joe and Rebecca decide to write the Chamber of Commerce in Park City (84060) for information about accommodations for the family, necessary arrangements for skiing, area sight-seeing spots, plus any other information that would convince them to come to Park City for a holiday skiing vacation.

The three children (Jessica, eight years old; Amanda, three; and Patrick, five) have never skied before; Joe and Rebecca have skied once or twice. None has skiing equipment or clothes. Joe and Rebecca assume that it will be possible to rent all the necessary equipment and clothes.

Place yourself in the shoes of Joe and Rebecca; plan the strategy for the request message; then write the request. (Use your own experience in creating the specific questions to ask. Keep this question in mind: "What information would I need in order to make a decision about going to Park City for the week?")

15. In the following situation, you will assume the role of Cynthia

Sweeten, owner of Mountain Sporting Goods, 203 Maryville Pike, Montgomery, Alabama 36101. You have been looking through the catalog offerings of Eastern Mountain Sports, Inc. (Vose Farm Road, Peterborough, New Hampshire 03458), and decide to place an order for several sporting items. When you look at the back of the catalog, you discover that all of the order blanks have been used, so you will have to use a letter to send in your order. Even though you realize you could use the toll-free number, you decide to send a letter to make sure that everything is accurate.

You select the following items to order:

5 Eureka Catskills tents (color: green floor and fly-gold canopy)—3 two-man tents, wt. 6 lbs. ea.; and 2 three-man tents, wt. 7 lbs. 14 oz. Catalog number for the two-man tents, 58-1827; for three-man, 58-1843; cost: two-man, $79.50 ea.; three-man, $109.50 (catalog page 88).

3 New Eureka Domension tents (color: tan/sandstone—catalog no. 58-1405, price $110 ea.; av. wt. 6 lbs. 1 oz. (catalog page 88).

10 sleeping bags: 4 regular (no. 50-4225) EMS Mt. Robson, price, $175; and 1 large (no. 50-4241) EMS Mt. Robson, price $185. Regular—av. wt. 4 lbs. 2 oz., large—av. wt. 4 lbs. 7 oz. Only color available: forest green with dark brown lining (catalog page 92).

5 new EMS Dhaulagiri Mummy type sleeping bags (no. 50-4282), price $210, av. wt. 5 lbs. 12 oz. Only color available: electric blue (catalog page 92).

You have ordered from Eastern Mountain Sports before and have been billed for the orders. Therefore, you can request this method for payment of the order.

As Cynthia, design the strategy for this case; then write the appropriate request message.

16. Joe Herndon is in charge of training seminars for personnel at the Norwood Utility Company, P. O. Box 42, Nome, Alaska 99760. In talking with a colleague several days ago, Joe learned about a training film entitled *Meanings Are in People, Not in Words.* The colleague indicated that the film was designed to improve oral communication skills for supervisors and managers. He searched and found a brochure that indicated that the film was available through Avco Company, 4041 North High Street, Dallas, Texas 75242, at a cost of $500. Since Joe isn't sure that it would be appropriate for one of his seminars, he wants to receive a review copy of the film along with any materials (the brochure mentioned class exercises and presenter's guide notes) so that he can evaluate the content for possible use at Norwood. From previous experience, Joe knows that companies nor-

mally charge a fee for this review and then apply this to the cost of the film if it is purchased.

Acting for Joe Herndon in this situation, use the strategy to plan your message; then write the message to request the film. Supply other facts that would be needed to make a decision. About 50 supervisors would be involved in a seminar using this film.

17. As Joel Marks, you need to write a letter that authorizes Thomas Hardingdon of the Hardingdon Insurance Agency (P. O. Box 124, Boulder, Colorado 80321), to make changes in your automobile insurance policy.

    When you discussed the changes with Thomas over the phone, he asked you to send a letter giving the changes; as soon as he gets your letter, he will process them. The changes include the following: removing the travel trailer coverage for a savings of $46; changing the comprehensive coverage from no deductible to $50 deductible and the collision coverage from $100 deductible to $200 deductible on the Oldsmobile, a savings of $16.20 on the comprehensive and $28.80 on the collision; and removing comprehensive coverage from the second car (Ford) that is now eight years old, a savings of $23.44.

    The Hardingdon Insurance Agency has handled your insurance for the past 20 years for the automobiles, trailer, and house. Thomas has given you very prompt and helpful service over these years. You feel you know him personally, and that you can trust his recommendations. Everyone in the community speaks highly of the Hardingdon Insurance Agency.

    As Joel Marks, plan the strategy components for this setting; then write the appropriate confirmation letter.

18. Assume the role of James Carson, chairperson of a local group called Citizens to Help Citizens (CHC). James is faced with writing a request to persuade a select group of local merchants to make donations of merchandise.

    Since people in general respond well to a raffle, the board for CHC has approved this mechanism for obtaining money to assist local needy individuals throughout the year. CHC was formed about four years ago to aid those who were not eligible to receive either state or federal aid. CHC is manned completely by volunteers—all funds collected are spent on persons with valid emergency needs. Your daytime phone number is 637-5041. Some of the individuals who received aid last year included: elderly persons who needed emergency medical assistance; elderly persons who needed transportation to the hospital, the doctor's office, or other essential places; individuals needing emergency funds for heating bills; persons who suffered a tragedy such as loss of family member or loss of a home by fire; and numerous others.

    As James, you have obtained a list of 10 local merchants who have been known for their community involvement in the past. You plan to write a draft copy of the message for one merchant and then adapt it for the other nine. So you select Proffit's Department Store, 101 Main Street, Saint Joseph, Missouri 64508, to request a food processor.

Now, plan the strategy for this first letter; then write the letter that will convince Proffit's to donate the food processor to your group.

19. In this case, assume the role of Shirley Kirkpatrick, an elementary music teacher at Cedar Springs Elementary School, 220 Arrogane Road, Little Rock, Arkansas 72210. Some time ago, Shirley received material from the Music Publishing House (P. O. Box 27143, Portland, Oregon 97232), about a new service for music teachers. According to the literature, each month she would receive a card with the name and description of the book-of-the-month selection. In addition, a listing and description of other music books for teachers would be included if she wanted to substitute or order others. If she did not want the book-of-the-month selection, she would be free to select another from the attached list. The brochure also indicated that the membership could be cancelled at any time—no minimum or maximum number of books was mentioned. The material indicated that each month she would receive a card; if the card wasn't returned within 15 days indicating that she didn't want the selection for that month or another book, then she would automatically receive the book-of-the-month selection along with the statement (cost of book plus a small handling charge).

    Since Shirley thought that this might be a good way to get additional learning materials helpful in teaching choral music to students in grades one through eight, she signed and mailed the initial application card. After receiving five selections, she decided that the offerings were geared toward high school rather than elementary students. She also thought if the company would start offering books geared to the elementary grades some time in the future, she would consider becoming a member again. After receiving the sixth set of materials, she decides to cancel her membership (there was no restriction as to the number of months one needs to belong to the club).

    Plan the strategy for this case; then write the appropriate message.

20. In this case, you will assume the role of Tracey Watson (2310 Highland Avenue, Laurel, Missouri 39440), who has a consulting office in her own home. Last month, she received a set of promotional materials on a cordless phone. Since the phone situation had changed because of the breakup of AT&T, she decided that the cordless phone might be just the right thing to place in her home office. She ordered the phone.

    The promotional literature included these statements:

    - This amazing Cordless Phone lets you take and receive calls from almost anywhere up to 700 feet of its base unit!

- □ Use it four ways—cordless phone, paging system, extension phone, intercom.
- □ Try it FREE for 30 days!
- □ Easy to use! Just plug the base unit into a phone jack and convenient AC outlet.
- □ Price: $122.89 plus $5.88 shipping and handling charges.

After using the phone about two weeks, Tracey was unhappy with it. Each time the phone was used, there was a lot of static; and calls were difficult to complete. She and other members of her household had used the phone at various distances from the base and at different times of the day—always with the same types of problems. Tracey decided to return the cordless phone by mail and ask for her money to be returned. She did not want a replacement!

Using this information, plan the strategy for this case; then write the message that will get Tracey's money returned.

21. In this case, you will assume the role of Mark Smith, a high school senior (224 Appleside Drive, Orlando, Florida 32812). Three weeks ago, Mark received a copy of *Gentlemen's Quarterly* and thought it strange since he had not ordered the magazine. He checked with his parents and found that they had not ordered the magazine for him either. He thought that perhaps the publisher had sent the magazine to him as a promotional effort.

    Today, he received a bill and a letter with the following excerpts:

> Thank you for your recent subscription order to Gentlemen's Quarterly, the world's top fashion magazine for men.
>
> P.S. If you haven't yet sent payment (as shown on the attached statement), for your subscription, won't you please take a moment to do so right now? Thank you.

Since Mark now knows that the magazine wasn't a promotion and that he didn't subscribe to it, he surmises that some of his buddies or a "friend" must have played a trick on him by filling out a subscription card with his name and address.

Anyway, he must now write a message to the publisher (*Gentlemen's Quarterly,* P. O. Box 2962, Boulder, Colorado 80321), and cancel the subscription. Since the first copy was received three weeks ago, he is sure that he will soon be receiving the next issue. In his message, he plans to ask whether or not he should mail back the two issues.

Assuming the role of Mark, plan the strategy for this setting; then write the appropriate message to accomplish the objective(s).

CHAPTER 8

WRITING POSITIVE LETTERS

Learning Objectives

After studying this chapter, you will be able to:

- ☐ Determine when to write a positive response.
- ☐ Understand the goodwill objective of positive response messages.
- ☐ Demonstrate the use of the "you" viewpoint and reader benefit.
- ☐ Evaluate the situation and plan an appropriate approach for positive-response messages.
- ☐ Understand and apply the basic concepts for effective positive messages.
- ☐ Write effective positive-response messages for different situations.
- ☐ Select the appropriate format for the situation.
- ☐ Evaluate and improve messages with poor viewpoint, tone, organization, and sales appeal.
- ☐ Appreciate the time and effort for creating a well-written positive-response communication.

Assume you are marketing director of a large retail chain and someone writes you with questions about the luggage you sell. You promptly send a reply with answers to all questions plus colorful brochures and an order form. Someone else writes and invites you to speak at this year's graduation ceremonies at your old high school; you are honored and write a letter accepting the invitation.

Each of these responses is positive since the inquirer receives the information requested. Each contains good news and the anticipated response. As you write positive messages, keep these basic concepts in mind:

Basic concepts for positive messages

- ☐ Reply promptly.
- ☐ Use "you" viewpoint.
- ☐ Emphasize the good news.
- ☐ Provide all the information requested or a reason for not including it.
- ☐ Use sales appeal—reader benefit; persuasion.
- ☐ Make it easy for the recipient to respond, if appropriate.
- ☐ Keep the tone positive.
- ☐ Use enclosures, when appropriate.

In addition to these basic concepts, you must also consider the techniques for achieving unity, clarity, conciseness, the proper level of words, and the proper tone discussed in earlier chapters. Each situation requiring a written response is unique. If you focus on the person receiving the message, the event, subject, and any other information about the reader's environment, you'll find that planning your communication strategy is easier. Remember that the use of the direct and indirect arrangements for the overall message is based on the type of message, objective, and previous relationship with the reader rather than some "recipe" approach.

This chapter illustrates a step-by-step process for applying the strategy for communicating to some typical types of positive messages:

Sample types of positive messages

- ☐ Accepting an invitation.
- ☐ Writing a letter of recommendation.
- ☐ Acknowledging a first order.
- ☐ Answering an inquiry about a product or service.
- ☐ Granting a request for adjustment.

Once you have gone through the process outlined for each of these five situations, you should be able to apply this same strategy to similar situations calling for positive responses.

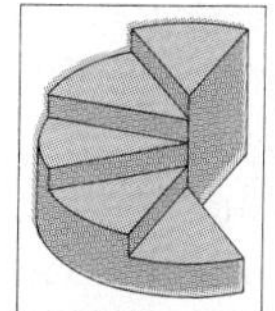

STRATEGY: THE ACCEPTANCE LETTER

Cassandra Noblett is a business consultant with expertise in employee job satisfaction/morale. She has just received a letter from Adam Lerner, executive director of the National Council of Private Schools and Colleges.

Figure 8.1 Letter: Accepting an invitation

MS. CASSANDRA NOBLETT

3001 John B. Dennis Hwy.
Kingsport, TN 37660
Telephone (615) 644-7711

September 23, 19__

Dr. Adam Lerner, Executive Director
National Council of Private Schools and Colleges
111 North Boulevard
Kansas City, MO 64100

Dear Dr. Lerner:

I am pleased to accept your invitation to speak at the National Council of Private Schools and Colleges on Thursday, March 12, 19__, in Chicago, Illinois. The honorarium of $500 and expenses are quite acceptable. The topic, "Curriculum Implications of the Changing Work Force," is a very timely one. Since rapid changes are taking place in business offices, there is a great need for schools to keep up with the changes. You are definitely on target to consider modifying your curriculum to meet these expanding needs.

To help me prepare for the presentation, will you please answer the following questions:

1. How much time will be allocated for the speech? What is the scheduled time for my speech? Will there be a question-and-answer session afterward?
2. What arrangements will be made for ground transportation from the airport? to the airport?
3. Do you need a copy of the presentation for the proceedings? Date needed?

It is an honor to be asked to speak to such a distinguished group. If you need to discuss any details concerning the presentation, you may call me at 615/644-7711.

Cordially yours,

Ms. Cassandra Noblett

He invites her to present the keynote speech at the national meeting to be held in Chicago, Illinois, on Thursday, March 12, 19__. The letter indicates that other members have heard her at an earlier regional meeting and recommended her as a speaker. The invitation letter also indicates that the council has authorized an honorarium of $500 plus expenses. Lerner suggests the following topic: "Curriculum Implications of the Changing Work Force." He indicates that approximately 1,200 people will attend. Hotel arrangements will be made if Cassandra accepts.

After reviewing her calendar, Cassandra decides to send a message to Lerner accepting the invitation to speak and confirming the date, topic, and other specifics about the engagement. She also wants to find out about the length of speech desired, whether someone will meet her at the airport, and whether the council wants copies of the speech for distribution.

PROBLEM
The central question for Cassandra is: How do I construct an appropriate letter of acceptance? Since Cassandra has decided to accept the invitation, she faces an easy task.

OBJECTIVES

General: To inform Lerner about the acceptance to speak.

Specific: To express appreciation for invitation.
To be courteous.
To confirm facts: date, group, honorarium, place, title.
To accept the invitation.
To give phone number for contact (615/644-7711).
To ask for more specific details about:
a. Length/format of presentation.
b. Time of speech.
c. Ground transportation from airport and back.
d. Council's need for copies of speech for proceedings.

At this point you merely list the specific objectives without concern for the appropriate sequence; you will decide on the exact sequence with the order component.

READER/AUDIENCE
With her objectives identified, Cassandra visualizes Lerner and his association members to help in drafting the message.

Characteristics: Lerner—someone who is experienced in managing conferences.
All are professional people.
Some have already heard me speak.

Reactions: Will be glad to learn of acceptance.
Willing to do other things necessary for speaker.
Will be cordial to speaker.

ORDER

OVERALL MESSAGE: DIRECT
Cassandra puts herself in the readers' place and realizes what they want is a positive response to their request. She is sure that Lerner and others will be glad to receive her acceptance. She believes that people value her

ideas, or they would not have suggested her for this event. So that the reader won't have to scan the message to find the answer, she uses the *direct approach* by starting with the good news.

SPECIFIC OBJECTIVES

1. To accept the invitation; express appreciation.
2. To confirm facts: date, group, honorarium, place, title.
3. To ask for more details about:
   a. Length/format of presentation.
   b. Time of speech.
   c. Ground transportation from airport and back.
   d. Need for copies of speech for proceedings.
4. To give phone number for contact (615/644-7711).
5. To express courtesy.

FORMAT

LETTER

With the strategy completed, Cassandra wrote the letter shown in Figure 8.1.

Listing the questions makes it easier for Lerner to read them and respond. Note in numbers 2 and 3 that a complete question is followed by an incomplete question phrase. This is an acceptable way to ask questions and avoid being repetitive. Even though the letter could end after the third question, Cassandra wanted her letter to have a "completed look," so she ended with courtesy statements. If she did not include this final paragraph, she would need to add a final sentence (giving her telephone number) to the opening paragraph.

LETTERS OF RECOMMENDATION

Business professionals routinely receive requests from former or current employees, colleagues, or acquaintances for recommendations on future employment, professional or civic honors, and promotions. In these instances, the information you supply should help the receiver evaluate the person in relation to the stated or implied criteria. In the next example, the writer recommends a person for a civic honor.

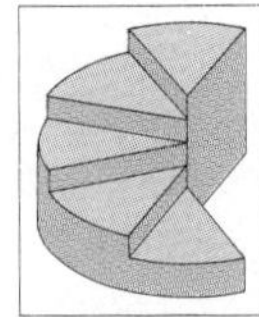

STRATEGY: WRITING A RECOMMENDATION

Amanda Lane, a former employee of Jones & Jones Advertising, has asked Dean Varlan, personnel director, to write a letter to the Selection Committee of the Houston Chamber of Commerce recommending her for the

Distinguished Community Achievement Award sponsored by the Houston, Texas, Chamber of Commerce. Dean believes that Amanda is very deserving of this award and is glad to write the recommendation. He remembers her superior performance at Jones & Jones as well as her work in such community projects as the United Way (local chairperson for two years and company representative for three years), Junior Achievement (sponsor for five years), and many other worthwhile organizations. In fact, Dean was always amazed at how Amanda was able to do such superior work at Jones & Jones and yet involve herself successfully with community projects. "If anyone deserves this award, it's Amanda," he thinks.

So he begins by planning his strategy.

PROBLEM

How do I write a convincing letter of recommendation that distinguishes Amanda from other candidates?

OBJECTIVES

General: To persuade the selection committee members to award the Distinguished Community Achievement Award to Amanda.

Specific: To recommend Amanda for the award.

To highlight Amanda's community activities:

Sponsor of Junior Achievement.

Company representative for United Way; local chairperson for two years, company representative three years.

To establish basis for my comments.

To convey sincerity of recommendation.

Dean examines his objectives again and decides that they are complete. He knows personally of Amanda's professional expertise and is aware of some of her community activities. Therefore, he feels that personal comments will provide evidence of Amanda's achievement. Dean realizes that specific examples of her qualifications are more likely to convince the readers than more general statements about her. He is glad to contribute these comments to help her obtain this coveted award.

READER/AUDIENCE

Characteristics: Committee members with responsibility for evaluating nominees.

Professional people.

Volunteers for Chamber Selection Committee.

Reactions: Glad to get recommendation.

Will be pleased with specific evidence of

Amanda's community projects.

Will carefully scrutinize the content and tone of message.

Dean realizes that each of the committee members will be reading several letters of recommendation and that his writing needs to be specific. He wants his letter to present Amanda's contributions in such a way that she will be the clear choice. His communication must be persuasive to place Amanda ahead of the others.

ORDER

OVERALL MESSAGE: DIRECT

By using the *direct approach* for this message, Dean leads the reader through a sequence from general to specific. To orient the reader, Dean feels his first sentence should contain the recommendation and a statement that conveys his sincere pleasure in recommending Amanda. He will then highlight her specific accomplishments.

SPECIFIC OBJECTIVES

1. To show sincerity of recommendation.
2. To recommend Amanda for the Distinguished Community Achievement Award.
3. To highlight Amanda's community achievements:
   United Way involvement.
   Junior Achievement sponsorship.
4. To reemphasize recommendation and Amanda's qualifications to receive award.

FORMAT

LETTER

With the five components of the strategy completed, Dean begins to compose his message; he revises it twice (see Figure 8.2, the final draft). Dean then reads the letter and is confident that he has achieved his general objective—to persuade the readers to award Amanda the Distinguished Community Achievement Award.

In Figure 8.2, note the use of Selection Committee as the first line of the inside address and the use of the simplified letter style—no salutation or complimentary close. Note also the use of "I" to provide a personal feeling throughout the letter. A letter such as this should emphasize two or three major points that justify the receipt of the award; the use of too many will detract from the letter and perhaps make it too long. A balance needs to be maintained between too few and too many accomplishments. Notice the repetition of Amanda throughout the letter to keep her name before the reader for emphasis; it appears again in the last sentence along with

Figure 8.2 Letter of recommendation

January 10, 19__

Selection Committee
Distinguished Community Achievement Award
Houston Chamber of Commerce
102 West End Boulevard
Houston, TX 77001

SUBJECT: Recommendation of Amanda Lane

What a privilege it is to write a letter supporting Miss Amanda Lane as a candidate for the Distinguished Community Award sponsored by the Houston Chamber of Commerce.

Having worked with the Chamber for six years, I am fully aware of this most significant honor and the caliber of individuals competing for this award each year. Miss Lane certainly meets your high criteria. As a person who exemplifies community involvement and leadership, she would bring honor to the award.

Miss Lane recognizes the importance of community service. She has demonstrated her concern by serving as the local United Way leader for two years. During this time, the campaign reached unprecedented goals.

Miss Lane also acted as chairperson of the United Way program at Jones & Jones for three years. Each year, she worked diligently to achieve the goals established by Jones & Jones--and with great success!

For five consecutive years, Miss Lane involved herself with the community through her sponsorship of a Junior Achievement Group. This program assists youngsters to learn about the free enterprise system.

In other words, Miss Lane has won the admiration of everyone in the community because of her caring attitude and unselfish dedication to others. I know of no one more deserving of the Distinguished Community Award than Miss Amanda Lane.

Dean Varlan
Personnel Director

dv/sp

123 Mockingbird Lane Houston, Texas 77121 Phone (713) 288-7023

the full name of the award. The final product is specific, sincere, and persuasive.

LETTERS OF ACKNOWLEDGMENT

In most businesses, only special occasions warrant a response to an order. Those special situations include a response to a first order or an especially large one, an appreciation letter at a seasonal time, or some other nonroutine event. Follow the activities of Marcee Whiteside as she plans her strategy and writes an appropriate message to acknowledge a first order.

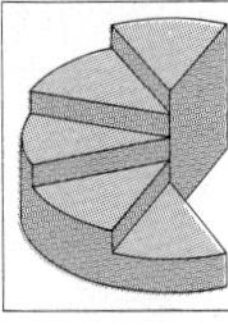

STRATEGY: ACKNOWLEDGING AN ORDER

Marcee Whiteside, the mail order manager for Whiteside Wholesale Supplies, has just received a letter from Christine Cooper of the Oberal Office Supplies Company (237 Colorado Avenue, Lincoln, Nebraska 68500), for the following items:

20 Glare Guard Filter Panels, no. 8447X, $27 ea.
5 PC Keyboard drawer slides, no. 74X, $49 ea., cream.
25 Micro Cleaning Kits, no. 923, $19.95 ea.
4 Anti-Static Mats, no. 627Y, 53"x45," $79.50 ea., clear.
25 Flip-and-Files, no. 347X, 5¼" size, $12.75 ea., color: smoke.

With the letter was a check for $1,920.50 for the first order. Marcee called the Credit Bureau in Lincoln about the Oberal Office Supplies Company; she found that the company was very reputable in the area and was noted for its quality products and personal service to its customers. Marcee surmised that Cooper probably had found a catalog (without an order form) and therefore used a letter for ordering. Marcee sees this as an opportunity to send a message to Cooper commenting on the quality of the items ordered plus an opportunity to gain a new continuing customer.

PROBLEM

How can I gain Oberal Office Supplies Company (via Christine Cooper) as a regular customer?

OBJECTIVES

General: To convince Oberal (via Cooper) to become a regular customer.

Since this is the first written contact, Marcee wants to create a message that will not only acknowledge the order but also sell the Oberal Company on the services of Whiteside and gain a regular customer. Because persuasion and goodwill are subjective in nature, Marcee realizes the outcome will depend on the makeup of the whole letter. Achieving her objectives depends on Cooper's reaction to the letter. If Cooper orders again, Marcee will know that she accomplished her general objective.

Without considering order at this time, she lists her specific objectives.

SPECIFIC OBJECTIVES

1. To encourage Oberal to apply for a credit account.
2. To acknowledge the first order.
3. To include sales appeal throughout message: benefits of carrying these products—use of Whiteside name throughout message, appropriate adjectives.

4. To tell how and when the first order is being shipped.
5. To acknowledge the check.
6. To enclose a midwinter sales flyer.
7. To suggest placing a second order.
8. To end letter with courtesty and goodwill.

To accomplish these objectives, Marcee realizes that she needs to watch the tone of this letter and not overdo the sales pitch. Therefore, she decides to emphasize the benefits Cooper can expect—customer recognition of the products and demand for the name-brand items. In addition, Marcee decides to repeat the Whiteside name throughout the message to build name recognition. She'll also use appropriate adjectives and sales content to convince Cooper to become a regular customer.

READER/AUDIENCE

Characteristics:	Purchasing manager of office supply company (primary).
	Other company officials (secondary).
	Eager to find products that have a high demand and good profit.
	Retail establishment.
	Already placed an unsolicited order.
Reactions:	Positive—will open an account; will reorder.
	Glad to know that someone will take the time to write a letter acknowledging the order.

Awareness of these characteristics and possible reactions helps in establishing a framework for completing the writing task.

ORDER

OVERALL: DIRECT
Since this is a good news letter, the *direct approach* will give the reader what she wants to hear first; this approach generates a mood for building a good customer relationship. Marcee knows that customer satisfaction and fair treatment will encourage additional orders. She then tackles the more time-consuming task of sequencing her specific objectives.

SPECIFIC OBJECTIVES

1. To acknowledge the first order.
2. To acknowledge the $1920.50 check.
3. To tell when and how the first order is being shipped.
4. To include sales content.
5. To encourage Oberal to apply for a credit account.

Figure 8.3 Marcee's first draft

Dear Ms. Cooper:

We thank you for your first order of January 2 for the versatile Whiteside microcomputer supplies and your check for $1,920.50. We are shipping the items to you on January 15 via Roadway Xpress. Our national advertising campaign now underway can help you increase sales because of the high demand for these quality office supplies.

I suggest that you can make ordering easier by applying for a credit account at WHITESIDE. Fill out, sign, and mail the enclosed background data form. As soon as we receive the completed form, we will review it carefully. We can guarantee that purchasing with a credit account will make future ordering more convenient.

Enclosed is our mid-winter sales catalog with exceptional savings. Look on page 10 at the end-of-season offer for microcomputer floppy disks. We are offering a special savings of from 10 to 40 percent on all orders placed soon.

I am glad that you ordered from Whiteside Wholesale Supplies. We offer 100 percent satisfaction! Welcome as a WHITESIDE customer.

Cordially yours,

6. To enclose a midwinter sales flyer.
7. To suggest sending in a second order.
8. To end letter with courtesy statement to promote goodwill.

Marcee wants Cooper to read her letter and conclude that Whiteside is the wholesale supplier for Oberal. Because Cooper has sent in a first order, Marcee has a contact point. Cooper already has enough confidence in Whiteside to place a first order. Marcee knows, however, that she needs

Figure 8.4 Marcee's marked-up first draft

Dear Ms. Cooper:

(We) thank you for your first order of January 2 for the versatile Whiteside microcomputer supplies and your check for $1,920.50. (We) are shipping the items to you on January 15 via Roadway Xpress. (Our) national advertising campaign now underway can help you increase sales because of the high demand for these quality office supplies.

(I) suggest that you can make ordering easier by applying for a credit account at WHITESIDE. Fill out, sign, and mail the enclosed background data form. As soon as (we) receive the completed form, (we) will review it carefully. (We) can guarantee that purchasing with a credit account will make future ordering more convenient.

Enclosed is (our) mid-winter sales catalog with exceptional savings. Look on page 10 at the end-of-season offer for microcomputer floppy disks. (We) are offering a special savings from 10 to 40 percent on all orders placed soon.

(I) am glad that you ordered from Whiteside Wholesale Supplies. (We) offer 100 percent satisfaction! Welcome as a WHITESIDE customer.

Cordially yours,

to reemphasize Whiteside's dependability as a supplier of needed items and to build on the confidence Cooper has already shown in Whiteside. Prompt service is a must!

FORMAT

LETTER

Having completed the initial planning, Marcee drafts the letter shown in Figure 8.3.

How do you feel about Marcee's draft? Before proceeding to Marcee's own evaluation, read the draft again and provide your own assessment.

Figure 8.5 Marcee's final acknowledgment letter

SUPPLIES
WHITESIDE
WHOLESALE

987 MEMORIAL DRIVE
GREENVILLE, SOUTH CAROLINA 29600
PHONE (803) 716-4217

January 5, 19__

Ms. Christine Cooper
Oberal Office Supplies Company
237 Colorado Avenue
Lincoln, NE 68500

Dear Ms. Cooper:

Thank you for your first order of January 2 for the versatile Whiteside microcomputer supplies and your check for $1,920.50. The items are being shipped to you on January 15 via Roadway Xpress. With the additional advertising campaign now underway, you can look forward to increased sales because of the high demand for these quality office supplies.

To make ordering easier, why not apply for a credit account at Whiteside? Fill out, sign, and mail the enclosed background data form. As soon as the completed form is received, careful attention will be given to your request. Purchasing with a credit account will make your future ordering more convenient.

Take advantage of the exceptional savings offered in the enclosed mid winter sales catalog. For instance, look on page 10 at the end-of-season offer for microcomputer floppy disks. You can enjoy savings from 10 to 40 percent by placing an order today.

You have made a wise choice in ordering from Whiteside Wholesale Supplies. At Whiteside, you can select from a wide assortment of dependable major brands. And you are guaranteed 100 percent satisfaction and prompt delivery! Welcome as a WHITESIDE customer.

Cordially yours,

Marcee Whiteside
Mail Order Manager

ct

Enclosures: Background Data Form
Mid-winter Sales Catalog

- ☐ What part(s) of the message do you feel will convince the reader to open an account?
- ☐ What weaknesses can you identify?
- ☐ How do you feel about the format—modified block; mixed punctuation; indented paragraphs?
- ☐ How could Marcee improve the viewpoint of this letter?
- ☐ What other changes would you make?

After reading the draft, Marcee felt that she had included all of her specific objectives but recognized that the viewpoint of the letter was "we" instead of "you." She also reviewed the letter to determine how well she had achieved her general and specific objectives. Changing several sentences to reflect a stronger "you" viewpoint would improve the letter and enhance the content. She, therefore, reread the draft and circled each of the "I-we-our-us" references as shown in Figure 8.4.

With a stronger "you" viewpoint and a slight modification in content, Marcee's much improved revision is shown in Figure 8.5.

LETTERS ANSWERING INQUIRIES

When a product or service is advertised, potential buyers may have numerous questions they want answered before they buy. These potential buyers usually write letters asking specific questions about the product or service. The information may or may not be covered in the advertisements. Since these are potential customers, it is important to provide the requested information and encourage them to buy—sometimes by sending in an order directly; sometimes by going to a local dealer; or perhaps through a representative of the company. Since the writer has already taken the time to write (or call), this type of letter needs to emphasize:

- ☐ The "you" viewpoint.
- ☐ Sales (reader benefits; persuasion).
- ☐ Action.

In this situation, you have an advantage since you have a prospective buyer: your response then can stress sales appeal and the important characteristics of the product or service as you provide answers to the questions raised. This example illustrates an answer to an inquiry about a service.

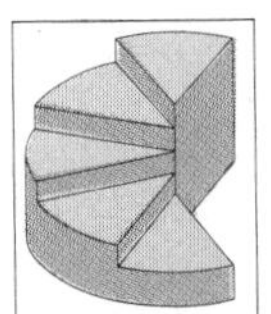

STRATEGY: ANSWERING AN INQUIRY

Martin Fellow is managing director of The Hideaway, a resort complex recently completed in the Rocky Mountains near Boulder, Colorado. Very soon he expects to receive numerous letters of inquiry about the facilities and accommodations at The Hideaway. The ultramodern resort offers both winter and summer vacation fun. Since the resort is almost finished, advertisements are now appearing nationally in magazines and newspapers and on television. In fact, Martin has received his first inquiry letter from Bernice and William Smuthers, who are eager to get information about The Hideaway. The Smuthers asked for the following information: types of accommodations available, with prices; the minimum length of stay; amount of deposit required; other facilities available; cost of ski passes; opening date; recommended types of transportation to the resort; and brochures.

Since Martin anticipates many such inquiries, he decides to use his letter to the Smuthers as the basis for a *model* response letter. He begins to plan his strategy.

LEGAL / ETHICAL ISSUES

Television advertisement is an effective means of selling products and services in our society. Some advertisements, however, are of a questionable nature. For example, TV commercials extol the importance of health insurance for persons aged 60 and over. Using well-known personalities, the commercials use these persuasive appeals: love and devotion of family members; high costs if not protected; and financial disaster for family members. After these appeals, most commercials end with something like this: "For only $3.75 a month, you can relax knowing that your hospital bills will be paid. And you can't be turned down for any reason!"

Sounds good and economical! But what does the subscriber get for the $3.75 a month? The $3.75 buys a very low level of coverage. To cover all the costs indicated in the ad, the person would probably have to spend $50 or more dollars per month to receive the stated coverage. This same tactic is used commonly in unsolicited sales letters.

How ethical is this type of persuasive sales message? Does this type of sales message generate goodwill on the part of the recipient? Is the American TV viewer really gullible to these types of ads?

PROBLEM
The lack of a model response letter to attract customers.

OBJECTIVES

General: To answer the questions contained in the inquiry letter.

Specific: To provide facts about:
- Types of accommodations available/prices.
- Minimum length of stay.
- Amount of deposit required.
- Other facilities available.
- Cost of ski passes.
- Opening date.
- Recommended types of transportation to the resort.

To include brochures.
To show appreciation for inquiry.
To request action.

Martin wants to make sure that he answers each of the questions posed in the inquiry letter. He gathers the appropriate brochures and other facts so that he can answer these questions easily and effectively. He plans to sell The Hideaway through the professionally prepared brochures he has just received. The brochures contain colorful pictures of the accommodations with prices and fees for ski passes.

READER/AUDIENCE

Characteristics:	Persons who like to ski in the winter.
	Financially able to pay for luxuries.
	Probably professional persons.
	May have small children.
	Familiar with snow areas.
Reaction:	Eager to get the information.
	Probably will book a vactaion.

Martin recognizes that later on he will need to add other ideas to this model letter to cover other inquiries. He plans to prepare different versions of the paragraphs so that he can select appropriate responses to the inquiries he is sure he will receive. For now, he thinks these will do.

ORDER

OVERALL MESSAGE: DIRECT

Since he has already received an inquiry letter from the Smuthers, Martin uses this letter to create the model response letter. The Smuthers have already seen an advertisement about The Hideaway; Martin feels that he needs to get right to the point and answer their questions. The *direct approach* seems best. He wants the Smuthers to open the letter, read the answers to their questions, and feel good about The Hideaway.

SPECIFIC OBJECTIVES

1. To show appreciation for the inquiry.
2. To promote goodwill.
3. To provide facts about:
   a. Opening date.
   b. Types of accommodations, available/prices.
   c. Amount of deposit required.
   d. Recommended types of transportation to the resort.
   e. Minimum length of stay.
   f. Cost of ski passes.
   g. Other facilities available (brochures).
4. To include brochures.
5. To request action.

Some of the information, such as the cost of the ski passes, will be too lengthy to include in the letter, so Martin decides to refer the reader to the brochures.

FORMAT

LETTER

Because the message will be going outside the company, he selects the *letter* as his format. He also thinks it would be good to present the answers to the questions in a list. Right now, all he wants is a draft of the *model* letter.

A draft of Martin's model letter to the Smuthers is shown in Figure 8.6.

Martin then examines the letter to make sure that it achieves his objective. As he looks at his draft, he realizes that he has in fact given the information requested but that the letter does not achieve what he really wants—to get the Smuthers to call and book The Hideaway. After all, the Smuthers have probably written to other resorts and will be getting responses from each. "What I have to do," he thinks, "is to persuade them that The Hideaway is the place for their vacation. My letter doesn't accomplish this objective."

He decides that the *problem* is still the same—the lack of a model response letter for inquiries. However, he knows now that his general and specific objectives need to be changed. After thinking about the draft, he decides on the following for his revised general objective:

General: To persuade ("sell") the reader to make arrangements to vacation at The Hideaway.

He recognizes that he will need to answer the questions, yet incorporate sales to convince the reader to book a vacation at the resort. Martin is aware that he must control the persuasive tone so that the reader doesn't feel that it is a hard-sell approach. Tone becomes very important in this type of letter. He plans to use action words to enhance the letter.

With these overall thoughts in mind, Martin then decides to use his three original specific objectives:

To show appreciation/goodwill for the inquiry.

To provide facts about The Hideaway.

To include brochures.

He *adds* the following *specific objectives:*

To provide other enticing features about the resort.

To include other appropriate brochures.

To suggest a call to book the vacation time.

To create a feeling that The Hideaway is *the* place.

He must go beyond simply answering the questions as he did in the first draft if he is to achieve his revised general objective—get the reader to book The Hideaway. The *specific objectives* just added will help him attain this objective.

Figure 8.6 Martin's first draft

Dear ____________

Thanks for your inquiry about The Hideaway. Below are answers to the specific questions you asked in your letter of September 10, 19__:

1. Opening Date for The Hideaway: November 1, 19__.
2. Accommodations/prices: See enclosed brochure.
3. Deposit: See enclosed brochure.
4. Transportation to The Hideaway: Airplane to Denver; special bus to and from the airport to The Hideaway.
5. Minimum Length of Stay: One week.
6. Ski Passes: See enclosed brochure.

If, after looking through the brochures, you have further questions about The Hideaway, please contact us.

Sincerely,

READER/AUDIENCE

No changes.

REVISED ORDER

Martin's first draft is direct. If he doesn't switch to the indirect approach, the reader may disregard the message once she/he reads the answers to the questions. If this happens, a prospective customer may be lost. By using the *indirect approach,* Martin can create an image of The Hideaway that will motivate the reader to call for a reservation without delay.

He then decides on the sequence of his specific objectives:

1. To create image of reader at Hideaway plus appreciation for inquiry (goodwill).
2. To refer to inquiry letter.
3. To provide facts about:
   a. Types of accommodations available/prices.
   b. Opening date.
   c. Recommended types of transportation to resort.
   d. Minimum length of stay.
   e. Cost of ski pass.
   f. Amount of deposit (deemphasized).
4. To provide information about other enticing features of the resort (fireplaces, nearby 1800s mining town, sidewalk cafes, sauna, exercise room, indoor and outdoor pool, hot tubs, cable TV; in summer—hiking, rafting, tennis, swimming, exploring mining ruins, golf.
5. To include brochures.
6. To include toll-free number for making reservations.

FORMAT

LETTER

After completing the planning and collecting all the specific information needed, Martin drafts the response letter shown in Figure 8.7.

Martin rechecks the order to make sure he is accomplishing his objectives. His first impression is that the letter is much too long. He needs to select a few major sales points and concentrate on those rather than try to include everything; after all, the letter is a response to a person who has already expressed interest in the resort.

Martin reads the draft and makes the marginal notes shown in Figure 8.8 for improving the message. The numbers on the letter correspond to Martin's thoughts:

1. The information about the townhomes and tower is important, but not important enough to occupy the opening part of the letter; perhaps it would be better just to leave these to the brochure and not include them in the letter, but just refer to the brochure.
2. This idea could present an effective opening to the letter; include some sales writing.
3. Numbering answers is OK; however, in this case, the content is rather flat. These answers don't stimulate the reader to want to book The Hideaway. Eliminate the numbering and use paragraph form—better for sales writing.

Figure 8.7 Martin's second draft

Dear ____________

Welcome to The Hideaway! The all-new, comfortable accommodations make The Hideaway an excellent choice for the value-conscious vacationer. You may choose accommodations that suit your family or business needs in the townhomes or tower units. Townhomes offer two and three bedrooms, up to three baths, a fireplace, and the privacy of an individual townhome. In the six-story Tower, you may choose from a studio and one- or two-bedroom units—some with fireplaces. You may select the accommodations and price range that fit your budget (see enclosed brochure).

Below are answers to the specific questions you asked in your letter of September 10, 19__:

1. Opening date for The Hideaway: November 1, 19--.
2. Transportation to The Hideaway: Airplane to Denver; special bus to and from the airport to The Hideaway.
3. Minimum length of stay: One week.
4. Ski passes: See enclosed brochure.

To hold space, a $100 a-person deposit is required within 30 days of verbal confirmation. Final payment is due when checking out.

Once you are here, you can enjoy the comfort of the luxurious sauna, exercise room, indoor or outdoor pool, cable TV, as well as the many other facilities at The Hideaway. You'll also be able to ramble through the nearby restored 1800s mining town with its narrow streets lined with soft gas lamps. You can browse through the quaint boutiques and century-old stores filled with antiques. If you become tired, you can rest at one of the many sidewalk cafes or restaurants and enjoy a festival of foods that will suit the most delicate palate.

Enjoy the miles of maintained ski trails that will challenge your ski techniques. And, if you desire, you may also engage in ice skating, snowmobiling, sleigh rides, and sledding. The Hideaway is a special place for that special Winter Vacation. (And in the summer, you can enjoy hiking, rafting, tennis, swimming, exploring mining ruins, as well as golf.) Tell your friends.

4. OK to express deposit and payment information in third person—this deemphasizes the money aspects.
5. Great sales writing; uses *you* effectively; use this paragraph in the letter.
6. Use ski action in the beginning of the letter; use the other snow action later in the letter. Omit the summer information since this model letter will be for winter.
7. Good close; use as is.

Figure 8.7 (*concluded*)

Look through the attached brochure to see some of the pictures of The Hideaway's facilities and highlights of its major attractions; then call our toll-free number (800/532-2346) and make your reservation today. Whatever your pleasure, you'll find the excitement and the relaxation you've been looking for at The Hideaway. Call today.

Sincerely

With these comments, Martin adds three specific objectives (nos. 1, 2, and 3 below) and revises the sequencing of the specific objectives for the model letter:

1. To create sales—Welcome.

Figure 8.8 Martin's second draft with comments

Dear ____________

Welcome to The Hideaway! The all new, comfortable accommodations make The Hideaway an excellent choice for the value-conscious vacationer. You may choose accommodations that suit your family or business needs in the townhomes or tower units. Townhomes offer two and three bedrooms, up to three baths, a fireplace, and the privacy of an individual townhome. In the six-story Tower, you may choose from a studio, one- or two-bedroom units; some with fireplaces. You may select the accommodations and price range that fit your situation (see enclosed brochure). (1)

Below are answers to the specific questions you asked in your letter of September 10, 19__: (2)

1. Opening Date for The Hideaway: November 1, 19__
2. Transportation to The Hideaway: Airplane to Denver; Special Bus to and from the Airport to The Hideaway (3)
3. Minimum Length of Stay: One week (4) NO "YOU"
4. Ski passes: See enclosed brochure

DEPOSIT; FINAL PAYMENT

To hold space, a $100 a-person deposit is required within 30 days of verbal confirmation. Final payment is due when checking out.

(5) "YOU" EXTRAS—IN AND AROUND AREA

Once you are here, you can enjoy the comfort of the luxurious sauna, exercise room, indoor or outdoor pool, cable TV, as well as the many other facilities at The Hideaway. You'll also be able to ramble through the nearby restored 1800s mining town with its narrow streets lined with soft gas

2. To answer questions about skiing at The Hideaway.
3. To refer to September 10, 19--, letter.
4. To create an image of the reader at The Hideaway.
5. To answer questions in paragraph form (accommodations, opening date, transportation to resort, minimum length of stay, amount of deposit, prices for accommodations, prices for ski

Figure 8.8 (*concluded*)

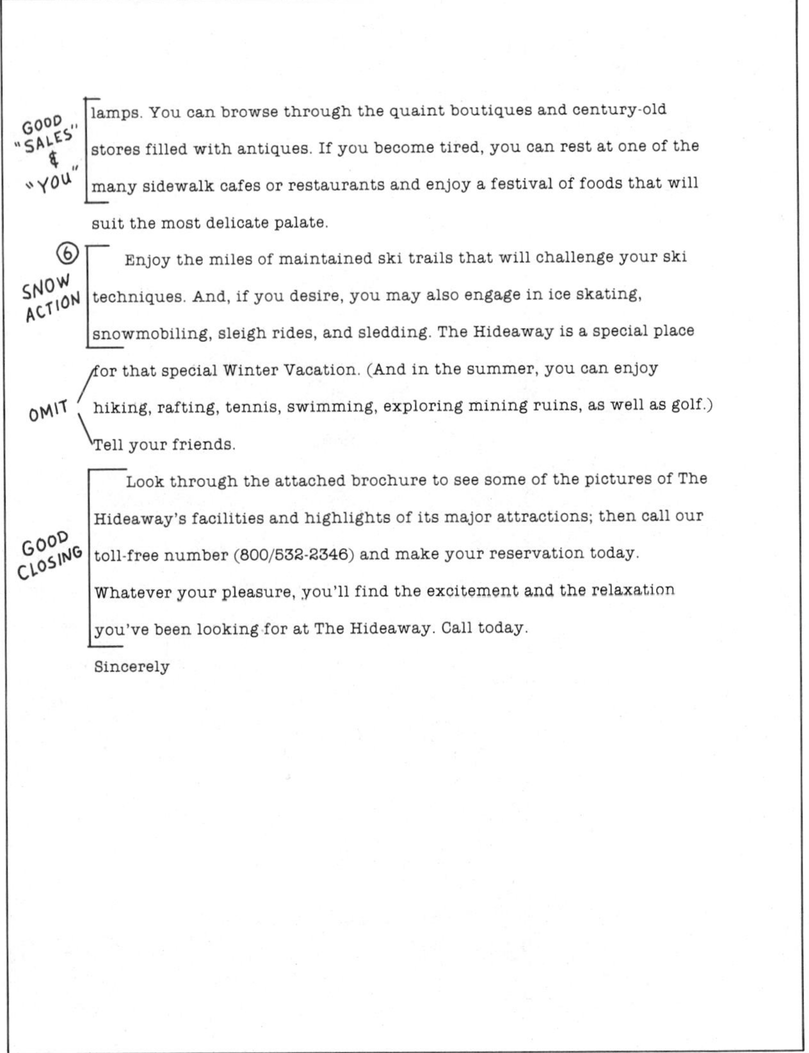
GOOD "SALES" & "YOU"
lamps. You can browse through the quaint boutiques and century-old stores filled with antiques. If you become tired, you can rest at one of the many sidewalk cafes or restaurants and enjoy a festival of foods that will suit the most delicate palate.
6 SNOW ACTION
Enjoy the miles of maintained ski trails that will challenge your ski techniques. And, if you desire, you may also engage in ice skating, snowmobiling, sleigh rides, and sledding. The Hideaway is a special place for that special Winter Vacation. (And in the summer, you can enjoy hiking, rafting, tennis, swimming, exploring mining ruins, as well as golf.) Tell your friends.
OMIT
GOOD CLOSING
Look through the attached brochure to see some of the pictures of The Hideaway's facilities and highlights of its major attractions; then call our toll-free number (800/532-2346) and make your reservation today. Whatever your pleasure, you'll find the excitement and the relaxation you've been looking for at The Hideaway. Call today.
Sincerely

passes, other enticing features—mining town, sidewalk cafes, indoor and outdoor pool).

6. To include enclosures: brochures with prices for ski passes and other accommodations.
7. To include toll-free number for making reservation.
8. To add action-oriented final request to call for booking.

With the additions and the new sequence for the major ideas, Martin then drafts the shorter but more effective letter shown in Figure 8.9.

Figure 8.9 Martin's final draft to inquiry letter

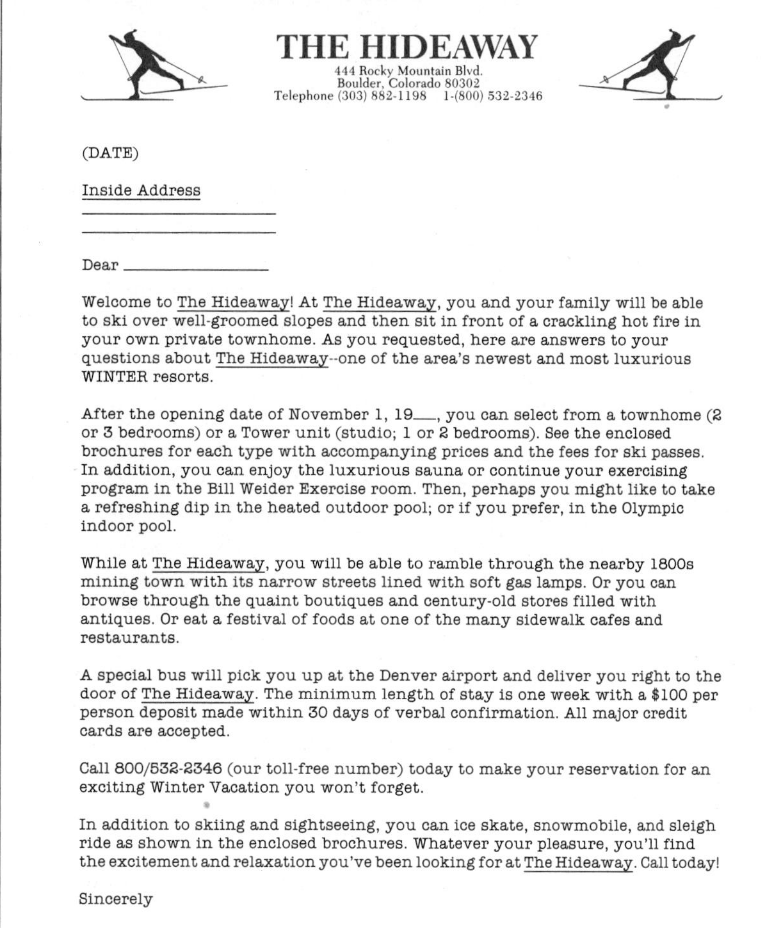
THE HIDEAWAY
444 Rocky Mountain Blvd.
Boulder, Colorado 80302
Telephone (303) 882-1198 1-(800) 532-2346

(DATE)

Inside Address
____
____

Dear ________________

Welcome to The Hideaway! At The Hideaway, you and your family will be able to ski over well-groomed slopes and then sit in front of a crackling hot fire in your own private townhome. As you requested, here are answers to your questions about The Hideaway--one of the area's newest and most luxurious WINTER resorts.

After the opening date of November 1, 19___, you can select from a townhome (2 or 3 bedrooms) or a Tower unit (studio; 1 or 2 bedrooms). See the enclosed brochures for each type with accompanying prices and the fees for ski passes. In addition, you can enjoy the luxurious sauna or continue your exercising program in the Bill Weider Exercise room. Then, perhaps you might like to take a refreshing dip in the heated outdoor pool; or if you prefer, in the Olympic indoor pool.

While at The Hideaway, you will be able to ramble through the nearby 1800s mining town with its narrow streets lined with soft gas lamps. Or you can browse through the quaint boutiques and century-old stores filled with antiques. Or eat a festival of foods at one of the many sidewalk cafes and restaurants.

A special bus will pick you up at the Denver airport and deliver you right to the door of The Hideaway. The minimum length of stay is one week with a $100 per person deposit made within 30 days of verbal confirmation. All major credit cards are accepted.

Call 800/532-2346 (our toll-free number) today to make your reservation for an exciting Winter Vacation you won't forget.

In addition to skiing and sightseeing, you can ice skate, snowmobile, and sleigh ride as shown in the enclosed brochures. Whatever your pleasure, you'll find the excitement and relaxation you've been looking for at The Hideaway. Call today!

Sincerely

Martin Fellow
Managing Director

rh

Enclosures

LETTERS GRANTING ADJUSTMENTS

When a product or service has been unsatisfactory or defective, it may be necessary to write an adjustment letter. Below is an example of a positive response to an adjustment. Even in this situation, it is necessary to rebuild confidence in the company and products. Emphasis should be placed on *what* is being done (sending a replacement or refund) and statements about the quality, demand, or some other appropriate feature of the company's products (sometimes called *resale*). Sometimes, you may want to provide the reason for making the adjustment. Tone, promptness, and fair treatment are important considerations for this type of letter. Follow Conrad Rhodes as he plans his strategy and drafts a message to grant an adjustment.

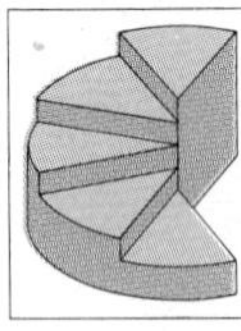

STRATEGY: POSITIVE RESPONSE TO AN ADJUSTMENT

Conrad Rhodes, manager of Video Wholesalers (212 Martin Pike Boulevard, Saint Paul, Minnesota 55100), has just received a package from Alexander Roman, owner and manager of The Best Video Shop (4321 Oak Ridge Drive, Los Alamos, California 93440), returning 10 video disks. Earlier, on March 6, Roman phoned Conrad and indicated that something was clearly wrong with the last shipment of video disks. Conrad requested that Roman ship them back (at Video's expense) for checking.

As soon as Conrad received the 10 video disks, he had his technician, Ted Knight, examine them. Ted confirms that the disks are in fact defective as indicated by Roman. (Ted speculated that the disks had been subjected to extreme heat.) Conrad, therefore, decides to rush another shipment of video disks to Roman by Overnight Express (but not before Ted has checked each one to make sure they are alright). Of course, Conrad will not bill for the shipping charges in this instance since he wants to retain Roman as a customer. (He has been a very good customer for the past three years.) He plans to keep the tone of the message positive to rebuild Roman's confidence in Video Wholesalers.

PROBLEM

Retain Roman (The Best Video Shop) as a customer.

OBJECTIVES

General: To inform Roman about the replacement.
To regain the goodwill of the customer.

Note that there are two general objectives. For Roman, the important news is the information about the replacement; however, from Conrad's perspective, the emphasis will be on convincing Roman that he can continue to depend on Video Wholesalers for quality goods and prompt services.

Specific: To grant request for replacement of video disks.
To acknowledge receipt of defective disks.
To refer to March 6 phone call (plus sales content).
To provide facts about what went wrong (plus resale content).
To rebuild confidence.

READER/AUDIENCE

Characteristics: Owner/manager of a retail store.

	Business-oriented.
	Very good customer for three years.
Reactions:	Positive—glad to get news of replacement.
	Will continue purchasing.
	Will consider defects as normal.

ORDER

OVERALL MESSAGE: INDIRECT

Conrad thinks that it would be a good idea to start first with a topic other than the replacement since this is a negative aspect—the *indirect approach.* So he decides to start with the idea of receiving the disks.

SPECIFIC OBJECTIVES

1. To acknowledge receipt of defective disks.
2. To provide facts about what went wrong.
3. To refer to March 6 phone call (plus sales content).
4. To grant request for replacement of video disks (plus resale content).
5. To rebuild confidence.

FORMAT

LETTER

With the strategy components complete, Conrad drafts the letter shown in Figure 8.10. After reading the letter, answer these questions:

- ☐ Does Conrad's letter meet his objectives?
- ☐ Put yourself in the reader's place. How will Alexander react to this letter?
- ☐ Do you think Alexander will buy from Video Wholesalers again? Why? Why not?
- ☐ What principles do you think Conrad applied best? What are its worst features?
- ☐ How would you improve this message?

After reviewing his draft (Figure 8.10), Conrad evaluated his message to see if he achieved his stated objectives. He concluded that opening the message with a discussion of the defective part emphasizes negative feelings. By switching to the direct approach, Conrad can tell the reader immediately the good news of the message. And this sets the stage for reselling the customer on Video Wholesaler's credibility as a supplier. Having had several conversations and exchanged letters with Alexander Roman over the past three years, Conrad feels at ease addressing him as Alexander. Based on this analysis, Conrad reorders the specific objectives as follows:

Figure 8.10 Conrad's initial draft

Dear Alexander:

As soon as your 10 video disks were received, our technician, Ted Knight, examined each disk. He confirmed the statements you made during our March 6 phone conversation about the 10 video disks being defective. Evidently, these video disks were subjected to extreme heat. Ten new video disks have been shipped to you today, March 10. Ted Knight has carefully checked each of these so that you can once again enjoy offering the best quality video disks available.

Over the past three years you have been one of our best customers. As you have learned, you are assured of buying only top quality products from Video Wholesalers. Our motto is prompt service with top-quality items.

Sincerely yours,

1. To grant request for replacement of video disks (plus resale content).
2. To refer to March 6 phone call (plus resale content).
3. To acknowledge receipt of defective disks.
4. To provide facts of what went wrong.
5. To rebuild confidence (resale).

Figure 8.11 Conrad's final version of adjustment letter

Video Wholesalers, Inc.

212 martin pike expressway
st. paul, mn 55100
phone (612) 387-4121

March 10, 19__

Mr. Alexander Roman
The Best Video Shop
4321 Oak Ridge Drive
Los Alamos, CA 93440

Dear Alexander

Ten new video disks were shipped to you today (March 10) by Overnight Express--shipping charges prepaid by Video. As you indicated in your March 6 phone call, these are among the best video disks on the market.

As soon as your 10 video disks were received, our technician Ted Knight found that the disks had been subjected to extreme heat. To assure you of the guaranteed quality you expect from Video, Ted checked to make sure the new ones are ready for use.

In two weeks, you will receive information about a special sales promotion of video equipment. The price plus high quality will make these items fast sellers at The Best Video Shop. Providing you with prompt and personal service over the past three years has been a pleasure. We value you as a customer.

Sincerely yours

Conrad Rhodes, Manager

om

Conrad uses this new approach and sequence to produce the letter shown in Figure 8.11. How would you evaluate the revision?

SUMMARY

When you write positive messages, keep these basic concepts in mind: reply promptly; use "you" viewpoint; emphasize the good news; provide all the information requested or a reason for not including; use reader benefit; make it easy for the recipient to respond if appropriate; and keep the tone positive. Use techniques to achieve unity, clarity, conciseness, and proper tone. The arrangement of the content depends on the type of message, objective, and previous relationship with the reader.

Each situation requiring a written response is unique. Five common types of positive messages are illustrated with the strategy for communicating. An acceptance-to-speak letter contains these ideas: acceptance; restatement of date, topic, place, and other specifics; questions that need answering; phone number for easy contact; courtesy.

Professionals routinely write recommendation letters. The letter presents information to help the reader assess the person's capabilities. Use these guidelines: topic statement; strengths and weaknesses of applicant; specific qualifications; sincerity; courtesy.

Letters of acknowledgment include a response to a first or an especially large order, an appreciation letter at a seasonal time, or some other non-routine event. In acknowledging a first order, show appreciation, state specifics, suggest credit plan, use persuasion and goodwill, encourage future ordering, enclose sales material, use positive tone.

When potential buyers request information about a product or service, your objectives are to provide the requested information and to encourage them to buy. Emphasize the "you" viewpoint, reader benefits, and action to obtain product or service.

In letters granting adjustment requests, rebuild customer confidence in the company and products through resale. Emphasize what is being done and major features of the product or service. Tone, promptness, and fair treatment are important considerations for this type of message. This letter has two general objectives—to provide the requested information and to regain goodwill. Use persuasive writing.

END-OF-CHAPTER ACTIVITIES

DISCUSSION

1. Define the term *goodwill* as it relates to positive response letters and memos.
2. What are the basic ideas to keep in mind when writing a positive response?
3. What is the "you viewpoint"? Discuss its importance in writing positive messages.
4. In what ways does the recommendation letter differ from the acknowledgment letter?
5. What three factors should the answer to an inquiry emphasize?
6. Discuss the importance of form letters and their usefulness in business writing.
7. "Granting-an-adjustment letter is a form of persuasive writing." Accept or refute this statement.

8. What are the three important characteristics to include in a letter granting an adjustment request?

ACTIVITIES

9. Using the strategy components, critique the following response letter to an inquiry about the price list for plumbing items. How well does this letter to Mr. Johnson achieve the objectives of a response letter? Offer suggestions to improve it.

Dear Mr. Johnson:

Per your request, please find enclosed our current price list regarding the Blandon line of plumbing hardware and supplies. This information has been distributed to the trade in general and is being passed on to you for your information.

Thank you for your cooperation in this matter.

Very truly yours,

10. Using the strategy components, critique the following message sent in response to an inquiry letter in which the writer asks for three copies of a magazine article. How well does the writer achieve the objective in this response letter?

Dear Ms. Jordan:

It is a pleasure to send you three copies of the article "The Impact of Technology on the Executive Suite" that appeared in the March 20, 19--, issue of The Executive. This article presents valuable information to the executive who is considering the addition of technology for better information management. You, like others, will benefit from the suggestions in the article.

Providing you with reprints is a pleasure.

Sincerely,

11. Using the strategy components, critique the following message that was sent in response to a letter asking about an error in a textbook. How well does the message achieve its objective? Is the tone appropriate? How would you revise the letter?

Dear Sir:

Your letter to the Bond & Ellis Business College in reference to an error in the text Everyday Accounting has been referred to me.

In reply, I would state that the cash footing on page 250, for the month of May, is an error. The correct total should be $153,244.38, as stated in your letter. There is also an error in the same edition on page 242. The amount set aside to the surplus account should be $1,001.11, and not $9,001.11, as given in the fifth line from the bottom.

Trusting the delay in answering this has not caused you any inconvenience, I remain,

Respectfully yours,

For each of the following case settings, plan your strategy; then write an appropriate message.

12. Assume the role of Lloyd Spain, an analyst with the Elliot Consulting Group, one of the largest consulting firms in the country (branches in most of the major cities in the United States). You have just received a letter from your alma mater inviting you to speak to a group of students majoring in economics. Of course, you are flattered by the invitation. After obtaining approval from your superiors, you are faced with the task of responding.

    You checked the invitation letter for the specifics and made a listing as follows: Time—7 P.M.; date—October 15, 19--; place—Hyatt Regency, Atlanta, Georgia 30303; dinner meeting; 30-40 minute speech, including question-and-answer session; about 40 people expected; topic—"Contemporary Issues in Economics." The writer of the invitation letter also asked if the Elliot Consulting Group would pay your expenses for your trip to Atlanta. Your supervisor approved this request. You do need a reservation for October 15 at the Hyatt—so this is a request that needs to be included. Also, you need an overhead projector for the presentation. You plan to drive your car and will arrive about 3 P.M.

    Write the letter for Lloyd, accepting the invitation to speak to the campus group of future economists.

13. For this case, assume the role of Eleanor Rose, who has just received an invitation to speak at the April 20, 19--, meeting of the Salt Lake City Chapter of the Management Society. Since it is now September 10, you decide to accept the invitation. During the past two years, you have spoken to several civic groups in the Southeast on "Stress Management"—your area of expertise. In the invitation letter you received, Joe Marable indicated that several people had heard you and had recommended you as an excellent speaker. This compliment partially persuaded you to accept the invitation. Other facts contained in the invitation letter included: meeting place—Holiday Inn, Central Avenue, Salt Lake City, Utah (look up the ZIP); meeting time—5:30 P.M.; social hour, 6:30 P.M.; dinner, 7:30 P.M.; program (about 30-40 minutes for speech).

    Of course, the invitation indicated that all expenses (travel, meals, and hotel) would be paid by the society plus an honorarium of $500. Marable stated that he would make hotel arrangements. And you'll have to let him know later about arrival plans (mode of transportation, date, and time). You will need a slide projector for your presentation.

    As Eleanor Rose, write the acceptance to speak at the April 20 meeting of the Salt Lake City Management Society.

14. As Robert James, customer relations director for TRAVEL ETC. (a wholesale company located at 2143 Farragut Street, Denver, Colorado

80200), you have just received a first order from Bryant Fowler, owner of The Leather Shoppe at 204 State Boulevard, Twin Falls, Idaho 83301, for the following:

4 American Tourister Series 6500 "Escort" garment bags (1 burgundy, 1 blue, 1 black, 1 gray), ea. $64.97.

4 30" Pullman with wheels (1 blue, 1 burgundy, 1 black, 1 gray), ea. $109.97.

2 24" Pullman (1 blue, 1 burgundy), ea. $74.80.

2 Cosmetic cases (1 blue, 1 burgundy), ea. $54.90.

5 Heritage leather attaché cases, ea. $84.25.

Prior to this order, your sales representative called on Fowler to present the items available from TRAVEL. Fowler was so impressed that he opened an account with TRAVEL and now is placing his first order. You are glad that he is ordering and want to welcome him as a new customer, confirming that the order will be shipped by State Express on September 15, 19--, shipping charges payable upon delivery. The total will be charged to his account. Since you want to stimulate future sales, you decide to mention the special upcoming sale on leather wallets and credit card organizers (include brochure with letter). For the wallets, include trifold model; woodgrain cowhide; oil-tanned; wholesale cost, $7.50; very popular sellers. For the credit card organizers, slim, ultrasoft glove leather in soft brown; wholesale cost, $14.35. Retail for wallets, $15.75; for Credit Card organizers, $29.95.

As Robert James, write an appropriate message.

15. As Professor Melanie Forbes (University of Kansas, Department of Information Systems), you have been asked to write a letter of recommendation for Marie Collins for a special summer internship program in records management with the Clarion Corporation. Since Marie took two classes with you (Management Information Systems and Records Management) and did well, you are glad to write the letter of recommendation. You remember that she did excellent work, was punctual, had her assignments in on time, went beyond the regular assignments to learn as much as she could, and got along well with her fellow students. In fact, her project in the records management class was the best that you have seen in a long time.

You also know that she has worked part time during her college years in several companies, assisting them with various information-related projects. She had approached each of these projects with enthusiasm and provided the appropriate insights to design each project that was needed to solve the problem. You, personally, have seen some of her work since she came to you to check out her recommended solution or to make sure that the proper procedure was followed. The letter of recommendation should go to Clark Higgins,

The Clarion Corporation, 741 Tazewell Pike, Richmond, Virginia 23234. Assuming the role of Melanie Forbes, plan your strategy for the situation; then write an effective recommendation letter.

16. Ann Green, a graduate student at the Medical College of Missouri, St. Joseph, Missouri, has requested that you (Thomas Lawrence, a professor at the Medical College) write a letter of recommendation for her to David Holder, director of City Hospital (904 Clinch Street, Sioux Falls, South Dakota 57100). Ann is applying for a position as assistant hospital administrator at City Hospital. You have worked with Ann for several years and have been impressed with her work both inside and outside class. You gather the following facts about Ann before attempting to write the letter of recommendation:
    a. Work experience. During the summers, she worked part time in offices; gained insights into business practices plus ability to work with people; experiences made Ann more mature in attitude toward studying.
    b. College experience. B.S. in Business Administration, June 1980, University of New Mexico; received master's degree in hospital administration, December 1986, from the Medical College—both degrees with honors.
    c. Residency. Completed residency at Petersville General Hospital, Petersville, Missouri—excellent report from hospital personnel and supervisor. Rotated among all departments within the hospital. Participated in a restructuring of the administrative offices and implementation of automated technology project. Very valuable experiences.

    You are very pleased that you can write this letter of recommendation for Ann. You are looking forward to hearing good things in a few years as she moves from the assistant level to that of the director of a hospital. As Thomas Lawrence, write an appropriate letter of recommendation.

17. Stephen Tipps (223 Ruby Lane, Pontiac, Michigan 48053), purchased a Redman Ice Chest to take on his special camping vacation. During the vacation, he noticed that the ice melted faster than he thought it should; near the end of the vacation he examined the chest more carefully and discovered that there was a slight warp in the lid; the space allowed warm air to come into the chest. He was surprised since the Redman name has meant quality for many years. So he felt the Redman Company should stand behind its product. He immediately wrote a letter to the home office requesting a replacement and giving all the details of his dissatisfaction with the warp and melting ice.

    Assume the role of Randall Grizzle, customer relations director for the Redman Company. You have just received the letter from Tipps about his disappointing experience with the Redman Ice Chest (the

45-quart model). Because Redman is the top-quality maker of ice chests and other vacation supplies, you want to write a letter to Tipps granting his request; you also want to restore the confidence he had in Redman.

To help ease the situation, you decide to replace the 45-quart model with a 54-quart model (you are providing him with additional storage space if he desires). Some of the features your advertisement lists for the Steel Belted 54 Model are steel-belted case—zinc coated for rust protection; durable backed enamel finish; big 54-quart size—room for everything; two-way handles—swing out or lift straight up for tight places; scuff-resistant base—steel reinforced for extra strength; hinged lid—built tough enough to sit on; polyurethane insulation—provides maximum cold-holding power; fast-flow drain—leakproof, can't rust or corrode.

You decide to write a message granting the request for replacement of the Redman Ice Chest with the Steel Belted 54 Model. All Tipps has to do is take the authorization form you are including with the letter along with the defective cooler to his local dealer. The dealer will replace the cooler. Write the appropriate message.

18. Robert and Mary Hatmaker, owners of the Sport Fitness Center, 2345 Lemay Boulevard, Colorado Springs, Colorado 80910, are interested in expanding their line of fitness equipment. They saw an advertisement in the *Home Gym & Fitness* magazine for the Cobble Home Fitness System. The unit consists of a padded bench, leg lift unit, and weight rack. They have written to you for the following information: makeup of the system; availability; cost; markup; future advertisements; process of becoming a dealer.

As Margaret Fifield, sales representative for the Cobble Sport Fitness Industries, 2324 Belview Avenue, Detroit, Michigan 48224, you need to answer this request letter and provide the necessary information to gain this new customer. You have brochures that you will include about the deluxe Cobble Home Fitness System. The advertisement for the system describes it as follows: it features a multipurpose unit that will readily meet the individual exercise requirements of all family members; quality-built for a lifetime of family fitness; easy weight selection from 22 lbs. to 198 lbs.; bench constructed of sturdy 1¼″ tubular steel; stack frame (2″ × 2″ × ⅛″) steel tubing; deluxe leg lift, leg curl with three cushions; ankle strap; can be set up in a minimum of time and space; exercises every major muscle group through progressive weight resistance. The unit mounts to the wall, requiring only 84″ of vertical space, folds for easy storage, and can also be used with the optional free-standing unit (sold separately).

Using the appropriate information, write a letter to the Hatmakers, stimulating them to become a dealer for the Cobble Home Fitness System, one of the most compact training systems available. Here are some of the facts you will need to answer the letter: the system is readily available for immediate shipment; its cost, $120; shipping charges extra; suggested retail price, $275; optional wall mount, $15 wholesale—$25 retail; the Cobble System will be featured in *Home Gym & Fitness* each month during the remainder of this year plus other nationally distributed magazines; TV spots are also planned for later this year.

You want to encourage the Hatmakers to become dealers for your gym systems—one of the most popular home gyms in the country; therefore, you want to include an application to establish an account with you. Write the appropriate letter that will answer the initial inquiry and convince them to place an order with you and complete the application for an account. Use your creativity to add other sales material that will convince them to handle your system. After all, they have probably written to your competitors. Your response needs to be better than the others they will receive.

19. Six months ago, Frederick Woods (223 Fourth Street, Newport News, Virginia 23608), bought an electric Weed Eater while visiting relatives in Missouri. The one-year guarantee covered defective parts. The unit has worked fine until now. Frederick is frustrated since he needs to trim the grass around his house and cannot. The Weed Eater just won't run. So he packaged the unit and shipped it to the address given on the guarantee label: Kilroy Industries, 223 South Street, Wichita, Kansas 67214.

Assume that you, Scott Davis, have just received the Weed Eater from Frederick Woods; you have had your service specialist examine the unit to see what the problem is. He found that the string had become wound around the top of the unit, and that the motor had burned out as a result. You feel that Woods should have stopped the unit, and then the motor would not have burned out. The guarantee voids the replacement in cases of carelessness. However, in this case, you decide to replace the unit to build goodwill.

Write an appropriate letter to Woods in which you include tactful advice on the use of the machine, particularly care of the cutting string. Don't forget to take this opportunity to try to resell Woods on the qualities of the Weed Eater. Remember, he's rather dissatisfied with his.

CHAPTER 9

WRITING NEGATIVE LETTERS

Learning Objectives

After studying this chapter, you will be able to:

- □ Identify situations that require negative messages.
- □ Determine the appropriate mix of persuasiveness and reader benefit in writing negative messages.
- □ Evaluate the situation and plan an appropriate strategy for negative communication.
- □ Determine when to state or imply the negative information.
- □ Understand the importance of keeping a positive tone when writing negative messages.
- □ Select the appropriate approach for the situation.
- □ Create effective negative messages.

Types of disappointing news

No one likes to receive disappointing news. Whether the news is in the form of a refusal, put-down, claim, delay in action, or some other unfavorable message, a negative impact is bound to result, even though it may be minimal. Readers of these messages probably won't feel good under any circumstances. But the blow will be lessened and goodwill maintained if readers are made to feel that:

Maintaining goodwill in negative messages

- □ They were dealt with fairly.
- □ They were treated in a professional manner.
- □ The writer was concerned about their feelings.
- □ They would probably have acted similarly under the same circumstances.

If you as a writer can achieve these results, you are on the right track and will probably accomplish your desired objectives and goals. But a lot will depend on how you go about this task and your:

Things to consider when writing negative messages

- □ Understanding of your reader/audience.
- □ Complete grasp of the situation.
- □ Understanding of human relations.
- □ Ability to use a positive tone under negative circumstances.
- □ Ability to choose words and sequence ideas to deemphasize the negative.
- □ Ability to empathize with the reader.
- □ Ability to determine when to use a strong, direct approach or a mellow, indirect one.
- □ Ability to buffer the bad news when appropriate.
- □ Ability to imply the negative.
- □ Understanding of resale techniques.

You have learned many of these techniques already as you developed your style of writing. But it is now time to pull out all stops and use all the principles of writing you've studied in earlier chapters to deal with some very difficult communication problems.

In this chapter you will apply the strategy for communicating to develop messages for six different situations, some of which are more difficult than others:

Types of negative messages

Incomplete order.
Order substitute.
Request refusal.
Adjustment.
Credit refusal.

For each of these types of situations, you will develop a strategy and draft a communication until you meet your objectives for each strategy component.

LETTERS ABOUT THE INCOMPLETE ORDER

People quite often leave out needed information when ordering—size, color, etc. As the recipient, you need to obtain the information before sending the product. The message is negative since the reader gets the message rather than the expected product.

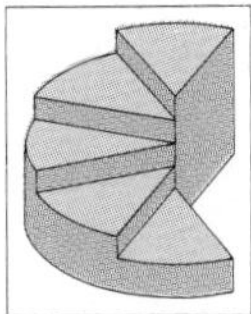

STRATEGY: REPORTING MISSING INFORMATION

Mark Allen, customer service representative, F. P. Dean Company (a mail-order house at 1123 Kingsley Road, Minneapolis, Minnesota 55400), has just been handed an incomplete order form mailed by Jonathan Willard, 203 Stockton Drive, Pueblo, Colorado 81001. The F. P. Dean Company specializes in quality products for camping, backpacking, and outdoor living in general.

For the two pairs of Khaki Hiking Trousers he ordered (stock no. 1848P), Willard forgot to indicate the desired inseam size and whether he prefers cuffs. He did mark a 32-inch waist size on the order form along with the correct price ($27 each). Page 11 of the catalog states:

Please specify inseam and whether cuffs are desired.

The catalog description of the Hiking Trousers is as follows:

Double stitched-down front pleats provide exceptional freedom of motion for hiking and climbing, yet are neat in appearance. Fabric is a sturdy twill weave of 100% cotton. Strong, abrasion-resistant, and comfortable against the skin. Straight legs with welted side seams. Two side pockets, watch pocket, and two flap-and-button rear pockets. Zipper fly front and 1¾″ belt loops. Washable.

In addition to the Hiking Trousers, Willard also ordered 1 navy, medium-sized lined parka (stock no. 1357P) at $80. The total amount charged to his American Express credit card was correct, $134.

Willard has been a customer for the past three years. Mark needs to get the missing information before sending his order by UPS.

Mark could send the order form back with a notation about the missing information; however, this might cause Willard to feel bad and even cancel the whole order. Therefore, Mark decides to send a letter.

To save time, Mark checks the files to see if there is a previous letter for a similar situation. He retrieves the following form letter:

You forgot to indicate the ____________________. If you will look at your order blank, there is a statement asking you to ____________________. We can't fill your order until you send us what you want. Send it at once.

Mark knows this will never do. There are too many obvious weaknesses:

The first sentence blames the writer; it makes reader seem like a dope!

The second sentence indicates information in the catalog, but it doesn't help get the right information; this sentence also blames the customer rather than focusing on a solution.

The last two sentences repeat the request for information.

The form doesn't provide space for the catalog stock number, which would give the information needed.

There is no effort to promote future sales.

Clearly the form letter doesn't help much. Mark must develop his own response; he plans his strategy.

PROBLEM
Lack of information to complete order for shipment.

OBJECTIVES

General: To get information for completing the mailing of the three items.

Specific: To obtain inseam size desired.
To know preference—cuff or no-cuff style.
To encourage further ordering.
To obtain information without belittling the customer.

READER/AUDIENCE

Characteristics: Mr. Jonathan Willard, customer for three years.

Reaction: Disappointed in not receiving the order but will understand and send back the desired information.

ORDER
Mark had no difficulty determining the problem, objectives, and reader/audience for this situation. They were pretty straightforward. He spent more time deciding how he would *order* the communication. By empathizing with the reader, Mark realizes that Willard expects to receive the merchandise any day now. To delay the objective of the message will only increase Willard's anxiety. The *direct* order will get right to the point.

OVERALL MESSAGE: DIRECT

SPECIFIC OBJECTIVES

1. Appreciation for ordering again (goodwill).
2. Information needed: inseam size; cuff/no-cuff.

Figure 9.1 Incomplete order letter, direct approach

February 27, 19__

Mr. Jonathan Willard
203 Stockton Drive
Pueblo, CO 81001

Dear Mr. Willard

Thank you for your January 10 order. Just as soon as we receive your inseam size and cuff/no-cuff preference for the two pairs of 100% cotton hiking trousers, your order will be sent immediately by UPS. Merely indicate at the bottom of this letter the inseam size and cuff/no-cuff preference and mail in the enclosed envelope.

The freedom of the double-stitched front pleats will give you many comfortable miles of hiking pleasure; and the sturdy twill weave with its abrasion-resistant feature will be comfortable against your skin no matter how long you hike. You have certainly made a wise choice in selecting one of the most popular hiking trousers offered by F. P. Dean.

The hiking trousers will be shipped along with the navy, medium-sized lined parka the day we receive your response. The total $134 will be charged to your American Express credit card as you requested.

Thank you for letting F. P. Dean Company supply your outdoor sporting needs over the past three years. Be sure to take advantage of the specials in the Spring catalog that you will receive shortly. Remember, you are guaranteed 100 percent satisfaction. Quality counts at Dean's!

Sincerely

Mark Allen
Customer Service Representative

MA:ct

Inseam Size Preferred: __ inches
Style Preferred: __ cuff __ no cuff

1123 Kingsley Road • Minneapolis, MN 55400 • Phone (612) 703-9470

3. To encourage further ordering.
4. Sales: 100 percent guarantee on all products.
   a. Convenience of ordering from Dean Company.
   b. Convenience of payment: check, money order, or credit card.
   c. Double-stitch front pleats—comfort.
   d. Sturdy twill weave/abrasion resistant.
5. Personalize: Mention past three years' experience.

LEGAL / ETHICAL ISSUE

Business people depend on others to provide job performance references. Because of law suits that other companies have experienced, some people now limit their letters of recommendation to basic facts such as dates of employment, job title, and similar objective facts.

Assume you have just read a letter from a business associate asking about a former employee. You remember quite vividly the trouble you had with that individual. In your thoughts, you consider the person incompetent, dishonest, and a hypocrite. In the past, you have always written these letters in good faith without fear of lawsuits. You are beginning to be concerned about making judgmental statements about employees or former employees since you have read several incidents of law suits recently in business magazines.

Should you use the descriptive words (*incompetent, dishonest, hypocrite*) in your reply? What could be the consequences? What should you say in the reply communication?

FORMAT

LETTER

To maintain goodwill and encourage future purchases, Mark begins his letter with a courteous acknowledgment of the order. Because he chose the direct approach, Mark must then ask Willard to supply the needed information—the main ingredient for this communication. The rest of the message emphasizes the strengths and reliability of F. P. Dean Company and mentions their past business relationship.

Mark then drafts the letter shown in Figure 9.1.

LETTERS ABOUT THE ORDER SUBSTITUTE

Sometimes a company receives an order for an item that is no longer available. In this situation, the person placing the order must be notified of the bad news. The general practice is to suggest another item similar to the one ordered.

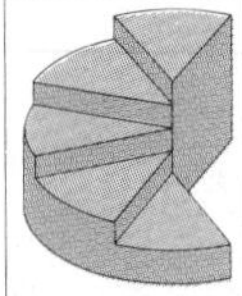

STRATEGY: SUGGESTING AN ORDER SUBSTITUTE

Mark Allen, the F. P. Dean Customer service representative, receives an order for one Lightweight Parka (women's size M: green color; catalog no. 123-09) along with a check for $125 from Sandra Johnson, 221 East End Boulevard, Youngstown, Pennsylvania 15696. This particular Lightweight Parka has been replaced with the much better Ultralight Gore-Tex Parka, but at a slightly higher price—$138. The catalog description for the new Ultralight reads as follows:

Ultralight Gore-Tex Parka: functional wilderness garment with easy on-and-off zippered feature; four generous outside pockets—all with stormflaps—two pockets with zipper, two cargo-hand-warmer pockets. Two inside zipped pockets. Waterproof, breathable Gore-Tex material; protects against rain, wind, snow, and moisture from body. Hood has contour fit with inner and outer drawstrings to allow full head movement and vision along with snug weather protection. Underarms have zippered vents for letting out excess heat. Waist drawcord. Catalog no. 124–10, color: Royal Tan, Stewart Mahogany, Forest Green with tan linings. Women's sizes: XS (6–8); S (10–12): M (14–16); L (18–20).

Mark recognizes the importance of handling this type of message with care since Johnson could refuse the substitute—especially since there is an additional charge. Clearly, he must also use effective sales strategies to convince Johnson that the Ultralight Parka is a better buy.

Mark plans his strategy.

PROBLEM

Unavailability of Parka ordered.

OBJECTIVES

General: To persuade Johnson to accept a substitute Parka.

Specific: To inform Johnson that the Parka ordered is no longer available.

To sell Johnson on the qualities of the Ultralight Parka.

To express appreciation for the order.

To present strengths/features of the Ultralight Parka.

To make it easy for Johnson to reply.

To retain the goodwill of Johnson.

To request an additional $13 for the substitute.

READER/AUDIENCE

Characteristics: Customer—outside company person interested in lightweight Parka probably for summer hiking or outdoor wear.

Person was willing to pay $125 for original order: probably will recognize the advantages of the Gore-Tex even though slightly higher in price.

Primary person to read letter for decision; secondary could be someone she asks for advice.

Reactions: Initial disappointment—receives a message instead of the Parka.

Probably can be convinced of Ultralight benefits.

ORDER

OVERALL MESSAGE: INDIRECT

The *indirect order* was chosen since Johnson will receive a letter instead of the Lightweight Parka she's expecting. She'll be disappointed at first, so the letter needs to be persuasive.

SPECIFIC OBJECTIVES

1. To express appreciation for the order.
2. To inform Johnson that the Parka ordered is no longer available.
3. To present strengths/features of the Ultralight Parka.
4. To sell Johnson on the qualities of the Ultralight Parka.
5. To make it easy for Johnson to reply.
6. To request an additional $13 for the substitute.
7. To retain the goodwill of Johnson.

FORMAT

LETTER

To achieve the general and specific objectives contained in the strategy, Mark decides to create three main parts for his message:

To convey the information that the Ultralight Parka has replaced the Lightweight, adding elements to promote goodwill and sales.

To highlight three outstanding features of the Ultralight and include facts about available colors and the extra charge.

To give directions for sending in the authorization and check; this point is most critical.

Since Mark wants to convince Johnson to authorize the Ultralight Parka, he barely plans to mention the Lightweight (stress the positive; put less emphasis on the negative).

Mark selects the following features to highlight: Gore-Tex fabric; hood; storage pockets; colors. He knows that he has to tell her that the Ultralight costs $13 more but will subordinate this unpleasant fact. His intent is to present the highlights so that Johnson will want the Ultralight and will not find the $13 extra charge objectionable.

Giving Johnson specific directions will make it easy to reply. If Johnson had to complete another order form or write an order letter, she might decide that responding is just too much trouble. If a special form is provided along with a return envelope, she will probably respond favorably.

Mark's review of his first draft (paragraph by paragraph) reveals a number of deficiencies:

Thank you for ordering a Lightweight Parka; also for your $125 check. The Lightweight Parka has been replaced with the Ultralight Parka made of Gore-Tex.

You will be able to enjoy those mountain hikes with the waterproof yet breathable Gore-Tex material.

Deficiencies

- □ Doesn't flow; lacks continuity.
- □ Impersonal.
- □ Improper placement of key idea ($125 check).
- □ Needs more sales content.

This parka is the latest style. The Gore-Tex fabric allows moisture and heat to pass through to the outside but does not allow rain and wind to penetrate; the hood with inner and outer drawstrings provides a contour fit against the wind and rain and allows full head movement and vision. There are four generous outside pockets—each with a zipper and stormflaps. The Ultralight comes in the following colors: Forest Green, Royal Tan, and Stewart Mahogany. The cost of the Ultralight is $138—$13 more than the Lightweight you ordered. A full-color brochure illustrating Ultralight's additional features is attached.

Deficiencies

- □ Lacks sales appeal.
- □ Lacks "you" viewpoint.
- □ Heavy on facts.
- □ Lacks persuasion.
- □ Confusing placement of cost figures.

Just complete and mail the attached card in the enclosed envelope along with your check for $13.

Deficiencies

- □ Lacks sales.
- □ Abrupt ending.
- □ No assurance of immediate response.
- □ Ends with negative point: $13 extra charge.

The number of deficiencies is quite a surprise. In his second draft (Figure 9.2), Mark concentrates on the content.

After reading his edited copy, Mark feels confident that this meets his objectives. He has:

- □ De-emphasized the negative by placing the additional cost in a subordinated position.

Figure 9.2 Order substitute: Indirect approach

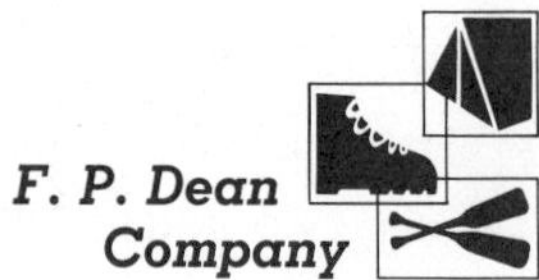

March 28, 19__

Ms. Sandra Johnson
221 East End Boulevard
Youngstown, PA 15696

SUBJECT: March 21 Order for Parka

Thank you for your March 21, 19__, order for one green, Lightweight Parka, Catalog No. 123-09, and your $125 check. Even though the Lightweight Parka has been very popular, we have had many requests for additional features. Therefore, the Lightweight has been replaced with the ULTRALIGHT--a far superior Parka made of Gore-Tex. You will be able to enjoy those mountain hikes with the waterproof, yet breathable, Gore-Tex material; the ULTRALIGHT is perfect for those summer outings.

You will like the latest style of this functional wilderness parka. The Gore-Tex fabric allows moisture and heat to pass through to the outside, but does not allow rain and wind to penetrate. The hood with inner and outer drawstrings will give you a contour fit to protect you against the wind and rain, yet allow full head movement and vision. Storage is easy with the four generous outside pockets--each has a zipper and stormflap for easy use and in addition to the Forest Green color, you may select the ULTRALIGHT in Royal Tan or Stewart Mahogany; and the price of the ULTRALIGHT is only $13 more than the Lightweight. A full-color brochure illustrating ULTRALIGHT's additional features is attached.

So we may ship your ULTRALIGHT Parka, just complete and mail the attached card in the enclosed envelope along with your check for $13. One medium-sized ULTRALIGHT will be shipped the same day we get your notification. The new Gore-Tex ULTRALIGHT will give you many hours of walking comfort on those wilderness outings.

Mark Allen
Customer Services Representative

kk

Enclosures: ULTRALIGHT Brochure
Return Card; Envelope

1123 Kingsley Road • Minneapolis, MN 55400 • Phone (612) 703-9470

- ☐ Emphasized the superior quality of the substitute product.
- ☐ Made it easy to respond.
- ☐ Used sales appeal to create awareness of and interest in the substitute product.
  - *a.* Action words suggest the pleasure that the reader can experience with the Ultralight.
  - *b.* Repetition of Ultralight.
  - *c.* Descriptive adjectives.

- □ Used a positive, forward-looking tone.
- □ Included specifics for reference: Johnson's order date, quantity, item, description, catalog number; $125 check.
- □ Identified enclosures
  a. Person who mails letter will know what to enclose.
  b. Reader can see what is enclosed.

LETTERS REFUSING A REQUEST

During the year, businesses receive requests from various organizations for contributions of gifts or money. Most companies maintain goodwill relations with the community through projects and specified contributions. At times, however, requests must receive a no response. When refusing the request, you need to give a legitimate reason and try to retain the goodwill of the reader/audience.

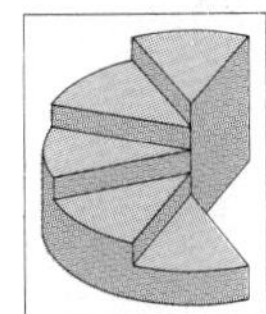

STRATEGY: REFUSING A CONTRIBUTION REQUEST

J. R. Roberts, director of customer services for Miller's Inc., a local department store in Charleston, West Virginia, has just received the following letter from the Northside Society:

Gentlemen:

The Northside Society, a local group of people interested in community improvement projects, is holding its annual bazaar as part of the RiverFest Festival. Would you donate a food processor to be auctioned off as a part of our annual fund-raising activities? All proceeds from the bazaar go toward improvement projects throughout our community. Your contribution will certainly aid in the further beautification of our area.

Sincerely,

Joella Sawyer

After getting the letter, J. R. checks with several people about the Northside Society. They do indeed fund many beneficial projects to beautify the community. But, in looking over the budget, J. R. finds that the funds allocated for community service ($2,500) have been disbursed for the current year. He must write Joella Sawyer and refuse the request. Since many of the members of the Northside Society are customers of Miller's, he wants to make a special effort to retain their goodwill.

J. R. checks and finds that he can add the name of the Northside Society to next year's list of donations to community groups. He now applies the components of the strategy to design his response to Joella Sawyer, keeping these thoughts in mind.

PROBLEM

Lack of funds to grant request.

OBJECTIVES

General: To refuse the request for a donation.

Specific: To imply or state the refusal for the request.
To present the reason for the refusal.
To retain the goodwill for the reader/audience.
To commend the society for its community projects.

READER/AUDIENCE

Characteristics: Primary—Joella Sawyer.
Secondary—Other community-minded members of the Northside Society.

Reactions: Displeasure at not getting the food processor.
Positive toward Miller's after the reason for the refusal is given.

ORDER

OVERALL MESSAGE: INDIRECT

SPECIFIC OBJECTIVES

1. To commend the society for its community projects.
2. To state the refusal of the request—funds have been disbursed this year.
3. To offer help next year by placing name of the society on list.
4. To retain goodwill.

Sometimes it is necessary to say no to many worthy requests. In this type of response, J. R. knows he may either state or imply the no. He recognizes that even though Sawyer is his primary audience, other members of this community group will also read and react to his communication. Even though J. R. is responding and the letter will contain his signature, he is concerned because the company's image is at stake with the group.

As a buffer to the bad news, this would be a good opportunity to emphasize what a worthy organization Northside is and to commend the members for their efforts. To deemphasize further the negative news, J. R. selects the indirect approach.

FORMAT

LETTER

J. R. feels confident as he reviews his communication (Figure 9.3) to Ms. Sawyer because he knows the letter:

Figure 9.3 Request refusal ("no" stated)

MILLER'S, INC.

May 10, 19__

Ms. Joella Sawyer, Secretary
Northside Society
Box 1221
Charleston, WV 25300

Dear Ms. Sawyer:

The Northside Society is to be commended for the many improvement projects it has sponsored in the community. Your efforts have not gone unnoticed.

Because your organization is so highly regarded, we checked to see if there were any way you could be included in this year's allocations. But funds set aside for worthy requests such as yours have already been disbursed; thus, I have to say "no" to your request for a food processor. However, I am personally placing the Northside Society on our contributory list for next year.

We at Miller's salute you and the other members of your group who take time to sponsor many worthwhile projects that benefit the whole community. Good luck in this year's bazaar and the RiverFest Festival.

Very truly yours,

J. R. Roberts, Director
Customer Services

sp

429 BROAD STREET
CHARLESTON, WEST VIRGINIA 25716
PHONE (304) 429-2614

- ☐ Recognizes the many contributions of this worthwhile organization (sure to create goodwill).
- ☐ Accentuates the positive/deemphasizes the negative (begins and ends positively; negative hidden in the middle).
- ☐ Says no in a positive way by expressing sincere admiration for the reader's community activities.
- ☐ Provides a good news option by placing the society on next year's list.
- ☐ Expresses desire for their success in the RiverFest Festival.

LETTERS REFUSING ADJUSTMENT

When refusing an adjustment request, you should avoid blaming the reader. Present the facts by writing in the third person—what is wrong, why adjustment can't be made (out of warranty, etc.), what can be done. To retain goodwill, businesses may repair a product at a reduced cost or offer some incentive to retain the goodwill of the customer. Examine this setting that results in a refusal.

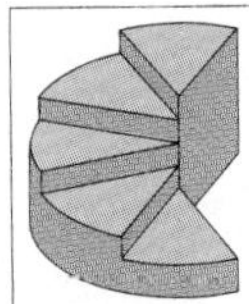

STRATEGY: REFUSING TO REPLACE AN ITEM

Basil Lloyd, owner of The Gourmet Supplier (1200 Davis Avenue, San Francisco, California 94102), has just received the following letter from a retailer who purchased 10 automatic drip coffee makers (model—My Cafe) for resale in Miss Sephena Nichol's specialty shop:

Dear Mr. Lloyd:

One of the 10 My Cafe automatic drip coffee makers ordered from you in September, 19__, purchase order no. 2-431B, is being sent to you by UPS because of malfunction. Please replace this unit with a new one. One of my customers purchased this coffee system and used it for six months; then the unit stopped working. I can't determine why.

Since the coffee unit carries a one-year warranty, please send a replacement.

Sincerely,

(Miss) Sephena Nichol
THE UNIQUE SHOP
P. O. Box 1211
Billings, MT 59101

After receiving the coffee maker from Nichol, Basil had his expert service technician, Joe Terrence, examine it to determine why it had malfunctioned. Terrence reported the following:

The internal unit has not been cleaned periodically with the vinegar-water solution as recommended in the instruction. This has allowed the buildup of material inside the coffee unit, which sealed the tube through which the water passed from the reservoir to the brew basket. The instructions accompanying the My Cafe unit state: "Once each month, the unit should be cleaned internally by pouring a solution of 2 parts vinegar and 2 parts water into the reservoir and operating the unit through a regular cycle. This regular maintenance will prevent residue from collecting on the internal portion of the unit and will ensure that your coffee maker will continue to make the same fresh, flavorful coffee you want. CAUTION: Lack of periodic, internal cleaning can result in damage to the internal system of the unit!"

With Nichol's letter from Unique and the service technician's report as background data, Basil reflects on the situation. He weighs all the evidence and concludes that this could be a "touchy" issue. If Nichol's reaction to his response is negative, it will reflect both on Basil and The Gourmet Supplier. "Tender care" is called for in this response. He plans his strategy.

PROBLEM
How to say no and keep the customer.

OBJECTIVES

General: To refuse the request.

Specific: To reemphasize quality/uniqueness of the coffee maker.
To acknowledge receipt of malfunctioning coffee maker.
To provide rationale for not replacing unit.
To build goodwill through removal of residue at no charge.
To indicate that the unit is being returned by UPS.
To suggest that Nichol point out the cleaning process to all customers.

READER/AUDIENCE

Characteristics: Customer for past two years.
Retailer whose customer was at fault.
Nichol is the primary audience; Nichol's customer is the secondary audience.
Nichol is familiar with regular business procedures.

Reactions: Probably depends on our service technicians for advice.
Will probably be pleased Lloyd repaired unit free.
Will feel Lloyd stands behind products.
Will be glad to have specifics; will probably continue ordering.

Since The Gourmet Supplier has been supplying Nichol with merchandise for two years, Basil has little trouble identifying the characteristics of his reader/audience. He knows Nichol very well, since they have developed a good business relationship during this time, and he can anticipate Nichol's reaction. As an experienced communicator, Basil knows, though, that he cannot presume on their past association. To take Nichol for granted could result in a lost customer. Given the circumstances, however, Basil can only offer Nichol an option to her request—repair of the unit.

ORDER

OVERALL MESSAGE: INDIRECT

Basil will imply the no near middle of his letter.

To determine the best overall order for the letter, Basil considers both the direct and indirect approach. Using the *direct* approach, he would have to say that the coffee maker is not being replaced near the beginning of the letter; with an *indirect* approach, he could place the statement near the end. After considering the alternatives, Basil decides to use the indirect approach with the denial of the request near the middle of the letter. To avoid emphasizing the negative, he decides also to *imply* rather than state that the request cannot be granted. On the basis of these decisions, Basil orders his specific objectives accordingly.

SPECIFIC OBJECTIVES

1. To acknowledge receipt of malfunctioning coffee maker.
2. To provide rationale for not replacing the unit.
3. To build goodwill through removal of residue at no charge.
4. To indicate that the unit is being returned by UPS.
5. To suggest that Nichol point out the cleaning process to all customers.
6. To reemphasize quality/uniqueness of coffee maker.

FORMAT

LETTER

Basil's first draft of the opening paragraph looks like this:

> The coffee maker you returned for replacement arrived on May 10, 19__. Our service technician examined the unit to determine why it did not function properly. His examination revealed that your customer was negligent and had not cleaned the internal units monthly as she was supposed to have done. Her negligence resulted in the buildup of residue, clogging the tube through which the water passes from the reservoir to the brew basket.

Basil recognizes that he has the ideas he wants to convey but that the tone of the paragraph needs work if he is to retain Nichol as a regular customer. Note how the revisions in the first sentence achieve greater concreteness and avoid blaming Nichol for the problem:

> The My Cafe Automatic Drip Coffee Maker returned to you by a customer and then sent to us for replacement arrived on May 10, 19__.

In his revision of the second sentence, Basil includes the name of the technician as a personal touch and the phrase *at once* to indicate his immediate attention to the request:

> Mr. Joe Terrence, our service technician, examined the unit at once to determine why it did not function properly.

In his original version, the next two sentences seem particularly harsh on Nichol's customer. Even though the customer was clearly negligent, Basil has already decided to remedy the problem by having the unit cleaned and restored. Thus he emphasizes what the technician found, and NOT what the customer did or did not do. In the revised version, he omits all references to the customer, reverses the ideas in the two sentences, gives the probable cause of the malfunction, and adds a comment about the varying mineral levels in different city water systems.

> His examination revealed that residue had built up, clogging the tube through which the water passes from the reservoir to the brew basket. This resulted from the lack of monthly internal cleaning with the recommended vinegar-water solution. Some city water systems have higher levels of minerals than others.

In the next section of the letter, Basil describes what action has been taken:

> Mr. Terrence thoroughly cleaned the inside of the coffee maker. The good-as-new coffee maker is being returned to you by UPS today.

The last sentence above implies that Nichol's request for replacement of the unit has not been granted. Even so, the phrase *good as new* suggests that the adjustment meets the customer's needs. Basil's revised version of the second paragraph reads as follows:

> Mr. Terrence thoroughly cleaned the inside of the coffee maker so that it once again brews the freshest, most flavorful coffee that your customer expects from and appreciates in the My Cafe unit. The good-as-new coffee maker is being returned to you by UPS today.

Finally, Basil must caution Nichol about proper cleaning procedures for the My Cafe unit. He decides to quote from the maintenance instructions that come with the coffee maker:

> Because you are one of our regular customers, there will be no charge for the special cleaning. Please be sure, however, to point out to your customers the cleaning instructions that appear on page 3 of "Maintenance Tips," the booklet that comes with each My Cafe unit.

Since Nichol might conclude from the first sentence above that she should

Figure 9.4 Adjustment refusal letter

The Gourmet Supplier
1200 Davis Avenue, San Francisco, California 94102, Telphone (818) 756-8145

May 12, 19__

Miss Sephena Nichol
The Unique Shop
P.O. Box 2112
Billings, MT 59101

Dear Miss Nichol:

The My Cafe Automatic Drip Coffee Maker returned to you by a customer and then sent to us for replacement arrived on May 10, 19__. Mr. Joe Terrence, our service technician, examined the unit at once to determine why it did not function properly. His examination revealed that residue had built up, clogging the tube through which the water passes from the reservoir to the brew basket. This resulted from the lack of monthly internal cleaning with the recommended vinegar-water solution. Some city water systems have higher mineral levels than others.

Mr. Terrence thoroughly cleaned the inside of the coffee maker so that it once again brews the freshest, most flavorful coffee which your customer expects from and appreciates in the My Cafe unit. The good-as-new Coffee Maker is being returned to you by UPS today.

Because you are one of our regular customers, there will be no charge for the special cleaning this time. Please be sure, however, to point out to your customers the cleaning instructions that appear on Page 3 of "Maintenance Tips," the booklet that comes with each My Cafe unit.

> "Once each month, clean the unit internally by pouring a solution of 2 parts vinegar and 2 parts water into the reservoir and operating the unit through a regular cycle. This regular maintenance will prevent residue from collecting on the internal portion of the unit. . . .
> CAUTION: Lack of periodic, internal cleaning can result in damage to the unit."

send in any unit that gets clogged, Basil adds the phrase *this time* to the end of the sentence.

Because you are one of our regular customers, there will be no charge for the special cleaning this time.

Having checked off all of his specific objectives except the last one ("re-emphasize the quality and uniqueness" of the My Cafe unit), Basil works on the closing paragraph of his letter. He is determined to end the letter

Figure 9.4 (*concluded*)

Top Margin 1 inch 7 Lines

Miss Sephena Nichol 2 May 12, 19__

The My Cafe model has proved to be one of the best selling utomatic drip coffee systems, as you have indicated through your repeat orders. Because the coffee mill is built right into the brew basket and because the 24-hour digital timer can be set for any time, the owner can wake up in the morning to the aroma of freshly ground and brewed coffee--a good way to start the morning! Because of these and other unique features, the My Cafe Automatic Coffee Maker will continue to be a BEST seller for THE UNIQUE SHOP.

Cordially yours,

Basil Lloyd

sp

with a strong, concentrated sales message. Though many of the outstanding features of the coffee maker have already been mentioned, Basil chooses two from this catalog description to emphasize the proven value of this model.

FROM BEANS TO BREW WHILE YOU SLEEP

Automatic drip coffee system with built-in coffee mill. Pour in whole beans and set the digital timer before you go to bed. In the morning, wake up to the aroma of freshly ground and brewed coffee.

10-function panel controls clock, 24-hr. timer, coffee strength (light to dark), bean mill (0–30 seconds), and two-hour "keep warm feature."

Brews preground coffee too. 1 to 8 cups capacity.

High-impact, heat-resistant plastic body with glass carafe, built-in stainless steel filter. Brews the freshest, most flavorful coffee.

My Cafe. No. E-308. One-year warranty. $129 (shipping charge, $4.50).

Basil highlights the "built-in coffee mill" and "24-hr. timer" in his closing paragraph.

The My Cafe model has proved to be one of the best-selling automatic drip coffee systems, as you have indicated through your repeat orders. Because the coffee mill is built right into the brew basket and because the 24-hour digital timer can be set for any time, the owner can wake up in the morning to the aroma of freshly ground and brewed coffee—a good way to start the morning!

In his final sentence, Basil creates a positive sales ending:

Because of these and other unique features, the My Cafe Automatic Coffee Maker will continue to be a BEST seller for THE UNIQUE SHOP.

Study Basil's polished letter to Nichol in Figure 9.4.

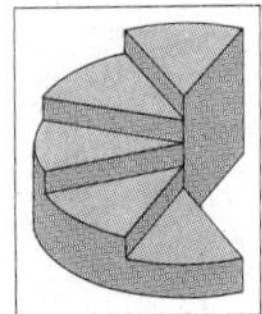

STRATEGY: REFUSING TO REPAIR AN ITEM

Now assume the *same setting* as the previous situation except that in this instance the coffee maker's interior tubing and heating element have been destroyed.

The problem and general objectives stay the same. Only one specific objective changes. The objective "To build goodwill through removal of residue at no charge" changes to "To build goodwill through prompt attention and examination of unit."

Reactions will include:

Probably depends on our service technicians for advice.

Probably will be disappointed but understand the company's position.

Will probably continue ordering.

Only the third specific objective changes—from "To build goodwill through removal of residue at no charge" to "To build goodwill through prompt attention and examination of unit." A letter is still the appropriate format.

The body of the letter will differ mainly in the middle and closing portions since the order for the communication remains the same. Basil

Figure 9.5 Adjustment refusals—No repairs possible

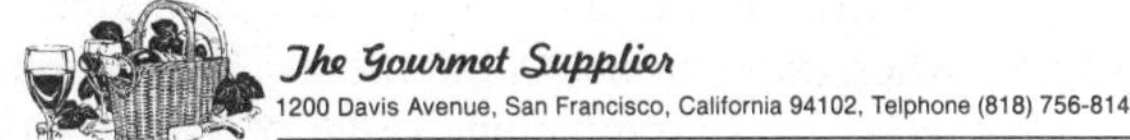

The Gourmet Supplier
1200 Davis Avenue, San Francisco, California 94102, Telphone (818) 756-8145

May 12, 19___

Miss Sephena Nichol
The Unique Shop
P. O. Box 2112
Billings, MT 59101

Dear Miss Nichol

The My Cafe Automatic Drip Coffee Maker that was returned to you by a customer and then sent to us for replacement arrived on May 10, 19___. I immediately gave it to our service technician.

Mr. Joe Terrence, our service technician, examined the unit at once to determine why it did not function properly. His examination revealed that build-up residue had destroyed the internal tubing and that the heating element was damaged beyond repair. This resulted from the lack of monthly internal cleaning with the recommended vinegar-water solution as explained on page 3 of the warranty booklet. The one-year warranty covers defective parts and workmanship only.

The coffee maker is being returned to you by UPS. As you know, the My Cafe Coffee Maker offers unique and dependable service when properly cleaned. CONSUMER REPORTS rates the unit as "Excellent."

Cordially yours

Basil Lloyd

gp

reasons that Nichol will probably be disappointed but will understand if the communication is fair and her feelings are considered. The letter for this situation is shown in Figure 9.5.

Since the customer is at fault, Basil concludes that about the only thing he can do is to return the coffee maker but assure the retailer that the unit is a quality product and is dependable when properly used. On the basis of his analysis, he feels the letter meets these requirements.

LETTERS REFUSING CREDIT

Even though you may refuse credit to an applicant, you want to retain the goodwill of the individual. Using preestablished written criteria is important when trying to make judgments about extending credit. You must conform to federal laws regulating credit; certain practices have been deemed discriminatory. If a letter contains certain information, the company can be held accountable. Use caution in what you say and how you express the reasons about refusing credit. Examine this setting.

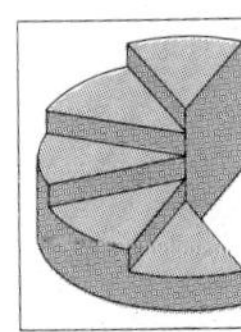

STRATEGY: REFUSING A CREDIT CARD APPLICATION

As applications manager of the Multi-Nation Credit Card Company, a well-established and recognized credit card organization, Nancy Bishop has received an application from Jack Lathers (Mills, Inc., P. O. Box 234, West Bend, Wisconsin 53095) requesting a corporate account. The completed application form contains all the required information.

After reviewing the application form, Nancy finds that the net earnings for Mills, Inc. don't meet the $50,000 minimum requirement of Multi-Nation for a two-year period. In addition, she circles the bank references section, which indicates only a checking account for Mills, Inc. Lathers requested two cards for him and his co-owner for business travel expenses.

Nancy now has the task of writing a letter to Lathers refusing credit. She decides to create a letter that she can use as a model for other clients who may request credit but do not meet the $50,000 minimum net earnings for a two-year period.

Nancy plans her strategy.

PROBLEM

How to refuse a credit request and still retain goodwill.

OBJECTIVES

General: To inform Lathers that Mills, Inc., does not qualify for the credit card.

Specific: To refuse credit.

To express appreciation for the application.

To provide reasons for refusal.

To retain goodwill of reader.

To resell customer on advantages of credit card.

To encourage customer to reapply when qualified.

As Nancy reviews the problem and objectives, she is thinking that perhaps at some point in the future the company could qualify for credit. As Mills, Inc., grows, it is sure to meet the criteria for a card from Multi-

Nation. She knows that the goodwill message and the tone of this refusal letter are important because the news will be disappointing.

READER/AUDIENCE

Characteristics: Lathers—co-owner of Mills, Inc.
Appears to be a new and relatively small business.

Reaction: Disappointment.

Figure 9.6 Credit refusal letter

MULTI-NATION, INC.

240 MILLEDGE AVE., COLUMBUS, OHIO 43081, TELEPHONE (614) 887-4130

August 26, 19__

Mr. Jack Lathers
Mills, Inc.
P. O. Box 234
West Bend, WI 53095

Dear Mr. Lathers:

Your application for a Multi-Nation Credit Card was received on August 23. To establish a corporate account at Multi-Nation, a minimum of $50,000 net earnings for each of the past two years and sufficient assets are needed. You indicated an annual net earnings of $20,000 for this past year, so at this time Mills, Inc., does not qualify for the corporate account from Multi-Nation.

As your business continues to grow, however, you may want to request the Multi-Nation Credit Card again. The Multi-Nation Card is welcomed by more than 200 airlines, all major car rentals, and a wide variety of leading restaurants, hotels, and fine department stores throughout the world.

Sincerely yours,

Nancy Bishop
Applications Manager

mr

Figure 9.7 Nancy's analysis of her letter

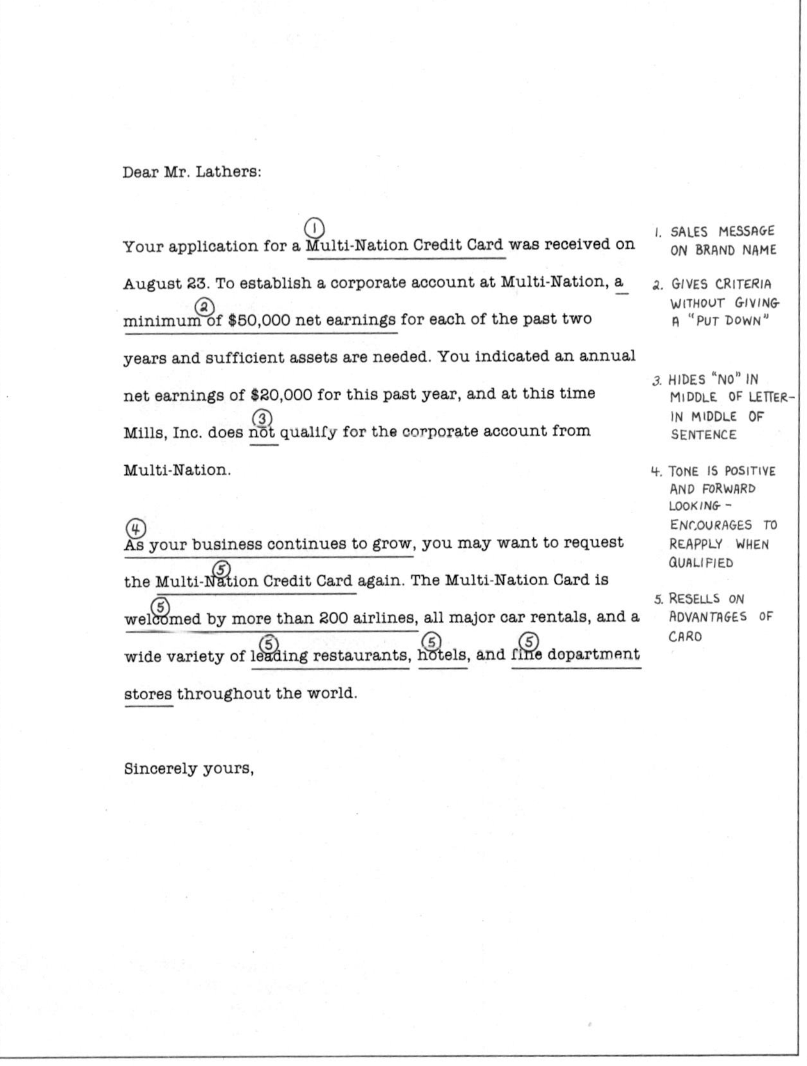

Dear Mr. Lathers:

Your application for a Multi-Nation Credit Card was received on August 23. To establish a corporate account at Multi-Nation, a minimum of $50,000 net earnings for each of the past two years and sufficient assets are needed. You indicated an annual net earnings of $20,000 for this past year, and at this time Mills, Inc. does not qualify for the corporate account from Multi-Nation.

As your business continues to grow, you may want to request the Multi-Nation Credit Card again. The Multi-Nation Card is welcomed by more than 200 airlines, all major car rentals, and a wide variety of leading restaurants, hotels, and fine department stores throughout the world.

Sincerely yours,

ORDER

OVERALL MESSAGE: INDIRECT

SPECIFIC OBJECTIVES

1. To express appreciation for the application.
2. To provide reasons for refusal.
3. To refuse credit.
4. To retain goodwill of reader.

5. To encourage customer to reapply when qualified.
6. To resell customer on advantages of credit card.

Since she must refuse the request because Mills, Inc., does not meet the $50,000 two-year minimum net earnings, Nancy uses the indirect approach:

A statement showing her appreciation for the application.
An explanation of company policy.
The credit refusal.
A statement encouraging Lathers to reapply later.

FORMAT

LETTER

As with all letters, Nancy must try to promote goodwill and confidence in her company. Her letter appears in Figure 9.6.

Nancy rereads her draft and makes the comments shown in Figure 9.7. Numbers and underscoring in the letter correspond to the numbered comments at the right of the letter.

She likes the letter and sends this version to Jack Lathers. She places a copy of the letter in a file to use as her model for future similar situations.

SUMMARY

Readers of disappointing (negative) news probably won't feel good under any circumstances. The blow will be lessened and goodwill maintained if readers are made to feel they were dealt with fairly and were treated in a professional manner.

To create an effective negative communication, you need to understand the reader/audience; collect facts about the situation; know something about human relations; know how to write with a positive tone under negative circumstances; select words and sequence ideas to deemphasize the negative; know when to use a strong direct approach or a mellow indirect approach; know when to imply the negative; and determine the appropriate degree of sales to use. Negative messages may be longer than other types since you present reasons for your action.

Emphasis is given to applying the principles of writing negative letters, using the strategy for communicating. When ordering goods or services, people sometimes leave out needed information—size, color, etc. The recipient needs the information to complete the order. The letter is considered negative since the reader gets the letter instead of the expected product. The message shows appreciation for the order, indicates what is needed, makes response easy, and convinces the reader that the product is worth the wait.

Messages that suggest order substitutions require special persuasive writing. The bad news may cause the reader to forget about the item. Use persuasion to overcome the expected negative reaction. The message informs the reader why the item isn't available with the suggested substitution. Most of the message presents sales about the substitution. Deemphasize negative ideas.

When you write a refusal of a request, give a legitimate reason and try to retain the goodwill of the reader. Make the reader feel the request received fair consideration. Keep the tone positive.

When you refuse an adjustment request, avoid blaming the reader. Use the third person to express what is wrong, why the adjustment can't be made, and what can be done. If possible, offer an acceptable alternative to retain the goodwill.

At times, companies must refuse credit requests. Even though credit is refused, the message strives to retain goodwill. Use a preestablished set of criteria for credit requests. You must conform to federal laws regulating extending credit. Use caution in what you say and how you express the reason for refusing credit.

END-OF-CHAPTER ACTIVITIES

DISCUSSION

1. What reader considerations are important when you write negative messages?
2. Explain how you can use a positive tone in a negative message.
3. How can the negative idea be deemphasized?
4. Under what conditions should you imply the negative idea?
5. What does *resale* mean in writing negative messages?
6. Define *buffer* and explain its use when writing negative messages.
7. Discuss how to maintain customer goodwill when writing a refusal adjustment letter.
8. What factors should be considered when writing a credit refusal letter?

ACTIVITIES

9. Read and critique the following letter refusing a request for a donation of merchandise:

    Dear Mrs. Joston:

    We are in receipt of your letter requesting merchandise samples, to be used in conjunction with the TASCOE Convention to be held in your area in the future.

    While we certainly appreciate that this represents a fine public relations opportunity and represents a very fine advertising potential, we are unable to supply the samples requested.

I am certain you will appreciate our position, Mrs. Joston; with nearly 200 stores across the country, we receive hundreds of requests similar to this one every month. Since it is financially impossible for us to comply with all of them, in all sincerity, we feel it is only fair that we contribute to none of them.

It is a regular part of our program each year to make very generous financial contributions to charity and welfare organizations which benefit many communities across the country. We feel that this is not only the best way, but the only way in which we can make philanthropic contributions. In addition, we contribute door prizes to all grand openings and anniversaries for our new and old stores, along with large quantities of sample merchandise available at the time. This is the limit of our activity in this area.

I am sure that the TASCOE Convention in your area is very, very worthy of the samples you have requested, and believe me, Mrs. Randles, we would certainly like to cooperate in compliance with your request, but we trust you will understand our position as I have tried to outline it above.

Thanks very much for giving us this opportunity to explain.

Sincerely yours,

10. Anthony Fisher (101 Main Street, Deerfield, Kansas 67838), has sent you an order for Weiser locks along with his $225.00 check for his December account; it is now February 1. Fisher has been purchasing from you for the past two years on a regular basis, but payments have been slow during the past six months. As a result, you are requesting that he send a check with his next order or have the items sent COD. You (Marsha Wade, credit manager for the RDI Distributors, Atchison, Kansas 66002), want to continue serving Fisher but feel that his slowness in paying in the past indicates some type of trouble; therefore, you want to request future payment by check or COD. Now, you want to write a letter thanking him for his order and check and indicating that he may send future orders with a check or have them sent COD. This process has been caused by his slowness in paying during the previous six months after having had a good-paying record over the past two years. You do, however, want to review the situation again within the next four months and hope at that time you will be able to grant him credit again, allowing him the convenience of receiving his orders on open-account terms again. In order to continue, you need a statement of his willingness to accept his current order and the next four months' orders for Weiser locks COD.

    Develop the strategy; write the appropriate message.

11. On April 10, 19--, you (James Strunk, national sales manager for Allied Conduit Corporation, 1400 Main Street, Houston, Texas 77012), sent a letter and accompanying *Distributor News Sheet* to all dealers listing a price increase on three items: EMT, IMC, and Galvanized Rigid Conduit. The letter indicated that the new price list would go into effect on June 1, 19--; it is now April 20, 19--, and you have found an error on one item—the 1″ EMT net; the April 10 *Distributor News Sheet*

shows $23.84—the correct net is $27.84. You have prepared a revised pricing sheet (goldenrod) and need to write a letter to accompany it. Write a model message to Broadway Electric Distributors (204 Walker Street, Montgomery, Alabama 36105). This model letter will be used for the other customers who also received the faulty price list.

Develop the strategy and then write the message.

12. Several weeks ago, Homer McGuire (Milliken Tube Corporation, 120 West Boulevard, Chicago, Illinois 60426), requested a booklet titled "The Effects of Video Display Terminals on Office Workers" from the National Business Bureau (2401 Lakeside Avenue, Washington, D.C. 20037). Homer saw a review of the study and mention of the availability of the report in booklet form in the January 19-- issue of *Today's Technology*. The following findings particularly attracted Homer's attention: "Research has not confirmed fears that VDTs emit harmful amounts of radiation"; and "There is no evidence that radiation emissions from VDT units harm fetuses." Since there has been some concern in his business about the installation of VDTs for the use of secretaries and managers, he is very eager to get the report. A check for $30 was included, as indicated in the magazine.

    Now, as Jon Strenk of the National Business Bureau, you must write a message informing Homer that the supply is exhausted. So many people wanted the report that your supply was gone within a week after the magazine review appeared. There is a possibility that the report will be reprinted, but it will be almost three months before it will be available. Of course, you will return Homer's check. Remind him to look at future issues of *Today's Technology* for announcements about the report.

    Develop the strategy for this situation; then write the appropriate message.

13. As head of the order department for the Global Microcomputer Supplies (6203 Martin Avenue, Woodbridge, New Jersey 07095), you have received a letter order from Olene Thayer (P. O. Box 102, Strasburg, Pennsylvania 17579), an established credit customer, for 4 Flip File Albums; however, she did not specify the color desired. Red, blue, and beige are available. Even though you could call, you decide to write a letter asking for the incomplete data and enclose a new spring catalog, price list, and order blanks. The description of the album on page 10 of the last catalog reads: "Handy flip-through binder displays 15 diskettes in durable vinyl jackets that are static-resistant; ensures data protection; organized filing and rapid retrieval possible through index tabs and see-through design; stock no. C3137, disk size, 5¼ in., price $20.50, each."

    Develop the strategy; then write the appropriate message that will get the necessary color information you need to ship Olene's order.

14. As head of the order department for the Global Microcomputer Sup-

plies (6203 Martin Avenue, Woodbridge, New Jersey 07095), you have received an order from Jim Dunham (204 Boonville Road, Albuquerque, New Mexico 87100), his first, for the following items:

10 boxes ORA Flexible Disks (5¼ in. for IBM PC; stock no. C1926V; double sided; double density; price, $4.25 per disk (10 disks per box)

5 File-by-Color Library Storage Boxes (stock no. C3113, 5¼ in. disk size; 1 ea. color: beige, blue, green, yellow, red; price, $3.90 ea.

1 Diskette Tub File (stock no. C3111)-5¼ in. disk size; putty color; price, $29.95.

You have the items to send except for the ORA Flexible Disks, which are no longer manufactured. Instead, you now have a far superior product: Verbatim Flexible Disks-Price, $3.35 per disk in boxes of 10; disks have five-year manufacturer's warranty, are individually tested and certified error-free; exceed all ANSI and ECMA specification governing flatness, stability, and torque of jackets; double sides; double density; disks have been chosen no. 1 for performance and price.

Develop the strategy for the message telling Dunham his order for microcomputer accessories will be shipped as soon as he approves the substitute for the Flexible Disks. As indicated on the original order, freight charges will be paid by Dunham upon arrival of the order. Keep in mind that this is his first order, and you want to convince him to approve the substitute.

After completing the strategy, write the appropriate message.

15. As customer service manager for the Idea Shopper, a convenient catalog ordering house of specialty items, you have just received a Sanyo rechargeable flashlight sent to Roberta Anderson (701 East Fourth Street, Parkersburg, Iowa 50656), about two months ago. The accompanying letter indicates that the flashlight does not perform satisfactorily and that she wants her $25 back. The flashlight unit is rechargeable; one charge of the built-in nicad batteries gives over an hour of continuous use; the unit only weighs 9 ounces and has a tough housing with a one-year warranty. The beam is very powerful, as a result of the polished reflectors. After you received the unit, you had your service technician examine it to find out why the flashlight malfunctions. She found that the unit had been smashed in some way since the tough housing had been cracked; in addition, it appeared that the unit had been submerged in water since there was water throughout the unit. Evidently, rough treatment or some type of accident had resulted in this damage. The warranty does not cover negligent treatment such as this.

Design the strategy for this case; then write the appropriate message to send to Anderson.

16. As the circulation manager for *Management World,* you have received a request from Elmer Chamber (221 Elkmont Road, Winchester, Oregon 97495), for a free copy of "Trends in Information Technology," as indicated in the February, 19--, issue of *Management World.* A reviewer writing in the February issue indicated that the report was available through local offices of Arthur Andersen & Company. Therefore, you need to write a message to Chambers indicating that he should contact his local Arthur Andersen office to request a copy of the informative report. Since Chambers is a member of the Administrative Management Society—publishers of the *Management World*—you want to use caution in your reply (you checked your membership records). You want to help him get a copy of the report. Develop the strategy to use in this case; then write the message.
17. As the Midwest regional sales manager for Super X Drug Company, 120 Oakland Avenue, Indianapolis, Indiana 46204, you (William Ozmand) have just received a request letter from Martha Randles (Mrs. J. R. Randles) asking for merchandise samples to use as auction prizes at the upcoming GALA Convention—a community effort to raise funds for worthwhile projects in the community. Although you recognize the opportunity for a fine public relations gesture and a good advertising potential, you are unable to provide the samples as requested for a number of reasons: hundreds of requests are made each month from across the country for similar items with nearly 11,000 store outlets. Since it is financially impossible to comply with all of them, the company feels it is only fair that we contribute to none of them; each year, generous financial contributions are made to charity and welfare organizations which benefit many communities across the country—this is the fairest way for us to make philanthropic contributions. In addition, door prizes are contributed at the time of grand openings and anniversaries for all Super X Drug stores along with liberal quantities of sample merchandise at these times.

    Develop your strategy; then write the appropriate communication for William Ozmand.

CHAPTER 10

WRITING OTHER TYPES OF MESSAGES

Learning Objectives

After studying this chapter, you will be able to:

- □ Recognize situations that require special types of messages.
- □ Plan a strategy for special-situation messages.
- □ Apply the appropriate degree of persuasion.
- □ Evaluate the effectiveness of different parts of letters.
- □ Create an appropriate tone for your messages.
- □ Write an effective message for special situations.

Given the scope of any textbook, there is no possible way to present every conceivable situation for writing. The types of letters you will typically encounter in the business world are presented in these chapters. The present chapter includes some other types of unsolicited messages you might occasionally have to write. Many of these messages require little attention to persuasive techniques or concern for the reader's possible negative reaction. The only goal of some letters is to generate goodwill. In some instances, the originator may feel an obligation to write. Nevertheless, since they represent the writer and the company as well, all letters, memos, and reports—whatever their initial purpose—function in part to promote goodwill.

Messages promote goodwill

In this chapter, you will use the strategy for communicating these types of messages:

Types of special messages

- □ Introduction.
- □ Special request.
- □ Notices of change.
- □ Follow-up letters.
- □ Order messages.
- □ Unsolicited sales letter.
- □ Transmittal of information.
- □ Congratulations.
- □ Sympathy.

At the end of the chapter, study and evaluate the additional examples of communications used by companies.

LETTERS OF INTRODUCTION

As people change positions in organizations, a need arises to introduce new personnel to established customers. Whether the new appointee is a recently hired operations manager, salesperson for a new territory, or someone recently promoted to president, the occasion offers an opportunity to build goodwill as well as to inform clients of new personnel.

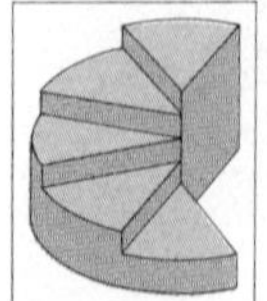

STRATEGY: INTRODUCING A NEW EMPLOYEE

Beginning June 1, 19__, Tom Weiser is assuming the position of president of the Western Division of Excelor Industries. Curt Walker, who has been president of the Western Division for the past 10 years, is retiring—a pleasant event since he has made the request.

Phil Whaley, senior vice president, must notify the customers of this change in leadership. In collecting background information about Weiser, Phil finds the following: Weiser has been an Excelor employee for 20 years—1965, sales representative in Boise, Idaho; 1967, territory sales representative in Portland, Oregon; 1969, territory sales representative in

Las Vegas; 1972, district manager, Portland; later, national sales manager, vice president of sales, and vice president of operations; most recently, executive vice president. His performance has been outstanding in each of these positions.

The Western Division of Excelor Industries includes Excelor Lock, continental U.S.; Excelor Lock Co., Ltd., Canada; and Excelor Overseas Division—Australia and Japan.

To aid in preparing the message, Phil identifies the components of the strategy as follows.

PROBLEM

To reduce as much as possible the negative effects of a change in leadership.

OBJECTIVES

General: To inform customers of the change.

Specific: To introduce Tom Weiser.

To indicate that Curt Walker is retiring.

To reassure customers that the retirement is a pleasant event.

To summarize positions held by Weiser (build confidence in him).

To reinforce goodwill with customers.

To mention the scope of the Western Division.

READER/AUDIENCE

Characteristics: Primary audience—all current customers in Western Division; others who may need the information.

Customers in the United States, Canada, Australia, and Japan.

Business people who are accustomed to changes in organizations.

Reaction: Some could have negative reaction if they had direct contact with Walker over the years.

Most probably not concerned since change would not affect their association with Excelor Industries.

Most would see the announcement as a courtesy and consider congratulations were in order for Walker.

Some could wonder if major changes might happen as a result of change in leadership—especially the overseas customers.

ORDER

OVERALL MESSAGE: DIRECT

Because the letter is to inform customers of a pleasant event, the opening can begin with the main objective—announcing the new president of the Western Division. You want to communicate this good news immediately.

SPECIFIC OBJECTIVES

1. To introduce Tom Weiser.
2. To indicate that Curt Walker is retiring.
3. To reassure customers that retirement is a pleasant event.
4. To mention the scope of the Western Division.
5. To summarize positions held by Tom Weiser (build confidence in him).
6. To reinforce goodwill with customers.

FORMAT

LETTER

Since the message goes outside the company, Phil uses a *letter*. He plans to use the mail-merge feature of his word-processing system to send a personally typed letter to each customer.

After preparing the strategy for the announcement, Phil begins to construct his message using the first three objectives:

The Western Division of Excelor Industries takes pleasure in announcing the appointment of Tom Weiser as president, effective June 1, 19__. Tom is replacing Curt Walker, who is moving into happy retirement.

Phil reviews the paragraph and jots down these thoughts:

1. The tone of the introductory statement is pleasant and shows that the change in leadership is a welcome event, not something to cause anxiety.
2. "Tom Weiser," "president," and "Western Division of Excelor Industries" are the key items that will require further development here for the reader.
3. The effective date is also important.
4. The clause "who is moving into happy retirement" should put readers at ease. Since Walker wanted to retire and is looking forward to it, this statement is honest and conveys the right attitude.
5. The use of "Tom" by itself conveys a more personal tone than does the title "Mr." with his last name.

Satisfied with the introductory paragraph, Phil drafts the next part of the letter, one that provides more facts about the scope of the Western Division (Specific Objective 4):

Figure 10.1 Introduction of new division president

Phil Whaley
Senior Vice President

Western Division
87918 Torrance Avenue
Los Angeles, CA 90741
Telephone (213) 573-2167

April 30, 19___

Inside Address

SUBJECT: New President of Western Division

The Western Division of Excelor Industries takes pleasure in announcing the appointment of Tom Weiser as president, effective June 1, 19___. Tom is replacing Curt Walker, who is moving into happy retirement.

The Western Division includes Excelor Lock in the continental United States; Excelor Lock Co., Ltd., in Canada; and the Excelor Overseas Divisions located in Australia and Japan.

Tom's 20 years of experience with Excelor at various locations and in various positions makes him well qualified to lead the Western Division. He began his career with Excelor in 1965 as a sales representative in Boise, Idaho. In 1967, he transferred to Portland, Oregon, and later to Las Vegas, Nevada, as a territory sales representative. He returned to Portland in 1972 as a district manager; later, he became national sales manager, vice president of sales, and vice president of operations in the Portland area; and most recently, he served as executive vice president of the Western Division. Tom certainly knows the business from bottom to top.

Won't you join me in wishing Tom success in his new assignment.

Thank you for your continuing support of Excelor products.

Phil Whaley
Senior Vice President

et

The Western Division includes Excelor Lock in the continental United States; Excelor Lock Co., Ltd. in Canada; and the Excelor Overseas Divisions located in Australia and Japan.

Now Phil writes a paragraph reviewing Weiser's previous experience to establish the idea that the new president is well qualified for the leadership role (Specific Objective 5):

Tom's 20 years of experience with Excelor at various locations and in various positions makes him well-qualified to lead the Western Division. He

began his career with Excelor in 1965 as a sales representative in Boise, Idaho. In 1967, he transferred to Portland, Oregon, and later to Las Vegas, Nevada, as a territory sales representative. He returned to Portland in 1972 as a district manager; later, he became national sales manager, vice president of sales, and vice president of operations in the Portland area; and most recently, he served as executive vice president of the Western Division. Tom certainly knows the business from bottom to top.

After reading these drafts, Phil thinks, "My major concern was to introduce Weiser to the customers; yet I have inserted the paragraph about the scope of the Western Division between the introductory paragraph and the information about Weiser. Even though it may appear that I am digressing here, I want to keep this paragraph arrangement. The information about the Western Division reflects the extent of Tom's new role. This makes the position more meaningful to the uninformed readers."

Now all Phil has to do is end the letter with courtesy. For emphasis, he places two ideas in separate paragraphs:

Won't you join me in wishing Tom Weiser success in his new assignment?

Thank you for your continuing support of Excelor products.

The completed model letter announcing Tom Weiser's appointment as president is shown in Figure 10.1.

SPECIAL REQUEST LETTERS

Occasionally, you might need to notify suppliers, employees, or customers about a change in procedure. For this type of message, you would not expect a response. Your main objective is to inform. Study this example.

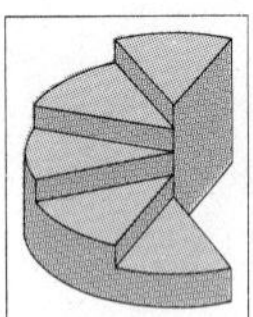

STRATEGY: EXPLAINING A CHANGE IN PROCEDURE

Alexander Bryne, purchasing manager for the Norris Companies, Inc. (Box 1120, Long Beach, California 90802), is reviewing the past few months' processing of invoices directly to the various branch stores (10 stores scattered through the United States) rather than directing them to the central office in Long Beach. This has resulted in some delays in checking the processing invoices in the central office. Alex has set up new procedures and wants to inform Norris's suppliers of the changes.

In this new procedure, purchase order numbers are issued to the branch store where purchase order forms are completed and sent to the supplier with a copy forwarded to Alex's office. In filling the order, the supplier ships the merchandise directly to the branch store and sends the invoice to the central office at Long Beach. The invoice should contain the purchase order number and, in the "ship to" column, indicate the store to which the merchandise was shipped. When the branch store receives the shipment, the order is checked and an approved form is completed, then forwarded to the central office in Long Beach. People in Alex's office check this form against the invoice before payment is made.

Alex has just received another invoice that was sent to the branch store in Ft. Collins, Colorado (invoice no. ST-7185-R10; date, September 10, 19__), by the Bartlett Construction Company (3810 Regal Street, Memphis, Tennessee 38117). Alex realizes he needs to tell Bartlett about the new process. He writes a message to Bartlett telling them to forward all billing and shipping invoices to the Long Beach office for Norris Companies, Inc. He plans to use this as a model to send to other companies to tell them of the change in procedures. Alex prepares the components of the strategy:

PROBLEM
Inaccuracies resulting from invoices sent to local branch stores instead of to the central office.

OBJECTIVES

General: To inform the company of the new procedure for mailing invoices and shipping merchandise.

Specific: To notify the company to send invoices to the central office in Long Beach.

To present the reason for the new procedure—all processing of invoices through central office.

To indicate that merchandise should be shipped directly to the branch store making the purchase.

To convey the idea that compliance will make payment more orderly.

READER/AUDIENCE

Characteristics: Primary—probably credit manager.

Secondary—others who may read message.

Reaction: Favorable action since the request is routine but with a valid reason.

ORDER

OVERALL MESSAGE: DIRECT
Since Alex assumes that this notification is a routine request to send all invoices to the central office, and that the recipient will take favorable action, the *direct approach* is appropriate. Consequently, Alex prefers a letter that will be relatively short and to the point.

SPECIFIC OBJECTIVES

1. To present the reason for the new procedure.
2. To explain why the company should send invoices to the central office in Long Beach.
3. To indicate that merchandise should be shipped directly to the branch store making the purchase.
4. To convey the idea that compliance will make payment more orderly.

FORMAT

LETTER

Alex plans to use the mail-merge feature of word processing to notify the suppliers. Using the specific objectives identified above, Alex writes the following letter to Bartlett and numbers each sentence:

1. I have noticed that your invoices are being mailed directly to each of our branch stores. 2. For example, invoice no. ST-7185-R10 was mailed to Norris in Ft. Collins, Colorado. 3. In the future, please submit all invoices to the central office at Norris Companies, Inc., Box 1120, Long Beach, California 90802. 4. Do not mail the invoices to individual branch stores. 5a. It is important that our purchase order number be referenced correctly on the invoice, as no invoice can be processed without this number; 5b. and in the "ship to" column please indicate to which of our stores the merchandise was shipped. 6. Your compliance will be appreciated.

After studying the draft, Alex makes the following assessment:

- ☐ The general objective is met.
- ☐ The specific objective about shipping the merchandise to branch stores is only vaguely indicated.
- ☐ Sentence 1 is "I" oriented.
- ☐ Sentence 3 really contains the main idea of the message.
- ☐ Sentences 1 and 2 add little to the message; they emphasize past action—eliminate.
- ☐ Sentence 4 is negative—eliminate.
- ☐ Sentence 5a is negative and also vague—revise.
- ☐ Sentence 5b is wordy—revise.
- ☐ Sentence 6 sounds like a rubber stamp—omit.
- ☐ The closing paragraph not needed in this letter; would just be extra words without any purpose.
- ☐ The tone of the message is demanding—revise.
- ☐ The organization and sequencing of ideas is weak—restructure to give emphasis to the procedures.

Based on this analysis, Alex rewrites the letter as shown in Figure 10.2.

Figure 10.2 Letter notifying recipient of new procedure

Norris Companies, Inc.

October 5, 19__

Bartlett Supply Company
3810 Regal Street
Memphis, TN 38117

Attention: Credit Manager

Gentlemen

To improve our process of invoice payment, please follow the new procedures outlined below. You will receive your money in a shorter time by

1. Sending your invoices to me at Norris Companies, Inc., Box 1120, Long Beach, CA 90802 (instead of to our individual branch stores).

2. Indicating in the "Ship To" column of your invoice the store where the merchandise is shipped.

3. Using our purchase order number on your invoice to expedite payment.

4. Continuing to ship the merchandise to the branch stores.

Yours very truly

Alexander Bryne
Purchasing Manager

jm

Box 1120
Long Beach, California 90802
Telephone (213) 288-5604

MESSAGES ABOUT CHANGES

During the year, stated prices, discounts, or other standard practices need revision. Customers need to know about the changes, the effective date, and the reason for the changes. Even though the information may be negative, convey this information promptly and provide the rationale to reduce any negative effects. Such is this situation.

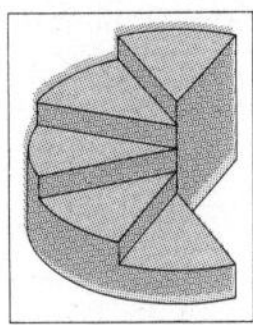

STRATEGY: ANNOUNCING A PRICE CHANGE

Isadore Fleetwood, general manager of the Ridgeway Window Grilles Company (P. O. Box 41, Jasper, Texas 75951), needs to communicate with all of Ridgeway's customers about a change in discounts allowed on future orders. In the past, jobber discounts of 50 percent and 10 percent were given as a regular practice; in addition, quantity discounts were provided as follows: 5 percent on all invoices between $1,000 and $4,999; 8 percent on all invoices $5,000 and over.

Beginning April 15, 19__, all shipments are subject to a new policy: jobber discounts of 50 percent only; no change in quantity discounts. The increased costs of pine lumber and labor require the change in jobber discounts. The huge increases in lumber and labor costs have been widely reported in business magazines. To stay competitive and provide quality products, Ridgeway changed its jobber discounts as described above.

Isadore Fleetwood needs to notify each of the customers of these changes. In addition, she also needs to send along brochures for two new products: MT1333, Grids for Sash Doors; and MT1431, Grilles for New Window Units by Anderson.

PROBLEM

How to communicate a change in discount policy.

OBJECTIVES

General: To inform customers about the new discount policy.

Specific: To indicate the change in discount policy—from 50/10 percent to 50 percent.

To provide a rationale for the change—increased costs in pine lumber and labor; the company must stay competitive; must provide a quality product.

To give the effective date—April 15, 19__.

To state that quantity discounts still apply:

$1,000-4,999: extra 5 percent discount.

$5,000+: extra 8 percent discount.

To express appreciation for business.

To send brochures for two new products.

Isadore realizes that the customers will not like the announcement of the higher cost of lumber products. She will deemphasize this negative news by explaining the economic conditions and increased competition.

READER/AUDIENCE

Characteristics: Some will be long-standing customers.

Some will be relatively new customers.

Some will be regular customers in business.

Reaction: Initial response will be negative since this will mean a higher cost.

Some may not continue to purchase from us.

Most will accept the increase in cost since prices are increasing in every facet of the business economy.

The prices are in line with competitors.

ORDER

OVERALL MESSAGE: DIRECT

Since this is a change in procedure, the recipients will want to know the subject first, even though it isn't good news. The customers will understand the reason for the change since they, too, are in business and understand the increasing prices of raw materials and labor.

SPECIFIC OBJECTIVES

1. To give the effective date.
2. To indicate the change in discount policy.
3. To provide a rationale for the change.
4. To state that quantity discounts still apply.
5. To send brochures for two new products.
6. To express appreciation for business.

In this instance, the direct approach is better since the objective of the letter is mainly to present the facts and other positive information—quantity discounts and new items.

FORMAT

LETTER

Since this message goes to all of Ridgeway's regular customers, Isadore plans to design a form letter in simplified style. Each will be personalized by adding individual names and addresses using the mail-merge feature of the word processor.

Her first draft looks like this:

SUBJECT: Change in Discount Rates, Effective April 15, 19__

Effective on all shipments as of (April 15, 19__), the jobber discount will change to 50 percent; formerly it was 50 percent and 10 percent. The increased costs for pine lumber and labor have made the above change necessary. To maintain the quality wood products you like, it is necessary to change the discount rate.

Figure 10.3 Announcement of price change (form letter).

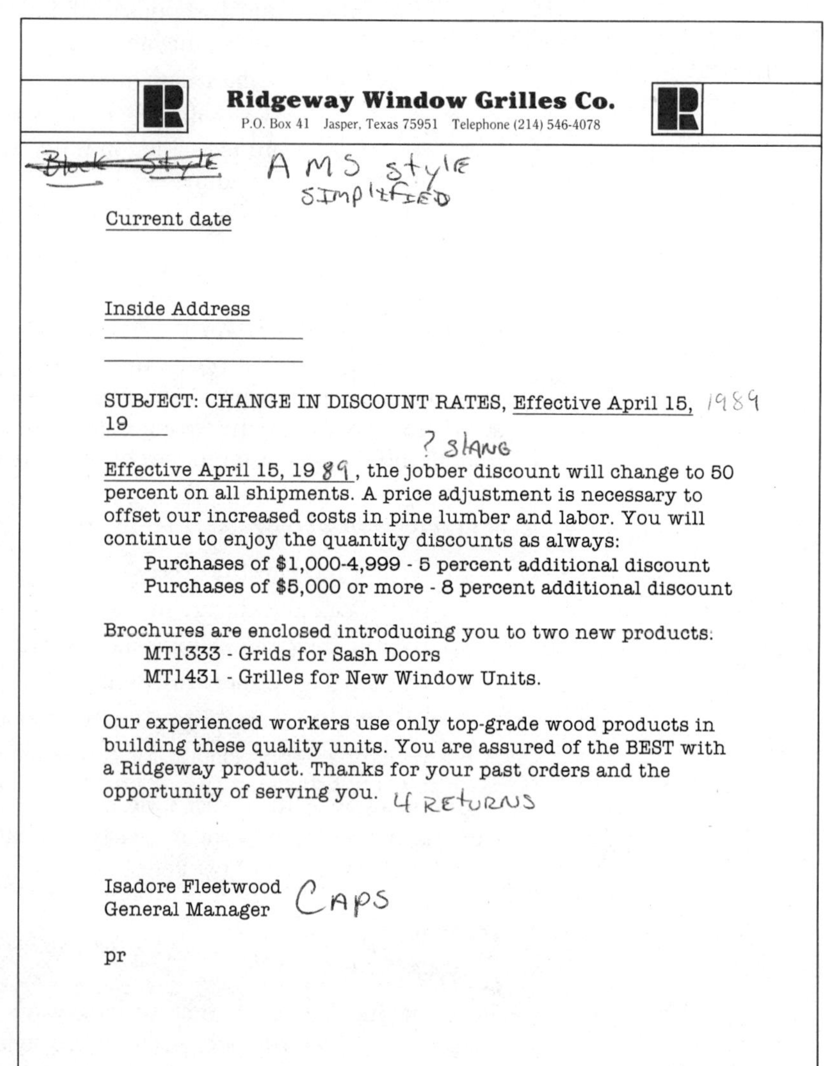

Ridgeway Window Grilles Co.
P.O. Box 41 Jasper, Texas 75951 Telephone (214) 546-4078

~~Block Style~~ AMS style SIMPLIFIED

Current date

Inside Address

SUBJECT: CHANGE IN DISCOUNT RATES, Effective April 15, 19__ 1989

Effective April 15, 1989, the jobber discount will change to 50 percent on all shipments. A price adjustment is necessary to offset our increased costs in pine lumber and labor. You will continue to enjoy the quantity discounts as always: ? slang

Purchases of $1,000-4,999 - 5 percent additional discount
Purchases of $5,000 or more - 8 percent additional discount

Brochures are enclosed introducing you to two new products:

MT1333 - Grids for Sash Doors
MT1431 - Grilles for New Window Units.

Our experienced workers use only top-grade wood products in building these quality units. You are assured of the BEST with a Ridgeway product. Thanks for your past orders and the opportunity of serving you. 4 RETURNS

Isadore Fleetwood
General Manager CAPS

pr

To continue providing you with quality wood products, we had to increase the price because of our inceased costs for pine lumber and labor.

On your next purchase, you can continue to receive quantity discounts as follows:

Purchases of $1,000–4,999—5 percent discount
Purchases of $5,000 or more—8 percent discount

Two new price lists are enclosed for your convenience:

MT1333—Grids for Sash Doors
MT1431—Grilles for New Window Units

Each of these units is built with quality products by experienced carpenters. You are assured of the best with Ridgeway Window Grilles. Thanks for your past orders; we look forward to serving you again soon.

Isadore examines the draft and then rewrites it to achieve the following goals:

- □ Combine ideas: *increased costs* and *quality products* to produce a positive effect.
- □ Use words that stress company *costs* versus customer's *price adjustment*.
- □ Emphasize the positive policy of continued quantity discounts with words *continue to enjoy* and *as always*.
- □ Emphasize the quality of these wood products and their fabrication in the closing paragraph.
- □ Express appreciation to the customer.

See Figure 10.3 for her completed letter.

Isadore checks to make sure she has included all specific objectives and given them the proper emphasis. The content of the letter is correct, and the tone is appropriate. The "you" and "your" references provide a balanced viewpoint. Indenting the material highlights the more technical facts, and underscoring the effective date makes future reference easier. She accepts the draft (Figure 10.3) as her final copy.

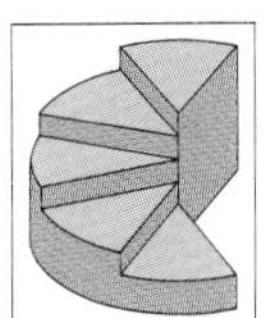

STRATEGY: TRANSMITTAL MEMO ON PROCEDURE CHANGE

The Data Processing Management Association (an international association of computer-related professionals) currently requires all new membership applications to be handled first by a local DPMA chapter. Over the past five years, people have mailed their membership applications directly to the Chicago headquarters; the applications were mailed back to the local chapter to maintain the right of refusal of a member by an individual DPMA chapter. An examination reveals rare use of the refusal. Therefore, a revised procedure for processing new member applications has been developed and approved by the DPMA Council. Headquarters will process all applications received and then notify the local chapter of the new member. Each person in the headquarters office and the local chapter membership chairperson needs to receive the new procedure. The executive director, Marsha Peres, needs to write the message to notify office staff and local membership chairpersons.

PROBLEM

People lack information about the revised procedure.

OBJECTIVES

General: To inform people about the revised procedure.

Specific: To indicate that applications received at headquarters will be processed; the names of new members will be sent to the local chapter.

To provide the reason for the revision.

To convey council approval of the revised procedure.

To specify the implementation date.

READER/AUDIENCE

Characteristics: Primary audience—professional staff at headquarters; membership chairpersons of local DPMA chapters.

Secondary—others who may read the message.

Reaction: Most people will welcome a revised procedure.

Some people will object to the change.

ORDER

OVERALL MESSAGE: DIRECT

The message that contains the revised procedure needs to be brief and to the point. The *direct* approach facilitates conciseness.

SPECIFIC OBJECTIVES

1. To provide the reason for the revision.
2. To indicate that applications received at headquarters will be processed; the names of new members will be sent to the local chapter.

Figure 10.4. Transmittal memo about procedure change

July 10, 19__

TO: Headquarter's Staff and Chapter Membership Chairpersons
FROM: Marsha Peres, Executive Director
SUBJECT: Revised Procedure for New Member Application, Effective September 1, 19__

Effective September 1, 19__, new membership applications received at the Chicago headquarters will be processed; the name of each new member will be sent to the local chapter. This revised procedure was approved by the DPMA Council at its July 19__, meeting. Inconsistent handling of membership applications in the past has resulted in loss of new members.

3. To specify the implementation date.
4. To convey council approval of the revised procedure.

FORMAT

MEMO
All people who will receive it are considered intracompany. Figure 10.4 presents the transmittal memo.

FOLLOW-UP LETTERS

To stimulate sales, marketing people write communications to follow up leads from phone conversations, face-to-face contacts, or from just informal chitchat with other professionals. These contacts make it easier to write unsolicited messages to remind the prospective customer about the product or service. An unsolicited sales letter without a previous contact is more complex and requires a more persuasive style of writing.

The setting below illustrates a follow-up message to a discussion about the use of a hotel for a group conference.

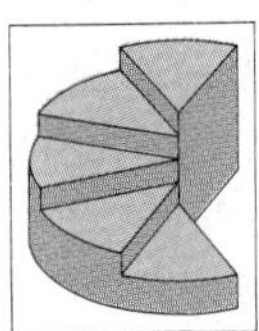

STRATEGY: FOLLOW-UP FOR GROUP CONFERENCE

Angela Shaefer, director of sales for the Regency Hotel, Jacksonville, Florida, has discussed the possibility of hosting the regional meeting of the American Association of Management (AAM) with Elizabeth Walker, the local chairperson. The conference is set for January 10-12, 19__. During their discussion, Angela gave Elizabeth a *Planning Guide* describing the Regency Hotel facilities. Other groups have praised the *Planning Guide* as a valuable planning tool. Prices as well as a list of all facilities (banquet meals, room rates, meeting rooms, overhead projectors, speaker systems, etc.) are provided in the *Planning Guide*. Many groups have used the Regency as a result of the information contained in the guide. Angela provided several different proposals for the AAM to consider. Elizabeth planned to meet with her program committee within the next two weeks.

After their discussion, Angela wants to send a follow-up letter. She plans to express appreciation for Elizabeth's consideration and to encourage her to book the Regency for the upcoming meeting. Angela does not want a hard sales approach in the message.

With these thoughts in mind, she begins to develop the message to send to Elizabeth. Angela realizes that a successful conference for the AAM (about 200 members) would certainly help attract other professional groups.

PROBLEM
How to persuade Walker to book the Regency for the conference.

Angela knows that a direct sales letter with a hard sales pitch will annoy Elizabeth and the committee members. Tact will be very important in this letter.

OBJECTIVES

General: To convince the AAM to book the Regency.

Specific: To express appreciation for the discussion about the AAM conference at the Regency.

To remind Elizabeth Walker of available facilities (excellent).

To highlight the use of the Regency by another professional group.

To give the phone number for easy response.

To stimulate Elizabeth to call and book the Regency.

READER/AUDIENCE

When examining the Reader/Audience component, Angela realizes that she will have to rely upon her meeting with Elizabeth and her own experience with other groups.

Characteristics: Elizabeth Walker, chairperson of the AAM Conference Committee; main person.

Other members of the conference committee who are also professional people.

Most have had experience with conferences before; their likes and dislikes.

Reaction: Most will probably agree to use the Regency because of its location, image in the community, good facilities, and assistance given by the Regency staff.

Some could oppose the Regency because of the slightly higher cost of meals and rooms.

Elizabeth can influence others since she has seen the facilities.

ORDER

OVERALL MESSAGE: INDIRECT

Angela decides on an *indirect* order since she plans first to thank Elizabeth and the committee members for considering the Regency. Her suggestion that the members of the committee should book the Regency for the conference will be delayed. In this way, Angela anticipates that she can tactfully convince them to use the Regency. The message will emphasize services and convenience.

SPECIFIC OBJECTIVES

1. To express appreciation for the discussion about the AAM conference at the Regency.
2. To highlight the use of the Regency by another professional group.
3. To remind Elizabeth of the excellent facilities available.
4. To give the phone number for easy response.
5. To stimulate Elizabeth to call and book the Regency.

FORMAT

LETTER

With the strategy completed, Angela begins her initial draft of the letter:

Thank you, Dr. Walker . . .

. . . for discussing with me the possibility of holding your American Association of Management Winter Conference at the Regency on January 10-12, 19__. When your conference is over, you, like the Chairperson of the National Engineering Association, can say, "I'm glad we selected the Regency!" Comments from attendees at the NEA Conference praised the excellent facilities at the Regency—spacious rooms, comfortable meeting rooms, and superb food.

After you present the plans to your Conference Committee, just call me at 525-0143 to have your group scheduled. To assure the January 10-12, 19__ dates, you will want to make a decision soon. Once you have made the Regency choice, you can relax knowing that our competent staff will take care of the details for the meeting facilities. Call me soon!

As you read the letter, note that Angela used a different way to begin the letter. She combined the appreciation and salutation; then continued with the letter. The quoting of the adjectives *spacious*, *comfortable*, *superb*, *excellent* creates a favorable image of the Regency. Note the balanced repetition of the name Regency. The reference to another group assists in stimulating the AAM to respond soon and positively. Mention of the need to make a decision soon to book the meeting is persuasive without being pushy. Ending on a positive note is also a good idea. She decided to use *Chairperson* instead of *Chairman* and to place the name Regency in caps. Angela's completed letter appears in Figure 10.5.

Figure 10.5 Appreciation—Follow-up sales stimulus letter

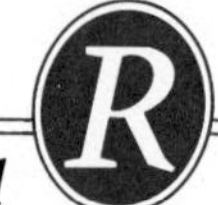

Regency Hotel

February 10, 19__

Dr. Elizabeth Walker
American Association of Management
213 Omaha Street
Jacksonville, FL 32209

Thank you, Dr. Walker . . .

. . . for discussing with me the possibility of holding your American Association of Management Winter Conference at the REGENCY on January 10-12, 19__. When your conference is over, you, like the Chairperson of the National Engineering Association, can say "I'm sure glad we selected the REGENCY!" Many who attended the NEA Conference praised our excellent facilities--spacious rooms, comfortable meeting facilities, and superb food.

After you present the plans to your Conference Committee, just call me at 525-0143 to schedule the REGENCY. To assure the January 10-12, 19__ dates, you will want to make a decision soon. Once you have made the REGENCY your choice, you can relax knowing that our competent staff will take care of the details for the meeting facilities. Call me soon!

Sincerely

Angela Shaefer
Director of Sales

dk

1717 Ocean View Drive • Jacksonville, Florida 32210 • Telephone (904) 313-2198

ORDER MESSAGES

Normally, businesses use an order form to obtain goods from suppliers. When a form is not available, a letter is needed for the order. In this case, you would use the listing format of the order form as a guide; add an introductory paragraph and perhaps a closing one if you have a special request. Follow this case, which requires an order letter.

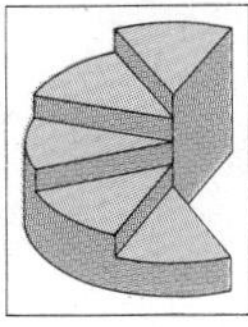

STRATEGY: REQUESTING AN ORDER LETTER

Jeanne and Gerald Jacobs are owners of the Mountain Ski Shoppe, specializing in wearing apparel, near Grand Father Mountain, North Carolina. They opened their shop near the end of the summer months in a newly developed snow ski area. They were pleasantly surprised at the rapid pace of sales. Jeanne and Gerald talked and decided to place another order for two fast-moving items. They checked through the supplier's catalog and decided on these items: 16 pairs (Dolomite Ski Boots, no. M41274, Men—2 pairs each in sizes 9, 9½, 10, 11, cost—$140 each; no. F41274, Ladies—2 pairs each in sizes 7, 7½, 8, 9; cost, $135 each; 6 pairs, Aris Gold Safety Gloves (no. 2431-A: Thinsulate; 1 each in small, medium, large sizes for Men; 1 each in small, medium, large sizes for Ladies; cost, $60 each).

Because of the newness of the Ski Shoppe, the supplier (Mava Skiing Headquarters, 5023 Riverside Avenue, Killington, Vermont 05751), requires that a 25 percent prepayment accompany each order. When Gerald checked the catalog, he did not find an order form.

PROBLEM

Additional ski items are needed; sales will be lost if they are not available.

OBJECTIVES

General: To request selected items.

Specific: To state request.

To identify items—catalog number, catalog description; quantity, price (each), total by item, total for order.

To indicate 25 percent payment enclosed as agreed.

To request order forms.

To indicate the popularity of the items and the success of the Ski Shoppe.

READER/AUDIENCE

Characteristics: Wholesaler-supplier of items for ski shop retailer.

Person accustomed to routine orders.

Reactions: Pleased to receive another order and down payment.

Will act promptly because of seasonal nature of articles ordered.

ORDER

OVERALL MESSAGE: DIRECT

The direct approach is correct since this is a routine request; they expect a positive reaction.

Figure 10.6 Order letter

430 Summit Avenue
Asheville, North Carolina 28800
Telephone (704) 687-1265

October 20, 19___

Mava Skiing Headquarters
5023 Riverside Avenue
Killington, VT 05751

Gentlemen:

Please send the ski boots and gloves listed below; a check for $640 (25% prepayment) is enclosed:

Item No.	Description	Size	Quantity	Amount
M41274	Men's Dolomite Ski Boot	9	2 pair @ $140	$280.00
M41274	Men's Dolomite Ski Boot	9½	2 pair @ $140	$280.00
M41274	Men's Dolomite Ski Boot	10	2 pair @ $140	$280.00
M41274	Men's Dolomite Ski Boot	11	2 pair @ $140	$280.00
F41274	Ladies' Dolomite Ski Boot	7	2 pair @ $135	$270.00
F41274	Ladies' Dolomite Ski Boot	7½	2 pair @ $135	$270.00
F41274	Ladies' Dolomite Ski Boot	8	2 pair @ $135	$270.00
F41274	Ladies' Dolomite Ski Boot	9	2 pair @ $135	$270.00
2341-A	Men's Gold Aris Safety Glove	M	3 pair @ $ 60	$180.00
2341-B	Ladies' Gold Aris Safety Glove	S	3 pair @ $ 60	$180.00

To make future ordering easier, please send a supply of order forms.

The Dolomite Ski Boot and Aris Glove are very popular with the skiers this season. Your quality products have helped the Mountain Ski Shoppe to have a profitable season.

Sincerely,

Jeanne and Gerald Jacobs

Enclosure

SPECIFIC OBJECTIVES

1. State the request.
2. Indicate the enclosed check (25 percent)—this item to be in a subordinate position.
3. Identify the items.
4. Request order forms.

5. Indicate the popularity of the items.
6. Establish the idea of the success of the Ski Shoppe.

FORMAT

LETTER

Since Jeanne and Gerald don't have an order form, the letter is the appropriate format. Also, the check for 25 percent of the order total will be attached. They used an old order form as a guide and listed the items. Figure 10.6 shows the letter for the order.

A critique of their letter offers these comments:

1. Because of its routine nature and the anticipated positive reaction, the more factual, straightforward content is appropriate. Listing the items ordered helps the reader act promptly. The overall tone of the letter is straightforward, yet courteous.
2. The closing paragraph provides feedback to the supplier—a good idea since the supplier might have other items that could also increase sales. The success of the Mountain Ski Shoppe also provides a basis for a later review of the payment plan. As the Ski Shoppe becomes established, Gerald wants a regular account without the prepayment requirement. The words ***rapid sales***, ***popularity***, and so on, achieve that specific objective.

UNSOLICITED SALES MESSAGE

Sales through direct mail is widely practiced—these letters are unsolicited. To be effective, you need to select carefully your recipients, use an appropriate sales appeal, and create an action-getting communication. With today's computer technology, you can purchase mailing lists to meet your desired audience (or prepare your own). For example, one bank offers a preapproved credit plan (with a gold card) to a select list of professionals with annual incomes of $40,000 or above for the past five years. Special appeals (sales) convince the recipients to accept the card by signing an authorization card. Identifying groups with specific characteristics makes the writing easier since you use a sales appeal oriented to that particular group. Preparing a strategy is also important for unsolicited sales messages.

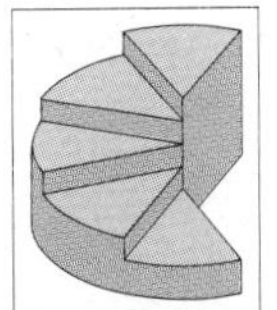

STRATEGY: DIRECT-MAIL SALES

In this situation, assume the role of Dorothy Ukes, owner of Ukes Mortuary (1400 Broadway, Boulder, Colorado 80321). People generally face major decisions about funeral expenses at a time of emotional upset. To overcome this unpleasant task and to provide rational decisions, the Ukes Mortuary has joined the Prepayment Plan program so people can prear-

LEGAL / ETHICAL ISSUE

As the owner of a local business, you are invited to the office of a city official to discuss the procedures for submitting a bid to provide office supplies for the city for the next fiscal year. Placing items out for bid is a common practice for governmental agencies. Both you and the city official belong to the same civic organization and know each other well.

The city official discusses the list of specifications and procedures and answers your questions. During the discussion, you notice three competitors' bids that have been strategically placed on the table—evidently so that you can see the bids. You leave the building feeling good that you can offer the low bid and still make a profit.

Should you use this information to submit the lowest bid? What are the legal and ethical implications of the city official's actions? Your actions?

range a funeral and prepay the expenses. Dorothy wants to use a direct-mail approach to a select group of area residents to generate interest in Ukes's service plan.

She realizes the difficulty of the task she is undertaking because of the unpleasant topic. "How can you get the readers to read the message when it is about death?" she thinks. Most people will throw away a letter of this type if death is mentioned. "How can I write so that the reader will return an attached card to receive more detailed information about the plan?" Tone and word selection will be very important. She sets out to accomplish her perceived objective by completing her strategy.

PROBLEM

How to generate sales.

OBJECTIVES

General: To persuade people to request the brochure on the Prepayment Plan (a nonthreatening message).

Specific: To inform people about the Prepayment Plan.

To mention situations under which the traditional decision is made:
The death of a loved one.
A sad time.
Emotional stress.

To establish the benefits of preplanning the funeral:

Peace of mind.
Lessen burden on relatives.
Financial payment already made.
Unique method of prearrangement for funeral.
Saves money.
Done without pressure of time/grief.

To identify action to be taken:
Return enclosed card for free brochure—"Funeral Arrangements in Advance."

READER/AUDIENCE

Characteristics:	People in the region.
	Adults—young, middle-age, older; some single, married, divorced; low-, middle-, and upper-income levels; mostly white-collar workers.
Reactions:	Most will react negatively at first.
	Some will throw the letter away because of its topic.
	Some will not want to face the topic but see a need for preplanning.
	The prepayment plan will appeal to some.

ORDER

OVERALL MESSAGE: INDIRECT

Since the subject is a sensitive one, the reader needs to be convinced from the start to continue reading. Special appeals are needed. The reader must be convinced of the benefits before any action is requested. Special attention needs to be given to avoid scare tactics or a too negative tone. This takes space in a letter.

SPECIFIC OBJECTIVES

1. To establish benefits of preplanning a funeral.
2. To inform people about the Prepayment Plan.
3. To mention situations under which the traditional decision is made.
4. To identify action for the reader to take.

FORMAT

LETTER

A form letter merged with a mailing list (on letterhead stationery) will reach the greatest number of people in the area.

After completing the strategy, Dorothy drafts the following form letter:

Dear ______________________________:

What would your family members do if you suddenly died? At one of their saddest times, they would have to make quick decisions about the plans for the funeral—and expenses. Do you want this stressful situation to occur?

You can eliminate this stressful situation by joining the Prepayment Plan through advance funeral planning. You can have peace of mind knowing that your funeral arrangements are taken care of while lessening the burden on your family.

The Prepayment Plan offers a way to plan for your funeral arrangements. The plan is economical and offers a sensible way for you to plan for your funeral—without the pressures of time and grief.

To obtain the free booklet, "Funeral Arrangements in Advance," fill out and return the enclosed postage-paid card.

Cordially yours,

Dorothy lays the draft aside to take care of several pressing activities. Two days later, she picks up the draft and rereads it. She is amazed at the tone of the letter—it doesn't create the right feeling she'd hoped for when she began the task. So she checks her strategy to make sure nothing was omitted. Her check reassures her that she has covered all her specific objectives with the facts—and in the right order. However, she decides that words such as *death*, *funeral*, *you*, and *your* create a morbid atmosphere. "Most people would probably throw that letter away after reading the first sentence," she surmises.

Dorothy revises the letter on the following basis:

- ☐ More of a buffer opening is needed to get the reader's attention; the tone should be nonthreatening.
- ☐ A more positive tone.
- ☐ Lessen the hard sales.
- ☐ Stress more benefits to the reader.
- ☐ Encourage action; use a nonthreatening tone in offering a get-the-facts booklet rather than a call from a salesperson.
- ☐ There should be less use of the "you" viewpoint.

With these ideas in mind, Dorothy rewrites the letter until she produces the model letter shown in Figure 10.7.

This version conforms to Dorothy's initial image:

- ☐ Opening establishes credibility of situation through experience.
- ☐ Uses soft sales approach.
- ☐ Creates proper tone—uses third person until the end of the second paragraph.
- ☐ Uses "you" in a nonthreatening way.

Figure 10.7 Unsolicited sales letter—Model

Dear ______________________________:

As funeral directors, we have been called upon many times to advise people in the period shortly after a beloved family member has passed away. It is without question one of the saddest hours of their lives.

But unfair as it may seem, it is also the time they are called on to decide about funeral expenses. Because of this fact, it is our firm conviction that advance planning gives you the peace of mind that comes with knowing your funeral arrangements are taken care of while lessening the burden on your survivors.

For this reason, we now offer the nationally known and advertised *Prepayment Plan*—an insurance-funded program.

Prepayment Plan offers a unique method for you to plan in advance for the inevitable. In addition to saving money, it offers a sensible way to face this issue without the pressures of time and grief.

To learn the facts about Prepayment Plan, return the enclosed reply card today. You can read the facts in the free brochure, "Funeral Arrangements in Advance," in the privacy of your own home. We know you will be pleased that you looked into this money-saving, sensible way of dealing with an inevitable expense.

By planning ahead now for your funeral, you can express wonderful love for the members of your family. What a comfort this can be.

Sincerely,

Dorothy Ukes

- ☐ Offers benefits of plan after establishing confidence.
- ☐ Delays unpleasantness by offering the brochure.
- ☐ Closing refers to "family and love" as appeals for action.

LETTERS THAT TRANSMIT

At times you will send a brochure, catalog, or some other item and need to write a letter of transmittal. The purpose is to indicate what is being sent, any facts the reader needs to know, and any action the reader needs to take. Sometimes no action is needed. An enclosure notation is added to the letter. The phrases "Please find enclosed" or "Enclosed please find" are trite; instead, say "Enclosed is." If the enclosure is fastened to the letter, then you may say "Attached." Follow Randy Allison as he creates a form transmittal letter.

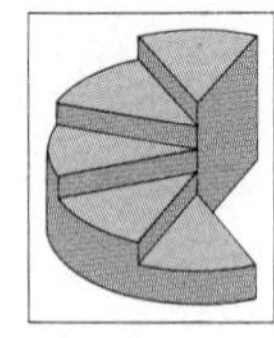

TONE Important

STRATEGY: A FORM TRANSMITTAL LETTER

Randy Allison is customer service manager for the HearthStone Builders, Inc. (Route 2, Box 434, Dandridge, Tennessee 37725; phone—615/397-9425). HearthStone specializes in manufacturing custom-designed log houses. Standard house plans are available, but most customers usually modify the standard plans.

The customer order process involves the following major phases: the customer signs a contract and makes a down payment; customer approves the custom plan; production blueprints are prepared; the log house is produced; the completed house is delivered; and the customer's home is erected.

After the draftspeople modify the standard blueprints, the customer must approve the plans. This phase requires sending a set of blueprints to the customer; the customer checks the blueprints and then if they are correct, signs and dates one set (one stamped APPROVAL PRINT) and returns it to HearthStone. If not, the customer marks any changes in red and returns the set to HearthStone. The other sets are included for the customer's use with bank financing and reference copy.

Randy recognizes that the letter is almost the same each time. Therefore, he decides to prepare a form transmittal letter to use each time the four sets of blueprints are mailed to the customer. This will speed up the process of mailing out the blueprints since he can use the mail-merge feature of word processing. Randy prepares his strategy.

PROBLEM

Saving time in getting the customer's approval of blueprints.

OBJECTIVES

General: To inform the customer about the APPROVAL PRINT.
To reinforce sales appeal.

Specific: To state that four sets of blueprints are enclosed.
To ask the customer to check the blueprint.
To sign and date the APPROVAL PRINT set if it is satisfactory, or
To mark changes on the APPROVAL PRINT in red if it is unsatisfactory.
To ask for the return of the APPROVAL PRINT.
To reinforce the wise choice of the purchase.
To provide a telephone number in case of questions.

READER/AUDIENCE

Characteristics: Primary person is the customer.
Eager to move into the house.
Established customer—purchases have been submitted.
Secondary—others to whom the customer might show the letter: financing institutions; another architect; salesperson; etc.

Reaction: Positive.

ORDER

OVERALL MESSAGE: DIRECT

Since there is an established relationship (the customer has signed a contract and made a down payment), the customer is expecting to receive the plans for approval. The receipt of the plans is good news since the customer is one step closer to having the house. Therefore, the *direct* approach is appropriate.

SPECIFIC OBJECTIVES

1. To state that four sets of blueprints are enclosed.
2. To ask the customer to check the blueprints.
3. To sign and date the APPROVAL PRINT set if it is satisfactory, or
4. To mark changes on the APPROVAL PRINT set in red if it is unsatisfactory.
5. To ask for the return of the APPROVAL PRINT set.
6. To provide a telephone number in case of questions.
7. To reinforce the wise choice of the purchase.

FORMAT

Letter

Randy goes to the file and retrieves a copy of the last transmittal letter that was sent (see Figure 10.8).

Randy makes these notes as he rechecks his strategy:

- □ The opening is slow; it needs to be more forceful/customer-oriented; "please find" is trite; the letter needs consistency in words—blueprints, plans, drawings.
- □ The opening paragraph is choppy.
- □ Opening paragraph: mentioning the salesperson—good.
- □ Middle paragraph: needs to be clearer about two options; it could use sales appeal.

Figure 10.8 Copy of previously used transmittal letter

Date

Dear ____________________:

Enclosed please find four sets of design drawings. One set of these plans is stamped APPROVAL PRINT. These plans contain the changes which you made in the standard plans for your HearthStone home at the time you signed the contract with your salesperson, Mr. Ernest Jones.

Following your review of these plans, please return the approval plans to us for our records and use in the preparation of production drawings. If you approve the plans as they are represented, simply sign, date, and return the prints to us. Should you wish to make any modifications to the plans, please make any corrections in RED ink on the APPROVAL PRINT and return for our review and consideration.

If you have any questions pertaining to these plans, or if you need assistance in any other area, please do not hesitate to call your sales representative.

Very truly yours,

Randy Allison

ct

HearthStone Builders, Inc. Route 2, Box 434, Dandridge, TN 37725 615-397-9425

- ☐ Closing paragraph: trite; it needs to be revised—doesn't include the specific objective of reinforcing a wise choice; it omits the telephone number.

Randy redrafts the form letter as shown in Figure 10.9.

Randy reads this version and decides that it fulfills his objectives for the transmittal letter. With slight changes to meet the situation, he can now use this form letter for transmitting the blueprints to customers. If no action is required from the customer, he can omit the middle paragraph.

Figure 10.9 Randy's redraft of transmittal letter

HEARTH STONE

______________, 19__

____
____
____

Dear ______________:

Enclosed are four sets of blueprints for your modified Americana HearthStone Log House. The customized blueprints reflect the changes you desire in the standard Americana model plan. ______________, your salesperson, indicated how pleased you were with the Americana.

Please review the modified blueprints. If they are satisfactory, sign and date the blueprint marked APPROVAL PRINT; if you desire further modifications, please mark any changes in RED on the APPROVAL PRINT. Return the blueprint to me.

Please call (615) 739-2200 if you have additional questions. Once your Americana model is completed on your site, your dream of owning an authentic, distinctive HearthStone Log House will become a reality.

Very truly yours,

Randy Allison, Manager
Customer Service

js

Enclosures: 4 sets of modified Blueprint for Americana Model

HearthStone Builders, Inc. Route 2, Box 434, Dandridge, TN 37725 615-397-9425

MESSAGES THAT CONGRATULATE

By expressing appreciation for others' accomplishments, you show the personal characteristic of consideration. Each of us likes to know that others recognize and appreciate our achievements. This type of message is usually short and positive. The form can be a memo, letter, or handwritten message on a special note card. You need to be sincere in expressing your congratulations. Avoid flowery language. Read this setting about Susan Chumley.

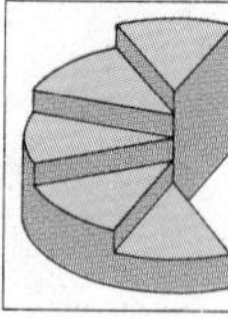

STRATEGY: WRITING CONGRATULATIONS

Susan Chumley, head of the research and development department at Hill Energy Systems, Inc. (a high-tech, energy-related firm), has just read in the company newsletter about Rudolph Lopez's promotion to head of the Office Automation Department at Hill. Susan is glad to see the promotion news since she vividly remembers working on a task force with Rudolph. She knows he is well qualified for the new position in the Computing and Telecommunication Division of the company.

Susan plans her strategy.

PROBLEM

How to communicate her sincere, positive feeling about Rudolph's promotion.

OBJECTIVES

General: To let Rudolph know you share the pride in his promotion.

Specific: To convey pleasure about the promotion news.

To refer to a specific past experience that supports the sincere feeling about the promotion.

To state the exact job title.

To offer congratulations.

READER/AUDIENCE

Characteristics: Primary—Rudolph; he is glad to know someone shares in the good news of his promotion; will feel good.

Secondary—others with whom Rudolph shares the letter.

Reaction: Positive.

ORDER

OVERALL MESSAGE: DIRECT

SPECIFIC OBJECTIVES

1. To offer congratulations.
2. To convey pleasure over promotion news.
3. To refer to a past experience that supports the sincere feeling about the promotion.
4. To state the exact job title.

Figure 10.10 Susan's memo of congratulations

November 28, 19__

TO: Rudolph Lopez, Head
Office Automation Department

FROM: Susan Chumley, Head
Research and Development Department

SUBJECT: Your Promotion

Congratulations, Rudolph, on your promotion to head of the Office Automation Department at Hill. Your promotion is well deserved. I remember vividly the contributions you made to the success of the Systems Task Force on which we both served. Hill can certainly benefit from your leadership in the Office Automation Department. Good luck!

FORMAT

MEMO

Susan decides on the memo format since they are both in the same company. Her memo is shown in Figure 10.10.

Susan likes the tone of the message and sends the memo to Rudolph. She is glad to show him this consideration. As an alternative, Susan could have sent a special card with a longhand message.

SYMPATHY MESSAGES

Messages that express sympathy are quite often difficult to write. Death is a topic most people prefer to push aside. In the work environment, professionals and coworkers need to express sympathy orally and in written form. Because of the finality of death, people generally are uncomfortable with the topic and tend to avoid conveying feelings of sympathy. At this unpleasant time, most people prefer to send a preprinted sympathy card from a card shop. Someone else has written the brief message—all you need do is sign your name.

At times, however, you will need to write a personal message—either typed or handwritten—to a colleague. If you know the person well, you may write a handwritten message on a special sympathy card; for others, you may prefer to type a short message expressing your sympathy.

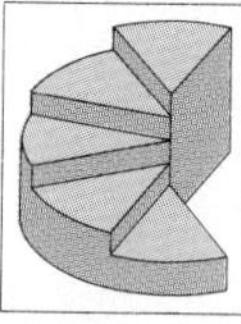

STRATEGY: HANDWRITTEN SYMPATHY MESSAGE

Robert Childers, a flight attendant, has been notified that his father died unexpectedly. His supervisor, Rebecca Ellington, wants to express her feelings of sympathy to Robert. Rebecca has supervised Robert for nine months. The strategy for communicating looks like this.

PROBLEM

How to convey feelings of support during this crisis.

OBJECTIVES

General: To let Robert know of sincere feelings of sympathy.

Specific: To express sympathy.
To create a feeling of support.

READER/AUDIENCE

Characteristics: Primary—Robert, a fellow worker and friend.
Secondary—Others who may read the message.

Reaction: He will be pleased that his supervisor thought enough to send a written message.

ORDER

OVERALL MESSAGE: DIRECT

SPECIFIC OBJECTIVES

Figure 10.11 Sympathy message—Note card

Robert,

I share your feelings of sadness at the loss of your father. At this time, remember his guidance and friendship in preparing you for your personal life. He did an outstanding job.

Rebecca E.

1. To express sympathy.
2. To create a feeling of support.

FORMAT

SPECIAL NOTE CARD WITH HANDWRITTEN MESSAGE
Rebecca's first thought was to send a sympathy card from the card shop. Because of their relationship, she rules out that option. She also rejects the idea of a typed letter since that would be too formal. She decides to buy a special note card with the word *Sympathy* on the front and write a short message on the inside. Rebecca's personal message is shown in Figure 10.11.

SUMMARY

Various conditions call for writing special types of business messages. Many of these messages require little attention to persuasive techniques or concern for the reader's possible negative reaction. The only goal of some messages is to generate goodwill. All messages, however, represent the writer and/or the company and should promote goodwill.

The strategy for communicating is applied to settings; a model communication is presented for each case.

As people change positions, a need arises to introduce new personnel to established customers. The occasion offers an opportunity to build goodwill. The message emphasizes the new person's name, special qualifications, and effective date. If appropriate, give a reason for the new position (retirement, etc.). Promote the company image throughout the message.

Over time, stated prices, discounts, and other standard practices need revision; customers and employees need to know about these changes. Convey this information promptly with the effective date indicated. Provide a rationale for the change. Develop goodwill throughout the message with a positive tone.

Follow-up letters from face-to-face or phone contacts are common in business. The personal contact makes writing this unsolicited sales letter easier than one without the contact. Quite often messages stimulate action based on the previous contact. Express appreciation for the contact, resell the product or service, emphasize the benefits, and suggest a specific action. Maintain the proper tone.

Normally, businesses use an order form to obtain goods from suppliers. When a form is not available, a letter is needed for the order. In the order letter, use the listing format; add an introductory paragraph and a closing paragraph for special information such as details of payment and shipment.

Sales through direct mail is practiced widely. To be effective, carefully select the recipients, sales appeals, and action-oriented statements. With today's computer technology, businesses commonly purchase mailing lists of specific groups. The unsolicited sales letter requires a high degree of persuasion and interest development. Use specific benefits to convince the reader.

Identify specific action needed to explain the product or service. Keep the tone positive and the sales pitch appropriate.

Letters and memos transmit brochures, catalogs, or some other information. The transmittal message indicates what is being sent, any facts the reader needs to know, and any action the reader needs to take. An enclosure notation is added to the letter.

Congratulation messages recognize others' accomplishments and create goodwill. This type of message is usually short and positive. The form can be a memo, letter, or handwritten message on a special card. Be sincere and specific in expressing congratulations.

Messages that express sympathy are quite often difficult to write because of the topic. People commonly use preprinted sympathy cards to avoid the unpleasantness of writing a personal message. The content of the brief message depends upon your relationship to the person. A special sympathy card with a handwritten message is also appropriate when you know someone well; a typed letter can also be used for someone you don't know well. Promptness in sending the message is important.

END-OF-CHAPTER ACTIVITIES

DISCUSSION

1. Based on the concepts you have learned about writing business communications, what is your understanding of the differences between solicited and unsolicited letters? Which is more difficult to write? Why?
2. Discuss the process for applying the strategy for communicating to solicited and unsolicited communications. Is there any difference? If so, describe.
3. What is the purpose of a letter of transmittal, and under what conditions would this type of letter be appropriate?
4. Which other types of messages listed in this chapter were probably written for the sole purpose of generating goodwill? Discuss.
5. How does a letter of introduction promote goodwill? A special request letter? Notices of change?
6. Contrast the complexity of writing an order letter and an unsolicited sales letter.

ACTIVITIES

7. Critique the following body of a letter that is used after a person becomes a new customer of the Home Savings and Loan Association; offer suggestions for its improvement.

It is a pleasure to welcome you to our savings/investment family. Attached to this letter is a receipt for the funds. Evidence of these accounts, together with signature cards, will be sent to you within the next few days. Earnings will be paid at the close of each calendar quarter.

As a new account holder, you will be very interested in our savings/investment program. It will provide comprehensive information about the strength and services of our branches of our association.

This new savings/investment concept offers the maximum safety, convenience, and rate of return. . . with the opportunity to have all of your accounts under one account name insured up to the maximum by the F.S.L.I.C.

It is our continuing aim to provide the best possible service ever to every account holder. Please contact me whenever you feel that I can be of any further assistance.

Cordially yours,

For each of the following, plan your strategy; then write an appropriate message.

8. As Verna McLain, chairperson of the State Library Association, you need to write a message thanking Lanoka Hadler (203 North Avenue, Springfield, Missouri 65804), for giving an excellent speech at the Spring meeting of the Library Association in Columbia, Missouri. The presentation on automating records and suggestions on ways to update learning about computerization were especially meaningful to the various members who attended. The ratings turned in by those attending the meeting were excellent (4.94 on a 5-point scale); typical comments included: "We need more information like this." "This is the best session I have ever heard!" "I know that I can adapt to the automation after listening to Dr. Hadler. I don't really fear the change that is going to take place." As you are aware, many librarians are extremely apprehensive as automation becomes more pervasive in libraries. You believe that the response from the attendees has indicated that some of these fears have been laid aside—thanks to Hadler. In the back of your mind, you hope that you can have Hadler back so that others may learn from her experience.
9. As president of the Subaru West dealership in Billings, Montana 59101, you want to prepare a model letter that can be sent to each person who buys a Subaru from you. Since you have a microcomputer with the software to merge the name-and-address information with the text, you plan to use a model letter. The following represents your thinking about the content of the letter: Opening—appreciation for buying; enclosure—owner identification card for customer to use each time car is serviced; service personnel—competent, factory-trained, work with modern facilities, friendly; Subaru—rates as one of

top five automobiles available; offers many years of driving pleasure, economical to operate. Closing—courtesy.

10. As credit manager of Alexander's Department Stores, you are interested in developing a letter to be sent to new residents of your area to welcome them and to encourage them to shop at your store. In order to stimulate the newcomers to try your store, you plan to offer a gift to each person presenting this letter at the Customer Service Department. You can use an idea like "to help make your new household chores a little brighter" as a reason for a gift of 10 G.E. light bulbs, which they will probably need in their new house or apartment. Of course, you are using this approach to get them into Alexander's, to get them acquainted with the store—convenient shopping, reasonable prices, a wide selection of brand name products, the place where everyone shops, etc. The nearest Alexander's is at 5431 Tipp Road in the Western Plaza Shopping Center. You also want to encourage people to apply for a charge account—so plan to enclose an application form and ask them to complete it and return it (a postage-paid envelope will also be enclosed). If the person desires, he/she may bring the completed form into the store and leave it with the Credit Department. (You want to be careful how you word this part since you do not want to give the idea that everyone who applies will be approved; you merely want them to apply; their credit record will determine whether they will actually receive the charge account privilege.) The offer for the bulbs will expire in 30 days (use today's date when writing the letter).

    Use Mr. and Mrs. Clifford Hunt, 6812 Eldon Drive, Knoxville, Tennesse 37911 for the model welcome letter.

11. In this case, you will assume the role of L. R. Daily, general manager of the Brooks Window and Door Distributors (P. O. Box 34157, Ashland, Nebraska 68003). Mr. Pat O'Brien has just been hired as the new operations manager for Brooks; you want to send a letter to all the area Brooks customers introducing him. Ideas for developing the letter of introduction include: O'Brien's responsible for all Brooks manufacturing operations and reports directly to the general manager; O'Brien is also responsible for the Materials Division, Plant Engineering, Industrial Engineering, Production Scheduling, and Quality Control areas. This position has been created to provide better support for the customers—to increase Brooks's production to meet customer needs. O'Brien has spent his entire adult life as a manager in modern manufacturing plants employing in excess of 1,000 persons; he brings much experience in manufacturing operations that are related to Brooks's needs; he has a wife and two children—a son, age 14, and a daughter, age 8. You hope that the recipients of your letter will also welcome O'Brien to the area and to Brooks.

    Use the Jefferson Company, Inc. (600 Evans Drive, Covington,

Kentucky 41011), a local customer, as you prepare your strategy and message.

12. Assume you are Steve Dover, credit manager for the Dover Construction Company (4704 Stage Road, Lincoln City, Indiana 47522). Your company will be moving to Indianapolis, Indiana (1615 H. Street, 46231) on the 30th of June (it is now May 1, 19__) and you want to notify each of your subcontractors and material suppliers of your upcoming move (21 names are on your list). You want all of the recipients of your letter to have their Application for Payment for June submitted by June 6 so that it can be processed before you make your move. You want to suggest strongly that they meet the June 6 deadline so that payment can be sent on time. Use Mr. M. T. Gardner, Mid-South Contracting Company, 204 Broad Street in Lincoln City, Indiana 47552, as the receiver of this model letter.

13. As Philip Julian, marketing consultant for ESC Computers, Inc., 500 Hill Avenue, Macon, Georgia 31203, you have designed a questionnaire to send to a carefully selected list of businesses to determine the needs of consumers in these industries who use office automation equipment and supplies. You want each recipient to complete and return the questionnaire by April 10, 19__. Since you know that many recipients do not respond to such questionnaires, you have planned to send a gift to all those who do respond—a ballpoint pen with a digital watch/calendar. The name and address of the recipient is requested on the questionnaire. You plan to use a salutation like "Dear Respondent" rather than individually typing in the name and address on each letter; you will use mailing labels for the envelopes. Therefore, you will duplicate the letter.

14. As the owner of the Odyssey Microcomputer Store (3620 Regal Boulevard, Fort Lauderdale, Florida 33304), you are in the process of preparing a letter to send to Katie Stevens (819 Lakewood Drive, Fort Lauderdale, Florida 33301), announcing that she has won first prize in the Grand Opening Contest for your new store. During the grand opening celebration, Mrs. Stevens registered for the special drawing. Her name was drawn as the winner of the grand prize: an IBM PC! All she needs do to receive her prize is to present this letter along with such identification as a driver's license or major credit card (Visa, MasterCard, etc.). Since this has been your grand opening, you want a picture of her receiving the microcomputer to use for publicity in the local newspaper, TV, and/or store bulletin board. It probably would be a good idea to request that she phone first to make an appropriate date and time for the event; too, you will want to have time to prepare the microcomputer for use and will need to know when she plans to come by to pick it up. You are very glad that she won the PC and want to give her exact instructions on how she is to receive her prize.

Figure 10.12

DATA PROCESSING MANAGEMENT ASSOCIATION

GATEWAY OF KNOXVILLE CHAPTER INC.

April 29, 19__

Dr. E. Ray Smith
Professor, Office Administration
The University of Tennessee
611 Stokely Management Center
Knoxville, Tennessee 37996

Dear Dr. Smith

Thank you for being the "drawing card" for one of the most successful seminars DPMA has ever had. The number of attendees indicates we identified a subject of interest to our members. I sincerely feel they left the seminar pleased that they had come.

Please let us know if we may ever reciprocate.

Sincerely,

Carol A. Willis

Carol A. Willis
Education Committee Chairman

CAW:tmg

THE ASSOCIATION OF DATA PROCESSING AND COMPUTER MANAGEMENT

As the program chairperson for the Administrative Management Society (AMS) (Lima, Ohio, chapter), you must write a message to the members of AMS to announce an upcoming seminar sponsored by the Lima chapter entitled "Microcomputers in the Modern Office." The special seminar will be held on September 11, 19__ (a Thursday) from one o'clock until 5 P.M. at the Holiday Inn (Central Avenue) in Lima; the topics include text processing, graphics, spreadsheet, and increasing productivity in the office. Two special speakers, Mr. Jack Waterford and Mrs. Eleanor Rose, will present the seminar—you plan to attach a sheet with biographical data about each. Each is well

Figure 10.13

How often have you been told,
"I tried to reach you but couldn't."

And you learned later that you'd missed
. . . an emergency call
. . . a social occasion
. . . a chance to catch up with an old friend.

There's no need to miss those important phone calls again.

Now with CALL WAITING and CALL FORWARDING services, you can get all your important calls . . . even when your line is busy or you're away from home.

Dear Customer:

Now you never have to worry about missing an important phone call because you're talking to someone else or you're not at home. With Call Waiting and Call Forwarding services, missing important calls can be a thing of the past for you and your family. With these great new services, you can be reached at all times.

How Call Waiting works:

Let's assumé you're talking on the telephone and someone is trying to reach you. If you have CALL WAITING service, you'll hear a gentle tone which tells you another person is trying to call you.

The person trying to call you will hear your phone ring, not a busy signal.

Then you just tell the person you're talking to that there's another call coming in, push down your receiver button for half a

known in the area for practical presentations and helpful suggestions for business professionals. The $45 fee for members should be sent with the reservation (attached form); deadline: September 1, 19__. The fee covers materials and a coffee/soft-drink break. Nonmembers are also welcome to make reservations.

16. Amanda Sumner has just learned that Mary Tempo's sister died. Amanda has worked with Mary for five years. Mary's sister lived 500 miles from her. Prepare an appropriate sympathy message.
17. Figures 10.12 to 10.16 on the following pages are real business letters. Based on the concepts you have learned thus far, evaluate their strengths and weaknesses. Rewrite them to eliminate the weaknesses.

Figure 10.13 *(continued)*

second, release it, and you are talking to the second caller. Meanwhile, your first caller is on "hold." * You can alternate between both calls, or, if you wish, continue one conversation and end the other.

It's that easy!

Imagine having CALL WAITING in an emergency. Suppose that second call were news of a family member involved in an accident – or an urgent call for help from a loved one. You'd be thankful to have programmed your phone for –

CALL WAITING!

In today's world, CALL WAITING is a necessity.

Your telephone is probably the fastest way for someone to reach you from anywhere throughout the world – provided your line isn't busy.

How many times have you tried to call home, only to run into an unwelcome busy signal? Probably more times than you are willing to count.

Perhaps your teenager is on the phone going over a homework assignment with a classmate. Maybe it is your wife on the phone with the school counselor – your husband trying to arrange a golf date – or maybe the babysitter is talking to friends. It doesn't matter who's on the telephone or for what reason; you are trying to get through, and the line is busy.

Think of how inconvenient it can be when you try to call home and someone is tying up your phone!

THE CAR WON'T START, so you call home hoping for a lift. But you get a letdown, because the line is busy ... busy ... busy ...

YOU LEFT HOME WORRYING ABOUT A SICK CHILD, and you are calling to find out if the fever is down. But each time you call, you get a busy signal.

Because CALL WAITING lets others reach you while you're on the phone, you can enjoy the freedom and convenience of talking on the telephone – without worrying that you may miss an important call.

*In the unlikely situation of a third caller trying to reach you while a second call is "on hold," the third caller would hear a busy signal.

Figure 10.13 *(continued)*

How Call Forwarding works:

Let's assume you're going to spend the afternoon with your mother, who is ill. If you have CALL FORWARDING service, you can automatically have your incoming calls transferred to your mother's phone. Before you leave home, you simply pick up your phone and dial a special code number along with your mother's phone number. Then your calls will ring on your mother's phone without your caller even being aware of it.

When you return home, you just dial another special code number and your calls will ring on your phone again.

How many times have you had to stay home, "trapped" waiting for a call?

ALL WEEK YOU HAVE BEEN PLANNING TO GO to your monthly dinner club get-together tonight. But today you receive a letter from your best friends. They'll be in town for a few hours tonight and will call you when they arrive. You cancel out on the dinner because you don't want to miss seeing your friends.

GRANDMA CALLS RIGHT AFTER LUNCH. Your family accepts her invitation to come over for a swim. You can't go because the chairman of next week's holiday cookout will call by 5 p.m. for your committee's report. You can't call him because he's running all over town to pick up supplies.

YOU'RE INVITED TO PLAY BRIDGE. But you're expecting a call from your son who left this morning on vacation. He is to call so you'll know he arrived safely. If you leave home to play bridge, you'll miss your son's call and worry if he doesn't remember to call again later.

Because CALL FORWARDING lets you transfer your calls where you can be reached, you won't have to stay home anymore and wait for an important call. You can go visiting and still "be home" when family or friends call.

Also, think of CALL FORWARDING as another security measure for your home when you're gone on vacation. Before you leave, transfer your calls to a friend or family member. That way, your phone won't go unanswered all the time you're gone.

Figure 10.13 (*concluded*)

You use CALL WAITING and CALL FORWARDING with your existing phone. No new equipment is needed.

There are no gadgets to install, no visits from telephone installers. We do everything from our central office. Once we hear from you, we'll do our best to have the additional services you request connected to your phone quickly.

Try CALL WAITING and CALL FORWARDING services and see how much convenience they give you for so little money.

You'll get a lot of convenience, peace of mind, and freedom with these new services. Yet they cost so little. Please refer to the accompanying rate sheet for information on the low monthly charge and the one-time service ordering charge. See how you can save valuable time and avoid worry for so little money. You'll not want to lose another day — or another call — without CALL WAITING and CALL FORWARDING.

How to get these two great services for your phone:

It's easy to get CALL WAITING and CALL FORWARDING services for your phone. The services are available separately, or you can save by ordering both services now. Call TOLL-FREE 1-800-633-4270 (in Alabama 1-800-292-4671) between 8 a.m. and 4:30 p.m., Central Time, Monday through Friday.

Or, if you prefer, mail us your order for these services. Just check the appropriate "Yes" box on the return card. Please be sure you have signed the order card, and included your phone number, before mailing it in the enclosed postage-paid envelope.

Add CALL WAITING and CALL FORWARDING services to your phone today. And give yourself — and your family — the most convenient phone services available.

Sincerely,

Stan Manning

Stan Manning

Figure 10.14

PHILLIPS 66 COMPANY

Dear Phillips 66 Credit Card Customer:

We hope you noticed our new neighborhood location at 7300 Middlebrook Pike which offers you:

* Phillips 66 New Superclean Unleaded Gasolines
* Four bay wand carwash
* A complete Deli facility
* 24 Hour Convenience Store
* Any size fountain drink for 49¢

In the near future, you will see some remodeling to make this facility more attractive and convenient. Additionally, we will be installing state-of-the-art equipment to serve you more efficiently. Following that - - - - - watch for our GALA GRAND OPENING!

As a Phillips 66 Credit Card Customer, there is no extra charge for using your Phillips 66 Credit Card. Bring this letter to 7300 Middlebrook Pike and receive $1.00 off on your next credit card purchase.

See you soon at MIDDLEBROOK 66.

Sincerely,

Scott Spencer

Scott Spencer
Phillips 66
Retail Representative

SS:jdk

Figure 10.15

Dear Customer:

Top quality service has always been our primary goal at Park National Bank. The requirements to provide quality retail banking services are constantly changing. In order to continue to provide high quality services, we have found it necessary to adjust our fee schedule.

The new fee schedule lists our services and the applicable service charge. Not all of our service charges have been increased, and those that have been adjusted will be implemented at different times. An effective date for each adjustment is indicated on the Schedule of Bank Services so that you may be aware of the timing of each increase. Please review this schedule to determine which of the adjustments will affect you.

Please note that the service charge for Regular Savings accounts with minimum balances less than $200 will not be assessed for minors (18 and under). If you are a minor or have children with a Regular Savings account, simply visit one of our twelve branches and inform any of the Customer Service Representatives that you would like to have the monthly service charge waived.

You may receive this notification in other account statements as we attempt to notify all our account relationships of current prices.

We regret having to raise fees at any time and have attempted to minimize the impact associated with these adjustments. We appreciate your patronage and look forward to serving all of your banking needs.

Park National Bank Post Office Box 511 Knoxville, Tennessee 37901 Telephone 615 521-5100

Figure 10.16

The Sporting News
100 STADIUM DRIVE ● MARION, OHIO 43305

ACTION DISPATCH

Dear Subscriber:

Our records show you have only two weeks left on your subscription. This is the last notice you will receive before your subscription to THE SPORTING NEWS runs out.

To renew, just check the number of issues you'd like sent on your renewal form and mail it back in the postage-paid envelope provided. We will process your order immediately.

D.B. Barrows, Jr.
Circulation Director

SP664

PART THREE

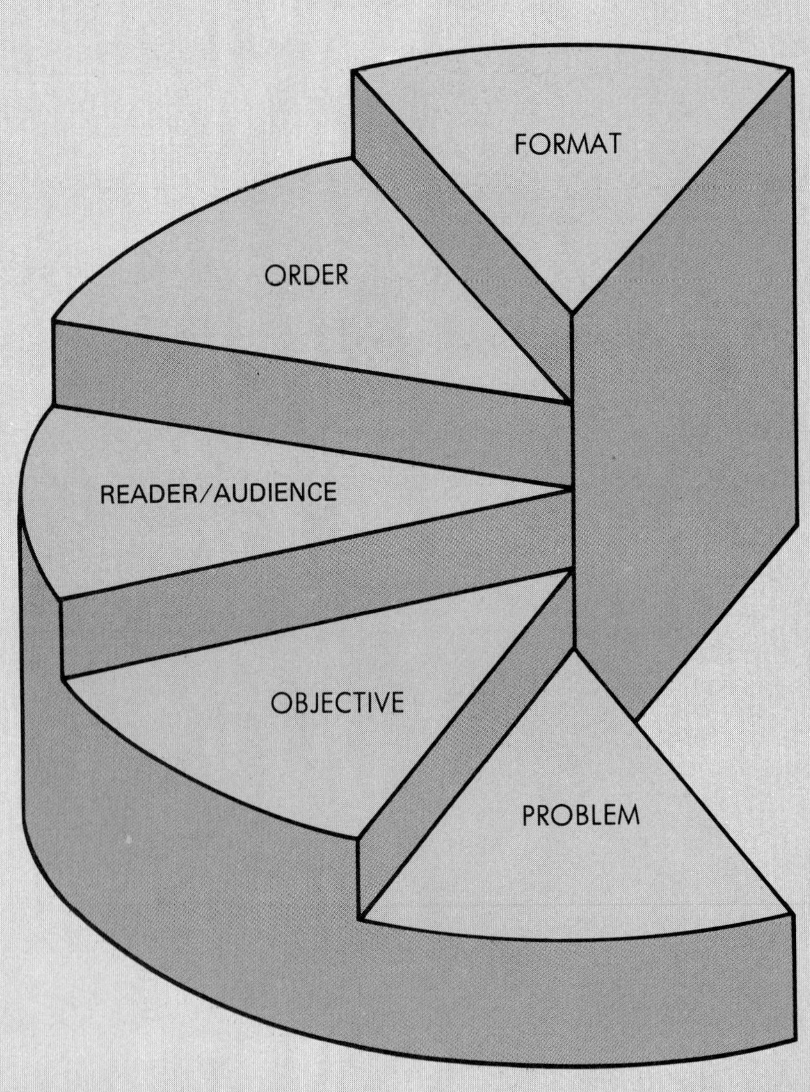

A PROCESS FOR COMMUNICATING BUSINESS REPORTS

11. INTRODUCTION TO REPORTS
12. SOURCES OF DATA
13. PRESENTATION OF DATA AND GRAPHICS
14. WRITING INFORMATIONAL REPORTS
15. INTRODUCTION TO THE ANALYTICAL REPORT
16. WRITING THE ANALYTICAL REPORT
17. ABSTRACTING

CHAPTER 11

INTRODUCTION TO REPORTS

Learning Objectives

After studying this chapter you will be able to:

- ☐ Understand the importance of writing business reports.
- ☐ Define business reports.
- ☐ Classify business reports, using the strategy for communicating in business.
- ☐ Distinguish between informational and analytical reports.
- ☐ Cite the characteristics of announcement reports, status reports, and proposal reports.
- ☐ Apply the strategy for communicating to the writing of announcement reports, status reports, and proposal reports.
- ☐ Understand the significance of using forms for writing business reports.

Importance of business reports

The written report is at the center of business activity. Most companies are organized into departments, such as production, service, finance, marketing, and administrative. Reports are one way for companies to unify their image and message in their communication with the company and outside audiences. Reports also help coordinate the activities of the departments.

Professionals who write business reports

Salespeople, accountants, personnel managers, management trainees, and other professionals write and use business reports daily. As an employee, you need to know how to digest the many reports you receive and be able to prepare clear reports for others. At times you will write reports for internal users; at other times, you'll write for external audiences.

NATURE AND DEFINITION OF BUSINESS REPORTS

Content of the business report

By its nature, a report is a record of something seen, heard, read, done, or considered. Because they are used for so many purposes, reports vary in content, organization, format, and style. For example, a departmental report showing the number of sick leave days by employee would be relatively short and direct. The content could consist of a lead-in sentence and a listing of the facts. In contrast an annual report to the stockholders of a corporation would be more formal and would contain narrative and statistical facts as well as pictures. Businesses usually want to project a high-quality image via their annual reports.

You usually base the content on an investigation or collection of facts. Facts can be obtained from a telephone survey of city residents, a search through company records, an experiment, or various other appropriate techniques. Before writing the report, classify, arrange, study, and analyze the data and information. Use a combination of narrative, tabular, and graphic presentations to communicate the meaning of the collected facts. Organizational aids for content presentation include headings and subheadings, indentations, underlining, and uppercase and lowercase letters.

As you would for memoranda and letters, select the direct or indirect approach on the basis of the objectives and your intended audience. Remember that the direct approach presents the most important idea(s) at the beginning of the message; the indirect approach, at or near the end.

Report formats

Because of the variety of uses, common report formats include a memorandum, bulletin, letter, fill-in form, formal or informal report, booklet, and special form. Memos, letters, reports, and forms are discussed in Chapter 4 on strategy for communicating. Sometimes information such as insurance coverage is communicated via a small booklet.

In this example, the booklet would contain the essentials about insurance coverage and limitations, how to process claims, the name of the contact agent, and other pertinent information. Bulletins generally announce current information such as job openings to all employees. Quite often these bulletins are placed on bulletin boards for general access. Companies that have implemented networked microcomputer systems use an electronic bulletin-board system for a rapid dissemination of employee-related information.

LEGAL / ETHICAL ISSUE

Salespeople, managers, executives and other business professionals must travel frequently as a part of their job responsibility. In addition, some of these professionals often entertain prospective and current business clients. To receive reimbursement for business-related expenses, these professionals submit *forms* to the appropriate accounting personnel of their respective companies.

Recently, someone brings to your attention the fact that one of your most valuable, trusted, and highly paid managers is padding his expense-account forms. The padding has occurred over a period of several months; the amount to date is 6 percent of the manager's salary.

You are shocked to learn of this manager's behavior. You think of several ways to handle this situation:

- ☐ Find out from the manager what really happened.
- ☐ Obtain the manager's point of view and an explanation.
- ☐ Determine the manager's past behavior and seniority.
- ☐ Determine how the actions you take will affect other employees.
- ☐ Determine the productivity level of the employee and his worth to the company.
- ☐ Study policies and procedures regarding reimbursement for business-related expenses.
- ☐ Determine the effects of your decision on the employees.
- ☐ Terminate the employee.

Assume that you are in charge of deciding what action to take to handle the unethical behavior of this manager. Would you select any of these alternatives? Are there other alternatives you would suggest? Defend your response on the basis of your beliefs about how to deal with such ethical issues. Does your defense have any legal implications?

The idea for this legal/ethical issue is based on an article by Barry Z. Posner and Warren H. Schmidt, "Ethics in American Companies: A Managerial Perspective," *Journal of Business Ethics* 6, no. 5 (July 1987), pp. 385-88.

Length (short versus long) varies according to the scope of the report. The actual makeup of a report (formal versus informal) depends on the following characteristics:

Basic characteristics of reports

- ☐ Complexity and scope of report objective.
- ☐ Relationship of report writer to the audience.

- □ Importance of report content for decision making.
- □ Permanence of the report content.
- □ Constraints of time and money.
- □ Company procedure.

Report Definition

Business reports defined

For purposes in this text, a business report is defined as *a factual presentation of data/information to fulfill an identified business objective for an intended Reader/Audience.*

Let's look at each element of this definition.

Emphasis on facts

Factual Presentation. The emphasis in reports is on facts rather than persuasion. The presentation is objective in nature; that is, it subordinates personal bias and opinions and relies on facts that are verifiable. Responses from a questionnaire survey would be recorded on a master sheet and perhaps included in the appendix of the report. In reading the data analysis, the reader could check the data from the master sheet (raw data) to verify the correctness of the summarized presentation.

Usually, you use the third person in writing reports to accomplish this goal. In some informal reports, however, you may use the first or second person. (Refer to the style chapter for a discussion of the use of the first, second, and third persons.)

Developing objectives

Identified Business Objective. You write business reports primarily to inform people about work-related matters or to analyze a situation so that people can make an informed decision. For example, assume each customer service representative in a retail department store is required to complete a daily report on returned merchandise. That report must include the name of the item returned, the reason for return, the department name, the name of the person returning the item, the date of return, and the date of purchase. The manager receives the reports from several service representatives; then he/she summarizes the results in a weekly report for the supervisor of buying. After assessing the summarized data, the supervisor makes recommendations to the buyers about defective or unsatisfactory items. The manager uses judgment and experience to formulate the recommendations.

Two purposes of business reports

This series of merchandise reports illustrates the two main purposes of most business reports: to inform and to analyze. The report from each service representative informs the manager; the manager combines the results, analyzes the results for trends, and makes recommendations to guide the buyers' future actions.

Identifying your audience

Intended Audience. Direct each report to an intended audience—internal or external. The audience may be an individual or a group to whom you are responsible. For instance, a junior manager may write a report at the request of a superior. Your relationship to the audience has a direct bearing on the degree of formality. For example, if you and the reader/audience know each other well, you would probably use a formal, impersonal style. The internal or external nature of the report also affects the degree of formality.

CLASSIFICATION OF REPORTS

How to classify reports

Because of the wide variety of uses, no single classification scheme for reports is appropriate. The most useful approach for writing purposes is to consider the content of the report as it relates to the strategy for communicating in business. For example, if you have a job opening, your Problem is to obtain a qualified person for the job. Your Objective is to inform an identified Audience (either external and/or internal) by way of an announcement. The Order would be direct, and the Format probably would be a memo or a bulletin. The identification of the strategy components aids you in selecting the appropriate format.

Figure 11.1 shows the relationship of the strategy to report characteristics. Keep in mind that the classification of reports is not cast in concrete but is relative to the perceptions of the writer. The way you classify reports is always open to interpretation, and at times the characteristics of the components may even overlap. This text uses the objective characteristic for report classification—to inform and to analyze.

Informational Reports

Informational reports defined

An *informational report presents a fact or related facts about a subject.* In informational reports, writers frequently notify the reader of policies and procedures, progress toward goals, proposals for some type of action, recommendations for future action, reports of sales, and a host of other types of business activities. For example, if you send a memo announcing a seminar on wellness, you present facts such as subject, time, place, instructor's name and qualifications, purpose, cost, etc. As the name suggests, informational reports present the facts about some particular occurrence or occasion. You make no attempt to analyze or interpret the facts. The reader will use the facts to make a decision or save for future use.

Analytical Reports

Analytical reports defined

In addition to presenting facts about a subject, an analytical report also includes an analysis of the facts. It leads the Reader from the Problem to the conclusions. The conclusions are based on the interpretation of the data. Some analytical reports go beyond the analysis of the facts and offer recommendations for future action. Findings and conclusions support these recommendations. Sometimes the writer presents implications. If you had customers fill out a 10-question form after eating at your restaurant, you would summarize the data and then draw conclusions about likes and dislikes. One implication might be that you need to change the menu items.

Figure 11.1 Relationship of Strategy for Communicating to Reports*

Problem	Objectives		Audience	Order	Format
(Why)	(What)		(Who)	(How)	(Type)
Solicited Report The problem is identified Unsolicited Report You must determine the problem	General To inform:	Specific Announcement Status report Proposal Progress report Policy statement Procedure report Minutes of a meeting Recommendation	Internal or External	Direct or Indirect Cause to effect Simple to complex Company procedure Least to most important Most to least important Time sequence	Memo Letter Report (formal/ informal) Booklet Bulletin Form
	To analyze:	Investigation Examination Feasibility study Research report			

* Report classification is open to interpretation. Characteristics may overlap.

FORMALITY AND LENGTH CHARACTERISTICS

Distinguishing features of informal reports

The distinction between the formal and informal characteristics of informational and analytical reports is not cut-and-dried. Rather, the degree of formality or informality is on a continuum between two extremes. Generally, informational reports are short and directed to people within an organization. However, some informational reports can also be long and formal depending on the problem, objectives, and audience. Examples are seminar announcements, minutes of meetings, and progress reports.

In contrast, analytical reports are generally formal and lengthy and use the direct approach; some, however, may be short and informal or short and formal or lengthy and informal and use the indirect approach. They may be directed to either internal or external audiences. The strategy components—Problem, Objectives, and Audience—determine the report makeup.

Formal reports may include some or all of these preliminary and supplementary parts:

Parts of a formal report

- □ Preliminary—title page; acknowledgments; table of contents; list of figures; list of tables.
- □ Body—initial; middle; ending.
- □ Supplementary—endnotes; bibliography; appendix.

Selection of formality on this continuum depends upon the report objective and the audience. General guidelines which apply to the writing of informational reports include these characteristics:

Guidelines for informational report

- □ Focus on one main objective—to inform.
- □ Emphasize facts.

- ☐ Contain what, who, why, when information.
- ☐ Use a positive tone.
- ☐ Use an appropriate style determined by the relationship of the writer to the audience.
- ☐ Use an appropriate Format determined by report subject and audience.
- ☐ Contain narrative, tabular, and/or graphic content.
- ☐ May contain subject, headings, and subheadings.
- ☐ Can be formal or informal and short or long.
- ☐ Can use the direct or indirect approach.

The next section of this chapter uses the strategy for communicating to illustrate various types of informational reports. In addition, the end of the chapter includes some sample forms commonly used in the simpler types of informational reports. Unique features of different reports are described with that particular report type.

ANNOUNCEMENT REPORTS

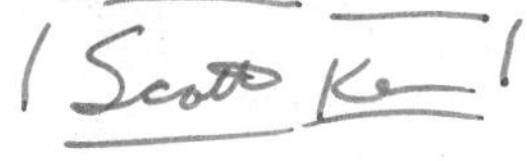

Examples of announcement reports

In business, you have numerous opportunities to write and receive announcement reports. *An announcement informs readers about something.* Some examples are reports dealing with prices and services, honors, favorable and good news, resignations, employment of key people in the organization, or changes in company policy.

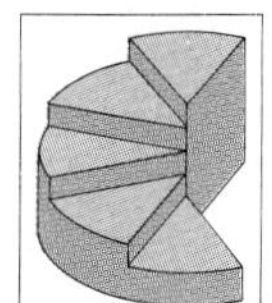

STRATEGY: ANNOUNCING A CHANGE IN MANAGEMENT

You are managing partner of Georgetown Village Apartments, a large complex of 50 two- and three-bedroom apartments located in Athens, Georgia. For 10 years, Mrs. Beverly Bradshaw served as resident manager of the apartments. Mrs. Bradshaw is retiring on May 1, 19... Her husband, Jesse, works for a company in Athens; he, too, plans to retire on the same date. They will continue living in their current apartment.

June and Russell Calhoun will become the new resident managers on May 1. Their present apartment, Number 119-1, will become the new office location for Georgetown Village. The Calhouns' telephone number is 353-2787. Apartment residents need to call this number to conduct apartment business or to report maintenance problems. As managing partner of the apartment complex, you must inform all the residents of the change in management.

PROBLEM

Residents do not know who is filling Mrs. Bradshaw's position.

OBJECTIVES

General: To notify the residents regarding a change in resident management.

Specific: To announce the new management team.

To indicate the location and telephone number of the new managers.

To announce Mrs. Bradshaw's retirement.

To welcome the new managers.

To wish the Bradshaws a happy retirement.

To indicate the retirement date.

To indicate the date the new management team will begin.

READER/AUDIENCE

Characteristics: Several residents know the Bradshaws personally.

Some residents are professional people, including lawyers, professors, and accountants.

Some residents are law and business students who attend the local university.

Some residents are retirees.

Reaction: Some residents will be surprised since they are unaware of Mrs. Bradshaw's impending retirement.

All residents have a high regard for Mrs. Bradshaw and will hate to lose her as manager.

Residents want the Bradshaws to have a good retirement.

Some residents will be apprehensive of the new management.

ORDER

OVERALL MESSAGE: DIRECT

You want the readers to know at the beginning of the report that Mrs. Bradshaw is retiring, so you begin with the direct approach.

SPECIFIC OBJECTIVES:

1. To announce Mrs. Bradshaw's retirement.
2. To indicate the retirement date.
3. To announce the new management team.
4. To indicate the date the new management team will begin.

5. To indicate the location and telephone number of the new managers.
6. To wish the Bradshaws a happy retirement.
7. To welcome the new managers.

FORMAT

MEMO (ANNOUNCEMENT)

You select the memo Format since your plans are to hand deliver copies to each of the respective apartments and to drop them in the mail slots of each apartment. The audience is within the "company."

Now that you have determined your strategy, you complete your first attempt at writing the report.

```
This memo informs you that a change in management is about to occur at
Georgetown Village Apartments. You will be interested to know that Mrs.
Beverly Bradshaw will retire on May 1, 19__.

Note these changes:
  New managers: June and Russell Calhoun
  When:         May 1, 19__
  Where:        Apartment 119-1
  Telephone no.: 353-2787 (call for apartment business and maintenance)
```

You reread your communication. Did you accomplish your objectives? For the most part, you did stay with the facts. You announced the retirement date, new management team, effective date, location and telephone number of the new manager. You failed, however, to wish Mrs. Bradshaw a happy retirement or to welcome the new managers. You conclude from the first draft that, if you just stay with facts, the communication sounds impersonal; and the tone is curt. You begin to rewrite the communication with a more personal tone. You decide to begin with a statement recognizing Mrs. Bradshaw's years of service as manager and her impending retirement date.

```
After serving as a resident manager for 10 years, Mrs. Bradshaw will retire
on May 1, 19__. Happily, Beverly and Jesse will continue to live at
Georgetown Village Apartments and enjoy a well-deserved private life.
```

Your rewrite looks fine. You have recognized Mrs. Bradshaw's many years of service, and you are glad that she and her husband will continue to live at the apartment complex. You have also achieved a positive tone and have implied a change in management.

Now you continue your communication to include the when, who, and what regarding the other specific objectives:

Figure 11.2. Announcement Report

TO:	All Residents
FROM:	Your name Managing Partner Georgetown Village Apartments
DATE:	April 15, 19__
SUBJECT:	Change in Management

After serving as resident manager for 10 years, Mrs. Bradshaw will retire on May 1, 19__. ~~Happily~~ However, Beverly and Jesse will continue to live at Georgetown Village Apartments and enjoy a well-deserved private life.

Effective May 1, 19__, June and Russell Calhoun will become the new managers. The Calhouns live in Apartment 119-1. Continue to use the same telephone number, 353-2787, when you need service.

Join me in welcoming the Calhouns as the new managers and wishing Mrs. Bradshaw a happy retirement.

Effective May 1, 19__, June and Russell Calhoun will become the new managers. The Calhouns live in Apartment 119-1. Continue to use the same telephone number, 353-2787, when you need service.

Your rewrite answers these questions:

When: May 1, 19__

Who: June and Russell Calhoun

What: Apartment and telephone number for receiving service

You want to end your communication accentuating the positive and maintaining a personal tone. You draft several rewrites and finalize your thoughts in this manner:

Join me in welcoming the Calhouns as the new managers and wishing Mrs. Bradshaw a happy retirement.

See Figure 11.2 for the completed report.

STATUS REPORT

Status report defined with examples

A *status report presents data or information about the present condition of some business situation,* such as the number of sales completed, advertising costs, level of inventory, or status of action items. The main objective of the status report is to inform the reader about selected facts at the current time. The status report assists the reader with decision making in the organization.

These are the unique characteristics of the status report:

Characteristics of status reports

- □ Is temporary in nature.
- □ Generally uses the third person.
- □ Generally responds to a request.
- □ Generally reports on an ongoing project.

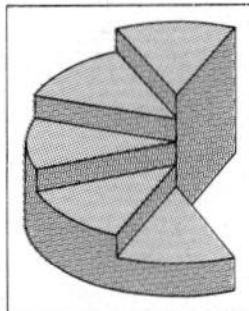

STRATEGY: SALES STATUS REPORT

Aleen DeMarco, manager of Volunteer Realty Company, wants to know which residential houses have been slow selling. She also wants to analyze why some of those houses are slow in selling. She thinks some of them are remaining on the market too long. Possible causes, she suspects, could be that some of the houses have an undesirable location, are overpriced, or have limited features. She asks her assistant, Lahr Huff, to extrapolate data on houses which have been on the market for three months or more. Specifics needed include:

House location (NE, SW, SE, NW, Central).
Seller's name.
List price.
Number of months listed.
Square feet in the house.
Number of bedrooms.
Number of baths.
House type (ranch or colonial; multilevel or one-level).

Huff knows he must access the property listings database file and use the criteria selection menu for receiving a printout on unsold homes which have been on the market for three months or more.

PROBLEM

Lack of selected data on slow-selling homes.

OBJECTIVE

General: To extrapolate data on unsold houses which have remained on the market for three months or more and prepare a report for DeMarco.

Specific: To provide data about each house:

House location (NE, SE, SW, NW, Central).
Seller's name.
List price.
Number of months listed.
Square feet in house.
Number of bedrooms.
Number of baths.
House type (ranch or colonial; multilevel or one-level).

READER/AUDIENCE

Characteristics: Your supervisor.
Well known.
One-to-one relationship.
Reaction: Anxious to get facts.
Will use for decision making.

ORDER

OVERALL: DIRECT
The audience is Huff's immediate supervisor; she has requested specific facts about each slow-selling house. Therefore, the direct order is appropriate.

SPECIFIC OBJECTIVES

1. To identify subject—listing of slow-selling houses.
2. To provide specific facts:
   Number of months listed.
   House location (NE, SE, SW, NW, Central).
   List price.
   Square feet in house.
   Number of bedrooms.
   Number of baths.
   House type
   (ranch or colonial; multilevel or one-level).
   Seller's name.

The order of facts is according to DeMarco's need in making a decision about each. If several unsold houses cluster in one geographic location, your firm may implement other marketing strategies.

Figure 11.3. Status report showing slow-selling houses

TO: Aleen DeMarco
FROM: Lahr Huff
DATE: May 10, 19__
SUBJECT: Slow-Selling Houses

Here is a listing of the slow-selling houses (those listed at least three months) as you requested:

Months listed	Site	Price	Square feet	Bed-rooms	Baths	Type	Seller's name
14	SE	$ 69,000	1,100	2	1	Brick	Andrews
11	SE	41,500	920	2	1½	Brick	Coder
7	SW	124,500	2,050	4	3	Colonial	Pope
7	NW	125,000	2,225	4	2	Brick	Gordon
6	SW	130,400	2,100	4	3	Contemporary	Corbitt
6	NW	350,000	4,700	5	3½	Contemporary	Reed
5	SE	49,900	1,000	3	2	Split level	Carlson
4	SE	45,700	950	3	1½	Brick	White
4	SE	54,800	1,100	3	2	Brick	Thompson
3	NW	205,500	3,050	4	2¾	Early American	Cochran

FORMAT

MEMO

Since this is an internal status report, Huff selects the memo format using a tabular form for presenting the facts.

Huff then generates the status report using the data from the database listings file. Figure 11.3 shows this report. Note the phrase "as you requested" in the opening statement. This phrase establishes the authorization to prepare the report and also gives evidence of the assignment completion.

PROPOSAL REPORTS

Proposal reports defined

A proposal is another type of informational report. *A proposal suggests, offers or declares a plan of action;* the reader/audience may accept, modify, or reject the proposal. Even though the major thrust of the proposal report is to inform, the facts are presented in a persuasive manner. For example, you may propose to retrain professional staff with supporting statements to justify the costs. You would also include estimated expenditures. Or you may write a proposal for renting company cars rather than owning them.

Other examples of proposals are the result of national, state, and/or local governmental projects where requests for grant proposals (RFPs) are regularly announced. Some agencies use special forms; others do not. The proposal Format depends on the funding agency requirements, the type of project, the size and type of the funding agency, and whether the agency is private or public. Each proposal is unique since the funding agency dictates the proposal guidelines.

These are the unique features of the proposal report:

Characteristics of proposal reports

- ☐ Answers a need.
- ☐ Includes a proposed plan of action.
- ☐ Describes implementation strategies or procedures.
- ☐ Delineates expected outcomes.
- ☐ Includes an estimated budget.
- ☐ Projects a time schedule for completion.
- ☐ Discusses the qualifications of key personnel.
- ☐ Describes evaluation measures used to support outcomes.

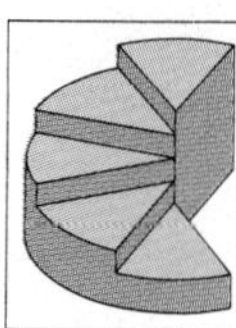

STRATEGY: A BID PROPOSAL

Culberson and Watson is a consulting firm specializing in information systems analysis and design. Recently, a 12-lawyer firm asked them to submit a bid proposal. So representatives of Culberson and Watson met with the co-owners of the law firm to gather preliminary information about the firm's needs for an information system. During the meeting, the two consulting partners took notes which they would use later when writing a bid proposal offering their services to the law firm. They also interviewed personnel to discover which operations are perceived to be problem areas. The following contains most of the information they gathered:

A successful law firm (Knief, Martinek, and Fain) in Macon, Georgia, has been experiencing some internal problems. The firm houses two separate law practices. Knief, Martinek, and Fain (KMF) specialize in general legal cases, while Rosenthal, Price, and Walden (RPW) specialize in asbestos and black lung legal cases. Knief and Rosenthal are co-owners of the 12-lawyer firm.

The breakdown of clerical and support staff is as follows: KMF has a legal secretary, an office manager, a clerk-typist, and a paralegal. RPW has two legal secretaries, a paralegal, a records management clerk, and an administrative assistant. KMF and RPW share a bookkeeper, a person to run errands and do copying, a word-processing specialist, and a receptionist.

Some very strong personalities work at KMF and RPW. This is true not only for the lawyers but also for the clerical and support staff as well. The workload is heavy for all personnel within KMF and RPW. Seemingly, everybody just goes along doing his/her own thing though griping, pressure, and stress seem to be common. The clerical and support staffs accumulate much overtime; turnover has increased significantly during the past year.

Oftentimes, KMF calls on RPW personnel for clerical and support services during rush jobs; likewise, RPW personnel call on KMF employees. But within this firm (which started out as a family business), all jobs are "rush."

Complaints among the lawyers include the following: "I cannot seem to get access to the word-processing specialist; it seems the other lawyers get their reports done before me." Price and Knief say, "The bookkeeper should not be keeping personal bank account information for Martinek and Fain." Walden, Martinek, and Price say that "they are not clear about their roles within the firm." According to some of the lawyers, "Knief wants to run the entire show."

The following are typical of comments among the clerical and support staff: "They're about to work me to death," says the word-processing specialist; the records management clerk vows, "The management of records is a horror story. They even have records on the floor." The errand runner loves his work, but lawyers, clerical, and support staff people complain that "he can never be found."

The bookkeeper says she really likes working for the firm. She contends that "freedom and flexibility in the firm are just great." The receptionist is rather negative: "None of the personnel think my job is important; it is like pulling teeth just to get someone to relieve me for breaks and lunch." The paralegals want to run the show, according to many of the clerical and support staff members. One of the most frequent complaints from the clerical and support staff is that they do not seem to know to whom they are responsible and exactly what their jobs entail.

When the consultants returned to their offices, they compared notes. Sorting through the notes and observations, they were able to visualize the types of problems within the law firm and, at least tentatively, frame their approach to several of these problems. Having been asked to submit a bid proposal to the firm, they plan their strategy for communicating.

PROBLEM

Worker morale at KMF and RPW is not conducive to productivity.

The consultants realize that a number of weaknesses related to worker morale and management are apparent at the law firm. Both are confident they can help the co-owners eliminate or reduce some of these problems.

OBJECTIVES

The consultants recognize that they need to resolve a number of issues and so proposed to examine several different factors in the firm's operations. Their preliminary meeting with members of the firm helped them identify several specific objectives.

General: To provide a framework for the proposed study.

Specific: To state the overall goal of the proposed study: an assessment of personnel, equipment, and procedures.

To identify the factors to be analyzed in the study:

- Determine whether automated equipment is being fully utilized.
- Determine which would be most appropriate—an electronic filing/retrieval system or a state-of-the-art manual system.
- Study work loads of clerical and support personnel.
- Study paper flow for possible improvements.
- Identify duties performed by lawyers.
- Identify duties performed by clerical and support staff.
- Document needs of lawyers as they pertain to origination, distribution, storage, and retrieval.
- Measure job satisfaction as it relates to human problems in administration.
- Develop organizational chart for the firm.
- Inventory equipment.

To indicate the best procedures and methods to use for conducting the study.

To indicate how much time is necessary to conduct the study.

To estimate the costs of conducting the study.

To refer to preliminary meeting and the request for a formal proposal.

To demonstrate how the firm would benefit from the study.

To request approval from the firm's co-owners to conduct the study.

Both consultants recognize that their tentative objectives are extensive. Nevertheless, they believe that the law firm will accept the proposal. In their preliminary discussions, they sensed that the co-owners were willing to work closely with the consulting team to eliminate problems. Their next step was to analyze their audience.

READER/AUDIENCE

Characteristics: Professionals—lawyers.
Have already made contact.
Primary—Knief and Rosenthal, co-owners.
Secondary—other lawyers and selected support personnel.

Reaction: Favorable.

The consultants already know much about the characteristics of their readers. Knief and Rosenthal are recognized in the Southeast for their expertise in the practice of law. Knief and Rosenthal are graduates of two of the country's top law schools, and each has practiced law for about 20 years. Knief and Rosenthal are also known for recruiting to their firm graduates from highly recognized law schools. Generally speaking, the potential primary and secondary readers are professional, legal experts, and have many years of experience. Thus, if other lawyers in the firm read the consultants' proposal, they will be able to identify with many of the characteristics of Knief and Rosenthal.

The reactions of Knief, Rosenthal, and the other 10 lawyers are a bit more difficult to predict. Colleagues think Knief is rather conservative. The proposed cost factor is sure to concern her. Rosenthal, on the other hand, will probably be pleased and welcome the services of the consulting team. Other lawyers, if they read the proposal, might make comments but will probably defer to the decision of their superiors, Knief and Rosenthal.

ORDER

OVERALL: DIRECT

Direct order is appropriate since the proposal has already been requested. The direct proposal will get to the point and save time.

SPECIFIC OBJECTIVES

1. To refer to preliminary meeting and request for proposal.
2. To state the overall goal of the proposed study.
3. To identify the factors for analysis:

   Personnel:

   Develop organizational chart.

   Identify duties performed by lawyers.

   Identify duties performed by administrative and clerical personnel.

   Evaluate work load of administrative and clerical personnel.

   Measure job satisfaction.

   Procedures:

   Document needs of lawyers.

   Identify and evaluate paper flow.

   Equipment:

   Conduct inventory.

   Evaluate use of automated equipment.

   Study present filing system and recommend appropriate system (electronic or manual).
4. To identify benefits for the firm resulting from the study.

Figure 11.4. Proposal Report—Letter Format

CULBERSON & WATSON
MANAGEMENT CONSULTANTS
407 Peachtree Blvd. Atlanta, Georgia 30317

August 30, 19__

Atty. D. D. Knief
Atty. R. A. Rosenthal
Attorneys-at-Law
224 Atlanta Court
Macon, GA 32109

Dear Attys. Knief and Rosenthal:

External audience

Presents a need

After we visited your office and interviewed you and your colleagues, you requested a bid proposal outlining the specifics of a study of your office operations. Based on our visit, discussions with you and others, and a tour of your offices, our proposal is presented as follows.

The overall goal would be to conduct a current needs assessment of personnel, equipment, and procedures within KMF and RPW. The scope of the study would include the following:

Proposed plan of action

Personnel
- Develop organizational chart.
- Identify duties performed by lawyers.
- Identify duties performed by administrative and clerical personnel.
- Study work load of administrative and clerical personnel.
- Measure job satisfaction.

Procedures
- Document needs of lawyers.
- Identify and evaluate paper flow.

Equipment
- Conduct inventory.
- Evaluate use of automated equipment.
- Study present filing system and recommend appropriate system (electronic or manual).

Convincing tone/outcomes

Improved worker morale will result in increased productivity. With our recommendations, your firm can realize improvements in organization, job design, and productivity.

Figure 11.4 (*concluded*)

Atty. D. D. Knief
Atty. R. A. Rosenthal 2 August 30, 19__

Implementation strategies and procedures

Evaluation measures

We will collect the data by personal interviews with all lawyers and support personnel. The Minnesota Satisfaction Attitude Questionnaire and the Position Analysis Questionnaire will be used to determine job satisfaction and role definitions of each position in the firm. Both are nationally validated tests and are widely used for the type of services needed.

Budget

We suggest this project start by approximately September 15 and end by December 31, 19__. The fee for the total project is $5,000.

"You" attitude throughout

After you have had an opportunity to study our proposal, may we have your approval to begin? We look forward to working with you.

Sincerely,

D. Dan Culberson
Management Consultant

Jeffrey A. Watson
Management Consultant

Qualifications of key personnel

DDC/JAW/DC
Enc. (Qualifications of Personnel)

5. To indicate what procedures and methods to use to conduct the study.
6. To indicate the time needed to complete the study.
7. To indicate cost of conducting the study.
8. To request co-owners' approval to conduct the study.

Specific Objectives 1 and 2 fulfill the direct order concept. Because Specific Objective 3 covers a number of factors, it is a good idea to classify and group these factors in some way. Placing related goals together makes it easier for the reader to understand them and for the investigator to analyze acquired data. Specific Objectives 3 through 6 address what, who, how, and when. These four objectives are appropriately grouped together. Cost isn't mentioned until the end of the communication; that placement is good psychology, especially under these circumstances.

FORMAT

LETTER

Based on their initial draft and their list of objectives, the consultants know that the document will be at least two pages long. They may use one of two styles: a short report with a cover letter, or a letter incorporating the proposal itself. They select the letter Format for the proposal report since the audience is external to the company.

Figure 11.4 shows the final draft of the proposal report they sent to the co-owners of the KMF and RPW law firm.

Note that the proposal report ends with positive comments. The consultants want the lawyers to have enough time to study the proposal, yet they say, "We look forward to working with you." Such a positive approach reduces any of the prospective clients' negative thoughts about the scope and cost of the proposal.

FORMS FOR REPORTING DATA

In routine business matters, professionals frequently use forms to transmit data. Figures 11.5, 11.6, and 11.7 illustrate how one may use a form to get business data. The content of each form relates to the specific objectives for each form.

Use of forms for business writing

Figures 11.5 and 11.6 show how an independent insurance agency transmits information to one or several offices represented by the agency. Forms provide rapid communication of vital data between the firms. Forms standardize data transmission, and so they help improve productivity. Data from forms can be computerized and thus provide a simpler means of interpreting the set of data.

Figure 11.7 illustrates a form used by a business consultant to record time and activity spent on a client's project. Note the different parts of the form and

Figure 11.5

Independent Insurance Agent

ATHENS INSURANCE CENTER, INC.
P. O. BOX 6545
ATHENS, GA 30604
353-7811

AGENT/COMPANY MEMO

DATE ______________________

ATTENTION ______________________

TO: ______________________

REFERENCE

INSURED ______________________
COMPANY & POLICY NO. ______________________
CLAIM FILE NO. ______________________
TYPE OF CLAIM ______________________
YOUR LETTER DATED ______________________
EFFECTIVE DATE OF CHANGE ______________________
REPLY REQUESTED PRIOR TO ______________________

CHECK HERE

☐ UNDERWRITING DEPARTMENT

- ☐ ENDORSE AS REQUESTED BELOW
- ☐ ☐ ADD ☐ DELETE LOSS PAYABLE CLAUSE AS SHOWN BELOW
- ☐ ☐ RENEW AS IS ☐ RENEW AS SHOWN BELOW ☐ SEND RENEWAL QUOTE POLICY EXPIRES ______
- ☐ ATTACHED ARE THE ITEMS LISTED BELOW
- ☐ CHANGE SCHEDULE AS SHOWN BELOW
- ☐ ISSUE CERTIFICATE OF INSURANCE TO PARTY SHOWN BELOW
- ☐ ASSIGN POLICY AS SHOWN BELOW
- ☐ SEND CLAIMS BREAKDOWN FOR PERIOD SHOWN BELOW
- ☐ ☐ INCREASE ☐ DECREASE AS SHOWN BELOW
- ☐ CANCEL ATTACHED POLICY ☐ S.R. ☐ P.R. ☐ FLAT
- ☐ SEND CANCELLATION NOTICE FOR REASON STATED BELOW
- ☐ POLICY CORRECTED BY ERASURE AS SHOWN BELOW
- ☐ BIND COVERAGE FOR ______ DAYS AS SHOWN BELOW
- ☐ COMPLETED APPLICATION ATTACHED

☐ PRODUCTION OR ENGINEERING DEPARTMENT

- ☐ ☐ SEND BUILDING APPRAISAL ☐ UPDATE APPRAISAL
- ☐ INSPECT RISK TO CHECK ☐ PUBLISHED RATES ☐ SCHEDULED RATES ☐ PROPER CLASSIFICATIONS

CHECK HERE

☐ CLAIMS DEPARTMENT

- ☐ CLAIM REPORT ATTACHED
- ☐ REPAIR ☐ ESTIMATES ☐ BILLS ATTACHED
- ☐ MEDICAL ☐ REPORT ☐ BILLS ATTACHED
- ☐ ENCLOSED ARE THE ITEMS LISTED BELOW
- ☐ SIGNED PROOF OF LOSS ATTACHED
- ☐ CLAIMANT'S CORRESPONDENCE ATTACHED
- ☐ FIRST REPORT SENT TO YOU ON ______
- ☐ PLEASE ADVISE STATUS OF CLAIM
- ☐ MAKE CHECK PAYABLE TO ______
- ☐ MAIL CHECK TO: ☐ AGENT ☐ INSURED ☐ REPAIR SHOP ☐ MORTGAGEE
- ☐ ______

fold ← back

☐ ACCOUNTING DEPARTMENT

- ☐ CORRECT COMMISSION AS SHOWN BELOW
- ☐ ITEMS BELOW WERE PAID ON DATE SHOWN
- ☐ ITEMS SHOWN BELOW ARE NOT INCLUDED IN OUR REMITTANCE FOR THE REASONS INDICATED BELOW
- ☐ ______
- ☐ ______

fold ← in

☐ VEHICLE CHANGE **☐ SUPPLY DEPT.: SEND ITEMS LISTED BELOW**

AUTO ADDED	YEAR	MAKE, BODY STYLE & MODEL	VEHICLE IDENTIFICATION NO.	CU/HP	SYMBOL
	PURCHASE DATE & COST	NEW/USED	CLASS CODE	RATE FACTOR	ANNUAL MILEAGE	TERRITORY

★ LOSS PAYEE NAME & ADDRESS

AUTO DELETED	YEAR	MAKE, BODY STYLE & MODEL	VEHICLE IDENTIFICATION NO.

MESSAGE

SIGNED

SAVE envelope addressing · fold at arrows to fit standard #10 window envelope · OHIO ENVELOPE CO., INC. · RIDGELY, MARYLAND 21685 · CAT. NO. 430-2 PART

Figure 11.6

SET TAB STOPS AT ARROWS

acord

CANCELLATION REQUEST / POLICY RELEASE

NAME AND ADDRESS OF AGENCY	COMPANY	
	KIND OF POLICY	
NAME AND MAILING ADDRESS OF INSURED	POLICY NUMBER	AGENCY CODE
	EFFECTIVE DATE/HOUR OF CANCELLATION MONTH DAY YEAR — HOUR OF CANCELLATION	
	POLICY PERIOD MONTH DAY YEAR TO MONTH DAY YEAR	

☐ CANCELLATION REQUEST (Policy attached)

☐ POLICY RELEASE (Policy not attached)

RELEASE STATEMENT

The undersigned agrees that:

The above referenced policy is lost, destroyed or being retained.

No claims of any type will be made against the Insurance Company under this policy for losses which occur after the date of cancellation shown above.

Any premium adjustment will be made in accordance with the terms and conditions of the policy.

WITNESS ______ DATE ______ SIGNATURE NAMED INSURED ______ DATE ______

WITNESS ______ DATE ______ SIGNATURE NAMED INSURED ______ DATE ______

☐ LIEN HOLDER ☐ MORTGAGEE ☐ LOSS PAYEE ______ AUTHORIZED SIGNATURE ______ TITLE ______ DATE ______

☐ LIEN HOLDER ☐ MORTGAGEE ☐ LOSS PAYEE ______ AUTHORIZED SIGNATURE ______ TITLE ______ DATE ______

FOR AGENCY/COMPANY USE

REASON FOR CANCELLATION

☐ NOT TAKEN

☐ REQUEST OF INSURED

☐ REWRITTEN

COMPANY ______

POLICY NUMBER ______ DATE ______

☐ OTHER (Identify)

METHOD OF CANCELLATION

☐ FLAT

☐ SHORT RATE

☐ PRO RATA

FULL TERM PREMIUM $	UNEARNED FACTOR	RETURN PREMIUM $

☐ PREMIUM CALCULATION SUBJECT TO AUDIT — PRODUCER'S SIGNATURE ______ DATE ______

ACORD 35 (11-77) COMPANY COPY

INSTRUCTIONS TO

☐ INSURED

☐ LOSS PAYEE

☐ MORTGAGEE

☐ LIEN HOLDER

☐ COMPANY

Figure 11.7

FORM MAS 70 12-78

MAS ENGAGEMENT STATUS REPORT

Client ______________________ **Engagement Number** ______________________

Supervising Partner ______________________ **Four Weeks Ended** ______________________

No.	Engagement Milestone	Completion Date	Met? Yes	Met? No
	Current Period			
	Next Period	**Scheduled Dates**		

Current Period Charges	Hourly Rate	Hours Charged	Services	Expenses
Totals as Shown on EO Run of				
Estimated Charges to Date				

Estimate To Complete And Billing Status

	To Date	Estimate To Complete	Total at Completion	Quote/Estimate Given Client
Services				
Expenses				
Total				
Billed Through		Percent of Std. Per. Eng. Memo Suggested Change		
Unbilled				
Suggested Billing				

Dates of Latest Discussions with Key Client Executives: ______________________

	Yes	No
1. Are any fee problems anticipated?		
2. Are scope or staffing requirements changing?		
3. Are any other problems foreseen?		

Prepared By:	Date	Reviewed By:	Date

the types of data that you can summarize on one sheet of paper. A form is only one part of the strategy for communicating; you will have an opportunity in later chapters to apply the strategy to the development of forms.

SUMMARY

Business reports are one way for companies to unify their image and message in their communication with company personnel and outside groups. Because they are used for so many purposes, reports vary in content, organization, format, and style. Before a report is written, the data are classified, arranged, studied, and analyzed. Reports are presented using a combination of narrative, tabular, and graphic aids. You can select the direct (most important idea near beginning) or indirect (most important idea near end) approach based on the objectives and your intended audience. Memos, letters, forms, and formal or informal reports are among the common Formats. The length varies according to the scope of the report. Business reports are defined as a factual presentation of data/information to fulfill an identified business objective for an intended reader/audience. The two main purposes of reports are *to inform* and *to analyze*. So, in this textbook, reports are classified as either informational or analytical. The strategy for communicating is applied throughout the chapter.

An informational report presents facts or related facts about a subject. In informational reports, writers frequently notify the reader of policies and procedures, progress toward goals, proposals for some type of action, recommendations for future use, quarterly sales, and other types of business activities.

An announcement informs readers about something. Common types of announcements deal with prices and services, honors, favorable and good news, resignations, changes in key people in the organization, or changes in company policy. The main purpose is to inform.

A status report presents data or information about the present condition of some business situation, such as the number of sales completed, advertising costs, level of inventory, or status of action items. The main objective is to inform the reader about selected facts at the current time. The status report helps the reader in making decisions about the project.

A proposal report suggests, offers, or declares a plan of action; the reader/audience may accept, modify, or reject the proposal. Even though the major thrust of the proposal report is to inform, the facts are presented in a persuasive manner.

Analytical reports present facts about a subject and include an analysis of the facts; informational reports just present the facts. Analytical reports lead the reader from the problem to the conclusions based on an interpretation of the data. Analytical reports may include recommendations for future action. These recommendations are supported by findings and conclusions. Analytical reports are generally formal and lengthy although some may be informal and relatively short. The report makeup depends on the Objectives, the Audience, and the Problem investigated.

In routine business matters, professionals frequently use forms to transmit data. Forms provide rapid communication of vital data between/among employees and other firms. Forms standardize data transmission, and so they help improve productivity.

END-OF-CHAPTER ACTIVITIES

DISCUSSION

1. Why are reports important to businesses?
2. Define a report.
3. What characteristics determine the actual makeup of a report?
4. What are the two main purposes of reports? How do these two reports differ?
5. How does the strategy for communicating relate to report writing?
6. Contrast the content of an announcement report and a status report.
7. How does a proposal report differ from other types of informational reports?
8. Why are forms important to businesses? Explain.

ACTIVITIES

9. Study the financial status report in Figure 11.8. Using the strategy for communicating and the characteristics for writing status reports, answer these questions:

   Group I—Strategy
   - *a.* What problem does this report address?
   - *b.* What is the general objective?
   - *c.* What are the specific objectives?
   - *d.* Who is the intended audience?
   - *e.* Is the order direct or indirect?
   - *f.* What type format does this report represent?

   Group II—Characteristics
   - *a.* What time period does this temporary report cover?
   - *b.* Is the report intended for an internal or external audience?
   - *c.* Did the report concentrate on factual data?
   - *d.* How limited is the content of the report?
   - *e.* Do you think this report was requested?

Figure 11.8

Price Real Estate
Property Management Division

Monthly Financial Status Report
Account: Southern Royale Partnership

Date: May 1987

Beginning balance:	$5,365.28	
Income: Mortgage Payments	Current Month	Year-to-date
Schmidt: Meadowlark Apts.	$3,407.63	$17,038.15
Nelson: Pleasantview Apts.	$406.92	$2,034.60
Total income	$3,814.55	$19,072.75
Total available funds	$9,179.83	
Expenses		
J. Abbott	$1,609.24	
Bookkeeping	$25.00	
Payments to partners	$1,637.66	
Price Real Estate	$527.51	
Total Expense	$3,799.41	$18,936.24
Reserves	$3,200.00	
Net income	$2,180.42	$10,420.82
Disbursements of this month's net income		
Price Real Estate	$532.05	$2,515.87
Total to partners	$1,648.37	$7,904.95
Cross, P.	$412.09	$1,976.24
Markham, L.	$412.09	$1,976.24
Miller, Z.	$412.09	$1,976.24
Paxton, D.	$247.26	$1,185.74
Harrison, N.	$164.84	$790.50

Notes:
1. Reserves include next month's Abbott payment of $1,609.24.

f. How lengthy is the report?
g. What other formats might be applicable for this type report?

10. Study the proposal report in Figure 11.9. Using the strategy for communicating and characteristics for writing proposal reports, answer the same questions as in Group I of question 9 above. In addition, answer these questions:
    a. What need does this report answer?
    b. Does the report have a convincing tone?
    c. Does the report apply the "you" attitude?
    d. What is the proposed plan of action?
    e. What are the expected outcomes?
    f. What is the estimated budget?
    g. Is the audience internal or external to the organization?

Figure 11.9

November 2, 19___

Dr. Sandra Price
Oakwood College
Oakwood Road
Huntsville, AL 35896

Dear Dr. Price:

The following information is provided per your phone request of November 2, 19___.

		Maintenance
1 forms tractor	\$ 250 less 15% = \$ 212.50	\$180/2nd yr.
1 sheet feeder	\$1550 less 15% = \$1317.50	\$180/2nd yr.
1 envelope feeder	\$1495 less 15% = \$1270.75	\$180/2nd yr.

SuperCalc \$295 price of one for sixteen originals with documentation.

Other purchases are guaranteed at same prices for 12 months as outlined in TDS's winning bid specifications; however, software purchases must be considered separately according to quantity orders and may or may not qualify for the same discount granted for your sixteen original systems.

Sincerely,

William B. Hill
Regional Manager

js

CORPORATE HDQTRS.

Parklane Bldg.	Osborne Office Center	Executive Park	Nonconnoh Office Ctr.	2227 Drake Ave.
6200 Maryland Way	Suite 102	D-415 9111 Cross Park Drive	2603 Corporate Avenue E.	Suite 11
Brentwood, TN 37027	Chattanooga, TN 37411	Knoxville, TN 37923	Memphis, TN 38132	Huntsville, AL 35805
615/373-3836	615/899-5500	615/690-5544	901/346-0088	205/882-1300

11. Collect a variety of announcement, status, and proposal reports from business, industry, or government (at least one sample of each type). Share these reports in a class discussion activity. Explain how these reports coincide with the characteristics and strategy components described in this chapter.
12. Dr. Joseph Steller is responsible for planning a conference for 10,000 executives attending the annual Management for Executives Conference to be held in San Francisco, from April 10 to April 13. As a convenience to the participants, he has decided to provide a shuttle

bus service to and from the major hotels in the downtown area and the Convention Center. Each person registered for the conference and staying in one of the major hotels will be able to catch a shuttle bus to go back and forth between the convention site and his/her hotel. A check with the local transportation service to be used indicates that there will be eight buses used daily to transport participants.

To communicate the times of departure, Dr. Steller decides to prepare a poster and place copies at various locations in the hotels and in the Convention Center. Below is the information that appeared on the poster:

Bus Schedule
Starting Time Each Day: 7:30 A.M.
Every 20 Minutes Thereafter
Stopping Time Each Day: 4:30 P.M.

a. Imagine you are one of the registered participants of the conference. If you arrived in the lobby of your hotel during the morning (say 7:40 A.M.), could you readily see the time for the next bus?

b. Design a better poster to provide information about the bus schedule times for the participants.

c. Using the strategy for communicating, write an appropriate communication about the transportation between the hotels and the Conference Center. Assume that this communication would have been included in the mailing participants received prior to arriving in San Francisco. You may also assume that a map with the hotels listed is printed on the reverse side of the message.

13. You are director of financial services for the American Express Company, P. O. Box 254, Wilmington, Delaware 19800. You need to send an announcement to American Express Company cardholders regarding certain provisions of the automatic flight insurance plan. Cite these details (which are not in the appropriate order and are not worded correctly) in your report:

- ☐ Enclose a new Description of Insurance to indicate an increase in lump sum benefits to $250,000.
- ☐ The Automatic $250,000 Flight Insurance Plan is an unusually good plan—the per flight premium of $3 has remained the same for 14 years.
- ☐ The effective date of the increase is July 1, 19__.
- ☐ Spouse receives the same coverage as you when you travel together at no additional cost.

- □ The plan is under the Master Airline Flight Accident Policy issued by Fireman's Fund American Life Insurance Company.
- □ Ticket must be charged to your American Express Card; when you and your spouse travel together, both tickets must be charged to your charge form.
- □ When you or your spouse travel alone, a $3 fee per ticket is charged; this must be charged to your card account.
- □ Make sure that you keep the Description of Insurance in a safe place; and you could keep this along with the $75,000 Travel Accident Insurance Certificate you received as a part of Cardmembership.
- □ American Express Company is constantly developing new ways to improve the value of your Cardmembership. The increase in insurance benefits is really good news.
- □ The $3 charge is automatically billed to your card when you charge airline tickets to the card.
- □ The charge is added to the monthly statement.
- □ If you charge the fee and do not use the ticket, you must notify American Express Company. A credit will be issued when you write to American Express Company, Card Division, Insurance Unit, Fort Lauderdale, Florida 33337. Or you may call the toll-free number shown on your bill.
- □ Enclose a question-and-answer brochure for further information on this entire plan.
- □ The described plan is not available to dependent children.

Using the strategy for communicating, write the appropriate communication for this situation.

14. As director of personnel services for the Acme Corporation located in Portland, Oregon, you have the responsibility of notifying eligible employees of an open enrollment period and a rate increase. The company has 150 employees. All of the following details are important to include in the communication:

- □ The underwriter for the dental insurance plan is Healthstream Corporation.
- □ The new insured rates effective July 1, 19__ are based on claims experience. The rates are: adult $14.40 monthly premium; child $4.80 with a maximum of $14.40 for all children in one family. However, the Prepaid Plan premium rates are going to remain at $12 adult and $4 child. Maximum family premium is $24.
- □ The month of June is open enrollment period under Acme's Dental Insurance contract. If employees want to apply for either the prepaid or the insured plan or make permitted changes during the month of June, they need to complete and sign the enclosed

application and submit it to the Personnel Services Department on or before June 30, 19__.

- The Personnel Services Department phone number is 321-8722.
- Two different plans exist: the insured and the prepaid.
- The month of June is the time to take action on changes in the dental plan. One cannot make changes at any other time during the year except in December.
- Action on the plan taken during June becomes effective July 1.
- If an employee is currently in the prepaid plan, he/she cannot make changes to the insured plan, according to the enrollment agreement. As an example, if an employee began the prepaid plan on January 1, (which was the inception date), she/he will not be eligible to change to the insured plan until December 30, another enrollment period.
- The open enrollment period permits one to enroll for coverage, add dependents, or change plans.

Using the strategy for communicating, write the appropriate communication for this situation.

15. Sterchi Bros. Stores, Inc. of Knoxville, Tennessee, has just been acquired by Heilig-Meyers Furniture Company of Richmond, Virginia. You are manager of the Knoxville store of Heilig-Meyers Furniture located at 7815 Kingston Pike. You need to announce the merger to your customers. In addition, customers with outstanding accounts need to know their balance and the procedure for paying accounts. One of your customers, Ms. Ann McMurray, has moved from the Knoxville area to 123 Whipporwill Lane, Decatur, Georgia 30034. You want to enclose a passbook noting the balance and monthly payment. You plan to enclose a sufficient number of preaddressed envelopes for the monthly payments.
Here are facts about Ms. McMurray's account:

- Her balance as of January 17, 19__ is $1,400.
- Her monthly payments during the past year were $133.80.
- She is to continue paying the same monthly amount.

Other background facts include:

- The merger of Sterchi Bros. and Heilig-Meyers assures that the combined operations of these two fine organizations will result in better service for the community.
- Helig-Meyers is a leader in the retail home furnishings industry.
- The company has served Southern communities for 98 years.
- The company brings to Knoxville the experience and success of a 10-state, 240-store operation.
- The company sells furniture, rugs, kerosene heaters, electronics, and related items.

Using the strategy for communicating, write the appropriate communication to announce the merger and information about the continued payment.

16. Holiday Inn, Inc. is interested in promoting a new Priority Club using the theme, "Make Every Trip Count." Among the special guest privileges are (*a*) guaranteed corporate room rate; (*b*) single corporate room rate for families (when staying in the same room as the member); (*c*) free daily newspaper (Monday-Friday); (*d*) express reservations and check-in; (*e*) $100 check cashing (with approved credit cards); (*f*) complimentary extended checkout until 2 p.m., and (*g*) free morning coffee or tea. The Priority Club assures the member not only of these privileges but also free and discounted airline and car rentals, travel packages and merchandise awards, and points redeemable for Holiday Inn Guest Certificates. These guest privileges will be available at all U.S. Holiday Inn hotels for a one-time enrollment fee of $10. All payments must be sent to Priority Club Service Center, P. O. Box 1729, Minneapolis, Minnesota 55440. A new member may enclose a check or money order for the $10 fee payable to Holiday Inn Priority Club or charge the fee to any of the listed credit cards:

    1. Holiday Inn Preferred Corporate Traveler Card (HT).
    2. American Express (AX).
    3. Citicorp Diners Club (DC).
    4. MasterCard (MC).
    5. Visa (VS).
    6. Discover Card (DS).

    If a potential customer desires, you may keep on file her/his credit card number in order to facilitate express reservations.

    You are a member of the Public Relations Department at the headquarters of Holiday Inn, Inc., in Memphis, Tennessee. You are asked to *design* a form for use with the Priority Club enrollment. Your instructions are to develop the form in such a way that eventually you can computerize the data submitted by present and potential customers. The form will appear in all Holiday Inns throughout the United States.

CHAPTER 12

SOURCES OF DATA

Learning Objectives

After studying this chapter, you will be able to:

- □ Understand the cyclical nature of report preparation.
- □ Distinguish between data and information.
- □ Define secondary and primary sources of data.
- □ Recognize numerous library and computer resources for collecting secondary data.
- □ Identify the appropriateness of various sources of primary data: observations, questionnaires, and interviews.
- □ State the advantages and disadvantages of the common techniques for collecting primary data.
- □ Write and critique data collection forms for observations, questionnaires, and interviews.
- □ Explain probability sampling (random, stratified random, cluster random) and nonprobability sampling techniques for business reports.
- □ Develop a bibliography using the traditional method or the American Psychological Association (APA) style.

Collecting data for your business reports

Report writing at times can be a fairly simple process. This is especially true if the information you need for generating the report is readily available. In Chapter 11 you were introduced to some examples of simple reports. For the announcement report about the resident manager's retirement, you did not need to search for any information. You had sufficient knowledge on the subject and could easily report the facts. You would consider this announcement a simple report.

Suppose, however, that you are asked to report on a subject for which you have very little or even no information at hand. In these instances, you would need either to search for the information or generate it yourself through a research process. These types of reports can at times involve a lengthy process and, depending on the research techniques or investigative methods used, become quite complex. Even for some fairly simple reports, your source(s) of information may come from somewhere other than your file cabinet or in-house database file. This chapter introduces you to a process for writing all reports, whether simple or complex, in which you use readily available information or generate information through research or investigative methods.

Report Preparation

Steps for researching a business report

The report writing process is cyclical in nature. As you solve one problem, other problems may become evident. You begin the process by applying the strategy for communication. The strategy provides the framework for the report writing cycle. Notice that the main focus of the cycle (as shown in Figure 12.1) is on the Problem and the Objectives in the strategy. These components provide the basis for your research. Your next step will be to determine what sources are available and the most effective procedures for gathering the information to solve the problem. You could decide to gather the data yourself or hire someone else. Before beginning the data collection process, you should develop the appropriate forms for collecting the data. These forms can be as simple as a few questions listed on 3 × 5 cards or as complex as a multipage questionnaire. Forms are an efficient way to organize and group data for further study or analysis. The analysis then gives meaning to data and applies it to the problem. Figure 12.1 illustrates this report writing cycle.

Data versus Information

Data defined

We use the words *data* and *information* frequently in this chapter. Let's establish their meanings. *Data represent the isolated facts collected about people, procedures, objects, or concepts.* Data are usually expressed quantitatively as percentages, averages, frequency counts, mathematical expressions, or statistical measurements. For instance, the data collected about real estate listings in Figure 11.3 had very little meaning by itself. Such isolated data as SE, 1050, $69,000 are useless unless analyzed and given meaning.

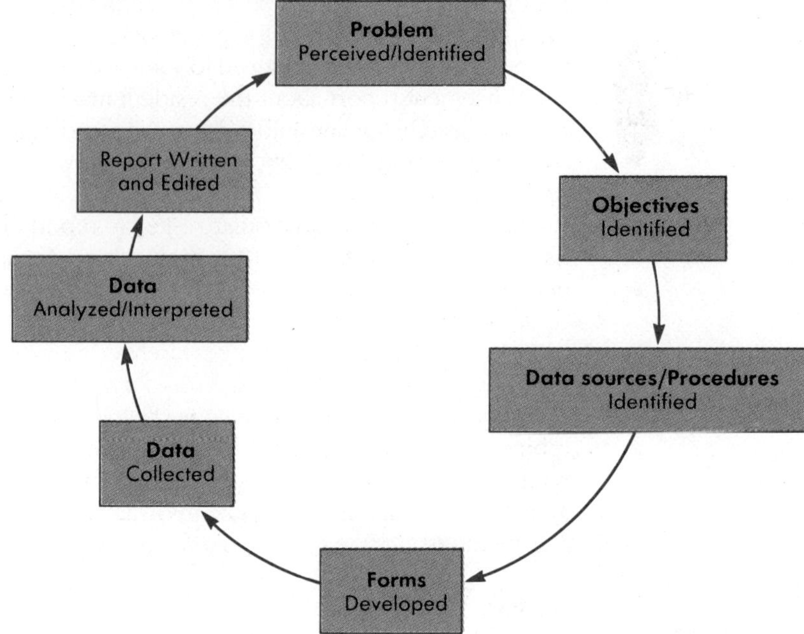

Figure 12.1
Cyclical nature of report preparation

Information defined with example

Information, by contrast, refers to meaningful data. The data are analyzed (grouped, processed, refined, interpreted, etc.) and then presented in an appropriate format for the decision maker, usually in a report or oral presentation. Normally, decision makers in business use the meaningful data to make informed choices among alternatives. Thus your tasks as a report writer include obtaining valid data, making intelligent and objective judgments about the data gathered, and then presenting the findings with your conclusions about the specific Problem/Objectives.

In reality, the process is not quite so straightforward. All the relevant data may not be available, even after you've done an extensive search. The decision maker may still face uncertainty, even after your best research efforts. Managers rarely have 100 percent of the needed information for making a decision. But, if you have provided the best information available, the decision maker incurs less risk.

Suppose you wanted to conduct a study on the location for a new retail outlet in a designated community. You'd begin by collecting a variety of raw data—possible locations, estimated land costs, zoning regulations, and numerous other types of data. You would then examine and arrange these materials according to preestablished criteria. Your next step would be to compare the advantages and disadvantages of each location by ranking each site in order of priority. Given this report, an administrator could then make an informed decision on the best location.

In many reports, you will collect data and interpret your findings; in other reports, you will merely summarize information from various sources; in still others, you may do both. The remainder of this chapter demonstrates how secondary and primary data are used in writing business reports.

SECONDARY AND PRIMARY SOURCES OF DATA

Secondary and primary sources defined

Sources of data can be grouped into two broad categories—secondary and primary. *Secondary data are those facts or information obtained from printed or published documents* such as you would find in your local library. *Primary data are those facts you derive from original research.*

Secondary Sources

Numerous sources are available for every conceivable area of business. In any large library, you will find publications targeted to specific industries (marketing, finance, insurance) or subjects (manufacturing techniques, computer technology, or management theory). Various almanacs, directories, periodicals, and a host of other publications provide general information on a variety of topics.

Secondary sources serve several purposes in business report writing.

Reasons for using secondary sources

- ☐ Using secondary data in the introduction helps to capture the Reader's attention and sets the stage for the report by providing background for the Reader.
- ☐ Secondary data give credibility to a report. They expand on or confirm present knowledge.
- ☐ Data provide a basis on which to build; data from one study can be compared with earlier data, for example.
- ☐ Your search helps you determine whether your proposed study has already been conducted by someone else. If it has, you may still want to replicate the study or take a different approach to the topic. Reviewing appropriate secondary sources helps you determine how previous studies relate to your proposed work.
- ☐ Secondary data provide factual background to use in developing strategic plans.
- ☐ Your research enables you to compare data from earlier studies with recently acquired data.

Commonly used library secondary sources

Some frequently used resources include the *Business Periodicals Index,* the *Index of Government Publications, Agriculture Index,* the *Reader's Guide to Periodical Literature,* the *Reader's Guide to Books, The Wall Street Journal Index,* the *New York Times, Funk & Scott Index of Corporations & Industries* as well as various dictionaries, encyclopedias, and other newspaper indexes. An annotated list of several business-related secondary sources is shown in Appendix A to this chapter. These references are available in most libraries. Consult a reference librarian for additional resources.

LEGAL / ETHICAL ISSUE

NEWSPAPER HEADLINE: "Candidate Quits Presidential Race—Plagiarism!" The newspaper article reported that a candidate running for the presidency frequently used parts of other people's speeches without referring to the originator; and he was caught plagiarizing a paper while in law school.

Once the press reported that behavior, the U.S. public no longer considered the person acceptable as a presidential candidate—and, therefore, the individual had to withdraw. Although the incidents didn't result in legal action, they show the severe consequence of unethical behavior.

Did the alleged plagiarism warrant the candidate's withdrawal from the presidential race? What can you do to protect yourself from being accused of plagiarizing?

Use of databases in report writing

Using the Computer to Access Secondary Sources. Another invaluable research tool is the computer. You can access over 400 databases or on-line information files through computer information services such as Lockheed, Dialog, System Development Corporation, and Mead Data Central Nexis. To use a database, you must first develop a profile of topic interests, that is, a list of keywords related to your research topic. When you enter these into an appropriate database, the computer searches for relevant materials, using authors' names, categories of information (book reviews, research abstracts, or periodical abstracts) or combinations of your keywords. If the search is successful, a printed bibliography on that specific topic, and, depending on the database you choose, brief summaries of specific articles are printed.

Variety of subjects available through database searches

On-line computer databases cover a wide variety of subjects in science, technology, the social sciences, health, business, education, and the humanities. Databases cite journal articles most frequently, but many also include references to books, newspapers, conference proceedings, patents, statistics, dissertations, research in progress, and foundation grants. Most databases correspond to printed indexes available in libraries. One called COMPENDEX, for example, is a computerized version of the *Engineering Index.* Others include AGRICOLA (*Agriculture* Index), BIOSEARCH (*Biological Abstracts*), and SCISEARCH (*Science Citation Index*).

Cost of computer database searches

Computer searches cost approximately $10 to $25 per database, but the cost may be higher or lower depending on the database used, the on-line search time, and the number of citations printed. Any researcher or formal report writer would be wise to check out these services. As a researcher or writer, you need to consider the cost in relation to the importance of the information obtained from a computer database search.

Sources available through Search Helper database

Search Helper. Search Helper, an inexpensive software package, makes it easy and convenient to run computer searches in six databases: Magazine Index, National Newspaper Index, Legal Resources Index, Trade and Industry Index, Management Contents, and Newsearch. These databases offer information from general magazines; newspapers; management, business and trade journals; law journals; and a file of current information from all these sources.

Usually, Search Helper will produce a list of up to 20 citations (author names, journal titles, article titles, pages, and dates) tailored to specific topics for $3.00.

Sources available through ERIC database

ERIC. ERIC is an acronym for Educational Resources Information Center, a nationwide information system supported by the National Institute of Education. ERIC consists of a coordinating staff in Washington and a number of clearinghouses located at universities or with professional organizations across the country. Each clearinghouse focuses on a specific field in education such as vocational education. Each acquires, evaluates, abstracts, and indexes educational information and makes it available through ERIC's database. Approximately 14,000 records are added each year to this database.

A manual entitled *Thesaurus* is the key to locating the indexing terms for ERIC materials. These terms, arranged alphabetically, are called descriptors. Using ERIC's *Thesaurus* assures you of correct and complete access to topics.

Determining your indexing terms through the use of ERIC *Thesaurus*

Contact a reference librarian for information about other databases and techniques for conducting computer searches.

You may find computer search services, Search Helper, and ERIC valuable sources of information. You should consider using them, when appropriate. (See Chapter 2 for additional information on databases.)

How to develop the bibliography for your business reports

Developing Bibliography Entries. When writing a research paper, you often must quote the work of other authors. Be sure to cite such works properly to give credit to these authors or sources. Appendix B at the end of this chapter provides sample entries for developing a bibliography. Common styles include the American Psychological Association (APA), Turabian, and others. To encourage uniform documentation, many disciplines have adopted a specific style manual. Note that this style may vary somewhat from the style explained in Appendix B. Consult several major scholarly journals in your field to determine whether your specific discipline has identified a preferred style manual.

Primary Data

Techniques for collecting primary data

Primary data are those facts you derive from original research. Data are not available; you must collect facts before making a decision. Since each project is unique, the writer has to decide on the appropriate techniques to use for collecting data. For example, you might search through company records. The most common techniques for gathering primary data include:

- □ Observations.
- □ Questionnaires.
- □ Interviews.

Select the technique that provides the data quickly and efficiently with the least amount of interruption and cost. In general, interviews and questionnaires provide data about people's opinions, attitudes, and knowledge; observations describe events or behavior patterns as they occur. You would not choose the interview or questionnaire techniques, for example, if you could obtain the appropriate data from existing company documents. Each data-collecting technique has individual characteristics.

If the project is extensive and time-consuming, you may even hire an outside agency to collect and analyze the data. For example, if you wanted to obtain opinions from people within a defined area (number of blocks from your store), you might hire a market research firm to obtain the needed information. Newspapers daily report opinion surveys about various topics: TV preferences, presidential candidate support, and numerous other topics. The use of an outside agency depends on money, time, and your expertise.

Observations as means of collecting data

Observations. Personal observations are especially helpful in situations where job tasks can be distinguished and quantified. For example, if your goal is to determine the types and the number of tasks that grocery clerks perform, you would likely use the observation technique.

Observations allow you to determine:

Characteristics of observations

- □ What is being done.
- □ How it is being done.
- □ When it is done.
- □ How much time it takes.
- □ Where it is taking place.
- □ Who is doing the activity.

Methods for conducting observations

An observation is made by walking through a designated area and observing people, objects, and activities at random and making notes or recording activities on a form. Or you might station yourself at a spot near an intersection and record traffic patterns. A special form is used. For certain studies, you may need to get permission from the individuals studied; the right to privacy needs consideration in these situations. During observations, you may interact with the people or perhaps not interact. This will depend on the situation.

Some guidelines for using the observation technique for collecting primary data are shown in Figure 12.2.

Advantages/disadvantages of using observations

Although the observation technique is well documented and widely used, this method is time-consuming and expensive compared with other techniques. Each person or thing in the study needs to be observed a designated number of times. Another disadvantage is that people dislike observations. People may behave differently when they know they are observed, and this

Figure 12.2
Guidelines for using the observation technique

Before the observation

1. Identify *what* you are going to observe.
2. Determine the time needed to observe.
3. Obtain appropriate management approval.
4. Tell subjects what you are observing and why (if appropriate).
5. Become familiar with physical layout and facilities in area observed.
6. Select or design an appropriate form for recording observations.

During the observation

1. Record predetermined facts.
2. Record predetermined time periods, if time is a factor.
3. Avoid judgmental or qualitative statements when interacting with subjects; emphasis should be on getting unbiased responses from the subjects.
4. Avoid interrupting the person performing the tasks you're observing.

After the observation

1. Organize notes and facts obtained.
2. Arrange data in appropriate order.
3. Check the accuracy of your notes with the person observed, if unclear.
4. Write final report.

can result in invalid data. Observing people without their knowledge presents both ethical and legal problems for the researcher.

Even though the observation technique has certain limitations, this method is a valid technique for collecting data. It may be the only way to get the needed data. A sample form for data collection using the observation technique is shown in Figure 12.3.

Questionnaire as a means of collecting data

Questionnaires. The questionnaire is recommended for situations when:

- ☐ Respondents are physically distant from the researcher.
- ☐ Potential respondents are many.
- ☐ Respondents' opinions on a variety of topics are needed.
- ☐ Reactions are needed to a specific set of questions identified by the researcher.

One example of a questionnaire for collecting data is the customer services survey that frequently is found in hotels and restaurants. Data from these questionnaires provide a basis for service improvement.

Questionnaires are a relatively inexpensive way to survey the opinions of a large group of people. In addition, questionnaires give you several other benefits:

Figure 12.3 Data collecting form for observation

Purpose: Identifying activities of two different groups of managers—top executives and middle managers

Procedure: Record activities of 300 executives (previously identified as top or middle managers) on random basis.

Date: ______________________

Office No. ______________________ ____ Top Manager
____ Middle Manager

ACTIVITY / TIME:	8:00	8:15	8:30	8:45	9:00	9:15	9:30	9:45		1:00	1:15	1:30	1:45	2:00	2:15	2:30	2:45	
Away from desk/office																		
Calculating																		
Conferring with secretary																		
Dictating to machine																		
Dictating to secretary																		
Filing																		
Handling mail																		
Meeting with group																		
Meeting with individual																		
Photocopying																		
Planning or scheduling																		
Proofreading																		
Reading																		
Retrieving filed information																		
Searching																		
Using equipment																		
Using telephone																		
Writing																		
Other (list)																		

NOTES:

Benefits of using questionnaires

- □ They put less pressure on respondents for immediate reactions.
- □ They protect the identity of respondents.
- □ They provide for uniformity in responses if structured questions are used.
- □ They can be analyzed by a computer if correctly designed.
- □ They provide a quick method for collecting factual information.

Closed- and open-ended questions defined

Two types of questions frequently used in questionnaires are the closed-ended type and the open-ended type. The closed-ended type consists of a question or incomplete statement with a set of alternatives; the respondent reads the question or incomplete statement and then chooses one or more of the alternatives. The open-ended type usually consists of a question and a space for the respondent to write in an answer.

Closed-ended example: multiple-choice

Closed-ended Questions. Closed-ended questions and the alternative responses to the question may be stated in a variety of ways. You may list several options similar to a multiple-choice question, a yes-no response, or a rating scale.

1. How many people does your company employ? (Check one.)
   A. 49 or fewer.
   B. 50 - 99.
   C. 100 - 149.
   D. 150 - 199.
   E. 200 or more.

Advantages of closed-ended questions

This question asks for a specific fact. In this type of closed-ended question, the researcher determines the categories rather than asking the respondent merely to fill in a blank. The advantage of predetermining the categories is that the researcher can easily tabulate the responses. Also, the respondent can quickly provide the facts, which greatly increases the number of responses received. Use care in identifying the categories so that they reflect the group surveyed. One disadvantage is that the actual thought of the respondent isn't obtained. He or she is forced to select from the choices.

Disadvantage of closed-ended questions

With this type of question, except for the first and last alternatives, each category should contain the same number of units so that the categories can be compared. In the example, each category has a range of 50. Note that alternative B ends with 99 and C begins with 100. Avoid using the same number in two alternatives. Also, although you should number the questions themselves, use letters (or some other scheme such as 1.1, 1.2, 1.3, etc.) for the responses to avoid confusion later when you analyze the responses.

A question with a yes/no response normally does not get the desired information.

Example: yes/no questions

2. Are microcomputers used in your company?
   A. Yes.
   B. No.

Responses to this question provide only the number of companies that use or do not use microcomputers. Use follow-up questions to obtain information about the use or expected use of microcomputers.

The yes/no-response question is improved by including more specific content as in question 3.

Example: follow-up of yes/no question

3. Which of the following microcomputer brands is most used in your company?
   3.1 None (Skip to question 10.)
   3.2 Apple.
   3.3 DEC.
   3.4 IBM.
   3.5 Wang.
   3.6 Xerox.

In this way, you can obtain more specific information from respondents. Those who work in organizations where no microcomputers are used are directed to other questions since the first alternative is *none.* All other respondents check the brands used in their companies. In this particular question, note that a respondent could check more than one alternative. You would need to give special attention to these multiple-responses when you interpret the data. Note the numbering scheme for the alternatives.

Example 4 asks for an opinion. Usually you want to use a rating scale of some type to get a high to low reaction. This rating scale is about the only way you can obtain the feelings from people about topics; respondents can react quickly to the questions, and the investigator can computerize the data for efficient analysis. One disadvantage is that respondents may interpret the degree of importance differently. They may also not give their true feeling by indicating a rating near the middle of the scale. However, this is true of all pencil-paper reactions.

Example: scale use

4. On a scale of 1 to 10, how would you rate the overall effectiveness of this training course? (Circle one.)

   Ineffective 1 2 3 4 5 6 7 8 9 10 Effective

The researcher assumes that the respondent is knowledgeable about the subject.

Question 5 illustrates a slightly different type of question. Note that the stem of the question provides a definition, then asks the question. Only a 5-point scale is used. The scale can vary depending on the writer's use of the data.

5. If grammar is defined as rules for "correct writing that includes usage, spelling, capitalization, punctuation, agreement, etc.," should a business communication course include a unit of grammar study?

   Strongly agree 1 2 3 4 5 Strongly disagree

Both 4 and 5 are closed-ended since the alternatives are provided.

Closed-ended questions are structured to allow for more than one selection as in question 6. This type response takes special caution since the total for the question is larger than the number of respondents; the total will depend on the number of responses. There isn't just one response—the respondent may check several categories.

Example: multiple response question

6. Which topic areas need more emphasis in the current MBA curriculum? (Please check all that apply.)

    ____ A. Accounting.
    ____ B. Business communication.
    ____ C. Business policy/strategy.
    ____ D. Economics.
    ____ E. Entrepreneurship.
    ____ F. Finance.
    ____ G. General management.
    ____ H. International business management.
    ____ I. Legal-political-social environment of business.
    ____ J. Marketing.
    ____ K. MIS (management information systems).
    ____ L. Organizational behavior/human resources.
    ____ M. Production/operations management.
    ____ N. Quantitative analysis (operations research/statistics).
    ____ O. (No topic areas ought to receive more emphasis.)

In question 7, rankings are requested. Specific directions are needed for the respondent.

Example: ranking question

7. When you purchased your last car, what features did you consider important? (Rank the three most important—1 = most important; 2 = next most important; 3 = next most important)

    ____ A. Comfort/convenience.
    ____ B. Cost.
    ____ C. Electrical/mechanical features.
    ____ D. Engine/transmission type.
    ____ E. Exterior workmanship.
    ____ F. Interior workmanship.

Specify the number of rankings; otherwise, some respondents may rank several items as 1, 2, or 3. Analyzing such mixed responses is difficult. Use this type question when you want to determine the importance of several items to the respondents. In this example, all features are potentially important; but which are the most important? The results from this question are applicable to marketing the automobile.

Open-ended Questions. The closed-ended questions numbered 1, 4, and 6 can be rewritten as open-ended questions.

Example: open-ended questions

8. How many people does your company employ? ______
9. How effective was this training course?

____

____

____

10. Which courses in your graduate program should have received more emphasis?

____

____

____

An analysis of responses to question 8 would take some time, but a grouping similar to the one used in question 1 could result. Responses to questions 9 and 10 are far more difficult to analyze and interpret. Each respondent could write almost anything. The researcher will find that summarizing and analyzing the responses is difficult and time-consuming. Because each respondent will use her/his own words, the researcher will need to devise some way to classify responses. The respondent is free to answer with her/his own words. Open-ended questions take less space on the paper but require more time to analyze.

In cases where the researcher does not want to indicate a direction to the respondent, the open-ended question is best. The respondent is "forced" to provide what is important to her/him. The open-ended question does not lead the respondent into a pattern of thinking. Question 11 illustrates a good open-ended question.

11. In a word or phrase, what do you consider the most important strength of your major?

____

____

A variation of the open-ended type question is the fill-in-the-blank type; less space is allowed for the response in question 12.

Example: fill-in-the-blank question

12. ______ is the brand name of my stereo.

Combination. Another strategy is to combine the closed-ended and open-ended type of question.

Example: combination closed-ended and open-ended question

13. Which of the following best describes your present job?

____ A. Top executive.
____ B. Middle manager.
____ C. Professional (engineer, accountant, etc.).
____ D. Supervisor.
____ E. Other; specify __________.

Figure 12.4
Comparison of open- and closed-ended questions

Open-ended questions	
Advantages	***Disadvantages***
Respondents can express motive or attitude.	Respondents may leave out important data.
Respondents can specify conditions for answer.	Require lengthy time to complete.
	Responses are difficult to analyze.
Closed-ended questions	
Advantages	***Disadvantages***
Easy to fill out.	Respondents are limited to choices provided.
Easy to administer.	May lack depth.
Focuses responses on subject of concern.	Respondents may select alternative that isn't true feeling.
Easy to tabulate and analyze.	Data might not be reliable.

Since the basic set of choices in question 13 might not cover all alternatives, respondents may specify other titles or job designations. Sometimes it is difficult to anticipate all alternatives when designing a questionnaire. Combination questions are a good way to find all possible responses to your questions.

To help you decide which type of questions to use for your particular needs, study the advantages and disadvantages of each given in Figure 12.4.

Guidelines for Wording Questions. Use these suggestions for effective wording when you write questions for a questionnaire:

Guidelines for developing the wording

- ☐ Define or qualify important terms to avoid misunderstanding (TWA = Trans World Airlines).
- ☐ Include appropriate alternatives: married, divorced, widowed, single, other as alternatives.
- ☐ Underline a word for special emphasis: What communication competencies do middle managers need?
- ☐ In rating or comparison-type questions, provide a point of reference: When you purchased your last car, what features did you consider important?
- ☐ Avoid descriptive adjectives and adverbs such as frequently, often, rarely; specify what "frequently" means such as times per week or times per month.
- ☐ Avoid double negatives: Do you object to not providing birth-control information to high school students?
- ☐ Avoid multipart questions: How many and which paid holidays does your company provide for its employees? Create

Figure 12.5
Guidelines for constructing questionnaires

- ☐ State the title, objective, and use of the results at the beginning of the questionnaire.
- ☐ Provide clear instructions for completing the questionnaire.
- ☐ Identify the questionnaire by the respondent's name, number, or some other type of identification (for follow-up purposes when using the mailed questionnaire).
- ☐ Use demographic or background factors, such as age or income level, to give more meaning to the data.
- ☐ Make the questionnaire attractive.
- ☐ Pretest the questionnaire with a select group to determine clarity of items.
- ☐ Use, where possible, a format for responses that allows computer analysis of data.
- ☐ Phrase specific questions in a clear, concise manner and provide for easy response.
- ☐ Arrange questions into two parts—demographic and content questions.
- ☐ Sequence the questions in a logical manner—group-related questions.
- ☐ Write the questions independent of one another; be sure one answer does not influence another.
- ☐ Make sure the questionnaire content will produce the data necessary to fulfill your objectives.
- ☐ Indicate at the end what the respondent is to do with the completed questionnaire—return to a specific area, mail to a specified address, etc. Include the name and address of the researcher.

independent questions—How many paid holidays does your company provide? Which paid holidays are granted to employees?

- ☐ Avoid assumptions: Do your children use the local library? The respondent may not have children.
- ☐ Avoid leading questions that imply the response: Don't you agree that communication is important to business people?

Figure 12.5 presents guidelines for constructing questionnaires.

Interviews as a means of collecting data

Interviews. Face-to-face interviews offer many benefits. They provide opportunities to inform the interviewee about various facets of the subject and offer a quick and convenient method to obtain data from the selected group. Face-to-face interviews offer a two-way communication to clarify any questions or to obtain other information by observing the respondent's reactions. Regardless of the level within an organization, this method provides an appropriate method for collecting valid data.

Benefits of interviews

Interviews may be structured, unstructured, or a combination of the two. For a structured interview (probably the most common type of interview), list all pertinent questions or topics before conducting the interview. Your results will be congruous and easy to quantify, even if you've interviewed a number of respondents. Unstructured interviews rely on no predetermined set of specific questions. To be of benefit, however, the unstructured interview requires a very skilled interviewer who uses predetermined general

Structured versus unstructured interviews

Figure 12.6
Guidelines for using the interview technique

Prior to the interview

- ☐ Obtain top management endorsement and announcement.
- ☐ Schedule interviews through appropriate managers.
- ☐ Obtain organizational chart with each person identified; get job duties and responsibilities for each person.
- ☐ Select place for interview.
- ☐ Set up convenient time with the interviewee.
- ☐ Determine type of interview and method for recording responses. If the interview is structured, prepare specific questions.

During the interview

- ☐ Identify yourself.
- ☐ Explain the purpose of the interview as it relates to the project.
- ☐ Identify value of input by interviewee.
- ☐ Assure the interviewee of the confidentiality of responses.
- ☐ Ask questions.
- ☐ Listen well. Allow sufficient time for interviewee to respond.
- ☐ Maintain control of interview to minimize the interviewees' rambling or introduction of unrelated material.
- ☐ Follow up on vague responses to questions.
- ☐ Ask for additional comments or suggestions that have not been covered.
- ☐ Indicate that there may be a follow-up if any questions arise.
- ☐ Thank the person.

questions. A combination interview is partly structured and partly unstructured.

The results from a structured interview and a questionnaire are similar. However, the selection of the data-collection method depends on the identified problem and the constraints of time, money, and trained personnel. In some situations, it may be critical to view the nonverbal reactions of the interviewee; at other times, it may be sufficient to get a response via a questionnaire. Select the method and forms to fit the objectives of the study.

Three different approaches are widely used to record the responses of the people interviewed:

- ☐ Recording the responses on a prepared form while interviewing.
- ☐ Recording the responses on tape for later analysis.
- ☐ Recording the responses at a later time following the interview.

The interviewer must assess available resources and capabilities to decide which of these three methods will work best in obtaining the desired data for a particular situation. Figure 12.6 lists guidelines for using the interview technique. A sample sheet for a structured interview is shown in Figure 12.7. This interview sheet could serve as a mailed questionnaire.

Figure 12.7
Interview sheet for grocery store customers

1. Which of the following represents your view of our store?
   ____ a. First in my mind when I need to shop for groceries.
   ____ b. Among three I consider when I need to grocery shop.
   ____ c. Last in my mind when I need to grocery shop.
2. How would you rate the overall appearance of our store? (5-point scale)
   Unattractive 1 2 3 4 5 Attractive
3. On a 5-point scale, how would you rate the availability of items?
   Available 1 2 3 4 5 Unavailable
4. On a 5-point scale, how do you like the electronic check-out device?
   Dislike 1 2 3 4 5 Like
5. What three features attract you to a grocery story? (Rank top 3)
   ____ a. Prices ____ e. Name brands
   ____ b. Wide range of merchandise ____ f. Quality of meat products
   ____ c. Check-cashing privileges ____ g. Store hours
   ____ d. Store atmosphere ____ h. Other; list ____________.
6. On a 3-point scale, how would you rate the store personnel?
   Helpful 1 2 3 Not helpful
7. Which of the following conveniences do you prefer at a grocery store? (You may indicate more than one.)
   ____ a. Cash-checking privileges ____ f. Nongrocery items
   ____ b. Carry-out help ____ g. Discount items
   ____ c. Trading stamps ____ h. Ready-to-eat items
   ____ d. Electronic check out ____ i. Fresh seafood
   ____ e. 24-hour shopping ____ j. Samples

Demographic information

8. Distance you live from our store:
   ____ a. Less than 1 mile ____ c. 3-4 miles
   ____ b. 1-2 miles ____ d. 5 or more miles
9. Type of dwelling for your primary residence:
   ____ a. Apartment ____ c. Condominium
   ____ b. Single-family house ____ d. Other; list ____________________.
10. Sex:
    ____ a. Male
    ____ b. Female
11. Age category:
    ____ a. Less than 21 ____ e. 51–60
    ____ b. 21–30 ____ f. 61–70
    ____ c. 31–40 ____ g. 71 or older
    ____ d. 41–50
12. Which customer classification fits you?
    ____ a. Regular
    ____ b. First-time
    ____ c. Once-in-a-while
13. What attracted you to this store?
    ____ a. Newspaper advertisements ____ c. TV advertisements
    ____ b. Store signs ____ d. Other; specify ____________
14. What is your family size?
    ____ a. one ____ d. four
    ____ b. two ____ e. five or more
    ____ c. three

SAMPLING

When collecting data, the researcher must decide whether to collect data from the entire population or from a representative sample. *Population refers to a designated group: for example, all employees in a company, all residents of a city, or some other classification of subjects.*

Population defined

Examples of population

If the entire population is relatively small, say 20 employees, including the total population in your research study presents no major problem. However, the results of the study apply only to this group. The findings are not assumed to apply to other groups. For instance, if you were surveying all employees of the Chamber of Commerce in Tulsa, Oklahoma, the findings obtained from this group may be totally unrelated to the findings of the Chamber of Commerce employees in Jacksonville, Florida.

Sampling defined

Collecting data from a selected group within the population is known as *sampling.* If conducted carefully, sampling of a population should yield results representative of that total population. Sampling is a manageable way to obtain data from the population at a reasonable cost and within a satisfactory time period. Sampling techniques are of two types—probability and nonprobability.

Probability Sampling

Probability sampling defined

Example of probability sampling

Probability sampling is the more scientific approach; statistical methods are used to select a representative sample. When using this approach, you must identify the population (such as the names of all customers of a particular store or all households within a given area). With a representative sample, each person or thing in the population has an equal chance of being included. The actual sample is selected using a random method. You would then use a statistical measure to determine the degree of error or risk in the sample. A table of random numbers is used to select the sample from the ordered list. The ordered list provides a check on the completeness of the list.

Types of probability sampling

You can use three basic types of probability sampling when writing reports—simple random sampling, stratified random sampling, and cluster random sampling.

Simple random sampling defined

Simple Random Sampling. In simple random sampling, a designated number of cases is chosen from the population on a purely chance basis. You could, for instance, place every name of the population in a fishbowl and draw out the appropriate number of cases. A table of random numbers (available in most statistics books) is useful in this process; however, you would still need an ordered list (alphabetical or numerical) of each of the units included in the population.

The systematic random sample is a variation of the simple random method. In this approach, you divide the total number of units in the population by the sample size, and then use every *n*th case. For example, if

100 cases constituted the population and the desired sample size were 10, then the 10th, 20th, 30th, etc. cases would make up the systematic sample. This variation also results in a representative sample.

Stratified random sampling defined

Stratified Random Sampling. When you know (or suspect) that certain characteristics of the population might influence the results, you should choose the stratified random sampling technique. You need to know the relevant characteristics of the population (age, gender, occupation, income level, etc.). In the stratified sample, each selected characteristic is reflected in the sample in the same proportion as it exists in the whole population. If, for example, 10 percent of the known population is in the 30-39 age group, you would select 10 percent of the sample from this age group.

Cluster random sampling defined

Cluster Random Sampling. In the cluster random sampling approach, the sample reflects the group rather than the individual cases in the population. Rather than listing all households in a city, you could list all the blocks in the city. From these blocks, you select at random a predetermined percent of the total blocks and then survey all households in those selected blocks. This type of sampling may produce results less representative than the other types because of the differences among individual clusters in the population. This method offers the advantage of using a concentrated geographic area for data collection.

Nonprobability sampling defined

Nonprobability Sampling. Nonprobability sampling is widely used in business with much success. Unlike probability sampling, however, the nonprobability sample is selected on the basis of convenience and judgment. You must still carefully select the method and sample size. But you have no scientific means to determine the sampling error.

Suppose you wanted to assess employees' attitudes on a proposed relocation. You could stand in the entrance lobby of your business and select people at random until you have interviewed a predetermined number of employees. The results would represent a convenient sample.

Or perhaps you want to determine the need for a day-care center at your business. You would want to interview only those who have children. In this case, you could also stand in the entrance lobby and ask each person entering whether he or she has children. Next you'd ask additional questions of those who indicated they have small children. You would continue to interview employees until you reached the predetermined number for the study.

Criteria for using probability or nonprobability sampling

Whether you use probability or nonprobability sampling depends on two criteria: *the nature of the problem studied and the intended use of the results.* As a general rule, the more significant the decision, the greater the need for scientific and precise sampling techniques.

SUMMARY

The report writing process is cyclical in nature. As a report writer, you identify the Problem, state your Objectives, identify your data sources and procedures, develop a data collection form, analyze your data, and then write and edit your report. Data, which represent facts collected about people, procedures, objects, or concepts, are usually expressed quantitatively. Information refers to meaningful data—that which has been analyzed (grouped, processed, refined, interpreted) and then presented in an appropriate format, oral or written, for the decision maker. Normally, the decision maker in business uses the meaningful data to make informed choices among alternatives.

When writing reports, you might use data from either secondary or primary sources. Secondary data are facts or information obtained from printed or published documents. Primary data are facts you derive from original research using any of a number of investigative procedures.

Secondary sources are almost limitless and are available for every conceivable area of business. Sources cited in this chapter include *Business Periodicals Index, The Wall Street Journal Index, Reader's Guide to Books,* and the *Index of Corporations and Industries.* You may also use the computer to access secondary source databases. When you enter a list of key words related to your research topic into a computer database, a bibliography on that topic (and sometimes abstracts) is printed. Most databases correspond to printed indexes available in libraries. Sample selected database sources cited in this chapter include Compendex, Biosearch *(Biological Abstracts),* National Newspaper Index, and ERIC (Educational Resources Information Center). When you quote secondary sources in your reports, include a bibliography which lists all the sources cited.

The most common techniques for gathering primary data include observations, questionnaires, and interviews. Select the technique that provides the data efficiently and quickly but with the least amount of interruption and cost. Interviews and questionnaires provide data about people's opinions, attitudes, and knowledge; observations describe events or behavior patterns as they occur.

Personal observations are helpful in situations where tasks of a job are distinguished and quantified. Observation allows you to determine what, how, when, where, and whom for a situation. Observation is a valid technique for collecting data, but this method is time-consuming and expensive. A main disadvantage of this technique is that people dislike being observed. They may behave differently in an observation situation. When this happens, you obtain invalid data.

Questionnaires are recommended for situations when the respondents are physically distant from the researcher, when you have many potential respondents, and when you need reactions to a specific set of questions identified by the reader. Questionnaires offer you an inexpensive way to survey the opinions of a large group of subjects. Questionnaires provide for uniformity in responses if structured questions are used, and they can be analyzed by computer if correctly designed. Among the disadvantages of the questionnaire are that the respondent is limited to the choices provided, and the questionnaire may take a long time to complete, if lengthy. Questionnaires are made up of two types of questions. Closed-ended questions are stated either as questions or incomplete statements and are followed with a specific set of alternatives. Open-ended questions leave a space for the respondents to write in an answer.

Interviews are a quick and easy way to obtain data from a selected group. Interviews allow for two-way communication so that the interviewer can clarify any questions and inform the interviewee about various facets of the subject. Interviews may be structured, unstructured, or a combination of the two. The interviewer must assess available resources and capabilities to determine which of these methods will work best in obtaining the data for a particular situation.

When collecting data, the researcher must decide whether to collect data from the entire population or from a representative sample. Sampling techniques are of two types—probability and nonprobability. Probability sampling refers to the more scientific approach in which statistical tools are used for selecting a sample. Three basic types of probability sampling are simple random, stratified random, and cluster random. Nonprobability sampling refers to selecting a sample on the basis of convenience and judgment. The use of probability or nonprobability sampling depends on two criteria: the nature of the problem studied and the intended use of the results.

END-OF-CHAPTER ACTIVITIES

DISCUSSION

1. Explain why the report writing process is cyclical in nature.
2. What is the relationship of data and information?
3. Define secondary sources of data. Define primary sources of data.
4. What are some secondary sources of data?
5. Discuss the advantages of using the computer for data collection.
6. What methods are common for collecting primary data?
7. Describe the differences in a closed-ended question and an open-ended question.
8. What guidelines are appropriate when constructing a questionnaire?
9. What is random sampling? Identify three common types of random sampling. Indicate a situation that calls for each type of sampling.
10. Give a brief description of Computer Search Service, Search Helper, and ERIC. How could each of these databases prove beneficial to the formal report writer?

ACTIVITIES

11. Evaluate the effectiveness of this questionnaire used by a senator to collect data from constituents (Figure 12.8). Discuss the strengths and weaknesses of the questionnaire.

Figure 12.8
Sample questionnaire
Used by permission.

The Sasser Poll

It is very helpful to Senator Sasser to have the benefit of your views on key issues. The completed questionnaire should be mailed to Senator Jim Sasser, 260 Russell Office Building, Washington, D.C. 20510.

1. Rank the following economic problems in the order of which should receive the greatest attention from the federal government.
   ____ Inflation ____ Declining productivity
   ____ Unemployment ____ Poverty
2. The administration is preparing to propose additional budget cuts to deal with a deficit which is expected to be much greater than original administration projections. Please rank the following according to which areas should be cut first.
   ____ Public works projects ____ EPA sewer projects
   ____ Defense ____ Alternative energy projects
   ____ Social Security ____ Veterans benefits
   ____ Public assistance and food stamps ____ Foreign aid
   ____ Urban development ____ Education
3. The administration has proposed a massive cutback in Social Security benefits. Do you believe this move is justified?
   ____ Yes ____ No
4. Do you believe there will be sufficient funds in the Social Security system to insure payment of your benefits when you retire?
   ____ Yes ____ No
5. The administration is considering a proposal to immediately decontrol the price of natural gas. This move would lead to a doubling of gas prices, and the energy companies contend they need the additional revenue to finance exploration and drilling for gas. Which of the following most accurately reflects your views with regard to natural gas decontrol?
   ____ The energy companies already have sufficient revenues to finance drilling and exploration, and decontrolling prices will only lead to higher prices, not additional supplies.
   ____ The price of natural gas is being held at an artificially low level by government price controls, and a free market will produce additional gas supplies needed by industrial concerns and residential users.
6. While it is clear that government has gone too far in many areas in intruding on private business activities and other matters, there are some important obligations which must be met by government. Listed below are some areas affected by government which can be rated according to whether the government is doing too little in this area, doing enough or doing too much.

	Doing too little	Doing enough	Doing too much
Veterans benefits	____	____	____
Care for elderly	____	____	____
Small business development	____	____	____
Oil company price regulation	____	____	____
Welfare	____	____	____
Foreign aid	____	____	____
Assistance to refugees from other nations	____	____	____

7. The Federal Reserve Board in November 1979 implemented a high interest rate policy to curb economic growth and fight inflation. However, some economists believe the policy has been a failure and that high interest rates contributed to inflation. Which of the following statements affects your view?
   ____ High interest rates have been harmful to the economy, have caused thousands of bankruptcies of small businesses, have contributed to inflation and should be abandoned as a means of combatting inflation.
   ____ Tight money and high interest rates are necessary evils in the fight against inflation and will help stabilize the economy in the long term.

You need to be familiar with useful business sources of information. These exercises give you an opportunity to obtain specific information from secondary sources; you will also assess the availability of resources in your library.

12. Using the *Fortune 500 Largest US Industrial Corporations 1984 Directory,* answer these questions:
    a. What company ranked number 1 in sales in 1983?
    b. What city is indicated in this directory as the home office for the company ranked number 1 in sales?
    c. What was the amount of sales indicated for this company in 1983?
    d. What was the average number of employees for this company in 1983?
    e. What company was ranked number 250 in sales in 1983?
    f. Where was the company located at that time?
    g. In 1983, how did Stokely Van Camp rank in the Fortune 500, and what were this company's sales in dollars?
    h. Based on total return to investors in 1983, what were the top three corporations?
13. Using *Dun and Bradstreet's Million Dollar Directory,* answer these questions:
    a. What types of business are listed?
    b. What address is indicated for Persepolis Oriental Rugs Company?
14. Using the *International Finance Handbook,* vol. 2, 1983, answer these questions:
    a. What is contained in Section 6.5?
    b. From the same source in a section entitled "Objectives of International Lease Financing," what are the two reasons cited for cross-border leasing?
15. Using *Standard & Poor's Register of Corporations, Directors, and First Executives,* vol. 3, 1985 Index, answer these questions:
    a. Cite two companies listed that manufacture steel springs, except wire. Include the locations of these companies.
    b. What is the Standard Industrial Classification (SIC) number assigned to the industries cited in *a.* above?
16. Using the *Rand McNally International Banker's Directory,* 1st ed., 1985, answer the following questions regarding the Bank of Commerce, Americus, Georgia:
    a. On December 31, 1984, what were the total assets?
    b. Who is listed as the chief executive officer (CEO)?
    c. To what parent company does the Bank of Commerce belong?
17. Using *Moody's Handbook of Common Stocks,* Summer 1985, answer these questions:

a. What predictions are made about prospects for the Martin Marietta Corporation?
b. When is the annual meeting of the Firestone Tire & Rubber Company held? The Chrysler Corporation?

18. Jeanette Sitton, manager of 10 Kroger Stores in a midwestern city, wants to increase sales and decides to implement a Price Patrol project. She plans to hire three people who, for the next six months, will visit competing grocery stores in the area once each week. The Price Patrol will record the prices of a list of grocery items and then report the results to Sitton. The results of these weekly visits are to be used in TV and newspaper advertisements.
a. Are the data collected in the case primary or secondary? Explain.
b. What technique would you use to collect the data: questionnaire, observation, or interview? Give reasons for your answer.
c. Design an appropriate form for use during the six-month study.

19. Since a nuclear waste disposal facility is planned for a site near Oak Ridge, Tennessee, one of the state senators seeks information on the opinions of residents. Because your company is a well-known consulting firm dealing with such studies, the senator asks you to undertake this project.
a. Will the project entail primary and/or secondary data? Explain.
b. What technique(s) would you suggest for collecting the data? Explain your rationale.
c. How would you obtain a representative sample?

20. For each of the following questions, identify whether primary or secondary data are needed. If primary data are required to answer the question, what technique is needed to collect the data: observation, interview, questionnaire? Why?
a. What are the opinions of area residents concerning prayer in school?
b. What reactions do customers have to shopping at a convenience store such as 7-11?
c. What are the TV viewing habits of teenagers?
d. What are the attitudes of people concerning selected bills before Congress?
e. What tasks do mail-room personnel perform?
f. What are the names of all textbooks on a selected topic?
g. How have the recent changes in federal legislation affected banking practices?
h. How can the local chapter of a professional association increase its membership?
i. How can the processing of a sale be improved?

21. Using the guidelines for writing questionnaire items in this chapter,

critique each question individually as it relates to the identified topic. How could each be improved?

a. From a workshop evaluation form:

(1) Please rate the value of the general information received in this workshop.
No value 1 2 3 4 5 6 Extremely valuable

(2) List some specific ideas you feel this workshop provided you with, which will assist you in your daily work. Be specific.
____

b. From a survey of lipstick preference by women:

(1) Do you buy the same color of lipstick over and over again?
____

(2) Is lipstick necessary to be well groomed? Y/N

(3) How many tubes of lipstick should a girl own? ________

(4) Would you like to see a lipstick that lasted several days on the market? ________ Would you buy it? ________

(5) Do you buy your lipstick to go with your complexion or with your clothes? ________

(6) Do you look for bargains in lipstick? Y/N

(7) Do you buy lipstick as a cosmetic? ________

c. From a survey of local chapters of a professional association about the use of Video Cassette Recorder equipment:

(1) Does your chapter have access to VCR equipment?
____

(2) If yes, is the equipment:
________ Owned by the chapter?
________ Rented/leased by the chapter?
________ Borrowed by the chapter?

(3) Are video presentations used in your chapter for professional development? ______ Yes ______ No

(4) Do you personally have access to VCR equipment?
________ Yes ________ No

(5) If you do, how do you get your video tapes?
________ Buy ________ Rent ________ Borrow
________ Other

(6) How often are video presentations made at your chapter meetings? ________ Rarely ________ Sometimes
________Often

(7) How would you rate the presentations of this type to your professional development?
________ Very beneficial ________ Somewhat beneficial
________ Not beneficial

d. From a mailed questionnaire about microcomputer printers:

(1) Do you use a microcomputer at work?

(2) _______ Yes _______ No (If No, skip to question 20)
What is the brand and model of this machine?

____

(3) Do you use a printer with this machine?
_______ Yes _______ No

(4) What kind of printing device does your printer use?
_______ Element
_______ Daisywheel
_______ Dot matrix
_______ Ink jet

(5) Where and when was your printer purchased?
_______ Computer store
_______ Office products dealer
_______ Direct from manufacturer
_______ Through advertisement in computer magazine

e. From a questionnaire containing demographic information:

(1) What is your household composed of?

____

(2) What is your income? ___________________________
(3) What level of education do you have? _______________
(4) What types of magazines do you subscribe to?
_______ *Sports Illustrated*
_______ *Time*
_______ *Life*
_______ *Playboy*
_______ *Reader's Digest*

(5) What is your age? _______
(6) Sex? _______

22. Design a form to be used by an observer in recording the traffic patterns at the intersection shown below. Be sure to include a way to record the movement of each car from any of the four directions.

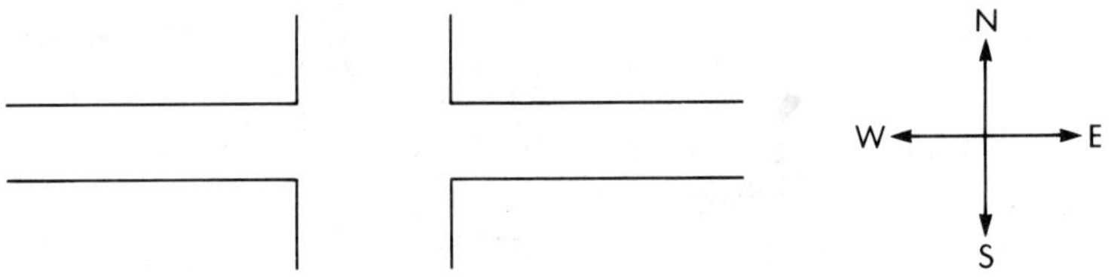

N
W E
S

23. Read the following questionnaire/checksheet provided by a restaurant for its customers to complete. Based on the chapter guidelines, list the strengths and weaknesses; then rewrite to overcome your identified weaknesses.

Dear Guest,
We welcome you to our restaurant, and we really hope that you have enjoyed your meal away from home. In order that we can continue to provide you with the best service, won't you kindly take the time to answer the following questions about our wonderful establishment.

Thanks,

Why did you select our restaurant?
_______ Area resident _______ Recommended by a friend
_______ Repeat guest _______ Television ad
_______ Radio ad _______ Radio ad
Would you dine with us again and bring a friend? _______________
How would you rate your meal?
Salad bar: _______ good _______ fair _______ poor
Entree: _______ good _______ fair _______ poor
Dessert: _______ good _______ fair _______ poor
Drink: _______ good _______ fair _______ poor
Would you agree that the service was good? _______ Yes _______ No
Time ____________ Date ____________
Location ____________
Your name and address
____
Your phone number ____________

24. Based on the guidelines you have learned about questionnaire construction, evaluate each of these questions that were used to survey college students about music preference.
    1. What is your overall? (From a survey of college students)
    2. Approximately what percent of your total budget was spent on music?
       _______ 0 percent
       _______ 1-5 percent
       _______ 6-10 percent
       _______ 10-20 percent
       _______ 20 percent or more
    3. Name your three favorite musical acts (single or group) not necessarily in order.
       ____
       ____
       ____
    4. How much musical background do you have?
       _______ None
       _______ 1-3 years
       _______ 3-5 years
       _______ over 5 years
    5. Which mode do you use when listening to music?
       _______ musical instruments _______ record player
       _______ radio—am _______ tape recorder
       _______ radio—fm

6. Which sex do you prefer?
   _______ Male
   _______ Female
   _______ Mixed
7. Do you own or plan to buy a record player, phonograph, or stereo?
   _______ Yes
   _______ No
8. Are you male or female?
9. Do you attend concerts, music festivals, or etc.?
10. Approximately how many times a day do you listen to the radio?
   _______ None at all
   _______ Less than three but more than one time
   _______ Less than six but more than three times
   _______ More than six times daily
11. If given a choice, which would you rather listen to: popular music or classical music?
12. Is there an opera house in your city or close by?
   _______ Yes
   _______ No

APPENDIX A: SELECTED REFERENCES FOR INDUSTRY DIRECTORIES

This list is not inclusive, of course, even for business-related publications. The intent is to provide names and descriptions of some commonly used business references, particularly those useful as industry directories.

Industry Directories[1]

***Million Dollar Directory* (Dun & Bradstreet).** Someone who is asked to locate information on a company will often head straight for this directory. While not by any means the most comprehensive general directory, it does offer such features as sales, number of employees, stock exchange, senior executive officers, and directors. To receive a listing in the directory a company must have a net worth of over $500,000.

This directory only lists headquarters locations, or addresses of a corporation's major subsidiaries. It does not list each plant location. A new version of the directory, the *Billion Dollar Directory,* lists all parent-subsidiary relationships and addresses for all companies with a worth of $500,000 or more.

***News Front: 30,000 Leading U.S. Corporations* (Year).** Public companies are ranked by sales, and privately held corporations are arranged by sales and

[1] Source: Fuld, Leonard M. *Corporate Intelligence: How To Get It: How To Use It.* New York: John Wiley & Sons, © 1985. (Reprinted by permission of John Wiley and Sons.)

geographic area. Tables include top performing companies by sales categories. Information contained on many of the companies includes assets, long-term debt, depreciation, P/E ratio, and stockholders equity.

North American Register of Business and Industry (Global Marketing Services). This text contains the 5,000 largest companies in North America. The companies are ranked by sales volume. In addition to sales, each entry lists number of employees.

Rand McNally International Bankers Directory (Rand McNally). This hefty tome contains information on 15,000 U.S. banks and 33,000 branches of U.S. banks, as well as on foreign banks and their branches. The text also contains economic and financial data for over 1,000 cities. Each entry offers amount of deposits held with that institution, other balance sheet information, the bank's principal officers, bank branches, and its directors.

Standard Directory of Advertisers (National Register Company). On the surface, this is a book meant only for the advertising industry. But in fact it is an excellent reference tool for general business research. The book has a roster of over 17,000 companies that are major advertisers. Each entry lists the company, its advertising agency, the products, and the media used. The Directory also comes with a complementary Geographic and Trademark volume, from which you can cross-check a company by its location or its product trademark names.

Standard & Poor's Register of Corporations, Directors and Executives (McGraw-Hill). There are three volumes in this excellent set. While it contains only one-half of the companies mentioned in D&B's *Million Dollar Directory,* the companies it does cover are covered well—with excellent indexing. The heart of the book, volume one, is an alphabetical listing of all the companies in the text. Each entry contains name, address, officers, directors, sales (where available), number of employees (also where available), and stock exchange. The other volumes index the text by geographical area and industry. It also has a parent-subsidiary directory, where the researcher can quickly spot who owns whom. The second volume sketches brief biographies of many of the key executives mentioned in volume one, under their company name.

Thomas Grocery Register (Thomas Publishing Company). If you ever have to find a food store or a food wholesaler, this is the book to turn to. It lists almost 6,000 companies in the food business. Aside from name and address, it also offers a company's estimated asset size and brief description of its product line. The types of companies mentioned are distributors, discount stores, food brokers, exporters, manufacturers, importers, equipment suppliers, and other services related to the food industry.

***Thomas Register of American Manufacturers and Thomas Catalog File* (Thomas Publishing Company).** Sixteen volumes long, it lists manufacturers' products and services by product. Companies are indexed by product. The product index itself serves two very important purposes: (1) it uses standard industry terminology, which will make looking up your industry group that much easier; and (2) the fact that Thomas uses industry lingo also makes the text a de-facto dictionary. You will find that the company advertisements, interspersed throughout the set, will quickly tell you how competitors are marketing their products and the extent of their product line. The last few volumes in the set are samples of company catalogs. Again, this will serve as a means to gauge the competition's product line. Another index, on yellow paper, has an extensive trademark listing. While not a true trademark register, it does cover thousands of commonly used manufacturers' trademarks.

Like the *Thomas Grocery Register,* this text will offer company name, address, telephone number, and an estimate of its asset size. Along with the Yellow Pages and *The Wall Street Journal,* you should consider Thomas a necessity for your research library.

APPENDIX B: BIBLIOGRAPHY ENTRIES

The first group of entries below illustrates the traditional method for citing secondary sources; the second group represents the style preferred by the American Psychological Association (APA).

Traditional Method

One author—book:

Ford, Gerald R. *A Time to Heal.* New York: Harper & Row, 1979.

Galbraith, John Kenneth. *A Life in Our Times.* Boston: Houghton Mifflin, 1981.

Whitney, David C. *The American Presidents.* Garden City, N.Y.: Doubleday, 1969.

Two authors—book:

Peters, Thomas J. and Robert H. Waterman, Jr. *In Search of Excellence: Letters from America's Best Run Companies.* New York: Warner Books, 1982.

N.B.: Include subtitle "Letters from . . ." in your bibliographic entry.

Three authors—book:

Stallard, John J., E. Ray Smith and Donald Reese. *The Electronic Office: A Guide for Managers.* Homewood, Ill.: Dow Jones-Irwin Incorporated, 1982.

Walgenbach, Paul H., Norman E. Dittrich, and Ernest I. Hanson. *Principles of Accounting.* 3rd ed. New York: Harcourt Brace Jovanovich, 1984.

N.B. In addition to having three authors, note this book is the third edition.

More than three authors—book:

Micheli, Linda et al. *Managerial Communication.* Glenview, Ill.: Scott, Foresman, 1984.

N.B. Rather than list all the authors, you may use et al. (or and others) after the name of the first author.

Editors—book:

Matteson, Michael T. and John M. Ivancevich, eds. *Classics.* Santa Monica, Calif.: Goodyear Publishing, 1977.

Weekly magazine:

Kirkpatrick, Curry. "Dingdong Duel in Dean's Dome." *Sports Illustrated,* 27 January 1986, pp. 22-25.

Monthly magazine:

Ellis, William S. "Queensland Broad Shoulder of Australia." *National Geographic,* January 1986, pp. 2-39.

American Psychological Association (APA) Style

One author—book:

Harris, Thomas H. (1969). *I'm ok—you're ok.* New York: Harper & Row.

Stigum, Marcia. (1978). *The money market—myth reality, and practice.* Homewood, IL: Dow Jones-Irwin.

Two authors—book:

Ayers, R. V., & Miller, S. M. (1983). *Robotics: Applications and social implications.* Cambridge, MA: Ballinger.

Hunt, H. A., & Hunt, T. L. (1983). *Human resource implications of robotics.* Kalamazoo, MI: W. E. Upjohn Institute for Employment Research.

Three authors—book:

Porter, Lyman W., Lawler, Edward E., III, & Hackman, J. Richard (1975). *Behavior in organizations.* New York: McGraw-Hill.

Smith, Allen N., Alexander, Wilma Jean, & Medley, Donald B. (1986). *Advanced office systems.* Cincinnati, OH: South-Western Publishing.

Book, second edition:

Dubrin, Andrew J. (1985). *Contemporary applied management: Behavioral science techniques for managers and professionals.* 2nd. ed. Plano, TX: Business Publications.

Book, revised edition:

Terry, George R. (1949). *Office management and control.* rev. ed. Homewood, IL: Richard D. Irwin.

Book—edited:

Crank, Doris & Crank, Floyd (eds.) (1963). *New perspectives in education for business.* Washington, DC: National Business Education Association.

Computer careers. (Editors of Consumer Guide) (1984). New York: Fawcett Columbine.

Book—no author or editor:

College-bound seniors. (1979). Princeton, NJ: College Board Publications.

Journal article, one author:

O'Connor, Bridget N. (1983). Administrative systems curriculum model. *Office Systems Research Journal.* 2 (1). 35-41.

Journal article, two authors:

Morris, R. I. & Biederman, D. A. (1985). How to give away money intelligently. *Harvard Business Review.* 63 (6). 151-59.

Journal article, more than two authors:

Gibbs, M., Hewing, P., Hulbert, J. E., Ramsey, D., & Smith, A. (1985). How to teach effective listening skills in a basic business communication class. *Bulletin of the Association for Business Communication.* 47 (2), 30-33.

Magazine article, author indicated:

Friedrich, O. (1983, January 3). The computer moves in. *Time.* 121 (1), 14-24.

Magazine article, two authors:

Encamation, D. J., & Vachani, Sushil. (1985, September-October). Foreign ownership: When hosts change the rules. *Harvard Business Review.* (5), 152-160.

Magazine article, no author indicated:

America rushes to high tech for growth. (1983, March 18). *Business Week,* 84-90.

Reference to an article or chapter in an edited book:

D'Onofrio, M. F. (1983). The office—today and tomorrow. In J. Rodenstein and R. Lambert (Eds.) *Microcomputers: Applications in vocational education,* pp. 193-211. Madison, WI: Vocational Studies Center, University of Wisconsin, Madison.

Technical report from a university:

Benton, O., & Branch, C. W. (1984). Robots, jobs, and education. (Report No. R01-1565-44-006-85). Knoxville, TN: University of Tennessee Office for Research in High Technology Education.

Proceedings of meeting:

O'Brien, F. O. (1984). Computer applications in professional writing: Systems that analyze and describe natural language. In R. D. Ramsey (Ed.), Professional Communication in the Modern World—Proceedings of the American Business Communication Association Southeast Convention. 293-297.

Unpublished doctoral dissertation:

Buero, C. S. (1979). Criteria for evaluating secondary consumer and homemaking programs in Tennessee. Unpublished doctoral dissertation, University of Tennessee, Knoxville.

Government publication:

Congress of the United States, Office of Technology Assessment (1982). Informational Technology and Its Impact on American Education. Washington: DC: U.S. Government Printing Office.

Book review:

Darian, Steven (1984). Review of how to prepare, stage and deliver winning presentations. *Journal of Business Communication* 21 (2), 58-59.

CHAPTER 13

PRESENTATION OF DATA AND GRAPHICS

Learning Objectives

After completing this chapter, you will be able to:

- □ Determine how various statistical techniques give greater meaning to the quantitative data in business reports.
- □ Understand meanings and applications of frequencies, central tendency (mean, median, mode), extremes (highest and lowest values), range, and mathematical relationships such as percents.
- □ Explain the importance of using graphics in business reports.
- □ Construct and explain the usefulness of tables, pie charts, various types of bar charts, and line charts.
- □ Develop several types of graphics and write appropriate interpretations of those graphics to support objectives of a business report.

Organizing data for meaning

Once you have obtained your raw data by using the appropriate research techniques (observations, surveys, questionnaires, interviews, or searches of company records), you must make them meaningful by classifying them, organizing related data, or developing appropriate calculations on the basis of the data. Only then are the data ready to be presented to the Reader. This chapter focuses on the various statistical techniques you may apply to raw data to make them more meaningful and useful. Some of the standard techniques for graphic illustrations of quantitative materials are presented.

Based on your general and specific objectives, you might, for example, select one or more of the following techniques to give greater meaning to the quantitative data you have collected:

Types of statistical tools for data interpretation

- ☐ Frequency (number of occurrences for a characteristic).
- ☐ Central tendency
  —the average (mean)
  —the middle score (median)
  —the most frequently occurring characteristic (mode).
- ☐ Extremes (highest and lowest values).
- ☐ Range (difference between the highest and lowest values).
- ☐ Mathematical relationship (percent, standard deviation, correlation).
- ☐ Trends—upward or downward change in variables over time.
- ☐ Changes—deviations from normal trends, patterns, etc.
- ☐ Exceptions—the absence of a characteristic; deviation from the average or generally accepted concepts; inconsistencies.
- ☐ Logical expectation—cause and effect, before and after.

Then once you have calculated whatever statistical measures you need, you are ready to decide on the most effective graphic format for presenting the data. Each graphic (table or figure) is normally accompanied by textual material that interprets or explains the major findings.

To help you in your selection process, let us focus on a discussion of the most common types of quantitative representations used in data analysis (frequency, percent, central tendency, dispersion, and correlation) and the most common types of graphics, along with their textual interpretations.

QUANTITATIVE REPRESENTATION

Your selection of the quantitative measure will depend on the nature of your general and specific objectives. (Refer to statistical textbooks for additional information on these or other statistical techniques.)

The raw data collected from individual subjects or respondents have little meaning in isolation. Meaning can be extracted only from data that reflect the responses of all subjects in the sample.

Frequency data

Frequency

One of the simplest means of expressing data is the frequency count: How many times does a particular characteristic occur in a given category? For example, if you were calculating data about the makeup of your communication course, you might want to classify the group in terms of student class level. The groups are freshmen, sophomores, juniors, seniors, and other. A simple way of obtaining the data for your class is to ask for a show of hands. The results might look like this:

College classification	Frequency
Freshmen	0
Sophomores	2
Juniors	15
Seniors	6
Other	2

Converting data to percents

Percent

Since numbers by themselves have limited meaning, we usually convert the raw figures into other numerical expressions. The frequency, for example, is often and easily converted into a percentage. To determine the percent, divide the frequency amount for each classification by the amount of units in the total sample and multiply by 100. You get the following results:

College classification	Frequency	Percent
Freshmen	0	-
Sophomores	2	8.0
Juniors	15	60.0
Seniors	6	24.0
Other	2	8.0
Total	25	100.0

The percentage figures for each group give a measure of the frequency of one item as compared to another. Adding the totals for each column helps the reader interpret the set of data. In this example, you can see that 60 percent of the students in the class were juniors.

Central Tendency

Sometimes data are more meaningful when interpreted by the central tendency of the measures or set of scores. The common central tendency measures are the mean, median, and mode.

LEGAL / ETHICAL ISSUE

In his book, *How to Lie with Statistics,* Huff adroitly points out how writers can distort numerical presentations to convey a misleading message.[1] Huff demonstrates how "averages and relationships and trends and graphs are not always what they seem."[2]

To illustrate, suppose you wanted to report your yearly sales to top management. This is how the graph might look:

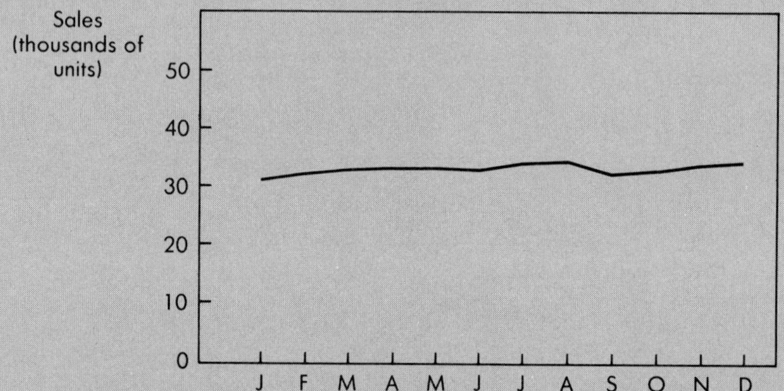

This figure reveals a flat sales image for the 12 months. You don't like this flat image because it makes your department look bad. If you wanted to convey a different image, you might use a different vertical scale and get this result:

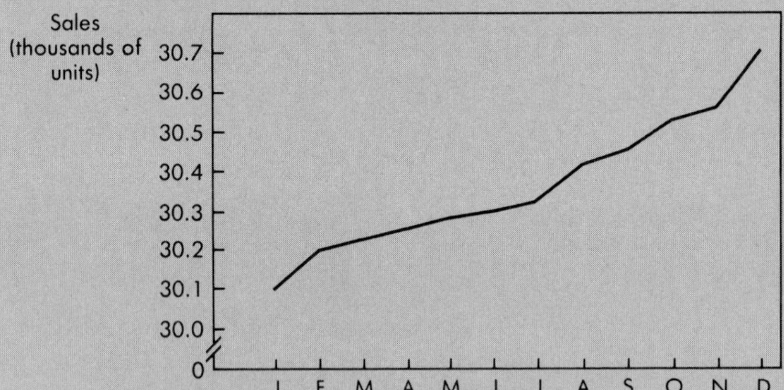

The sales image looks much better since sales appear to increase steadily. As a report writer, which of the examples would you use? Is it ethical to present data in a visual form such as this to convey this bent image? What might be the consequences? What basic principles should you follow in presenting visual data?

---

[1] Darrell Huff, *How to Lie with Statistics* (New York: W. W. Norton, 1954).

[2] Ibid., p. 8.

Arithmetic average

Mean. The mean is the arithmetic average of a numerical set. To obtain the mean, just add all the measures in the set of data and divide that total by the number of cases. For instance, look at this set of salaries for seven employees:

Employee	Salary
A	$73,000
B	18,000
C	23,000
D	21,000
E	25,000
F	15,000
G	21,000

The total salary, $196,000, divided by the number of employees, 7, yields a mean (or average) of $28,000.

Midpoint

Median. The median is the midpoint of the set of numbers. To find the midpoint, arrange the numbers in sequence—high to low or low to high—as shown:

Employee	Salary
A	$73,000
E	25,000
C	23,000
D	21,000—median
G	21,000
B	18,000
F	15,000

In this case, the midpoint is the fourth salary from the bottom or the top ($21,000); three salaries are above and three below this point. The median is based on the number of cases and ignores the numerical value of the salary.

Use the median to represent the central tendency of a set of numbers when there is an extremely high or low number that may distort the average. The mean for the set of data is $28,000; the median, $21,000. If you were reporting information about the salaries in a newspaper, the mean could distort the central tendency of the data since six of the seven people earn below the mean; the one high salary ($73,000) affected the mean. In this case, the median is probably a better measure of the central tendency of this set of numbers since three people made more and three made less than the median salary.

Most frequently occurring characteristic

Mode. The mode is the most frequently occurring characteristic in a set of data. In the preceding example, $21,000 is the mode; it is the same as the median. The mode is infrequently used in data representation but may from time to time be helpful in expressing the central tendency of a numerical set.

Dispersion

Central tendency measures for comparison purposes

The central tendency measures are one way to compare an individual's score with the tendencies of the overall data set. As you can see in the following data about salaries, however, these measures can provide limited information when you want to compare one whole set with another.

	Group A	Group B	Group C
	$20,000	$35,000	$39,000
	20,000	30,000	25,000
	20,000	20,000	20,000
	20,000	10,000	15,000
	20,000	5,000	1,000
Mean:	$20,000	$20,000	$20,000

Here the mean for each group is the same; yet there are great differences among the salaries for the three groups. These variations mean that sometimes you may need to look at the values using measures other than central tendency. By using dispersion measures, you can examine how much variation occurs, that is, how the scores spread out. Two of the most useful dispersion measures are range and standard deviation. Refer to a statistics textbook for other such measures.

Range

Range. The range is the simplest measure for the spread of a set of scores, because it uses the highest and lowest scores. The crude range is simply the difference between the highest and lowest values in the data set. In the preceding example, the range for Group A is zero ($20,000 minus $20,000); for Group B, $30,000 ($35,000 minus $5,000); and for Group C, $38,000 ($39,000 minus $1,000). The range offers a rough measure of the variability of the salaries. A larger spread exists between the highest and lowest salaries for Group C than for any of the others; Group A has no spread at all since all salaries are the same.

Standard deviation

Standard Deviation. Since the crude range ignores all scores other than the highest and lowest, using a dispersion measure such as the standard deviation is better. This measure accounts for each score and its variation from the measures of central tendency. Normally, the standard deviation offers the best measure of variability, because it reflects the deviation of each score from the mean in the data set. This method offers the most reliable measure of dispersion.

Assume that the following list represents 30 employees' scores on a computer literacy test:

Employee	Score	Employee	Score	
A	59	P	47	
B	55	Q	47	
C	54	R	47	
D	54	S	43	
E	53	T	43	
F	52	U	43	
G	52	V	43	
H	50	W	42	
I	49	X	42	
J	49	Y	40	
K	49	Z	40	
L	48	AA	39	
M	48	BB	37	
N	48	CC	37	
O	47	DD	30	N = 30

The formula for the standard deviation is:

$$\text{S.D.} = \sqrt{\frac{\Sigma d^2}{N}}$$

where:

S.D. = Standard deviation
d = Score minus mean
d^2 = Sum of deviations squared
N = Number of scores

Calculating standard deviation

The steps for calculating the standard deviation are shown in Figure 13.1. Keep in mind, however, that today most researchers use either a computer or calculator to compute statistical data.

The standard deviation for this set of scores is 6.23. In a normal distribution, 68.26 percent of the scores fall between one standard deviation above and below the mean. In this example, one standard deviation below the mean is 40 (46.23 − 6.23); one above, 52.46 (46.23 + 6.23). Of the 30 scores, 70 percent fall within this band. Consequently, this grouping is very near that of a normal distribution. Therefore, you could say the scores spread out from the mean in a normal fashion.

If another group of employees were given the same test and the results

Figure 13.1
Calculation of standard deviation

(1) Employee	(2) Score	(3) d	(4) d^2
A	59	12.77	163.0729
B	55	8.77	76.9129
C	54	7.77	60.3729
D	54	7.77	60.3729
E	53	6.77	45.8329
F	52	5.77	33.2929
G	52	5.77	33.2929
H	50	3.77	14.2129
I	49	2.77	7.6729
J	49	2.77	7.6729
K	49	2.77	7.6729
L	48	1.77	3.1329
M	48	1.77	3.1329
N	48	1.77	3.1329
O	47	.77	.5929
P	47	.77	.5929
Q	47	.77	.5929
R	47	.77	.5929
S	43	−3.23	10.4329
T	43	−3.23	10.4329
U	43	−3.23	10.4329
V	43	−3.23	10.4329
W	42	−4.23	17.8929
X	42	−4.23	17.8929
Z	40	−6.23	38.8129
AA	40	−6.23	38.8129
BB	39	−7.23	52.2729
CC	37	−9.23	85.1929
DD	37	−9.23	85.1929
EE	30	−16.23	263.4129
Total 30	1,387		1,163.3670

Calculations

1. Determine the mean for the set of scores
   Total of column 2 (1,387) divided by the total number of employees (30) = mean (46.2333 or 46.23).

2. Subtract the mean from each score to get the difference, using a negative sign for scores below the mean. Each score in column 2 minus 46.23 = column 3.

3. To get rid of the negative signs, square each entry in column 3. Each number in column 3 times itself = the amount shown in column 4.

4. Total all figures in column 4 to obtain the sum of the squared deviations (Σd^2).

5. Insert the appropriate numbers into the formula for the standard deviation ($\sqrt{\Sigma d^2/N}$) and solve the problem:

   a. Divide the sum of deviations squared by N (the number of scores). In this case, 1,163.367 divided by 30 = 38.7789.
   b. Extract the square root of this number:
   $$\sqrt{38.7789} = 6.227.$$
   c. Round off: (2 digits in this example): 6.23.

showed that the standard deviation was 1.44, you would know that more variability exists within the first group; members of the second group must be more nearly alike because less variability exists.

The standard deviation is a reliable means of determining similarities or dissimilarities within a group. The standard deviation is frequently used with other statistical techniques for giving meaning to a set of data.

Correlation

Correlation defined

Another statistical technique used in data analysis is correlation. Sometimes you may need to compare measures of one variable with another. For example, you might want answers to the following questions: How does performance compare with attitude? What is the relationship between ability and performance? How do scores on a pretest compare with scores on a posttest?

Correlation is a statistical technique that summarizes the degree of relationship between two sets of scores for the same group of persons. The two sets of scores can have different scales. You can select from several different statistical methods to determine the relationship between two sets of scores (variables).

Figure 13.2 illustrates one type of correlation—the Pearson Product-Moment Correlation. Again, statistical computations of this type are usually calculated on a computer. The computer will use the formula shown in Figure 13.2 and, in that particular instance, compute the correlation of .913.

What does the correlation .913 mean? The highest possible value for a correlation is ±1.00, which would occur if each employee's score were in the same relationship in both sets of scores. Since +.913 is very close to perfect

Figure 13.2
Relationship of two sets of scores using the Pearson Product-Moment Correlation

Employees	Performance	Attitude Scale
A	95	36
B	55	10
C	72	26
D	94	30
E	80	25
F	60	20
G	90	28
Maximum score	98	40

The formula for calculating the Pearson Product-Moment Correlation is:

$$r = \frac{\Sigma xy}{\sqrt{\Sigma x^2 \times \Sigma y^2}} = .913$$

Use of the Pearson Product-Moment Correlation

positive correlation, you could say that correlation is extremely high. Each employee performed at about the same level on both tests.

Using the Pearson Product-Moment Correlation, you can determine the relationship between two sets of scores—performance and attitude scores—for each person in the group. You can use this formula with measures on two different scales.

The steps for calculation of the formula are shown in Figure 13.3.

GRAPHICS

Why is it important to use graphics as a part of your business reports? You have probably heard the statement "A picture is worth a thousand words." In business reports, effective graphics can provide this picture and:

Figure 13.3 Calculation of Pearson Product-Moment Correlation

Employee	(1) Performance X	(2) Attitude Y	(3) x	(4) y	(5) x^2	(6) y^2	(7) xy
A	95	36	17	11	289	121	187
B	55	10	−23	−15	529	225	345
C	72	26	−6	1	36	1	− 6
D	94	30	16	5	256	25	80
E	80	25	2	0	4	0	0
F	60	20	−18	− 5	324	25	90
G	90	28	12	3	144	9	36
	546	175			1,582	406	732

Calculations

1. Determine the mean for each set of scores:
   Total column 1 (546) divided by number of employees (7) = performance mean (78)
   Total column 2 (175) divided by number of employees (7) = attitude mean (25)
2. For each set, subtract each score from the mean for that set of scores:
   column 1 minus 78 = column 3
   column 2 minus 25 = column 4
3. Square each value for x and y to get rid of the negative values:
   column 3 times column 3 = column 5
   column 4 times column 4 = column 6
4. Multiply each value for x by y to obtain column xy: column 3 times column 4 = column 7
5. Total columns x^2, y^2, and xy
6. Substitute the appropriate values in the formula for

$$\sqrt{\Sigma x^2 \times \Sigma y^2}$$

   a. Multiply column 5 total by column 6 total (1,582 times 406) = 642,292
   b. Extract the square root of that number (642,292) = 801.43
   c. Divide the total of column 7 by the square root (732 divided by 802.43) = .913 or .91

Importance of using graphics in business reports

- ☐ Hold the reader's interest.
- ☐ Break up the written material into manageable units.
- ☐ Organize the presentation of data.
- ☐ Help the reader form a quick mental image of data.
- ☐ Focus on specific data.
- ☐ Facilitate oral presentation of key points.

After collecting the raw data from a study and selecting the statistical technique, you must then decide how to present the data to your readers. Data are summarized best in either tables or figures. Tables present data in row-and-column format; figures present data in pie, line, bar, or other chart formats. Other visual forms include pictures, diagrams, and maps. Generally, the raw data are included in the appendix of the report. The main content of the report is the grouped or summarized data presented in the analysis section.

Use these overall guidelines for graphics:

Guidelines for use of graphics in business reports

- ☐ Place on the next page after its first mention or as soon as possible. Short graphics may be integrated within text itself.
- ☐ Number tables consecutively throughout the report.
- ☐ Number figures consecutively throughout the report.
- ☐ Use consistent form for placement of figure numbers, titles, etc.

The analysis section of most reports contains graphic representations, and the accompanying text explains the significance of accumulated data. As a report writer, you have an obligation to examine the data and interpret the results so that a reader can understand their significance.

Tables

Use of tables in business reports

Writers frequently present data in their reports in tabular form. The content can range from simple to complex. The table format is flexible enough so that you can present large amounts of detailed data efficiently. Figure 13.4 is a model of a typical table used in business reports. Notice that this table, and in fact most tables, consist of three basic parts: heading, body, and footer.

Table heading

Heading. The heading includes a table number and title. As long as you are consistent, you may use Arabic or roman numerals or a decimal system. Figure 13.4 uses Arabic. If the first table in the report is numbered 1, the next table is 2, etc. Number the tables consecutively throughout the report including those in the appendix.

Developing the table title

Normally, express the title as a phrase, which answers all or most of these questions: What? Who? Where? When? To create an effective title for a table, just jot down answers to these questions, using prepositions and appropriate

Figure 13.4
Example of simple table

TABLE 1
Major field of study for Communications 101 students at Southwestern University, May, 19--

Heading

Body

Footer

Major	Number	Percent
Accounting	7	2.3
Business education	5	1.6
Computer science	8	2.7
Finance	49	16.1
General business	63	20.7
Management	24	7.9
Marketing	88	29.0
Transportation	34	11.1
Other	26	8.6
Total	304	100.0

Source: John M. Penrose, "A Discrepancy Analysis of the Job-Getting Process and a Study of Resume Techniques," *Journal of Business Communication* 21 (Summer 1987), p. 8.

punctuation marks to provide the necessary connectives. For the example in Figure 13.4, the answers to these questions are:

Elements of a table title

What? Major field of study
Who? Students in Communications 101
Where? Southwestern University
When? May, 19--

By adding the prepositions *of* and *at* and the comma, you can easily complete the title. Also try to sequence these facts for the best effect. Generally, the *what?* will be placed first since it is the most important, though other arrangements can also yield effective titles. You usually arrange the multiline heading in inverted pyramid style with the top line longer than the bottom line. Some companies may specify other forms. At least one other alternative arrangement of table headings is presented in this chapter (see Figure 13.9).

Table body: column headings, facts (data), totals

Body. The body usually consists of column headings, the facts in columnar form, and totals. Some tables, however, may not include totals. Since the leftmost column normally is considered the primary position, present the major first. Arrange the number and percent columns from left to right; percent is a representation of the number column. Numbers are converted into percentages rounded off to one decimal place.

In the list in Figure 13.4, the majors are alphabetically sequenced. (Note that the *other* is placed last. Many times you will have an other or miscellaneous entry in this primary column.) You may use numeric, geographic, or some other logical sequencing depending on what data you want to emphasize. For example, if you wanted to emphasize the numbers in each category, you would arrange the data according to frequency from high to low or low to high. If you used this numeric arrangement, however, locating a specific major would be more difficult. Thus, the alphabetical arrangement used in Figure 13.4 probably presents the best arrangement if you want to focus on majors.

Table footer defined

Footer. The footer may include information about the sources of primary and secondary data. Footers may also explain items in the table, as shown in Figure 13.10. When you're writing a report, you may or may not choose to list sources at the bottom of every table, especially if the same source was used for most or all of the tables. Keep in mind, though, that many times you may use tables in an oral presentation. If you have lifted them from the report without the footers, the readers won't know the sources. To be on the safe side, you may prefer to give the source on every table. You need to indicate a reference for all lifted material. For primary data, you have an option to list or not to list. Each secondary source needs a reference.

Table Interpretation

Guidelines for narrating or interpreting tables

Now that we have examined the makeup of the table (heading, body, and footer), let's look next at the narrative or text that accompanies the table. When you write a narrative or interpretation, be sure that when you first introduce the narrative you use the table reference (table number) and subject idea. Then use a lead-in to introduce a new table or other graphic. Examples of lead-in statements include:

"As shown in Table 1, . . ."
"Table 1 shows . . ."
"As illustrated in Figure 7, . . ."

Some writers prefer to describe the content of a graphic first and then show the reference at the end: ". . .of the 304 students (Table 1). . . ." A key point to remember is that you should be consistent in the way you introduce or reference tables and other graphic material. For example, if you begin with "As shown in Table 1, . . ." and then describe its content, introduce your next graphic in the same manner: "As shown in Table 2, . . ."

To complete the lead-in statement, use the information in the title. To complete the interpretation, select the major points that the reader will need to understand the meaning. Present these points using the same sentence structure and consistent wording; changing the sentence pattern hinders the understanding. Use the third person.

Using these guidelines, you could introduce Figure 13.4 as follows:

As shown in Table 1, of the 304 students surveyed at Southwestern University concerning their reactions to résumé preparation, . . .

Note that the table reference, title information, the subject of the study, and one bit of data (304 students), were used to begin the interpretation.

How do you know what to include in the interpretation? From Figure 13.4, just look at the types of data that are available:

Points to consider when interpreting tables

Highest value: marketing with 29.0 percent

2nd highest: general business with 20.7 percent

3rd highest: finance with 16.1 percent

Top three majors (marketing, general business, finance) account for 64.8 percent

Remaining majors (transportation, management, computer science, accounting, business education) account for 25.6 percent

Business majors: 91.4 percent (278); nonbusiness majors: 8.6 percent (26).

Analysis of data

Note the regrouping of data in the last three items above. After listing the major points, decide on the best sequence for the findings. Normally, a general-to-specific arrangement works best for this type of writing. Adding this information to the introductory part produces the following interpretation:

As shown in Table 1, of the 304 students in Communications 101 surveyed at Southwestern University concerning their reactions to résumé preparation; 91.4 percent (278) were business majors and 8.6 percent (26) were other majors. Three majors accounted for 64.8 percent of the students—marketing with 29.0 percent, general business with 20.7 percent, and finance with 16.1 percent. The other five majors accounted for 25.6 percent—transportation, management, computer science, accounting, and business education.

When you interpret a table, carefully study its content and select the major points. The interpretation above ignores the other majors. Instead, the emphasis is on the top three—marketing, general business, and finance. An alternative interpretation is shown below. Which do you prefer?

As shown in Table 1, 304 students in Communications 101 were surveyed at Southwestern University concerning their reactions to résumé preparation. Of the 304 students surveyed, 88, or 29.0 percent, were marketing majors; 63, or 10.7 percent, general business majors; 49, or 16.1 percent, finance majors; 54, or 25.6 percent, other business majors; and 26, or 8.6 percent, other majors.

No one correct way exists for writing the interpretation. Each table presents a different set of circumstances and meets a different set of objectives. Study the table data, review your objectives, use the guidelines, then write an appropriate interpretation.

Figure 13.5
Sample of cross-referenced table

TABLE 2
Major field of study for Communications 101 students classified by sex at Southwestern University May 19__

Major	Female Number	Male Number	Total
Accounting	2	5	7
Business education	5	—	5
Computer science	1	7	8
Finance	12	37	49
General business	20	43	63
Management	10	14	24
Marketing	40	48	88
Transportation	20	14	34
Other	4	22	26
Total	114	190	304

Cross-referenced table

Cross-referenced Table. Now, let's look at a more complex table with interpretation. Starting with the data shown in Figure 13.4, assume that you want to examine the distribution of female and male students in the sample. This view produces a cross-referenced table. Figure 13.5 shows the effect of adding data on female and male students. The total for each major is now cross-referenced by two variables—gender and major.

Of course you need to modify the title to reflect the new ingredient. That is, the title should answer an additional question: How is the data classified? A revised title reflects this new view of the data:

Title for cross-referenced table

Major field of study for Communications 101 students classified by gender at Southwestern University, May, 19__

Before completing the table, you will need to consider its purpose. Any of these questions might need answering.

1. What percentage of students in each major is female? Male?
2. What percentage of the total female student population is in each of the majors? What percentage of the total male student population is in each of the majors?
3. What percentage of the total number of students is female? Male?
4. What percentage of the total number of students in each major is female? Male?

Organizing tabular information

Each question presents a different view of the data. When you are organizing tabular data for a business report, you'll need to decide which data is important and what type of presentation is most appropriate for the objectives of your report. The more you know about statistics, the more you'll understand the numerous options available for organizing and calculating tabular information. For example, the tables in Figures 13.6, 13.7, and 13.8 illustrate three different ways to view the same data, based on gender and major distribution for business students at Southwestern University.

Figure 13.6
What percentage of students in each major is female? male? (question no. 1)*

Major	Female		Male		Total	
	Number	Percent	Number	Percent	Number	Percent
Accounting	2	28.6	5	71.4	7	100.0
Business education	5	100.0		—	5	100.0
Computer science	1	12.5	7	87.5	8	100.0
Finance	12	24.5	37	75.5	49	100.0
General business	20	31.7	43	68.3	63	100.0
Management	10	41.7	14	58.3	24	100.0
Marketing	40	45.5	48	54.5	88	100.0
Transportation	20	58.8	14	41.2	34	100.0
Other	4	15.4	22	84.6	26	100.0

* Note: Incomplete table—it shows only the body of the table.

Notice that Figure 13.6 presents the percentage of female and male students in each major based on the total number of students in each major. Thus, the table tells you that out of the total number of finance majors (49), 24.5 percent are female and 75.5 percent are male. These percentages are arrived at by dividing the number of female or male finance majors by the total number of finance majors (12 ÷ 49 = 0.245; 37 ÷ 49 = 0.755).

Figure 13.7 uses the same set of data, but the percentages are based on the total number of each gender who have declared a business major. Thus, out of the total number of females declaring a business major (114), 10.5 percent have declared a finance major (12 ÷ 114 = 0.105).

In Figure 13.8, the percentages are based on the total number of business students, both male and female. So the 12 females declaring a finance major represent 3.9 percent of the total number of business students.

Depending on the purpose of the report, the writer might include the first,

Figure 13.7
What percentage of the total female student population is in each of the majors? What percentage of the total male student population is in each of the majors? (question no. 2)*

Major	Female		Male		Total	
	Number	Percent	Number	Percent	Number	Percent
Accounting	2	1.7	5	2.6	7	2.3
Business education	5	4.4	—	—	5	1.6
Computer science	1	0.9	7	3.7	8	2.6
Finance	12	10.5	37	19.5	49	16.1
General business	20	17.5	43	22.6	63	20.7
Management	10	8.8	14	7.4	24	7.9
Marketing	40	35.2	48	25.2	88	29.0
Transportation	20	17.5	14	7.4	34	11.2
Other	4	3.5	22	11.6	26	8.6
Total	114	100.0	190	100.0	304	100.0

* Note: Incomplete table—it shows only the body of the report.

Figure 13.8
Percentage of total students who are female; percentage of total students who are male; percentage of total students classified by major*

Major	Female		Male		Total	
	Number	Percent	Number	Percent	Number	Percent
Accounting	2	.7	5	1.6	7	2.3
Business education	5	1.6	—	—	5	1.6
Computer science	1	0.3	7	2.4	8	2.7
Finance	12	3.9	37	12.2	49	16.1
General business	20	6.6	43	14.1	63	20.7
Management	10	3.3	14	4.6	24	7.9
Marketing	40	13.2	48	15.8	88	29.0
Transportation	20	6.6	14	4.7	34	11.1
Other	4	1.3	22	7.3	26	15.4
Total	114	37.5	190	62.5	304	100.0

* Note: Incomplete table—it shows only the body of the table.

the second, or all three of these tables. What would be the objectives of a report using the percentages supplied in the first table? The second table? The third table? Which tables the writer uses and how the data are interpreted depend on the objectives of the report.

Rating scales as a means of collecting and interpreting data.

Rating Scales. Previous examples used only frequency data for selected characteristics. Some survey data are in the form of rankings. In this section of the chapter, we'll discuss an example where responses are ranked from highly pleased to highly displeased.

Assume that you wanted to survey 32 managers in a company about their level of satisfaction with current support services. Information from this survey would be used to improve support services so that managers could be more productive. As a follow-up, the same survey could be sent out again to help measure improvement. The tabulated responses shown in Figure 13.9 are for one support area included on a questionnaire: the telephone/receptionist support service.

To make the data in Figure 13.9 meaningful, convert the frequency of responses into a different form. A rating scale is one way to obtain a weighted total for each service. For example, assign the following weights to the five ratings:

Use of a rating scale for data collection

5 = Highly pleased
4 = Moderately pleased
3 = Neutral
2 = Moderately displeased
1 = Highly displeased

Multiply the frequency by the assigned weight; for the first service, placing phone calls, the weighted frequency is 151 (26 × 5) + (4 × 4) + (1 × 3) +

Figure 13.9 Table showing rating-scale response

TABLE 3.1
Management personnel satisfaction with telephone/receptionist, support services, Excello Corporation, July 19__*

Telephone/ receptionist	**Highly pleased**	**Moderately pleased**	**Neutral**	**Moderately displeased**	**Highly displeased**
Placing phone calls	26	4	1	1	0
Answering phone calls	26	4	1	1	0
Obtaining directory assistance	29	2	0	0	0
Receiving/directing visitors	15	17	0	0	0
Acting as receptionist	16	5	1	1	1
Messenger/errand running	0	15	1	1	16

* An alternative arrangement for a table heading.

Use of weighted totals for table interpretation

(1 × 2). Figure 13.10 presents the frequencies and weighted totals. The weighted totals by themselves don't mean much. You need some criteria against which you can compare the weighted totals. The following is a common method to give meaning to the weighted frequency data. If all 32 managers indicated a neutral level of satisfaction, the weighted total is 96 (32 times the assigned weight of 3). Any weighted total more than 96, therefore, would indicate a favorable response. Likewise, a weighted total of 64 or less would indicate an unfavorable response (32 times the assigned weight of 2 for moderately displeased). Anything between 64 and 96 is neutral.

Using these criteria, you might interpret the table shown in Figure 13.10 as follows:

As shown in Table 3.1, in July 19__, 32 Excello Corporation managerial personnel rated their level of satisfaction with six telephone/receptionist support services. Managerial personnel indicated a favorable response to five of the six telephone/receptionist support services as indicated by the weighted averages: obtaining directory assistance (156), placing phone calls (151), receiving/directing visitors (143), answering phone calls (139), and acting as receptionist (100); and an unfavorable response to only one support service, messenger/errand running (77). Although the support service "acting as a receptionist" received a favorable response (100), the degree of satisfaction is slight.

Group Comparison. You may use the rating scale to interpret responses from two groups for the same support services. A survey of 32 managers and 103 engineers about their satisfaction with secretarial support services reveals the responses shown in Figure 13.11. You suspect there is a difference between the levels of secretarial support services provided for the two groups.

To identify the differences in responses and to make the data meaningful

Figure 13.10 Example of Likert-Scale Table

TABLE 3.1

Management personnel satisfaction with telephone/receptionist, support services, Excello Corporation, July 19__

Service telephone/receptionist	Frequency[a]					
	Highly pleased	Moderately pleased	Neutral	Moderately displeased	Highly displeased	Weighted total[b]
Placing phone calls	26	4	1	1	—	151
Answering phone calls	20	4	7	1	—	139
Obtaining directory assistance	29	2	1	—	—	156
Receiving/directing visitors	15	17	—	—	—	143
Acting as receptionist	8	6	6	6	6	100
Messenger/errand running	—	15	0	1	16	77

[a] Thirty-two management personnel surveyed.
[b] Total = Sum of value scale times frequency; highly pleased = 5; moderately pleased = 4; neutral = 3; moderately displeased = 2; highly displeased = 1.

for top management, you must separate the responses of engineers and managers for each category, as shown in Figure 13.12. For engineers, the number 309 (scale value of 3 × 103 frequency), can serve as a reference point; thus, a weighted frequency total above 309 would show a tendency toward agreement. A weighted frequency below 206 (scale value of 2 × 103 frequency) would show a tendency toward disagreement. For managers, a weighted frequency total above 96 (scale value of 3 × 32 frequency) would show a tendency toward agreement; 64 (scale value of 2 × 32 frequency) and below, a tendency toward disagreement.

With this statistical set of data, you could write the following information to accompany the table:

Sample table interpretation using weighted averages

Table 15 shows that satisfaction of managers and engineers differed on three of the four document processing support services. Weighted averages above 309 for the engineers and above 96 for the managers indicate agreement. Engineers tended to agree that documents take too long before they are passed along and mailed (377), while managers were neutral (94); engineers tended to agree that a one-page document requires at least one day to be put in final form (336), while managers were neutral (71). On the topic "length of time needed for revised document versus the first draft," engineers were neutral (285) and managers were displeased (51).

Report writers prefer to use the weighted frequency method because of its simplicity in interpreting the data. The combined value for each category makes comparison clear.

Figure 13.11 Comparison of two groups

TABLE 4
Engineer and manager satisfaction rating of secretarial support services, Excello Corporation, July 19_

Support service	Rating[a] 5	4	3	2	1
Documents take too long before they are ready to be mailed or passed along.					
Engineers	35	31	8	25	4
Managers	3	12	2	10	5
A one-page document requires at least one day to be put in final form.					
Engineers	26	24	14	29	10
Managers	4	2	1	17	8
Getting a revised document takes just as long as getting the first draft.					
Engineers	13	20	8	54	8
Managers	2	1	1	16	12
Once a document is typed, it is delivered to me immediately.					
Engineers	14	45	3	34	7
Managers	6	14	3	7	2

[a] Highly agree = 5; moderately agree = 4; neutral = 3; moderately disagree = 2; highly disagree = 1.

Pie Charts

Pie charts defined

Use the pie chart when you want to show the proportion of the parts to the whole, such as microwave oven features in a sales presentation. The components of the pie chart must equal 100 percent. Follow these guidelines for developing pie charts to use in your business reports:

Guidelines for developing pie charts

- ☐ Limit the chart to six components to avoid clutter.
- ☐ Begin with the largest component at the 12 o'clock position. Other components follow in order of magnitude moving clockwise.
- ☐ Label components and show percentages for each. Put percentage and label inside the large components and outside the smallest components.
- ☐ Use color or cross-hatching for emphasis.
- ☐ Refer to each pie chart as a figure in the report.
- ☐ Use the same style for figures throughout the report, such as either boxed or not boxed titles at the top or bottom.
- ☐ Give a complete title for each chart.
- ☐ Indicate the source, if known.

Examine the sample pie chart and its interpretation shown in Figure 13.13.

Even though pie charts occur frequently in business reports, they do have certain limitations. Pie charts generally do not show the specific amounts for each segment. For example, if you need the specific amount of revenue for IBM, you (the reader) must multiply the total revenue ($69,333.3 million) by 70 percent. If you had another pie chart for a second year, comparison is

Figure 13.12 Weighted frequency total table

TABLE 15

Attitudes of engineers and managers with document processing support services, Excello Corporation, July 19_

Support service	Weighted frequency	
	Engineer[a]	Manager[b]
Documents take too long before they are ready to be mailed or passed along.	377	94
A one-page document requires at least one day to be put in final form.	336	71
Getting a revised document takes just as long as getting the first draft.	285	51
Once a document is typed, it is delivered to me immediately.	289	111

[a] Value above 309 indicates agreement; below 206, disagreement.
[b] Value above 96 indicates agreement; 64 and below, disagreement.

more difficult than it is with other forms. A line or bar chart is better for showing comparisons.

Bar Chart

Bar charts defined

When you want to compare items in your business reports, select the bar chart. Since they are easy to construct and understand, bar charts are among the most commonly used visual aids in reports and presentations. You can construct bar charts either vertically or horizontally. As a variation, you might also subdivide each bar into segments. As a report writer, you have a great deal of flexibility in determining how you will use these three types. Follow these guidelines for developing bar charts to use in your business writing:

Guidelines for developing bar charts

- ☐ Use two axes. Label the item (subjects) and the value scale (dollar, quantity, etc.). Always begin the quantitative axis with zero.
- ☐ Select meaningful labels to ensure that the content items are clear.
- ☐ Sequence items logically, using a numerical (high to low or low to high), an alphabetical, a degree of importance, or other logical sequence.
- ☐ Assign color or cross-hatching for emphasis.
- ☐ Construct each bar in proportion to a specific scale.
- ☐ Make space between bars smaller than the bars themselves.
- ☐ Make bars equal in width.
- ☐ Round off numbers; omit decimals.
- ☐ Refer to each chart as a figure.
- ☐ Use consistency in form—boxed or not boxed; titles at top or bottom.
- ☐ Give a complete title for each.
- ☐ Indicate a source, if known.

Figure 13.13
Sample pie chart and interpretation

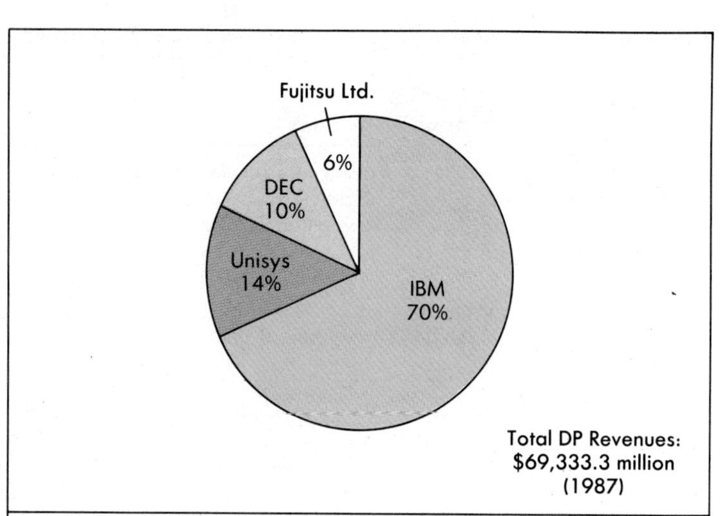

Figure 7. The Top Four Worldwide Data Processing Companies

Source: *Datamation* 33, no. 12 (June 15, 1987), p. 42.

As shown in Figure 7, the top four worldwide data processing companies accounted for data processing revenues of $69,333.3 million. IBM ranked first with 70 percent of the data processing revenues; the next closest was Unisys (merger of Burroughs and Sperry) with 14 percent.

When to use vertical bar charts in business reports

Vertical and Horizontal Bar Charts. Avoid using both the scale and the number at the end of the bars in the same chart. When you want your Reader to get a quick image of the contrast of items, use a scale. When you want to give the specific amounts of the items, indicate the number at the end of the bar. Figure 13.14 shows how to use specific numbers to identify the quantities for each bar. Bar height should reflect the differences in bar totals. Figure 13.15, a horizontal bar chart, illustrates the use of a scale.

Multiple-bar charts as an alternative

Multiple-Bar Chart. Figure 13.16 is a multiple-bar chart together with a sample interpretation. This example reflects top-level and middle-level mana-

Figure 13.14
Sample vertical bar chart and interpretation

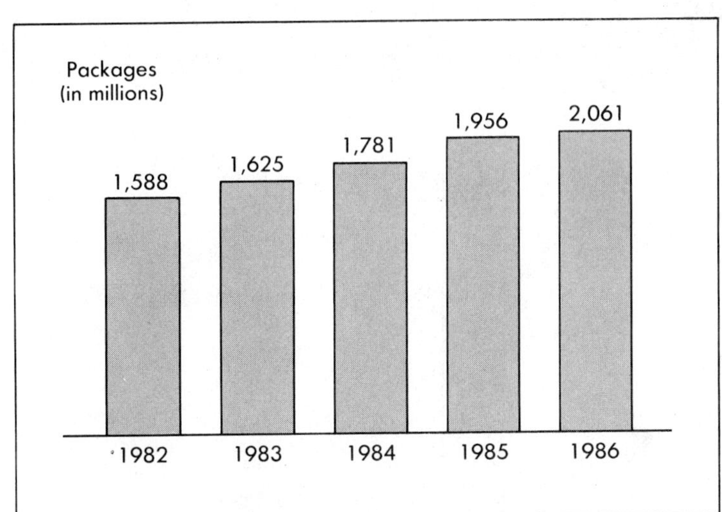

Figure 12. Volume of Packages Delivered by Dual Corp., 1982–1986.

Source: Company records.

As shown in Figure 12, the volume of packages delivered by the Dual Corporation increased by 473 million packages between 1982 and 1986. In 1982, 1,588 million packages were delivered; in 1984, 1,781 million; and in 1986, 2,061 million.

gerial use of personal computers. Note the legend at the top middle of the figure.

Use of stacked and segmented bar charts in business reports

Variations of Bar Charts. A stacked bar chart and a segmented bar chart are variations of the regular bar chart. Instead of placing the bars side by side, the stacked bar chart places the smaller bars in front of the others, as in Figure 13.17. The segmented bar chart differs from the stacked bar chart since the whole bar represents 100 percent; each segment is shown in proportion to the whole. Although similar to the pie chart, the segmented bar chart is useful

Figure 13.15
Sample horizontal bar chart and interpretation

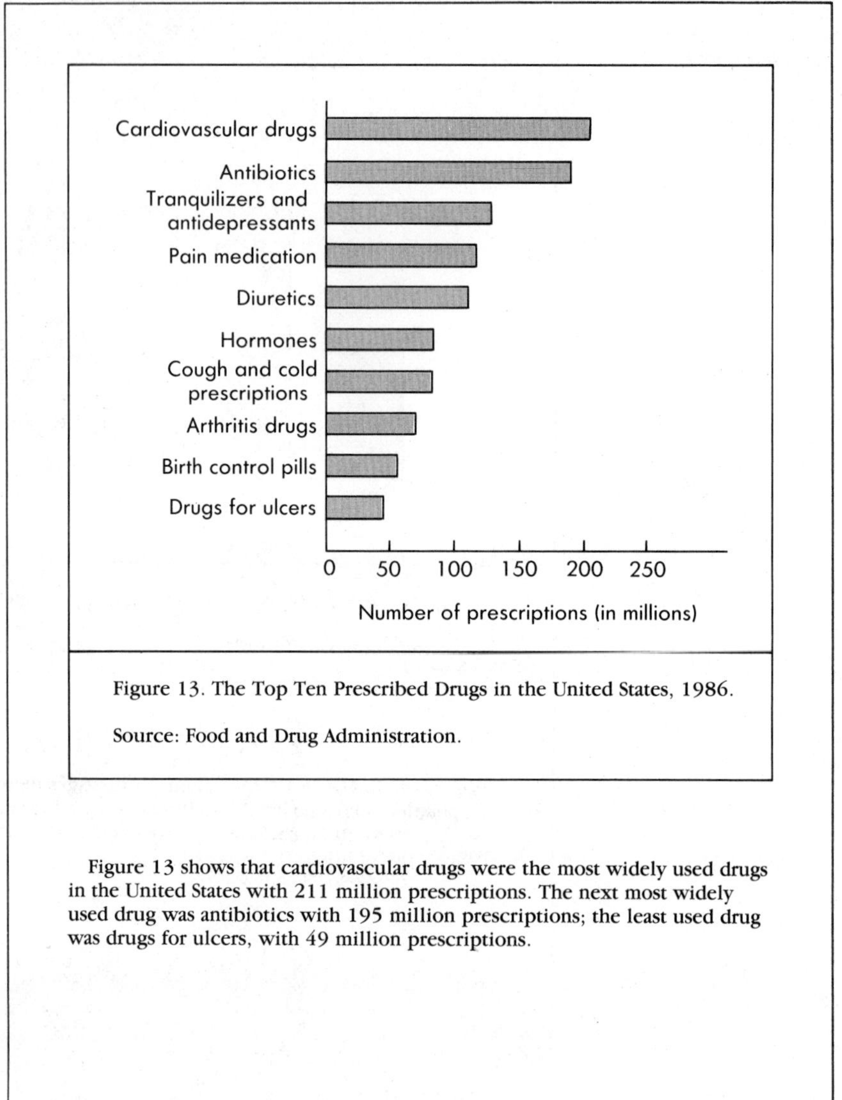

Figure 13. The Top Ten Prescribed Drugs in the United States, 1986.

Source: Food and Drug Administration.

Figure 13 shows that cardiovascular drugs were the most widely used drugs in the United States with 211 million prescriptions. The next most widely used drug was antibiotics with 195 million prescriptions; the least used drug was drugs for ulcers, with 49 million prescriptions.

in comparing more than one set of data as shown in Figure 13.18. Numbers or percents are included to communicate the meaning of the data.

Line Charts

Line charts defined

Line charts, which are used to illustrate trends over time (increases, decreases, fluctuations in some value), are easy to create. Follow these guidelines to develop effective linear charts for your business reports:

- □ Use horizontal scale lines for easier reading.

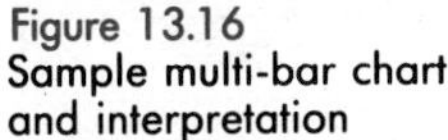

Figure 13.16
Sample multi-bar chart and interpretation

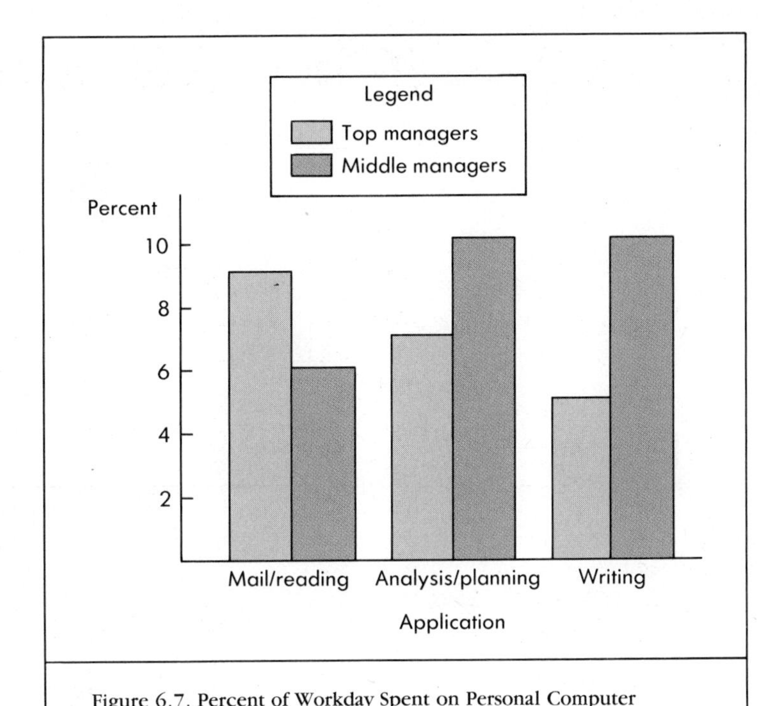

Figure 6.7. Percent of Workday Spent on Personal Computer Applications by Managers.

Figure 6.7 shows that top managers spent 9 percent and middle managers spent 6 percent of their work day using the personal computer for mail/reading. Top managers spent 7 percent and middle managers spent 10 percent of their work day using the personal computer for analysis/planning. Top managers spent 5 percent and middle managers spent 10 percent of their time using the personal computer for writing. Top managers spent the most time using their personal computers for mail/reading, while the middle managers spent the most time using their personal computers for analysis/planning and writing.

Guidelines for developing line charts

- ☐ Show the time periods at the bottom of the chart.
- ☐ Limit the number of lines to no more than four.
- ☐ Use legend (what the line represents) for multiple-line charts.
- ☐ Use color or symbols for emphasis, especially with multiple-line charts.
- ☐ Use consistent form.
- ☐ Give a complete title.
- ☐ Indicate source, if known.
- ☐ Refer to as a figure in the report (number consecutively).

Figure 13.17
Sample stacked bar chart

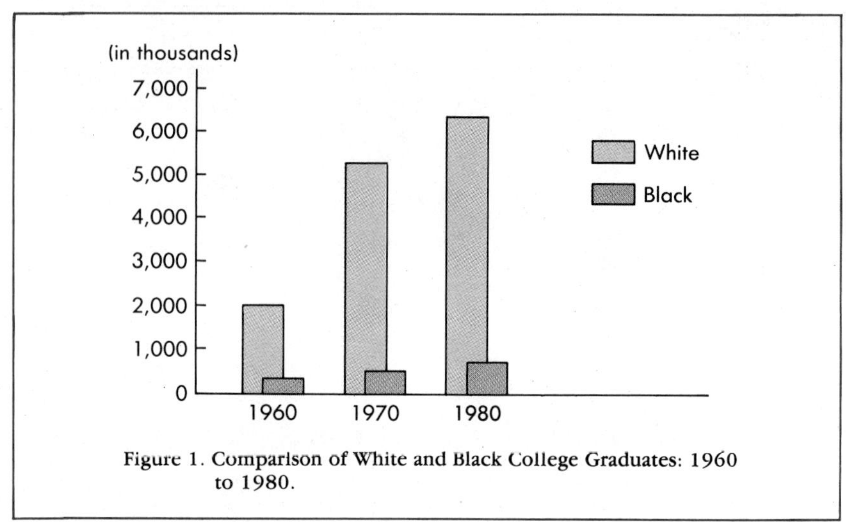

Figure 1. Comparison of White and Black College Graduates: 1960 to 1980.

Figure 13.18
Sample segmented bar chart

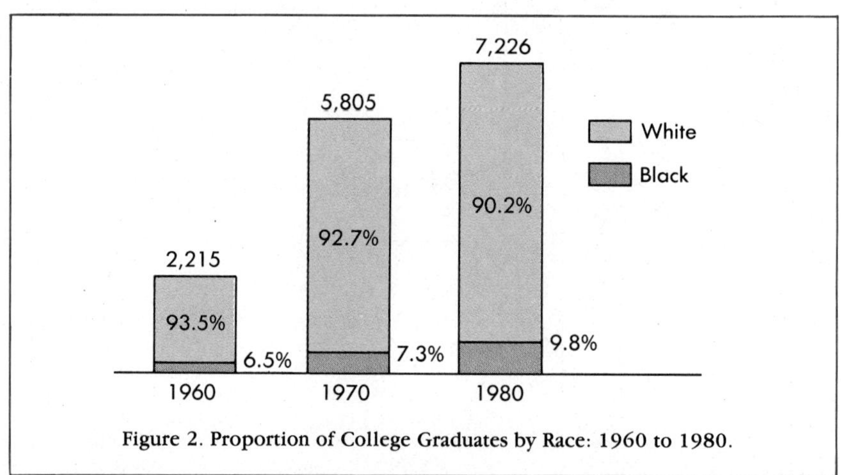

Figure 2. Proportion of College Graduates by Race: 1960 to 1980.

Figure 13.19 is a sample line chart with its interpretation. Figure 13.20 illustrates a multiline chart.

Other Graphics

Other graphic aids for business writing

Other types of visual aids you may use in your business writing include maps (see Figure 13.21) and organizational charts (see Chapter 4).

Use of the computer and graphics

With the advanced computer technologies available today, you can obtain selected software packages to create a variety of computer graphics. With a special printer called a plotter or color laser printer, you can prepare multicolor graphics for written or oral presentations. The key point to keep in

Figure 13.19
Sample line chart and interpretation

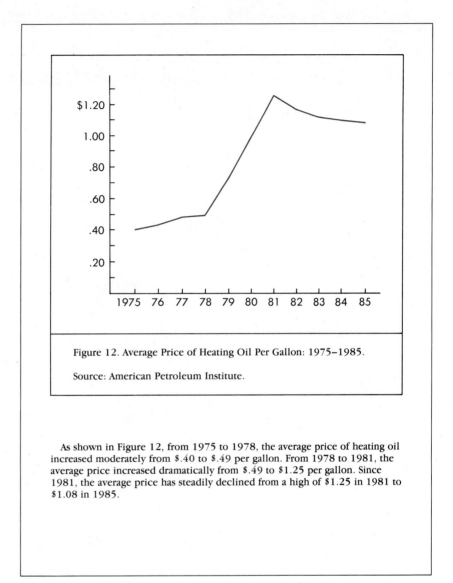

Figure 12. Average Price of Heating Oil Per Gallon: 1975–1985.

Source: American Petroleum Institute.

As shown in Figure 12, from 1975 to 1978, the average price of heating oil increased moderately from $.40 to $.49 per gallon. From 1978 to 1981, the average price increased dramatically from $.49 to $1.25 per gallon. Since 1981, the average price has steadily declined from a high of $1.25 in 1981 to $1.08 in 1985.

mind when using any visual aid is that you must select the graphic that most nearly portrays the meaning you want to convey. Graphics are an important part of any written or oral business presentation, but use judgment. Keep these thoughts in mind when designing and using them:

A word of caution regarding use of graphics

- ☐ Don't overdo.
- ☐ Some data do not require the use of visual aids.
- ☐ Present the data in the most appropriate form.

Figure 13.20
Sample multiple-line chart and interpretation

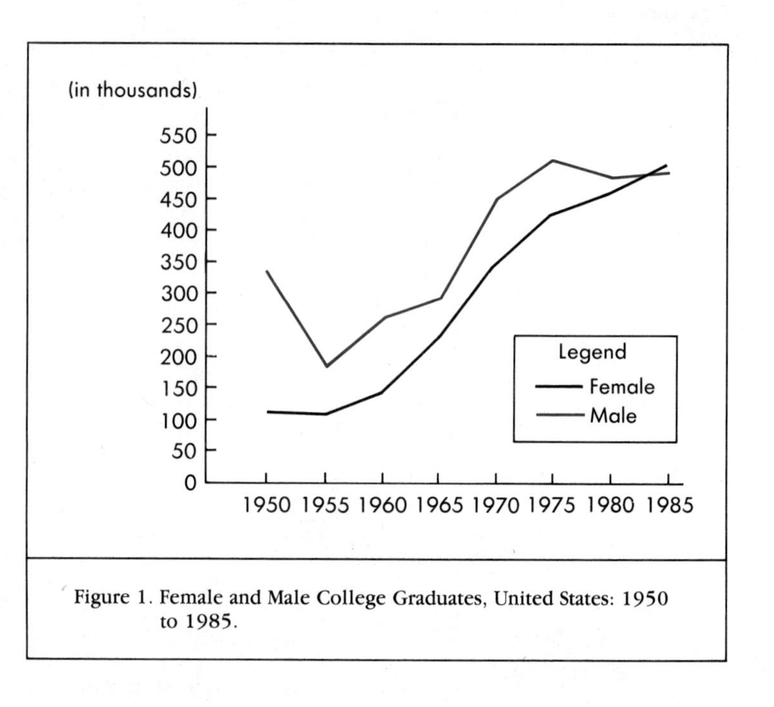

Figure 1. Female and Male College Graduates, United States: 1950 to 1985.

As shown in Figure 1, the number of female and male college graduates increased overall between 1955 and 1985. Male college graduates decreased from 329,000 to 183,000 (44.4 percent) between 1950 and 1955; female college graduates remained the same. By 1985, female college graduates outnumbered male college graduates by 10,000. The most rapid increase in the number of college graduates for both female and male students occurred during the 1960–1975 period. While the number of male college graduates has leveled off, the number of female college graduates continues an upward trend.

SUMMARY

On the basis of your general and specific objectives, you may need to collect quantitative data to present in your report. These quantitative data are usually presented in the form of frequencies, central tendency, extremes, range, and mathematical relationships. The statistical measures you use help determine the most appropriate graphics for presenting the data.

Graphics are frequently used in business reports. Graphics help hold the

Figure 13.21
Map showing zip code zones

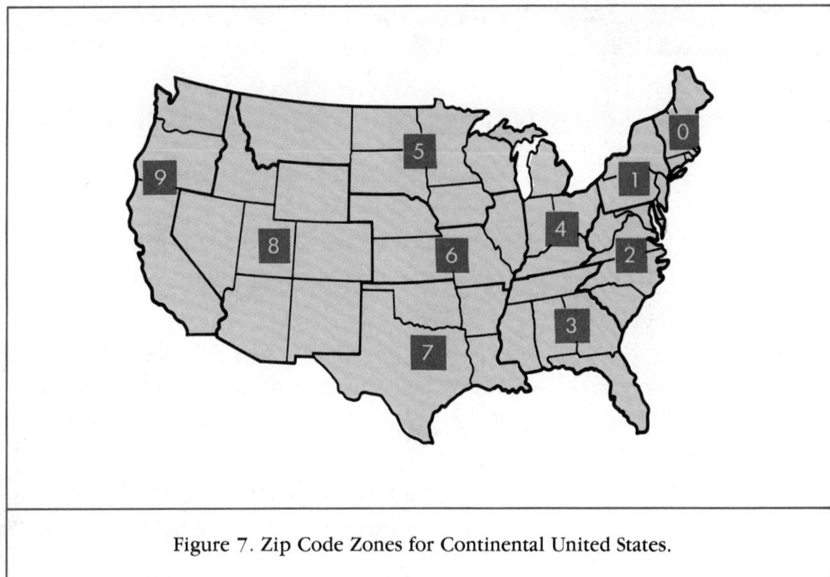

Figure 7. Zip Code Zones for Continental United States.

interest of the reader, divide the material into manageable units, organize the presentation of data, and enhance the meaning of the content.

When you use graphics in your reports, place them on the page immediately after they are first mentioned; if the graphics are brief, you may integrate them within the text. Number tables consecutively throughout the report; number figures consecutively throughout the report. Use consistent form in the placement of figures, numbers, and titles. As a report writer, you should narrate and interpret all graphics for your readers.

Writers often present data in tabular form because tables allow them to present large amounts of detailed data efficiently. Tables consist of a heading, body, and footer. When you interpret tables, select the major points the reader will need to understand the meaning. Present these points using the same sentence structure and consistent wording: use the third person.

Other types of graphics for use in business reports are bar charts, pie charts, and line charts. Use the pie chart when you want to show the proportion of the parts to the whole. The components of the pie chart must equal 100 percent. When you want to compare items in your business reports, select the bar chart. Line charts illustrate trends over time (increases, decreases, fluctuations in some values).

With advanced computer technologies available today, you can obtain many graphics software packages to create a variety of computer graphics. Even though graphics are an integral part of business reports, you need to use judgment in selecting them for your writing projects.

END-OF-CHAPTER ACTIVITIES

DISCUSSION

1. Define frequency, central tendency measures, relational measures. When is each used?
2. How do the mean, median, and mode differ?
3. How does a dispersion measure differ from the central tendency measures?
4. For what situation might you use the standard deviation statistic?
5. For which situation might you use the correlation statistic?
6. What is the difference in tables and other types of visuals used in reports?
7. What is the value of graphics in a report?
8. What is a cross-referenced table? How does it differ from a frequency table?
9. Explain the makeup of an interpretation that accompanies the table or figure.
10. What can you do with data from a rating-scale question to give meaning to the data?

ACTIVITIES

11. A survey conducted in 1986 showed that 79 percent of the U.S. population had credit cards. The "buy now, pay later" concept is a popular one in the United States as indicated by the numbers of credit cards used. The survey revealed the following: 34 percent of the population carry gasoline cards, 3 percent carry airline cards, 26 percent carry telephone cards, 3 percent carry car rental cards, 68 percent carry retail cards, 12 percent carry third party cards, and 56 percent carry bank cards.

    Develop an appropriate graphic and interpretation for these data.
12. The arts continue to get a rising share of corporate philanthropy. Note the difference between grants for the arts and for other categories in 1976 and 1986. In 1976 the arts accounted for 7.4 percent; education, 36 percent; other, 7.7 percent; civic activities, 10.4 percent; and health and education services, 38.5 percent. In 1986, health and education services accounted for 27.7 percent; other, 3.9 percent; education, 38.9 percent; civic activities, 18.8 percent; and the arts, 10.7 percent.

    Develop an appropriate graphic and interpretation for these data.
13. According to the 1986 Census Bureau, Americans born between 1946 and 1964 are not as rich a market as some people think. For example,

70 percent of baby boom women work. Baby boom incomes by percent for 1986 were:

Women	Percent	Income
	7.5	$20,000–29,999
	0.3	50,000+
	63.7	Less than $10,000
	0.4	40,000–49,999
	26.6	10,000–19,999
	1.4	30,000–39,999

Men	Income	Percent
	$40,000–49,999	2.8
	20,000–29,999	19.9
	50,000+	2.5
	Less than 10,000	35.3
	30,000–39,999	8.2
	10,000–19,999	31.4

Develop an appropriate graphic and interpretation for these data.

14. The annual report presented by the executive board of Marketing International (MI) includes memberships and new chapters chartered from 1982 to 1986:

Membership	New chapters
1986–15,000	1982– 70
1985–15,500	1983– 90
1984–14,000	1984–100
1983–12,500	1985–110
1982–11,000	1986–120

Using one figure to show these data, develop an appropriate graphic and interpretation.

15. Expenses in 1986 for Marketing International (MI), which were also included in the annual report, included 17 percent merchandise and publications; membership services, 13.9 percent; executive board project, 4.9 percent; (INFOE 86-14.3 percent); rebates to chapters, 9 percent; headquarters, 4.9 percent; data processing, 4.6 percent; promotion, 3.4 percent. Revenues for 1986 for MI: interest income, .3 percent; membership dues, 45.3 percent; rental income, 1.7 percent; INFOE 86, 34.3 percent; publications and merchandise, 18.4 percent.

The 1985-86 fiscal year income for MI was $1,800,056; expenses, $1,873,080 (loss $72,324).

With the revenues and expenses provided, develop a financial statement illustrated with appropriate graphics. Provide an interpretation.

16. Assume that you need to show in a business report how six major stock market indexes fared in the first quarter of 1987. You have collected these data:

Standard & Poor's 500	+8.02 percent
AMEX market value	+12.40 percent
Dow Jones Industrials	+4.56 percent
NASDAQ composite	+12.88 percent
NYSE composite	+8.53 percent
Value line	+9.29 percent

Develop an appropriate graphic and interpretation for these data.

17. U.S. merchandise trade deficits continue to increase. In May 1986 alone, the trade deficit was $14.2 billion. Data for a 10-year period as reported by the Office of Management and Budget are as follows:

1980–$38*	1976–15
1982–40	1974–11
1981–38	1975–11
1978–41	1985–14.8
1977–38	1984–120

* All figures are in billions of dollars.

Develop an appropriate graphic for these data.

18. You would like to show in graphic Format the total number of employees for Slant Inc. for the years 1983-87. In 1985 there were 124,200 employees; in 1987, 152,400 employees; in 1983, 114,300 employees; in 1986, 141,100 employees and in 1984, 117,800 employees. Your data were collected from Slant, Inc. annual reports for the years shown.

Develop an appropriate graphic and interpretation.

19. The Census Bureau has compiled wholesale trade figures for sales and inventories for January-September 19__. You would like to illustrate in graphic Format these data for selected months:

Sales		**Inventories**	
January	$114.7	January	$132.2
February	114.3	April	134.0
May	118.8	July	135.8
June	110.8	September	135.3
August	116.9		
September	115.0		

These data are seasonally adjusted in billions of dollars. Prepare the appropriate graphic.

20. Assume that your superior at Highland, Inc., a retail chain of television retail outlets in the Southeast, has asked you to collect and compare your annual sales with those of two other competitors—the City TV Outlet and the Home TV Shoppe. You work very hard and obtain the following data for each of the regional sales offices:

    Region A—Highland sold 2,400 units; City 3,600; Home 1,200.
    Region B—Highland sold 5,000; City 5,200; Home 2,400.
    Region C—Highland sold 250; City 5,000; Home 800.
    Region D—Highland sold 50; City 300; Home 3,000.
    Region E—Highland sold 2,500; City 2,000; Home 2,800.

    Present the data in the most appropriate graphic (or graphics). Interpret the graphic(s).

21. Information presented in narrative form is sometimes confusing. Read the paragraph; then prepare an appropriate graphic and interpretation for these data.

    The stereo system manufactured by Florida Company costs $605.00 whereas $640.95 for a comparable High-Tech unit. The AM/FM stereo receiver is priced at $154 for the Florida and $125 for the Hi+Tech. Florida is lower on both the cassette player/recorder and phonograph turntable ($120.25 and $125) as compared to $130.65 and $150.55, respectively for the Hi+Tech. Hi+Tech is lower on speakers at $159.75 as compared to $200.25 for Florida. Whereas the speaker cabinet is free from the units from Florida, it costs $75 at Hi+Tech.

22. You are assigned to compare the U.S. advertising expenditures by medium at 10-year intervals (1960, 1970, and 1980). With the data below, prepare an appropriate graphic and then interpret the graphic.

    Newspapers—1980, $15.5 billion; 1970, $5.8 billion; 1960, $3.7 billion
    Magazines—$3.1 billion; $1.3 billion; $.9 billion
    Business Papers—$1.7 billion; $.7 billion; $.6 billion
    Radio—$3.7 billion; $1.3 billion; $.7 billion
    Television—$11.4 billion; $3.7 billion; $1.6 billion
    Direct Mail—$7.6 billion; $2.7 billion, $1.8 billion
    Outdoor—$0.68 billion; $.2 billion; $.2 billion
    Miscellaneous—$10.9 billion; $3.9 billion; $2.4 billion

23. On the basis of the guidelines for developing graphics in this chapter, evaluate Figures 13.22, 13.23, and 13.24.

24. According to the Corporate Design and Realty Company in Atlanta as of January/February 1987, the following data show Atlanta's largest design firms, along with their respective rank in the United States, in 1986 and 1987. Projects are measured in terms of millions of square

Figure 13.22

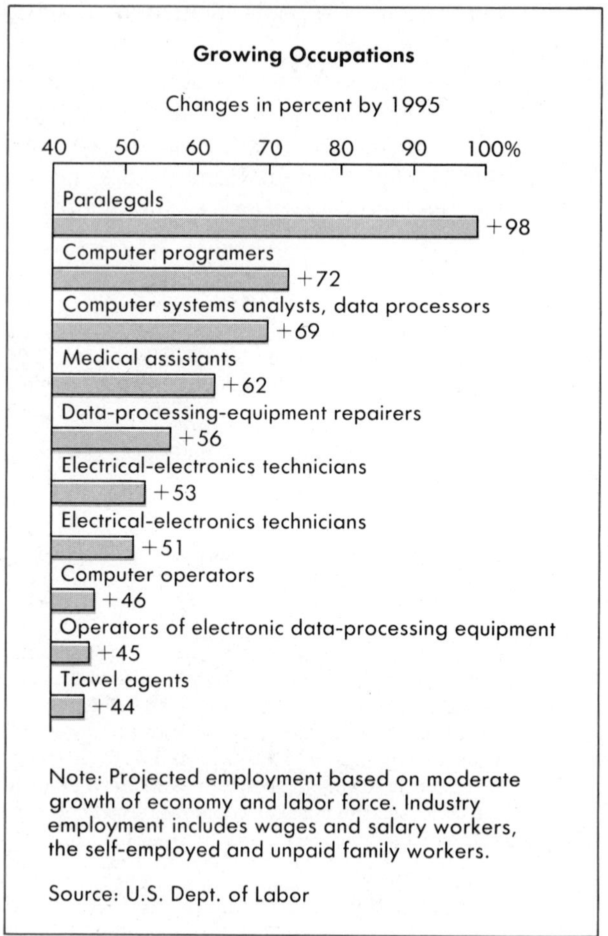

feet of building design and millions of dollars. Rank is for all design firms in the United States. Gorman & Associates, Inc., 8.7 millions of dollars volume of business; rank in United States 1986, 190; 0.40 (million) square feet; rank in United States 1987, 174. Quantrell Mullins & Associates, rank in 1987, 95; rank in 1986, 101; projects in square feet 0.60 (million); volume of business in million dollars, 25.5. Carlston Associates had 0.85 (million) square feet projects; 4.5 million dollars in business; ranked 192nd in 1987. Associated Space Designs, business volume $110.4 million; rank 55 in 1986, 49 in 1987; 2.63 (million) square feet. Godwin & Associates ranked 105 in 1987; 86 in 1986; $7.5 million in business and 1.20 million in projects. Cooper Carry Interiors Group, Inc. 1.85 (million) in square feet; 99.2 million dollar volume, 109 rank in 1986 and 130 in 1987. Herry Interiors, Inc., rank

Figure 13.23

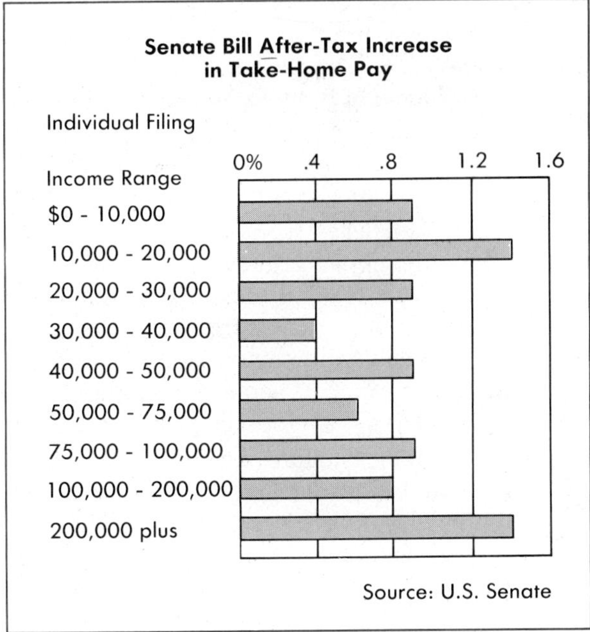

Figure 13.24

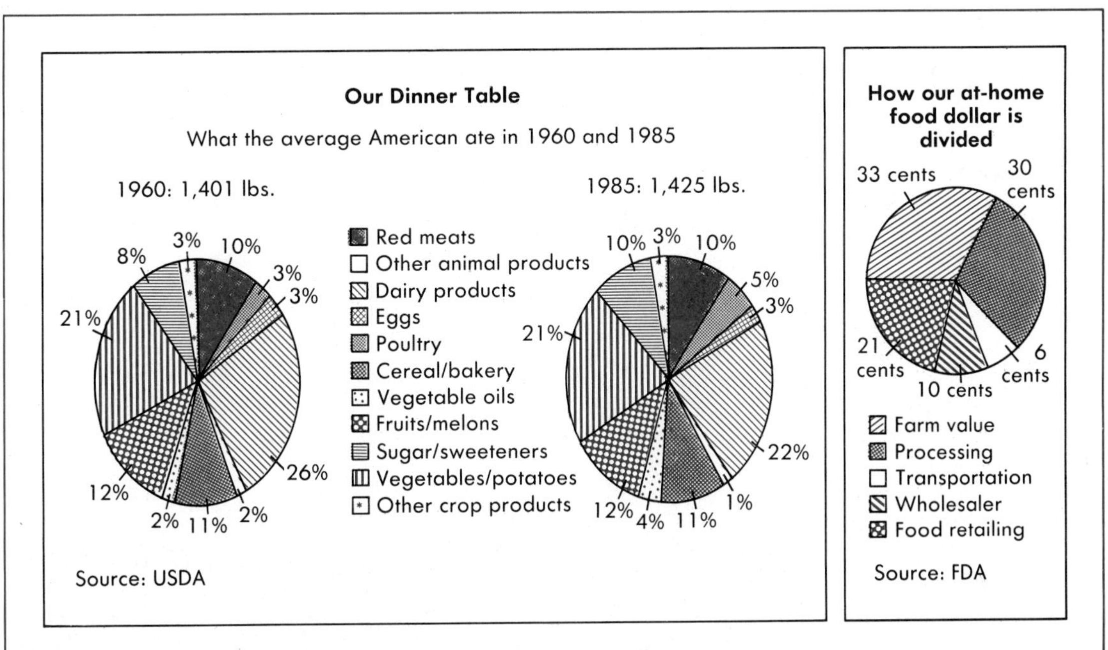

112 in 1987; rank not indicated in 1986; 111.8 million dollar volume of business and 2.36 million in square feet. Thompson, Ventulett, Stainbuck & Associates, ranked 57 in 1987 and 84 in 1986; $68.5 million volume of business and 3.30 (million) in square feet. Stevens & Wilkins, Inc. rank in 1986, 54; in 1987, 56; 0.47 projects in square feet (millions); dollar volume of business 23.5 million.

Develop an appropriate graphic for these data.

25. The United States Travel Data Center reported that summer vacations are on the upswing. In 1985, there were 82 million person-trips in June; in July 1985, 91 million; and in August 1985, 105 million. In 1986, 80 million person-trips were taken in June; 91 million in July and 109 million in August. June 1987 had 84 million person-trips; 100 million in July 1987 and 115 million in August 1987.

    Develop the appropriate graphic for these data.

26. Based on expenditures at the 1986 Republican Convention in Dallas (Source: Dallas Chamber of Commerce), the projections are that conventioners will spend $30 million at the 1988 convention in this manner: 50 percent, hotel rooms; 6.7 percent, other restaurants; 4.5 percent, entertainment; 18 percent, hotel restaurants; 8.4 percent, retail purchases; 6.9 percent, other expenditures; and 5.1 percent, transportation.

    Develop the appropriate graphic for these data.

CHAPTER 14

WRITING INFORMATIONAL REPORTS

Learning Objectives

After studying this chapter, you will be able to:

- ☐ Consider alternative types of informational reports.
- ☐ Understand the characteristics of an informational report.
- ☐ Understand the characteristics of a progress report and periodic report.
- ☐ Apply the strategy for communicating to the writing of periodic reports and progress reports.
- ☐ Explain how factual data are reported through additional types of informational reports: recommendation for future action report, biweekly summary report, and quarterly transactional report.

Variations of the informational report

You have already examined informational reports in the form of announcement reports, status reports, and proposal reports. You have also considered forms as an alternative method for reporting factual data. For the most part, these informational reports were simple and easy to write. This chapter is a continuation of informational reports and illustrates how report writing can vary greatly in form, style, and content depending on such factors as company policies, procedures, size of organization, and environment of the organization (formal or informal), and many other company characteristics. You will begin by applying the strategy for communicating to writing periodic and progress reports. You will then examine a variety of informational reports without using the strategy for communication.

Generic characteristics of the informational report

Our purpose is to show you the diversity of informational reports. These reports will range from a one-page summary report in tabular form to a multiple-page quarterly transactional report. Some reports are based on available data; others require data collection and depict graphics.

PERIODIC REPORT

Periodic report defined

A *periodic report is prepared at specific time intervals—daily, weekly, monthly, quarterly, or annually.* Professionals use these scheduled reports to adjust future actions or to confirm planned courses of actions. For example, if a sales manager receives weekly sales reports from departmental supervisors, he could increase advertising to stimulate sales for particular items on the basis of information from those weekly reports. Items selling at or below a predetermined level would not require managerial time. Thus, a periodic report helps personnel keep informed about and make decisions in response to periodic changes. Periodic reports sometimes also point out critical areas that require decisions. The annual report, another periodic report, presents information to stockholders and employees. Quite often periodic reports are generated by the computer. This approach is highly recommended, since much of the data from the previous report is usable by editing the report to make the information current.

These are the unique characteristics of the periodic report:

Characteristics of the periodic report

- □ Summarizes activities for a specific time period.
- □ Is ongoing; submitted at a predetermined time interval.
- □ Can take a standard form—the writer fills in facts and figures.
- □ Is temporary in nature.

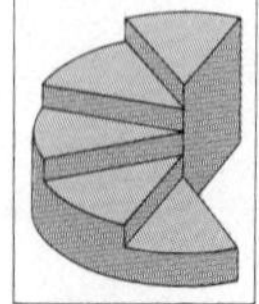

STRATEGY: MONTHLY PRODUCTION REPORT

HearthStone Corporation, a builder of customized houses, offers thirty different models. To keep informed about production and sales, the president requests a monthly report on work in process. He wants to be able to answer these questions: How long does it take from production

LEGAL / ETHICAL ISSUE

Janice Frederick worked as an assistant to the purchasing agent of a large furniture manufacturing company in the Northwest. When her boss took a higher paying job with a competitive firm, Janice was promoted to purchasing agent. She was excited over the opportunity of proving her capabilities in the new position.

In addition to purchasing all supplies and equipment, Janice was responsible for preparing two monthly periodic reports—one comparing vendor purchases with year-to-date budget allocations, and another comparing current monthly expenditures with those for the same month a year ago. To ensure that her monthly reports were impressive, Janice decided to contact some of the major suppliers and negotiate new purchasing contracts. Her goal was to cut expenditures.

In negotiation procedures, Janice found most suppliers followed company policy where prices were based on quantities ordered; they were reluctant to budge from policy. To encourage a lower price, Janice exaggerated incidents about defective materials the company had received in the past. To maintain the goodwill of the furniture company, most of the suppliers submitted better prices or made concessions.

Janice felt that these negotiating tactics were ethical since ethical behavior is really a function of context. She had observed her former boss practicing similar tactics and reasoned that suppliers really expect hard tactics in price negotiations. Was Janice ethical? Why? Why not? Do you agree that ethical behavior is always a function of context? Since the new contracts are inconsistent with suppliers' company policies, are they legal? Why? Why not?

start to shipping for each model? Who are the customer and salesperson for each house sold? Mike Elliott, who is in charge of customer orders, is responsible for preparing this monthly report. Assume that Elliott is now planning to prepare the first of these reports for the current month, January.

PROBLEM
President needs data about work in process (production). Mike has been recording each order in a note pad as each house is placed into production. His current form includes these headings: job numbers, model, date, salesperson's name.

OBJECTIVES

General: To summarize facts about house models placed into production for the month.

Specific: Date placed into production.

Figure 14.1 Mike's form for periodic reports

In Process Production Report
Month ending January

Job Number	Salesperson	Customer	Model	Date into Production	Shipping Date
1271	Munsey	Coffee	Elkmont	1–2	1–20
2887	Giles	Cooper	Elkmont	1–4	1–24
2854	Tucker	Murray	Cedar	1–13	2–21
2837	Flanders	Childers	Custom	1–14	2–2
2617	Beck	Johnson	Macon	1–15	2–4
2959	Vine	Winnegar	Custom	1–20	2–10
2942	Testerman	Ware	Pioneer	1–21	2–24
2916	Thompson	Maddox	Belle	1–23	2–2
2900	Beck	Rohan	Belle	1–24	2–2
2983	Giles	Sanders	Cumberland	1–27	2–15
2913	Tucker	Stafford	Greenbrier	1–28	2–11
2984	Beck	Radcliff	Custom	1–28	2–2
2946	Flanders	Underwood	Macon	1–30	2–8

To indicate time interval—month ending January 31, 19...

To present facts by model:

- Salesperson's name.
- Job numbers.
- Customer's name.
- Model name/number.
- Shipping date.

To indicate subject.

READER/AUDIENCE

Characteristics: Primary—president; secondary—other officers who may read report.
President has requested report.

Reactions: Positive.
Will use information for decisions.

The report is assigned by the president and is an ongoing report. The president will use the results to gauge the financial operation of the company.

ORDER

OVERALL MESSAGE: DIRECT

Since the president has requested the monthly report, the direct approach is appropriate.

Figure 14.2 An example of computerized information regrouped to produce other reports

Sales Honor Roll
Month Ending January

Job Number	Salesperson	Customer	Model	Date into Production	Shipping Date
2617	Beck	Johnson	Macon	1–15	2–4
2900	Beck	Rohan	Belle	1–24	2–2
2894	Beck	Radcliff	Custom	1–28	2–2
2837	Flanders	Childers	Custom	1–14	2–2
2946	Flanders	Underwood	Macon	1–30	2–8
2887	Giles	Cooper	Elkmont	1–4	1–24
2983	Giles	Sanders	Cumberland	1–27	2–15
2854	Tucker	Murray	Cedar	1–13	2–21
2913	Tucker	Stafford	Greenbrier	1–28	2–11
1271	Munsey	Coffee	Elkmont	1–2	1–20
2942	Testerman	Ware	Pioneer	1–21	2–24
2916	Thompson	Maddox	Belle	1–23	2–2
2959	Vine	Winnegar	Custom	1–20	2–10

SPECIFIC OBJECTIVES:

1. To indicate subject.
2. To indicate time interval—month ending January 31, 19__.
3. To present facts by model:
   Salesperson's name.
   Customer's name.
   Job number.
   Model name/number.
   Date placed into production.
   Shipping date.

FORMAT

SPECIAL FORM

Because this is a monthly report, Mike decides to create a special form that will contain the needed information. Each month he can complete the form by filling in the sales and production data for that month, and submit the form to the president. Mike also knows that he can use this same form on the new microcomputer system that is planned. With the new computer system, he can generate a weekly report from these facts, thus keeping the president and other officers even more up-to-date.

Mike drafts a preliminary form in his note pad. He decides to use a simple form with a heading and a section for columns. The completed form and the first month's report appear in Figure 14.1.

Mike looks at the periodic report and rereads his memo from the president. He concludes that, by looking at this report, the president can obtain the answers to his questions. Mike also thinks of the ease of retrieving and rearranging the needed information from this form when he starts using the microcomputer system. Instead of having to group data manually from this table, he can give a report to the president grouped by any of the identified column headings. For example, the data could be sorted by the computer and grouped so that each salesperson would have his/her job numbers grouped together. This report could be called *Sales Honor Roll.* This type of report will keep the president informed about who is doing the most selling. Figure 14.2 illustrates this report.

PROGRESS REPORT

Progress report defined

The *progress report details the work completed or the status of a project.* The main purpose of a progress report is *to inform others about the progress to date on a project* and how close you are to your projected goal. An important objective of a progress report is to identify problems and correct them while the project is under way, thus affecting time and cost savings.

Phases of progress reports

During the project, three different types of reports are written depending on the time period—initial, intermediate, and final. The initial progress report indicates activities completed, problems encountered, and projected activities. The intermediate progress report summarizes the activities completed to date plus the three sections included in the initial report. Several intermediate reports are prepared for most projects. The final progress report summarizes the activities of the entire project. The initial and intermediate reports quite often provide the material for the final progress report. Because of the nature of progress reports, some companies use a special form for the progress reports to save time for the reader and writer.

These are the unique characteristics of the progress report:

Characteristics of a progress report

- ☐ Consists of a series of reports—initial, intermediate, and final.
- ☐ Contains four areas of information in the report body: summary of previous activities, activities completed during period, problems encountered, projected activities.
- ☐ Terminates when the project is completed.
- ☐ Can take a special form—the writer fills in facts and figures.
- ☐ Is temporary in nature.

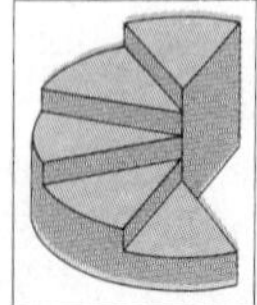

STRATEGY: MONTHLY PROGRESS REPORT

Jim Callahan, an insurance agent, purchased an older six-story building in the downtown area at 17 Broadway in a midwestern city (population 150,000). The building was vacant for a number of years and was in need of complete renovation. The basic wall structures were sound. Jim wants his offices to occupy the top two floors; he will lease floors 1-4 to other

diagonal diagonally

professionals. To meet the deadline of his loan agreement, Jim must move into his suite by October 1. He signed the contract in January; work began on February 1.

The project proposal first calls for complete renovation of the top two floors—removal of all interior walls, ceilings, outer wall coverings, and old wood floors. The new design will use an open-landscaped system. Plans call for:

- □ An elevator in the central part of the building.
- □ Removal of the outside stairs.
- □ Sprinkler system on each floor.

After an architect designed the interior, Jim hired Allen Contractors, Inc., to refurbish the building. When he hired Allen, Jim requested a monthly progress report. Eleanor Graves, the chief contractor, prepares her first progress report at the end of February. Eleanor's crew cleaned out the old papers, boards, furniture, and other junk from all six floors, removed all inside walls (except the main supports), and removed the coverings on the inside of the brick outer walls. Eleanor checked all features of the architect's plans and determined that the supporting structure would not allow for the placement of the elevator in the middle of the building. The best placement is near the front in the center of the building. In addition, she knows that fire regulations stipulate stairs at the front and back of each floor—the original plans called for steps at the back of the building only.

Eleanor prepares her strategy.

PROBLEM

Jim Callahan doesn't know the status of the project.

OBJECTIVES

General: To inform J. Callahan of the progress toward project completion.

Specific: To identify work completed during February.
To list the next activities to complete.
To introduce the subject of the report.
To identify problem areas.
To offer suggestions for problem areas.

READER/AUDIENCE

Characteristics: Primary—Jim Callahan.
Secondary—Architect (redesign).
Others to whom Jim Callahan may show report such as possible renters or loan officers.

Reaction: Positive as to activities completed to date.
Negative about redesign work (elevator, stairs).

Even though Jim Callahan will react negatively to the redesign work for the extra set of stairs and relocation of the elevator, he will be glad to know this early. This timely information will prevent costly reconstruction.

ORDER

OVERALL: DIRECT

Since Jim Callahan expects monthly progress reports, he is eager to obtain the specifics. He needs to get the message immediately.

SPECIFIC OBJECTIVES

1. To introduce the subject of the report.
2. To identify work completed during February.
3. To identify problem areas.
4. To offer suggestions for problem areas.
5. To list the next activities to complete.

FORMAT

MEMO WITH SPECIAL SUBSECTIONS

Since Eleanor will prepare several of these progress reports, she decides to use the memo format with a lead-in statement followed by sections with side headings. The memo format is appropriate since Eleanor now works for the company as a contractor. She thinks a list will be adequate to report on the completed and planned activities. The problem area section, however, needs some explanation.

Eleanor jots down the information for the memo heading:

To: Jim Callahan From: Eleanor Graves, Chief Contractor Date: March 1, 19__ Subject: Progress Report No. 1 on Building Renovation, February 1-28, 19__

Eleanor prepares the lead-in statement:

Here is the first progress report on the renovation of your six-story office building (17 Broadway Street). The report shows the completed activities for February 1-28, 19__, problem areas needing your attention, and planned activities for March.

Note the lead-in statement repeats the ideas contained in the subject line. This appears redundant at first. Keep in mind, however, how the reader uses the entire report. Most likely, Jim Callahan will glance at the subject line to determine the priority of the message when he first gets it.

Figure 14.3 Initial progress report

To: Jim Callahan
From: Eleanor Graves, Chief Contractor
Date: March 1, 19__
Subject: Progress Report No. 1 on Building Renovation, February 1-28, 19__

Here is the first progress report on the renovation of your six-story office building (17 Broadway Street). The report shows the completed activities for February 1-28, 19__, problem areas needing your attention, and planned activities for March.

Activities Completed—February 1-28, 19__

1. Items on floors 1-6 (papers, boards, old furniture, junk) removed.
2. Interior walls (except main supports) removed from floor 6.
3. Wall and ceiling coverings on inside of brick walls removed from floor 6.

Problems Encountered

1. Placement of Elevator—Building support structures are unsound for placement of the elevator in the center of the building. Structurally, the elevator must be positioned near the front, center of the building.
2. Addition of a front set of stairs—Fire regulations require a set of stairs at the front in addition to the back of each floor. Plans already call for a set of stairs at the back.

Activities Planned for March

1. Remove the interior walls (except main supports) for floor 5.
2. Remove the wall coverings and ceiling for floor 5.
3. Remove the wooden flooring for floors 5 and 6.

He will either read the message at once or place it aside for later reading. Upon returning, he will begin reading the body. Repeating the ideas from the subject line aids the reader in understanding the remainder of the report. The subject line and lead-in serve different purposes. They are, therefore, not redundant.

The rest of Eleanor's progress report is presented under three subsection headings:

Activities Completed—February 1-28, 19__

1. Items on floors 1-6 removed (papers, boards, old furniture, junk).
2. Interior walls (except main supports) removed from floor 6.
3. Wall and ceiling coverings on inside of brick walls removed from floor 6.

Problems Encountered

1. Placement of elevator—Building support structures are unsound for placement of the elevator in the center of the building. Structurally, the elevator must be positioned near the front, center of the building.
2. Addition of a front set of stairs—Fire regulations require a set of stairs at the front in addition to the back of each floor. Plans already call for a set of stairs at the back.

Activities Planned for March

1. Remove the interior walls (except main supports) for floor 5.
2. Remove the wall coverings and ceiling for floor 5.
3. Remove the wooden flooring for floors 5 and 6.

Note the listing Format under the subsection headings. This provides fast information to the reader. You also need no closing paragraph. The main Objective is to simply inform Jim Callahan. The entire progress report is shown in Figure 14.3.

The second and succeeding progress reports need add only one other section—a summary of all previously completed activities. Thus, the second and succeeding progress reports can use these subsections:

Activities Previously Completed: (Inclusive dates from start of project)
Activities Completed: (Month)
Problems Encountered:
Activities Planned for (Name of next month)

SAMPLE INFORMATIONAL REPORTS

This section presents three informational reports which merely serve as examples of how various organizations report factual data. Note the diversity in report makeup.

Recommendation for Future Action

Recommendation report

Figure 14.4 is an example of one company's method of writing a report which offers recommendations for future action. In this case, the management of the company is concerned about productivity in the accounting department. The report provides factual information about probable criteria for evaluating performance and outlines the award system for motivating employee performance.

BIWEEKLY COMPARATIVE SUMMARY REPORT

Summary informational report

Figure 14.5 is an example of a biweekly summary report used by a consulting firm. The data in this report deals with information pertaining to the Electronic Data Processing Audit Unit. The purpose of the report is to compare current consulting procedures with those projected at the beginning of the fiscal year. The left column shows comparisons for the two-week period ending May 2. The right column depicts year-to-date comparisons. Note how so much factual data is compressed into a one-page informational report.

This type of report is a variation of the status report.

Figure 14.4
Recommendation report

Georgia Power 

January 28, 19___
Athens, Georgia

TO: ATHENS DIVISION ACCOUNTING PERSONNEL

Ref: 19___ Accounting Performance Awards

We have just completed a very successful year and are proud of the achievements of all of our Accounting offices. We realize that many of you had excellent records this year but were never a quarterly winner. With this in mind the contest rules will be changed for 19___.

This year offices will not compete against each other but will compete against a division goal. Any office obtaining this goal will be a winner. This will allow performance at a high standard to be recognized.

Attached is an explanation of this year's contest.

Thanks again for the fine job last year and good luck in this year's contest.

Sincerely,

R. Ernest McClure, Jr.
Division Accounting Manager

REM:wr
cc: Mr. Ben Williams
Mr. Tommy Hollingsworth
District Managers
Local Managers

QUARTERLY TRANSACTIONAL REPORT

Use of the quarterly informational report

Figure 14.6 is an example of a quarterly transactional report to notify policy holders of the status of their annuities. The quarterly report is one of the most frequently used informational reports. Note how effectively a coding system (1, 2, 3, etc.) defines and describes the content of the graphic illustrations provided in the report.

Remember, the major thrust of informational reports is to inform. You can exercise a great deal of creativity when writing these types of reports as long

Figure 14.4 (*continued*)

ATHENS DIVISION 19__ ACCOUNTING PERFORMANCE AWARDS

Purpose: Boost morale, improve performance, provide positive recognition for people achieving excellence in Customer Accounting.

1. Criteria

   A. Athens Division Monthly Activity Reports

      1. Meter Reading Efficiency
      2. Transaction Processing
      3. Final Bill Collections

   B. Division Goal

      1. Each office competes against a performance indicator
      2. Each office's performance will be calculated as described in D."
      3. An office must have a composite score of 105% or better of goal to be a winner.

   C. Employees Eligible to Win Group Awards

      1. District Accounting Supervisor
      2. Accounting Supervisor - District
      3. Special Service Representatives
      4. Senior Customer Representatives
      5. Customer Representatives
      6. Field Service Representatives
      7. Local Managers
      8. Cut-In/Cut-Out Linemen who read meters

   D. Calculation to Determine Quarterly Winners

      1. Monthly totals by category will be added together and divided by three months to determine quarterly winners.
      2. All calculations will be carried out two decimal places to be consistent with other reports.

as you stay within the framework of the strategy for communicating and apply the guidelines for informational reports. Study your data and carefully select the design that best meets your objectives and solves your company's problem.

SUMMARY

Informational reports can vary greatly in form, style, and content depending on such factors as company policies, procedures, size of organization, the environment of the organization, and other characteristics. This chapter presents several alternative methods for reporting factual data.

Two of the most common types of informational reports are the periodic

Figure 14.4 *(concluded)*

2. Awards

   A. A meal for eligible employees in each office that has a composite score of 105% or more for the quarter.

   B. A plaque for the office in each of the following office groups with the highest composite score over 105%

   C. Breakdown by Office Group

      1. One Customer Representative Local Offices
      2. Two or more Customer Representatives Local Offices
      3. Hartwell, Madison, and Cornelia District Offices
      4. Gainesville, Athens, and Gwinnett District Offices

report and the progress report. A periodic report is prepared at specific time intervals—daily, weekly, monthly, quarterly, or annually. Professionals use these scheduled reports to adjust future actions or to confirm planned courses of action. A periodic report includes these characteristics: main objective—to inform; summary of activities for specific time period; ongoing; submitted at a predetermined time interval; statistical data—graphic and/or tabular form; narrative—presents explanation of the content; standard form optional; subject headings and subheadings; format—determined by subject and audience of report.

A progress report details the work completed or the status of a project. The main purpose is to inform others about the progress to date on a project and

Figure 14.5 Sample informational report

038 MAS1038 — 09/28/_ 13:46 PAGE 1

SORTED BY: PRACTICE UNIT
106—COMPUTER ASSURANCE SERVICES
SOUTH CM

MAS PROFITABILITY REPORTING
UTILIZATION REPORT—ACCOUNTING PERIOD SUMMARY

Period 4 — Period Ending: 09/19/_

CURRENT PERIOD								FISCAL YEAR TO DATE								
															Headcount	
Avail.	Service	EO Proj	Total	Util.	Target	Var.	Consultant	Avail.	Service	EO Proj	Total	Util.	Target	Var.	Plan	Var.
160	28	0	28	18%	45%	27%–	COWLES E T	640	220	0	220	34%	45%	11%–		
160	28	0	28	18%	45%	27%–	TOTAL SENIOR MGR	640	220	0	220	34%	45%	11%–	1	0
160	67	0	67	42%	58%	16%–	OLSSON R R	640	369	0	369	58%	58%	0%		
160	67	0	67	42%	58%	16%–	TOTAL MANAGERS	640	369	0	369	58%	58%	0%	4	3–
160	141	0	141	88%	65%	23%	BELL J H	640	467	0	467	73%	65%	8%–		
0	0	0	0	0%	0%	0%	KENNEDY J R	240	88	0	88	37%	60%	23%–		*
160	116	0	116	73%	65%	8%	SERCOMBE M R	640	535	0	535	84%	65%	19%		
160	84	2	86	54%	65%	11%–	TWOMEY T J	640	483	2	485	76%	65%	11%		
480	341	2	343	71%	65%	6%	TOTAL SENIOR CONS	2160	1573	2	1575	73%	64%	9%	4	1–
160	105	0	105	66%	74%	8%–	BROOKS K L	640	479	0	479	75%	74%	1%		
160	50	0	50	31%	74%	43%–	NEWTON A O	610	206	176	382	60%	74%	14%–		
160	113	0	113	71%	74%	3%–	TIMMERMAN S	480	218	0	218	45%	74%	29%–		
160	98	0	98	61%	65%	4%–	YEE Y C	480	222	0	222	46%	65%	19%–		
640	366	0	366	57%	72%	15%–	TOTAL CONS—24	2240	1125	176	1301	58%	72%	14%–	6	2–
1440	802	2	804	56%	65%	9%–	P. U. TOTAL	5680	3287	178	3465	61%	65%	4%–	15	6–
2400	1060	0	1060	44%			PLAN	7360	2730	0	2730	37%				
960–	258–	2	256–	12%			VARIANCE	1680–	557	178	735	24%				

HEADING DESCRIPTIONS

Avail. reflects the total hours *available* for the four-week accounting period (40 hrs/wk × 4 wks = 160 hrs. available).

Service shows the total *Service* hours, those hours charged to a client engagement, by employee.

EO Proj denotes the total hours charged to an *Executive Office* (in-house consulting) *Project.*

Total combines the *Total* service and EO Project hours accumulated for each employee. Both of these categories "make money" for the consulting firm. All available hours not charged to either of these categories represent *overhead.*

Util. shows the percentage of *utilization* for each employee (computed by dividing available hours by (Service and EO Project) total hours

Target represents the utilization goal for the practice unit for the year. This *Target* is determined and stated by the practice unit leader in his/her business plan at the beginning of the fiscal year.

Var. reflects the *Variance* of the current period's actual vs. target utilization.

Consultant shows (by employee classification: Senior Manager, Manager, Senior Consultant, Consultant) the names of each employee in this practice unit.

Headcount shows the actual number of employees *planned* vs. actual or *variance.* When creating their business plans, practice unit leaders determine the period in which new personnel will be hired.

Figure 14.6
Quarterly transactional report

TIAA-CREF Retirement Annuities
Quarterly Report of Transactions

This sample report, prepared and distributed with the March 31, 1987 inauguration of TIAA-CREF's quarterly reporting program, is designed to assist you in interpreting your enclosed personalized report.

Beginning with the enclosed TIAA-CREF Report of Transactions for the calendar quarter ending March 31, 1987, TIAA-CREF launches a new program of personalized reporting to provide you with more current information on your TIAA-CREF annuities throughout the year. These Quarterly Reports are in addition to your annual Report of Annuity Benefits which you will continue to receive once each year but in a revised format that will no longer provide an itemized listing of monthly premiums as it has done in the past—only a summary year-end total of all premiums paid during the year. Thus you will want to retain your Quarterly Reports for your records.

Following the close of each calendar quarter, you will receive this comprehensive accounting of all annuity transactions for the quarter indicated, showing their effect on your accumulation in the TIAA and/or CREF annuities identified at the top right portion of your Report. You will receive under separate cover a Quarterly Report for each set of TIAA-CREF annuities you own.

This initial quarterly reporting process required implementation of extensive new data-based accounting systems. With these systems now fully operational, future Reports will be issued on a timely basis following the close of each quarter. We hope that you will find these new reports helpful and informative.

If you have questions about your Report, please feel free to write us or call our Policyholder Information Center, toll-free, at 1 800 842-2776. When calling, it may be helpful for you to call during "off-peak" times. Typically the busiest day is Monday, and the busiest hours each day are between 12:00 and 2:00 (ET). This telephone center is open between the hours of 9:00 AM and 5:00 PM (ET) Monday through Friday.

how close you are to your projected goal. The characteristics of a progress report are: heading—project title; time period; person submitting report; date; main objective—to inform; a series of reports—initial, intermediate, and final; report body—four areas of information (summary of all completed activities to date, completed activities for current period, problems encountered, and projected activities; project completion terminates the progress report; narrative, listing and/or graphic/tabular content; special form optional.

Samples of other informational reports in this chapter include a recommendation for future action report, a biweekly summary report, and a quarterly transactional report. These are presented as alternative methods for reporting factual data from the perspective of various companies and situations.

Figure 14.6 *(continued)*

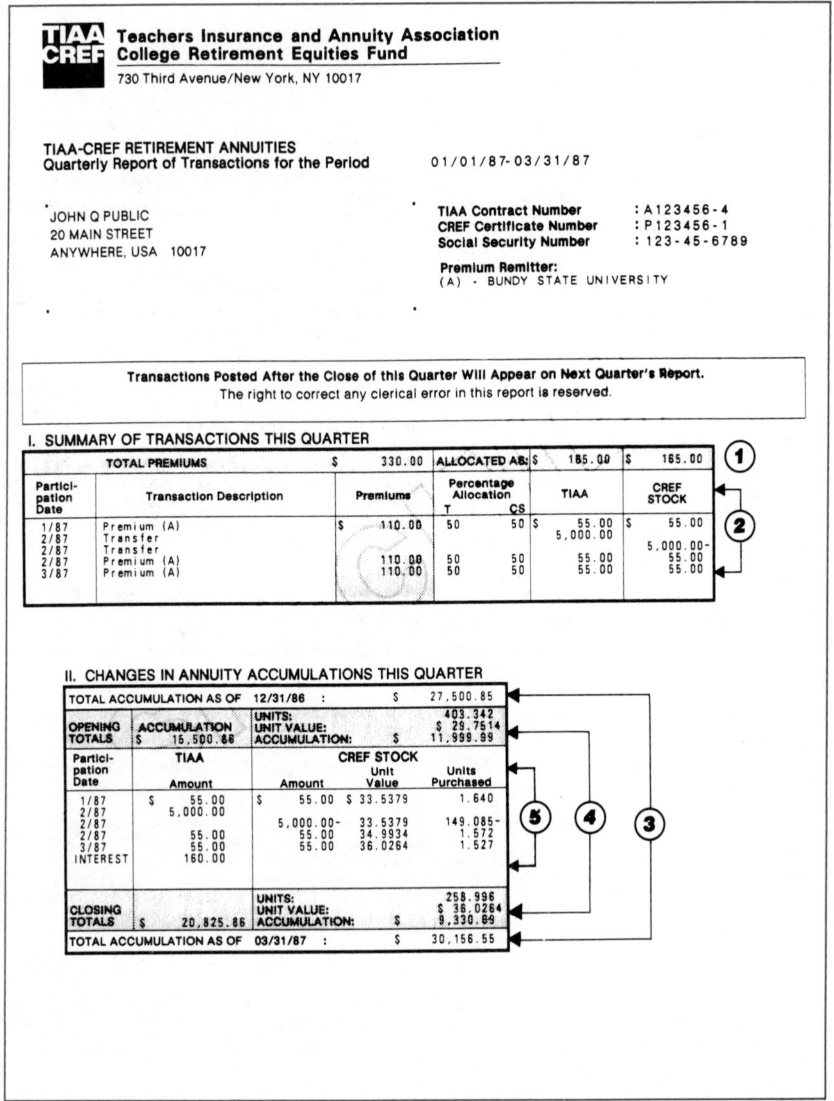

TIAA CREF **Teachers Insurance and Annuity Association**
College Retirement Equities Fund
730 Third Avenue/New York, NY 10017

TIAA-CREF RETIREMENT ANNUITIES
Quarterly Report of Transactions for the Period 01/01/87-03/31/87

JOHN Q PUBLIC
20 MAIN STREET
ANYWHERE, USA 10017

TIAA Contract Number : A123456-4
CREF Certificate Number : P123456-1
Social Security Number : 123-45-6789

Premium Remitter:
(A) - BUNDY STATE UNIVERSITY

Transactions Posted After the Close of this Quarter Will Appear on Next Quarter's Report.
The right to correct any clerical error in this report is reserved.

I. SUMMARY OF TRANSACTIONS THIS QUARTER

TOTAL PREMIUMS		$ 330.00	ALLOCATED AS:		$ 185.00	$ 165.00
Partici-pation Date	**Transaction Description**	**Premiums**	**Percentage Allocation T**	**CS**	**TIAA**	**CREF STOCK**
1/87	Premium (A)	$ 110.00	50	50	$ 55.00	$ 55.00
2/87	Transfer				5,000.00	
2/87	Transfer					5,000.00-
2/87	Premium (A)	110.00	50	50	55.00	55.00
3/87	Premium (A)	110.00	50	50	55.00	55.00

II. CHANGES IN ANNUITY ACCUMULATIONS THIS QUARTER

TOTAL ACCUMULATION AS OF	12/31/86 :		$	27,500.85
OPENING TOTALS	**ACCUMULATION** $ 15,500.86	**UNITS:** **UNIT VALUE:** **ACCUMULATION:**	$	403.342 $ 29.7514 11,999.99
Partici-pation Date	**TIAA Amount**	**CREF STOCK Amount**	**Unit Value**	**Units Purchased**
1/87	$ 55.00	$ 55.00	$ 33.5379	1.640
2/87	5,000.00			
2/87		5,000.00-	33.5379	149.085-
2/87	55.00	55.00	34.9934	1.572
3/87	55.00	55.00	36.0264	1.527
INTEREST	160.00			
CLOSING TOTALS	$ 20,825.86	**UNITS:** **UNIT VALUE:** **ACCUMULATION:**	$	258.996 $ 36.0264 9,330.69
TOTAL ACCUMULATION AS OF	03/31/87 :		$	30,156.55

END-OF-CHAPTER ACTIVITIES

DISCUSSION

1. Define a periodic report and give some examples of this type of reporting.
2. What is the major purpose of a periodic report?
3. Briefly describe the characteristics of a periodic report.
4. Define a progress report.

Figure 14.6 (*continued*)

Your Quarterly Report presents data in two sections. Please read the following explanation of Sections I and II using the key numbers to refer to the sample report on the opposite page.

SECTION I: Summary Of Transactions This Quarter

The only entries in this section for most reporting periods will be premium transactions, although non-premium transactions, such as CREF-to-TIAA transfers, are also reported in this section. For each of these non-premium transactions, you will receive an individual confirmation statement shortly after the transaction occurs.

(1) shows the combined total amount of all TIAA and CREF premiums posted during the quarter, and the portions allocated to TIAA and to CREF. These amounts include plan premiums remitted by your employer and premiums you contributed either through your employer or by direct remittance to TIAA-CREF.

TOTAL PREMIUMS	$ 330.00	ALLOCATED AS:	$ 165.00	$ 165.00

(2) details each transaction, including premiums, posted during the quarter, showing the Participation Date, a description of the transaction and the TIAA and CREF dollar amounts. Additionally, for each premium the combined TIAA-CREF amount and the percentage allocation to TIAA and to CREF are shown.

Partici-pation Date	Transaction Description	Premiums	Percentage Allocation T	Percentage Allocation CS	TIAA	CREF STOCK
1/87	Premium (A)	$ 110.00	50	50	$ 55.00	$ 55.00
2/87	Transfer				5,000.00	
2/87	Transfer					5,000.00-
2/87	Premium (A)	110.00	50	50	55.00	55.00
3/87	Premium (A)	110.00	50	50	55.00	55.00

The Participation Date is the month in which the premium or non-premium transaction was effective. For example, the premium shown with a 1/87 Participation Date was received in January; the TIAA premium began earning interest and the CREF premium began participation in investment experience in that month. For CREF-to-TIAA transfers, the Participation Date refers to the month that the amount transferred begins participation in TIAA; it ceases participation in CREF at the end of the prior month. For example, the $5,000 CREF-to-TIAA transfer is shown on two entry lines, both with a 2/87 Participation Date. The first 2/87 transfer entry represents the transfer amount being credited to TIAA and starting to earn interest in TIAA as of February 1. The second 2/87 transfer entry shows the amount transferred out of CREF, and includes CREF investment experience through January 31.

A transaction that occurs near the end of a quarter and is not shown in the report for that quarter will appear in the next quarterly report, reflecting the correct Participation Date for the prior quarter.

5. What are the unique characteristics of a progress report?
6. What are the major distinctions between a periodic and a progress report?
7. What other types of reports could be generated from the computer-stored information contained in Figure 14.1?
8. What major recommendations are included in Figure 14.4?
9. If you were planning to improve Figure 14.4, what would you suggestions include? Why?
10. Answer the following questions that relate to Figure 14.5:
    a. What is the Problem of the report?

Figure 14.6 (*concluded*)

SECTION II: Changes In Annuity Accumulations This Quarter

This section reports your accumulation at the close of the prior quarter and the current quarter being reported, and the effect each transaction listed in Section I had on your accumulation. It also reports the total TIAA interest credited during the quarter.

(3) shows the dollar amount of your combined opening and closing TIAA and CREF accumulations for the current quarter reported. (The current quarter's opening accumulation is, of course, the accumulation at the close of the prior quarter.)

TOTAL ACCUMULATION AS OF 12/31/86 :	$	27,500.85
TOTAL ACCUMULATION AS OF 03/31/87 :	$	30,156.55

(4) shows your opening and closing TIAA and CREF accumulations for the current quarter separately. For CREF, it also shows the number of accumulation units owned and the then-current value of each unit, which establish the dollar value of your CREF accumulation.

	ACCUMULATION		
OPENING TOTALS	$ 15,500.86	UNITS: UNIT VALUE: ACCUMULATION:	403.342 $ 29.7514 $ 11,999.99
CLOSING TOTALS	$ 20,825.86	UNITS: UNIT VALUE: ACCUMULATION:	258.996 $ 36.0264 $ 9,330.89

(5) shows the dollar amount of each transaction reported in Section I, presented in the same order as in Section I. The last entry for TIAA is the total amount of interest credited during the quarter. For CREF, the accumulation unit value and the number of accumulation units applicable to each transaction are also shown. In the 2/87 CREF-to-TIAA transfer example, the prior month's accumulation unit value is shown because the amount transferred ceased participation in CREF as of January 31.

Partici-pation Date	TIAA	CREF STOCK		
	Amount	Amount	Unit Value	Units Purchased
1/87	$ 55.00	$ 55.00	$ 33.5379	1.640
2/87	5,000.00			
2/87		5,000.00-	33.5379	149.085-
2/87	55.00	55.00	34.9934	1.572
3/87	55.00	55.00	36.0264	1.527
INTEREST	160.00			

The opening and closing totals are balanced for TIAA by reading down the TIAA "Amount" column; for CREF they are balanced by reading down the CREF "Units Purchased" column. CREF accumulations are expressed in terms of the number of accumulation units owned, and the accumulation unit is revalued at the end of each month to reflect CREF's common stock investment return—market value changes and investment income.

TEACHERS INSURANCE AND ANNUITY ASSOCIATION • COLLEGE RETIREMENT EQUITIES FUND
730 Third Avenue, New York, New York 10017

F5829(5/87)

b. What is the general objective of the report?
c. What are the specific objectives of the report?
d. Who is the intended Reader/Audience?
e. How would you describe the Format?
f. Evaluate the report with regard to organization, clarity, conciseness, format, and achievement of objectives.

ACTIVITIES

11. Assume the role of Kendra Macomb, who is responsible for finding a suitable location in your city for a new outlet for Lite-Lite, a restaurant specializing in fast foods for diet-conscious people. Foods contain low

Figure 14.7
Interoffice correspondence

Georgia Power

October 24, 19___

Mr. V. N. Rose	Mr. H. M. Lanier
Mr. J. A. Dunn	Mr. R. D. Brown
Mr. C. D. Moss	Mr. J. A. Gordon
Mr. R. E. Newton	Mr. R. A. Credilk
Mr. E. L. Carter	

RE: 198___ Division Accounting Goals

In follow-up to our meeting on October 24, 198___, in which 198___ Division Accounting goals were discussed, the following goals and goal weights were agreed upon:

	GOAL		WEIGHT
1.	Meter Reading Efficiency		
	—Read-on-Schedule	6.25%	
	—No-Bills	6.25%	
	—Estimates	6.25%	
	—Billed Correctly	6.25%	
	Total Meter Reading		25%
2.	Transaction Processing		
	—Correction of Unpostables (present measure)	12.5%	
	—Overall Cash and Noncash Processing Efficiency (additional measure)	12.5%	
	Total Transaction Processing		25%
3.	Collections		25%
4.	Materials and Supplies		
	—Service Level	5%	

cholesterol, natural ingredients (no preservatives), whole grain breads, salads, etc. You undertake a study to find a suitable location. Collect the following facts for three locations in your local community: general location; price per acre; taxes; availability to and from freeway; traffic count; competition; availability of hotels/motels; traffic congestion; other comments about sites. Use the strategy to plan your study; collect the facts; then write a report presenting your first, second, and third choices. Make sure your findings support your rankings.

12. Alan Jordan, the president of Litton Log Houses, has asked Judy Litton, a sales representative, to prepare a weekly report of prospective cus-

Figure 14.7 *(continued)*

Division Accounting Managers
Page 2
October 24, 19___

	—Transmission and Distribution Inventory Turnover	5%	
	—Transformer Inventory Turnover	5%	
	Total Materials and Supplies		15%
5.	Presentations		10%

Also, the following specific goal amounts were discussed and agreed upon:

1.	Meter Reading Efficiency	
	—Read-on-Schedule	70.0%
	—No-Bills	
	• Atlanta	99.15%
	• Outside	99.50%
	—Estimates	
	• Atlanta	98.9%
	• Outside	99.3%
	—Billed Correctly	99.7%
2.	Transaction Processing	
	—Correction of Unpostables	99.85%
	—Overall Cash and Noncash Processing Efficiency	99.3%
3.	Collections	
	—Atlanta	99.62%
	—Outside	99.80%
4.	Materials and Supplies	
	—Service Level	98.0%
	—Transmission and Distribution Inventory Turnover	2.5 Annual Turnover Ratio

tomers. Judy's responsibilities include showing prospective customers through a model log house and telling them about the quality features of the log houses. During the initial contact, Judy obtains the person's name, address and phone number. After each visit, she jots down in a notebook customer information along with a comment about their interest in the house. She gives the card to the sales department; and a few days later, the sales department does a follow-up mailing to each visitor.

Figure 14.7 *(concluded)*

Division Accounting Managers
Page 3
October 24, 19___

—Transformer Inventory Turnover	1.0 Annual Turnover Ratio
5. Presentations	4/District

The rationale for the overall revised goal methodology and amounts is to reflect proper business practices and allow for flexibility and creativity in meeting the demands of our operation. Specifically, the rationale for the revised meter reading goal is to ensure a proper allocation of resources and to ensure adequate cash flows to the Company. The rationale for the revised transaction processing goal is to reflect increased statewide rerouting and to afford initial flexibility in dealing with the new revised goal. The rationale for decreasing the collection goal is to reflect the anticipated impact of billed deposits and to more accurately reflect actual performance. Presentations and materials and supplies goals are at their 19___ levels.

With regard to Atlanta Division restructuring and associated recycling, it was agreed that they be exempt of the cash and noncash processing efficiency component of the transaction processing goal until 30 days after the total recycling process has been completed. This exemption will only affect those locations actually involved in recycling. This exemption will accommodate Atlanta Division in an equitable manner given the magnitude of the Atlanta Division restructuring process.

Attached is information that provides historical actual performance versus goal amounts using the revised goal methodology and amounts.

J. A. Johnson

jm

Attachment

cc: Mr. J. G. Watts
Mr. F. W. Perkins
Mr. J. R. Stout
Mr. J. W. Howard

Assume the role of Judy. You have just shown a model log house to several visitors at a home show in the local civic arena. Design a report you can adapt for use as a weekly report to the president, Alan Jordan. Supply five sets of data for five fictional customers.

13. Using the Georgia Power report (Figure 14.7) regarding Division Accounting Goals, answer the following:
    a. How would you classify the report as to type?
    b. What Problem does the report address?

Figure 14.8
Sample survey

	Not Important				Very Important
Communication theory	16	29	328	426	530
Oral communication	16	210	319	431	533
Letter format	13	210	320	425	543
Collection letters	14	216	334	424	512
Claim letters	18	29	326	432	525
Clear writing principles	1	2	34	415	581
Goodwill techniques	13	24	317	427	550
Meetings	111	215	335	428	512
Business reports	16	26	318	425	545
Rules of order	134	225	330	49	52
Telephone guidelines	123	227	331	412	57
Small groups	116	217	332	419	516
Interviewing	110	213	320	426	531
Appearing on TV and videotape	128	222	327	414	59
Writing style	12	21	37	424	567
Grammar and mechanics	13	26	329	423	540
Instructions	15	29	324	437	526
Policies and procedures	16	214	336	430	515
Manuals	112	219	338	420	511
Negative messages	14	22	39	425	560
Performance appraisals	111	222	341	418	59
Office technology	113	220	333	422	511
Ethics	15	212	328	431	525
International business communication	110	217	334	426	514
Feasibility studies	119	220	337	418	56
Articles for lay audience	127	227	327	413	56
Articles for trade journals	129	228	327	411	54
How to do primary research	113	218	322	428	519
How to do secondary research	112	216	320	429	524
How to document sources	19	214	322	427	529
Routine inquiries	14	26	315	429	546
Routine letters	14	24	314	430	548
Persuasive letters	13	22	37	432	556
Refusals	14	23	37	430	557
Job applications	13	21	313	426	556
Sales	112	211	324	425	528
Grants	119	225	333	418	55
Proposal writing	113	219	327	428	513
Nonverbal communication	17	213	322	425	533

c. What are the General and Specific Objectives?
d. Who is the intended Reader/Audience?
e. Describe the Format of this report. Is this Format appropriate for the intended purpose? Why or why not?
f. Identify the specific characteristics of this report.
g. How would you improve this report?

14. A nationwide survey of business communication instructors was conducted to assess teachers' perceptions about what should be included in a business communication text. These tabulated data in Figure 14.8 represent one portion of the survey. Numbers to the right of the scale

(1-5) indicate the frequency of responses. Assume that the results will be reported in the *Journal of Business Communication.* From the data provided, write a report using the strategy for communicating.

15. Based on your understanding of what constitutes an informational report, collect a minimum of three different types of informational reports from local businesses. Share the reports in a class activity. Compare and contrast the varieties of the reports according to company size, procedures, style, form, and content. In addition, discuss these points:
    a. Problem identification.
    b. General and Specific Objectives.
    c. Reader/Audience—primary and secondary.
    d. The "you" attitude.
    e. Possible reactions of the reader.

CHAPTER 15

INTRODUCTION TO THE ANALYTICAL REPORT

Learning Objectives

After studying this chapter, you will be able to:

- ☐ Recognize the importance of using analytical reports in business.
- ☐ Construct a framework for writing the analytical report.
- ☐ Develop the parts of the preliminary section of the analytical report.
- ☐ Prepare the parts of the initial section of the analytical report.
- ☐ Describe what is involved in the analysis of data section of the analytical report.
- ☐ Understand the concepts needed to develop the final section of the analytical report.
- ☐ Recognize what to include in the supplementary section of the analytical report.

Now that you have learned how to write informational reports using the strategy for communicating, let's examine the analytical report. The purpose of this chapter is to present an overview to the analytical report. Then in Chapter 16, you will use the strategy for communicating to write an analytical report.

Analytical report defined

Analytical reports usually follow a systematic method of defining the Problem, gathering data, discussing the data, and reaching conclusions and recommendations for solving the stated Problem. Because of the nature of analytical reports, they are usually written in the direct approach. After the report is completed, the writer may prepare a synopsis of the report and use the indirect approach (place the conclusion first so that the reader gets immediate results of the study). You will most likely use the analytical report when the decision can have major consequences. For instance, if you were searching for a new building site, you would gather and analyze detailed information about possible sites before reaching a conclusion. The data collected would help you make a more intelligent decision.

Management's use of reports

Managers report they frequently use *analytical* and *informational* reports in business. A group of University of Texas researchers sought an answer to the question, "What types of internal and external business communications are used in today's business environment?" The responses of top executives representing 100 randomly selected corporations indicated that 80 percent frequently used analytical reports; 72 percent frequently used informational reports.[1]

Need for the development of report writing and other communication skills

A *Harvard Business Review* article cited in Chapter 1 can be cited again here. The statement points out the significance of several types of business communication. Note the inclusion of *formal report* in this quotation:

> Provision must be made for significantly greater development of oral and written communication skills, including advocacy, elocution, formal report preparation, extemporaneous speaking, oral response under pressure, and group leading.[2]

Chapters 15 and 16 deal with the process for writing the analytical report. Other chapters in this textbook will assist your development of oral and other written communication skills. To be marketable and promotable in today's highly competitive corporate environment, strive to develop and enhance your competencies in each of the skills discussed in this quote.

ORGANIZATION OF THE ANALYTICAL REPORT

Content of the analytical report

An analytical report generally consists of the following major sections: preliminary, initial, middle, final, and supplementary.

[1] James C. Bennett and Robert J. Olney, "Executive Priorities for Effective Communication in an Information Society," *Journal of Business Communication* 23 (Spring 1986), p. 16.

[2] Behrman and Levin.

LEGAL / ETHICAL ISSUE

A serious problem faced by businesses is that of reporting on wrongdoing by employees. The dilemma is whether insiders should report on wrongdoing, known as *whistle-blowing,* or wait until someone outside the organization reports on the wrongdoing. The issue involves situations that could be harmful to others.

Many people do not like to report on incidents of wrongdoing because they feel that such an act shows a lack of loyalty to their fellow employees or their supervisors. Those who are aware of wrongdoing must decide whether to leave their jobs as a means of protest or to stay with the job and attempt to correct the problem.

An example of whistle-blowing took place at the Long Island Lighting Company's (LILCO) drill for emergency evacuation. Frank Petrone, an official of the Federal Emergency Management Agency, said that on the basis of the drill run by LILCO on February 13, 1986, he could not "give reasonable assurance that public health and safety" would be protected in the event of an accident at the plant. The head of the agency in Washington asked him to delete his conclusions from the report that was to be issued soon. Mr. Petrone chose to resign rather than to delete his statement. He objected to the test evacuation procedure that did not have the participation of local police, fire, and medical services.*

Do you think Mr. Petrone should have deleted his written conclusion from the report? Defend your response.

* Jane Perlez, "U.S. Aide Quits, Charging Pressure over LILCO's Drill," *New York Times,* April 15, 1986, p. B5. (Cited in Karen Gillespie, *Business Ethics,* Alpha Chapter, Delta Pi Epsilon Annual Peter L. Agnew Memorial Lecture, New York University, 1986).

Preliminary

Preliminary section

The preliminary section precedes the body of the analytical report. A letter of transmittal and an executive summary often accompany the report. (Executive summaries are discussed and illustrated in Chapter 17.) The preliminary section includes:

Content of title page

- Title page.
- Acknowledgments (optional).
- Table of contents.
- List of figures.
- List of tables.

Examples from one report illustrate the *preliminary* parts of a report. Note that each page of the preliminary section except for the title page is numbered with small Roman numerals at the bottom of the page.

Title Page. Figure 15.1 shows a sample *title page* for an analytical report. Note these characteristics of the four parts:

- ☐ Title (centered and all caps).
- ☐ To whom submitted/address (centered).
- ☐ By whom written/address (centered).
- ☐ Date (centered).

Content of acknowledgment(s) part

Acknowledgment. Figure 15.2 shows a sample of an *acknowledgment* placed on a separate page. Actually, this part is included at your discretion. Should you want to give someone or several people recognition for assistance with some phase of a report or research study, you may insert such an acknowledgment page. In the sample shown here, the authors of the report believed that several groups of employees deserved a special "thank you."

Makeup of a table of contents

Table of Contents. The table of contents (see Figure 15.3) is a listing of the preliminary parts, the main divisions of the analytical report, bibliography, if applicable, and any appended material. Note the typing of the various divisions, the placement, and the leaders (horizontal dots). Listing page numbers for each of the divisions of the report helps readers find the particular sections they need to read. Entries in a table of contents are in order of page reference numbers. The table of contents is the key to a complex report.

Listing of figures and tables

Figure 15.4 lists by title all figures used in the sample analytical report with their respective page numbers. Figure 15.5 lists all tables used in the sample analytical report with their respective page numbers. If the listings are few in number, you may combine tables and figures into a single listing, identifying each. On the other hand, if listings are numerous, you may need more than one page for figures and/or tables.

Initial Section

The initial section is the beginning of the text portion or body of the analytical report. The components of this section comprise the *introduction* of the report and may include the following:

Initial section (introduction)

The problem.
Objectives.
Procedures.
Limitations/delimitations.
Definition of terms (optional).
Related studies (where applicable).
Organization of the study.

Figure 15.1
Analytical report title page

Title

EFFECT OF THE INSTALLATION OF A WORD PROCESSING

SYSTEM ON JOB SATISFACTION

AND PRODUCTIVITY

For whom prepared

Prepared for

Mr. Gary Dempster
Union Carbide Corporation
Oak Ridge, Tennessee 37830

By whom prepared

Prepared by

Helen A. Northcutt
Sue Y. Luckey
C. Steven Hunt
School of Business and Economics
Morehead State University
Morehead, KY 40351

Date

April 18, 19__

Developing the problem statement

Writing the problem statement

Problem. The problem statement is derived from the setting and reflects the reasons for the study. Whereas in business letters you might consciously underplay the *problem* to avoid being too negative, in a business report you actually focus on the problem. Of all the sections of the analytical report, the problem statement itself is one where conciseness matters most. Write the problem in one sentence—either as a question or a statement. The problem statement explains the overall reason for conducting a study and indicates which issue is to be addressed. These are good problem statements:

Figure 15.2
Analytical report acknowledgments

Acknowledgments

The authors of this report are indebted to the managers, engineers, and secretaries who participated in this study.

ii

- ☐ Personnel absenteeism is excessive.
- ☐ Has resistance to change resulted in declining morale among members of the technical staff?

Objectives or factors of the problem

Objectives. Analytical reports may contain several specific objectives. Sometimes these are referred to as the factors or elements of the problem. Specific objectives may be written as null hypotheses, infinitives, or questions. Ordinarily, if you are not going to treat your data statistically, then use the question or infinitive format. State research statements as hypotheses when

Figure 15.3
Analytical report table of contents

TABLE OF CONTENTS

	Page
Acknowledgments	ii
Figures	iv
Tables	v
Introduction	1
Position Analysis Questionnaire	2
Managers	3
Secretaries	5
Word Processors	7
Managers—Satisfaction	13
Statements with Significant Difference	13
Statements with No Significant Difference	17
SSRQ Statements with Significant Difference	24
Engineers—Satisfaction	32
Statements with Significant Difference	41
Statements with No Significant Difference	43
Bibliography	44
Appendix: Data Collection Instruments	46
SSRQ	48
PAQ	50

iii

Writing the objectives for the analytical report

statistical treatment of the data is necessary. The types of data needed to solve the problem determine the expression of the objectives.

The null hypothesis is an objective statement of the relationships between the variables studied.

Null hypothesis

☐ There is no significant difference between the size of the organization and managerial assessments of regulatory relationships.

In analytical reports, investigators take an unbiased approach by expressing

Figure 15.4
Analytical report list of figures

FIGURES

Figure		Page
1	Job Profiles for Secretaries and Word Processors Using Mean Scores for the Six Main Divisions of the Position Analysis Questionnaire, January 19__	8
2	Job Profiles for Secretaries and Word Processors Using Mean Scores for Subparts of the Six Main Divisions of the Position Analysis Questionnaire, January 19__	9

iv

the hypothesis in the null (no difference) form. When the statistics show that there is a significant difference, you reject the statement; when the difference is not significant, you accept the hypothesis.

You may also use infinitive and question objectives. Objectives expressed in infinitive or question form are commonly used for survey research.

Infinitive

- ☐ To identify current practices for writing international business letters among northeastern companies.

Question

- ☐ What empirical data exists in the current research literature regarding the content of the résumé?

Figure 15.5
Analytical report list of tables

TABLES

Table		Page
1	Comparison of PAQ Scores Using the Mann-Whitney U Test for Managers before and after WP Installation	4
2	Comparison of PAQ Scores Using the Mann-Whitney U Test for Secretaries before and after WP Installation	6
3	Comparison of PAQ Scores Using the Mann-Whitney U Test January 19__ Data for Secretaries and Word Processors	11
4	Responses to the User Statisfaction Questionnaire by Management Personnel	20
5	Attitudes Concerning Selected Aspects of Secretarial Support by Management Personnel	30
6	Responses to User Satisfaction Questionnaire by Engineers	37
7	Attitudes Concerning Selected Aspects of Secretarial Support Services by Engineers	46

v

Describe procedures used

Procedures. Since the collection and analysis of data are an important part of the analytical report, much attention is given to the procedures or steps used to collect and analyze the data. The procedures include a step-by-step presentation of how you conducted the study. The procedures also give details about the means used to collect data (i.e., questionnaires, interviews, experimentation, examination of historical records), the sampling process, and, if hypotheses are used, the statistical treatment of the data. The pro-

Means of collecting data

cedures should be so well described that the process could be replicated, if necessary.

☐ The authors mailed questionnaires to the accounting department chairpersons of the 210 accredited schools of the American Assembly of Collegiate Schools of Business. An additional 84 questionnaires were sent to the managing partners of firms listed by the AICPA among the 105 largest accounting firms in the United States. Ninety academics (42.9 percent of those surveyed) replied; among the 84 accounting firms surveyed, responses were received from 38 companies (45.2 percent). Of these, 74 percent of the replies came from firms employing between 51 and 200 or more accountants.

Because the questionnaire had a relatively high response rate and was distributed on a national basis, the findings are fairly representative of the universe surveyed.

Chapter 12 presents an in-depth discussion of secondary and primary sources of data and sampling.

Limitations/delimitations defined

Limitations/Delimitations. *Limitations* are those constraints over which you have no control; *delimitations* are the constraints you place on the study.

Setting boundaries

Some of the more common boundaries that exist when conducting analytical reports are geographical, numbers surveyed, time, and financial resources. Reports are on specific topics and therefore place definite boundaries on the report writer. Consider these examples and these questions. Your report could be on a specific survey of businesses in the Southeast. Or you may need to conduct some facet of research that involves New York City residents. As you can see in these examples, because of the vast numbers of businesses in the Southeast and the millions of New York City residents, sampling procedures must be used to collect manageable data for such studies.

Important questions to answer before conducting study

You must be aware of the time necessary to collect data, whether by questionnaires, interviews, historical records, or scientific experimentation. Ask yourself, "Do I have sufficient time to mail or hand deliver 100 questionnaires to collect the necessary data for my study?" "How about the follow-up of nonrespondents?" Or "How much time would it take to interview 25 middle managers to obtain the necessary data?" Or "Is there enough time to conduct an experimental study to obtain the necessary data?" Then, once you've determined your time constraints, use a timetable as a roadmap for achieving the goals of your analytical report. A good maxim to keep in mind is "Do not bite off more than you can chew." Above all, "Are adequate financial resources available to complete the study? Do the benefits warrant the cost?" Other important considerations are the capabilities of the researcher, availability of statistical programs, and the ease of access to a computer.

These factors illustrate limitations:

- ☐ The economic conditions at the time of the study.
- ☐ The expertise of the individuals who respond to the survey.

These statements clearly define the delimitations of the study:

The following were delimitations of the study:

1. The study was limited to written communications in the form of letters and memorandums.
2. The concepts used in this study were identified as essential by business managers and employees rather than by educators or teachers of business communication courses.
3. This study was limited to 150 students attending business communication classes at State University during second semester, 19__.

Placement of definition of terms

Definition of Terms. In a report, it is a good idea to define all terms that may be unfamiliar to your reader/audience. You may define terms in three different places in the analytical report:

- ☐ A special portion in the initial section.
- ☐ Where they are first introduced (text or footnote).
- ☐ At the end of the report.

The advantages and disadvantages of each technique are indicated in Figure 15.6.

This example shows the form you may use.

The following are definitions of important terms used throughout this study:

1. Competency—the requisite knowledge, skills, and values to perform a job successfully.
2. Central processing unit—the portion of a computer that consists of a core memory component, a calculations component, and an operating control component.
3. Reprographics—a photocopy or reproduction of graphic materials.

No standard placement exists for the definition of terms section. Some business reports even include definitions in footnotes; this style is an acceptable method as well. Keep in mind, however, that your goal—wherever you decide to place definitions—is to help the reader understand the material and to simplify the task of reading the report.

Referencing related studies

Related Studies. Quite often, you may choose to use secondary sources which contain information related to your research study. For example, you may want to inform the reader/audience about the results of previous research studies. Your references may include journal articles, proceedings, technical reports, and reviews of applied and basic research. When you include reviews of related research in your analytical report, use these questions as a guide in writing a meaningful *abstract* (a shortened form of a work that retains the general sense and unity of the original).

Figure 15.6 Three possible locations for the definition of terms

Location	Advantages	Disadvantages
Special portion in the initial section.	*a.* Identifies each term in some logical order in a specific place. *b.* All definitions are grouped in one place. *c.* Easy to get meaning before reading remainder of report.	Not always convenient for reader to locate the special portion within the initial section when reading the body of the report.
When first mentioned.	Reader has immediate access to meaning of term.	Least desirable because reader may have trouble locating where item was first mentioned.
End of report.	*a.* Similar to special section except placement of terms is in appendix. *b.* More appropriate for exceptionally long sets of definitions. *c.* Reader may prefer this placement.	Some readers say they never read appended material.

Writing an abstract of a research study

Who conducted the study?

What is the name of the study?

Where was the study completed?

When was the study completed?

What was the problem addressed by the study?

What were the objectives of the study?

What procedures were used to conduct the study?

What were some of the major findings, conclusions, and recommendations of the study?

How does the study relate to your study?

Further illustrations of abstracting are presented in Chapter 17. Depending on the study, the abstracts of secondary sources are placed in a special portion of the initial section or in the appendix. Note how these questions are covered in this example of an abstract of a comprehensive research study.

Abstract of a research study

The purpose of the Gump study was to identify and evaluate the concepts pertinent to a basic business communication course at the college level as viewed by business professors and business executives.

Through the analysis of five major textbooks in business communication, data were collected and a checklist developed for validation by communication professors; by professors of accounting, finance, management, and marketing, who were known as the noncommunication business professors; and by business executives.

The professor groups represented 54 colleges and membership in AACSB in the states of Illinois, Indiana, Kentucky, Michigan, and Ohio. The executives represented 82 businesses with over 100 employees located in 14 metropolitan areas in the same five-state region.

The three main groups of respondents were then asked to rate each of 46 concept statements according to its importance—very important, moderately important, slightly important, or unimportant.

Statistical measures used in the study included the Spearman rank-order correlation coefficient, the critical-ratio Z test, the F distribution, Duncan's Multiple-Range Test for Nearly Equal Numbers, and Chi Square.

The 45 concept statements were classified according to the following categories: business writing theory, business letters, business reports, oral communication, and communication theory. From the ratings received by the three groups of respondents, none of the concepts averaged a mean rating below slightly important.

The concepts identified by business executives as being the most important were eliminating unnecessary words; effective messages free from error; matching the message with the reader; vivid and natural writing; an appropriate writing environment; the physical appearance and general style of a letter or memo; the purposes of business reports; the problem-solving approach in report writing; all of the oral skills; the three-step process in communication of symbolizing, transmitting, and interpreting; and a communication environment that promotes trust, loyalty, and interest between management and the employer.

The major conclusions of the Gump study were:

1. Communication professors, noncommunication professors, and executives generally do not agree on the relative importance of specific communication concepts in terms of their value to success in a business career.
2. The noncommunication professors and the executives are closer in agreement concerning the relative importance of the concept categories than the communication professors with either of the other two groups.
3. The main areas of disagreement on individual statement comparisons between the communication professors and either of the other two groups involved the statements in the letter category and the oral communication category.
4. Communication professors, noncommunication professors, and executives most frequently disagreed at a significant level on individual statement comparisons within the business writing theory category and the letter category.
5. The 16 subgroups within the sample of communication professors, noncommunication professors, and executives tended to agree on their perceptions concerning the importance of concepts.
6. The communication professors appear to be meeting the needs of executives in all areas except oral communications.

The Gump study and the present study are related in that both studies are concerned with including in the business communication course those concepts and/or competencies relevant to today's business offices as viewed by business executives.

Preview of the entire study

Organization of the Study. The last component of the initial section includes the organization of the study. You may show an overview of what the remaining sections of the analytical report covers. This is especially helpful if the study is quite comprehensive and if the study includes several major parts or chapters. Consider these examples.

The study is organized as follows:

Chapter 1 includes the introduction, the problem, the objectives, the hypotheses, limitations and delimitations, definition of terms, review of related studies, and the organization of the study.

Chapter 2 includes the review of the literature.

Chapter 3 includes the methodology for conducting the study.

Chapter 4 includes the analysis of the data.

Chapter 5 includes the summary, findings, conclusions, recommendations, and implications.

The supplementary section includes the bibliography and the appendices.

Another example is that of dividing the study into sections as follows:

- Introductory statements.
- Sources of data.
- Corporate performance and outlook.
- Corporate recruiting for college graduates—class of 19_.
- Employer screening practices.
- Corporate campus recruiting trends.
- Manpower planning.

The scope of the study will help you to determine how to organize the sections within your report.

MIDDLE SECTION

The middle section of the analytical report focuses on one major component—analysis of the data. Sometimes referred to as interpretation of data, the middle section is probably the most important of all sections of the analytical report.

Middle section (interpretation)

Analysis of the data (narrative discussion of data grouped by objectives and presented through the use of tables and figures).

Completing the data analysis

Analysis of Data. When collecting data in support of your objectives, you must classify, regroup, or derive calculations from the data to provide meaning. Present your data logically to coincide with the order of your specific objectives.

Developing graphics and statistical measures

Because of the length and complexity of the analysis section, you would normally include graphic aids. For the most part, you can present the data to support responses to the specific objectives using tables, figures, charts, pictograms, or other aids. These graphics help the reader grasp the content more easily. Based on the type of data gathered in the study, you can use statistical measures such as means, medians, modes, percentages, and other complex methods to give greater meaning to the data. (Chapter 12 gives more detail on the use of statistical measures for report writing.) Some data are placed in appendices, especially if they interfere with the flow of the analysis. In the body of your report, refer to all graphics and appended materials to alert the Reader to their existence and to give the Reader a sense of the context of that material.

FINAL SECTION

The final section of the text of an analytical report should synthesize or summarize the first two sections and make logical conclusions and/or recommendations. A person should be able to read this final section and understand the study. Writers should never introduce new information, examples, or data in the final section of the analytical report. The writer of the report should make his/her case before reaching the findings, conclusions, and recommendations section.

The components may include the following:

Final section (synthesis)

- Lead-in.
- Major findings.
- Conclusions.
- Recommendations.
- Implications (optional).

Writing a lead-in statement

Lead-in. The analytical report may contain a summary statement which serves as a lead-in to the other parts of the final section. The summary reorients the Reader to the Problem and objectives of the study and provides a brief review of the procedures. This lead-in presents a clear statement of the material covered in the initial section of this full report.

Lead-in statement

The question addressed in this study was "How can the business communication course be updated and/or improved to meet the needs of the modern and future business environment?" The objectives of the study were to identify the principal writing skills needed in business, as perceived by business managers, and to develop teaching materials for large business communication classes that use a lab with modern electronic office equipment.

To acomplish the objectives of the study, concepts considered essential for effective letter writing were identified through related literature and were categorized into major areas of learning. A conceptual framework was developed for incorporating a writing laboratory into the learning cycle for business communication classes. An outline of the laboratory exercises was then developed to ensure that the concepts identified by the survey were included in the syllabus.

The laboratory learning materials were developed to incorporate specific con-

cepts perceived by managers as essential for effective letter writing. These materials were tested at State University with 150 students during the second semester, 19__. Based on the test and student perceptions, revealed in the exit survey, the materials were revised and refined to reflect the needed changes.

Developing major findings

Major Findings. The major findings are an essential part of the analytical report. This section summarizes the important findings from the analytical middle section. Arrange your findings logically to coincide with the order you used to present the specific objectives in the initial section. Since the arrangement for analyzing the data is also presented according to the specific objectives, the findings are presented in the same way to ensure uniformity and ease of reading.

From the findings, you make conclusions relevant to the objectives of the study. Use these guidelines for stating major findings in a report:

Guidelines for writing major findings

- ☐ Use *Major Findings* as a side heading.
- ☐ Use a lead-in statement.
- ☐ State one or more findings for each specific objective.
- ☐ State the findings in the past tense since findings were true at the time the data were collected.
- ☐ Be specific; incorporate numerical data (numbers, percents, statistical results, etc.) to reveal concrete facts.
- ☐ List findings in the order of the specific objectives of the report.
- ☐ Derive major findings from interpretation of data.
- ☐ Enumerate the major findings for ease in reading.
- ☐ Avoid the terms *some, almost, majority, most, least,* etc. when writing major findings.

The following example clearly states the major findings covered in the middle section of the full report.

Major findings

The findings of the study were as follows:

1. **Fifty-three concepts considered essential to writing effective letters and/or memos by business managers were identified. (Concepts were based on research studies by Gump, Hergenroeder, Hixon, and Stine-Skarzenski.)**
2. **One evaluation instrument assessed students' perceptions on the effectiveness of large-group instruction using simulation learning matierals in small-group labs equipped with modern office technology. The overall weighted mean score of the 14 statements about the laboratory process was 4.1 on a 5-point scale indicating total agreement.**
3. **Another evaluation instrument assessed students' perceptions about the laboratory learning materials. The high-agree areas were: (1) Statement 14—the use of modern office technology with immediate feedback (4.7); statement 11—immediate feedback through the use of CRT's (4.5); and (3) statement 10—the use of a simulation for teaching letter writing concepts (4.4).**

4. Another evaluation instrument assessed student perceptions about the laboratory materials interfaced with modern technology. The mean scores of the other 11 statements (3.8 to 4.2) ranged in the agree area.

Developing conclusions

Conclusions. Probably one of the most important parts of the analytical report is the conclusions section; yet this area is also one of the most difficult for many writers. Conclusions are a synthesis of the findings developed through inferences; they are not restated findings. Each finding does not require a conclusion; rather, conclusions are based on one or more findings. Through practice you will build skill in writing valid conclusions. Some guidelines for stating conclusions in a report are:

Guidelines for writing conclusions

- ☐ Use *Conclusions* as a side heading.
- ☐ Use a lead-in statement.
- ☐ State at least one conclusion for each of the specific objectives.
- ☐ State conclusions in the present tense.
- ☐ Use one or more of the major findings as the basis for stating the conclusion.
- ☐ Enumerate the conclusions.
- ☐ Place in parentheses the number of the major findings that support the conclusion—for the reader's reference.
- ☐ *Avoid* the use of words like *some, almost, majority,* etc., when writing conclusions.

The following example assembles the major findings of the data into a few points stated as conclusions:

Conclusions

The following conclusions are based on the findings of the study:

1. Identified concepts considered essential by business managers for effective written communications can be incorporated into simulated learning materials.
2. A lab setting provides an experience to make large-group instruction effective.
3. Modern electronic office technology facilitates the students' ability to compose written communication.

Developing recommendations

Recommendations. When you have completed the findings and conclusions, you may want to make some recommendations on the basis of your study. Recommendations are derived from the whole study and entire set of conclusions and suggest needed courses of action or additional data. Recommendations for action essentially answer the question regarding application of results. Your communication may raise such questions as:

- ☐ How may the conclusions of the study be applied?
- ☐ What possibilities exist for further study with reference to the study being researched?

Or you may recommend action, for example, that Company A produce an additional 5,000 specially designed convertibles during the next year. Here are some basic guidelines for stating recommendations in a report:

Guidelines for writing recommendations

- ☐ Use the word *Recommendations* as a side heading.
- ☐ Number the recommendations.
- ☐ Use a lead-in statement.
- ☐ Use one or more recommendations that emerge naturally from the study.
- ☐ State recommendations in the future tense.

In the following example, the recommendations clearly state the possible directions that the report reader—the decision maker—should consider.

Recommendations

The following recommendations are based upon the findings and conclusions from this present study:

1. Because this pilot testing of materials was limited to a sample of 150 students enrolled in Business Communication: Letters at State University during the second semester, 19__, the study should be replicated at other institutions to provide a means of comparison.
2. A study should be conducted to compare the effectiveness of the traditional method with that of the simulated approach interfaced with modern technology.
3. Further research should be conducted to determine what impact electronic office equipment is having on other related business courses.
4. This study should be replicated every 10 years to ensure that as concepts of writing business letters change, they are still relevant to practices of contemporary businesses.

Developing implications

Implications. The writer of the analytical report may also discuss implications. Basically, implications are narrative statements based on your insights about what contributions your study may make. Here you can state what your perceptions are about the outcomes of your research effort. Or you may indicate in more detail than in the recommendations what possible actions and alternatives are available to carry out a proposed course of action based on the content of the report. Implications are an indirect indication of the results of the study—to say or express indirectly. Implications are not straightforward; they are judgmental. Implications may offer suggestions for possible action or alternatives available to carry out the recommendations. Guidelines for stating implications are:

Guidelines for writing implications

- ☐ Use the word *implications* as a side heading.
- ☐ Use a lead-in statement.
- ☐ State implications in the present or future tense.
- ☐ Base implications on the insights gained from the preparation of the study.

Here are examples of implications.

Implications

The following are implications for future teaching as a result of this study:

Students who use the laboratory learning materials developed in this study in an electronic office environment look at information processing from a systems approach rather than a skills-oriented approach to job entry-level skills.

Students have numerous opportunities for group work during the simulation. Team work and participative management are practiced. The simulated laboratory learning materials developed for this study use an informal group atmosphere to promote the development of cooperative working relationships. The outcomes of these types of activities help develop the necessary human relations skills that are necessary for growth on the job.

The use of electronic office equipment promotes computer literacy. According to this study, students using microcomputers acquire relevant training that helps to promote decision making and productivity on the job.

SUPPLEMENTARY SECTION

Supplementary section

Business writers frequently use a supplementary section in analytical reports. This section includes:

- Endnotes.
- Bibliography.
- Appended material.

Endnotes

Referencing quoted material

Source notes for quoted material, when collected in the supplementary section, are labeled as endnotes. Citations appearing at the bottoms of the text pages are termed footnotes. Some writers prefer to cite quoted references in the body of the report with a reference number following the quote. The full source note entries are shown in the order in which they appear in the report. These source notes would be collected in the end notes section as follows:

Source notes

1. Booz, Allen, and Hamilton (management consulting firm), "Are You Ready for the Telecommunications Revolution?" Industry Week 182, no. 2 (July 8, 1974), p. 42.
2. Jerry L. Salvaggio, Telecommunications: Issues and Choices for Society (White Plains, N.Y.: Longman, 1982), p. 3.
3. Ibid., p. 3.
4. L. Parker, Introduction to Teleconferencing: A Training Program, (Madison, Wisc.: University of Wisconsin, Madison Extension, 1976).
5. "Telecommute: Making a Shortcut to the Work Place," Communications Update (Spring 1982), p. 15.

The style of documentation you choose is usually dictated by company policy or by a particular style manual, depending on the specific discipline.

Choosing a style for referencing material

Civil engineers, for instance, use the *MLA Style Manual;* chemical engineers use the *Council of Biology Editors Style Manual.* You should learn which style manual is recommended for the discipline and learn the conventions for documentation your colleagues will expect.

Bibliography

Developing the bibliography

The bibliography contains a complete listing of all reference sources cited in the report. These sources are listed alphabetically by author. Some writers prefer the term *List of References.* Consult the style manual appropriate for the discipline. Remember, this is the form your colleagues will know and expect of you.

Traditional bibliography style

Ashby, W. R. An Introduction to Cybernetics. New York: John Wiley & Sons, 1956.

Attneave, F. Application of Information Theory to Psychology. New York: Holt, Rinehart & Winston, 1959.

Baker, E. J., and E. A. Alluisi. "Information Handling Aspects of Visual and Auditory Form Perception." Journal of Engineering Psychology 1 1962, pp. 159–79.

Barlow, H. B. "Sensory Mechanism: The Reduction of Redundancy and Intelligence." In Mechanization of Thought Process. Vol. 2. National Physical Laboratory, Symposium no. 10. London: Her Majesty's Stationery Office, 1959, pp. 535–74.

Levine, M. M. "The Role Redundancy in the Assessment of the Effectiveness of Teacher Communication." National Institute of Education, Department of Health, Education, and Welfare, U.S. Office of Education, 1973.

Wenberg, G. M. The Psychology of Computer Programming. New York: Van Nostrand Reinhold, 1971.

Appended Material

Developing appended material

Supplementary appended material, other than the end notes and the bibliography, should be labeled Appendix A, Appendix B, etc. Appended material may include:

- □ Copy of survey form.
- □ Complex multipage tables.
- □ Other pertinent supplemental data such as raw data.

Placement of forms

If you use a questionnaire or other type of data collection device (such as an interview guide), place a copy in the appendix. The data collection form gives the reader insight into the specific questions asked as well as the way in which you constructed the survey form. An example of a data collection form is shown as Figure 15.7.

Placement of complex tables

Should your report require complex, multipage tables, it is a good practice to place them in the appendix. Such placement will not detract from the reader's understanding of the analysis section of the report.

Figure 15.7
Copy of survey form

APPENDIX C

STUDENT EVALUATION FORM

This survey gives you a chance to anonymously express your views concerning the simulation materials used in the laboratory. Please give your thoughtful consideration to each statement. DO NOT SIGN YOUR NAME.

Key: SA = Strongly Agree   U = Uncertain   SD = Strongly Disagree
A = Agree   D = Disagree

1. The objectives of the laboratory materials were made clear to me at the beginning of the course.	SA	A	U	D	SD
2. I understood what was expected in the jobs and exercises.	SA	A	U	D	SD
3. I found the laboratory materials to be written in a manner that provided a variety of writing experiences similar to "real life" situations.	SA	A	U	D	SD
13. To me, the "letter tests" reflected the objectives of the laboratory jobs and exercises.	SA	A	U	D	SD
14. I was given ample time for completing the letters during the assigned laboratory hours if I had adequately prepared prior to lab time.	SA	A	U	D	SD
15. I prefer using the electronic equipment with immediate feedback rather than preparing the letters at home and handing them in for a grade the next day.	SA	A	U	D	SD

COMMENTS

____

____

Placement of supporting materials

You may also place other materials in the appended section. A listing of raw data, for instance, used to prepare the report might be placed in an appendix. A computer printout, engineering specifications, or a schematic would probably impede the reader's progress if they were placed in the body of the report. They, too, should go in an appendix.

SUMMARY

According to research, managers frequently use analytical reports in business. Analytical reports involve a systematic method of defining the problem, gathering data, discussing the data, and reaching conclusions and recommendations for solving the stated problem.

The analytical report generally consists of the following major sections: preliminary, initial, middle, final, and supplementary.

The preliminary section of the analytical report contains a title page, acknowledgments (optional), table of contents, list of figures, and list of tables. The title page includes the title (centered and all caps), to whom submitted and address (centered), by whom written and address (centered), and the date (centered). Should you include an acknowledgment page, you will give credit or recognition for those who have assisted with some phase of the study. The table of contents is a listing of the preliminary parts, the main divisions of the analytical report, the bibliography, and any appended material. A listing of figures and tables used in the report is desirable.

The initial section is the beginning of the text portion or body of the analytical report. The components of this section comprise the introduction of the report and may include the problem, objectives, procedures, limitations/delimitations, definition of terms (optional), related studies (where applicable) and the organization of the study. The problem statement is derived from the setting and reflects the reasons for the study. Analytical reports may contain several specific objectives, which may be written as null hypotheses, infinitives, or questions. The procedures include a step-by-step presentation of how you conducted the study. Limitations are those constraints over which you have no control; delimitations are the constraints you place on the study. The definition of terms are the terms that may be unfamiliar with the reader/audience. These terms may be placed in a special portion in the initial section, when first mentioned, or at the end of the report. You may choose to use secondary sources which contain information related to your research study. Such related studies may include previous research studies, journal articles, proceedings, technical reports, and reviews of applied and basic research. The last components of the initial section include the organization of the study, an overview of all sections of the report.

The middle section of the analytical report contains the data you collect to support your objectives. These data are classified, regrouped, and calculated to provide meaning to your reader/audience. For the most part, you can present the data to support responses to the specific objectives using tables, figures, charts, pictograms, or other graphic aids. Based on the type of data gathered in the study, you can use statistical measures such as means, medians, modes, percentages, and other complex methods to give greater meaning to the data.

The final section of the text of an analytical report includes the lead-in, major findings, conclusions, recommendations, and implications (optional). The lead-in reorients the reader to the problem and objectives of the study and provides a brief review of the procedures. The lead-in reveals what is included in the initial section of the full report. The findings are specific, concrete facts derived from the analysis of data to answer the specific objectives. Conclusions are a synthesis of findings developed through inferences. Recommendations are derived from the whole study and the entire set of conclusions, and suggest needed courses of action. Implications are narrative statements based on your insight about what contributions your study may make.

The supplementary section of the analytical report may include endnotes, bibliography, and appendices. Source notes for quoted material, when collected in the supplementary section, are labeled as endnotes. The bibliography contains a complete listing of all reference sources cited in the report. These sources are listed alphabetically by author. Appended material may include copies of survey forms, complex multipage tables, or other pertinent supplemental data, such as raw data.

END-OF-CHAPTER ACTIVITIES

DISCUSSION

1. Define an analytical report.
2. Briefly describe each of the components of the preliminary section of an analytical report.
3. Briefly describe each of the components of the initial section of an analytical report.
4. Briefly describe what is included in the content of the middle section of an analytical report.
5. Briefly describe each of the components of the final section of an analytical report.
6. Briefly describe each of the components of the supplementary section of an analytical report.
7. Distinguish between a finding, a conclusion, a recommendation and an implication.
8. Interpret the *Harvard Business Review* quotation on page 435 and show how you may apply the content of the quotation to your professional development.

ACTIVITIES

9. Read the limitations from a research study which appears below. Comment on their readability, accuracy, and completeness.

   The study was limited to:

   a. A sample of public high school teachers of the accounting course.
   b. Postsecondary accounting courses.
   c. Those accounting concepts included in selected accounting textbooks.
   d. Authors of accounting textbooks.
   e. Data collection methods.
10. The following data were excerpted from a research study. The data

were jumbled in such a way that the material lacks any semblance of effective organization. Rewrite the abstract using the nine questions which appear in this chapter on page 445 and the Gump study illustration on pages 445–46.

The present study also utilized a modified Delphi technique as a means of validating the criteria for evaluation. Two conclusions of the study were: (1) the two probe-Delphi technique was a valid means of identifying the evaluation information necessary for secondary institutions and community/junior technical-occupational programs; (2) present evaluation theory explicitly for technical-occupational education is inadequate.

The statements considered necessary for accountable technical-occupational program evaluation were selected on the basis of an interquartile range no larger than 1.99 and a median no lower than 5.00. From 117 statements, 93 met the criteria as necessary for technical-occupational program evaluation.

The Kienast study was related to the present study in that the purpose of the study was to identify the types of information needed for evaluating occupational-technical programs while the purpose of the present study was to identify the criteria for evaluating consumer and homemaking education programs.

The evaluation statements were grouped into six categories: personnel and employer information, placement and follow-up information, cost information, student and parent information. Additional evaluation information suggested by panel members was grouped together at the end of Questionnaire II. Two other groupings were: community information and institutional information.

Other conclusions were as follows: There is apparently a lack of professional preparation concerning program evaluation, and there is a lack of trained evaluators for technical-occupational programs.

The present study also utilized a modified Delphi technique as a means of validating the criteria for evaluation.

The purpose of the Kienast study was to identify the types of information needed for evaluating occupational programs as perceived by community/junior college technical-occupational deans and/or directors and secondary vocational directors.

A modified Delphi technique was used to identify the needed evaluation information by eliciting and refining the opinions of experts in the field of technical-occupational education. A panel of 16 community/junior college technical-occupational deans and/or directors and 41 secondary vocational directors within a 100-mile radius of Dallas responded to a two-probe Delphi questionnaire. A second purpose was to determine the differences in the types of information needed for evaluating secondary programs and community/junior college programs.

The study was completed by Kay Earlene Kienast as a doctoral dissertation at East Texas State University in 1976. The abstract appeared in *Dissertation Abstracts,* p. 4318-A.

Questionnaire I consisted of 109 evaluation statements which panelists rated on a Likert scale of one (disagree) to seven (agree). Questionnaire II was identical to Questionnaire I with the addition of eight statements provided by the panel members and the statistical data relative to the group's response to each statement.

The study was entitled "The Identification of Evaluation Information for Technical-Occupational Programs."

11. Gather several analytical reports. Attempt to obtain reports that reflect a diversity of types of businesses such as sales, hospital administration, banking, insurance, and manufacturing. Make comparisons using these questions:
    a. Is the Problem clearly stated?
    b. How are the objectives expressed—questions, infinitives, or hypotheses?
    c. Are the conclusions supported by the findings? Why or why not?
    d. How well do the findings answer the questions expressed in the discussion?
    e. Are the procedures expressed so that you could replicate the study?
    f. Are the terms adequately defined?
    g. How effective is the organization?
    h. How does the report relate to the strategy for communicating?
12. Study the analytical report entitled "Survey of Institutions in Knoxville, Tennessee, Offering Individual Retirement Accounts, Spring 19_." Evaluate the content based on the principles of effective report writing and the strategy for communicating. Write a report to your instructor regarding your analysis of the report. You may use the questions stated in activity 11 as a part of your evaluation. In addition, you may address these points (plus others of your own):
    a. Appropriate construction, use, placement, and interpretation of graphics.
    b. Organization of the report.
    c. Relevancy of information/data contained.
    d. Ease of comprehension.

SURVEY OF INSTITUTIONS IN KNOXVILLE, TENNESSEE OFFERING INDIVIDUAL RETIREMENT ACCOUNTS

Spring, 19_

INTRODUCTION

In *Newsweek,* December 1981, Jane Bryant Quinn defined an Individual Retirement Account as a tax shelter wherein an individual may invest $2,000 a year from his earnings ($2,250 if the IRA covers his nonworking spouse). This contribution is deductible on his federal income tax and accumulates interest until time of withdrawal—usually after 59 1/2 years of age. A survey was conducted by University of Tennessee Business Communications students to determine the most desirable institutions in the Knoxville area for opening an IRA.

Purpose

The purpose of this study was to determine the most desirable institutions in the Knoxville area in which to invest money in IRA accounts. Answers were sought to the following questions:

1. What type of institutions offer the IRA?
2. What is the minimum deposit to open an IRA?
3. What is the interest rate on the investment?
4. What penalty is involved for early withdrawal from the account?

Source of Data and Method of Procedure

To determine the best institutions for investment in Knoxville, the following steps were taken:

1. Designed a questionnaire using closed-end questions.
2. Made copies of the questionnaire.
3. Made a list of all the financial institutions in Knoxville who were likely to offer IRAs.
4. Collected the data on each institution using telephone interviews.
5. Narrowed the list of institutions by removing the ones not offering IRAs.
6. Made evaluations of the remaining institutions using frequency tables, pie charts, and bar charts.
7. Chose the best institutions in terms of interest rates, penalties, insurance, and other advantages.

Preview

The following section presents the findings of the survey and the last section presents the summary.

FINDINGS

To determine the most profitable institutions for an investment (IRA), a questionnaire was developed and a telephone interview completed. Sixty institutions were surveyed and out of this total, 11 did not offer IRAs. As shown in Figure 1, of the 49 institutions surveyed, the highest number of institutions offering IRAs were insurance companies; that is, 20 companies or 41 percent of those institutions surveyed. The lowest number of institutions offering IRAs were banks. Five banks were listed, a percentage of 10 percent. Savings and loan companies numbered nine at 18 percent, and there were eight brokerage firms at 16 percent. Credit unions totaled seven, or 14 percent.

Figure 1

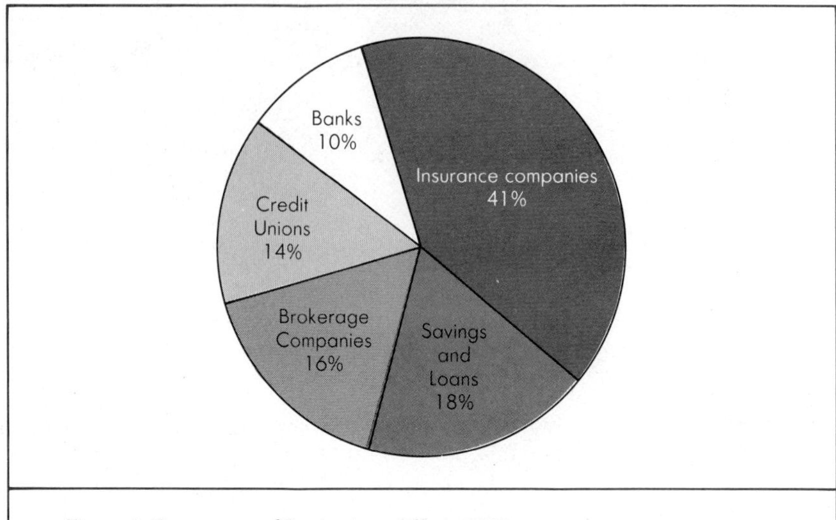

Figure 1. Percentage of Institutions Offering IRAs.

Minimum Deposit

Thirty-six out of the 49 institutions surveyed required a minimum deposit of less than $500. As shown in Figure 2, 10 institutions required a deposit of $500 to $1,000, and only two required $1,001 to $2,000. These two were Security Trust Savings and Loan and Special Plans of Tennessee. None required $2,001 or more. Some institutions require that you have another account with their firm before opening an IRA account; however, of the 49 surveyed, only 7 required another account, and these were credit unions.

Figure 2

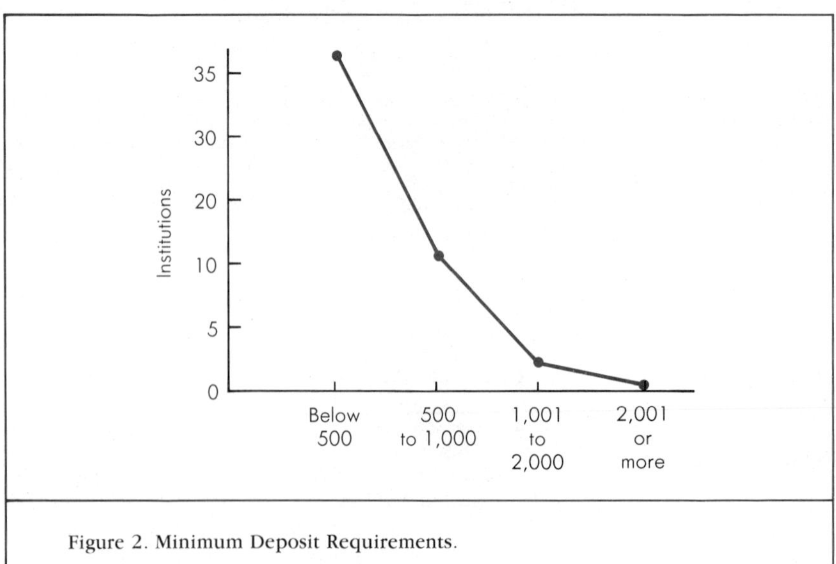

Figure 2. Minimum Deposit Requirements.

Figure 3

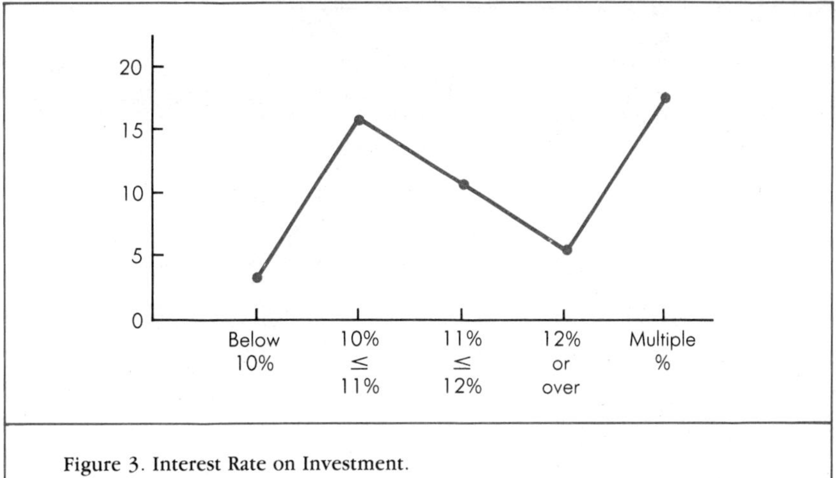

Figure 3. Interest Rate on Investment.

Interest Rate Paid on Investment

In the survey, most institutions paid at least 10 percent and less than 11 percent. This number consisted of 15 out of the 49. As shown in Figure 3, 10 institutions paid over 11 percent interest and 6 paid over 12 percent. Fifteen institutions offered a multiple percentage. For example, at one firm, if you purchased a five-year certificate, your interest rate would be as follows:

First year	11.40%
Second year	11.65
Third year	11.95
Fourth year	12.05
Fifth year	12.20

Penalties for Early Withdrawal

Of the eight institutions charging no penalty for early withdrawal, three were insurance companies, three were brokerage firms, one was a credit union, and one a savings and loan. There is usually some type of penalty for early withdrawal; however, most institutions base the penalty on the amount and several charge six months' interest for early withdrawal. Also, the Federal Government taxes the amount withdrawn at 10 percent. Heritage Federal charged one year's interest and Farm Bureau Insurance Company charged more than one year's interest. These penalties are reflected in chart number one.

SUMMARY

To determine the most desirable institutions for IRAs in Knoxville, a questionnaire was developed and a telephone interview completed. Evaluations were made using bar charts, pie charts, and graphs.

Major Findings

1. Of the total institutions surveyed, the majority of IRAs were offered by insurance companies.
2. Thirty-six of the 49 institutions had a minimum deposit of less than $500.
3. Fifteen out of the 49 paid at least 10 percent interest on the investment. Ten institutions paid over 11 percent interest and six paid over 12 percent.

Chart No. 1

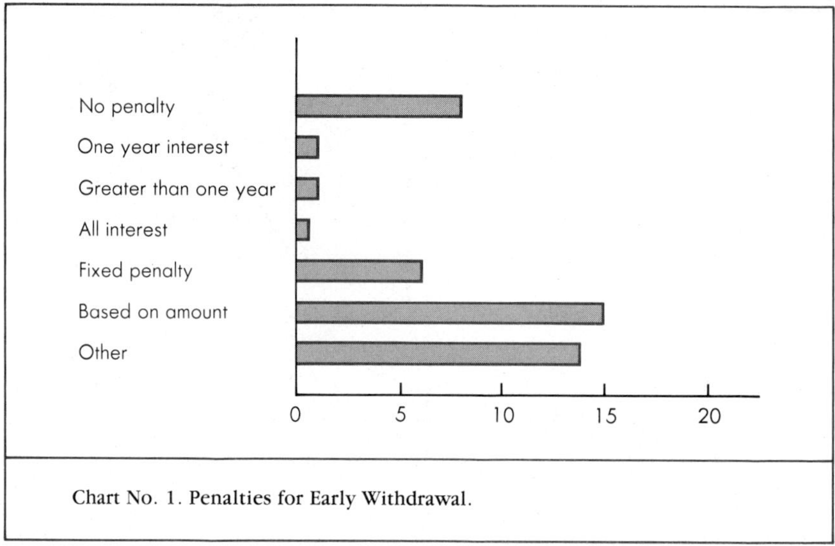

Chart No. 1. Penalties for Early Withdrawal.

4. There is usually some type of penalty for early withdrawal; however, most institutions base the penalty on the amount and several charge six months' interest. Of the eight institutions charging no penalty for early withdrawal, three were insurance companies.

Conclusions

The following conclusions are based on the major findings of this study:

1. The insurance companies are more competitive in the IRA market. There are more insurance companies offering IRAs, and the minimum deposit at 15 of the 20 companies is less than $500.
2. Eight of the insurance companies paid over 11 percent interest rate on the IRA investment; the other 12 paid 10 percent.
3. Of the eight institutions charging no penalty for early withdrawal, three were insurance companies. The penalty for early withdrawal is usually based on the amount of the investment.

Recommendations

The following recommendations are made concerning an IRA.

1. The insurance companies have the most desirable IRA account based on our findings.
2. The banks and savings and loan companies do offer some attractive IRA plans, and it is possible that a better plan could be negotiated if you are already a customer.
3. It is always wise to conduct a personal investigation in order to find an IRA to meet your personal needs.

CHAPTER 16

WRITING THE ANALYTICAL REPORT

Learning Objectives

After studying this chapter, you will be able to:

- □ Plan and write all sections of an analytical report.
- □ Apply the strategy for communicating to all sections of an analytical report.
- □ Develop an appropriate background of the study for an analytical report.
- □ Develop the appropriate organization for analyzing the specific objectives of an analytical report.
- □ Narrate specific objectives for an analytical report and use correct graphics for your data analyses.
- □ Develop major findings, conclusions, recommendations, and implications for an analytical report using concrete guidelines.

Points to consider when writing an analytical report

In this chapter you will study the *process* for writing the analytical report. Even though there is no one best way to write reports, it is good to know how to approach the writing. Individual preference, instructor preference, and company policies for reports are some of the factors that help determine which method you use.

Now, we will walk you through planning and writing all sections of a sample analytical report. Keep in mind that the principles of writing an analytical report on any topic are similar. The intent here is to teach you how to write an analytical report using the strategy for communicating. After learning this process, you can easily adapt it for any type of business report.

KNOW THE SETTING

Developing the problem of the study

When writing an analytical report, you must first determine the Problem in the context of your particular setting or situation. In business, you will understand the setting and the problems that need solving simply because you've worked directly with them. In this textbook, however, the settings are provided for you to determine the Problem. Our topic is "Perceptions of The University of Tennessee (UT) Students Regarding Various Effects of the 1982 Knoxville World's Fair."

Remember, the strategy for communicating includes the Problem, general and specific Objectives, Reader/Audience, Order, and Format. The setting includes background for you to identify the problem of the study.

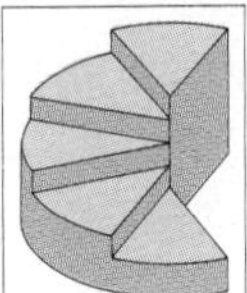

STRATEGY: THE WORLD'S FAIR REPORT

Tennessee hosted the 1982 World's Fair at a site directly adjacent to The University of Tennessee campus in Knoxville. Before the fair, some of the general public were not only interested but enthusiastic about the world exposition. Others were more concerned about negative effects. Rumors abounded as well as suggestions that hotels, restaurants, and other businesses would gouge area residents with extremely inflated prices. Some feared that apartment landlords would evict tenants and rent that space to fair goers at exorbitant prices. Traffic in Knoxville would indeed be difficult to handle with an expected 12 million visitors during the six-month fair. Many UT students feared their parking spaces would be used by fair goers.

Not all of the general public and students dwelled on the possible negative impact. Numerous members of the general public and some students anticipated greater employment opportunities, more cultural opportunities and exposure to international pavilions and visitors, and opportunities to hear some of the world's greatest musicians.

Because she was concerned about the effects of the World's Fair on students, Dr. Clara Templeton, vice president for student affairs, has di-

rected you, a professional staff member in her office, to survey the students.

You are to design an appropriate study, collect the necessary data, and submit a report within three weeks. The vice president for student affairs plans to take corrective action on the negative aspects of the fair, where possible. She plans to publicize the positive aspects. The fair opened one month ago.

After studying the setting, you define the *Problem* and identify the *general* and *specific Objectives:*

PROBLEM

How is the 1982 World's Fair affecting The University of Tennessee students?

OBJECTIVES

General: To identify the positive and negative effects of the World's Fair on UT students.

For specific objectives, you need to consider how students are being affected in the following areas:

Specific: Student housing.
Employment.
Parking.
Entertainment.
Prices (on-site and off-site).
Traffic.

READER/AUDIENCE

The *primary Audience* for your report is the vice president of student affairs, since she requested the study. Possible *secondary* readers may include the student affairs staff and the university students.

Characteristics: Well educated.
Holds high administrative post on campus.
Former professor of English.

Reactions: Will be glad to get the results of the study. She hopes to use the study to assist administration with minimizing or eliminating problems associated with the fair.

Other staff members and students want the study to help them to make positive recommendations.

ORDER

Even though you have much work to do before you can write the report, you turn your attention to the Order of the communication. Normally, analytical reports follow a conventional structure which may include the following sections:

- □ Preliminary.
- □ Initial.
- □ Middle.
- □ Final.
- □ Appendices, as necessary.

Direct style. At this point, you could defer organizational decisions until you have collected your data. The length and the variety of readers for this report suggest that the most appropriate Order will be *introduction, analysis section,* and then *conclusions.* Since the purpose is written immediately after the introductory paragraphs, you use the direct Order. You sequence the specific objectives as follows:

1. Student housing.
2. Employment.
3. Parking.
4. Entertainment.
5. Prices (on-site and off-site).
6. Traffic.

Once you start writing the report, you may decide on some other Order. Because of the complex nature of any analytical report, determining the most appropriate Order early in the planning process is not always easy. You must remain flexible enough to adapt the Order as you begin writing the report.

FORMAT

Your last task is to decide on the Format of the report. Because your investigation covers six separate objectives, you can anticipate that the formal document will be quite long. Thus the conventional *analytical report* seems appropriate. You'll need preliminary, initial, middle, final, and supplementary sections.

WRITING THE INITIAL SECTION

Components of the initial section of the analytical report

Typically, the introduction of an analytical report contains a statement of the problem, general and specific objectives of the study, procedures, limitations/delimitations, definitions of key terms, a review of related literature, and an optional organization of the study.

LEGAL / ETHICAL ISSUE

As a member of the telecommunications faculty for three years at a major land-grant university, Josh Hunt knows the importance of doing well in teaching, research, and service. Administrators evaluate the faculty on the basis of their performance in these areas. Josh consistently receives very fine teaching evaluations from his students; he was nominated for an outstanding teaching award during the past academic year. Josh's service performance is ranked among the top three faculty in a 15-member department. The administration is highly pleased with Josh's work in teaching and service.

Josh is now beginning to sense the need to do research that will result in publication in a well-known journal. His department head Steven Hayes told him recently that he must have at least one research-related article published in a major journal by the end of his fourth year of teaching.

The pressure is on! Since Josh knows that he does not have the time to conduct any type of survey or experimental research, he decides to develop a fictional research study. He assumes a fictional problem, a fictional objective, three fictional specific objectives, and a fictional database for analysis purposes. Josh has always been recognized for his creative abilities. He developed a very forward-looking fictional study related to telecommunications and managed to get a major publication in a leading journal.

Actually, Josh fabricated all the parts for his entire research study. He has slipped below any accepted standard for collecting and analyzing data.

If you were Josh's department head, what action would you take for this unethical behavior? Is the university liable for Josh's conduct? Elaborate.

Developing the background for the study and the problem statement

As you begin to write the analytical report, you need to develop a background for the study. An appropriate heading might be "The Setting and Problem." You then develop a list of the items to include in this section:

- ☐ Set the stage for the entire report.
- ☐ Capture the reader's interest.
- ☐ Include possible secondary sources to help justify or support the topic.
- ☐ Include possible internal and external environmental conditions that give rise to the problem.
- ☐ Include possible historical data.

- ☐ Include possible report topic.
- ☐ Incorporate problem statement.

With these ideas in mind, you can begin collecting the necessary secondary sources and background information. The example shows a model of the setting and problem of the analytical report. Comments in the left-hand margin highlight the various segments.

PERCEPTIONS OF UNIVERSITY OF TENNESSEE STUDENTS
REGARDING VARIOUS EFFECTS OF THE 1982
KNOXVILLE WORLD'S FAIR

INTRODUCTION

Setting the stage for the report

World's Fairs have been a source of entertainment for millions of people for over a century. The magic of World's Fairs began in 1851 with the Crystal Palace Exposition in London. Many inventions and new ideas have come out of World's Fairs of the past. The Eiffel Tower in Paris was built for the World's Fair in 1889, and the first Ferris wheel was introduced at the 1893 Chicago Fair. Such inventions as ice cream, television, and telephones were introduced at different World's Fairs.[1]

Capturing the readers' attention

Much controversy exists in Knoxville and the surrounding communities regarding what impact the fair will have on the area. Some people say that Knoxville's interstate system will improve, employment will rise, and the downtown section will be revitalized. Knoxville will gain international attention.

Since the 72-acre site for the World's Fair is directly adjacent to The University of Tennessee campus, students have many concerns. They are aware of both the negative and positive rumors that abound. Possible strains on campus parking, housing, employment, price increases for on- and off-site entertainment, and increased traffic are issues that concern the students.

Developing the problem statement

Problem

How is the 1982 World's Fair affecting University of Tennessee students?

---

[1] U.S. News & World Report (April 1982), p. 76.

General and Specific Objectives

Writing the general and specific objectives

Referring to your strategy planning, you will now write the second part of the *initial section*—general and specific Objectives. These are sometimes referred to as factors or elements of the Problem.

Side heading

General Objective

Infinitive phrase

The general objective of this study is to identify the positive and negative effects the World's Fair is having on University of Tennessee students.

The specific objectives are discrete factors for a study. (Discrete factors refer to the types of data needed.) In this case the report is to include data relating to housing, employment, etc. Specific objectives are written in the form of infinitives, questions, or hypotheses. In the World's Fair study, data from students will be collected and analyzed. Since descriptive statistics will be used, the infinitive form is appropriate. The question form would also be appropriate. The way you sequence the specific objectives determines the order of discussion and presentation for the middle section of the analytical report. This example shows the specific objectives for the World's Fair study.

Side heading

Lead-in to enumeration

Objectives

Infinitive form

Parallel construction

Specific Objectives

The following specific objectives will be addressed in this report:

1. To determine student perceptions of the fair's effect on student housing.
2. To determine student perceptions of the fair's effect on student employment.
3. To determine student perceptions of the fair's effect on student parking.
4. To determine student perceptions of the fair's effect on off-site entertainment.
5. To determine student perceptions of the fair's effect on on-site and off-site prices.
6. To determine student perceptions of the fair's effect on traffic.

Procedures

Developing the procedures section of the analytical report

The next part of the initial section, the procedures, describes how you will complete the study. The procedures for the World's Fair study include the following steps:

1. Development of closed-ended questionnaire to survey the students. (A time constraint precluded other methods of data collection.)
2. Pretest of questionnaire with five students.
3. Revision of questionnaire based on pretest.
4. Completion of questionnaire by 100 UT students.
5. Tabulation of questionnaire responses.

Procedures are usually written in narrative form (or narrative plus an enumeration of steps.) Write the procedures in the past tense. The next example shows the procedures used to conduct the World's Fair study.

Side heading

Lead-in objective restated

Procedures

UT students provided their perceptions of the effects of the 1982 World's Fair in questionnaire form. The process involved developing, pretesting by five students, and revising. (See pages 472–473 for copy of the questionnaire.) A convenient sample of 100 students completed the questionnaire. Data were collected, tabulated, and analyzed.

Limitations/Delimitations

Developing the limitations/delimitations of the analytical report

The next part of the initial section describes the limitations/delimitations. This section establishes the boundaries of the study.

Refer to the procedures you have just developed. A convenient sample of 100 students completed the questionnaire. This becomes one of your primary limitations. The time available to conduct the study was another major limitation. The subjects of the study were University of Tennessee students.

Because of the ease in communicating these limitations to the reader, you decide to write this section with enumerated items. An alternative is to omit the numbering system and write in a narrative form.

Side heading

Lead-in

Enumeration

Limitations/Deliminations

The limitations of the study were as follows:

1. Subjects were University of Tennessee students.
2. Data were collected from a convenient sample of 100 students.
3. Three weeks were allotted to complete the report.

Definition of Terms

Developing the definition of terms section of the analytical report

Most analytical reports include specialized terms. Terms are added as the study progresses. For the World's Fair study, four terms are especially appropriate: on-site, off-site, commuter, and noncommuter. Include the terms as a separate part in the initial section and number them for ease of reading. Since you envision the report to be approximately 25-30 pages in length, you decide to group the definitions in one place in the early part of the report. Your reader/audience can obtain meaning of the terms in the early stages of the writing.

Side heading

Lead-in

Enumeration

Terms underlined

Parallel construction

Definition of Terms

The following terms are applicable to this study:

1. <u>On-site</u>. Refers to the 72-acre grounds of the 1982 Knoxville World's Fair.
2. <u>Off-site</u>. Refers to the downtown Knoxville area and the surrounding metropolitan communities.
3. <u>Commuter</u>. Refers to students who live off campus and who pay to park in UT parking lots.
4. <u>Noncommuter</u>. Refers to students who live in residence halls, campus apartments and fraternity houses who pay to park in UT parking lots.
5. <u>UT</u>. Refers to the University of Tennessee campus.

Review of Related Literature

Citing appropriate secondary sources

The last component of the initial section is the review of related literature. Other than the incorporation of appropriate secondary sources presented earlier, library searches revealed no related literature was available for the World's Fair study. Therefore, the inclusion of a review of related literature was not necessary for this study.

MIDDLE SECTION OF ANALYTICAL REPORT

Developing the analysis of data for an analytical report

The middle section of the analytical report includes one major component—analysis of the data. Sometimes referred to as interpretation of data, the middle section is probably the most important section of the analytical report. The final section of the report (findings, conclusions, and recommendations) is derived from the middle section.

Data from 100 UT students were collected by a questionnaire, designed so that the data could be analyzed on a computer. The questionnaire is shown in Figure 16.1 with the computer tabulated data of 83 respondents indicated by color. You will refer to the questionnaire and the raw data responses in developing the analysis of data section.

So the big job here is to make some sense out of the raw data. You must classify and regroup the data to provide meaning to the six specific objectives listed in the initial section.

Organization

Guidelines for writing the middle section of the analytical report

The middle section contains several parts—an introduction and subparts corresponding to each specific objective. This pattern alerts the reader to the topic covered and provides quick and easy access to specific segments within the report. The introduction for the middle section *briefly* summarizes the general and specific objectives and the procedures to reorient the reader to these important components. You may think this is repetitious, but the length makes some redundancy necessary. The repetition helps orient many readers who, because of differing interests, may not need to read each segment entirely.

Within each subpart, integrate the graphics with interpretation. The order for your presentation of data is the same as the order for the specific objectives given in the initial section of the report.

Use centered and side headings for divisions. The headings commonly used for the middle section include Analysis of Data, Interpretation of Data, or some other descriptive word or phrase.

For each of the specific objectives, use a side heading positioned at the left margin and underscored. Use a descriptive word or phrase for each objective. You will see examples in this chapter.

Now let's look at the World's Fair study. To write the introduction for the middle section, use these guidelines:

- ☐ Use centered heading, all in capitals, for the middle section name.
- ☐ Use an introduction which briefly summarizes the general and specific objecives and procedures.

Present data according to the order of the specific objectives

The order or sequence of presentation of data is dependent on the listing of specific objectives in the initial section of the report. The analysis begins with the first specific objective.

Study the model introduction to the World's Fair report on page 474.

Figure 16.1
Questionnaire and tabulated data for analytical report (83 respondents)

Questionnaire—Perceptions of the World's Fair

Directions: Please complete the following questions about your perceptions of the impact of the World's Fair.

1. How has the World's Fair affected your housing? (Check all that are applicable.)
   - 66 a. Has not affected me.
   - 2 b. I was evicted.
   - 13 c. My rent increased.
   - 2 d. Other; specify ______________
     - 1 Hard to find one.
     - 1 Condemnation of apartment building.
2. How has the World's Fair affected the availability of affordable housing?
   - 14 a. Increased.
   - 42 b. Decreased.
   - 27 c. Unaffected.
3. Which factors influenced the employment situation of UT students?
   - 78 a. Increased availability of work.
   - 1 b. Decreased availability of work.
   - 2 c. No change in availability of work.
   - 12 d. Increased wages.
   - 5 e. Decreased wages.
   - 23 f. No change in wages.
   - 23 g. Increased workload.
   - 3 h. Decreased workload.
   - 3 i. No change in workload.
4. Which of the following best describes your feeling about this statement: "In the long run, the World's Fair temporary employment may be a detriment to the Knoxville economy."
   - 8 a. Strongly agree.
   - 24 b. Agree.
   - 24 c. Undecided.
   - 24 d. Disagree.
   - 3 e. Strongly disagree.
5. In your opinion, do you feel there is a parking problem due to the World's Fair?
   - 34 a. Yes. 1 c. No opinion.
   - 48 b. No.

   If yes, rank in order how you would solve the problem (1-first choice; 2-second; etc.) **Weighted average*
   - 67* d. Build additional parking lots for UT students.
   - 97* e. Impose heavy penalty for any illegal use of present facilities.
   - 97* f. Intensify the use of alternative mode of transportation, such as bus.
   - 69* g. Stop issuing any parking permits to persons other than UT students and personnel.
6. Do you feel the World's Fair has brought entertainment to Knoxville that otherwise would not have been available?
   - 79 a. Yes.
   - 4 b. No.
   - 0 c. Undecided.

Figure 16.1
(*concluded*)

7. Many off-site entertainment events have had poor attendance. Rank in order the following to show what you believe to be the problems associated with the off-site entertainment (1-first choice; 2-second, etc.).
   15 *a.* Too many shows scheduled too close together.
   5 *b.* Too little variety.
   20 c. Tickets too expensive.
   8 *d.* Shows not properly advertised.
   35 e. Too many kinks in Ticketron System.
8. Check the areas in which you feel UT students have had to pay higher prices because of the World's Fair. (You may check more than one.)
   8 *a.* Not affected.
   56 *b.* Restaurants.
   23 c. Grocery items.
   26 *d.* Gas products.
   44 e. Entertainment.
   50 *f.* Housing.
9. Which do you feel is true about prices on the Fair site?
   36 *a.* Higher than expected.
   39 *b.* Lower than expected.
   7 c. Same as expected.
10. Since the World's Fair started, what has been the effect on your daily time spent in traffic?
    31 *a.* Increased.
    38 *b.* Decreased.
    13 c. Remained the same.
11. How would you solve the traffic congestion due to UT football and the World's Fair? (Check only one.)
    41 *a.* Shuttle bus.
    17 *b.* Arrive early.
    6 c. Car pool
    7 *d.* Do not attend.
    8 e. Other; specify ______________________.
        2 Boat.
        4 Walk.
        2 Special rides.

Demographic Data

12. Are you a
    44 *a.* Commuter?
    39 *b.* Noncommuter?
13. What is the driving distance from your place of residence while attending UT to the World's Fair site?
    25 *a.* 0–5 miles.
    13 *b.* 6–10 miles.
    4 c. 11–15 miles.
    1 *d.* 16–20 miles.
    1 e. More than 20 miles.

ANALYSIS OF DATA

To determine the effects the 1982 World's Fair is having on UT students, a questionnaire survey of 100 students was conducted in July 1982. The specific objectives were to determine students' perceptions about student housing, employment, parking, off-site entertainment, on-site and off-site prices, and traffic.

Of the 100 students surveyed, 17 gave incomplete responses. Therefore, the following is an analysis of the data from the 83 students who gave complete responses to the questionnaire regarding the six specific objectives.

Analysis of the Specific Objectives

Use these guidelines for developing the remainder of the middle section of the report:

Sequencing the specific objectives

- ☐ Use a side heading positioned at the left margin for each specific objective.
- ☐ Underline the side heading.
- ☐ Provide an appropriate lead-in for each objective.
- ☐ Present the specific objectives as ordered in the strategy for communicating and listed in the initial section of the report.
- ☐ Present the interpretation with appropriate graphics.

Specfic Objective 1. The analysis begins with the first specific objective: "to determine student perceptions of the fair's effect on housing." Note that questions 1 and 2 in the questionnaire deal with housing.

How has the World's Fair affected your housing? Check all that are applicable.
How has the World's Fair affected the availability of affordable housing?

Now, the big question is, "How will you present these data in the analytical report?" To show how the responses (shown in Figure 16.1 in color) compare to one another, you might select the bar chart to illustrate the data. *Housing* is the most appropriate side heading for this segment of the analytical report. Based on this information, you could complete the analysis of data for Specific Objective 1—*housing*—as shown in the narrative in Figure 16.2.

Specific Objective 2. The second specific objective is "to determine student perceptions of the World's Fair's effect on student employment." Question 3 of the questionnaire deals with employment.

Which factors influenced the employment situation of UT students?

Again, how should you present these data in the report? (See Figure 16.1 for the tabulated responses.) Three variables make up this question—availability of work, wages, and work load. Since there are degrees of each of these variables, the data become somewhat complex. Because of its complexity, the data lend themselves more to a formal table than to other graphic forms.

The interpretation should include a lead-in statement and the highlights of each of the three variables: availability, wages, work load. Students could respond to more than one item for question 3 as indicated at the bottom of the table. The example shows the interpretation for Table 1, which relates to the side heading of *Employment* and presents the analysis of the data for Specific Objective 2.

Employment

Table 1 shows the students' perceptions of the effects of the World's Fair on the availability of employment, level of wages, and workload.

Of the 81 students responding to the question concerning the availability of employment, 78, or 96 percent, indicated an increase in job possibilities. Of the 40 students responding to the portion of the question concerning the effect of the World's Fair on wages, 23, or 57.5 percent, indicated no change in wages; 12, or 30 percent, indicated an increase. Of the 29 students responding to the portion of the question concerning the effect of the World's Fair on workload, 23, or 80 percent, indicated an increase in the workload.

TABLE 1
PERCEPTIONS OF UT STUDENTS ON THE EFFECTS OF THE WORLD'S FAIR ON EMPLOYMENT

	Availability		**Wages**		**Workload**		**Total**	
Response	**Number**	**Percent**	**Number**	**Percent**	**Number**	**Percent**	**Number**	**Percent**
Increase	78	96.3	12	30.0	23	79.4	113	75.4
Decrease	1	1.2	5	12.5	3	10.3	9	6.0
No change	2	2.5	23	57.5	3	10.3	28	18.6
Total	81	100.0	40	100.0	29	100.0	150*	100.0

*Not every student responded to all of the three categories. If they had done so, the total for each category would have been 83; and the total of the category totals would have been 249.

Question 4 from the questionnaire is also somewhat related to employment:

In your opinion, do you feel that there is a parking problem due to the World's Fair?

As you can see, this is an evaluative statement. The logical way to present these data would be to compare the different responses. A bar chart is appropriate for these data; the interpretation for these data would be very similar to the data presented in Figure 16.2.

Specific Objective 3. The third specific objective is "to determine UT students' perceptions of the fair's effect on parking." Note that question 5 deals with parking.

Figure 16.2
Specific Objective 1

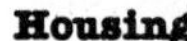

Housing

Figure 1 shows the students' perceptions of the effect of the World's Fair on housing. Of the 83 students, 66 indicated that the World's Fair did not affect their housing; 13 indicated that their rent had increased; and 2 indicated that the World's Fair was responsible for their eviction. Of the 2 students who checked Other, one indicated that housing was hard to find; and one indicated that the World's Fair was instrumental in the condemnation of an apartment building.

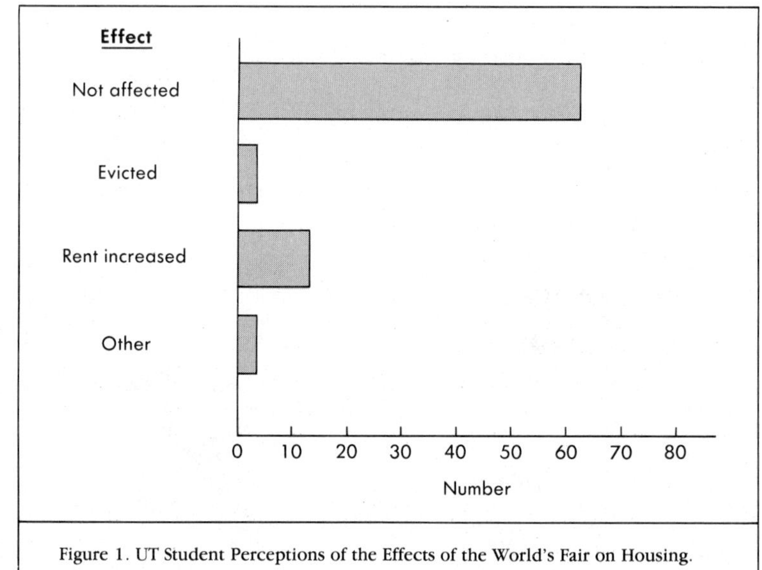

Figure 1. UT Student Perceptions of the Effects of the World's Fair on Housing.

In the long run, do you feel that the World's Fair may be a detriment to the economy of Knoxville?

From the raw data shown in Figure 16.1, rankings are calculated on a worksheet, then summarized in the graphic. How will you present these data in the report? For the first part of question 5, you could provide just a narrative statement like that shown in the next example.

The 83 students were asked to give their perceptions as to whether the World's Fair caused parking problems. Of the 83 students, 34 indicated yes, 48 indicated no, and 1 indicated no opinion.

Figure 16.2
(*continued*)

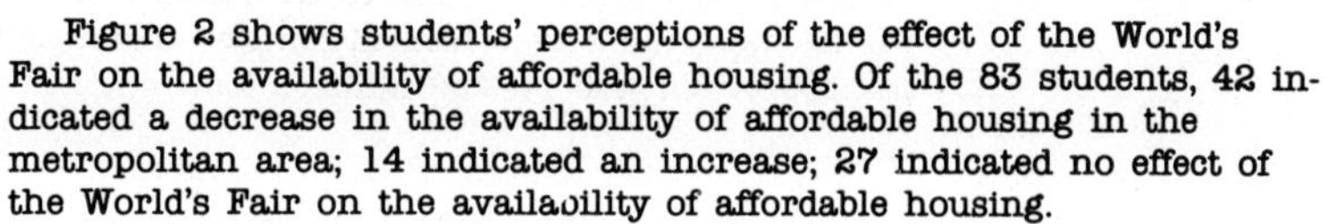
Figure 2 shows students' perceptions of the effect of the World's Fair on the availability of affordable housing. Of the 83 students, 42 indicated a decrease in the availability of affordable housing in the metropolitan area; 14 indicated an increase; 27 indicated no effect of the World's Fair on the availability of affordable housing.

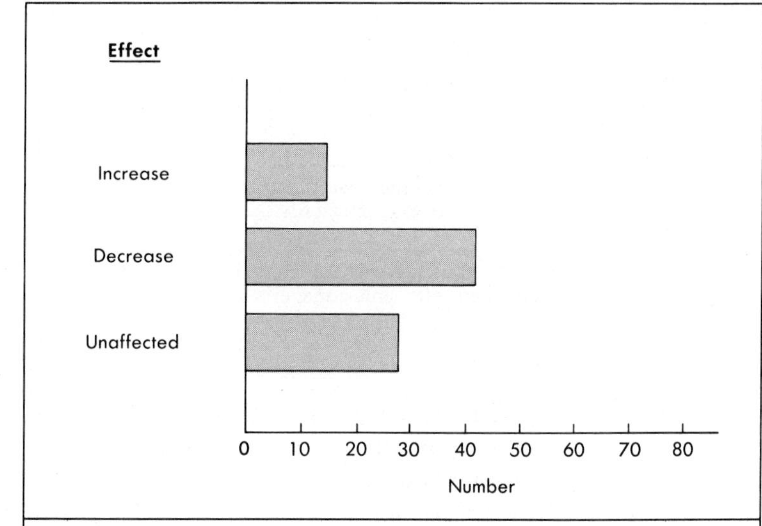

Figure 2. UT Student Perceptions of the Effects of the World's Fair on Availability of Affordable Housing.

For the first part of question 5, you may write the responses in narrative rather than using a graphic. Remember, not all data need to be put into graphic format. For the second part of question 5, a table is the most appropriate because of the complexity of the data. This example shows this interpretation and table. Frequency times weight yields the overall rating.

Parking

Of the 83 UT students surveyed, 34 indicated parking problems as shown in Table 2. Four possible solutions to the parking problems were to build additional parking, impose heavy fines, increase use of other transportation, and issue permits only to UT students and staff.

According to students' responses, building additional parking was ranked number one; issuing permits to UT students and staff ranked number two; imposing heavy fines was ranked number three; and increasing use of other transportation was ranked number four.

TABLE 2
UT STUDENTS' RANKING OF SOLUTIONS TO PARKING PROBLEMS CREATED BY THE WORLD'S FAIR

Solutions	**Weighted Frequency***	**Ranking**
Build additional parking	67	1
Issue permits only to UT students and staff	69	2
Impose heavy fines	93	3
Increase use of other transportation	97	4

*Frequency was multiplied by rank: 1, 2, 3, or 4; a total of students responded with solutions.

Specific Objective 4. The fourth objective is "to determine students' perceptions of the fair's effect on off-site entertainment." Questions 6 and 7 of the questionnaire deal with entertainment. The types of results are similar to the results for previous questions. A bar chart is appropriate for the data from question 6; a table is appropriate for question 7.

Specific Objective 5. The fifth specific objective is "to determine students' perceptions of the fair's effect on the on-site and off-site prices." Questions 8 and 9 deal with prices.

Check the areas in which you feel UT students have had to pay higher prices because of the World's Fair. (You may check more than one.)

Which statement do you feel is true about the prices on the fair site?

Why not exercise some creativity and originality by developing a pictogram for these data? Create some drawings to represent items such as housing, gas products, etc. Figure 4 includes the data from questions 8 and 9 in the form of a pictogram. The side heading appropriate for this segment is *Prices* (see Figure 16.3).

A bar chart is appropriate for question 9. The interpretation for these data is similar to those of earlier figures presented in this chapter.

Specific Objective 6. The final objective is "to determine students' perceptions of the fair's effect on traffic." Questions 10 and 11 deal with traffic.

Figure 16.3
Specific Objective 5

Prices

Figure 4 shows the perceptions of UT students as to whether higher prices in various areas have occurred because of the World's Fair. The five areas of concern mentioned in the questionnaire were restaurants, grocery products, gas products, entertainment, and housing.

Of the 83 students surveyed, 56, or 67 percent, indicated that restaurants were charging higher prices because of the World's Fair; 50, or 60 percent, indicated that housing prices had increased. Only 23, or 16 percent, indicated that grocery prices had increased.

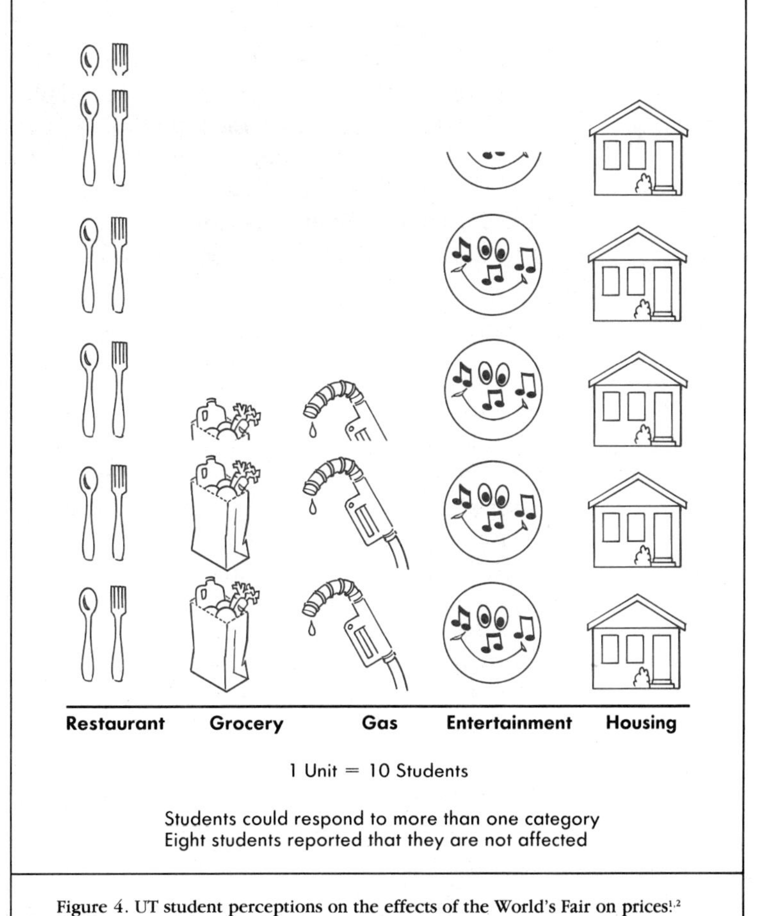

Figure 4. UT student perceptions on the effects of the World's Fair on prices[1,2]

Since the World's Fair started, what has been the effect on your daily time spent in traffic?

How would you solve the traffic congestion due to UT football and the World's Fair?

The responses of the three categories in question 9 are appropriate for a pie chart. Convert the raw data to percentages to equal 100 percent. One person did not respond (see the interpretation and the pie chart in Figure 16.4). A bar chart is appropriate for the data from question 11.

Now refer to questions 12 and 13 in the questionnaire, which deal with demographic data. To show the relationship between the distance commuters travel to get to campus and their perceptions of the change in traffic caused by the World's Fair, data from two questions were contrasted. The first part of question 12, "Are you a commuter?" was contrasted with question 10, "Since the World's Fair started, has your daily time spent in traffic increased, decreased, or remained the same?"

Some very interesting results can be derived from analyzing such cross-classified data. (See Chapter 13 for instructions on preparing cross-referenced tables). Table 4 shows the data and interpretation resulting from this specific contrast, as shown in Figure 16.5.

FINAL SECTION OF ANALYTICAL REPORT

Components of the final section of the analytical report

In this section of the report, the summary, findings, conclusions, recommendations, bibliography, and supplementary section are presented. Study the guidelines for developing each component of the final section of the analytical report presented in Chapter 15. Selected portions of the World's Fair report illustrate how to write major findings, conclusions, and recommendations. Sometimes, writers add an *implications section* to their reports. This is left to the discretion of the report writer. The implications area gives the writer an opportunity to state what is perceived as the outcomes of the research effort. The writer is free to be highly creative in writing implications, which are statements about the contributions of the study in the marketplace. Or the writer may choose to detail possible alternatives in a proposed course of action.

Now that you understand these concepts, let's complete each of the components as they relate to the World's Fair report.

Report Summary

Developing the lead-in for the summary

The opening paragraphs of the final section should summarize the report objectives and procedures to reorient the reader. Even though doing so may seem repetitious, you may even repeat some of the same phrases and sentences from the initial section of the report. Ideally, the reader could read

Figure 16.4
Specific Objective 6

Traffic

Figure 6 shows how the World's Fair affected the amount of time students spent in traffic daily. Of the 83 students surveyed, one did not respond. Of the 82 students who did respond, 46 percent indicated a decrease in the time spent in traffic daily; and 38 percent indicated an increase.

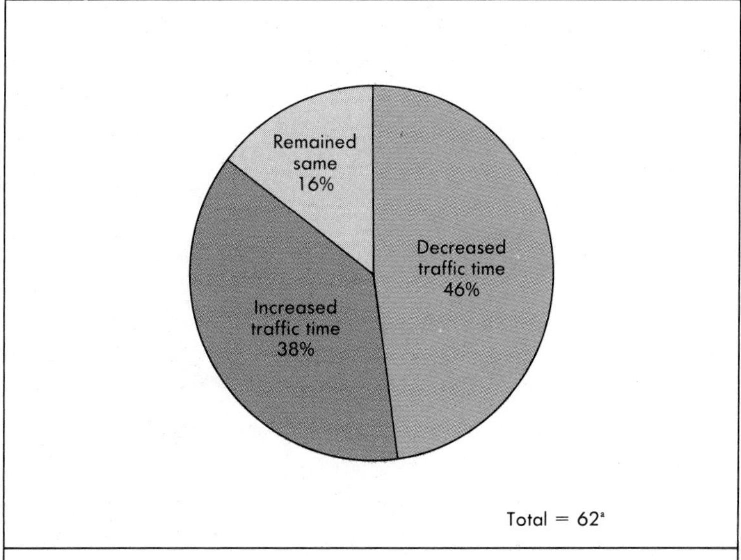

Figure 6. UT Student Perceptions about the Effects of the World's Fair on Daily Time Spent in Traffic.

[a]One student did not respond.

only the final section and get the essence of the whole report. Most readers, particularly executive managerial personnel, read reports selectively. In fact, many readers want only the most basic information. Others will want to refer to the specifics.

With this in mind, look again at the lead-in statements for the World's Fair report in the initial section. You can excerpt the necessary information from the general and specific objectives and the procedures. Thus the summary for the report would resemble that shown in this example.

Figure 16.5
Cross-Classified Data

Table 4 relates commuter students' driving distance from campus to their perceptions of change in daily time spent in traffic due to the World's Fair. Of the total 44 commuters, 46 percent indicated no change in daily time spent in traffic; 36 percent indicated an increase. Of the 25 commuter students who drove up to 5 miles, 44 percent indicated daily time spent in traffic increased; 44 percent indicated no change. Of the 13 commuter students who drove between 6 and 10 miles, 54 percent indicated no change; 31 percent indicated an increase.

TABLE 4

Commuter student perceptions of changes in time spent daily in traffic caused by the World's Fair classified by driving distance from residence

Change in traffic	0–5 Miles		6–10 Miles		11–15 Miles		16–20 Miles		Over 20 Miles		Total	
	Number	Percent	Number	Percent	Number	Percent	Number	Percent	Number	Percent	Number	Percent
Increased	11	44.0	4	30.8	1	25.0	—	—	—	—	16	36.4
Decreased	3	12.0	2	15.4	1	25.0	1	100.0	1	100.0	8	18.2
No change	11	44.0	7	53.8	2	50.0	—	—	—	—	20	45.4

MAJOR FINDINGS, CONCLUSIONS, AND RECOMMENDATIONS

The general objective of this study was to identify the positive and negative effects of the World's Fair on University of Tennessee students. The specific objectives of the study were to determine students' perceptions of the effects on student housing, employment, parking, off-site entertainment, on-site and off-site prices, and traffic. Data for the study were collected from a nonprobability sample of 100 students by means of a questionnaire. Data for the report were based on 83 usable questionnaires.

Major Findings

Developing the major findings for the analytical report

The intent of this section is to summarize the major findings from the analysis of data. From these major findings, you make conclusions relevant to the objectives of the study. Use the guidelines shown in Chapter 15 for stating major findings in a report.

With these guidelines, let us proceed to determine the major findings for the World's Fair study. We use Specific Objectives 1 and 2 to illustrate the process for writing major findings, although the process is the same for the other objectives.

The major findings for Specific Objective 1 are taken from the interpretation and narrative developed under the heading *Housing* in the middle section of the report. This material can be extracted as shown in findings 1 and 2 of the next example.

The major findings for specific objective 2 can be extracted from the interpretation and narrative under the heading *Employment.* These major findings are 3, 4, and 5 in the following.

Major Findings

The major findings of this study are as follows:

1. Of the 83 students, 66 indicated that the World's Fair did not affect the cost of their housing; 13 indicated that their rent had increased.
2. Of the 83 students, 42 indicated a decrease in the availability of affordable housing in the metropolitan area.
3. Of the 81 students responding to the question concerning the availability of employment, 96 percent indicated an increase in job possibilities.
4. Of the 40 students responding to the portion of the question concerning the effect on wages, 57.5 percent indicated an increase.
5. Of the 29 students responding to the portion of the question concerning the effect on workload, 80 percent indicated an increase.

Conclusions

Developing conclusions for the analytical report

Conclusions are a synthesis of the findings developed through inferences; they are *not* restated findings. Each finding does not require a conclusion; rather, conclusions are based on one or more findings. Use the guidelines shown in Chapter 15 for stating conclusions in a report.

To draw conclusions from the major findings, look at all data. Ask yourself the following questions: "What do the major findings reveal about housing? About employment?" "What is significant about the major findings?" Here you need to use logic and your judgment. No cut-and-dried rules exist for writing conclusions. What matters most is how well you can justify the conclusions by using your major findings. The following lead-in and conclusions for the first two specific objectives are stated as shown in items 1 and 2 of the next example. Since major findings 3, 4, and 5 relate to employment, you can draw one major conclusion as shown in item 3 of the example.

Conclusions

The following conclusions are based on the major findings of this study:

1. The World's Fair is not adversely affecting UT students (major finding 1).
2. UT students perceive that affordable housing in the metropolitan area has decreased (major finding 2).
3. Students indicate increased job possibilities but with increased workloads and unchanged wages as a result of the World's Fair (major findings 3, 4, 5).

You have now applied the guidelines for writing conclusions for two of the specific objectives of the World's Fair study. The process is similar for developing conclusions for the remaining specific objectives of the World's Fair report.

Recommendations

Developing recommendations for the analytical report

Recommendations are derived from the whole set of conclusions and suggest needed courses of action or additional data. Recommendations for action essentially answer the question regarding application of results. Use the basic guidelines shown in Chapter 15 for stating recommendations in a report.

Recommendations are based on the whole study and the entire set of conclusions. This example shows the first part of the Recommendation part of the report.

Recommendations

Based on a study of the effects of the World's Fair on UT students, the following recommendations are made:

1. Further study is needed to find solutions to the on-campus parking problem.
2. Further study is needed to consider offering shuttle bus service to campus from outlying parking areas to reduce traffic congestion.
3. No further study is needed on the effects of the World's Fair on student employment, housing, entertainment, or prices for goods.

Implications

Developing implications for the analytical report

The implications section is optional. Implications are indirect and are an extension of the recommendations. Implications offer suggestions for possible action or alternatives available to carry out proposed courses of action. Guidelines for stating implications are shown in Chapter 15.

The World's Fair study does not include an implications section. When the vice president for student affairs gets the completed report, she will decide whether to proceed with various recommendations.

This completes the body of the report—the initial, middle, and final sections.

Bibliography

Developing the bibliography

The bibliography for the World's Fair report lists the secondary sources quoted in the report. The *U.S. News & World Report* article cited on page 468 is the only secondary source for the sample report.

Appended Section

Developing the appended section

The appended section usually consists of a copy of the data collection form, summary sheet(s) of the raw data, and any other data too bulky for the analysis section of the report. Usually a cover page with the word *Appendix* identifies this part. Each item included in the appendix is given a title: "Appendix A—Questionnaire Used in the Study"; "Appendix B—Sample Calculations Showing Statistical Significance of Responses", etc. Using these titles (or the letters identifying each separate appendix), you can easily reference these materials in the body of your report.

SUMMARY

Before writing the analytical report, you must do adequate planning. One of the most effective plans is the strategy for communicating. You must first determine the Problem which emanates from the setting. Then you develop your specific Objectives, identify your Reader/Audience, determine the Order, and establish the Format.

When you begin the initial section of the analytical report, you need to develop a background for the study, which may be entitled "The Setting and Problem." This section sets the stage for the entire report and captures the reader's interest. This section may cite secondary sources to help justify or support the topic; may describe internal and external environmental conditions that give rise to the problem; may include historical data about the subject studied; may mention the report topic; and incorporate a problem statement.

Specific objectives for the analytical report are written in the form of infinitives, questions, or hypotheses. The way you sequence the specific objectives determines the order of discussion and presentation of the middle section of the analytical report. Write the procedures for conducting the study in the past tense using narrative form. At your discretion, you may enumerate the procedures or steps. Write your limitations/delimitations (the boundaries for the study) in narrative form with or without enumeration. Most analytical reports include specialized terms. Define terms that are unique to the study and include them so that your Reader/Audience can obtain the meaning of the terms in the early stages of the writing. A review of related literature is sometimes included in certain types of analytical reports. The scope and complexity of the report determine whether a review of related literature is necessary.

The middle section of the report includes one major component—analysis of the data. The middle section contains several parts—an introduction and subparts pertaining to each specific objective. The introduction for the middle section briefly summarizes the general and specific objectives and procedures to reorient the reader to the important components. Within each subpart, integrate graphics with interpretation. You determine which type of graphic to use on the basis of the type of data you have collected in support of your specific objectives. Use centered and side headings for the various divisions within the analysis of data. You may use a side heading for each specific objective positioned at the left margin.

The summary section of the analytical report should begin with the report objectives and procedures to reorient the reader. Some readers want only the basic information and read reports selectively; therefore, a little repetition is necessary. The summary includes the major findings, conclusions, recommendations, implications (optional), and bibliography. Summarize the major findings from the analysis of the data and make conclusions based on the findings. Recommendations are derived from the whole set of conclusions and suggest needed courses of action or additional data. You may decide to include implications in your analytical report. Implications are indirect and are an extension of the recommendations. Be sure to include a bibliography which shows all secondary sources cited in the analytical report.

You may append various material to your analytical report such as data collection forms, summary sheets of raw data, or multipage tables.

END-OF-CHAPTER ACTIVITIES

DISCUSSION

1. What is involved in the writing of the background for the study?
2. Why does the World's Fair study include objectives stated in infinitive form rather than question form or hypotheses? Defend your response.
3. Discuss the content of the questionnaire "Perceptions of the World's

Fair." Critique the content based on the guidelines for questionnaire construction shown in Chapter 12. Share your comments with other class members.

4. Explain the relationship of graphics and interpretation.
5. What is the relationship of the analysis section and the initial section?
6. How is the final section related to the initial section? The middle section?
7. The summary section of an analytical report could be omitted. Accept or refute this statement. Defend your response.
8. Identify a situation where the indirect approach is appropriate for the analytical report.

ACTIVITIES

9-14. For each of the settings in Activities 9-14:

a. Develop a Problem statement.
b. Identify the Objectives.
c. Identify the Reader/Audience.
d. Outline the procedures.
e. Indicate the limitations.
f. List any special terms that need defining.

9. The Carter Manufacturing Company is behind in filling orders for its customers. The rate of lost sales has increased daily. Some customers have lost confidence in the company. Because inventories of Carter's products are inadequate, customers are beginning to turn to Carter's competitors to obtain the products and services needed.

10. The high incidence of deaths and serious injuries because of the detrimental effects of alcohol on driving has alarmed the general public. Estimates indicate that over half of all traffic deaths are alcohol-related. In fact, most studies indicate that at least half of the drivers killed in fatal automobile accidents have over 0.05 percent blood alcohol, a fact which suggests that the current minimum limit for legal intoxication (0.10 blood alcohol) is inadequate.

    State legislators have reacted to the increased public concern over alcohol-related accidents. Most states have recently reviewed and revised their statutes. Since the intake of alcohol is a totally voluntary act, it is conceivable that such a high incidence of deaths and serious injuries could be brought under control through stricter legislation, which would restrict under penalty of arrest the amount of alcohol intake allowed prior to driving. Some contend, however, there is no evidence that such arrests will prevent traffic deaths. As the public becomes increasingly aware of this issue, it is important to analyze current perceptions of the effectiveness of increased legislation against drunk driving.

11. For several weeks, many employees of the Cole Company have been reporting late for work in the mornings and are extending their midmorning and midafternoon breaks. The personnel director has become aware of the situation from casual observation when he's tried to locate various employees at different times.
12. Trucking costs for the Jackson Supply Company, a coffee packer in St. Louis, are rising. Managers of some coffee companies in other parts of the country have decided to rent rather than purchase trucks to reduce costs.
13. From day-to-day observation, one can see that many persons violate the parking regulations on the campus. Each day campus police give tickets to persons who are illegally parked. Professors have indicated that students are frequently late for classes and use "no parking space" as the excuse. Recently, a construction firm started using part of a major parking area to store supplies.
14. Housewives banded together to demand that food costs be lowered. Just prior to their action, food costs increased by 4 percent. Several women indicated that trading stamps used by most of the food stores caused prices to increase.
15. Assume the specific objective, "What brand name watches are popular?" An excerpt from the interpretation of data is shown below:

    Eight respondents included brands of watches other than the six brands which were listed in the questionnaire. This was 3 percent of those who answered the questionnaire. Seventy-one percent of the watches owned were of two brands–Timex and Bulova. Sixty-four people said they owned Bulova watches; 105 stated that they owned Timex watches. Six brands of watches were listed on the questionnaire. There were 237 people who responded to the questionnaire; 27 percent said they owned Bulova watches; 44 percent said they owned Timex.

    From this description, construct an appropriate graphic and rewrite the interpretation.
16. Assume the specific objective, "What were the brand names of watches owned by respondents by sex?" The results are shown below:

    7 males owned brands of watches other than the six brands listed on the questionnaire.
    132 respondents were male.
    105 respondents were female.
    9 percent of the females owned brands of watches in the other category.

Figure 16.6

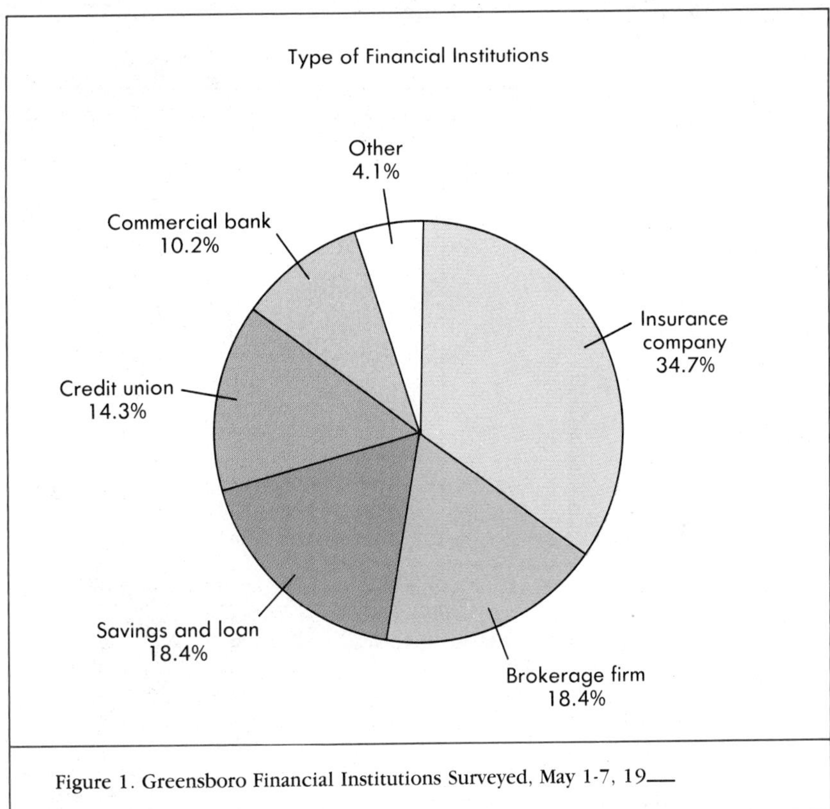

Figure 1. Greensboro Financial Institutions Surveyed, May 1-7, 19__

237 people responded to the questionnaire.
81 males owned Timex watches.
103 females owned Timex watches.
19 percent of the males owned Bulova watches.
37 percent of the females owned Bulova watches.

Prepare an appropriate graphic for these data; write an interpretation of the data.

17. Write an appropriate interpretation of data for the graphics provided in Figures 16.6-16.10. The graphics are part of a report which included a survey of financial institutions in Greensboro concerning Individual Retirement Accounts (IRAs).

Figure 16.7

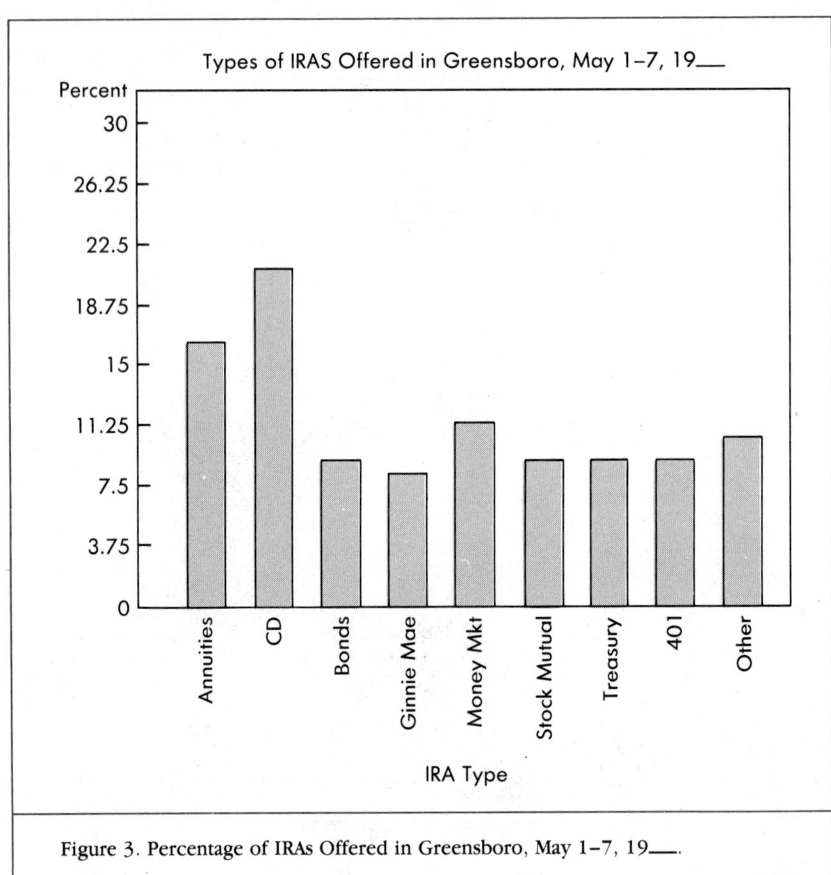

Figure 3. Percentage of IRAs Offered in Greensboro, May 1–7, 19__.

18. For Figures 16.6-16.10, develop findings and conclusions from the interpretations of the Greensboro IRA study.
19. The following are suggested topics for analytical reports. You may use a given topic in whole or in part, as directed by your instructor.

    TV viewing habits.

    Price comparison of selected items.

    Restaurant dining preferences.

    Comparative cost of domestic and foreign travel.

    Advertising costs for different media (TV, radio, newspaper, etc.)

    Employment opportunities for a specific college major.

    Alternative means for financing a:

    - ☐ Home.
    - ☐ Automobile.
    - ☐ Other consumer item.

Figure 16.8

Interest Rate on IRAs in Greensboro
May 1–7, 19__

Type	Below 10		10–11		11–12		12+		Other		Total	
	Number	Percent	Number	Percent	Number	Percent	Number	Percent	Number	Percent	Number	Percent
Annuities	3	9.0	9	27.2	11	33.3	7	21.2	3	9.0	33	100.
Certificates of deposit	5	13.5	11	29.7	12	32.4	6	16.2	3	8.1	37	100.
Corporate bonds	2	10.0	4	20.0	6	30.0	5	25.0	3	15.0	20	100.
Ginnie Maes	2	10.5	4	21.0	5	26.3	5	26.3	3	15.7	19	100.
Money market mutual funds	3	11.1	7	25.9	7	25.9	7	25.9	3	11.1	27	100.
Stock mutual funds	3	13.0	5	21.7	6	26.0	6	26.0	3	13.0	23	100.
Treasury receipts	2	10.0	4	20.0	6	30.0	5	25.0	3	15.0	20	100.
401 (k) plans	2	10.0	4	20.0	6	30.0	5	25.0	3	15.0	20	100.
Others	5	19.2	7	26.9	5	19.2	8	30.7	1	3.9	26	100.

Source: Survey

Figure 16.9

Comparison of Fees Charged by Greensboro Institutions, May 1–7, 19__

Institution	Total Surveyed		No Charge	
	Number	Percent	Number	Percent
Brokerage firm	21	100.0	3	14.2
Commercial bank	5	100.0	5	100.0
Credit union	9	100.0	5	55.5
Insurance company	23	100.0	11	47.8
Savings & loan	9	100.0	8	88.8
Other	4	100.0	1	25.0

Source: Survey

Figure 16.10

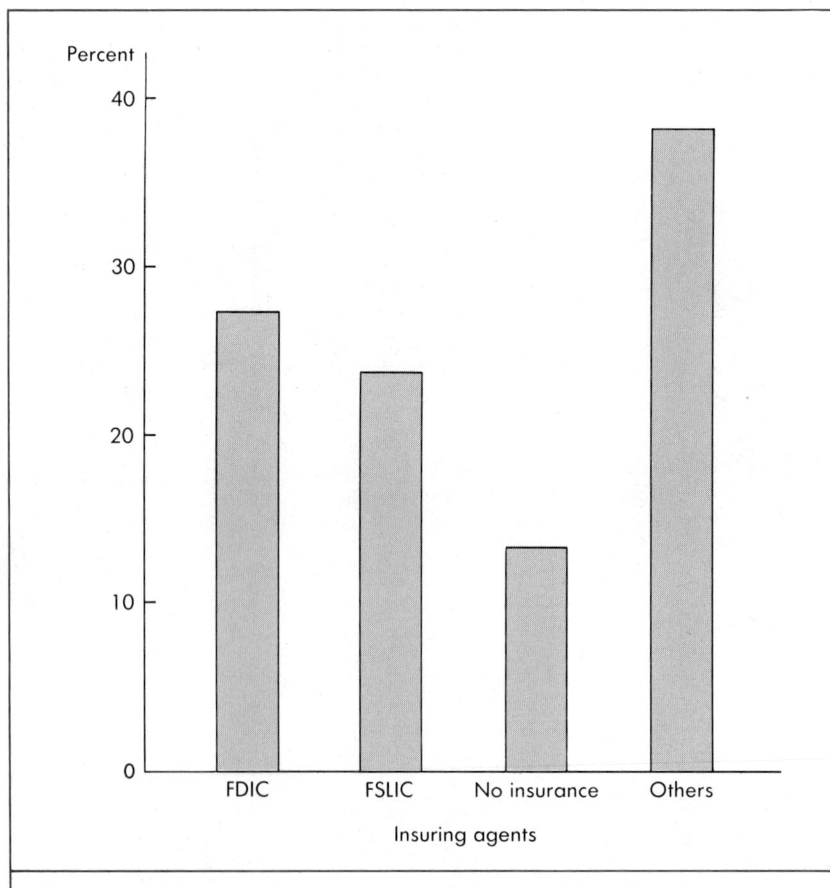

Figure 4. Percentage of IRAs Insured in Greensboro, May 1–7, 19___.

Comparison of fringe benefits available for selected companies.

Assessing employee morale in selected companies.

Effectiveness of participative management in selected companies.

Benefits of a company wellness center.

Book store purchasing—which store is best?

Video cassette top movie rentals for past six months.

Services and types of loans/accounts available at savings and loan banks.

Comparative costs of obtaining Visa/MasterCard from various lending institutions.

Comparative interest rates on $5,000 and $10,000 certificates of deposit.

Management advisory services offered by Big Eight accounting firms.

Financing a home through Federal Housing Administration (FHA), Veterans Administration (VA), Farmers Home Loan Administration, and local savings and loan company.

Status of use of electronic mail in 10 corporations.

How companies tackle health costs.

Advantages/disadvantages of travel on five major airlines.

The management of change related to:

- ☐ Company growth.
- ☐ Innovation.
- ☐ Technology.
- ☐ International competition.
- ☐ Mergers.
- ☐ Management turnover.

Automation in:

- ☐ Manufacturing.
- ☐ Retail businesses.
- ☐ Office environments.

Human aspects of retraining and smoothing the transition to office automation.

Software applications for sales management and product and distribution planning.

Software—buy or lease?
—packaged or tailor-made?
—what are the suppliers' obligations?

Guidelines for building beneficial relationships with customers.

Management by objectives—current use in selected companies.

Opportunities for middle managers in selected companies.

Means of conducting market research in:

- Small organizations.
- Large organizations.
- Nonprofit organizations.

Employer rights and employer programs.

Types and availability of organizational development programs in selected businesses.

Corporate giving.

Business team approach to problem solving.

CHAPTER 17

ABSTRACTING

Learning Objectives

After studying this chapter, you will be able to:

- □ Understand the reasons for using abstracts in business.
- □ Define *abstract.*
- □ Distinguish between indicative and informative abstracts.
- □ Understand the guidelines for writing a book abstract, an abstract of a journal article, and an executive summary.
- □ Apply the strategy for communicating to the writing of a book abstract, a journal article, and an executive summary.

With the barrage of letters, memos, long reports, short reports, and other written communication they receive, professionals in business can become overwhelmed by paper. Even in a modest local business, the volume of letters, reports, and memos can sometimes seem overwhelming. Imagine how difficult it must be to cope with the demands of paperwork in a multinational corporation such as General Motors or Westinghouse.

Need for abstracts in business

Busy executives simply do not have the time to read the volumes of information that cross their desks. To save time and expense, most decision makers prefer their written communication in abstract form. The conventional abstract of a major report, the executive summary, and other types of condensed forms allow decision makers to review the contents of much longer reports and memos in a fraction of the time required to read entire documents.

Advantages of using abstracts in business

You can easily see how useful such abstract forms are to professional organizations. The savings in cost alone would justify the use of abstracts in business today. But perhaps more important are the savings in time. With effectively condensed versions of many of the materials they must consider, executives can make timely, informed decisions. Abstracts also allow for a convenient storage of thousands of related documents in a computer database. Using such a computerized data system, an executive can review contents of dozens of reports, articles, and even books in the time it might take just to collect copies of original documents. Because of the growing use of condensed forms for summarizing information, developing your skill in writing abstracts will prove invaluable to you in the world of business.

Definition of an abstract

Just what is an abstract? Some synonyms reflect something of the nature of abstracts: a brief; a condensation; a digest; a distillation; a summary; and an epitome. Abstracts, in many ways, are similar to these other kinds of abridgments. Basically, *an abstract is a shortened form of a work that retains the general sense and unity of the original.*

Indicative abstract

Informative abstract

Examples of informative and indicative abstracts

Abstracts are grouped into two types: *indicative* and *informative.* An indicative abstract describes the topics discussed but contains little else. An informative abstract describes the topics but also gives specific information on these topics. Sometimes a combination of the two types of abstracts is possible. This chapter presents guidelines for abstracting several different types of communication. The first example is an indicative abstract. The other examples are informative and include examples of a book abstract, a journal article, and a sample executive summary. Some general techniques for abstracting all types of communications apply to both the indicative and informative methods. When preparing an abstract, you should:

- ☐ Identify the strategy components—Problem, Objectives, Reader/Audience, Order, and Format.
- ☐ Scan each paragraph and jot down the key ideas based on the document's topic sentences (or check the table of contents if topic sentences were not used).
- ☐ Group the key ideas in a logical order.

LEGAL / ETHICAL ISSUE

Jerry Hornbeck and Kathy Maxwell have written a new economics textbook for the introductory course. The book is now ready for distribution in the marketplace. All of the publicity materials sent by the publishers indicate that Hornbeck and Maxwell have developed a unique approach to the study of economics.

An economics association journal contains reviews on books published in this discipline. Collegiate professors of economics have a high regard for these quarterly book reviews. In fact, a majority of economics professors base their book adoptions on the reviews.

The editor of the journal asks June Starnes, an economics professor at a major university in the Midwest, to review the Hornbeck and Maxwell book and give an objective opinion on its content. After reviewing the first three chapters, Dr. Starnes is "turned off" by the unique approach of the book. She is so influenced by what she perceives as an acceptable approach to the study of economics that her review emphasizes only negative points. From her comments, it is evident that she has not done a thorough review of the entire book. She basically centers her comments around the content of the first three chapters.

Was the book review handled in an ethical manner since only negative factors were presented? Should the association have a policy for conducting book reviews to assure legal and ethical considerations? Do the authors of the book have any legal recourse against the reviewer? Against the association?

- ☐ Condense material to a manageable size.
- ☐ Do not include the bibliography, tables, or illustrations in an abstract or refer to them.
- ☐ Draft the abstract in one of two ways:
    1. Present key ideas condensed in your own words.
    2. Use verbatim key sentences from the work, but be sure to indicate the authors of the document you are abstracting.

AN INDICATIVE ABSTRACT

Because most people prefer that some explanation accompany an outline, an indicative abstract is not used in business as frequently as the informative abstract. However, at times an indicative abstract is appropriate. Examples of indicative abstracts include pending action items, a proposal for a study, a list of topics covered in a meeting, or the contents of a conference.

Indicative abstracts can be as short as one or two sentences as long as those few sentences describe the contents. See Figure 17.1 for an example of an indicative abstract.

Figure 17.1
Indicative Abstract

Abstract[1]

This paper examines recent occupational projections to determine how new technologies will affect future job growth in the United States. The first part of the paper reviews the methodologies used to derive occupational projections, focusing on how adjustments for technological change are incorporated into the forecasts. The second part of the paper reviews the most recent projections produced by the U.S. Bureau of Labor Statistics and compares them with projections produced by other organizations.

[1] Russell W. Rumberger and Henry M. Levin, "Forecasting the Impact of New Technologies on the Future of the Job Market." Project report 84–4A, Institute for Research on Educational Finance and Governance, School of Education, Stanford University (February 1984).

INFORMATIVE ABSTRACTS

Characteristics of the informative abstract

Informative abstracts are sometimes called *summaries* because they contain more information than do indicative abstracts, and they stress the conclusions and recommendations contained in the report. They are the most frequently used abstract form in business. Therefore, the remainder of the chapter is devoted to techniques for writing effective informative abstracts.

Writing a Book Abstract

Guidelines for abstracting a book

What is involved in abstracting a book? Obviously, an entire book cannot be included here for you to read and abstract. However, we can include some basic guidelines and helpful hints to assist you in writing a book abstract.

Begin by introducing the subject. Be sure to comment on all chapters. If a book contains 10 chapters or less, you can refer to each chapter in your abstract. If a book is quite lengthy (11, 20, 30, or more chapters), you may need to group related topics and then comment on the grouping of chapters. Actually, the scope of the book might limit the depth of coverage in your abstract. If your abstract is to be published in a journal or some other medium, you may have a limit of 250 words or less. When such limitations exist, you must exercise great care to present an abstract that is meaningful to the reader.

Include a summary of the major highlights for each chapter or grouping of chapters. Studying the topic sentence for each paragraph should help you prepare the abstract. Centered or side headings can also help you identify the major classifications of material in the chapters. Dividing the chapters this way creates a framework, or big picture, of the contents. Summarize the various sections of the chapters and include strengths and weaknesses of each, where possible. You may discuss the implications of the different chapters or groups of chapters if appropriate.

In essence, a book abstract should contain:

Content of a book abstract

- ☐ General content of the book (introduction).
- ☐ Overall purpose of the book.
- ☐ A description of the applicable Reader/Audience.

- □ Explanation of the book's usefulness for the specific Reader/Audience.
- □ Deficiencies in content coverage.
- □ Strengths of the book.
- □ Evaluative value judgments about the book's content (comments are interspersed throughout the abstract or given at the end of the review).
- □ An identification of the intended readers.
- □ Bibliographic data.

The following setting illustrates the strategy for developing a book abstract.

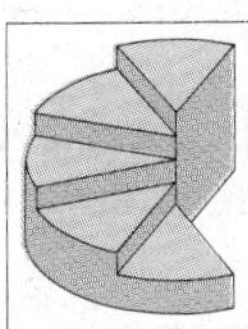

STRATEGY: A BOOK ABSTRACT

During the early and mid-1980s, an abundance of literature on the automated office appeared. Practically every magazine, journal, newspaper, and most books contained some reference to automation. This literature reflected the enormous impact of microcomputers in the business environment. Some scholars predicted that in a few years computers would practically take over the majority of routine tasks such as maintaining files, preparing payrolls, developing sales lists, and keeping employees' time cards.

Because of the volume of the literature published on the automated office, many people in different occupations needed to disseminate abstracts of books published on the subject. (Abstracts are more than just book reviews; they also contain statements regarding content. Book reviews, on the other hand, may contain only a reviewer's critical assessment of the published work without describing the book's contents.) Such abstracts, if properly placed in leading journals, would help educate the general public. The administrative board of *Modern Office Technology* decided to include a monthly review of selected books to meet this need. Joe Jones is responsible for the reviews and abstracts in the journal.

Follow Joe as he prepares his strategy to develop an abstract for this publication.

PROBLEM

A need exists for concise reviews of current literature pertaining to the automated office.

OBJECTIVES

General: To inform readers of *Modern Office Technology* about the content and value of major published works related to the automated office.

Specific: To indicate a book's overall purpose.
To indicate its general content.
To reference source(s).
To evaluate content.
To show how the Reader can use the book.
To evaluate deficiencies.
To identify the intended readers.
To indicate the book's strengths.

READER/AUDIENCE

Characteristics: *Primary Audience*—computer experts who manage automated records centers or word-processing centers or who specialize in information management.

Secondary Audience—educators specializing in information management who read current literature in their field.

Industry training directors working to upgrade the competencies of their personnel.

Reactions: Mixed reactions from the primary and secondary audiences.

Some will be pleased and will order copies of the book to use in their businesses.

Some educators will order the book for their classes.

Some will read the article and simply say, "That's interesting."

ORDER

The direct approach is appropriate for this communication. Following the guidelines for a book abstract, Joe lists the specific objectives in the following order:

SPECIFIC OBJECTIVES

- □ To indicate a book's general content.
- □ To indicate its overall purpose.
- □ To identify the intended Readers.
- □ To show how the Reader may use the book.
- □ To indicate strengths.
- □ To evaluate deficiencies.
- □ To evaluate content.
- □ To reference source(s).

Figure 17.2 Book abstract example

The Electronic Office

Review by: John M. McQuillan

What is the electronic office, anyway? So much nonsense is written on this subject daily that it is easy to lose track of what's important. The authors of The Electronic Office have done a fine job combining the business issues with the technological questions and the practical points. Their book is, as the subtitle says, A Guide for Managers, and well worth reading for office managers who are new to the job and looking for some basic pointers on how to get started. It offers a bit less to experienced office systems planners, who may be familiar with many of the concepts.

As the authors say in their preface, "(This book) has been written to assist managers and other professionals in the transition from a traditionally manual office setting to one that is automated. (It is) designed primarily for the manager who has little knowledge of the entire concept of the electronic office." The authors begin by describing the traditional office setting and the automated office setting, drawing parallels and contrasts as they go. It might have been better to include more punchy statistics and photos of equipment in the introduction, to further assist first-time office automation managers.

The next two chapters discuss in detail feasibility studies and word processing. The authors present a wealth of practical information on how to analyze an office's word-processing requirements and how to synthesize the best technical and organizational approach to meeting those requirements.

I especially welcomed the focus on business issues: how much WP will cost, how much it will save, and how it should be organized so a company gets the most for its investment. Position descriptions are explained in detail, with several examples. This material would be quite valuable for a company that has not yet truly automated its word processing, or for the office managers of smaller branches or divisions.

The next chapter examines written communications in the office—why there is so much of it and why it costs so much. The authors advocate dictation as an easy way to control costs. I agree completely, yet I have found that many managers resist the idea and have never become comfortable with the process. This book suggests reasons for trying it again and offers some helpful hints to make dictation work for you.

Next, we turn to electronic mail, a more complete and more radical answer to the question of what to do about all that office paper. This treatment is quite broad, covering such topics as communicating word processors, telex, computer-based message systems, and facsimile. On the other hand, it is a little too brief to be really helpful in deciding what to do next.

The following two chapters are a bit uneven. The section on records management is very good and very thorough. It delivers almost too much information on this rather specialized subject, unless this function falls within your responsibility. This in-depth treatment is followed by a very high-level overview of computer technology. It provides a quick glimpse of the technology and a useful introduction to the terminology.

The final chapter covers organizational change and development. This subject cannot be overemphasized.

Give the authors credit. They have their eye on a particular audience: office managers who need to understand thoroughly word

Figure 17.2 (*concluded*)

processing and records management and who want an introduction to advanced office systems technology, organizational development and other managerial practices. They succeed admirably in reaching this audience.

The Electronic Office by John J. Stallard, E. Ray Smith, and Donald Reese. Copyright © 1983 by Dow Jones-Irwin, Homewood, Ill. 223 pages, $19.95.

Dr. John M. McQuillan is president of McQuillan Consulting, Cambridge, Mass., and a frequent contributor to Modern Office Technology. "Reprinted from the July issue of Modern Office Technology, and copyrighted 1984 by Penton Publishing, a subsidiary of Pittway Corporation."

FORMAT

The professional journal requires a special format for the abstract.

Using the preceding strategy outline, study the example of an abstract published in a professional journal that reviewed a 223-page book (Figure 17.2). Study the following comments and their relationship to the specific objectives applied to the book abstract:

1. Paragraphs 1 and 3 meet the objectives "to indicate general content."
2. Paragraph 2 meets the objectives "to indicate overall purpose" and "to identify the intended readers." Paragraph 9 reinforces the fulfillment of the audience emphasis.
3. Paragraphs 5 through 8 meet the objectives "to show how the reader may use the book"; "to indicate strengths"; and "to indicate deficiencies."
4. The objective "to evaluate content" is addressed throughout the abstract. For example, paragraph 4 contains the statement, "I especially welcomed the focus on business issues." This is an evaluative statement. Another example in this same paragraph is the statement which reads "This material would be quite valuable . . . ." These types of value judgments meet specific objective number 7.
5. The reference at the bottom of the first page of the article meets the objective "to reference source(s)." This reference contains a complete citation for the work.

WRITING AN ABSTRACT OF A JOURNAL ARTICLE

Characteristics of the journal article abstract

Occasionally, business managers need to have abstracts of magazines or journal articles. A journal article abstract is short, and the scope is limited. When professionals have access to journal abstracts, they can keep up with the latest information in their area of expertise without reading masses of literature. With all the demands on a professional person's time, these journal abstracts become quite an asset. As a future professional in business, you'll find the following guidelines for abstracting journal articles beneficial.

Guidelines for abstracting a journal article

- □ Cite author of the article, title of article, volume number, publication date, and page numbers.
- □ Purpose of article (main focus of article; synthesize your reasons for writing article).
- □ Major sections or components of article (use side headings to state these). Describe the significant points for each section in capsule form; do not restate everything in the article.
- □ Include possible application of material as it relates to some phase of your company's operations.
- □ Relate the strengths and weaknesses of the article.
- □ Develop evaluative comments.

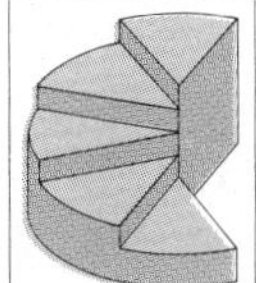

STRATEGY: ABSTRACT OF CURRENT LITERATURE

Kitts Industries, Seattle, Washington, is a wholesale distributor of food products in the Northwest. The company employs 190 people in a variety of jobs within the professional and semiskilled categories.

Kitts Industries, whose employees and customers have been extremely loyal over the years, is known as a highly reputable company. However, in the past 13 months, 3 typewriters, 2 microcomputers, 2 microfilm machines, 12 desk chairs, and several floppy disks have been stolen. Since Kitts Industries is planning to acquire 30 new microcomputers within the next three months Deborah Sweetwater, CEO, is concerned about the security of the computer hardware/software and company records. She asks you, as manager of information systems, to review current literature for possible security measures to protect computer hardware/software and company records. Security of high-tech equipment and data is her main concern. Ms. Sweetwater prefers that you give her abstracts rather than the entire articles. You agree to review the literature, abstract pertinent articles, and complete the assignment within two weeks. You'll use the strategy for communicating to prepare an abstract of a journal article.

PROBLEM

Lack of security at Kitts Industries has become acute during the past 13 months.

You are thankful for all the resources available. Your office subscribes to several journals dealing with technology and office furniture. Other good sources within easy driving distance are the Seattle public library and the University of Washington library.

OBJECTIVES

General: To review pertinent literature related to methods of protecting company hardware/software and company records.

Specific: To write abstracts of articles related to security of high-tech equipment and data.

Your goal is to complete the review of literature within a three-day period. You plan to do the literature search in about 10 to 15 hours.

Imagine that one week has passed. You've completed the computer searches within your proposed time period. You located five articles that may include some workable ideas for remedying security problems at Kitts. You will write one abstract as a model for the other abstracts.

One article you located is shown in Figure 17.3. Before abstracting the article, your first step is to read it carefully to get the "feel" of what it contains. Then you will reread the article after making some mental notes of what to include in the abstract. Sit back, relax, and begin your reading.

After reading the article, you must decide on a few other points to complete the strategy.

READER/AUDIENCE

The primary Audience is Ms. Deborah Sweetwater, CEO, Kitts Industries. She is a highly intelligent, perceptive, well-trained person with extensive management experience. She holds academic degrees in computer sciences and mathematics and an MBA. Her reaction to your work probably will be positive since Ms. Sweetwater has requested your advice to correct a major security problem. If she decides to use any of the suggestions presented in the abstracts, she may ask you or another management person to implement some of your findings.

Should this happen, possible secondary audiences could include other managers at Kitts. They, too, would be considered experts in the various functional areas of business they represent. The suggestions you give in the abstract for combatting some of the security problems should please these managers, too.

ORDER

How about the Order? The Order can vary, but the following is a guideline:

- ☐ Bibliographic data.
- ☐ Introduction.
- ☐ Overall purpose.
- ☐ Possible application.
- ☐ Deficiencies.
- ☐ Strengths.
- ☐ Evaluative comments.

FORMAT

The Format of the abstract is written in narrative. If you prefer, you may write a cover memo to accompany the abstract and send them to the

Figure 17.3 Article from Journal

Security: Protecting Information Resources and Media

William A. J. Bound
Lt. Cmdr., Royal Navy

Many office automation systems are being implemented without much regard for the security of the information being processed. Smaller systems are more vulnerable to attack simply because of their size and processing power. There are many headlines regarding computer abuse, error, waste, fraud and negligence. How long will it be before the OA systems make crime news?

We are currently at the tip of an iceberg with regard to office automation. Most major computer exhibitions and conferences are concentrating on the marketing of these systems, and any security discussion must look to the future. User-friendly software is growing and gradually functional managers are beginning to gain hands-on experience to support their decision-making process. The diskettes and small magnetic tapes are gradually becoming the "locked filing cabinets," and "cupboards" in terms of physically storing the information. Microcomputers will replace minis and their applications and some of the questions that must be answered are as follows:

- ☐ How will we interact with the home worker from our office systems?
- ☐ How will we distribute the relevant data to the correct people in our organization?
- ☐ Will we need a data Czar in control of all this electronic information?
- ☐ How can we control the protection of all this electronic data?
- ☐ Will we connect to a vast information network in order to mail our messages to the outside world?

Whatever the answers, automated office security and the protection of the office resources has to be considered.

Some Applications and Problems

Manufacturers and software organizations are producing many useful automated office applications. However, it is essential to look at some of these applications from the security point of view.

Consider electronic mail: Suppose you automate all your in- and inter-office memoranda and some of that information is sensitive. Do you communicate them in the clear or do you use some type of encryption code? Are these plug-in-the-wall office communication systems secure? Unfortunately, we do not realize that almost all methods of communication transmission are insecure and can be compromised.

Consider the electronic calendar: Suppose an executive automatic calendar is created for your organization. Here important meetings can be easily scheduled and you can see exactly what everyone is supposed to be doing in their business hours. Do you need to have some user access limitations on certain parts of the information stored or do you want everyone to see what the directors' schedule is? This schedule may well be critical in times of takeover or contract bidding.

Consider the maintenance of business or common directories: Suppose you implement a system so that every system user has access to electronic directories, bulletin boards, etc. If this common system also holds on-line sensitive company information which must only be accessed by certain members of the organization, then you are immediately putting the system at risk. You cannot guarantee full protection to this data even if the information was stored on a mainframe with a sophisticated operating system so your small

Figure 17.3 (*continued*)

office system can become an "open door." Personnel can browse through and exploit data, as well as "masquerade" as someone else.

Consider access to corporate data bases. In some cases it can cost as little as $100 to connect your word processor or office system to your larger mainframe system. It can be very useful and convenient to establish this link but what controls will you need to apply?

Consider budget preparation: Even the home microcomputers have cheap easy-to-use packages that enable projections, management summaries, and statistics to be produced. More often than not, combinations of ordinary data can produce sensitive results, which before automation would have been manually handled with care. The loss of a single word processing diskette (holding, say, 256,000 characters) could be sufficient to break or bankrupt a company. What if the user leaves that diskette, by accident, in their system? How long would it take to copy or erase the information? Not long. What if the user does not switch the system off after use? What can be gained from the memory contents?

Consider the stand-alone word processor. This system can be easily transformed into a small computer. How? Quite simply. Change the diskette and you then leave the programming capability to produce a useful data base retrieval update system or a small application just right for your company's needs. What controls will you place over the development and implementation of this software? Many unsuspecting functional users are accessing office systems. What if this in-house developed software has a "trap door" which stores or updates another copy of the sensitive information somewhere else in the system? Remember that by allowing the development of software you could be letting the wooden horse into Troy and encouraging the destruction or compromise of your "secure" system.

These are some of the problems you are likely to encounter. The stolen typewriter crimes of today will be the automated office equipment crimes of the future.

Office Automation Countermeasures

What then can be done to prevent some of the previous problems? Systems are now using some password or lockword controls imposed upon files and areas of sensitive data; more often than not this "security package" is available at a significant extra cost. Be wary, though, as some of these can be easily compromised.

Control the backup of the office storage media. Do not allow the users to copy their diskettes, but place this feature under a central organization. Also, control the physical storage of these small diskettes.

Look carefully at the transmission of your sensitive data. Encrypt, if necessary, and select a good safe algorithm. The cost of encryption and decryption can in most cases far outweigh the result of unauthorized disclosure.

If the office system is linked to the mainframe then it must be regarded as a remote site or in-house intelligent terminal. Therefore, all the terminal controls that are implemented (if any) for the mainframe must be applied to the office system. This could include the physical access methods, card entry, terminal identification or automatic alarms and disconnection.

In some cases the automated office is an integral application of a mini or mainframe. Here the operating system security features such as passwords and user and group identification are available. Also, some of the data base management systems, with their different user views of the information, provide further levels of protection.

The problems of electromagnetic emanations from the processor, power leads, and terminals of the office systems are now being addressed by the

Figure 17.3 (*continued*)

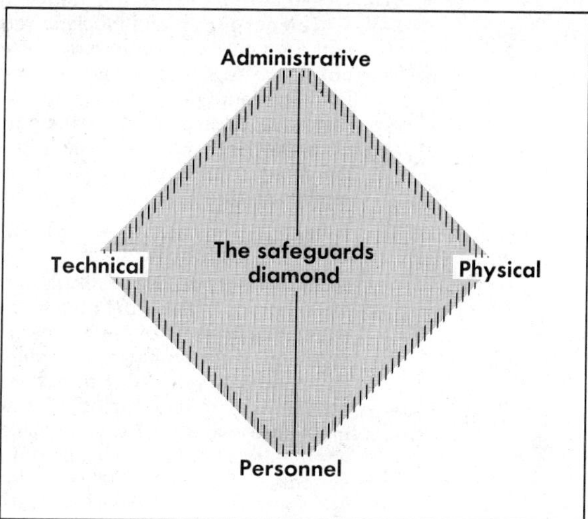

specialized vendors, especially for the needs of the Department of Defense. The cost of this protection can be significantly greater than the "ordinary" systems. However, more and more commercial businesses are showing interest in this countermeasure.

One major weakness of a stand-alone office system is that it can be powered up, a compromise performed and powered down, and nobody has a record of what happened. A countermeasure to this weakness could be the journal or logging capability, and this must be strictly enforced. It is bound to add overhead to the system, but it cannot be dismissed lightly.

The Management Approach Solution

A major awareness program is needed for OA security. Many managers are unaware of the vulnerabilities of their systems and the scope of their protection problems. Most regard the problem as a technical one. It is not: effective management and an analysis of the risks are the key. Someone must be designated responsible for the security of the systems: it should not be a small part-time task, especially in the systems analysis and development stages.

The vulnerabilities of a system can lie in four general categories—physical, technical, administrative and personnel. In developing an office system security program the manager must consider the following safeguards to counteract the vulnerabilities.

☐ Personnel: an attitude by the staff that security is important and the job of everyone working with the system.
☐ Physical: locked doors, uninterruptable power supplies.
☐ Administrative: policies, procedures, regulations on access.
☐ Technical: hardware and software mechanisms.

The manager will realize that there are fundamental principles that an office system must meet for "secure" processing. First, the resources in the

Figure 17.3 (*concluded*)

system must be identified. Ideally this identification must be unique.

Tamper-proof, and machine-readable. Second, access to files, programs and data must have a formal mechanism. Third, the system must have the capability to separate resources, users and information from each other. Fourth, integrity must be assured. This involves the logical correctness, completeness, and reliability of the hardware/software and the consistency of the data structures. Finally, some form of surveillance must be available so that the detection and reporting of unauthorized attempts to break into the system may be ensured.

Is OA Security Different?

Most of what has been described in this article applies not only to the automated office systems but also to the automated information systems (AIS), especially in terms of the countermeasures. We cannot obtain absolute security but we can integrate a comprehensive program into the systems development cycle. We can define the integrity of the process, the quality of the information, the disclosure restrictions and the backup requirements. In most cases we have been imposing security on operational AIS after their implementation. Let us try and not make the same mistakes with the new OA systems.

A sound security system must identify resources; create a formal mechanism to access programs and data; separate resources, users and information from each other; develop reliable hardware/software structures; and a form of surveillance.

Republished with permission from *Office Administration and Automation*, copyright 1984, by Dalton Communications, Inc., New York.

person who requested the communication. Using the guidelines shown in this section, Figure 17.4 shows the abstract of the article on "Security."

Figure 17.4 Journal article abstract

Abstract—Journal article

William A. Bound. "Security: Protecting Information Resources and Media," *Information Management*, August 1984, pp. 18–19.

Many office automation systems are implemented without much regard for the security of the information processed. Smaller systems are more vulnerable to attack because of their size and processing power. There are many headlines regarding computer abuse, error, waste, fraud, and negligence.

Automated office applications where security needs are most pressing include electronic mail; electronic calendar; business directories; corporate data bases; budget preparation; and stand-alone word processors. The stolen typewriter crimes of today will be the automated office equipment crimes of the future.

Countermeasures to secure information resources and media include the following:

1. Use password or lock-word controls for sensitive data.
2. Control backup of the office storage media; place responsibility for copying and storage of diskettes under control of central organization.

Figure 17.4 (*concluded*)

3. Encrypt sensitive data for second transmission.
4. If the office system is linked to the mainframe, control the physical access methods, card entry, terminal identification, or automatic alarms and disconnection.
5. Log the use of stand-alone office systems.

A major awareness program is needed for OA security. Make someone responsible for the security as a major part of her/his responsibility.

The vulnerabilities of a system can lie in four general categories—personnel, physical, administration, and technical. Fundamental steps for securing office systems include the following:

1. Identify the resources in the system.
2. Prepare formal mechanism for accessing files, programs, and data.
3. Separate resources, users, and information from one another.
4. Assure the integrity (logical correctness, completeness, and reliability of the hardware/software and the consistency of the data structures).
5. Develop a surveillance method to report and detect unauthorized attempts to break into the system.

We cannot obtain absolute security, but we can integrate a comprehensive program into the systems development cycle. We can define the integrity of the process, the quality of the information, the disclosure restrictions, and the backup requirements.

Concepts in the article are mainly related to security of databases and records management. Some pertinent concepts are applicable to Kitts operations.

WRITING AN EXECUTIVE SUMMARY

Characteristics of an executive summary

An increasingly popular abstract is the *executive summary.* CEOs and other top-level professionals have a high regard for such abstracts. Usually, executive summaries are based on long documents that may range from approximately 25 pages to several volumes in length. The executive summary is just as useful, of course, for reports of less than 25 pages. Executive summaries are developed from such studies as the feasibility of changing a company's total computer systems from one type of system to another; the number and rationale of alternative sites for relocating a company; the need for merging various functions within a corporate environment; and personnel reduction due to a host of reasons.

As with all types of business writing, no definite prescriptive model of rigid rules apply to writing an executive summary. However, these types of guidelines, not intended to be inclusive, are useful in determining the general makeup of an executive summary:

Guidelines for writing an executive summary

- ☐ State the purpose of the executive summary.
- ☐ Include a request for board approval (if some project requires funding).
- ☐ Summarize management recommendations with a brief justification for request(s).

- ☐ Summarize benefits to the company.
- ☐ Show the methodology used to conduct the study.
- ☐ Indicate who is affected by the implementation of the recommendations.
- ☐ Relate how the study may affect policies and procedures within the company.
- ☐ Project the scheduling (timetable) for completion of some project.
- ☐ Summarize cost estimates (if applicable).
- ☐ Include supporting documents (when appropriate).

The following setting illustrates the strategy for developing an executive summary.

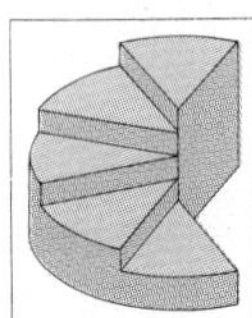

STRATEGY: AN EXECUTIVE SUMMARY OF RECOMMENDATIONS

The New York City headquarters of a major utility firm employs 1,200 professional and technical staff members. The utility firm has branch operations in four northeastern states. The combined branches employ another 1,800 employees. The entire utility operations are headed by Kevin Nunley, CEO. The management staff in New York City includes 5 vice presidents and 10 senior managers; 20 branch managers are located throughout the four-state area.

In October 1988 Mr. Nunley appointed a Current Diversion Task Force to study some major problems associated with reducing losses from theft and intentional damage to metering equipment. These situations are causing millions of dollars revenue losses for the utility firm. The task force chairperson is Lisa Carter, manager of branch operations. In addition, the task force includes these members: C. E. Starnes, manager of accounting; Gail Ousley, manager of personnel; two branch managers, Darla Hunt, Syracuse, New York, and Jack Henson, Newark, New Jersey. The chairperson requests the task force to submit recommendations to her by May 1, 1989. She asks that you study and make recommendations regarding who should have responsibility for all phases of current diversion; what goals should be established; training possibilities; impact on policies and procedures; the legal aspects of current diversion; and means of publicity.

Assume that six months have passed. As chairperson, you have the responsibility for synthesizing 90 pages of documentation that your task force developed during your investigation. You realize that Mr. Nunley prefers an abstract of your recommendations rather than the entire report. You begin to plan your strategy for communicating.

PROBLEM

The utility firm is losing millions of dollars in revenue from residential service.

OBJECTIVES

General: To prevent theft of electric service and intentional damage to metering equipment.

Specific: To make recommendations from the Task Force to resolve the Problem, addressing the following areas:

- ☐ Policies and procedures.
- ☐ Overall objective and goals.
- ☐ Training needs.
- ☐ Publicity requirements.
- ☐ Legal implications.

READER/AUDIENCE

Primary: Kevin Nunley, CEO.

Secondary: All vice presidents, senior managers, and branch managers.

Characteristics: Mr. Nunley is an effective administrator; he holds an MBA from the Wharton School of Finance and has 20 years of successful experience in corporate management. The vice presidents, senior managers, and branch managers are well educated. These managers are experts in their specific areas of responsibility.

Reactions: Both the primary and secondary audiences will be happy to receive the recommendations of the Task Force. They will be supportive of their implementation.

ORDER

The most logical order for this communication includes:

- ☐ Objective.
- ☐ Goals.
- ☐ Organization.
- ☐ Policies and procedures.
- ☐ Training.
- ☐ Legal considerations.
- ☐ Publicity.

FORMAT

Executive summary.

Write the abstract in narrative using the preceding objectives as major categories within the report. The executive summary is shown in Figure 17.5.

Figure 17.5 Executive Summary

Redding Utilities Company
Current Diversion Task Force Recommendations
September 4, 19__

Executive Summary

Current Diversion continues to be a growing problem throughout the electric utility industry. Recent estimates indicate average annual revenue losses of 0.5 to 2.5 percent, which is four (4) to twenty (20) million dollars of residential service for Redding Utilities Company. Our existing program needs to be strengthened in order to be more effective in reducing losses from theft and intentional damage to metering equipment. A stronger program will also be a deterrent to additional theft, will present a good public image, and will promote high employee morale and interest.

The program needs a clearly defined objective and goals; some organizational changes to enable more effective management of the function; well-defined policies and procedures consistently applied throughout the state; personnel assigned full-time to current diversion activities; a comprehensive, ongoing training program; some Public Service Commission orders and local ordinances; and increased employee and public awareness regarding the company's resolve to control current diversion.

The following is a brief summary of recommendations:

Objective

To prevent theft of electric service and intentional damage to metering equipment.

Goals

- ☐ Conduct an effective program of detecting current diversion.
- ☐ Consistently prosecute cases in accordance with management approved policies and procedures.
- ☐ Aggressively pursue restitution for diverted service and damaged equipment, including investigative charges.

Organization

The current diversion function should be the responsibility of the customer accounting organization. Daily activities should be managed by the division accounting managers. General office staff support should be provided by the security department's current diversion investigations and training sections, accounting methods and procedures, and revenue accounting.

All investigations should be conducted by well-qualified, full-time current diversion investigators. A current diversion field supervisor classification should be installed in the East Metro and West Metro divisions.

Policies and Procedures

Current diversion policies and procedures should be determined by the senior vice president, division operations, and the vice president, customer accounting and accounting services. They should be incorporated into the customer accounting procedures. Major policies include the following:

Investigations Field Service Representatives will closely inspect each meter and meter seal monthly. Broken seals will be replaced after the meter is pulled and inspected. Accounts will be coded to indicate a broken seal was

Figure 17.5 (*concluded*)

found. Any detected current diversion will be corrected and/or reported to a Current Diversion Investigator (CDI).

A follow-up inspection of nonpay disconnects will be required. Employees who detect current diversion (including unauthorized reconnects) will correct and/or report the diversion to a CDI.

All unauthorized reconnects, meters found to have a broken seal twice within six months, and all other reported incidents of suspected current diversion or intentional equipment damage will be investigated by a CDI.

Incentive Awards Certain employees detecting current diversion will be awarded $15 for each confirmed case. A confirmed case is determined by a CDI, and the employee becomes eligible for the award when a revenue adjustment for theft of service is processed, excluding cases from nonpayment disconnect follow-ups.

Prosecution A case will not be prosecuted for the first offense if full restitution is made. Prosecution will normally be pursued in all other cases, either under local ordiances or Georgia state law.

Training

An intensive technical training program should be required for all new investigators. It should be developed and coordinated by the security department. Reinforcement training should be conducted in the field on a regularly scheduled basis.

Legal

The Public Service Commission should be requested to issue a declaratory order regarding their disconnect rule. A $70 tariff for an investigative charge should also be filed with the PSC. Large towns without an ordinance on theft of utility services should be asked to establish such an ordinance.

Publicity

The company should frequently utilize internal publications and public information's normal external communication methods to publicize state law and the penalties for current diversion.

SUMMARY

Many business decision makers prefer their written communications in abstract form. Reports in abstract form save time and expense for professionals within the corporate environment. With effectively condensed versions of long documents, professionals can make timely, informed decisions. Abstracts also allow for convenient storage of thousands of related documents in a computer database. Using such computerized database systems, professionals can review dozens of reports, articles, and even books in the time it might take to collect copies of the original documents. Such abstracts and the convenience of the database systems are tremendous assets to decision makers.

An abstract is a shortened form of a work that retains the general sense and unity of the original. An indicative abstract tells what topics are taken up in the report but gives little information on what the report says concerning these topics. An informative abstract tells what topics are taken up in the report and gives specific information on these topics. Combinations of the two types of abstracts are possible and acceptable.

Examples of indicative abstracts are pending action items, a proposal for a study, topics covered in a meeting, or the contents of a conference. Examples of informative abstracts include a book abstract, a journal article, a formal report, and an executive summary.

You may cover the following topics in a book abstract: general content of the book (introduction); overall purpose of the book; explanation of how the reader may use the book; deficiencies in content coverage; strengths of the book; evaluative judgments concerning the book's content; and bibliographic data.

You may cover the following topics in an abstract of a journal article: cite the author, title of the article, name of the journal, volume number, publication date and page numbers; state purpose of the article, and show significant points relating to major sections of the article; include the possible application of the content as it relates to some phase of your company's operations; relate strengths and weaknesses of the article; and develop evaluative comments.

You may cover these types of topics in an executive summary: purpose of the executive summary; request for board approval (if some project requires funding); summary of management recommendations with brief justification for requests; timetable for completion of the project; summary of cost estimates (when applicable); methodology used to conduct the study; who is affected by the implementation of the recommendations; how the study may affect policies and procedures within the company; and support documents.

END-OF-CHAPTER ACTIVITIES

DISCUSSION

1. Define an abstract and cite examples of the various types of abstracts.
2. What are some of the major advantages of using abstracts for business purposes?
3. Distinguish between an indicative and an informative abstract.
4. Discuss the major factors involved in abstracting a book.
5. Compare and contrast the writing of a book abstract, a journal abstract, and an executive summary.
6. Discuss the major factors involved in abstracting a journal article.
7. Discuss the major factors involved in developing an executive summary.
8. Accept or refute this statement: "An abstract is more meaningful to a business professional than the report from which the abstract is derived." Justify your response.

ACTIVITIES

9. List all the synonymous terms you can locate for the concept *abstract.* Write a definition for each of these terms to see how closely the terms are allied.
10. Write an executive summary based on the World's Fair report discussed in Chapter 16.
11. Respond to the following memo:

    Date: ____________
    To: Students Enrolled in Business Communication
    From: Business Communication Instructor
    Subject: Report on Magazine Article

    Select an article from a recent issue of the *Harvard Business Review* pertaining to your major field of study. Prepare an abstract of this article set up in the following order:

    - ☐ Complete reference.
    - ☐ The purpose of the article.
    - ☐ A brief summary of the article.
    - ☐ Evaluate the article in terms of its relative merit, its contribution to your major field of study, and its effectiveness.

    The abstract should be no longer than three double-spaced typewritten pages. Use headings.

12. Read the executive summary shown in Figure 17.6. Answer these questions:
    a. What is the Problem of the study?
    b. What are the Objectives of the study?
    c. Who is the intended Reader/Audience?
    d. How are the topics included in the executive summary related to the guidelines shown in this chapter?
    e. How would you improve this executive summary on the basis of the concepts you have learned about writing effectively? Give a brief written rationale for each suggestion you make.
    f. Could you further condense this summary without losing the intended meaning?
13. From the executive summary referred to in Number 12, prepare an indicative abstract.
14. Write an abstract of one of the following books or some other book assigned by your business communication instructor: *Megatrends; In Search of Excellence; Re-Inventing the Corporation; The Third Wave; Information Payoff.*
15. Using the forms provided by your instructor for extracting data from a research study, complete an abstract of a major research study which applies to your area of interest.
16. As a group activity, obtain an executive summary from some local company and critique the content using the strategy for communicating.

Figure 17.6

Executive Summary: MIS Career Patterns Study

The purpose of the research proposed here is to create a database that will enable researchers from a network of academic institutions to conduct longitudinal studies dealing with the career patterns of students currently majoring in Management Information Systems (MIS). The database will contain information obtained from 2,000 to 2,500 MIS majors from a national sample of colleges and universities regarding their career expectations, priorities, and goals. This information, when combined with demographic characteristics of the students and profiles of their programs of study, will be used to analyze career attainments and job satisfaction at selected intervals after graduation. Such research is needed because of the relative recency of the MIS major, the proliferation of institutions offering it, mushrooming student demand, expanding employment opportunities, high turnover rates among MIS personnel, the dynamic nature of the discipline, and the present lack of longitudinal career research in MIS.

Participants

A national sample of colleges and universities will be invited to participate in the study. Participating institutions must:

- ☐ Have an undergraduate and/or graduate program of study for MIS majors.
- ☐ Agree to gather survey data from graduating MIS majors (up to a maximum of N = 100) during their last term of enrollment.
- ☐ Agree to transmit survey instruments to follow up samples at one-, three-, and five-year intervals after graduation.
- ☐ Be AACSB member schools.
- ☐ Provide a profile of the MIS programs from which the students are being graduated.
- ☐ Agree to safeguard the confidentiality of the students in accordance with the study's methodology.

Invited participants represent both public and private institutions of higher education and vary in terms of size and degree offerings.

Methodology

During the 1986–87 academic year, MIS majors in participating institutions will be asked to complete a survey instrument during their last quarter or semester of enrollment. The instrument, requiring 20–30 minutes for completion, will include:

- ☐ Requests for demographic information with demonstrated relevance to career patterns.
- ☐ Ratings of the importance of selected job, location, company, and personal goals variables.
- ☐ Job preferences for entry level positions, and career goals for 5 and 10 years later.

Follow-up surveys will be conducted on subsamples of one-third of the students at one-, two-, and three-year intervals after graduation. The entire sample would be surveyed at five years after graduation. The follow-up surveys would ask for the completion of the *Job Descriptive Index* and solicit present job information such as job title, principal responsibilities, city of employment, time in position, etc. Location data (city) will, in turn, be related to selected Census data. The follow-up requests will be limited to 15 minutes of response time.

Figure 17.6 (*concluded*)

Confidentiality will be maintained in the following manner:

- ☐ Students will be coded by Social Security number and a research number designating the school (A, B, C, etc.) and the subject number (001, 002, 003, etc.) The participating schools will retain a confidential list that relates Social Security numbers and research numbers.
- ☐ Instruments will be administered and mailed by the participating schools, but the responses will be returned with research numbers as identifiers to the database developers, where a parallel database code number will be entered.

The participating institutions will not have access to response data except through the database code number, and the database developers will not have access to the Social Security numbers or names of the students.

The data collection schedule will be as follows:

Academic Year	**Activity**
1986–87	Pretesting of MIS majors Acquisition of program profiles
1987–88	Follow-up testing of first 33.3 percent of students
1988–89	Follow-up testing of second 33.3 percent of students
1989–90	Follow-up of remainder of students
1991–92	Follow-up of entire sample

Accumulated data will be analyzed as new data are being collected for the database and research reports will be issued.

Expected Benefits

The longitudinal analyses of the database are expected to contribute valuable information on the career patterns of MIS majors, thereby enabling educators to improve their programs of study and employers to maximize the use of this valuable human resource. In addition, participating institutions will benefit by having access to the database for faculty and graduate student research projects.

Prepared by Stanley J. Smits and John R. Tanner in consultation with Robert J. Vandenberg, December 11, 1985.

PART FOUR

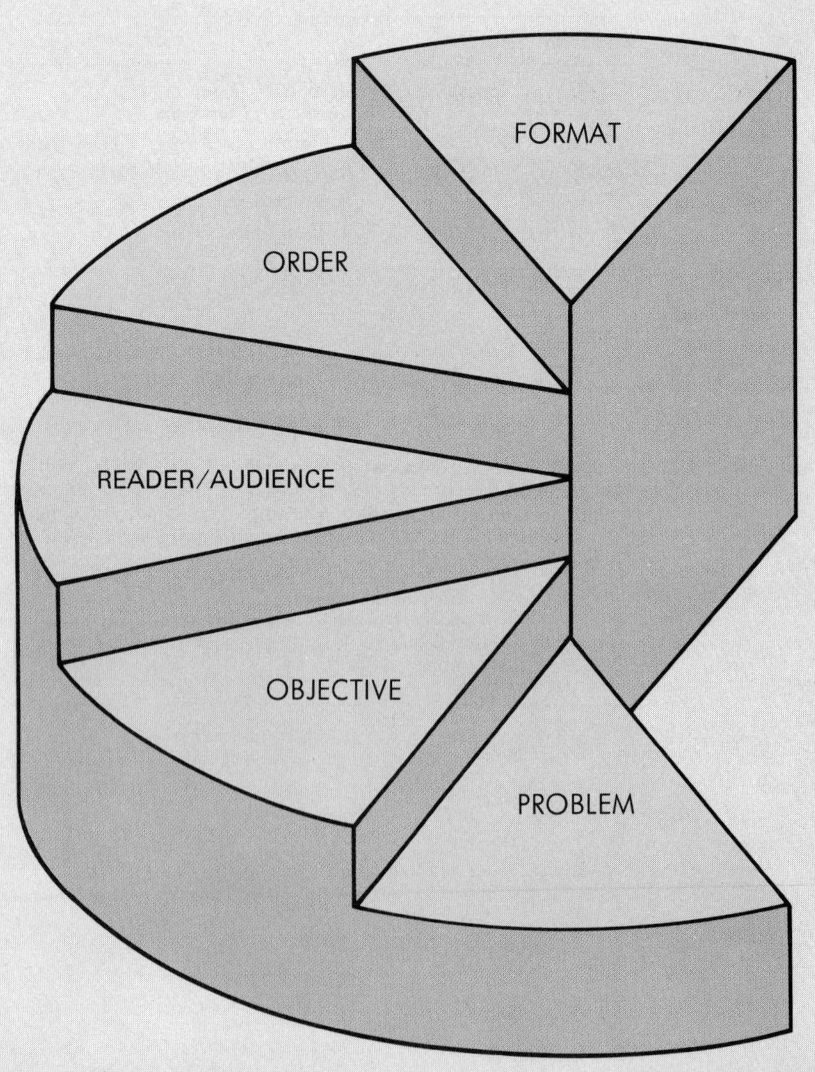

A PROCESS FOR COMMUNICATING OTHER SPECIAL APPLICATIONS

18 UNDERSTANDING THE EMPLOYMENT PROCESS

19 PREPARING FOR THE INTERVIEW

20 SPEAKING IN BUSINESS

21 WRITING POLICY AND PROCEDURE STATEMENTS

22 WRITING CASE ANALYSES

CHAPTER 18

UNDERSTANDING THE EMPLOYMENT PROCESS

Learning Objectives

After studying this chapter, you will be able to:

- □ Analyze your job qualifications and match these qualifications to the right job.
- □ Understand how and where to begin looking for a job.
- □ Use library resources for research on a prospective employer.
- □ Recognize a variety of résumé formats and identify the strengths of each.
- □ Explain and follow established guidelines for developing an effective résumé.
- □ Apply the strategy for communicating to the development of a résumé.
- □ Apply the strategy for communicating to writing a letter of application.
- □ Employ the necessary steps for soliciting and obtaining letters of recommendation.
- □ Plan and employ a follow-up process after the résumé and cover letter are sent.

Job hunting in a competitive market

You would think that with the 20 million new job openings predicted for the next decade, you, as a job seeker, would have little trouble finding the job for you.[1] But the fact of the matter is that the job market today is fiercely competitive. Personnel managers are scrutinizing job applicants to make sure that the employee and employer will be well matched.

Important factors in securing a job

Because first-time applicants don't have a track record to give them a competitive edge, they must depend on other factors. They must understand the importance of first impressions and develop employment savvy. They must be able to *sell* their qualifications and abilities to strangers, and they must be able to communicate effectively, both orally and in writing. Both skills can profoundly affect an applicant's chances in the job market. Based on your résumé and cover letter, interviewers will evaluate your writing skills before the interview. During the interview itself, they will weigh your oral communication skills. These skills very often determine who gets the job.

In this chapter and the next, you will be guided through a sequence of steps designed to help you understand the job market. The key word in the strategy is preparation. Your goal is to select, analyze, and compete for the job that is right for you. Then you need to demonstrate that you are right for the employer. The step-by-step-process includes:

Steps prior to the interview

- ☐ Knowing yourself.
- ☐ Looking for a job.
- ☐ Knowing your employer.
- ☐ Preparing your résumé.
- ☐ Writing your letter of application.

KNOWING YOURSELF

Job hunting can be an agonizing experience. Even after hours of planning, writing letters, writing a résumé, and setting up appointments, you may still be nervous. The moment you set foot in the interviewer's office, you will be on "center stage." Remember, the questions that plague you also plague every other job candidate:

Comparing yourself with other job seekers

- ☐ Will I make a good impression?
- ☐ Will I be able to convince the personnel director of my capabilities?
- ☐ Will my résumé stand up against those of hundreds of other candidates applying for the same position?
- ☐ How can I handle questions about job experience when I just completed my education and have not worked in a full-time position?

---

[1] Snelling and Snelling, Inc., *Jobs! What They Are . . . Where They Are . . . What They Pay!* (New York: Simon & Schuster, 1985), p. 23.

But even more difficult than going through the rigors of job hunting is taking a job that is inappropriate for you or one that does not satisfy your career goals. This disappointment need not happen, though, if you proceed logically by assessing who you are and where you want to go with your life, and then by seeking a job offer that's right for you.

First step in seeking a job

Power from Within

The power to obtain the right job depends on knowing yourself and being able to capitalize on your strengths and the positive aspects of your own personality. The better you know yourself, the clearer your perception will be when you try to match your qualifications to the right position.

Know yourself

Begin by taking an inventory of yourself. Figure 18.1 is an example of a personal analysis inventory. A form like this one helps you organize and order, in terms of importance, your own qualifications, the requirements of your "ideal job," and the requirements of an actual job opening.

Know your qualifications

Under the category "Personal Qualifications and Training," list your experience, educational training, interests, personal qualities. Under "Desired Job Requirements," indicate in order of importance those job characteristics and recommended or required skills which best reflect your goals. Then, when you actually locate the jobs you are interested in, you can record in the column "Actual Job Requirements," the training or skills actually required to qualify for each job.

Completing this type of analysis helps you see on paper your strengths and weaknesses as measured by the requirements for a specific job. You will also be able to compare your assessment of the skills needed for a position to the actual requirements for the job opening you have found.

Benefits of self-analysis

In addition, your analysis provides actual details and information for your letter of application and résumé and the basis for discussion during your interviews. Knowing how your training and skills fit the job for which you are applying will impress a prospective employer and perhaps help you get the job.

Skills and Abilities

Do you type, cook, draw or sketch, sew, work math problems, sing, operate calculators or microcomputers, program in BASIC or Fortran? These and many other skills may be marketable. Did you gain these skills through training or experience? As you fill out your inventory, list only those skills you feel confident about. You could also list activities for which you are only minimally qualified, indicating, of course, that you would need additional training or experience to use them on a job.

Prioritizing your skills

Under "Very Important," list the ones you feel you are qualified to do. Then, list as "Important" those you can do fairly well. Finally, under "Not So Important," list all the other skills and abilities you have identified.

If you have difficulty identifying specific skills and abilities, you may want

Figure 18.1 **Personal analysis inventory**

	Personal Qualifications and Training	Desired Job Requirements	Actual Job Requirements		
			Company 1	Company 2	Company 3
	Skills and experience		Omaha Mutual	First Federal	IBM
1.	Programming - BASIC	**Very important**			
2.	Type 60 wpm	Good conceptual skills	Good conceptual skills	Good with figures	Use microcomputer
3.	Track star	Working with figures			
4.	Microcomputer user	**Important**	Good communication skills		
5.	Good communication	Good communication skills		Use microcomputer	Good communication
6.	Good with figures	Use microcomputer program			
7.	Good conceptual skills	**Not so important**			
8.	Swimming honors	Typing			
9.	Pianist				
	Education and training				
1.	High school graduate	**Very important**			
2.	Community College - 1 year	B.S. Degree in Finance	B.S. Degree in Finance	B.S. Degree	B.S. Degree
3.	2-week computer training course				
4.	Will obtain B.S. degree next May	**Important**			
5.	Major: Finance	2-week computer course			2-week computer course
6.	Minor: English				
7.	Drivers training course	**Not so important**			
8.		High School			
9.					
	Job preferences				
1.	Bank Officer	**Very important**			
2.	Financial Planner	Financial Planner			
3.	Business Manager				
4.	Stockbroker	**Important**			
5.		Bank Officer			
6.					
7.		**Not so important**			
8.					
9.					
	Personal qualities				
1.	Work well with people	**Very important**			
2.	Keep confidentialities	Working with people	Keep confidentialities	Persevere until successful	Listen carefully
3.	Extrovert	Listening carefully			
4.	Listen carefully	**Important**			
5.	Persevere until successful	Keeping confidentialities	Persevere until successful	Listen carefully	Follow directions
6.	Use initiative				Work well with people
7.	Personable	**Not so important**			
8.	Dependable	Extrovert			
9.					

Page 1

to consider taking a series of aptitude tests. These tests help you identify skills and abilities you didn't know you had. For example, tests are available to determine aptitude for almost any area, including social skills, logic, management, clerical ability, mechanical skills, or mathematics, to name a few. Most schools and employment facilities provide aptitude testing as a part of their employment assistance.

Identifying qualities and skills

Educational Training

Educational training defined

As you review your educational training, include any degrees you have received, areas of emphasis, majors and minors, home study and evening school programs. Don't neglect any employee training programs you've completed. If you have completed military training schools or specialized vocational training, list these also. While you are cataloging your educational experiences, rate them as well—very important, important, or not so important.

Job Preference

Identifying job preferences

You should include in your personal inventory your preferences for certain jobs. These preferences may be very general ("jobs dealing with people"), or you may be well acquainted with specific jobs, such as clerk-typist or salesclerk. You can probably identify some of your preferences based on past experiences. Even though you may not have prior work experience, you have probably thought about the kinds of work you would prefer doing—working in a bank, in retail sales, in a hospital. Don't eliminate something from your evaluation sheet just because you haven't had a job doing that kind of work.

Personal Qualities

Identifying unique qualities

What unique qualities do you have? What sort of personality would you say you have? Your friends and family can help by reminding you of qualities that stand out. The following questions should help you get started on your list of personal qualities:

- ☐ How well do you work under pressure?
- ☐ Do you prefer to work alone or with others?
- ☐ Do you like consistent work hours, or do you prefer variable hours?
- ☐ Are you a workaholic, or do you want time at home, too?
- ☐ Do you like supervising/management duties?
- ☐ Do you prefer work that is mostly physical or work that is mostly mental?
- ☐ Are you an optimist or a pessimist?
- ☐ Do you like your work duties spelled out completely for you, or do you like to develop and organize your own work duties?

*LEGAL / ETHICAL ISSUE**

Rick is a part-time undergraduate marketing-management major working full time for an import-export company at the World Trade Center in New York City. His boss, Rutherford Koberg, wants to transfer him to the company office at Kennedy Airport. Rick's apartment and school are near the World Trade Center, and the transfer would involve a lot of time and energy wasted in commuting to the new job location. Rick doesn't want this hassle even though the only alternative to the transfer is losing his job. Mr. Koberg is sorry to see Rick go, as he was a good worker and they got along well. Koberg, however, agreed formally to "fire" Rick rather than have him quit, so that Rick would be eligible for unemployment insurance. Rick was pleased with this arrangement and began to collect the insurance, saying nothing, of course, about the perfectly good job he turned down.

a. Rick's behavior is illegal. Is it unethical? Why?

b. Was it ethical of Koberg to "fire" Rick under these circumstances? Why?

* Edward Stevens, *Business Ethics* (New York: Paulist Press, 1979), p. 127. (Reprinted with permission.)

- □ Can you take constructive criticism, or do you take it personally?
- □ Do you do well in quantitative subjects such as mathematics and computer science, or do you prefer subjects such as English and history?

These questions suggest some ways of identifying your personal characteristics on your analysis sheet. Try to classify these traits according to how important each seems in your search for a job.

Comparing personal qualities with desired traits

As a final check, you may want to compare your personal characteristics against those found in a recent poll taken by the *New Accountant.* Figure 18.2 illustrates what characteristics recruiters stressed most often in job interviews at 47 colleges.

Establishing Career Goals

Career goals defined

Now that you understand yourself a little better, it will be easier to set realistic career goals. These goals must be spelled out precisely. When you prepare your résumé and go for a job interview, having precise goals will assure that the job you select will either meet those goals or be a stepping-stone toward your ultimate objective. Imagine how much frustration you'll avoid when you are moving up the corporate ranks rather than hopping from job to job trying to find satisfaction.

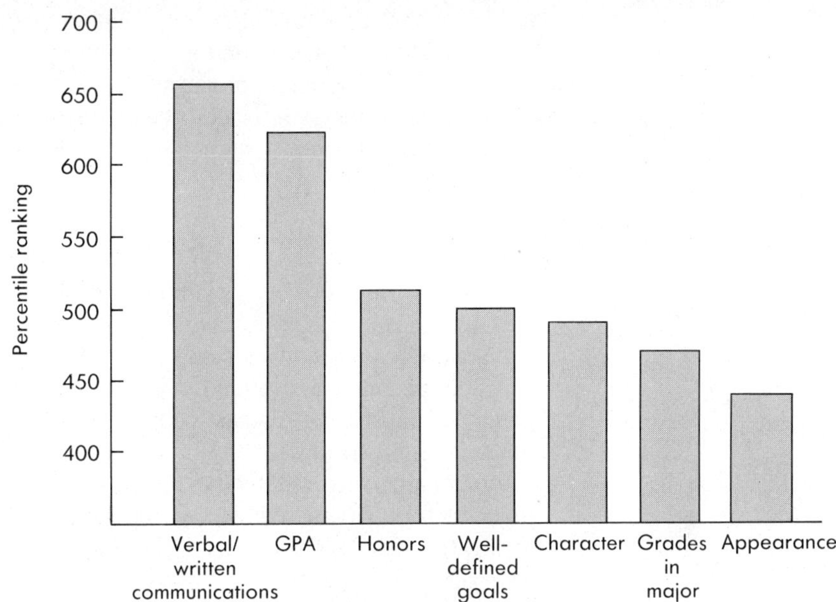

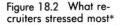

Figure 18.2 What recruiters stressed most*

Each category (Verbal/Written Communication, GPA, etc.) was rank ordered on a scale from 1 (highest) to 8 (lowest), then weighted: 8 points for a "1" and 1 point for an "8." Cumulative scores for each category were then compared, providing an overall ranking of Verbal/Written Communications as #1, GPA #2, etc.

* Morris Helitzer et al., eds., "Popularity Poll Results," *New Accountant* 2, no. 1 (September 1986), p. 20.

Since you spend at least half of your life on the job, you will be a lot happier if your work is enjoyable, challenging, and rewarding. Give careful thought to choosing your career goals. Know what you want to do with your life and why. By completing a personal analysis inventory, you will be able to pinpoint tasks you do best as well as the ones which are more important to your satisfaction and self-fulfillment. Understanding your career goal is the most important aspect of your self-analysis. All other information relates to this goal.

Are You Qualified?

Qualifications defined

Once you have set your goals, you need a clear understanding of the qualifications that might encourage employers to offer you the job over other applicants. If you are just getting out of school and have little or no experience, you are probably worried about your qualifications. Keep in mind that qualifications include more than just job experience. You need to concentrate on attributes that employers want. Are you dependable? Are you a self-starter? Do you have a good attitude? Do you get along well with other people? Do you stick to the job until it's done? Are you fast, yet accurate? Are you willing to learn or receive additional training if necessary? Do you listen attentively and ask questions?

And what about education? Formal training plays an important role in the selection process. Capitalize on the training you have received that prepares you for a particular job. Emphasize all the skills, abilities, talents, and education you possess that employers need and want. Believe in yourself first before trying to convince someone else to believe in you.

LOOKING FOR A JOB

Attitude of a job seeker

When looking for a job, begin with an attitude that you are ready to spend whatever time is necessary to obtain a position that is compatible with your career goal. Begin by considering some statistics that are rather interesting concerning the methods used in looking for a job. Figure 18.3 shows findings from an Administrative Management Society (AMS) study on job search techniques. In this study, AMS found that a difference exists between perceptions of persons involved in the hiring process. For example, employers responsible for hiring stated that the standard résumé and cover letter are the most effective means of obtaining a job interview. Management employees on the other hand rated contacting a business associate as the most effective. But when asked about their own experience in terms of their initial contact with their current firm, they stated referrals as the number one method.

Job-seeking methods

Since you don't know which method will prove productive for you, start with the ones considered most effective in the AMS survey. Use as many methods as required to be successful. Tell everyone that you are looking for a job.

Electronic searches defined

If you know the specific type of job you want, try one of the computer databases now available. By keying in your specialized field, you can obtain a computer printout of companies employing these specialties. Employment agencies and local libraries should be able to help you. (See Chapter 2 for an example of electronic searches.)

KNOWING YOUR EMPLOYER

So far you have come to grips with who you are and where you are going. You have looked over the job market and matched up your expertise with various companies that hire people with your skills and training. You are now ready to go after a particular job.

Researching the Organization

Before writing a résumé and letter of application, you need to do some research on the companies to which you are applying. At this point, it would be well to concentrate on 7 to 10 companies for which you would most like to work.

Techniques for researching the organization

- ☐ Check with the Chamber of Commerce in the city where the companies are located.

Figure 18.3
AMS job search findings*

Table 1
Employers Rate:
WAYS TO GET AN INTERVIEW

Q: Which of the initial contact methods listed below do you find are most effective in obtaining a job interview with your firm?

Standard résumé and cover letter	36%
Referral from another employee in organization	22
Referral by search firm, employment agency, college placement office	17
Referral from friend, relative or other person	7
Information interview	5
Telephone call	5
Standard résumé without cover letter	4
Walk-in cold call	3
Letter without résumé	0

Table 2
Employees Rate:
WAYS TO LAND A JOB

Q: What approach have you found to be most successful in obtaining jobs?

Approach	%
Contacting business associates	30%
Employment agencies/search firms	18
Responding to classified ads	16
Unsolicited contact of potential employer	11
Professional/trade associations	3
College placement centers	3
Contacting friends, relatives & others	1

Table 3
Employees Rate:
INITIAL CONTACT WITH CURRENT FIRM

Q: For your latest full-time position, what was your initial mode of contact with your employer?

Mode of contact	%
Referral by search firm, employment agency or college placement office	23%
Referral by friend, relative or other contact	22
Sent letter and résumé in response to ad	17
Referral by source within company other than personnel	11
Other (unspecified)	9
Walk-in cold call	6
Called firm in response to ad	4
Sent unsolicited letter and résumé	3
Referral from personnel department	2
Sent letter or résumé only in response to ad	2
Unsolicited letter, résumé or phone call	0

* Reprinted from *Management World,* September 1984, with permission from AMS, Trevose, PA 19047. (Copyright 1984) AMS.

- ☐ Request an annual report and/or proxy report from those companies listed on the stock exchange. All large publicly held companies produce annual reports.
- ☐ Request information from each company's public relations department or comparable department.
- ☐ Contact people you already know who work for the various companies and get information from them.
- ☐ Do research in the public library.
- ☐ Contact an investment broker if the companies sell stock and ask for information and track record of stock for each.
- ☐ Read the trade journals for employment listings.

Find out what types of employees each company is seeking. If possible, obtain a job description of the position you seek before writing your résumé and application letter. Figure 18.4 lists sources of corporate information available in most libraries.

Additional sources for researching companies

Sometimes you can obtain information about a company directly from the personnel department. Students sometimes overlook the fact that they can gain a lot of information on specific jobs from campus recruiters. Even if you have no interest in the company because of the location, reputation, or other factors, the people representing these companies can provide valuable information.

Company executives are impressed with people who research their organizations and know something about how the job for which they are applying fits in with the goals of that company. One such executive stated, "More often than most people realize, this is the deciding factor in offering an applicant the job."

Research Questions

As you research the companies in which you are interested, answer these types of questions before requesting an interview.

Key questions when researching companies

- ☐ Who are the key people in the organization?
- ☐ What are the major products or services produced by this company?
- ☐ How large is the organization both in terms of annual sales and employees?
- ☐ What is the company's profit and loss record for the past ten years?
- ☐ Where are other divisions of the company located?
- ☐ How is the company organized?
- ☐ How is the company viewed by its clients, suppliers, and competition?
- ☐ Is this a company for which my goals are compatible?
- ☐ Would my skills be fully utilized?

Figure 18.4
Corporate information sources

American Encyclopedia of International Information
American Register of American Manufacturers
Bernard Klein's Guide to American Directories
Business Week Annual Report
The College Placement Annual
Directory of Professional and Trade Organizations
Dun and Bradstreet's Middle Market Directory
Encyclopedia of Associations
Fitch's Corporation Reports
Forbes Magazine Annual Listing of 2,500 Major Companies
Fortune Magazine's Annual List of the 1,000 Largest Industrial Corporations, Financial Institutions, Overseas Corporations
Macrae's Blue Book—Corporate Index
Moody's Industrials
The Standard Periodical Directory
Standard and Poor's Register of Corporations, Directors, and Executives
Stores Annual List of Leading Department Stores (A National Retail Merchants Association Publication)
The Wall Street Journal Annual Report

- ☐ What about the geographic area of the company?
- ☐ Are the salaries of this company comparable to the economic norm?
- ☐ Are opportunities available for advancement?
- ☐ What type of job pressures would there be?
- ☐ In what type of environment would I be working?

In addition to the above answers, knowing the turnaround rate of each company would be helpful. Another area of interest is the attitude of the employees. The more you find out about each company, the better prepared you are to write a résumé and letter of application and to answer interview questions.

PREPARING YOUR RÉSUMÉ

One way to introduce yourself to potential employers is to send them a well-prepared résumé accompanied by a cover letter or letter of application. Once you have completed the Personal Analysis Inventory, identified the prospective job, and researched the company, you will have a useful body of information for preparing these materials.

Developing a Résumé that Works

By now, you probably realize that most communications can't be "whipped out" in just a few minutes. This especially holds true for something as important as a résumé. Think of your résumé as an advertisement. You know that some ads are so ridiculous they turn you off completely. Others are so mundane, they are boring. But those ads which seem honest, sincere, and factual are the most convincing. Your résumé advertises you and your ability to be of service to the organization to which you are applying. Make your résumé sincere and convincing, and it will help you get the job you want.

Résumé objectives

A well-prepared résumé can do more than serve as an admission ticket for obtaining an interview. The résumé also serves as a reminder of accomplishments which you may forget unless they are written down. In addition, you may use your résumé as an introduction to other members of the organization, as a time-saving device for you and the interviewer, and as a reinforcement device for what is discussed orally.

Common characteristics of a résumé

All résumés contain types of information which are basic for any format: vital statistics (personal data), career objective, experience, and education. Later you will see how to add other categories which uniquely describe you. First, consider the following guidelines which apply to all résumés:

Guidelines for preparing résumés

- *Include only relevant data.* Executives are too busy to wade through material that has little bearing on your career.
- *Be concise.* If possible, limit the information to one page—two at the most. If you have a wealth of background and experience, include the data that will have the most impact.
- *Make sure grammar, spelling, and punctuation are all correct.* You want to show that you are accurate, careful, and attentive to detail.
- *Use only high-quality paper.* Use at least 50 percent rag content paper.
- *Prepare your résumé on standard 8 1/2 by 11-inch paper.* High-quality copies are acceptable. Never send carbon copies.
- *Place data on one side only.* Even if the résumé is commercially prepared, most people prefer one side.
- *Avoid using abbreviations.* Spell out important information. Exceptions include two-letter state abbreviations and academic degrees (B.A. or B.S.).
- *Include only positive information.* The résumé is not a confessional.
- *Save salary requirements for the personal interview.* Salary is usually a negotiable item and should be discussed face to face *after* you receive an offer—not stated in a résumé.
- *Do not include sex, age, religion, race, and national origin.* These should have no bearing on your qualifications for the job.
- *Do not make false statements.* A false claim could later wreck your whole career.

A convenient way to begin your résumé is to use a worksheet similar to the one shown in Figure 18.5. Most of your data can be pulled from your personal analysis inventory and other material you have gathered. Include everything

Figure 18.5
Résumé worksheet

Worksheet for Résumé Preparation

____
Name

____
Street Address

____
City, State, Zip

Home phone: ____________________

Job objective: ____________________

Education: ____________________

Experience summary: ____________________

Optional category: ____________________

Optional category: ____________________

Good résumés begin with a planning sheet

you can think of. You can "weed out" later. Notice that this worksheet includes the four basic categories—vital statistics, objective, education, and experience. There are also blank areas for categories pertinent to your qualifications. Some suggested optional categories are:

Résumé categories

- ☐ Extracurricular activities.
- ☐ Languages.
- ☐ Special accomplishments.
- ☐ Research.

- ☐ Publications.
- ☐ Awards/honors.
- ☐ Community service.
- ☐ Military service.
- ☐ Professional memberships.
- ☐ References.
- ☐ Accreditation and licenses.

After completing the worksheet, you are ready to construct a résumé that works. Go over all the information you have listed and pull out the data that best describe your qualifications, achievements, and experience, as well as your highest levels of education.

Vital statistics defined

Vital Statistics should include your name, address, and phone number. Make sure your name appears on each page. Such information as height, weight, birthplace, marital status, and state of health take up unnecessary space and may pose a basis for legal action. If this information is relevant to job performance, save this data for the company application form.

Job objective defined

Job Objective should clearly state the functional area in which you seek employment. Don't specify the job title unless you want to limit the résumé to one specific job. Begin with your area of expertise and state your objective in terms of what you have to offer the company:

Objective: To work as an administrative assistant for a firm interested in using my effective communications skills, word processing efficiency, and human relations capabilities.

This objective is realistic because it is specific to your area of expertise, yet broad enough to apply to several positions for various firms.

Education defined

Education should emphasize all important academic experiences, including institution attended, degrees, honors, class standing, and leadership positions. Include only courses that are especially relevant to the objective. List your highest degrees. Leave out details about secondary education unless you wish to emphasize some extraordinary accomplishment.

Experience defined

Experience should cite specific on-the-job skills and/or accomplishments. Especially pertinent to this section are skills in which you have already demonstrated competence. Do not exaggerate here by using a lot of superlatives or meaningless adjectives. On the other hand, be honest about any noteworthy accomplishments or skills. Do not be bashful about listing your competencies. Your résumé should convey a positive message of potential leadership and past success.

Use the alternative categories listed above to describe yourself and what makes you special. These will not be the same for each person. For example, maybe you have not received many awards or honors, but perhaps you worked part-time during the school year or each summer to pay all your educational expenses. Or perhaps you were involved in a co-op or internship program. Have you done any volunteer work? If so, you should definitely mention this service. Such information distinguishes your special qualities. Place this important data in a category called "Additional Facts" or "Summary Statement."

References may be included on a résumé in one of two ways:

References defined

- ☐ Listed on a separate page and furnished on request.
- ☐ Listed right on the résumé itself in a separate category.

When stating the references, include the name of the person, title, full address, and telephone number. The best references are those persons who have a knowledge of your qualifications. Suggested references include former supervisors, co-workers, teachers, bankers, and others. Obtain permission in advance from all persons you wish to list as references.

Follow-up on references

Smart interviewers will follow up on these references. Some applicants make the mistake of thinking that no employer will follow up since any references furnished will most likely be positive. But studies reveal that this follow-up is well worth a company's time and energy, and more firms today routinely check references.

In addition to checking out your qualifications, managers are looking for discrepancies or outright falsifications in their investigations. According to Robert Half, an often quoted authority on hiring practices, these unethical practices are prevalent. One of his latest studies reveals that:

> roughly one-third of all job applicants either doctor their résumés or misrepresent their accomplishments. The only way to sort through these attempts to look good is by digging deep for a broad representative sample of people who can verify or deny claims.[2]

Make sure your claims, both in the interview and in the résumé, can bear this scrutiny, or your application could be dropped without any explanation.

Résumé Format

No specific format is required for a résumé. As in other written communications, the résumé expresses "you." All the concepts you have learned about style in previous chapters also apply to résumés:

Résumé style

- ☐ Employ a positive, courteous tone.
- ☐ Use active sentences or statements.
- ☐ Avoid technical jargon.
- ☐ Use the "you" approach.
- ☐ Eliminate boring details that waste the reader's time.
- ☐ Use a conversational yet professional style.
- ☐ Arrange material for easy reading.
- ☐ Arrange material attractively, employing "white space" to separate categories.

[2] Robert Half, "How to Really Check an Applicant's References," *Office* 102, no. 5 (1985), p. 90.

Since you are discussing yourself, use the first person in both your résumé and letter of application. However, avoid the overuse of the word *I*, especially at the beginning of each sentence. Statements describing job activities on the résumé, for instance, should begin with action verbs such as *completed, prepared, performed, organized, implemented, quoted, tested, planned, etc.* Repeating the word *I* for each statement would certainly get tedious. Instead, tell how you accomplished these or the result of the action.

Importance of verbs in résumés

You may choose one of three commonly used formats—the *basic résumé,* the *chronological résumé,* or the *functional résumé,*—or you may create one to fit your particular situation. Just keep in mind that the purpose is to *convince* the Reader that you qualify for the job you are seeking. As we discuss the different formats, be aware that you can vary the Order of the categories, except for your name, address, and phone number, which should go at the top of the page. An effectively ordered résumé should list categories in order of importance, with your objective near the top. If you are just getting out of school, education is probably more important. Later, your experience or special accomplishments might be more important. Choose the Format that best suits you.

Résumé formats commonly used

The Basic Résumé

The basic résumé is most often used by students with little or no experience. This Format emphasizes your objective, education and personal characteristics, achievements, or qualifications. Include those traits which indicate job success. For instance, good grades usually indicate high standards, motivation, and intelligence. Scholarships, awards, or honors suggest leadership. Long-term progress toward an objective may indicate commitment and perseverance. Extracurricular activities such as volunteer work, participation in sports, work on a school newspaper, class offices held, or participation in school clubs or activities show community interest and could be viewed as an indication of human relations skills. An example of a basic résumé Format is illustrated in Figure 18.6.

The basic résumé defined

The Chronological Résumé

Reverse chronology is quite common because it emphasizes most recent data. Although education and experience are arranged in the order they occurred, the most recent information is listed first. Figure 18.7 shows a chronological résumé

The chronological résumé defined

Some employers favor this type of résumé, because they can easily detect career gaps, job hopping, or other irregularities. This format is also easy to prepare and easy to read. Just be sure to highlight your skills in some way through underscoring or marginal notations or by identifying a special category in the résumé.

Figure 18.6
A basic résumé

CALVIN RICHARDS
137 Main Street
Birmingham, AL 35294
(205) 381–9298

OBJECTIVE
To obtain an entry-level position in a marketing firm.

EDUCATION
College:
Graduate of The University of XXXXXX, August 1987
Bachelor of Science in Business Administration
Major: General Business
GPA: 3.57
High School:
Graduate of XXXXXXX High School, XXXXXX, XX, June, 1983

EXPERIENCE
University of XXXXXXX Book and Supply Store, XXXXX,XX
Beginning: August, 1986, through June, 1987
Duties: Responsible for closing the store and overseeing student employees at night
XXXXXXX Landscaping and Design, XXXXXXX, XX
Beginning: June, 1985 through August, 1986
Duties: Landscaping residential homes and businesses
H and R Block, XXXXXXX, XX
Beginning: December, 1984, through March, 1985
Duties: Delivering tax forms

ACTIVITIES
College:
Pi Kappa Alpha fraternity, intramural official, Pi Beta Kappa honor fraternity, resident hall assistant, and campus police assistant
High School:
Key Club, Spanish Honor Society, and Fellowship of Christian Athletes

The Functional Résumé

The functional résumé defined

If you want to emphasize your talents, qualifications, or other assets, the functional résumé is an excellent choice, because it allows you to organize information according to job functions. You can design a résumé to emphasize how your talents, education, and experience directly relate to the position for which you are applying. Your résumé is actually a sales presentation of your unique qualifications for the job. This Format is especially appropriate for persons with varied skills and talents. For the most part, this Format is appropriate for a person with full-time work experience. Figure 18.8 is an example of a functional résumé.

Abbott Smith Associates, a recruitment firm specializing in training person-

Figure 18.7
Chronological résumé

Résumé
of
MARY E. SMITH
XXX XXXX XXXX XXX
Pine Bluff, Arkansas 71601

Home Phone:	(501) 233-5861
Job Objective:	To work in your firm as an apprentice appraiser with the eventual aim of becoming a member of the American Institute of Real Estate Appraisers.
Education:	Bachelor of Science degree in Real Estate and Urban Development with an emphasis in Finance and Economics University of Arkansas, 1988 Selected Courses: Real Estate Appraisal; Investment Analysis Real Estate Finance; Regression Analysis Urban Economic Analysis; Financial Management Urban Growth and Land Use; Data Processing
Employment History:	
March 1986 to September 1987	Red Lobster Restaurant, Pine Bluff, Arkansas Title: Hostess/Cashier
Summers of 1984-1985	Theif Neck Marina, Little Rock, Arkansas Title: Boat Maintenance Person
January 1985 to March 1985	University of Arkansas Cafeteria, Pine Bluff, Arkansas Title: Food Service Personnel
1982-1984	Little Rock Medical Center, Little Rock, Arkansas Title: Volunteer

nel professionals, developed this example to illustrate what a simple, one-page, functional résumé might look like. They state:

> That is, in many ways, the ideal form. Not only does it sell on one page, but it states an objective simply and clearly, and describes John Doe's experience in a way that makes the objective seem very reasonable. Note that each short paragraph in the "experience" section hits some salient points that further validates the objective.
>
> The section describing Doe's work history simply lists the various positions he has held, with dates and titles. Memberships in appropriate professional organizations should be listed, but not too many; don't give the impression of being a professional joiner.[3]

[3] David Brinkerhoff and Abbott P. Smith, "Write a Resume, Not an Obituary," *Training* 23, no. 7 (July 1986), p. 37.

Figure 18.8
A functional résumé*

JOHN DOE
47 Main Street
Plainfield, NY 16789
(914) 765-4321

Functions:

OBJECTIVE: I seek a position with challenge and advancement potential in management development, organizational development or training.

Counseling

Training

EXPERIENCE: While at XYZ Electronics, I have counseled individually the general managers (in charge of 500+ people) and section managers (100+ people) in organization development, management development, and individualized skills training. These sessions involved techniques such as those in Kepner-Tiegoe's "Managerial Problem-Solving & Decision Making," Dr. Fear's "Evaluation Interview Training," and elements of team building. In addition, I have led various seminars in effective presentation techniques, communication and the management process, managerial development via effective listening, and interpersonal skills training.

Design and implementation

I also assisted in the design of formal identification and personnel review procedures so that promotable/high-potential personnel were selected and developed through both individualized coaching sessions (which I conducted) and meaningful rotational assignments. In addition, I maintained liaison with XYZ's corporate personnel development operation and served on its staff on several occasions in all XYZ plants, providing time management and systems training concepts. I also performed these functions while at ABC Electronics.

Management

In addition to the preceding, I have had the responsibility of directing the managerial and professional development program for the XYZ government function.

POSITIONS:

19__-Present	XYZ Electronics	Plainfield, NY. Director of Management Development, Design Technology Division.
19__-19__	ABC Electronics	New York, NY. Supervisor, Managerial and Professional Development; Education and Training Analyst.
19__-19__	Dun & Bradstreet	New York, NY. Credit Reporter.
19__-19__	U.S. Army	Lieutenant, Corps of Engineers.

EDUCATION: B.S. 19__, Purdue University, Industrial Psychology. M.B.A. 19 , New York University. Related studies programs at XYZ Electronics.

* Reprinted with permission from the July 1986 issue of *Training,* The Magazine of Human Resources Development. Copyright 1986, Lakewood Publications, Inc., Minneapolis, MN (Area Code) 612-333-0471. All rights reserved.

The Creative Résumé

A creative résumé defined

Even though the three formats mentioned (basic, chronological, and functional) are the most popular, you don't have to use any of them. Perhaps you are a scientist and would like a research position in a certain type of research lab. You may want a Format that provides more detail. No prescribed approach for résumés exists. The job you seek and your unique qualifications should dictate the Format. You may create a customized résumé to highlight special points. The quality of the résumé determines the effectiveness. Creativity is merely a unique use of paragraphing, layout, color, type of paper, or whatever other feature you choose to vary. As long as the uniqueness enhances your chances, it's perfectly appropriate.

Figure 18.9 is an example of a creative résumé. Burdette E. Bostwick, a consultant specializing in marketing and organization, evaluates Ms. Langtry's creative résumé:

A creative résumé analyzed

> Ms. Langtry's résumé is an excellent example of much relevant and attractive material condensed for presentation on one page. Ms. Langtry, a successful writer, was able to describe 20 years of experience in about 200 words while expressing a competence that might easily have required several pages. She has effectively made use of the words of others, permitting discussions of talents that would be ill-received if expressed subjectively.
>
> The résumé does not follow a formal pattern and is therefore a *Creative Résumé*.[4]

Applying the Strategy to the Résumé

Now that you understand important concepts associated with the process of employment, you are ready to apply the strategy for communicating.

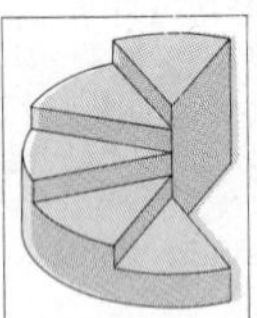

STRATEGY: THE BASIC RÉSUMÉ

Eileen Butler has had a tremendous interest in the retail profession since she was a little girl. She has always enjoyed all the activities that take place in the shopping malls and big department stores. Eileen especially delights in all the hustle and bustle associated with the retail industry during the holiday seasons. Such activities generated her enthusiasm and interest to pursue a career in the retail field.

Eileen is now a senior at Wayne State University and is ready to enter the job market. She is about to complete a degree in home economics with a major in merchandising. She has already completed a personal analysis inventory, and from this information jotted down relevant information on

[4] Burdette E. Bostwick, *Résumé Writing* (New York: John Wiley & Sons, 1985), pp. 97-99.

Figure 18.9 A creative résumé*

90 Divine Towpath
Stage, CT 12345
(000) 456-7890

RESUME
LILY LANGTRY
MAGAZINE EDITORIAL DIRECTOR-EDITOR

Qualifications: Twenty years of successful experience as Managing Editor with unusually broad responsibilities embracing three successful magazines with a largely female readership; and as Executive Editor, Managing Editor, Features Editor, Assistant Editor in reverse chronology; with three different publishers.

Publishers Weekly said: "The most knowledgeable woman's editor in the field" (June 1988).

Magazine Writer's Digest said: "Miss Langtry has helped more aspiring writers than anyone I know" (January 1987).

Magazine Guild said: "Miss Langtry has identified her markets and hit them in the bull's-eye; without question one of the most talented editors in her field" (November 1986).

Objective evaluation by Corporate Manpower Development Committee on Executive Evaluation: COMPETENT in all areas of manuscript selection and purchase, production, control, organizational and administration, wide author contacts and excellent reputation for judgment, decisiveness and creativity.

Possesses in high degree ability to lead, supervise, train and gain loyalty and dedication of staff. Oriented to profitable operations.

SENSITIVE to editorial and reader needs; capable of bringing them together to gain optimum circulation and to make changes quickly as need appears (Dec. 19--).

Employment history:
1987-Present National Publications, New York, NY
1986-1987 Hillside Publishing Company, New York, NY
1985-1986 Rex Magazine Company, New York, NY

Education: B.S., Journalism, University of Syracuse, Syracuse, NY, 1984

Personal data: Single, excellent health, no dependents, willing to relocate.

REFERENCES AND FURTHER DATA ON REQUEST

* Burdette E. Bostwick, *Résumé Writing*. (New York: John Wiley & Sons, 1985), pp. 97–99. (Reprinted with permission).

a résumé worksheet. She has also researched companies offering positions in her field. Based on this research of seven companies, Eileen narrows her focus to three major retail firms. She chooses these three because they each offer positions related to her expertise, provide upward mobility for reaching her long-range goal of sales manager, exhibit challenging job descriptions, and are located in her hometown. She obtains employment information on these firms from the *Stores Annual List of Leading Department Stores.* She also calls the telephone numbers of the firms and obtains the names of key personnel from the public relations departments. Eileen is now ready to plan her strategy for communicating to the development of a résumé.

PROBLEM

Eileen's assistantship position with the university's Pediatric Language Laboratory will terminate upon graduation. Eileen will soon be unemployed.

OBJECTIVES

General: To prepare a résumé that will result in a retailing position with a firm that can use her expertise.

Specific: To highlight educational background pointing out college major, supportive courses, and relevant activities.
To highlight avocations.
To state a job objective.
To show employment experience.
To provide a statement concerning references.
To include vital statistics data.

READER/AUDIENCE

Primary: Personnel manager.
Ultimate supervisor/manager

Secondary: Other managers.

Characteristics: Is an expert in personnel management.
Is highly educated.
Will view résumé from the company standpoint.
Is an effective interviewer.

Reactions: Will be impressed by a well-prepared résumé.
Will be hesitant to hire on basis of résumé alone.
Will need to verify accuracy of the résumé content.
Will compare the applicant with other candidates.

ORDER

To include vital statistics data.

To state a job objective.

To highlight educational background, pointing out college major, supportive courses, and relevant activities.

Figure 18.10 Résumé example

Résumé
for
EILEEN BUTLER
XXXX XXXXXXXXXX XXX.
Detroit, MI 48201

HOME PHONE:	(313) 663-0124
OBJECTIVE	To obtain a career in retailing within a firm that provides opportunity for growth and advancement.
EDUCATION:	WAYNE STATE UNIVERSITY, Detroit, MI. B.S. Degree, Home Economics, 1988
Major:	MERCHANDISING
Supportive Courses:	Marketing, Economics, Advertising, Journalism, Acccounting
Activities:	Merchandising Student Association Honors: Spring '86; Winter '87; Summer '87 Academic
EXPERIENCE:	
September 1987 to Present	Teacher's Aide, Pediatric Language Laboratory, Detroit, MI. Lead children in various activities; assist in snack lunches and naps.
September 1987 to December 1987	Assistant Area Sales Manager, Dillard's Department Store, Memphis, TN. Internship Program. Supervised sales staff, assisted customers in personal shopping and display. Received and checked in merchandise.
PART-TIME 1983-1987	Sales Clerk, Goldsmith's Department Store, Memphis, TN. Assisted customers, arranged displays, received and checked in freight, and conducted inventory.
AVOCATIONS	Sewing, bowling, reading, skating, and modeling.
REFERENCES	Available upon request.

To show employment experience.

To highlight avocations.

To provide a statement concerning references.

FORMAT

Since Eileen has had no previous full-time experience, she selects the **basic résumé Format** to emphasize her qualifications. Figure 18.10 shows Eileen's completed résumé.

WRITING YOUR LETTER OF APPLICATION/COVER LETTER

Cover letters defined

Résumés are basically statements of supporting data which demonstrate your qualifications for the job you want. However, the résumé alone is not enough; a cover letter or letter of application must accompany the résumé. In fact, you can write a letter of application without a résumé and save the résumé for the interview. However, you should never send a résumé without an accompanying cover letter that introduces you to the employer and provides convincing evidence that you are the person for the job. The following tips should help you in writing the letter.

Guidelines for writing cover letter

- ☐ *Give each letter a personal touch as if each employer is the only one receiving the letter.* This means you must type separate letters directed specifically to each company. A word processor can be a helpful tool in accomplishing this task.
- ☐ *Write to the department head in whose department you seek employment.* Address the person by name and use her/his correct title. Never send a letter "to whom it may concern." If the name of the employer is unknown, use the AMS Style, omitting the salutation and complimentary close.
- ☐ *Send a copy of the letter and application to the head of personnel.* If you wish to write directly to the director of personnel, this is totally acceptable; in most companies, however, personnel directors usually only recommend applicants to relevant department heads. They seldom have the power to hire. *In all cases,* however, make sure they receive a copy. Failure to do so could result in a negative recommendation or selection of another applicant who extended this courtesy.
- ☐ *Customize the letter by mentioning specifics which apply only to the particular company addressed.* Use information you obtained during the research portion of the employment process.
- ☐ *Keep the letter short and to the point.* If you want your letter singled out for further consideration, this is a good tip to remember. It is not unusual for companies of any size to receive between 100 to 300 résumés (or more) a week. Put yourself in their place; and you will understand their appreciation of short, *pointed* letters.
- ☐ *Adapt the letter to the information listed in the résumé.* Since the cover letter is intended to stimulate the reader to investigate your application further, draw attention to descriptions of special skills or training in your résumé.

Here are some additional pointers for developing the content in a letter of application.

Opening

Introduce yourself in the opening

Open your letter by introducing yourself and mentioning the benefits you can bring to the organization. This will arouse the employer's interest and create a desire to learn more about you. The opening orients the reader by giving your reasons for writing.

Middle

Address specifics in the middle

Describe specific achievements or special qualities you possess. Unless they are applicable, a list of duties from past employment won't interest most employers; they want facts which substantiate your ability to benefit the company as described in the opening portion of your letter. These facts should emphasize two or three of the most important achievements or qualities which make you special. Don't write a biographical sketch of your life's attainments. The résumé contains a complete list of all you have to offer. In the cover letter, few specifics will stimulate the reader to study the résumé for further details.

Ending

Close expectantly in the ending

The ending of your letter needs only two or three sentences, but it should have an expectant tone. Ask for an appointment at the employer's convenience. Request an answer or suggest a follow-up call to arrange for an appropriate time to discuss the particulars of the job. Give your telephone number and ask the employer to call you.

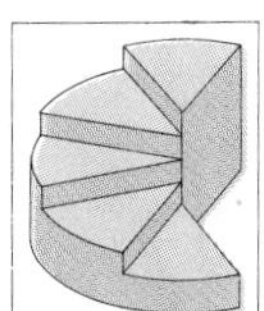

STRATEGY: THE LETTER OF APPLICATION

Using these guidelines and the résumé shown in Figure 18.10, Eileen Butler is ready to apply the strategy for communicating to the development of a letter of application to accompany her résumé. The setting for this communication is the same as the one used for developing Eileen's résumé.

PROBLEM
Eileen's assistantship position with the university's Pediatric Language Laboratory will terminate upon graduation. Eileen will soon be unemployed.

OBJECTIVES

General: To prepare a letter of application that will result in an interview with a retailing firm.

Specific: To ask for an interview.

To emphasize selected important achievements.

To indicate how her special qualifications meet the job requirements.

To introduce herself to the prospective employer.

To arouse the employer's interest.

To request an answer.

To stimulate the reader to study her résumé.

READER/AUDIENCE

Primary: Mr. John Cox, personnel manager.

Secondary: Relevant department head and other managers.

Characteristics: An expert in personnel management for a well-known national chain.

Has been with the company for 13 years.

Reviews approximately 100 résumés per week.

Has extensive expertise in analyzing résumés and letters of applications.

Reactions: Favorably impressed with applicant's research on company.

Favorably impressed with the letter of application and invites applicant for an interview.

Favorably impressed but has no openings that match the applicant's qualifications and does not invite for an interview.

Favorably impressed but receives applications from better qualified candidates.

ORDER

Since this is a persuasive message, Eileen will develop the communication similar to a sales letter. In reality, Eileen will be selling herself. Based on this approach, Eileen orders her specific objectives.

To introduce herself to the prospective employer.

To arouse the employer's interest.

To indicate how her special qualifications meet the job requirements.

To emphasize selected important achievements.

To stimulate the reader to study her résumé.

To ask for an interview.

To request an answer.

Figure 18.11 Letter of Application

XXXX XXXXXXXXXX XX
Detroit, MI 48201
June 10, 19__

Mr. John Cox
Personnel Manager
XXXXX XXXXXXXX XXXXX
XXXXXXXXXX XX XXXXX

Dear Mr. Cox:

Your policy concerning employee upward mobility for those who are hard-working and "get things done" greatly interests me. I would like to become a team member of your firm.

My education, internship, and part-time experiences provide me with retailing skills which could be beneficial to your firm. Some of my major accomplishments include:

- ☐ Creating window displays for one of the largest department stores in the Memphis, TN area. These displays received special commendation from top management.
- ☐ Supervising a 10-member sales staff, zeroing in on human development skills.
- ☐ Focusing on customer needs with special emphasis on effective public relations.
- ☐ Conducting an inventory in a responsible manner.

The attached résumé details my objective, education, experience, and avocations. As a graduate right out of college, I have researched some of the latest techniques used in retailing and marketing.

Please call (313) 663-0124 or contact me at the address shown above to let me know when I can come for an interview. I will be happy to meet with you at your convenience.

Sincerely,

Eileen Butler

Enclosure

FORMAT

Letter and accompanying résumé.

Figure 18.11 shows Eileen's completed letter of application.

Some Precautionary Measures

Even a very good letter can fail if the writer ignores some simple precautions. Before mailing your letters, check to see that you've met these requirements:

Premailing guidelines

- ☐ Proofread! Proofread! Proofread! In addition to checking all spelling, grammar, and punctuation, verify all figures and dates.
- ☐ Is your letter easy to read and easy to follow? Your letter should proceed from who you are to the request for an interview.
- ☐ Make sure everything in the letter is related to the job you seek.
- ☐ Is your letter prepared on a letter-quality printer or typewriter? As with the résumé, appearance is extremely important.
- ☐ Check to see if every sentence is positive. Delete any negatives—including salary expectations.
- ☐ Does your letter sound convincing enough to warrant an interview?

When your letter is ready to mail, post it to arrive sometime in the middle of the week. Mondays are often hectic, and Fridays are wrap-up-for-the-weekend days.

LETTERS OF RECOMMENDATION

Identifying sources for letters of recommendation

Many prospective employers require letters of recommendation prior to granting an interview. Therefore, obtaining letters of recommendation should also be a part of job preparation. The list of persons from whom you should solicit letters is identical to the list of references: former employers, co-workers, professional people, teachers, school counselors, bankers, or others who are acquainted with you and/or your work.

If you solicit several letters of recommendation, ask each writer to stress a different set of qualifications. For instance, your teacher could stress your integrity, leadership, responsibility, or personality. A letter from a former employer would probably stress your job performance. A co-worker could stress both your work skills and human relations skills. Figure 18.12, a letter of recommendation from an advisor/supervisor, focuses on the candidate's work performance.

Letters of recommendation make a better impression when addressed specifically to the company to which you are applying. A good practice is to have the writers mail the letters directly to the personnel manager. Ask for copies to place in your portfolio in case the manager misplaces the ones mailed. Sometimes letters of recommendation are requested after the interview is conducted. If so, follow the same procedures for requesting and obtaining these letters of recommendation.

Figure 18.12.
Letter of recommendation

June 2, 19__

Mr. John Cox
XXXXXXXXXXXXXXXXXXXXX
XXXXXXXXXX XX XXXXX

Dear Mr. Cox:

I understand Eileen Butler is applying for a position in your firm. This letter is a recommendation in support of that application.

As Eileen Butler's advisor for the past three years, I have worked closely with her in all aspects of her academic program. I am also acquainted with her work performance as a computer lab assistant, since she has worked under my supervision for the past nine months in this capacity.

The following comments describe my perceptions of Eileen's capabilities:

1. She has done superior work in all phases of her academic program. She will complete a B.S. degree in home economics next week.
2. She is an outstanding worker. The labs which she assists run smoothly and orderly. She is always on time and stays late if necessary to ensure that the lab is left orderly and ready for the next session.
3. Other students appreciate her assistance because of her helpful attitude and because of the impartial service she provides in the lab.
4. If you have had the opportunity to interview Eileen, I am sure you have been impressed with her communication abilities. She is a good listener and follows directions well. At the same time she is an able thinker and makes sound decisions on her own.

In other words, Miss Butler would be a tremendous asset to your firm. I highly recommend her.

Let me know if I can supply other information about Eileen. I will be happy to discuss any of her qualifications in detail.

Sincerely,

XXXXXXXXXXXX XXXXXXX

Following Up

When to follow up

Employers are impressed by candidates who are assertive and show initiative, not only by researching the company, but also by following up once the résumé and cover letter are sent.

Plan to follow up on your letter after about five to seven days (a phone call is usually appropriate). If you call too soon and the employer hasn't yet received your letter or hasn't had a chance to review it, you'll just have to call again. Too many calls may brand you as a pest. On the other hand, don't wait too long, or the employer may forget you. Persistence pays off many times.

SUMMARY

As a recent graduate, you can compete in the job market if you possess the necessary skills and know how to market these skills through effective communication. To identify what skills you possess, you begin by analyzing yourself, using a personal analysis inventory. Completing this inventory documents your strengths and weaknesses in meeting the requirements of a specific job.

Once you have identified and classified your specific qualities and interests, you compare these with traits that recruiters stress. Such information is helpful in establishing a realistic career goal—a goal that is compatible with your qualifications, interests, and identified company needs.

Begin looking for a job using a method that has a proven track record. Continue to use as many methods as necessary to gain success. Using campus recruiters is a good starting place. Before applying for a position, however, make sure you know something about the employing company and how your qualifications meet the organization's goals.

The next step in the employment process is to prepare a well-written résumé. Using established guidelines, you apply the strategy for communicating to the process of writing an effective résumé. Based on your objectives and Reader/Audience, you can Order your résumé to highlight your strengths, using optional categories where relevant. To keep the résumé to a manageable length, furnish references on request. These references are becoming increasingly important to prospective employers interested in verifying application data, so make sure all claims are true.

When preparing the résumé, choose a Format that fits your particular situation. The common types are the basic, the chronological, and the functional; but you may combine these categories or create one of your own to express uniquely your qualifications.

Never send a résumé without an accompanying letter of application. This letter introduces you to the employing firm and provides the convincing evidence that you are the right person for the job. If requested, obtain one or more letters of recommendation from persons acquainted with your qualifications.

If the company does not respond to your application within five to seven days, you may follow up with a phone call or a second letter. Persistence is an important way to set yourself apart from others.

END-OF-CHAPTER ACTIVITIES

DISCUSSION

1. Discuss the three most commonly used Formats for résumés. What are the strengths and weaknesses of each? Which Format do you prefer? Why? Which Format do you feel the employer would prefer? Why?

2. According to concepts presented in this chapter, which method(s) in the job search process has/have proven to be most effective? Least effective?
3. Discuss how you feel about the importance of job "matchup?" Is it more important just to get whatever job you can and then move around as necessary until matchup is achieved, or should you hold out for something directly related to your primary goal?
4. Discuss the meaning of the concept *power from within.*
5. Discuss the importance of GPA as a criterion for prospective employment.

ACTIVITIES

6. Using a form similar to the one illustrated in this chapter, conduct a self-analysis inventory to determine your job marketability. After you complete this form, analyze the information; and from an employer's perspective answer the following questions:
   a. What motivated you to choose your major?
   b. What special skills and/or qualities would you bring to my firm?
   c. Why should I hire you?
   d. What would you like to do five years from now?
   e. Do your grades adequately reflect your capabilities? Why? Why not?
   f. What are your primary goals?
   g. Would you approve of a full background investigation subject to hiring? Why? Why not?
   h. Do you belong to any professional organizations? Which ones? Why did you join? Why not? Do these reflect your primary goals? Secondary goals?
   i. What makes you think you're qualified for the job?
7. Research a *Fortune 500* company. Answer the questions listed in the chapter under the heading "Research Questions." Your reference librarian will help you find available sources of information.
8. Based on the guidelines in this chapter, prepare a winning résumé. Use whichever format best highlights what you have to offer. Using the guidelines presented in this chapter, analyze your résumé to determine its effectiveness.
9. *a.* Select an employment ad from the local newspaper. Plan a strategy for communicating for a résumé and letter of application. Then answer with a résumé and cover letter of application. (Be sure to conduct research to obtain information on the company. Secure the names of all important personnel.)
   b. Use the Precautionary Measures checklist before submitting 9*a* to your instructor.
10. Write an unsolicited letter of application to a major company in your community, applying for a position in the field of your choice.

Figure 18.13

Personal Résumé of:

XXXXXXXXXXXXXXXXXXXX
XXXXXXXXXXXXXXXXXXXXXXXXXXXXX
XXXXXXXXXXXXXXXXXXXXXXXXXXX
XXXXXXXXXXXXXXXX

PERSONAL DATA: Age: 20 Single
Height: 4 feet 9 inches
Weight: 100 pounds
Health: Excellent

EMPLOYMENT RECORD:
September 1987 - Present
Secretary/Customer Service Representative/Receptionist for Casualty Insurance Agencies

December 1986 - June 1987
Guardian Insurance Company of Canada
Mississauga, Ontario, Canada
Receptionist/Claims Department Secretary

February 1986 - December 1986
Thomson Newspapers Limited
Toronto, Ontario, Canada
Secretary to Manager Administration

EDUCATION:
Graduated from Gordon Graydon High School, June 1986
Graduated from Shaw Business College, August 1988
1 year Executive Secretary Program

Typing: 55 words a minute
Speedwriting: 110 words a minute
Accounting: two semesters

Graduated with honor grades

HOBBIES: Member of Ninth Street United Methodist Church
Camping, Reading, Skiing, Swimming, Tennis

REFERENCES: Mr. Gil Terry, District Sales Manager
Nationwide Insurance (205) 350-6142

Mr. Jim Gregory, President
First American Bank (205) 350-6111

11. Refer to the résumés in Figures 18.13, 18.14, and 18.15. (These are actual samples received by prospective employers.) Answer the following questions:
    a. What Format was used for each?
    b. Does the Format best emphasize the applicant's qualifications?
    c. Do the résumés meet the criteria listed on pages 532 and 535?

Figure 18.14

XXXXXXXXXXXX
XXXXXXXXXXXXXX
XXXXXXXXXXXXXXXXXX
XXXXXXXXXXXX

EDUCATION

College

Attended XXXXXXXXXXXXXXXXXXXXXXXXX, majoring in Business Management with a minor in Computer Science.

Business Courses Completed

Personal Finance
Accounting 121
Economics
Introduction to Data Base Systems

High School

Graduated from XXXXXXXXXXXXXX in May 1984. I followed the business curriculum, which included typing, personal development, bookkeeping, and accounting.

Scholastic Honors and Activities

Orange Grove (Institute for Handicapped) .... College
Band .... College
Typing Award .... 80 wpm
Girls' Club President .... High School
Treasurer (Senior Class) .... High School
Band (Award—Outstanding member) .... High School

EXPERIENCE

XXXXXXXXXXXX Nursing Dept., XXXXXXXXX, TN — August 85 - February 86

Held the position of student secretary. I did general office work and operated basic office machinery including a mimeograph machine and IBM word processor.

Figure 18.14
(*concluded*)

XXXXXXXXXXXXXX, Estes Park, CO May 85 - August 85
Served as part of Food Service team both in restaurant and for special catered parties. Also acted as a substitute for the housekeeping staff when needed.

Tupperware, Huntsville, AL May 84 - August 84
Self-employed as a sales representative. This position required self-motivation as well as time management and interpersonal communication skills.

SPECIAL INTERESTS

Enjoy working with the hearing-impaired and handicapped. I am proficient in sign language and have done voluntary work as an interpreter. Hobbies include working on my pilot's license, snow and water skiing, horseback riding, reading and photography.

PERSONAL DATA

Birth Date: June 12, 1966
Physical: Weight, 120; height, 5′5″
Health: Good

REFERENCES

XXXXXXXXXXXXXXXXXXXXXXXXX, 333 Wonderview, P. O. Box 1767, Estes Park, Colorado 80517
Telephone: (303) 586-3371

XXXXXXXXXXX, Office Manager, Nursing Department of XXXXXXXX XXXXXXXXXXXXXXXXXXXXXXXXXXXXXXXXXXXXXXXX
Telephone: (615) 238-2940

XXXXXXXXXXXXXXX, Route #1, P. O. Box 272A, Arden, NC 28704
Telephone: (704) 684-3422

Figure 18.15

XXXXXX
XX
XXXXXXXXXXXXXXXXXX

PERSONAL

XXXXXXXXXXXXXXXXXX
XXXXXXXXXXXXXXXXXXXX
XXXXXXXXXXXXXXX

CAREER GOAL

I am seeking a responsible position where I will contribute to the progress of the company as well as my self-development. My educational background, self-motivation, and ability to interact with people at all levels, qualify me for a challenging and demanding position.

EDUCATION

Columbia University Columbia College, New York, NY September, 1984 to May, 1988	Graduated with a B.A. degree in Economics

EXPERIENCE

January, 1988 to May 1988	John Jay Dining Services, Columbia University. Worked on catering staff.
September, 1986 to May 1987	Various part-time jobs for Columbia University Physical Education Department.
September, 1985 to May 1986	Student Refreshment Agency, Columbia University. Comanager in charge of various aspects of selling refreshments at Columbia University football games.
Summers 1987 and 1988	Teledyne Brown Engineering, Huntsville, Alabama. Draftsman in the Design Drafting Department.

Figure 18.15
(concluded)

Summer 1986	Huntsville Country Club, Huntsville, Alabama. Pool Manager responsible for all segments of pool operation including pool maintenance and scheduling and supervising of staff.
Summer 1985	Monte Sano Pool, Huntsville, Alabama. Assistant Manager and Swim Team Coach. Assumed manager's duties in his absence. Coached swim team consisting of 80 members ages 5–17.
	Note: The above jobs helped to finance more than half of my college education.
ACTIVITIES	
1984–1988	Columbia University Swimming and Diving Team. Four-year major letter winner. Cocaptain 1987–1988 season. University recordholder in 50 yard freestyle.
1986–1988	Charter Member of the Kappa Delta Rho Fraternity at Columbia University. Officer 1987–1988.
1982–1984	Huntsville High School Physics Club President.
1982–1984	Huntsville High School Mu Alpha Theta (National Math Honor Society).
1984	Elected Most School Spirited by peers at Huntsville High School.

CHAPTER 19

PREPARING FOR THE INTERVIEW

Learning Objectives

After studying this chapter, you will be able to:

- □ Understand the types of questions interviewers ask before and after the job offer.
- □ Analyze interviewer's questions from a legal point of view.
- □ Develop a portfolio to use for prospective employment.
- □ Write these types of communications as they relate to the employment process: confirmation letter, follow-up letter, acceptance letter, declining a job offer letter, and resignation letter.
- □ Understand how to prepare for the interview: what to wear, what to take, what to expect, when to arrive.
- □ Develop expertise for conducting yourself in the interview process—reception stage, interview stage, and departure stage.
- □ Assess the advantages and disadvantages of video interviewing.
- □ Evaluate employment documents.

Criteria for passing the interview

Up to now, you have been involved mainly with homework, preparing to look for a new job. The most important test in securing a job is still to come. You must pass the interview test, where your oral, listening, and nonverbal skills are assessed.

Interview advertises you

When you send a résumé and letter of application to a firm, your written communication is the focal point for assessing your capabilities. If you pass the test, you get an interview invitation. But how can the employer know for certain that you were the one who wrote the letter and prepared the résumé? Before purchasing, the buyer wants to make sure the merchandise is as good or better than its advertisement. In the interview process, you are the merchandise. The interview allows the employer to make a final assessment.

Elements associated with the interview

In this chapter, all phases of the business interview are discussed. Samples of recommendation, thank you, acceptance, rejection, and resignation letters are included.

PREPARING FOR THE INTERVIEW

As a result of your job hunt, assume you have just secured an interview appointment. The purpose of the interview is to find out if your goals and the goals of the organization are compatible. You should assume they are and go prepared to sell yourself, because you most likely won't get a second chance. Other goals are:

Goals of the interview

- ☐ To answer successfully any questions the interviewer may have.
- ☐ To obtain information about the organization to help make a wise decision.
- ☐ To establish a positive relationship with the interviewer.
- ☐ To be confident; to be positive about the opportunity to become a successful employee in the organization.
- ☐ To present yourself as someone whom this firm would be lucky to get on its team.

Assessing the interviewers

Keep in mind that several persons may interview you once you arrive. Do some more homework. Study again the information you have obtained on this company. Gather additional materials, if needed, to help you determine what the interviewers are like. Some possibilities would include: name, male/female, number of years with the organization, universities attended, and primary interests.

Anticipating Questions

Interviewers have in mind what qualifications they are seeking in job candidates. Even though the interviewer may not ask these questions directly, he or she may need to supply this type of information to others in the company. The list of needed information will probably look something like this:

LEGAL / ETHICAL ISSUE

Angie Good has just received her Bachelor of Science degree in Business Administration with a major in Management Information Systems (MIS) from Baylor University. She maintained a 3.2 GPA during her four years of study. In addition to her MIS courses, Angie took a number of elective courses in accounting and management. She was active in numerous societies and extracurricular activities. Her long-range goal is to become a manager of information systems with a Big-Eight accounting firm.

Angie is now in the process of interviewing. She has already interviewed with six well-known firms. She is scheduled to interview with a seventh firm two weeks from today. This firm is really the one Angie has her heart set on—ideal location, excellent salary and benefits, and good promotion potential. Angie is just sure that a few years' experience with this company will assist her with moving into a managerial position in a Big-Eight firm.

When Angie interviewed with the firm of her choice, she was asked some of the standard questions one would expect in an interview. She was taken aback, however, when the personnel manager subtly asked these questions: How soon do you expect to be married and raise a family? What is your religious affiliation? Have you ever been discharged by an employer?

Are there legal or ethical improprieties with asking these types of questions during an interview? If so, what are they? Discuss.

Interviewers assess your qualifications for their company

- ☐ Why should I hire you?
- ☐ What kind of person are you?
- ☐ What kind of employee will you be? Are you willing to take responsibility as well as directions? Will you be productive, loyal, creative, entrepreneurial, enthusiastic?
- ☐ Have you demonstrated a sustained interest in this work?
- ☐ Do your credentials demonstrate that you are a purposeful individual who gets things done?
- ☐ How much will you cost us?
- ☐ What haven't you told us about yourself?
- ☐ Will you work well with your supervisors and other employees in this organization?
- ☐ How long will you stay with us before you start looking for another job?

Figure 19.1

The 50 Questions Most Often Asked in an Interview

Your Career Goals

- ☐ Why did you want to join our organization?
- ☐ Why do you think you are qualified for this position?
- ☐ Why are you looking for another job?
- ☐ Why do you want to make a career change?
- ☐ What ideally would you like to do?
- ☐ Why should we hire you?
- ☐ How do we know you can produce practical results, meet deadlines, tend to details?
- ☐ How would you improve our operations?
- ☐ What is the lowest pay you will accept?
- ☐ How much do you think you are worth for this job?
- ☐ What do you want to be doing five years from now?
- ☐ How much do you want to be making five years from now?
- ☐ What are your short-range and long-range career goals?
- ☐ If you could choose your job and organization, where would you go?
- ☐ What other types of jobs are you considering? Other companies?
- ☐ When will you be ready to begin work?
- ☐ How do you feel about relocating, traveling, working overtime, weekend work?

Your Educational Background

- ☐ Describe your educational background.
- ☐ Why did you attend State University?
- ☐ Why did you major in communications?
- ☐ What was your grade point average?
- ☐ What subjects did you enjoy the most? The least?
- ☐ What leadership positions did you hold?
- ☐ How did you finance your education?
- ☐ If you started all over, what would you change about your education?
- ☐ Why were your grades so low? So high?

Types of questions interviewers ask

Place yourself in the role of the interviewer and develop a list of questions that would secure that information. As an interviewer, you may want to put the applicant on the defensive to see how she/he can handle questions under fire. You may want to ask some tricky questions to get the applicant to open up and discuss areas unrelated to the question. Figure 19.1 can serve as a guide for the general questions interviewers ask. Add to this list specific questions related to your particular field.

The interview works two ways—as a fact-finding mission for the *interviewer* and as a fact-finding mission for *you*. With every interview, strive for a job offer. Even if the position is not ideal, you should proceed as if it were, because it could very well lead to your ultimate goal. The interviewer can be acquainted with professionals in other organizations who can use your skills if this interview does not result in a matchup.

Figure 19.1
(*concluded*)

Your Work Experience

- ☐ What were your major achievements in each of your past jobs?
- ☐ Why did you change jobs?
- ☐ What is your typical workday like?
- ☐ What functions do you enjoy doing the most?
- ☐ What did you like about your boss? Dislike?
- ☐ Which job did you enjoy the most? Why? Which job did you enjoy the least? Why?
- ☐ Have you ever been fired? Why?

Your Personality and Other Considerations

- ☐ Tell me about yourself.
- ☐ What are your major weaknesses? Your major strengths?
- ☐ What causes you to lose your temper?
- ☐ What do you do in your spare time? Any hobbies?
- ☐ What types of books do you read?
- ☐ What role does your family play in your career?
- ☐ How well do you work under pressure? In meeting deadlines?
- ☐ Can you adapt to change—especially unplanned change—in a dynamic work environment?
- ☐ Tell me about your management philosophy.
- ☐ How much initiative do you take?
- ☐ What types of people do you prefer working with?
- ☐ How creative or analytical, tactful, etc. are you?
- ☐ If you could change your life, what would you do differently?
- ☐ Who are your references?

Stressing the positive when answering questions

Your answers should reflect how you can best serve the organization where you are interviewing. Don't say anything negative about yourself, your past jobs, past bosses, problems at home, your fears, or failures. Your objective is to inspire confidence in your ability to handle the job, and you do this by having confidence in yourself.

Develop two groups of questions for which *you* want answers:

Types of questions you ask before and after job offer

- ☐ Questions *before* a job offer.
- ☐ Questions *after* a job offer.

The first group of questions is aimed at finding out how well your career goals match the needs of the organization. The second is aimed at determining whether the salary and benefits of the organization are compatible with your expectations. Figure 19.2 includes some openers to help you get started.

Figure 19.2

Questions You Might Ask Prior to Job Offer

- ☐ What duties and responsibilities does this job entail?
- ☐ Is this a new position?
- ☐ For what kind of person are you looking?
- ☐ When was the last person promoted in the department?
- ☐ To whom would I report? Tell me a little about these people.
- ☐ Would I seem to fit in with them?
- ☐ What are your expectations for me?
- ☐ May I talk with present and previous employees about this job and organization?
- ☐ What problems might I expect to encounter on this job? (Efficiency, quality control, declining profits, internal politics, evaluation.)
- ☐ What has been done recently in regard to (example: turnover rate)?
- ☐ How long have you been with this company?

Questions You Might Ask after a Job Offer

- ☐ What is the normal pay range for this job?
- ☐ Based on my qualifications and/or experience, do you think a higher salary could be justified?
- ☐ Can you tell me about promotions and advancements with your company?
- ☐ Please explain the company benefits.
- ☐ I appreciate your offer. When do you need my decision?

After the interview, the company may respond with any one of several reactions. Be prepared for all possible responses:

Reactions from the company after the interview

- ☐ The company wants you to begin work immediately in the position which most interests you.
- ☐ The company wants you to begin work immediately, but in a position that is less than what you anticipated.
- ☐ The company wants you to begin work immediately in the position which most interests you, but at a salary less than you expected.
- ☐ The company wants you to begin work immediately in the position in which you are most interested, but for a probationary period of six months or a year.
- ☐ The company is interested in you as a possible employee, but wishes to interview several other applicants before making a decision.
- ☐ The company is interested in you as a possible employee, but is concerned about your ability to handle certain phases of the job.
- ☐ The company is interested in you as a possible employee, but needs additional information, references, evidence of your qualifications, etc.
- ☐ The company feels you are not the person for the job.

Your Right to Privacy

The legality of interviewer questions

The law does not allow employers to discriminate on the basis of race, age, sex, religion, or national origin. Be aware that any questions relating to these or other personal areas such as marital status, child-care arrangements, spouse, health condition, etc. are illegal, unless they are job-related. For example, employers do not have the right to ask your age, but they can ask if you meet the minimum requirement for a job for which all applicants must be 18 years old. They cannot ask you how much you weigh unless weight is a requirement for the job, such as that of a horse jockey or a position requiring heavy manual labor.

If an interviewer should infringe on your right to privacy, the best answer would probably be "Mr./Mrs. ______________, how does that question relate to this position?" Always be tactful. The interviewer may just be nervous and groping for some questions to ask.

The Rehearsal

Ideas for practicing an interview

The final rehearsal helps give you confidence. You can smooth some remaining rough edges; and you will be less nervous, having practiced for the real thing.

Practice with a tape recorder, in front of a full-length mirror, or with a family member or friend. Answer each question on your list. If someone else is interviewing you, have them ask you some unplanned questions, not on your list. See if you sound sure of yourself or if you hesitate in places which might indicate a weakness. Be aware of your facial expressions, the way you sit, and any annoying gestures. Keep practicing until you sound and look convincing.

MANAGING YOURSELF IN THE INTERVIEW

Role of the interviewee and the interviewer

Keep in mind that you are responsible for managing yourself in the interview. You decide how you will respond to the questions asked, how you will look, what you will say, how much you will reveal about yourself, and what image you will present. Even though the interviewer determines the style, length, and time of the interview, the meeting will center on you. You are the one in control.

Stages of managing the interview

This self-management procedure is divided into four stages: the before stage, the greeting stage, the consultation stage, and the departure stage.

The Before Stage

Confirming the interview by letter

Whether you were contacted for the interview by phone or letter, write a short letter to confirm the date, time, and place and state that you look forward to the meeting.

Major points to consider when preparing for the interview

Concentrate on your appearance. Wear conservative clothes, such as a tan, gray, or blue, wrinkle-free suit with a light shirt for men and an appropriate blouse for women. Hair and nails should be well-groomed. For the impor-

What to wear

tance of dress and nonverbal behavior, review Chapter 20 entitled "Speaking in Business." Business executives want people whose looks will enhance their firm's image.

What to take

Go prepared with a portfolio—a collection of related documents placed loosely in a cover or folder. This collection may include a brief one-page list of notes describing selling points about yourself, the company, and/or the person who will interview you; a notebook; two pens; extra résumés; a transcript of your grades; written samples of your work (reports, printed articles, sketches); list of references; and letters of recommendation from past employers. Impress the interviewers by producing these materials on request.

What to expect

Go to the interview with a time schedule that does not pressure you in any way. The interviewer may ask you to stay for additional interviews with other officers, to take a written test or fill out appropriate application papers. Be ready to respond to such requests positively and courteously; take whatever time they request to evaluate properly your skills.

When to arrive

Arrive at the interviewer's office at least 15 minutes before the scheduled appointment. If you get there 20 minutes ahead of schedule, spend 15 minutes relaxing and going over your notes. If you are traveling by plane, arrive in plenty of time, looking fresh and energetic.

Don't make the mistake of being off guard with the company driver who picks you up or with the receptionist who greets you in the waiting room. *Every employee is a representative* for his/her company. The impression you make with these representatives *is part of the interview* and is almost certain to be passed along.

The Greeting Stage

You and the reception area

Greet everyone courteously with a warm smile and a friendly hello. Don't underestimate the influence each person in the organization has in the decision-making process. Use some waiting room smarts. Keep your notebook handy and write down the names of all persons you meet, including those who assist you with the interview process. If you do read, pick up only professional journals. Again, this would be a good time to review your notes.

Meeting key employees

Once you are announced, thank the secretary and then greet the interviewer with a firm handshake. Stand tall and wait until you are asked to be seated. Use a title—Miss, Ms., Mr., Mrs., Dr.—unless you are invited to do otherwise. Don't assume anything.

The Consultation Stage

Principles regarding dialogue with the interviewer

Be responsive and enthusiastic during the interview but don't take over. Establish eye contact with the employer and *read* her/his reactions. Know when to interject key points about yourself and about the company. Be yourself and display sincere interest in how you can contribute to the goals of

Figure 19.3
Managing yourself in the interview

Do

- ☐ Establish eye-to-eye contact.
- ☐ Show positive attitude.
- ☐ Express interest and desire for job.
- ☐ Ensure that the interviewer knows what you can offer.
- ☐ Listen.
- ☐ Answer questions directly and quickly.
- ☐ Be positive.
- ☐ Speak clearly, enthusiastically.

Don't

- ☐ Smoke, chew gum or tobacco.
- ☐ Give one- or two-word answers.
- ☐ Lie—just accentuate the positive.
- ☐ Look at your watch.
- ☐ Be nervous.
- ☐ Take over the interview.
- ☐ Ask "what's-in-it-for-me" questions (benefits—vacations—holidays).
- ☐ Discuss personal, home, money problems.
- ☐ Appear hostile or defensive.
- ☐ Read or touch anything on the interviewer's desk.
- ☐ Overuse "ma'am" or "sir."
- ☐ Interrupt.
- ☐ Criticize former employers or bosses.
- ☐ Use profanity.

that organization. Let the interviewer know that you are a hard worker and what skills you have to offer. You have a right to be proud of your past performance. Listen intently. Part of the evaluation will be an assessment of how well you listen and directly answer questions.

The guidelines presented in Figure 19.3 are key considerations for managing this stage of the interview.

The Departure Stage

Expressing appreciation for the interview and desire to work for the company

Leave on a positive note. Express appreciation for the interview. Let the employer know you are extremely interested in the job and that the interview only further substantiated your desire to work for this company. There is nothing wrong with stating that "I'd really like to be part of this growing organization." Shake hands again. Then leave promptly and courteously.

Immediately after the interview, make notes that will help in the follow-up process. While ideas are clear in your mind, write down key points and the names of persons associated with these points.

The Video Interview

Interviews via satellite

An alternative to the face-to-face interview is the interview conducted via satellite and videophone. For example, in 1987 Video Placement Co., Pembroke, Massachusetts, signed five-year contracts with 25 universities for conducting on-campus satellite/videophone interviews with recruiters of major companies throughout the country.[1] This type system allows full-motion teleconferencing and is comfortable to use. Direct eye contact with the interviewer by satellite provides the feeling that you are sitting in the same room. Some researchers think this may soon be a common way of conducting initial interviews.

Benefits of video interviews via satellite

The benefits of such a service include a lower interview cost because of reduced travel, lodging, and dining expenses; better screening of applicants by more company officials; better access to qualified persons in remote areas; and easier conduct of follow-up interviews.

Interviews by videotape

The techniques for managing satellite/videophone interviews are the same as those for face-to-face interviews. Your verbal, nonverbal, and listening skills are evaluated the same as if you were physically present.

In another method of interviewing, an agency videotapes a candidate according to employer specifications. Corporate Interviewing Network (CIN), based in Fort Lauderdale, Florida, currently operates such a system for 20 locations throughout the United States and plans to expand to 120 locations. With offices located in major cities, CIN will conduct interviews in the candidate's hometown or near locality. The videotape is then sent to the prospective employer for evaluation. The employer pays a fee based on the length of the interview, the degree that the interview is customized, and whether the employee is hired. Again, the main benefits are savings in time and money and the convenience for prospective employers. Major drawbacks of videotape interviews are the lack of personalization in the interview and the employer's inability to evaluate the candidate objectively.[2] Check with your university's placement office to see if training is offered for video interviews. In the future, selling yourself may depend on your ability to be at ease in front of a camera.

Advantages and disadvantages of videotapes

FOLLOWING UP

On the same day as the interview, if possible, write a letter and thank each person who interviewed you. If someone helped you get the interview, write to this person also.

---

[1] Therese R. Welter, "Interviewing for a Job—by Satellite," *Industry Week* 233 (May 18, 1987), p. 94.

[2] William G. Flanagan, "Interview—Take One!." *Forbes* 136 (November 18, 1985), pp. 244-46.

Saying "Thank You"

Points to include in your follow-up letter

The letter should be short and typed on quality paper. Thank the interviewer for the time and consideration given, reaffirm your interest in the position, and add one or two selling points gently to encourage them to consider you further. Consider this example:

Dear Ms. Hopson:

Simple "thank you" for the interview letter

Thank you for taking the time to discuss the Financial Assistant position available in your company. After carefully weighing the points you made about the key elements of this position, I am confident that my competencies, training, and experience qualify me for the job.

As we discussed during the interview, I enjoy a challenge and working under pressure. Those quarterly analysis reports would pose no problem to me.

May we discuss further my qualifications for the various tasks required in this position? I look forward to hearing from you soon.

Sincerely,

Making a "Call-Back"

What to expect from a second interview

Companies usually inform candidates of the outcome of the interview within a week or 10 days. Some candidates are asked to come in for a second interview, since the interview process is a narrowing down of the candidates under consideration. For instance, out of 100 candidates applying, 10 might be selected for the first interview. If you are selected for a second interview, you're among the final candidates. For a second interview, concentrate on what took place during the first one. You should have a better idea of the position and exactly what the company wants. This final interview is a matter of how well you sell yourself in comparison with the other final candidates.

Assess the situation when you do not hear from a company

Determine why you were not selected for a job

If you don't hear from the company within two weeks, call back or write another follow-up letter and inquire about the status of your application. If a decision has not been made, ask if you can provide any further information. If a selection has been made and you were turned down, try to find out the deciding factor. Approach the interviewer with a sincere desire to find out the reason the company decided to hire someone else. You may gain valuable information that will assist you in future job interviews. Every piece of information you can acquire about yourself is part of the strategy for succeeding.

Accepting a Job Offer

Accepting a position by letter

Once you receive a job offer, take a few days to consider all elements of the offer before accepting. Go over your personal analysis inventory and check the actual job requirements against the desired job requirements.

If the job isn't really what you want, chances are you will look again in a

Figure 19.4
Sample acceptance letter

XXXXXXXXXXXXXXXXXXXXX
XXXXXXXXXXXXXXXXXX
March 26, 19__

Mr. Jonathan Cherne
XXXXXXXXXXXXXXXXXXXXXXX
XXXXXXXXXXX XX XXXXX

Dear Mr. Cherne

Thank you for your offer to become a Systems Analyst II for your firm. The offer and beginning date of April 1, 19__ are acceptable.

As requested in your letter, the necessary paperwork will be completed in your office on Monday, March 31. At that time, I will bring in the report from my physician, Dr. Howard.

Mr. Cherne, your confidence in my abilities is very much appreciated. I am eager to accept the challenges of the position and to use my talents to work for your organization.

Sincerely,

XXXXXXXXXXXXXXXX

few months. Don't jump at the first offer that comes along unless, of course, this really leads to your ultimate objective.

If you do decide to accept, call the interviewer right away. Then write a letter of acceptance within five to seven days. Figure 19.4 is a sample acceptance letter. Notice the writer of this sample uses the direct approach, assuming that the manager wants to hear the good news first.

Figure 19.5
Sample letter declining a job offer

XXXXXXXXXXXXXXXXXX
XXXXXXXXXXXXXXX
July 3, 19__

XXXXXXXXXXXXXXXXXXXXXX
XXXXXXXXXXXXXXXXXXXX
XXXXXXXXXX XX XXXXX

Dear XXXXXXXXXXXXXX:

Thank you for your July 2 letter offering a position as Marketing Representative for your firm. Your firm has much to offer applicants interested in pursuing a marketing career.

Based on a careful analysis of your offer in light of my career objective to research and analyze consumer needs, I must decline the position at this time. Since my expertise is mainly in the area of market analysis, work in this area would enable me to progress more quickly in my career goals.

Mr. ______________, thank you for the confidence you have expressed in me. Should a market analyst position become available in your firm, please keep me in mind.

Thank you again for your consideration.

Sincerely,

XXXXXXXXXXXX XXXXXX

Declining a Job Offer

If your personal analysis inventory suggests that an offer is not a good matchup or the salary is inadequate, write a letter declining the offer.

Expressing your intent to decline the job offer

This letter should express your appreciation for the offer and for the courtesies extended by the interviewer. In Figure 19.5 the writer uses an indirect approach and tactfully expresses the reasons for declining. If your reasons for not accepting the offer are valid and you express these reasons tactfully, you leave the door open for further negotiations should other positions open up for which you are qualified.

Resigning Your Present Job

Writing the letter to announce your resignation

If you are now employed and receive a job offer from another firm, a letter of resignation will allow you to leave the firm on a positive note. Departing with a positive relationship is important, because your present firm can serve as a good reference for later positions. You might even want to return someday if the right position opens up. Figure 19.6 is a good example of a letter of resignation.

In this type of letter, give the firm as much advance notice as possible to obtain a replacement. With a little courtesy, you can resign a position and still maintain good relationships with your former colleagues.

SUMMARY

The purpose of the interview is to find out if your goals and the goals of an organization are compatible. Other goals of the interview are: to answer questions successfully, obtain any additional information needed to make a decision, accent your special strengths, establish a positive relationship, show confidence, and to sell yourself. Based on these goals, place yourself in the role of the interviewer and develop anticipated questions and answers to three categories: company data, personnel data, and specific job data. You also develop questions which you will ask to determine how well your career goals match the needs of the organization. These questions include both those you would ask before a job offer and those you would ask after a job offer.

Prior to the interview, acquaint yourself with the laws pertaining to job discrimination. This knowledge will enhance your chances of being considered on an equal standing with other applicants.

To develop confidence, adequately prepare for the interview. Focus on how you can best serve the organization to which you are applying. Then rehearse until the rough edges are smoothed and you sound convincing to those with whom you have practiced.

Since the interview will center on you, proper self-management will greatly enhance your chances of being extended an offer. The self-management process is divided into four stages: the before stage, the greeting stage, the consultation stage, and the departure stage. The before stage includes writing a confirmation letter, concentrating on appearance and nonverbal communication, developing your portfolio, anticipating questions with positive responses, and arriving early. The greeting stage includes greeting everyone courteously, using waiting-room smarts, using your time wisely, and applying proper protocol when meeting the interviewer. The consultation stage includes responsiveness and enthusiasm, knowing when to interject key points, showing sincerity, highlighting your strengths, and listening

Figure 19.6
Sample letter of resignation

November 20, 19__

XXXXXXXXXXXXXXXXXXXX
XXXXXXXXXXXXXXX
XXXXXXXXXXXXX XX XXXXX

Dear XXXXXXXX:

Thank you for allowing me to work for one of the finest firms in the XXXXXXX area. As you know, without this job, the completion of my educational goals would not be possible.

In three more weeks, I will graduate with a degree in computer science. As a result, I have been offered a position with XXXXXXXX where my computer skills will be fully utilized. Therefore, please accept my resignation effective Friday, January 6.

The experience and insights gained from my present office management position are invaluable. I am grateful for the numerous skills you have taught me, many of which have direct application to my new job duties.

Let me know if I can assist you in training a replacement. My services are available.

Thanks so much for the opportunity to work with such a fine group of people.

Sincerely,

XXXXXXXXXXXXX

intently. The departure stage includes leaving on a positive note, expressing appreciation, expressing interest, leaving promptly, and making notes immediately after departure.

To save time and money and offer convenience to prospective employees and employers, video taping and satellite videophones may become a common method of interviewing. Being at ease in front of a camera would be important for these types of interviews.

Following the interview, write thank-you letters to each person who interviewed you and to those who helped you get the interview. When invited for a second interview, go prepared by using your notes and feedback from the first interview to zero in on what the company wants. If the company doesn't respond in two weeks, call back or write a follow-up letter. You may get turned down. If so, try to find out why as a means of self-improvement.

Following a job offer, take a few days to consider all elements and then call or write a letter either accepting or declining the offer—whichever is appropriate. If you accept and you are presently employed, write an effective letter of resignation, departing on a positive note.

END-OF-CHAPTER ACTIVITIES

DISCUSSION

1. Discuss the importance of finding out the names of the personnel who may interview you for a prospective job.
2. Discuss your perceptions of the five most difficult questions to answer from "The 50 questions most often asked in the interview." Defend your choices.
3. Discuss how much control the interviewer and the interviewee each has in the employment process.
4. Do you believe that a prospective employer should have the right to ask questions concerning such factors as race, religion, age, child care? Discuss and support your comments.
5. Do you believe that a prospective employer should have the right to an interviewee's personal and employment history? Discuss.
6. What are the factors involved in managing yourself in the interview? Discuss and elaborate on each.
7. Compare and contrast an interview which uses the traditional method with that of the video technique medium.
8. What characteristics differentiate these types of letters: thank-you letter, letter of acceptance, declining a job offer, and letter of resignation? Discuss.

ACTIVITIES

9. Assume you secured an interview as a result of a previously submitted letter of application. Supply your own details and write a thank-you letter to the interviewer.
10. You have not heard the results of the interview above and two weeks have passed. Supply your own details and write a follow-up letter.
11. Check with your placement office and set up a meeting with the next recruiters on campus. Supply your own details and write a thank-you letter to both the recruiter and the placement office.

12. Assume you have just been offered a position for which you have applied. Supply your own details and write a letter of acceptance.
13. Assume you are now employed and must write a letter of resignation to your present employer. Supply your own details and write an effective resignation letter.
14. Go to the library and research information pertaining to the latest discriminatory practices related to job employment. Present a report in written and/or oral form.
15. Go to the library and research video interviewing. Defend the pros and cons of this method of interviewing.
16. Select a classmate and role play the interview process. Using the content of Figure 19.1 as a basis for this simulation, conduct the interview; then reverse roles so that each of you has the opportunity to serve as the interviewer and the interviewee.

CHAPTER 20

SPEAKING IN BUSINESS

Learning Objectives

After studying this chapter, you will be able to:

- □ Assess the value of oral communication for a business environment.
- □ Apply the strategy for communicating to an oral presentation.
- □ Understand how to obtain listener feedback, both formally and informally.
- □ Deliver an oral presentation from a prepared manuscript from memory or extemporaneously, using notes or cue cards.
- □ Prepare an effective presentation applying the elements of the PMM concept.
- □ Develop oral communication skills for one-on-one meetings, small-group meetings, and large-group meetings.
- □ Apply the strategy for communicating to conducting a meeting.
- □ Understand what constitutes good listening.

Oral communication skills—the great human connector

Effective speaking is one of the most powerful skills you can possess. In fact, this skill could be called the *great human connector* since it serves as a connecting link for you to share and discuss ideas, interests, and opinions and form relationships with others.

Oral communication skills preferred

In the past few years, business executives have begun to realize how vital effective oral communication is in building confidence, trust, and commitment between organizations and people in general. Corporate executives no longer trust the written report as the primary way to convey information. Instead, they deliver speeches to the general public on everything from problems affecting the economy to specific issues which influence their thinking. Some executives spend half their time giving speeches, according to recent reports.

Oral communication within the organization

Even though business executives make speeches for all types of occasions to all types of audiences, most speeches are given within the organization. Some examples are a board of directors meeting, a sales presentation, and a marketing meeting. Given these facts, what do you think your chances are for delivering a speech once you enter the marketplace? You will probably begin performing this art *before* you reach that point—either at school, in church, for clubs, or for special functions.

THE ORAL PRESENTATION

Whether speaking at a board meeting or campaigning for office, you must first understand the *why* of the communication. To determine the why of an oral presentation, ask yourself these questions: "What am I expecting to achieve by delivering this speech? Do I want action? Feedback? Sympathy? Support? Sales? Sharing of ideas?"

All steps in the planning process derive from this first step. Without a plan that addresses the why, your first impulse is immediately to begin developing the message itself. Speakers who begin in this way tend to concentrate on what they are going to say more than on the results they hope to attain. Ignoring the why might cause the audience to become restless and the message to fail in meeting its purpose. Always plan for an oral presentation around the why or the desired outcome.

Understanding the desired outcomes (the why) and understanding the objectives (the *what*) complement each other. People who stand up to speak and don't fully understand the central idea they are to get across, tend to ramble. They may know everything there is to know about the subject, but unless they understand the objective, the message will have little meaning.

Most messages you deliver will have one of three specific objectives: to *celebrate,* to *inform,* or to *persuade.* Let's consider the meaning of these words:

Celebrate—to recognize or acknowledge a person, an event, an occasion, or an organizational theme. This category includes those messages used to inspire or entertain: commencement awards,

LEGAL / ETHICAL ISSUE

Techtronics Company is a large manufacturer of telecommunications equipment. The company is known for its interest in employee development through in-house training programs and free tuition for job-related courses at local educational centers.

Doris Johnson has worked as a secretary at Techtronics for three years. Her work has always been of the highest quality. She is well liked by her superiors and peers. Doris recently discussed with her supervisor Thomas Walker the possibility of pursuing the Certified Professional Secretary (CPS) status with hopes of promotion to an administrative assistant position within the company. She also requests CPS review courses at the expense of the company.

Doris's supervisor recognizes her potential and approves her request. He further promises orally that he will see that she receives a promotion within the next year if she passes the CPS exam. The next week, Doris receives in writing her approval to take the CPS review courses plus an approval form for submission to a local university offering the review courses. Nothing was indicated concerning a promotion.

After Doris successfully completed the exam and received notification of her CPS status, she reminded her supervisor Mr. Walker of the promised promotion. Mr. Walker acted surprised and stated he recalled no such promise.

Since Mr. Walker stated the promise of promotion orally, what legal action, if any, can Doris take? What ethical issues are involved? Discuss.

retirement addresses, achievement awards, founder's day speeches, and other congratulatory speeches.

Inform—to present facts, issues, events. This category also includes instructional and training presentations. Most messages probably are in this category.

Persuade—to convince or motivate listeners to think or act in accordance with the speaker. Examples of this category include messages used to sell products or services, support political candidates or issues, or to motivate listeners to change some behavior.

Understanding Your Listeners

Your message should address the needs, interests, and experience levels of your listeners. The same concepts for the Reader apply to a *Listener*. To understand better who your listeners are, ask yourself these questions:

- □ Are my listeners clients, potential customers, colleagues, strangers, supervisors?

Understanding your Listener/Audience

- □ Are they similar in age and background, or are they widely varied?
- □ What do they want to hear from me?
- □ What questions will they probably want answered?
- □ What are their social, political, economic, and ethnic backgrounds? Will they be friendly or hostile?
- □ Is the audience composed mostly of women or men?
- □ How many people will be listening to me?
- □ Where will the meeting be held?

By answering these questions, you can anticipate how your audience will respond to what you say. Learn as much as you can about your listeners. The clearer your perceptions of the audience, the better are your chances for success.

Getting Feedback

Feedback defined

You really don't know if you have met all your objectives until you receive *feedback* from your listeners. You can obtain this feedback either formally or informally. However, not all presentations need feedback. Speeches delivered primarily to celebrate an event, recognize an achievement, or acknowledge a milestone, will probably need no feedback, because you achieve your desired outcome by delivering the speech itself. In contrast, for those messages intended to inform or persuade, you need some feedback. Otherwise, you have no way of determining if you achieved the desired outcome.

Ways to obtain informal feedback

You can obtain *informal feedback* by chatting with the listeners after the presentation. Reactions and comments from the listeners are measures of how well they understood the message, providing valuable insight for future presentations.

Ways to obtain formal feedback

Formal feedback can be in writing or orally, as in the question-and-answer phase of many speeches. To save the listeners' time, provide a checklist of key elements of the presentation. Leave a space for additional comments on your handout to give your listeners some latitude in responding.

In the question-and-answer session, plan carefully so that you do not lose control of the meeting. Here are some suggestions for maintaining control:

1. Plan for this session by anticipating the questions your listeners will most likely ask.
2. If the outcome of the presentation is vital to the organization, conduct a dry run by delivering the presentation to a group of key corporate personnel with a question-and-answer follow-up. Many of the questions asked will probably be similar to the ones asked by the listeners.
3. Come to the question-and-answer session with additional backup materials, all relevant statistics, technical and financial data, supporting documents. Convince an audience of your preparedness.

Planning for a question/answer session

4. If you anticipate technical questions which might require additional expertise, ask a couple of technical people from your organization to assist you at the session to provide the data needed.
5. If you don't know the answer, say so. You can offer to send an answer or you may state that "additional study is needed before providing a clear answer."
6. Come with a list of questions as backup. Use these at the beginning of the session while waiting for audience response. Begin by saying, "The question I am most often asked is . . . ." or "Last week someone asked . . . ."
7. If the listeners react negatively to your response, be ready to shift gears when necessary to obtain the desired results. This step would be relevant to sessions where the desired outcome is a signed contract, a sale, a job, a political goal.
8. If the audience is large, repeat the question for all to hear. Then answer the question directly. Don't ramble or give the impression of uncertainty.

Failure to handle the question-and-answer session could result in a lost sale, a lost job, a lost raise, or a lost election.

Methods of Delivery

The most common methods for delivering speeches include *reading from a prepared manuscript, delivering from memory,* or *delivering extemporaneously* by relying on brief notes or cue cards. Which method you choose depends on the Problem, Objective, and Audience as well as your own preferences.

A *prepared manuscript* is especially appropriate when your goal is to deliver an exact, structured message. Suppose that you are chosen to deliver a 30- to 35-minute keynote address at this years annual meeting of the National Association of Students in Management (NASM). In addition to your role as principal speaker, you're responsible for introducing three other speakers and the six officers elected for next year. If you have an excellent memory, you could deliver your address and the introductions extemporaneously. Few speakers, however, would trust their memory alone on such an occasion. Because you want to get everything right, you'll probably choose to use a prepared speech or, at the very least, an excellent set of notes.

The prepared manuscript presentation defined

What if your task is to deliver an expert opinion before a body of scholars on a highly controversial subject? What if the audience is hostile or highly skeptical? You'll probably feel more confident having exact quotations, statistics, or other materials at your fingertips.

Because their speeches can have long-range effects, many government officials choose to deliver them from a *prepared manuscript.* Scripts often are approved prior to the presentation or made available to members of the press. The President of the United States often does this, especially if the issues addressed are controversial. If you choose to read your speech, it's wise to practice it well and to keep it as short as possible. The longer the speech, the more likely you are to lose portions of the audience. A 30-minute speech read to a group of tired business people who've just eaten lunch, or are eager to do so, will probably not be a raging success.

The memorized presentation defined

Some speakers *memorize* the presentation word-for-word. Politicians, prominent executives, government officials, and other public personalities sometimes use this Format. If one has a good memory, and if the speech is well organized to begin with, such a strategy is very effective. Unfortunately, many inexperienced speakers also choose to memorize a presentation. Barring any unforeseen occurrences, many survive the ordeal. Others might forget a line or sentence, lose their place in the speech, and become flustered.

The extemporaneous presentation defined

The extemporaneous presentation is the most popular and most desirable of the three. Here, materials are organized either in outline form or on note cards. Using these devices allows the speaker to monitor audience reactions and slow down, elaborate on a difficult point, provide additional examples, or cut material as necessary. The extemporaneous format has built-in flexibility; the speaker can more easily accommodate time constraints or interruptions. Speakers who depend neither on memory nor a prepared manuscript, but instead respond to and encourage audience involvement, have a greater chance for building trust, confidence, and commitment.

THE PMM CONCEPT

The three basic components which speakers address when preparing oral presentations are:

Person—individual making the oral presentation.

Message—the presentation itself.

Media—the presentation aids.

The PMM concept defined

This is called the *PMM concept. Message* is the heart of this concept, but you must support it with the vanguards—*person* and *media* (see Figure 20.1). This concept is the basis for the strategy for communicating orally.

The Person

Developing the person

Every society has an unwritten standard by which its citizens are measured. So the first step toward improving your professional image is to determine what constitutes that standard in our society. One of the best ways to do this is to study a person who stands out in a crowd and then ask yourself:

- □ What makes that person stand out?
- □ What would I guess that person's profession to be?
- □ What do I perceive his/her educational background to be?

Figure 20.1
PMM concept

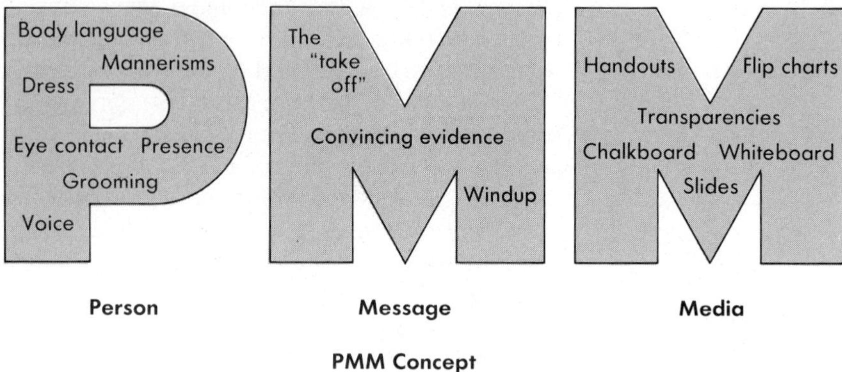

PMM Concept

- ☐ What is the probable intelligence level of that person?
- ☐ Do I think that person is a leader or a follower?
- ☐ On what characteristics am I basing my opinions?

The importance of nonverbal elements

In our society, some of the most important nonverbal elements used as standards for determining success include good grooming, appropriate dress, natural mannerisms, effective body language, a pleasing voice, good eye contact, and an authoritative presence. Before your Listeners ever hear your message, they have formed an opinion of you on the basis of these silent communicators.

According to Susan Bixler, founder and president of The Professional Image, Inc., "In this country, fifty-five percent of what we believe about one another—whether or not a person is well-educated, intelligent, competent, important, prosperous—is based on our observation and interpretation of nonverbal signals."[1]

There will always be characteristics about ourselves that we don't like. Some people feel they are too tall; others feel they are too short. Some don't like the size of their feet, and still others complain about the shape of their faces. But most people will not judge you by those features over which you have no control. Instead, they will judge you on those traits that you can develop and control, those characteristics which reveal how you feel about yourself: your self-confidence, your personality, your determination, your self-control. No one is born with these traits; but, fortunately, you can develop them relatively quickly with little effort.

Natural Manner. Stress is a natural part of public speaking. Even experienced speakers confess to some anxiety when standing before a large audience. Practice your presentation until you convince yourself you are ready. The more you go over the presentation, the more self-confident you will

[1] Susan Bixler, *The Professional Image* (New York: Putnam Publishing, 1984), p. 18.

become. As soon as you feel more confident about what you are going to say, you will begin to relax.

Overcoming anxiety

An alert audience will detect how confident you are by observing your mannerisms. Such annoying habits as knuckle rapping, scratching, fist clenching, nail biting, foot tapping, and coin jingling are all distracting quirks that lead to distrust. Experts also tell us that it is wrong to fold your arms across your chest, or to lean against a wall, lectern, or other object. Additional "no-nos" include folding your hands behind you or placing them in your pockets. People like a natural, self-confident manner. Standing straight with arms and hands hanging loosely at your sides and feet firmly planted and spread naturally is known as the *professional speaker's stance.* Practice developing this stance. You will find that it feels natural and makes you feel more at ease and comfortable.

Importance of image

Appropriate Attire. A desirable professional image begins with good grooming and appropriate dress. Use the guidelines in Figure 20.2 to help you present a professional image. Following these guidelines is especially important when you are giving an oral presentation and are in the spotlight.

Body language defined

Body Language. For effectiveness, use natural gestures to emphasize a point, such as hand, head, and eye movements. When done in a natural, unconscious and unplanned manner based on the speaker's enthusiasm and sincerity, these body movements are very effective. The key word is *natural.*

Ways to develop the voice

The Voice. Good voice quality is another attribute that promotes an effective presentation. You probably have developed this quality to some degree ever since, as a toddler, you began practicing your speech. To reach your fullest potential, use a tape recorder to practice your presentation and then evaluate the recording to determine your effectiveness. The voice development and evaluation checklists in Figure 20.3 also will help you make that evaluation. If a tape recorder is not available, a friend, family member, or teacher can also provide valuable feedback.

Use eye contact to establish audience rapport

Eye Contact. Your eyes are the most prominent feature of your face. Their expression can convey warmth, feeling, sympathy, interest, or sincerity. Use them to make contact with your audience. Try not to single out a particular person but make eye contact with many people in the audience. Begin by looking ahead and then rotate slowly from side to side, making eye contact with a number of different people. Lock eyes for a few seconds, but never long enough to complete more than 8 to 10 words.

By watching the audience's facial expressions, whether smiles, frowns, puzzled expressions, or bored looks, the speaker can determine the audience's reaction. Using this feedback, the speaker can adjust the message to meet the needs of the situation.

Girl Scout Elizabeth Brinton lets her eyes do the talking. In 1985, she sold

Figure 20.2
Business attire basics*

Women	Men
☐ Tailored clothing only. No frills, ruffles, straps, or plunging necklines. People won't take you seriously if you affect a "feminine" style.	☐ Dark or gray suits, solid, pinstripe, or shadow plaid. Navy blazer and gray trousers.
☐ Suits and blazers in plain, neutral colors or understated plaids.	☐ Dress shirts in solid colors, mostly white, pale blue, or yellow.
☐ Dresses in dark colors, worn with or without blazers.	☐ Variety of ties in muted colors but in contrast to the suit. Solids, stripes, or small patterns.
☐ Scarves for color accents.	☐ Calf-length hose in dark colors to match suits.
☐ Skirts that are pleated, straight, or dirndl, with no extreme slits.	☐ Black or brown 1-inch belt.
☐ Basic dark pumps with medium or low heels.	☐ Tassle loafers, wingtips, or laceup shoes.
☐ Stud earrings, gold or pearl necklaces. Avoid dangling bracelets.	☐ Avoid flashy cuff links, rings, or neck chains.

* J. Robert Connor et al., eds., *"Business Week's Guide to Careers"* 4, no. 3 (Spring/Summer 1986), p. 27. (Reprinted with permission.)

11,200 boxes of Girl Scout cookies, which is over 215 boxes a week. Her secret, she says, is "to look people in the eyes and make them feel guilty."

Because eye contact puts you in tune with your audience, let your eyes do some of the talking. This practice is an important part of gaining the confidence of your Listener/Audience. People trust a speaker's eyes more than they trust his or her words.

Presence defined

Presence. When some people walk into a room, they command attention by their very presence. Because they display a positive visual image, these are the individuals with whom other people like to associate. These are the winners. You achieve this visual presence by integrating the nonverbal elements into a professional image. The dress, the mannerisms, the smile, the handshake, the natural ease and style of the total person all contribute to this presence.

Effects of a good visual presence

Ronald Reagan, our fortieth President, exhibited good visual presence. With an acting background, he seemed an unlikely candidate for President of the United States. Yet he won the election. His smile, his self-control, his impeccable dress, his professional mannerisms, and the natural ease with which he carried himself all conveyed a message of integrity and consistency. Add to this his voice control, flawless grammar, enthusiasm, and wit; and it becomes apparent why he has been called the *great communicator*.

The Message

Developing the message

Every message contains three basic parts: the takeoff, the convincing evidence, and the windup. The takeoff gains the audience's attention and introduces the theme. The convincing evidence includes the data, facts, and

Figure 20.3

Voice Development Techniques

1. Stand or sit up straight and take deep breaths.
2. Relax! Being nervous tends to raise the pitch level.
3. Select a sentence and repeat it several times varying the tone, volume, and pace of the delivery. Adjusting your delivery to emphasize important points will help you achieve desired outcomes.
4. Practice some tongue twisters to improve articulation. Overemphasize the word sounds until you achieve clarity.
5. Write down the words that were pronounced incorrectly and practice repeating them until they flow easily.
6. Learn to be enthusiastic. A zestful presentation and a warm smile can accomplish what the words themselves cannot.
7. If correct grammar is a problem, go over the parts of speech and then study the appropriate rules.

Voice Evaluation Checklist

1. How distinct were my words? Could I understand each one clearly?
2. Was the tone pleasing, or did it sound shrill and harsh?
3. Did my voice crack at any point? Was it objectionable?
4. Did I sound enthusiastic? Authoritative? Warm and friendly? Or did I sound monotonous? Bossy? Cold?
5. Was my voice weak at times? Too loud at other times?
6. Did I pronounce the words correctly?
7. Did I use correct grammar?

information used to support the claim. The windup closes the message either with a dramatic impact or a summary of key elements.

Getting off to a good start

The Takeoff. The takeoff of the message sets the stage for audience response. The audience may be present for a variety of reasons. Depending on the purpose of the message, some members of the audience may be present because they desire information; others may be there because they are required to attend.

Regardless of the purpose of your presentation, an effective takeoff is vital. You must achieve impact at the very first if you are to capture the attention of your listeners. Here are some of the more popular techniques for achieving an effective beginning.

- *Startling Information.* The intent of this beginning is to jolt the audience into a listening mood. This can take the form of a question, a shocking fact, a quotation, or any form which jars or surprises the listener. (Example: Did you know that we as city dwellers are twice as likely as rural residents to become victims of violent crime?)

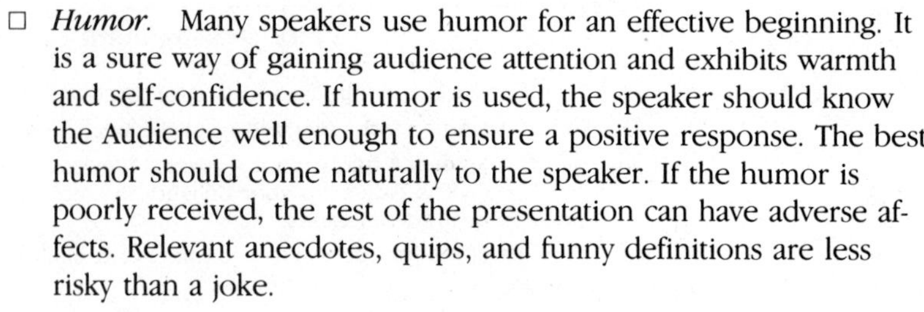

- *Humor.* Many speakers use humor for an effective beginning. It is a sure way of gaining audience attention and exhibits warmth and self-confidence. If humor is used, the speaker should know the Audience well enough to ensure a positive response. The best humor should come naturally to the speaker. If the humor is poorly received, the rest of the presentation can have adverse affects. Relevant anecdotes, quips, and funny definitions are less risky than a joke.
- *The Unusual.* People like to hear something new and unusual. Speakers often use this approach in persuasive presentations. If a new or better way is available, people want to know about it.
- *Suspense.* Paul Harvey's use of suspense is impressive in "The Rest of the Story." First he creates interest and then leaves the audience in suspense until the climax or end of the presentation.
- *The Message Core.* Begin immediately with the core of the message. (Example: We are here to discuss the parking problems on the university campus.)
- *Courteous Beginning.* Using courtesy at the beginning is always effective. Express your appreciation for the honor of speaking, and then commend the listeners for any accomplishments relevant to the speech topic.
- *The Inside Scoop.* Everyone likes to feel she/he has a line on the inside track. This approach can have a powerful impact as a beginning, especially if the message is coming from a high public official or corporate executive officer.
- *Dramatic Story.* A dramatic story is another approach that is sure to get attention. Once you complete the story, however, you need to introduce the central theme of the message. The audience should have a clear purpose of the presentation and the relevancy of the story. No listener should leave wondering "What was that all about?"

Providing sound, relevant data

Convincing Evidence. The middle section of the oral presentation is where you present all the sound, relevant data to prove your introductory statements. Begin this section with concepts that are familiar to your Audience, especially if you're speaking on a controversial subject or if the theme calls for technical, sophisticated language. Gradually introduce the more complex concepts. Group important elements in logical sequence. Support ideas with cases and incidents. Illustrations and examples help the audience connect ideas. Use jargon sparingly, unless you give a brief explanation or definition of the terms used. If the Audience doesn't understand the message, your presentation is in vain. Provide enough information to give the presentation the necessary depth and substance, but avoid boring, irrelevant details that will lose the audience.

Whether your presentation is intended to celebrate, inform, or persuade, the middle section contains the material that determines the outcome. The lawyer presents the evidence; the researcher explains his/her methods and findings; the salesperson describes the benefits to the consumer.

Options for ending an oral presentation

The Windup. For the windup of the oral presentation, restate the central theme, summarize the evidence, or propose some type of action. Do not introduce new evidence. The Format you select depends on the objective of your message. For an informative presentation, a summary of key points is appropriate. If the objective is to entertain, a punch line that restates the central theme is effective. In a persuasive presentation, you could use the ending to propose action. Regardless of the Format, use a brief windup.

The technique you select for the windup should complement the one used in the takeoff of the message. For instance, if you used suspense in the beginning, you must now come back to the cliff-hanger and give the ending of the story or anecdote.

Example of combined techniques

Suppose you are a speaker for the national organization, Mothers against Drunk Driving (MADD). Your audience is a civic group concerned about the dangers of driving under the influence. Your takeoff could include startling information, suspense, a direct statement of the problem, or a dramatic story. Your convincing evidence would be the data on deaths attributed to drunk driving. Your evidence would also include examples and cases to support the facts. In the windup you could then restate the startling information, resolve the cliff-hanger, summarize key points, or introduce a dramatic incident or case, depending on your introduction. You might also invite the listeners to sign a petition to civic authorities for action against convicted drunk drivers.

A dramatic close is more likely to stay with the listener. The powerful endings of historical speeches such as Patrick Henry's "I know not what course others may take, but as for me, give me liberty or give me death"; or Dr. Martin Luther King's "Free at last! Free at last! Thank God almighty, we are free at last!" we will long remember even though we may forget the rest of the speech.

The Media

Media are any aids used to enhance an oral presentation. Aids can be as simple as photocopied handouts or as elaborate as tape-programmed, multi-slide displays in four or more colors. Use media if they will enhance the presentation and add impact to the oral message.

Advantages of transparencies

Varieties of Media. Many types of media are available today. With the technological advances in today's information world, new types are always being developed. Here are some of the simplest and most commonly used media for oral presentations.

Transparencies are among the most popular visual aids available today, because they are effective and inexpensive. They provide color and a sharp image, even in a well-lit room. You can also write or draw on a transparency while it is being projected and still maintain eye contact with the audience. You can use this equipment almost anywhere. The projector is portable and very easy to operate. When using transparencies, consider these suggestions:

Guidelines for using transparencies

- ☐ Use colored felt tip marking pens to emphasize key points.
- ☐ Make sure the images are large and clear enough to be seen by each member of the audience. Avoid making reproductions from books and reports. These materials are almost always difficult to read.
- ☐ For a special effect, use overlays to display stages of development. For example, use an initial transparency of the human body with only the skeleton visible, then enhance this with an overlay showing veins, then arteries. For another effect, cover part of the transparency with a card and view different segments of the image in sequence, as the discussion warrants.
- ☐ Use a commercial artist if you need an elaborate or splashy visual. Since this procedure could prove to be quite expensive, make sure the benefits justify the costs.

Advantages of slides

Slides (regular 2″ × 2″) are also very popular. If you place the slides in a tray, you can use a push-button control to focus, move forward, move in reverse, or set at automatic intervals. This medium is quite versatile. Use slides to display photographs, diagrams, graphs, illustrations, or just a few key words. As with transparencies, you can use slides effectively without turning your back on the audience. When using slides, consider these guidelines:

Guidelines for using slides

- ☐ Use slides if you want a really professional look. According to some people, you will achieve the greatest impact using this medium because of the high quality and attractive appearance.
- ☐ Slides are a good choice for sales programs, training programs, and exhibits that are repeated.
- ☐ Where quality, simplicity, and mobility are demanded, slides should be a serious consideration. Slide trays are easy to transport and protect the slides as well.
- ☐ A few slides are good; fewer slides are better. Constantly flipping through slides without giving the viewers much chance to study them detracts from the message. Also a room darkened too long may put someone to sleep, regardless of how interesting you are.
- ☐ If you need brilliant color, slides are the answer. Film can achieve this effect as no other medium can.
- ☐ Make sure the slides are right side up and in the correct order. Otherwise, you'll be tagged as an amateur.

Advantages of the chalkboard/whiteboard

The *chalkboard* has been for years the number one device for educators. It is probably the simplest visual aid available. In addition, many speakers now use portable whiteboards which are similar to chalkboards, except that the speaker writes with special colored markers instead of chalk. Using whiteboards eliminates chalk dust and adds color contrast to enhance the visual presentation. Here are some tips for developing good chalkboard and whiteboard techniques.

Guidelines for using the chalkboard/whiteboard

- ☐ Even if the chalkboard/whiteboard is provided, be prepared by bringing additional chalk or colored markers and an eraser.
- ☐ Beforehand, write or draw out on note cards what you intend to present on the board to avoid making mistakes or omitting key elements.
- ☐ Do not write pertinent information on the board beforehand since this will divert the audience's attention to the board.
- ☐ Since you will be writing while you talk, limit the amount of information on the board to as few words as possible. Turn sideways and glance at your audience as you speak and write.
- ☐ Good writing on the board takes practice. Make boardwriting practice part of your preparation. Make letters large so that they are legible from any point in the room and clear enough so that no one has to guess what's on the board.

Advantages of using flip charts

Flip charts are similar to whiteboards. A large pad of paper is attached to a board or easel. You can write information on one sheet at a time. You could also write information ahead of time and flip the sheets as you discuss the data. You can still use color markers to gain impact. Flip charts are especially useful for small group presentations. Businesses use this medium extensively for internal work sessions. Some points to remember when using flip charts are:

Guidelines for using flip charts

- ☐ Apply all guidelines for chalkboards/whiteboards.
- ☐ Make sure the quality of the paper and pens is such as to avoid the bleeding through of colors from one sheet to another. These stray marks are distracting to the listeners.
- ☐ Practice beforehand using the same easel or mounting stand to make sure that it remains upright when you flip the pages. By practicing, you can determine where to hold the mount if necessary to ensure stability.

Advantages of handouts

Handouts are useful at times as a way of complementing your presentation. Usually, you will distribute handouts at the end of the speech. This leaves the audience free to concentrate on you and not on the handout. Nothing is more distracting than looking at an audience with bowed heads and trying to compete with the noise of paper shuffling.

When deciding on a handout, ask yourself what you want the audience to do. If you want them to take home some idea, then include a handout of the presentation or a summary of its key points. If you want them to take some type of action, then use some type of ballot. If you want feedback, then provide a checklist to make it easy for them to respond. Some guidelines for handouts are:

Guidelines for using handouts

- ☐ When the time alloted for the presentation is insufficient for getting vital information to the listeners, a handout can help. Such a handout might include most frequently asked questions and answers about the topic, a complete report on the topic, or detailed information on the key points covered.
- ☐ If you expect a follow-up response, a handout is a visual reminder for listeners once they leave the facility. In corporate environments, for instance, audience participants are sometimes expected to follow up with an action.
- ☐ If the speaker wishes to leave a memento of the occasion, a handout is appropriate. If you are delivering a presentation on "The Benefits of Microwave Cooking," for instance, you might want to give members of the audience a booklet of microwave recipes as a memento.
- ☐ If you need an immediate response, a handout provides an organized way of obtaining information. This handout could be in the form of a ballot, a checksheet, an evaluation form, a card for comments, or any device appropriate for obtaining the information in the simplest manner.

Impact. To ensure that the medium you select will achieve the intended impact, apply the FAST test, an acronym for the following four criteria:

Use the FAST test to help choose a medium

- ☐ *Feasible.* Cost is probably the most important factor in the feasibility of a medium. The goals of the presentation should justify the cost of a particular piece of equipment. Other factors include the availability of equipment and/or mobility of equipment; the accommodations of the facility in which the speech is given; size of the audience (handouts for 2,000 listeners will cost a great deal); appropriateness of the medium for the audience (age, educational level, sophistication).
- ☐ *Audible/visible.* Nothing is more frustrating to an audience than not seeing or hearing what is presented. Consider the size of the audience: a microcomputer screen may be large enough for a demonstration to five people but would be completely inappropriate for an audience of twenty-five. Make sure that the person who sits in the last seat on the back row can both hear and see what is going on.
- ☐ *Simple.* Many presenters overuse visuals, especially slides or transparencies. Keep the presentation simple. A visual should contain only key elements and be designed so that the message is conveyed clearly. Remember the visual *supplements*, it does not *supplant* the oral message. Simplicity also applies to the equip-

ment itself. If it's too elaborate, your audience may pay too much attention to the media and lose your key points. Choose media that promote simplicity.

- *Timely.* Choose media that contain up-to-date material and can be synchronized to the pace of the speaker. A film with out-of-date hair and dress style would lose credibility with your listeners. Even if the material in the film is appropriate, the impact of the message is still somewhat diminished. Neither is the visual timely if it lags behind the oral message or stays on the screen after the speaker has finished. Correct pacing of all visual materials is a must. To ensure synchronization, indicate in the margin of your notes where to present each visual. If you use an assistant, practice the presentation several times to avoid confusion or error.

Media Selection Principles. After you use the FAST test and before you make your final decision, consider these important principles:

Guidelines for choosing media

1. Make sure there are electrical outlets and sufficient extensions to handle audio/visual equipment.
2. Make sure the facilities allow you to face your audience at all times while using the device. Maintain eye contact.
3. Be in control of your visuals. Visuals should enhance what you say, not detract from your message.
4. Whatever equipment you choose, make sure it works properly before you begin the presentation. Nothing kills a presentation more quickly than fumbling to get equipment in working order.
5. Be responsible yourself for seeing that all equipment and materials are ready ahead of time. Go prepared and arrive early enough to make any adjustments. Not even a host can be depended on for this task.
6. Check the facilities for light control when using slides or transparencies. If light-level adjustments are not available and the room needs darkening, make sure a podium lamp is available for reading notes.
7. Prepare to make your presentation without any visuals should unforeseen circumstances prevent their use.

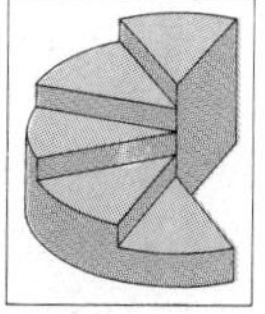

STRATEGY: THE ORAL PRESENTATION

Jack, an extremely bright and knowledgeable young executive, has worked for a large high-tech company in the Southeast for five years. He is articulate and well-groomed. No one was surprised when he was selected to make a presentation to NASA officials that could win a $20 million contract for his firm. Jack has made formal presentations since the first year he was hired by the firm. He thought he knew what to do.

After carefully going over NASA guidelines to make sure that no details were overlooked, Jack discussed technical aspects of the project with several engineers and researched every phase of the proposal. He prepared his presentation and delivered it at the specified time. Jack had done his homework, and he felt confident that the contract was a certainty.

Jack's company executives were shocked a few weeks later when NASA awarded the contract to another firm. With technology far ahead of any competitor in the field, Jack's company should have easily won the contract. What could possibly have gone wrong? When company executives traced the steps which led to NASA's decision, they discovered that the bid was lost because of Jack's presentation. In planning his strategy, Jack had concentrated so heavily on the presentation itself that he had failed to prepare for what followed. During the question-and-answer session, his statements seemed so rigid that the NASA officials felt that Jack's firm could not offer the flexibility needed to complete the project. What could Jack have done to handle the final phase of this presentation?

The point is, Jack's case is not an isolated incident. Far too many people fail as public speakers because they don't follow a strategy. By applying the strategy for communicating, let us see if we can help Jack identify his weaknesses and plan for future successes.

PROBLEM

Jack's company must compete and win contracts for survival.

OBJECTIVES

General: To obtain the NASA contract.

Specific: To persuade his Listener/Audience to award the NASA contract to his company.

To use effective media to enhance the oral presentation.

LISTENER/AUDIENCE

Characteristics: NASA officials responsible for awarding the contract.

Experts in their field.

Well educated.

Highly perceptive individuals.

Have awarded numerous contracts previously.

Reactions: NASA officials will put Jack on the hot seat.

NASA officials will critically analyze Jack's proposal.

NASA officials expect Jack to be able to defend the proposal as well as to incorporate suggested alternatives.

Some officials will react positively; some negatively; some will be neutral.

NASA officials will compare Jack's proposal with others on the basis of his presentation.

ORDER

DIRECT

The fourth element of the strategy—the Order, or organization of the message, addresses the *how* of the communication. Jack chose a direct order since the NASA guidelines were already spelled out, and the committee was anticipating a direct response.

FORMAT

ORAL

Jack delivers his message face-to-face from a prepared manuscript.

In this case, Jack did come prepared. Because of several dry runs with company officials, he anticipated the right questions and was ready with the evidence. But he failed to react to the verbal and nonverbal reactions of his Listener/Audience. When he began receiving some negative responses, he was not prepared to shift gears to meet customer needs. Because he was inflexible and too narrow in his thinking, Jack was not ready with alternative measures. If Jack had planned his strategy for communicating by analyzing Listener/Audience reactions, the outcome might have been different.

FORMAL AND INFORMAL SPEAKING

The strategy for oral communication discussed in this chapter applies to all forms of oral speaking: a one-on-one meeting, a small-group meeting, or a large-group meeting. But consider some additional factors for each of these special types.

One-on-One-Meetings

One-on-one meetings defined

Some people feel that because the one-on-one meeting is generally informal, they do not need to plan the strategy as carefully or as precisely. But consider the significance of the following one-on-one sessions:

- ☐ *The interview* determines whether you get the job.
- ☐ *The employee/employer session* determines your success in getting your points across whether you are the employee or the employer.

- *The sale* determines whether the product or service is purchased.
- *The confidential interchange* depends on the confidence and trust the speaker and the Listener have in each other.

Since these are all pretty important reasons for taking time to plan, consider the following points for the one-on-one meeting.

Guidelines for one-on-one meetings

- *Go prepared.* Even if the environment is informal, remember that time is one of the most valuable resources available. No one wants to waste it. Have your key points ready and be brief. If you are interrupted by a phone call or someone walking into the room, use this pause to reassess the conversation. Make your point when the conversation resumes. You can usually make your point in three or four sentences.
- *Observe nonverbal reactions.* Show sensitivity to the Listener's reaction. If the Listener seems in a hurry or bored, stop talking and give the Listener a chance to react and get involved in the conversation. You may come back later to finish the discussion. In all cases, adhere to a time schedule. If the appointment was for 15 minutes, make your point(s) and then leave before the 15-minute period has expired.
- *Involve the Listener.* In an informal environment, it is quite easy to involve listeners. Watch their eyes, and you will probably know when they want to react. If you don't receive an indication, ask a question or solicit a response by saying, "I would like your feedback on the idea."

Small-Group Meetings

Small-group meetings defined

Small-group sessions usually take place with people we know—colleagues, co-workers, comembers. Many times, however, these meetings are the most frustrating. The informality of the small-group business session does not lend itself to a prescribed order. In discussing ideas, people who know one another well will often ask questions, respond, comment, introduce new ideas, argue, or interrupt. Yet such meetings can have long-term effects. How people perceive you in this environment can affect your career advancement. Consider these techniques for effective leadership and speaking in small-group meetings:

Guidelines for small-group meetings

- *Show sensitivity.* There is a time to speak and a time to listen. People appreciate a person who is a leader and can stimulate discussion, but they also like a good listener who is sympathetic to their ideas and tactful. Many articles and books on communication group dynamics apply to the small group meeting.
- *Use opportunities wisely.* In the small group, your job is to listen as well as to speak. Watch for opportunities—a lull in the conver-

sation, an interruption such as a phone call, or when someone asks a direct question—and be ready to respond. However, do not change the subject unless the group seems ready. You will know when the group is ready—the subject is exhausted and people are becoming restless.

- ☐ *Be brief.* There is a cliché that goes something like this: "The best pitch a salesperson can give is the one that says all that *should* be, but not all that *could* be." This certainly applies to the small-group meeting. Don't pour out all your ideas, arguments, or convincing evidence at once. Make your one best point to get the group's attention. If the idea is worthy, the group will allow you more time to support it with evidence.
- ☐ *Use language discreetly.* This is not the place for profane language. Even slang is out of order. An informal atmosphere does not mean the relaxation of all barriers. Correct English, eye contact, sincerity, knowledge of the subject, and a positive professional image apply in all business environments.

Large-Group Meetings

Large-group meetings defined

Large-group meetings are usually more formal. The age we live in is highly specialized and technologically dynamic. Large-group meetings offer an excellent way to provide additional information and specialized training when needed. At these meetings, the speaker should:

Guidelines for large-group meetings

- ☐ *Speak slowly.* Slow your speech down so that your tones are clear and easily understood. Some experts even recommend a 30 percent reduction in pace when speaking to a really large group. A slower pace allows the audience to assimilate information and allows you a chance to place emphasis where needed.
- ☐ *Be time-conscious.* For any speaking appointment, a certain amount of time is allotted. Make sure that you stick to this agenda. In conferences where several speakers are scheduled, one long-winded person can disrupt the whole timetable. If this happens, however, and you are last on the program, adjust your presentation so that you finish on time. Failure to do this will reflect on you, even though the cause rests with someone else.
- ☐ *Use the microphone judiciously.* Adjust the microphone before the meeting begins. Place the microphone approximately eight inches from the mouth. Never begin your presentation by tapping the mike and asking "Is this on?" or "Can you hear me?" This will immediately brand you as an amateur. If the mike screeches or you hear popping sounds when speaking words beginning with a *p*, back off. Move slightly to the side so that you speak at an angle rather than directly into the mike.

CONDUCTING MEETINGS

How to conduct a meeting

Managers know that meetings are time-consuming and costly. However, they sometimes need to bring individuals together to solve problems, make decisions, transmit information, or provide training. Since most objectives are achieved through group effort, you will at some time probably have the responsibility for conducting or chairing a meeting.

Group meetings are especially effective for solving controversial, complicated problems where alternative solutions are generated and scrutinized. In this setting, managers depend on employees who can plan, organize, direct, and control these meetings to meet specific objectives.

Preparing the Listening/Speaking Audience

Selecting the meeting participants

The audience should be made up of participants who know and trust each other. Such a group can concentrate on the objective of the meeting rather than on trying to impress or vie for control. Prior to the meeting, inform each group member of the meeting objective; and if possible, provide each with a copy of the agenda. Furnish each group member with relevant materials—statistics, reports, list of customer complaints, etc.—for review prior to the meeting. This will speed the meeting process. When determining the number of group participants, consider the objectives of the meeting and follow these guidelines:

Problem solving	5 or fewer members
Decision making	5 or fewer members
Information	30 or less
Transmission	30 or less
Training (depending on type of training)	15-20 members

Good planning is a part of any business function. This is especially true for a meeting that could get out of hand if discussion is uncontrolled. Good planning includes the following duties:

Guidelines for conducting a meeting

- ☐ Determine the date, time, and place of the meeting.
- ☐ Plan, organize, and distribute the agenda.
- ☐ Place an estimated time limit on each agenda item.
- ☐ Determine ahead of time how you will involve each member in the discussion. You might allow each member 10 minutes to address the problem with possible solutions.
- ☐ Ask each member to write out one key strategy she/he wishes the group to address, collect strategies, run copies, then distribute ideas to all, etc.
- ☐ Review *Robert's Rules of Order,* so that you can follow parliamentary procedure or protocol when necessary.
- ☐ Plan for breaks if meetings last more than 90 minutes.

Preparing for the Meeting

Preparing the meeting room

When selecting the meeting room, consider the size of the committee. Room size can have a significant impact on productivity. Prepare the meeting room ahead of time. Arrange for adequate chairs, pad/pencils, presentation materials, and refreshments. If presentation aids are used, follow the principles outlined earlier in this chapter.

Using an oval or round table is also a good idea. This arrangement promotes equal involvement and a team approach.

Managing the Meeting

How to keep the meeting on track

Begin on time even if some members have not yet arrived. A tight agenda targeted to specific objectives is the most effective.

At the outset make sure each participant is clear on the objective(s) of the meeting. Reduce tunnel vision by promoting dissenting views and alternative strategies and ideas. Keep the group on track and encourage participation by all members. Some members may tend to take over. If this happens, use your oral communication skills to cut in and steer the meeting back on target.

Watch the nonverbal communication. If voices fall in volume or people begin slouching in their chairs, take a break.

At times you may need to ask for clarification on where the group stands. After full discussion, seek to move the group to a consensus for solving the Problem(s) by summing up elements of agreement. Before leaving the meeting, make sure everyone is clear on decisions about recommendations and solutions reached. Then convert these into action items such as:

- ☐ How recommendations will be implemented.
- ☐ Who is responsible for what recommendation.
- ☐ When is action due.
- ☐ Who will follow up on progress.

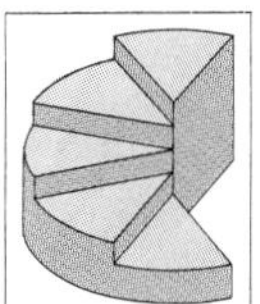

STRATEGY: CONDUCTING AN INFORMAL MEETING

Don Miller works for a company that sells small appliances. Periodically his company offers rebates to boost sales. Lately, however, sales have dropped and customers have lost interest in the rebate system. They don't want to wait four to six weeks for a rebate check from the manufacturer. Don has been asked to chair a committee for solving the sales slump problem.

As Don considers a strategy for conducting this meeting, he decides on an informal, small-group meeting made up of people who are familiar with company policy and procedures. They also hold positions responsible for implementing any outcomes of the meeting. Since this is a problem-solving meeting, he chooses five key company persons—the director of sales and marketing, three regional sales managers, and the comptroller.

Prior to the meeting Don sends each committee member background information, copies of customer complaints, and a planned agenda.

PROBLEM
Sales are lost because the rebate checks are slow.

OBJECTIVES

General: To increase sales.
Specific: To speed up the process of rebate checks or recommend alternative marketing strategies.

LISTENING/SPEAKING AUDIENCE

Characteristics: Director of sales and marketing.
Regional sales managers (three major regions).
Comptroller.
Knowledgeable professionals who can make a contribution.
Employees interested in company image and success.
Employees who are strong in oral communication and listening skills.

Reaction: Participants will be pleased they were asked to help solve the problem.
Participants want to do all they can to maintain the company's good image.
Participants have a positive attitude for solving the problem.

ORDER
A set agenda with open discussion.

FORMAT
Small-group meeting.

The success of the meeting is mainly dependent on your ability to direct the discussion and to assist the group in reaching a decision. You have identified each of the elements in your strategy for communicating; you are now ready to prepare for the meeting on the basis of these elements.

THE LISTENING PROCESS

Listening defined

Most people confuse listening with hearing. *Listening includes not only hearing, but three other equally important processes as well: decoding, evaluating, and reacting* (see Figure 20.4).

Figure 20.4
The four links of listening

Hearing—the sensing or perceiving process in which the human brain responds to noises or tones.
Decoding—the process of translating sounds heard into meaningful information.
Evaluating—the appraisal process which places a value on the decoded information.
Reacting—the process of responding based on how the information was decoded and evaluated.

Each of these is important to the act of listening. To illustrate how listening takes place, suppose you are watching "The Cosby Show" on TV. You are able to *decode* the sounds you *hear*, because the program is taped in a language you know. Once you understand the message, an *evaluation* process takes place; and depending on the value you place on the program, you will *react* in one of three ways: continue to watch the program, switch the channel to another, or turn off the TV.

Active versus passive listening

This sounds simple enough, but listening is not that easy. The above illustration is an example of what is known as passive listening. Passive listening takes place when you are reacting to most forms of entertainment like "The Cosby Show" on TV, music on the radio, or table talk with a friend. We call this passive listening, because it is almost unintentional. Active or critical listening is performed when you listen for the purpose of comprehending, remembering, discriminating, synthesizing, evaluating, or applying what you hear in productive ways.

Importance of listening compared to other communication skills

Active listening is what people in business want. Poor listening costs businesses millions of dollars. Administrators are becoming increasingly aware of the need for developing good listening skills. This is understandable when you consider that listening accounts for almost half (45 percent) of the working day, according to researchers. In other words, we spend almost as much time listening as we do speaking, reading, or writing combined.

To promote effective listening, many companies now sponsor listening seminars and are even developing whole programs for training their personnel in this art. Sperry Corporation stands out as a leader in the development of such programs. One of the outgrowths of its efforts is a listening chart that lists guidelines for effective listening skills (see Figure 20.5). This chart gives 10 keys to effective listening and demonstrates how bad listeners, as well as good listeners, score on each item.

How to be a good listener

As noted in this chart, good listeners constantly work at the listening process by asking themselves such questions as: What is the speaker trying to say? How can I use this information? What is the speaker leading to? A good listener is able to discriminate between relevant and irrelevant information, gestures, and attitudes and makes judgments on the overall content of the

Figure 20.5
Ten keys to effective listening

These keys are a positive guideline to better listening. In fact, they're at the heart of developing better listening habits that could last a lifetime.

Ten Keys to Effective Listening	The Bad Listener	The Good Listener
1. Find areas of interest.	Tunes out dry subjects.	Opportunitizes, asks "what's in it for me?"
2. Judge content, not delivery.	Tunes out if delivery is poor.	Judges content, skips over delivery errors.
3. Hold your fire.	Tends to enter into argument.	Doesn't judge until comprehension is complete.
4. Listen for ideas.	Listens for facts.	Listens for central themes.
5. Be flexible.	Takes intensive notes using only one system.	Takes few notes, uses 4 or 5 different systems depending on speaker.
6. Work at listening.	Shows no energy output, fakes attention.	Works hard; exhibits active body state.
7. Resist distractions.	Is easily distracted.	Fights or avoids distractions, tolerates bad habits, knows how to concentrate.
8. Exercise your mind.	Resists difficult expository material, seeks light, recreational material.	Uses heavier material as exercise for the mind.
9. Keep your mind open.	Reacts to emotional words.	Interprets color words, does not get hung up on them.
10. Capitalize on fact—thought is faster than speech.	Tends to daydream with slow speakers.	Challenges, anticipates, mentally summarizes, weighs the evidence, listens between the lines to tone of voice.

message itself. Good listeners are then ready to react in ways that will best serve the organizations.

SUMMARY

Effective speaking is a powerful skill for communicating in business. Executives are choosing this method of communicating as a way of building confidence, trust, and commitment between their organizations and people in general.

Planning a strategy for communicating orally is similar to that of communicating in writing. The components are identified based on the problem or *why* of the communication. When delivering a message orally, you usually have one of three specific objectives: to celebrate, to inform, or to persuade. Your success in meeting your objective(s) is determined by how well you understand your *Listener/Audience.* Therefore, anticipate how your Listener/Audience will react by asking yourself key questions about the profession, age, gender, background, and needs of members of your audience. Unlike written communication, oral communication allows you to obtain immediate feedback from your Listener/Audience. You obtain this feedback either informally through verbal or nonverbal responses or formally through question/answer sessions, written evaluations, or checklists. The way you order the communication will vary based on the Objective(s). At times, the Order will be direct; at other times, indirect; or at times, persuasive, beginning with an attention getter, adding facts and details, and ending with a climax or appeal. The Format of delivery involves reading from a prepared manuscript, memorizing, or delivering extemporaneously.

Once you have planned your strategy and know what you intend to accomplish, you are ready to begin preparing for the event. In written communication, you concentrate on one component—the document. In oral communication, you concentrate on three components—yourself (person), the communication (message), and presentation aids (media). These three components are called the PMM concept.

To improve the person component, you concentrate on natural mannerisms, appropriate attire, nonverbal signals, the voice, eye contact, and presence. When preparing the message, you develop the three parts—the takeoff, the convincing evidence, and the windup. Some of the most common types of media used for presentations are transparencies/overhead projectors, slides, chalkboard/whiteboard, flip charts, and handouts. When choosing the media, apply the FAST test; then consider the principles for media selection outlined in this chapter.

Oral communication skills are required for both formal and informal settings. Be prepared to speak effectively at one-on-one meetings, small-group meetings, or large-group meetings. You may be asked to manage or conduct a meeting. if so, plan your strategy for communicating so that you solve problems and/or achieve objectives.

Almost half of the working day is spent in listening. This communication skill is developed through training. A good listener will hear, decode, evaluate, and react to messages in a critical and responsible manner. This type of listening is called active listening. Another type of listening—passive listening—requires little thinking and takes place when we listen almost unintentionally.

END-OF-CHAPTER ACTIVITIES

DISCUSSION

1. Do you think it is possible for a shy person to become an effective oral communicator? Discuss and defend your position.
2. Do you think it is possible to develop effective listening skills, or do you think listening skills are innate? Discuss and elaborate on your position.

3. Distinguish among the major objectives for communicating orally—to celebrate, to inform, to persuade.
4. Compare and contrast the elements of oral communication with those of written communication. Discuss.
5. Accept or refute this statement: "Nonverbal communication is the most powerful ingredient in a formal presentation." Defend your position.
6. What are the distinguishing features of formal and informal speaking?
7. Discuss the various situations when communicating in a formal environment where feedback is appropriate.
8. What elements are associated with the PMM concept? Discuss.
9. Differentiate among what is involved with delivering an oral presentation from a prepared manuscript, from memory, or extemporaneously.
10. How would you apply the strategy for communicating to conducting a meeting to facilitate the outcome of the meeting? Discuss.

ACTIVITIES

11. The university you are attending has a critical parking problem. As a student, you find getting around campus a frustrating experience. Based on the present enrollment, only one parking space is available for every 50 students enrolled at the school. Apply the strategy for communicating orally and plan a five-minute class presentation to gain student support for a petition to send to the college administration.
12. Prepare an oral presentation based on a written report you developed in the report writing section of this book. Plan for a question-and-answer session following the presentation. Evaluate yourself using the suggestions in this chapter for initiating follow-up.
13. Listen to six TV advertisements—three local and three national. Based on the strategy for communicating orally and on the PMM concept, how effective were these advertisements? Defend your answer to each question.

    What was the problem or the *why* of the advertisement?
    What was the general objective? Specific objectives?
    What type audience was appealed to?
    Was TV the correct mode for this message?
    Were the right people chosen for this ad?
    Was the message well organized?
    What form of takeoff was used for the message?
    Identify the convincing evidence.
    Identify the windup.
    Was impact achieved? How?

14. Divide into small groups. In an informal, roundtable setting, select an issue and have two group members each give a 10-minute presentation on resolving the issue. Convince the group of your position. Defend your position in a question-and-answer session. Evaluate the effectiveness of the presentations.
15. Select a famous personality who has a reputation for exceptional communication skills. Based on the PMM concept, evaluate this person's strengths and weaknesses. What does this individual do to capitalize on his/her strengths and to minimize weaknesses? (Examples: Willard Scott, Barbara Walters, Jeane Kirkpatrick, Sam Donaldson, Dan Rather, Oprah Winfrey, Lee Iacocca, Bill Cosby, etc.) How do you think this individual reached a level of national recognition?
16. Spend a few minutes identifying and forming a list of problems on campus—parking, food service, registration lines, etc. Divide the class into groups and assign one problem topic to each group. Have each group role-play a meeting designed to solve the problem, using the following elements:

    - ☐ Assume the role of campus administrators.
    - ☐ Plan a strategy for communicating in a meeting.
    - ☐ Plan an agenda for a 30-minute meeting.
    - ☐ Select a group leader or facilitator.
    - ☐ Assign homework for researching a problem topic.
    - ☐ Reassemble and conduct a 30-minute meeting.

    Gain consensus and orally present solutions to the problem.
17. Prepare and deliver a five-minute extemporaneous speech on "The Ideal Teacher."
18. Interview one or more professional sales persons.
    Find out:

    - ☐ What techniques they use to analyze the Listener/Audience.
    - ☐ The role of nonverbal communication skills in sales.
    - ☐ What feedback mechanisms, if any, are used and how oral communication is adjusted on the basis of feedback.
19. Apply active listening skills to one major TV news program. Outline the key points of the news broadcast and write a one-page critical analysis.
20. Invite a local business owner or executive to the class to address the impact of listening skills on job success.

CHAPTER 21

WRITING POLICY AND PROCEDURE STATEMENTS

Learning Objectives

After studying this chapter, you will be able to:

- □ Recognize the importance of policies and procedures to business operations.
- □ Distinguish between a policy and a procedure.
- □ Plan strategies for writing policies and procedures.
- □ Evaluate this situation and create effective policy statements.
- □ Write effective procedures for a variety of situations.
- □ Assess the setting and select forms and graphics for certain types of procedures.
- □ Choose the appropriate Format for policies and procedures.

Importance of policies and procedures

Policies and procedures provide the framework for the work activities in a company and its relationships with customers and suppliers. Top executives are responsible for establishing overall policies for the firm; others at various levels in the firm may write procedures, which must conform to the intent of the broader policy statements.

Well-written policy and procedure statements are essential to any company's successful operations. Employees need to understand the thrust of the organization and how their efforts contribute to the continuity of the business. New employees, especially, need to know what procedures to follow as they perform their work. Similarly, consumers of services and goods need an awareness of the policies that affect them.

POLICY STATEMENTS

Definition of policy

A policy statement explains executive decisions about the company's organization, physical plant, personnel activities, budget, or other company goals. Employees or other interested people are informed about policy statements and changes. Policies are general or specific. Administrative policies tend to be broad and general and are long-range in nature; operative policies, in contrast, are more specific and may deal with short-range projects. Policies guide decision makers as they strive to attain organizational goals.

A complete list of subjects addressed in policy statements is several pages long. Here are a few of the typical subject areas:

Policy areas

- ☐ Authority and responsibilities of headquarters and satellite divisions.
- ☐ Basic lines of business products.
- ☐ Computer purchases.
- ☐ Warranty of products and services sold.
- ☐ Service to customers.
- ☐ Quality control.
- ☐ Safety.
- ☐ Types of acceptable vendors.
- ☐ Inventions, patents, and trademarks.
- ☐ Contributions and donations to community groups.
- ☐ Replacement of facilities.
- ☐ Collective bargaining and union relations.
- ☐ Equal opportunities.
- ☐ Training and educational opportunities.
- ☐ Working conditions.
- ☐ Compliance with the law.

Example of policy

A policy furnishes a broad guideline for managers as they make decisions. By adhering to the intent of the policy, managers help maintain consistency in attaining organizational goals.

For example, the top executives of a regional service station company want to expand business by enticing Canadian and other foreign visitors to use the company's stations. The executives, therefore, decide to modify their written credit policy to include all foreign credit cards. To communicate the policy to the targeted group, large posters containing the following message are prepared and displayed at each station:

ALL FOREIGN
CREDIT CARDS
WELCOMED!

Foreign visitors will feel delight at seeing this sign although most of them would not recognize it as a policy statement. In addition to publicizing the new policy to the station's visitors, the poster also reminds all station personnel of the new guideline—*accept all foreign credit cards.*

Consider a second example. As the business environment changes with the use of microcomputers and networks, executives at many companies may have to establish a personnel policy like the following:

Example of policy

> The use of microcomputers and networks has decreased our need for clerical/secretarial and middle-management personnel. Our organization will offer retraining opportunities for all affected employees. All displaced employees who complete the retraining program will be offered continued employment opportunities.

This statement actually contains two policies: one, the provision for retraining; and two, the continued employment of retrained employees.

After formulating these statements, managers need to communicate with all affected employees. Then, they must establish specific procedures to carry out the policies. Employees should understand the rationale for the decisions and the alternatives they can choose. The strategy for communicating helps in writing a policy statement.

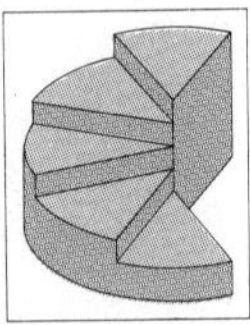

STRATEGY: A POLICY STATEMENT

Smoking was permitted in general areas at St. Mary's Hospital for years. No formal written policy appears in the policy manual. The top executives of St. Mary's have debated the topic of banning smoking from the hospital areas for some time. What was once accepted as commonplace is restricted. Over half of the U.S. population is now nonsmoking; in 1986, only 28 percent of women and 33 percent of men smoked.[1] Research showing

[1] R. C. Bates, "Smoking and Health Implications for Smoking Cessation Program," *Health Education* 18, no. 3 (June/July 1987), pp. 14-17.

the negative effects of smoking on health have changed our society's attitude toward smoking. After careful consideration, the top executives decide to ban smoking from all areas of the hospital for everyone's health benefit.

If you were responsible for writing the policy statement, your strategy might look something like the following.

PROBLEM

Need for a no-smoking policy statement.

OBJECTIVES

General: To provide a healthful atmosphere.

Specific: To provide a rationale for the policy—health, research findings, negative impact on nonsmokers.

To express in writing the no-smoking policy.

READER/AUDIENCE

Characteristics: Employees, patients, visitors, and others of varied ages and backgrounds (Primary—employees, patients; secondary—visitors and others who enter the building).

Smokers and nonsmokers.

Reactions: Most will be pleased. Some, primarily smokers, will be very displeased.

ORDER

OVERALL DIRECT

Policy statements are given first, according to the policy manual, followed by the rationale.

SPECIFIC OBJECTIVES

1. To express the no-smoking policy.
2. To provide a rationale for the policy.

FORMAT

SPECIAL FORM FOR POLICY STATEMENT

Figure 21.1 shows a draft of the policy statement.

To implement this policy, each unit head is sent a memo stating the new policy with the rationale. In this example, the first statement gives the policy, and the remainder presents the rationale. Each unit head, in turn, communicates the new policy to employees. No-smoking signs are prepared and displayed throughout the hospital.

Figure 21.1 Policy statement—No smoking

Policy on Smoking at St. Mary's Hospital

Beginning January 1, 19__, smoking will be banned in all areas of St. Mary's Hospital.

Today, more than 50 percent of the U. S. population is nonsmoking. Research studies confirm the health hazard to smokers and to nonsmokers who inhale smoke secondhand. Adherence to this policy will provide an atmosphere more compatible with St. Mary's goal—good health.

This policy is not intended to keep employees from smoking when away from St. Mary's facilities.

PROCEDURE STATEMENTS

Definition of procedure

A procedure is a logical arrangement or a series of related actions that must be completed to accomplish a specific task. A procedure provides a sequential description of who does what, when, where, and how. Like the policy, the procedure guides employees as they perform their work activities. Procedures, however, are more specific and action-oriented. Training sessions for new employees rely heavily on established procedures. To assure consistency, procedures should be in writing.

From the employee's perspective, procedures provide information and instructions for satisfactory job performance. They answer the questions:

What steps are involved?

When do I do that?

How does this contribute to the business?

From management's perspective, procedures unify the efforts of people and departments to achieve organizational goals and objectives. For both employees and managers, procedures offer the following major benefits:

Major benefits of procedures

- □ Assist in the delegation of responsibility and authority for work activities.
- □ Relieve the manager/supervisor of having to give detailed directions repeatedly.
- □ Provide organization and continuity for all work performed in the company.
- □ Identify the physical resources, people, and time requirements needed for efficient and effective job performance.
- □ Establish a basis for training and retraining.
- □ Provide a basis of control—comparison of actual performance with established standards of performance.
- □ Serve as references for nonroutine activities and operational questions.

Regardless of where you work in an organization, you will follow procedures as you perform your work activities. As you follow the steps in a

LEGAL / ETHICAL ISSUE

Software Piracy! Satellite Messages Intercepted! Hacker Intrusion! Implanted Bugs Discovered!

These white-collar crimes are common newspaper and TV headlines today. Computer fraud is reported to be widespread as evidenced by an Ernst & Whinney study. Of 562 Computer Security Institute members surveyed, 51 percent reported computer fraud within their business.* A growing concern is the loss of money through electronic fund transfers from one bank to another.

The computer is essential to the continued growth and management of business information. More and more microcomputers and networks are added to business offices to manage the vast amount of data and information; the potential for economic loss and invasion of sensitive data and information multiplies.

How can businesses continue to harness the power of the computer but avoid economic disaster as the result of invasions of corporate information? What are the implications for company policies and procedures?

* "Fraud Taking a Bite out of Business," *Security,* 24, no. 10 (October 1987), p. 63.

procedure, you will become aware of its weaknesses and strengths. At times, you will probably offer suggestions for improving a particular set of steps. You may need to write procedures or instructions for a new activity within your department. Since procedures and instructions affect the daily work activities of individuals, use care in preparing specific guides for accomplishing work.

The guidelines for writing procedures include the following:

Guidelines for writing procedures

- ☐ Identify the start and stop points and the in-between steps.
- ☐ Identify the forms and people involved at each step.
- ☐ Give the procedure an appropriate name.
- ☐ Number each step sequentially.
- ☐ Divide the steps into sections.
- ☐ Use action verbs for each numbered step.
- ☐ Include visuals if appropriate.
- ☐ Add headings and notations as needed.
- ☐ Introduce special terms gradually; provide definitions where appropriate.
- ☐ Use a set of symbols such as those developed by the American National Standards Institute for flow charts.

This chapter focuses on the preparation of written procedures and instructions for a variety of situations. In each situation, the strategy provides the planning guide for writing the message.

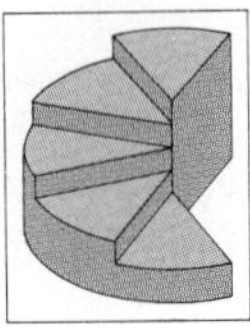

STRATEGY: PROCEDURE MEMO

Heidi Pennery, vice president of a marketing research firm, has managed the planning and implementation of a new telephone system. The new phone system resulted from a study which showed that on-line service centers would provide more flexibility, convenience, and save time and money. Six months ago, a memo announcing the installation of the new system was sent to all employees. Now the installation is almost complete, and Heidi is concerned about the transition from the old system to the new. To help, she has completed a procedures booklet for each type of telephone use.

Because approximately 30 people are affected by the change at this location, Heidi must instruct the employees on how to handle the most common types of calls: an outside local number; a long-distance number; and operator-assisted calls. A written message to the 30 people will help smooth the transition to the new system.

Heidi identifies the strategy components as follows:

PROBLEM

Lack of information on using new phone system.

OBJECTIVES

General: To provide information on basic types of phone use.

Specific: How to place local calls.
How to place long-distance calls.
How to place operator-assisted calls.
How to call the information operator.
To announce change and the effective date.

READER/AUDIENCE

Characteristics: 30 people in firm—managers, professionals, secretaries, other support personnel will each receive a copy.

Reactions: Some will like the new system because of its benefits.
Some will resent the change.
Some will be gone when the actual change takes place.

ORDER

OVERALL MESSAGE: DIRECT

The direct approach applies since the employees had previous information about the change in the phone system. Employees now need to know the procedures; the direct approach will provide basic information for using the system. A reference booklet is available for additional information.

SPECIFIC OBJECTIVES

1. To announce the change and effective date.
2. To describe the following:
   How to place local calls.
   How to place long-distance calls.
   How to place operator-assisted calls.
   How to call the information operator.

FORMAT

MEMO

Because the message goes to the 30 people in the firm, Heidi decides to use a memo.

With the strategy completed, Heidi drafts this memo message:

Effective April 20, 19__, the dialing procedures for making all calls will change; so be prepared! Instead of dialing 9, as you have done in the past, you will need to change to make sure that you conform to the new way of making calls. You will need to dial 99 and the local telephone number if you have to make a local call; if you want to make a long-distance call, you must first dial 98, then 1 and the area code (AC), followed by the telephone number (you don't have to dial the area code if it is the same as ours); dial 97 plus zero, plus area code (again, if different from ours), plus the telephone number for operator-assisted calls (collect, person-to-person, operator-assisted). If you need to get a number from the operator, dial 98 and 1 and AC and 555-1212. I am providing a booklet for easy reference for all phone use.

After completing the draft and making sure that the message contains all of the information identified in the strategy, Heidi gives the message to a person in her office for his reaction. Ted reads the message and suggests these changes:

1. The first two sentences are wordy and do not get to the point.
2. To reduce the frustration caused by changing the phone system, you might indicate a benefit in the opening sentences: the new system will be easier to use.
3. Indicate that the procedures listed in the memo are the more com-

Figure 21.2 **Procedure for using new phone system**

MEMORANDUM

TO: All Employees
FROM: Heidi Pennery, Vice President
DATE: April 17, 19__
SUBJECT: New Telephone Procedures, Effective April 20, 19__

Our new, easy-to-use phone system will go into service on April 20, 19__. Please use the following procedures when making your phone calls:

To place a call . . .	Dial:
Local	99 + local number
Long distance with	
same Area Code (AC)	98 + 1 + number
different AC	98 + 1 + AC + number
Operator-assisted	98 + 0 + AC + number
Operator information	98 + 1 + AC + 555-1212

You will receive a complete reference booklet shortly.

mon ones; more detailed procedures for other uses of the phone system are contained in a booklet that each person will receive.

4. List the information in two columns ("To place a call" and "Dial") rather than using the sentence form.

Heidi examines the message and agrees that it needs improvement; she uses Ted's suggestions. Her revised message looks like this:

Our new phone system will go into service on April 10, 19__, and will make your phone use easier; therefore, please use the following procedures when making your phone calls (you will receive a complete reference booklet shortly):

1. To place a *local* call	Dial 99 + local number
2. To place a *long-distance* call with—	
same area code (AC)	Dial 98 + 1 + phone number
different AC	Dial 98 + 1 + AC + number
3. To place an *operator-assisted* call (collect, person-to-person, operator)	Dial 97 + 0 + AC + number

Heidi reads the message and likes the introduction but feels that the list still needs revising. Each item begins with *To* plus a verb; and the second column begins with *Dial.* She places these as headings of the two columns. The revised listing is shown in final draft of the memo (Figure 21.2). Heidi directs her secretary to prepare the memo for distribution.

Step-by-Step Procedures

Procedures are very important in businesses because they direct workers' activities. Once you have written a set of procedures, have someone test them for clarity. This is the best way to assess their effectiveness.

The situation below focuses on developing a step-by-step procedure for learning to operate a microcomputer. A visual aid is used to assist the reader in performing the tasks. Read the following setting first.

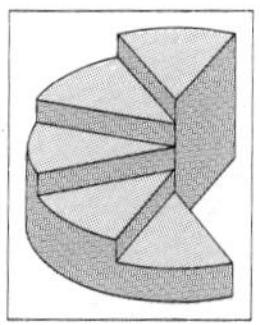

STRATEGY: WRITING STEP-BY-STEP INSTRUCTIONS

Clifford Warren, the owner and manager of a successful insurance company located in Ames, Iowa, has just purchased a new microcomputer, screen, and letter-quality printer for his growing business. The computer unit has two disk drives and a 512K memory. He purchased the following software for his office: a text-processing program (including a mail-merge feature, a spelling checker, and records processor), a spreadsheet, and a database management system.

After a brief training session at the vendor's office, Clifford returned to his office eager to begin automating various functions. He also planned to train the two secretaries and four agents in his office. He obtained manuals for the computer system and each of the software packages at the training session. From comments made by the vendor, Clifford was confident that the manuals could serve as training aids.

But once he returned to his office, he became shocked as he studied the manuals. He wanted to send a form letter to a list of potential customers plus another form letter to each of his established customers as a goodwill gesture. While looking through the manuals, he discovered that the procedures for developing form letters were filled with technical jargon. The manuals focused on the equipment itself and offered little instruction on specific tasks.

Clifford was thankful he had taken the training session at the vendor's. Using the information he had learned at the session, he prepared a set of basic instructions for the office personnel. He knew he would save much supervisory time if he prepared a step-by-step written guide for basic office applications.

So Clifford set out to prepare a good set of procedures. He wrote an introductory step-by-step procedure and tested it before writing the other procedures. The first session explains the computer components; in addition, it shows the user how to create and print a short paragraph.

As he prepared to write the instructions for the first session, Clifford completed the strategy components.

PROBLEM
Need for instructions for using hardware/software.

OBJECTIVES

General: To provide a step-by-step set of procedures for performing text processing.

Specific: To identify the parts of the microcomputer.

To identify the necessary supplies.

To construct easy-to-follow procedures for:

Turning on the microcomputer.

Loading the software.

Preparing/naming a document.

Making changes in the copy.

Saving the copy on a floppy disk.

Printing a hard copy.

Ending the session.

READER/AUDIENCE

Characteristics: Two secretaries; four agents (all novices in computer use).

Knowledgeable about insurance business.

Intelligent people.

Reaction: Positive since each has been involved with the decision to use a microcomputer system in the office.

Eager to learn how to use the micro.

ORDER

OVERALL: DIRECT (SIMPLE TO COMPLEX)

SPECIFIC OBJECTIVES

1. To identify the necessary supplies.
2. To identify the tasks to complete the session.
3. To identify the parts of the micro.
4. To construct easy-to-follow procedures for:

   Turning on the computer.

   Loading the software.

   Preparing/naming a document.

   Making changes in the copy.

   Saving the copy on a floppy disk.

   Printing a hard copy.

   Ending the session.

FORMAT

SPECIAL FORM

With the strategy components identified, Clifford writes the set of instructions beginning with the necessary supplies. Having the supplies first will alert the person to the needed items. The person will not have to interrupt the session to find the needed supplies.

Necessary Supplies

1. Two floppy disks—word-processing disk and one blank disk (5 1/4 in.; double density; double-sided).
2. Set of procedures for Session 1.
3. Paper in the printer.

Clifford completes the next specific objective; he identifies the tasks to be completed. Note the action-oriented writing style. Listing the individual steps make it easy to follow.

Session Tasks

When you finish the FIRST Session, you will know how . . .

a. To get the microcomputer ready for use.
b. To load the text processing program disk.
c. To insert the formatted disk for storing your document.
d. To name a document.
e. To input a message.
f. To make changes (correct spelling, delete errors, make other basic changes in content).
g. To save the message on your formatted floppy disk.
h. To print out a hard copy.
i. To end the session (store your disks; leave the microcomputer in the proper manner).

Clifford turns his attention to the next objective: to identify the parts of the microcomputer. This section identifies the parts of the microcomputer for the reader; these can be used later for reference. Clifford decides to use a schematic with numbered parts for easy reference.

Microcomputer Parts

Look at the basic parts of the microcomputer shown in Exhibit A; locate each part on your microcomputer before you continue:

(1) Keyboard (alphabetic and numeric/special).
(2) Screen (called a video display terminal).
(3) Disk drives (A is left drive; B is right).
(3A) Gates for disk drives.
(4) Printer.
(5) On/off switch.

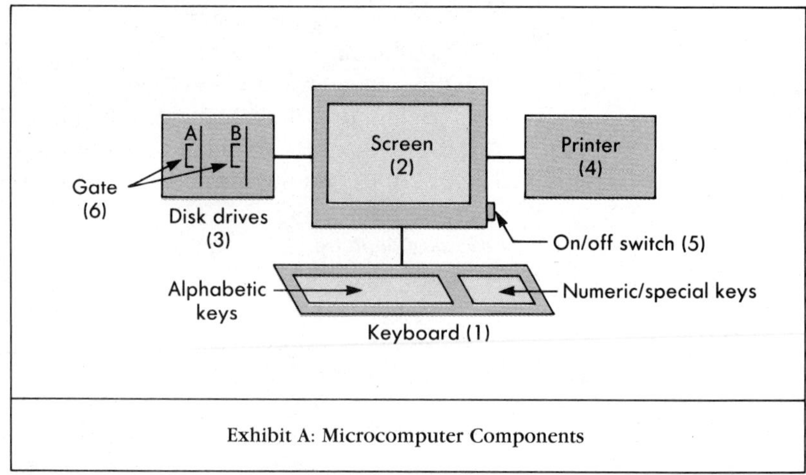

Exhibit A: Microcomputer Components

Clifford writes the following step-by-step procedures for getting started and uses the numbered parts shown in Exhibit A for a backup. Note the ease in using the steps with the coded graphic aid. Each function uses an infinitive phrase as a lead-in; then the steps are numbered for the step-by-step procedure. After the procedure, a summary statement is used. (See the summary/transition statement between Steps 8 and 9.)

To get started . . .

1. Be sure the video display terminal (VDT) and printer are plugged in to a grounded electrical outlet.
2. Turn the VDT and printer on by touching the on/off switches (no. 5 in Exhibit A).
3. Insert the *text processing* disk into Drive A (no. 3) (note arrows on disk for correct position).
4. Close the gate to Drive A (no. 3A).
5. Insert the formatted disk into Drive B (no. 3).
6. Close the gate to Drive B (no. 3A).

You're now ready to transfer the information on the *text processing disk* into the computer memory.

To load the text processing software . . .

7. Type: WP.
8. Touch the return key.
(*Note:* Wait a few seconds; you will hear the disk spin as it transfers the instructions into the computer memory. When this process is completed, you will see a Directory Menu on the screen with various options.)

You are now ready to select the option to work on a document and to give a name to the document; so . . .

9. Check to see that the Directory Menu is on the screen.

10. Touch the A key to select the *work on a document.*

FILE option; touch the return key.

(*Note:* You have selected this option from those listed on the screen since you want to create a new document.)

After touching the A and return keys, you will then see some instructions which you may read. Notice that the *cursor* (the small, white rectangle) appears after the words, *name of file to use:*

11. Type: B:Para (no space between).

(*Note:* This document will be known as *Para* from now on; you will name other documents to distinguish them from each other—you are limited to a maximum of seven characters for each document name.)

12. Touch return key.
13. Wait until Main Menu appears on screen.

At this point, you have completed these steps:
Getting the microcomputer ready for use.
Loading the text processing program into the computer.
Naming a document.

You are now ready to begin typing (keyboarding) Exercise 1 (blue copy) located at the end of the procedures for Session 1.

At this point, Clifford rereads the procedures and asks a secretary to test them. The secretary completes the steps with ease. Clifford feels he has made a good start. Writing the procedures for other specific objectives will be quite similar: to type in the message; to correct errors; to save the completed message; to print a saved document; and to end the session.

Information Procedures

This section presents a different type of procedure—one created by an information manager for use by engineers and administrative employees in a high-tech company. The procedure provides information for using the copying services (reprographics) available in the company. The guidelines presented earlier apply here also.

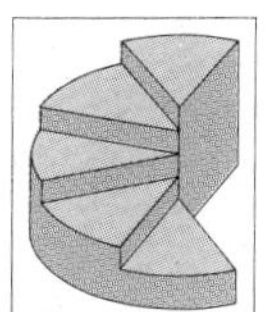

STRATEGY: INFORMATIVE GUIDELINES

The ZT Corporation is a designer and manufacturer of electronic equipment for industry. Joyce Wallace, the information manager, is responsible for designing and implementing the Information Center for ZT Corp. After getting the center underway, she has been busy writing procedures. She wants the various employees to know what center services are available and how to use the support services (document production, copying, electronic mail, regular mail, and related support services).

PROBLEM

Users need information (administrators, engineers, support personnel).

OBJECTIVES

General: To inform users about procedures for using the copying service.

Specific: What materials to submit to the Information Center.

What materials to copy at convenience machines.

How to submit materials to the center.

When materials can be submitted.

Priority of work submitted.

Turnaround time.

Location of copiers—Information Center buildings 100, 300, and Corporate Headquarters have convenience copiers.

Extension number of the Information Center.

How work is returned.

READER/AUDIENCE

Characteristics: Engineers and administrators who are technically minded and intelligent but uninformed.

Support personnel who are experienced with copying process/machines.

Reactions: Some will expect immediate turnaround of copies.

Most engineers and administrators will rely on a secretary or other support person for processing.

Some users will appear at center demanding that their work be completed while they wait.

Most users will conform to the written procedures.

ORDER

OVERALL MESSAGE: DIRECT

Reader/Audience will want to know the procedure without reading a lot of material.

Because she needs additional information before ordering the specific objectives, Joyce writes each of the specific objectives on a sheet of paper and collects the following facts:

1. What materials to submit to the Information Center:
   a. Reports and proposals of 10 or more pages (all others are to be done on the convenience copiers located throughout the buildings).
   b. Documents that require multiple copies and collating.
   c. Documents that require two-sided copying.
   d. Documents requiring binding.

   e. Microfilm copying.
   f. Computer printouts.
   g. Books that can be removed from their bindings (all bound book copying should be done through individual's secretary or clerk typist).

2. How to submit materials:
   a. Authorized person (engineer, administrator, secretary, clerk typist) fills out top portion of work order request form.
   b. Authorized person submits work to center supervisor.
3. When materials can be submitted:
   a. Daily: 8:30 A.M. to 5:30 P.M. (except for the lunch hour—12:00–1:00 P.M.).
   b. Evening or weekend: schedule in advance with center supervisor (extension 2234).
4. Priority of work submitted:
   a. Work completed in order of submission unless there is an emergency.
   b. Emergency work—complete as requested when possible; if time is inadequate to meet the requested deadline, the author's secretary/clerk typist assists them; any deadline not met will result in notification to the author.
5. Turnaround time:
   Generally within eight hours; depends on length and number of emergency requests.
6. What work to be completed at convenience copiers:
   a. All documents less than 10 pages in length,
   b. Copy sizes: 8 ½ × 14 inches; 11 × 17 inches.
   c. Bound books.
   d. Other short-run items.
   e. Reduction.
   f. Enlarging.
   g. Collating (on Canon 400s in Building 300).
7. Reprographic services available from the Information Center (Xerox 9400 copier):
   a. Binding of copies with automatic electric three-hold punch.
   b. Copying of continuous forms computer sheet printout without bursting.
   c. Enlarging.
   d. Reduction.
   e. Duplicating both sides of paper.
   f. Sizes: all regular sizes.
   g. Color paper (variety).
   h. Collating.

8. Location of copiers:
   a. Convenience copiers—located in Buildings 100, 300, and throughout the Corporate Headquarters Building.
   b. Xerox 9400—located in the Information Center, Room 101, Corporate Headquarters Building.
9. Extension Center phone number: 2234, center supervisor.
10. How work is returned:
    a. Author's secretary/clerk typist will call when work is ready for pick up.
    b. Completed work released only to authorized person submitting the work (control of completed work).

FORMAT

SPECIAL FORM

This form contains a listing of directions grouped under two sections: convenience copiers and center copying (Xerox 9400).

Joyce now considers the Order. The procedural steps will focus on the use of the copying services from the Information Center, but she must provide information about the convenience copiers also. She decides to use Specific Objective 6 (what work to be completed at convenience copiers) and Specific Objective 8 (location of copiers) as the introductory material. The opening section of the procedure appears below.

INTRODUCTION

At ZT Corporation, you may have copies of your documents made by either of two methods: by convenience copiers located throughout Buildings 100, 300, and Corporate Headquarters; or by the Xerox 9400 copier located in the Information Center, Room 101, Corporate Headquarters Building. The following information explains the use of the convenience copiers and the Information Center services.

With the specific directions grouped under the two section titles, Joyce's first section is as follows:

Convenience Copiers

Document types:	All documents less than 10 pages. Bound books. Other short-run items. *Note:* All other work should be submitted to the Information Center for processing.
Copier features:	Size reduction. Size enlarging. Document collating. Size selection: 8½ × 11 inches 8½ × 14 inches 11 × 17 inches
How to use:	Take the original to the convenience copier and copy. Record name/number of copies in the log.

After rereading the introductory part, Joyce concludes that this is enough information about the convenience copiers. She then orders the other specific objectives:

1. What materials to submit (Objective number 1)—change wording to *Document Types/Requirements.*
2. Services available (Objective number 7)—change to *Features* to be consistent.
3. How to submit materials (Objective number 2)—use only *How to Submit.*
4. When materials are submitted (Objective number 3)—use *When to Submit* only.

At this point Joyce examines the remaining specific objectives number 4—priority of work submitted; number 5—turnaround time; number 9—extension number for the Information Center; and number 10—how work is returned) and recognizes that these additional facts are needed in the procedure. The order is:

5. Priority of work submitted (Objective number 4)—change to *Work Priority.*
6. Turnaround time (Objective number 5)—capitalize *Time.*
7. How work is returned (Objective number 10)—change to *Completed Work Pickup.*
8. Extension number for Information Center (Objective number 9)—change to *Center Phone Extension.*

Joyce follows this order for the remainder of the procedures.

Center Copying (Xerox 9400)

Document types/requirements:	Reports and proposals with 10 or more pages.
	Documents that require multiple copies and collating.
	Documents requiring binding.
	Microfilm copying.
	Computer printouts.
	Books that can be removed from their bindings.
	Size reduction.
	Size enlarging.
	Document collating.
	Size selection: wide variety.
	Color selection: variety.
	Duplication on both sides of paper.
	Binding of copies with electric 3-hole punch.
	Copying of continuous forms computer sheet printouts without bursting.

How to submit:	*a.* Authorized person (engineer, administrator, secretary, clerk typist) fills out top portion of work order request form (sample attached). *b.* Authorized person takes form and originals to center supervisor: Room 101, Corporate Headquarters.
When to submit:	Monday through Friday: 8:30–11:50 A.M. 1:00–5:30 P.M. Evening or weekend: Schedule 24 hours *in advance* with center supervisor.
Work priority:	*a.* Work completed in order of submission except for emergency. *b.* Emergency work: When possible, completed as requested; if time allowed is to meet deadline, the author's secretary/clerk typist is requested to assist the center employees. *c.* Author phoned for any deadline not met.
Turnaround time:	Generally, 8 hours (may depend on length and number of emergency requests).
Completed work pickup:	*a.* Author's secretary/clerk typist will call when work is ready for pick up. *b.* To provide control of documents, completed work released only to authorized person submitting the work.
Center phone:	Ext. 223—Center supervisor, Room 101, Corporate Headquarters.

Joyce is pleased with her procedure statements.

Procedure in Flow Chart Format

Flowchart definition

A flow chart presents in picture form the logical steps and sequence of a procedure. The flow chart helps the reader see the relationship of the various steps in the whole process. What may appear to be an invisible process can be pictured and then studied for improvement. The guidelines presented earlier apply to the flow chart development.

Because it provides a simple outline of the steps in a task, a flow chart saves time. Procedures written in a flow chart format are especially helpful in the training of new employees. The employee can follow the steps to perform the needed tasks and also to understand the system concepts of the procedure. Presenting procedures as flow charts also helps managers analyze the steps and/or forms and perhaps improve the procedure.

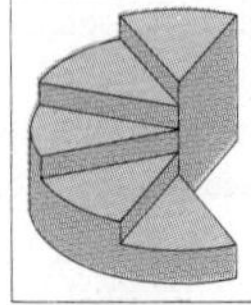

STRATEGY: FLOW CHART PROCEDURES

Mike Todd (co-owner of a successful law firm in Stillwater, Oklahoma), has just been informed by his personal secretary, Larry Ellis, that the receptionist is leaving in two weeks. The receptionist is responsible for taking and routing phone calls, greeting clients, preparing a file for new clients, and numerous other clerical duties. The law firm is relatively small, consisting of Mike Todd, his co-owner, two other lawyers, one legal assistant, two secretaries, one word-processing specialist, one file clerk, and the receptionist.

In the past, Mike orally instructed new employees about their job activities; however, this training process has been time-consuming and unsatisfactory. Because Mike is responsible for training new personnel, he asks the receptionist to write down each of the steps for the receptionist's job activities. From this material, he then develops a flow chart to outline those steps in the procedure.

Since the law firm specializes in health-related issues, the receptionist must be ready to collect background information from the clients. In addition, the receptionist must collect medical facts for each of the clients where appropriate. Finally, the receptionist directs clients to send disability forms and other information to the relevant federal office.

Mike uses the strategy for implementing his plan of action.

PROBLEM

Need for a written statement of procedures.

OBJECTIVES

General: To document the major activities of the receptionist.

Specific: To document the procedure for setting up a new client's file—steps and forms.

READER/AUDIENCE

Characteristics: New employees.
Not familiar with procedure.
Will need to adjust to a new environment.

Reactions: Will appreciate having the steps for reference.
Will have to ask questions if procedure is incomplete.

ORDER

OVERALL MESSAGE: DIRECT

The title of the form indicates the objective of the message; logical order.

SPECIFIC OBJECTIVES

To document the procedure for setting up a new client's file—steps and forms (arranged in logical sequence of steps performed).

FORMAT

SPECIAL—FLOW CHART WITH EXPLANATION

With the strategy complete, Mike considers the alternatives of getting the needed information so that he can document the procedure. The receptionist provides these written comments for setting up a new client's file:

> I will go into detail as to my routine chores in setting up a client's file. Setting up a file is probably one of my least favorite things to do. After the new client is interviewed, I get the file (which reminds me that before we interview the client I set up blank files, which means making sure that every one of our forms to fill out or be signed by the client is in a file folder so an initial interview can be performed. This is almost 30 forms, along with brochures, etc., which are also kept in my office.) Anyway, I'll get a new file and it has to be sorted into four- to five-odd files, these labels typed up and put on new file folders which have to be stamped with our firm name and address, holes have to be punched and Acco fasteners put in and the correspondence put in order chronologically. The medical has to be copied and the personal history to make up a medical file for Peggy and Rosemarie. The social security printout has to be ordered and the order form copied and put in each file. Then a form including name, address, responsible lawyer, statute date, etc., has to be typed up for my tickler notebook, which is another thing.

After reading the explanation, Mike is glad that the receptionist was still at the office so that he could ask some questions about specifics. Although he instructed her when she started with the firm four years ago, he is a bit rusty on the procedure—he even wonders about his own ability to communicate orally. Then, Mike realized that the flow chart approach would certainly be a good one for this activity, especially, and for documenting the other office procedures. Mike analyzes the description and prepares his outline. (Note the use of verbs to identify the main steps.)

1. Interview the client (initial interview).
2. Get the file.
3. Sort the file into four- to five-odd files.
    a. Type labels.
    b. Place labels on the file folders.
    c. Stamp file folders with the name and address.
    d. Punch holes.
    e. Put in the Acco fasteners.
4. Put correspondence in chronological order.
5. Copy the medical (medical file).
6. Copy the history (medical file).
7. Order social security printout.
    a. Copy order form.
    b. Put in each file.
8. Type form for tickler notebook: name, responsible lawyer, statute date, etc.

Even though this is a good basic outline of the procedure, Mike determines that he needs additional facts. He then lists questions for the receptionist to clarify. The questions with her responses are:

1. **Q:** What is contained in the file after the initial interview?
   A: The client's medical record, personal history record, and notes made by the lawyer during the initial interview.
2. **Q:** Isn't a form completed after the interview?
   A: Yes, it is Form 100; and it has five copies (original, yellow, pink, blue, and green).
3. **Q:** What is meant by "sort into four- to five-odd files"?
   A: Four or five file folders are created; depends on the type situation as to whether there are four or five.
4. **Q:** What happens to the original and four copies of Form 100 and the completed five folders?
   A: They are transferred to the central file room after the material in each folder is arranged chronologically: Form 100, notes.
5. **Q:** Is another file created for the medical file? Or is this one of the four/five already created?
   A: It is one of the four/five.
6. **Q:** Does the social security order have a special form?
   A: Yes; it is called the Social Security Order Form.
7. **Q:** Is only one copy made of the Social Security Order Form?
   A: No; the form has five copies already attached; we send one to the Social Security Administration and file the others in the client's folders.
8. **Q:** Is the social security copy placed before the notes in each file?
   A: Yes.

With this added information, Mike uses a flow chart template and converts the steps in the procedure into the flow chart shown in Figure 21.3

The receptionist then verifies the accuracy of the document. She indicates that it is all right, but suggests the following attachments: a supplementary list of the substeps involved in preparing the file folder (see Figure 21.4); and a completed copy of each form (Form 100, Social Security Order Form, Control Form) for convenience. Mike agrees. The entire package consists of the flow chart, the supplementary steps for preparing the file folders, and samples of completed forms. Mike feels sure that the new receptionist can set up a file for new clients with little or no assistance from him. When all the procedures are as well documented, breaking in a new receptionist will be quite easy.

Figure 21.3 Flow chart of procedure for setting up a new client's file in a legal office

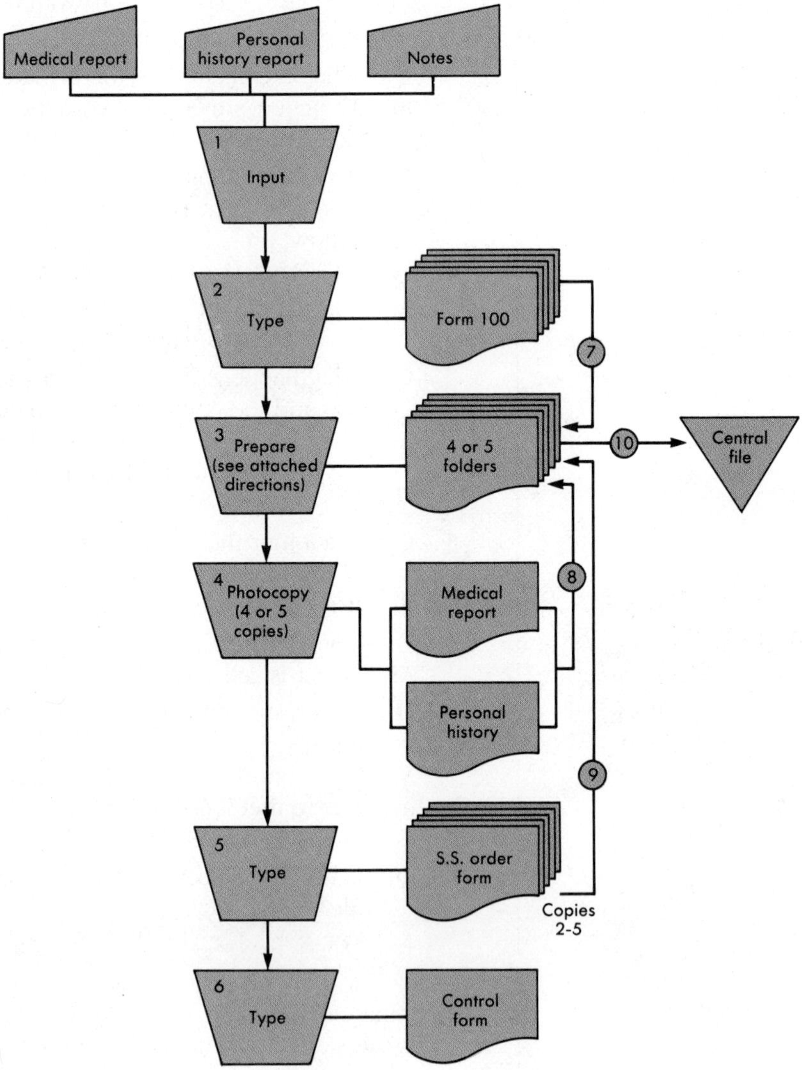

Medical report
Personal history report
Notes
1 Input
2 Type
Form 100
7
3 Prepare (see attached directions)
4 or 5 folders
10
Central file
4 Photocopy (4 or 5 copies)
Medical report
8
Personal history
9
5 Type
S.S. order form
Copies 2-5
6 Type
Control form

Figure 21.4 Supplementary directions for opening a new client's file

To Prepare File Folder:

1. Type labels in upper case starting on line two space three; client's last name given first.
2. Place labels on file folders.
3. Stamp firm's name and address on file folders.
4. Punch holes in folder and papers.
5. Place fasteners in folder.

Writing Directions

Sometimes in business it is necessary to gather information from a client, employee, job applicant, or business associate. In this message, specify *what* is needed, *why* the information is needed, and *when* it is needed. In addition, specify *how* the steps and/or facts are supplied. A convenient format for obtaining this type of information is a blank form along with a list of directions. Filling out a blank form can be confusing; therefore, clear directions are needed, especially for multiple-information forms. Use the guidelines given earlier in the chapter for writing the directions (directions are similar to procedures).

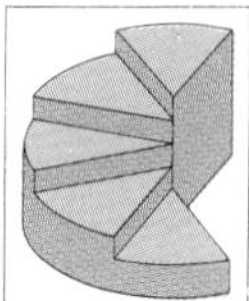

STRATEGY: DIRECTIONS FOR COMPLETING A FORM

Teresa Gambell is in charge of the group insurance for the French Manufacturing Company, New Bedford, Massachusetts. Blue Cross has asked her to obtain specific information about the dependents of each employee who has family coverage under the group Blue Cross program. Before this time, Blue Cross required the information only about the employee, not the dependents.

Teresa must get the full names (first name, middle initial, and last name) of each eligible dependent, the relationship, sex, date of birth, and whether each has other group insurance. If the spouse is also covered by the Blue Cross insurance program at another firm, then the spouse's name, social security number, and place of employment are also needed. Teresa's records already include the following information: employee's name, social security number, type of coverage (family, individual, etc.), and account number.

Because she must send the information to Blue Cross by January 1, 19--, Teresa estimates that she will need the information back from all employees by December 1, 19--. After January 1, 19--, Blue Cross will require this information before they honor a claim. Also, if any changes are made after the employee completes and files the initial form, he or she must file a revised form with the necessary changes, additions, and/or deletions within 30 days of the change.

Figure 21.5 Sample of special form "Eligible Dependent Form"

Employee name: ____________ Eligible Dependent Form
Social security no. ____________
Type of coverage: ____________
Responsible account: ____________

Eligible dependents (include spouse if family coverage)

① Name a. First	b. Middle Initial	c. Last	② Relationship Code	Description	③ Sex M/F	④ Date of birth MM/DD/YY	⑤ Other group insurance Yes/No

⑥ Please complete the following if your spouse is employed by the state but at a different agency.

(6a) Spouse name	(6b) Spouse social security no.
(6c) Agency name	

⑦ Misrepresentation constitutes fraud and may result in loss of benefits through the state group plan.

⑧ ____________ Signature ⑨ ____________ Date

A special form mailed with a memo is appropriate for this in-house communication. The memo will provide the necessary background information and encourage each recipient to complete and return the special form. Teresa plans to number each segment of the form and to explain each segment with step-by-step directions.

Teresa first develops the form shown in Figure 21.5. Then she determines the following strategy components for the directions portion of the memo.

PROBLEM

Need for dependent information for Blue Cross insurance coverage.

OBJECTIVES

General: To write clear directions for getting the needed information.

Specific: A. To request specific information:

A.1—eligible dependents (first name, middle initial, last name).

A.2—relationship of each dependent.

A.3—sex.

A.4—date of birth (month, day, year).

A.5—other group insurance coverage?

A.6—employee signature and date.

B. To provide definitions and/or examples where necessary.

READER/AUDIENCE

Characteristics: A mixture of blue- and white-collar workers.

Each will need to complete the form to have coverage.

Each will be concerned about insurance coverage.

Reactions: Some will resent having to take the time to fill in another insurance form.

Majority will complete and return the form since their coverage is dependent upon their doing so.

Some will be confused about filling out the form.

ORDER

DIRECT ORDER

A direct order will be used for the overall message because items will be arranged logically.

FORMAT

SPECIAL FORM AND MEMO

The memo gives directions on completing the required form.

With the form completed, Teresa writes directions for completing the form. Her draft of the directions for completing the Eligible Dependent Form appears below.

Directions for Completing the Eligible Dependent Form

1. List first name, middle initial, and last name for *each* dependent included on your insurance policy (see definition below to determine who qualifies as a dependent):

Eligible dependent

- ☐ Spouse.
- ☐ Children (unmarried dependent children who are living with you in a regular parent/child relationship; stepchild; foster child) from birth to the month of their 19th birthday.
- ☐ Unmarried children who are attending school on a full-time basis (through the month of their 23rd birthday).
- ☐ Incapacitated children (mentally or physically) who meet the plan's guidelines for continuation of coverage.

2. Relationship
Use the numbers and descriptions shown below to complete segments 2a and 2b on the form:
   - ☐ Spouse.
   - ☐ Dependent child.
   - ☐ Dependent child—permanently disabled (either mentally or physically).
3. Sex
Using M for male and F for female, enter the sex of each dependent.
4. Date of birth
Using numbers, enter the date of birth by month, day, year. Example: 12/20/35.
5. Other group insurance:
If the dependent has additional group medical coverage, enter YES.
If French's group insurance is the dependent's only group medical coverage, enter No.
6. Spouse's coverage at another agency
If your spouse is covered by another Blue Cross group plan at another place, supply the following:
   6a. Your spouse's name.
   6b. Your spouse's social security number.
   6c. Your spouse's agency name.
7. CAUTION! Read the misrepresentation statement.
8. Sign your name.
9. Indicate the date you signed the form.

To check the procedure, Teresa gives the form and directions to a fellow employee. The procedure was satisfactory; so Teresa then turns her attention to completing the memo that will accompany the form.

SUMMARY

Top executives are responsible for establishing overall policies for a firm; others at various levels in the firm may write procedures.

A policy statement explains executive decisions about the company's organization, physical plant, personnel activities, budget, or other company goals. A policy furnishes a broad guideline for managers as they make decisions. Policies can be general or specific. Policy statements are prepared to describe such things as the authority and responsibilities of headquarters and satellite divisions; basic lines of business products; service to customers; safety; collective bargaining and union relations; working conditions. Managers who adhere to the intent of the policy help maintain a consistency in attaining organizational goals.

A procedure is a logical series of steps in accomplishing a specific task. The procedure statement provides a sequential description of who does what, when, where, and how. The procedure can guide employees as they perform their work or as they complete a requested action. Well-written procedures help relieve supervisors from giving detailed direction, provide continuity of work performed in the company, and help identify the physical personnel and time resources necessary for efficient and effective job performance.

Write procedures as factual, step-by-step instructions. An outline Format is sometimes appropriate. Procedures can also be presented in flow chart Format. A flow chart presents in picture form the logical steps and sequence of a procedure. The reader can see the relationship and sequence of the various steps. The flow chart is accompanied by a brief explanation.

Sometimes in business it is necessary to gather information from a client, employee, job applicant, or business associate. Giving directions for completing a form is a common practice in this information-gathering activity. In writing directions, arrange sections logically, use a listing format with action verbs, provide definitions where appropriate, and include all actions you must take.

END-OF-CHAPTER ACTIVITIES

DISCUSSION

1. What role do policies and procedures play in a business?
2. Define a policy. Define a procedure.
3. What is the relationship of a policy and a procedure?
4. How do the strategy components relate to the development of policy and procedural statements?
5. Identify essential characteristics of procedure statements.
6. What contribution can graphics make to a procedure?
7. How are the writing of directions and procedures similar?

ACTIVITIES

8. Obtain sample procedure and policy statements from a variety of businesses. How are the policies and procedures communicated to employees?
9. Survey local businesses about their policies and procedures. Are they written? How are they developed? Who is responsible for corporate policies and procedures?

10. The following set of directions was part of a memo sent to find out employees' expenses of driving to work either in their own cars or in a bus or vanpool. Read the directions and evaluate their weaknesses and strengths. How would you improve their effectiveness? Rewrite for an improved version.

Directions

Complete the following:

Line 1. Cost of driving.
(If you do not drive your car, put 0 on line 1*d* and on line 1, page 5.)

a. Take the number of miles to work one way. (Enter on line 1a.) 1a.____
b. Multiply amount on line 1*a* by amount on line 2. 1*b*.____
c. Multiply amount on line 2*a* by 24¢ per mile (as figured by 6.9¢ per mile for depreciation, 4.2¢ per mile for maintenance and parts, 9.3¢ for gas and oil, 2.4¢ for insurance, and 2.2¢ for taxes). 1*c*.____
d. Multiply amount on line 3a × 5 to get a weekly total for travel (or by the number of days you drive if you are in a carpool). Put this number on line 1*d* and line 1, page 5. 1*d*.____

Line 2. Cost of bus or vanpool.
(If you do not take the bus, put 0 on line 2*c* and line 2, page 5.)

a. Figure the cost of a one-way bus fare. 2a.____
b. Multiply the amount on line 2a × 2 for a round-trip fare; enter this amount. 2*b*.____
c. Multiply amount on line 2*b* × 5 to get fare for an entire week; enter this amount on line 2*c* and on line 2, page 5. 2*c*.____

11. *Instructions for Baggage Pick-up.* Edward Holiday had just deplaned from a Delta 231 flight at a U.S. airport and had walked to the baggage claim area to pick up his two bags. As he came into the baggage claim area, he read the following message on an overhead TV monitor:

PASSENGERS ARRIVING ON . . .
ALL ODD NUMBER FLIGHTS
CLAIM BAGGAGE ON CAROUSEL NUMBER ONE (1)

– –

PASSENGERS ARRIVING ON . . .
ALL EVEN NUMBER FLIGHTS
ALL DC10 FLIGHTS
ALL DELTA AIRLINES FLIGHTS

CLAIM BAGGAGE ON CAROUSEL NUMBER TWO (2)

THANKS FOR FLYING **** 11:35 a.m.

Edward read the displayed message, looked at the flight number on his ticket, and then went to Carousel number 1 to wait for his baggage. While waiting, he noticed that baggage was beginning to appear on Carousel number 2 and thought he had made a mistake. So he went back and reread the TV monitor message. This time he read the whole message—and found the Delta flight information. Even though he finally retrieved his bags, Edward was a little upset since he was in a hurry to get to an important meeting.

Critique the weaknesses and strengths of this message as it appears. Then design the strategy for this case; and rewrite the message for clarity.

12. Assume the role of Tim Alexander, supervisor of the new duplication center for the TV & A Corporation. Tim needs to develop a form and write directions for using the duplication services. On the form, Tim needs this information: date; requester's name and department; number of copies desired; use of front only or front and back; paper color—white, blue, pink, green, yellow; date needed; whether to be collated; whether to be stapled.

    Plan the strategy components for this case. Design an appropriate form, and then write a set of directions for the users of the duplicating service.

13. *Procedure for Handling Mail.* Morris Starnes, manager of administrative services, is just now completing a revised procedure for handling the mail for Building Z-2110. Assuming the role of Morris, read the following facts that he has gathered; then write an appropriate message to the Transportation Division managers and engineers in that building, informing them about the mail service:

    Three different rooms for mail stops have been identified—MS-191, MS-194, MS-196. MS-196 will be used by all 2nd-floor personnel; all 1st-floor personnel except those using the MS-191 stop will use the MS-194; Landon Good and G. A. Dorton will be using the MS-191 stop. Mail drops will be located at the floor vaults on the 1st and 2nd floors. Mail delivered between 8 and 10 a.m. each morning; between 12 and 2 p.m. in the afternoon. Mail sorting will be performed by: MS-191, Tracey Smith; MS-194, Janice Butler; Jess Jones and Carol Ann Starnes for MS-196. These sorters will place the mail for each area in designated folders each time; then place the designated folders in the mail carts that will be located at the floor vaults for each administrative secretary to pick up. The administrative secretary must be regular and timely in getting the mail from the vaults for their people. Note to *new employees moving in:* Form ORA 422 should be completed; send one copy to main office payroll, one to telephone services (MS-703), and one to the receptionist in Z-2110. Correct building number and mail drop information are needed on the form.

    Use the strategy components, plan the message, and then write the appropriate message to send to these employees.

14. *Flowcharting.* The retail store where you work follows a consistent procedure for processing BankAmericard purchases. Your immediate

superior has asked you to show this process visually so that she can evaluate the procedure. Read the following description of the procedure and plan the strategy for this case; then prepare the visual that shows the various steps in the procedure.

When a purchaser makes a purchase from a BankAmericard merchant, the merchant must fill out a sales draft. Sales drafts are composed of three sheets—one for the customer, one for the store's records, and one for the bank. The copy sent to the bank is used for determining the merchant's gross sales and for making charges to the purchaser's account. The merchant has the responsibility of making sure that the purchaser is the rightful holder of the BankAmericard. Lists of lost, stolen, and cancelled cards are sent to the merchant regularly. After the merchant fills out the sales draft, which consists of three copies, the first copy is given to the purchaser. The second copy is kept for the store's records, and the third copy is sent to the Sequoia Bank (local bank). If the amount of the purchase is higher than the merchant's floor limit, the merchant must call the BankAmericard office (1-800-xxx-xxxx) for authorization to extend the limit. If permission is granted, the merchant enters a special authorization code number on the sales draft and completes the sale. A sale over the floor limit which was not authorized by the bank may be charged to the merchant's account if the debt is not paid within 90 days.

15. Joseph and Marian Collins are co-owners of a small enterprise that manufactures thermostat control devices. They now employ 10 people in their business.

Since they started business, they have relied on oral communications to their employees about sick days, vacation, and holidays. Because there have been some misunderstandings, they want to create a written policy concerning these three areas. They'll allow five sick days (with a doctor's statement) per year without any loss of pay. A person who has been employed for a period of two years or more receives one week's vacation with pay. After five years' employment, one additional week's vacation with pay is granted. Employees with less than two years' experience with the company can have one week's vacation without pay. The major holidays will be given without pay loss—New Year's Day, July 4, Labor Day, Thanksgiving (Thursday and Friday), and Christmas.

Assume the role of Joseph and Marian Collins. Plan the strategy, write a policy statement, and write the message to give to each employee.

CHAPTER 22

WRITING CASE ANALYSES

Learning Objectives

After studying this chapter, you will be able to:

- □ Define conceptual skills.
- □ Recognize the importance of developing your conceptual skills.
- □ Understand principles applicable to the case method of learning.
- □ Differentiate major areas of questions for use in case analyses.
- □ Apply the strategy for communicating to the analysis of questions at the end of cases, using the underline procedure, coding, outlining and going-beyond-the-question procedures.
- □ Understand the guidelines for using the four-part elements method of case analysis.

In developing your oral and written communication skills, you have analyzed the situation and determined the Problem, Objectives, Reader/Audience, Order, and Format. In writing case analyses, you will again go through this process, but because the situations are much more complex, they will require considerably more problem-solving skills.

The problem in these situations is not always readily apparent, and there may be several alternative solutions. You must assess the problem by considering all factors involved, then recommend a solution with appropriate support.

Developing your conceptual skills

The primary goal of this chapter is to help you develop your conceptual skills. Writing case analyses is one of the best ways to develop this skill.

The ability to do case analyses will make you a much stronger candidate for professional positions. Many consultants can demand lucrative fees for just this type of analysis. How can case analyses increase your professional skills? Typically, practice with demanding case studies:

Benefits gained from learning how to do case analyses

- Helps you to see things from a systems approach.
- Aids in developing real-world, problem-solving capabilities.
- Assists in developing logical thinking—similar to fitting the parts of a puzzle together.
- Develops divergent thinking for solving problems where there is no one right answer.

When analyzing cases, the key is to support your judgments with appropriate justification (qualitative and quantitative, where applicable).

BACKGROUND INFORMATION

Development of marketable skills

Research shows that individuals who get ahead in any organization possess three major competencies: technical skills, conceptual skills, and human relations skills. What do these terms mean?

Technical skills are simply the ability to do things—to run a machine, to operate a computer, to paint, to do mathematics, and so on.

Conceptual skills are usually equated with imaginative ability: being able to see the whole picture, to recognize how various functions of an organization fit together or depend on one another, or how changes on one level affect activities on another.

Human relations skills refer to the ability to communicate effectively with other people, to motivate or counsel others, to function well in a group.

During your academic training, you have had opportunities to develop these skills, some to a larger degree than others. Since research indicates that students need more opportunities to improve conceptual skills, this chapter includes many exercises to help you strengthen these skills.

LEGAL / ETHICAL ISSUE

Janice Hackler has worked for a national insurance company for five years. After completing her B.S. degree in insurance and real estate, Janice joined this company as a salesperson who primarily was responsible for acquiring commercial accounts. Within two years she was promoted to director of commercial accounts. Just this past month, she accepted a promotion as head of commercial accounts for the Northwest. This promotion is an important step in her career path to top management.

When the directors convene from all regions of the country to establish long-range goals for the company, however, she finds her input is not taken seriously. Her colleagues are courteous but patronize her; she feels unaccepted as an equal. This is further evident following the meeting when she tries to enter into their informal network at a directors' reception.

As time goes on, Janice becomes very frustrated with her position. Even though the directors established realistic, attainable goals, Janice has difficulty implementing these goals, because she is not taken seriously. Her productivity begins to diminish as a result.

Analyze the legal and ethical issues involved in this case. Does Janice have any recourse with this situation? Discuss.

THE CASE METHOD APPROACH

Scope of case situations

Cases range from simple mental exercises to comprehensive, complex situations calling for extensive analysis and synthesis. In some of your academic courses, you may analyze case material ranging from one-half page exercises to some that are 25 or more pages long.

In business you will use this conceptual ability for solving problems arising from actual situations. Quite often business professionals go through retraining to update their competencies in their areas of expertise. Seminars and leadership training utilize the case analysis method for developing these skills. A heavy emphasis is placed on the interrelationship of management and communication for such retraining. In this context communication and management are inseparable.

Key considerations regarding the case method of learning

Keep in mind some important points as you analyze cases. Here's a partial list of cautions:

1. Most cases are not intended as examples of *right* and *wrong* or *good* and *bad* situations. Cases are representative of actual situations where you recognize and deal with problems as they are. The case analyst assumes the role of a consultant and looks at the

situation as it is. Then the analyst must formulate a plan of action to solve existing problems, address specific issues, and communicate possible solutions.

2. The case method presents simulated activities where you learn by doing. The case method is an experiential activity, providing opportunities to transfer and apply textbook knowledge to realistic situations.
3. The case method does not necessarily produce *the answer* to specific problems. Effective communication is vital to the discussion and analysis for determining alternative solutions, pro and con. You evaluate several alternatives. In most instances you can communicate a good argument for one plan of action or another.
4. *Written discussion* is a key ingredient of case analysis. The *opposing views of others* through oral communication will challenge you to support your analysis and plan of action with concrete detail.
5. Ideally, in solving a problem, you should gather all the facts and then make a decision. Recognize, however, that often all facts are not available, whether in a case or in an actual situation.

The systems approach to case analyses

As a student of the case method, you will have opportunities to diagnose and form judgments about a company's situation. Since the firm is considered as a system existing within a larger environment and consisting of many subsystems, it is logical to assume that problems can exist on any of these levels. Thus, implicit in a systems approach to business problems is the concept of an organization as a hierarchy of systems. Figure 22.1 may help you assess situations from this systems perspective.

The level of problem within the hierarchy does not necessarily indicate its importance. A problem on a low level may be of major importance, while one on a higher level could be less critical. Usually, low-level problems cannot be solved, however, until related problems on higher levels are corrected.

In addition to using the conceptual framework of systems levels shown in Figure 22.1, put yourself in the role of a consultant when analyzing cases and develop answers to these questions:

Relevant questions to guide you in completing case analyses

What factors in the past have contributed to the organization's success or failure?

What internal problems are evident? (Consider both strengths and weaknesses.)

What external environmental factors exist?

Do competition, creditors, political, or other social factors affect the direction a company should take?

Once you've assessed the internal and external factors, what long-range or short-range objectives are relevant?

What are your recommendations for solving the problem?

What actions should the organization take? What evidence justifies such action?

Figure 22.1
Systems levels

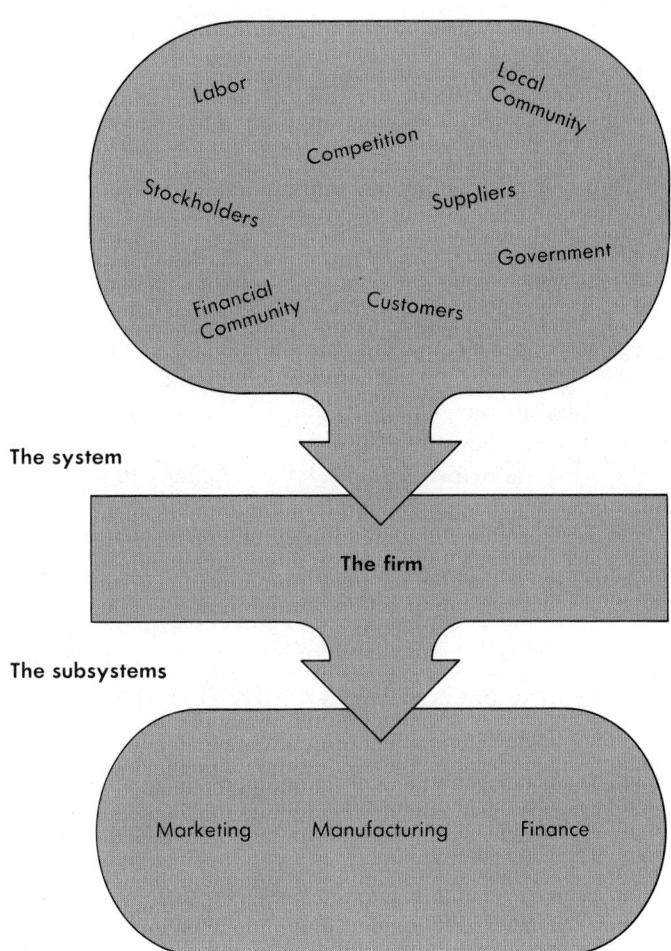

In a classroom setting, you usually have a number of days to reach a solution, depending on the length of the case. Usually, case analyses are typed. If you are requested to present the analysis orally, use the same pattern as that required for the written solution.

METHODS OF CASE ANALYSES

Approaches to case analyses

You may use several methods to complete your investigation or analysis of a case. The objectives of the course, the complexity of the case, and the preference of the individual who will evaluate the written product determine the method to use. The key is *flexibility* and *adaptability* to whatever Format is requested. Keep in mind that you are learning a *process* for developing and enhancing your conceptual skills. Two common methods of case analysis are the *questions-at-the-end-of-case* method and the *four-part-elements* method.

Questions-at-End-of-Case Method

Advantages of using Questions-at-end-of-case method

Many authors who write case material supply end-of-case questions. When you analyze such a case, those questions serve as an effective *plan for organizing* your written project. As a result, the method is easily followed. Usually, *questions at the end of cases* are thought-provoking and may include those pertaining to problem identification, symptoms or problem(s), causes of problem(s), and recommended solutions.

Before producing a final written project based on a case, read and analyze the case thoroughly. Study the facts of the case. Read the case two or three times before writing your analysis. As you read, take notes. These same ideas apply whether you are writing up an analysis individually or as part of a group. Distinguish between facts and opinions, recognize complex human relationships, and search for qualitative as well as quantitative support for your recommendations.

Do not be satisfied with your first draft. Actually, the final product may require three or four drafts. Refining and polishing the final product is critical if you want to achieve a quality case report.

Study the setting for the Stanleytown Paper and Packaging Company, Part I (SP&P Company). Then study the strategy and the sample answer for an application of the questions-at-end-of-case method.

STANLEYTOWN PAPER & PACKAGING COMPANY, PART I

Stanleytown Paper & Packaging Company (SP&P Company) is a wholesaler specializing in the distribution of various types of paper products, including plates, cups, napkins, towels, bathroom tissue, hospital gowns, and school supplies. The paper products are distributed throughout the country. Colleges, universities, and hospitals constitute at least 85 percent of the SP&P customers. The company is located in Stanleytown, Virginia, and has 50 employees, five of whom are at the management level. SP&P Company continues to prosper. Sales increased from $1 million in 1987 to $9 million in 1988.

Since its inception in 1982, Roger Davis, president and general manager of SP&P Company, has recruited the top management staff. When he hired the members of his management team, his first concern was that they have technical expertise in their particular areas. He would then further develop their talents. The other managers and their respective titles are as follows: Tim Fields, vice president (reports directly to Mr. Davis); Roger Carter, manager of sales; Terry Fields, manager of shipping; and Paula Pruitt, manager of personnel and office systems.

In addition to the manager, the sales department has 8 salespeople. The shipping department has 20 employees, including 8 dock workers, 5 truck drivers, and 7 stock clerks. The personnel and office systems department has 16 employees, including 4 accountants, 2 purchasing agents, 3 computer operators, 2 personnel officers, 4 secretaries, and 1 receptionist. The secretaries work for the president and general manager, the vice president, the manager of sales, and the manager of personnel and office systems. Ms. Pruitt, however, coordinates all secretarial assignments.

The educational background of SP&P Company's management personnel presents an interesting picture. Mr. Davis, 62, a retired military man, was trained in management and economics at the University of Georgia. Tim Fields, vice president, holds an M.B.A. from the University of Virginia. His twin brother, Terry, has a B.S. degree in marketing from East Tennessee State University. The twins are 48 years old. Roger Carter, 42, is working toward an M.B.A. at Virginia Polytechnic Institute and State University (VPI) in its evening program. Paula Pruitt, 43, completed a B.S. degree in office systems management at the University of Tennessee.

Tim Fields has been with SP&P since it started. The other managers have an average of three years' service with the company. Mr. Davis was able to recruit the managers from other Stanleytown industries. Even though SP&P is doing well financially, recent events indicate that some personnel problems are brewing. Tim and Terry Fields are spreading the word that Davis has become a tyrant to work for. Both men say that Davis should retire. His military retirement combined with his SP&P pension and social security would yield a substantial monthly income. Other managers and employees think that Tim just wants to become "chief honcho" and that he has elicited Terry's support for his own cause.

News travels fast at SP&P. Mr. Davis has heard the rumors about his supposed impending departure. He knows that Tim and Terry Fields are responsible for most of these rumors. Davis is becoming somewhat defensive and rigid in his management style. He issues a memo to all employees:

> The responsibility for all major decisions which affect all SP&P Company personnel and its operations lies with the president and general manager. My office is responsible for controlling and making major decisions. My secretary will record and file all actions. Please proceed through proper channels to obtain approval for all decisions and actions. Because of the position I hold, your compliance with my request will be appreciated.

Questions/Statements

1. Develop an organizational chart for SP&P Company showing the communication channels as they relate to management.
2. What communication issues do you see in this case? Base your response upon a critique of your original organizational chart.
3. Based on the study of the development of management thought, how would you characterize the management of SP&P Company? Be specific as you relate concepts to action and personalities.
4. Develop an alternative organizational chart for SP&P Company. Defend your position. (The new structure should address ways to alleviate some of the issues already identified.)

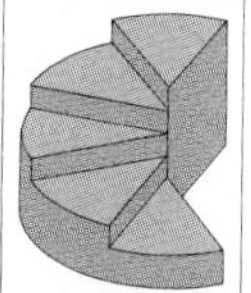

STRATEGY: CASE ANALYSIS

Assume the role of a consultant and, based on the content of the case, prepare your analysis.

The strategy for analyzing cases includes the same components as other types of business communication described in this book: Problem, general and specific Objectives, Reader/Audience, Order, and Format. The processes for analyzing the questions-at-end-of-case method include the:

- □ Underline procedure.
- □ Coding procedure.
- □ Outlining procedure.
- □ Go-beyond-the-questions procedure

PROBLEM

A lack of appropriate communication channels and leadership.

OBJECTIVES

General: To improve SP&P Company's total operations.

Specific: The questions shown at the end of the case are your specific objectives. Simply transform the questions/statements to specific objectives:

1. Develop an organizational chart for SP&P Company showing the communication channels.
2. Determine communication issues as they relate to management.
3. Characterize the management of SP&P Company based on a development of management thought.
4. Develop an alternative organizational chart for SP&P Company and address ways to alleviate some of the issues already identified.

READER/AUDIENCE

Cases such as the one for SP&P Company are typically used in various academic courses. Thus the audience might include the professors of such courses as well as the students enrolled in the courses. Cases are also often included in seminar courses designed to upgrade the skills of supervisory and executive personnel. In that setting, your audience would be seminar leaders of management development training programs and the participants in such programs. Assume that you are assigned the SP&P Company case in your communication class taught by Dr. Lisa Spalding.

PRIMARY AUDIENCE: DR. SPALDING, PROFESSOR

Dr. Spalding has used the case method for several years. She received her doctorate from an institution that trained its Ph.D.s primarily through the use of the case approach, so she is unusually perceptive in all facets of case analysis. Dr. Spalding is also a prolific writer and definitely can apply the red ink to your written assignments.

ORDER

Because of the scope and depth of some business cases, the Order component becomes quite complex. One logical means for ordering the case report is to respond to the questions in sequence (the Specific Objectives).

SPECIFIC OBJECTIVE NUMBER 1

Develop an organizational chart for the company showing the communication channels.

An organizational chart shows names and titles of management personnel, line and staff relationships, and channels of communication. It sometimes includes the number of persons in a department, their classifications, and to whom they are responsible. (Line of authority refers to the vertical structure, which shows superior-subordinate relationships. Staff indicates that someone has a supporting or advisory role within a company.)

Suggestions/Guidelines for Questions-at-End-of-Case Method. You may use four types of analyses to complete the questions-at-end-of-case method. These types may be used independently or collectively. A description and some basic principles of each type are described next.

Underline Procedure. As you read the case, underline key concepts regarding questions you would like to answer. The underline procedure is quite popular and relevant to almost any type of case analysis. Use this method at your discretion.

For the SP&P Company case, read the material at least twice to get a perspective on the entire situation. Then use the underline procedure to indicate those parts of the case that depict the channels of communication from top management to personnel employed in the various departments. Note how the underline procedure is used to determine these relationships within a company (Figure 22.2). These details of company structure are easily transformed into an organizational chart as shown in the sample answer in Figure 22.3.

The process for completing Specific Objective No. 1 using the underline procedure is as follows:

1. Underline appropriate sections of case.
2. Draft organizational chart showing channels of communication for employee relationships.
3. Refine the chart.
4. Produce polished copy.

Coding Procedure. Actually, the coding procedure resembles the underline procedure. You simply use a numbering system or an alphabetical system to identify answers to various parts of the questions. You could use the coding or the underline procedure to achieve Specific Objective No. 1.

For the SP&P Company case, read the case at least twice to get a perspective on the entire situation. Then use the coding procedure to depict channels of communication from top management to personnel employed in the various departments. The coding procedure involves the use of a numbering system (1-2-3) or an alphabetical system (A-B-C) to identify various parts of a question. For example, the circled 1 shown in

Figure 22.2 Underline procedure

Since its inception in 1987, Roger Davis, president and general manager of SP&P Company, has recruited the top management staff. When he hired the members of his management team, his first concern was that they have technical expertise in their particular areas. He would then further develop their talents. The other managers and their respective titles are as follows: Tim Fields, vice president (reports directly to Mr. Davis); Roger Carter, manager of sales; Terry Fields, manager of shipping; and Paula Pruitt, manager of personnel and office systems.

In addition to the manager, the sales department has 8 salespeople. The shipping department has 20 employees, including 8 dock workers, 5 truck drivers, and 7 stock clerks. The personnel and office systems department has 16 employees, including 4 accountants, 2 purchasing agents, 3 computer operators, 2 personnel officers, 4 secretaries, and 1 receptionist. The secretaries work for the president and general manager, the vice president, the manager of sales, and the manager of personnel and office systems. Ms. Pruitt, however, coordinates all secretarial assignments.

Figure 22.4 indicates key personnel; the circled A relates to the numbers of people and classifications for whom the key personnel are responsible. You can see the similarities for extracting material needed to answer questions. The coded material in the example provides the data needed for the organizational chart shown in the sample answer in Figure 22.4.

The process for completing Specific Objective No. 1 using the coding procedure is as follows:

Figure 22.3 Sample answer

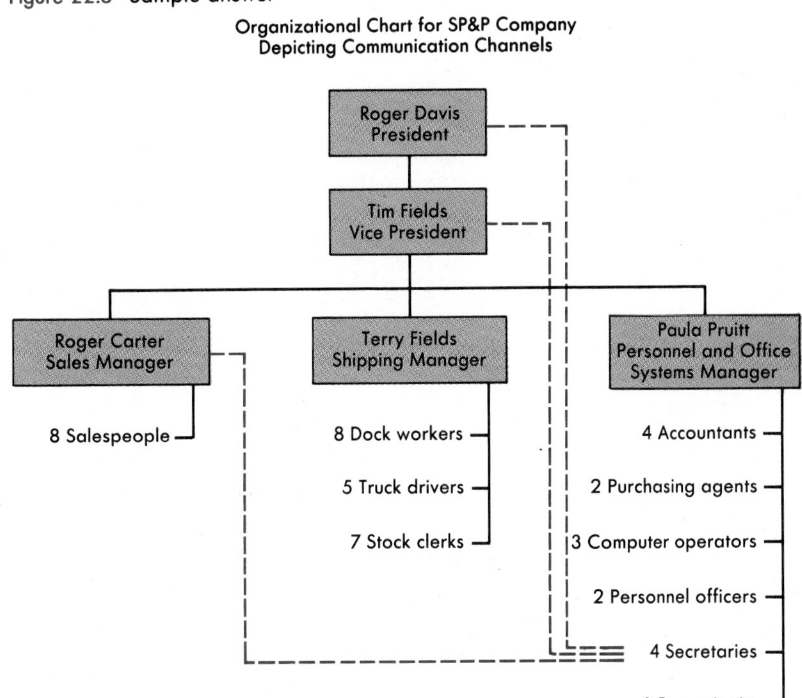

1. Code appropriate sections.
2. Draft organizational chart showing channels of communication for employee relationships.
3. Refine the chart.
4. Produce the polished copy.

SPECIFIC OBJECTIVE NUMBER 2

Determine communication issues as they relate to management.

This objective addresses communication as it relates to various principles of management. Essentially, you need to be perceptive to such issues as who works for whom, how many people report to each manager, and the formal and informal communication network.

Outlining procedure

Outlining Procedure. Another method of case analysis is the use of the outlining procedure. With the ideas in mind that you want to extract from a case, you may develop a sketch or detailed outline of key points. Read the

Figure 22.4 Coding procedure sample answer

Since its inception in 1987, Roger Davis,(I) president and general manager of SP&P Company, has recruited the top management staff. When he hired the members of his management team, his first concern was that they have technical expertise in their particular areas. He would then further develop their talents. The other managers and their respective titles are as follows: Tim Fields,(I) vice president (reports directly to Mr. Davis); Roger Carter,(I) manager of sales; Terry Fields,(I) manager of shipping; and Paula Pruitt,(I) manager of personnel and office systems.

In addition to the manager, the sales department has 8 salespeople.(A) The shipping department has 20 employees,(A) including 8 dock workers, 5 truck drivers, and 7 stock clerks.(A) The personnel and office systems department has 16 employees, including 4 accountants, 2 purchasing agents, 3 computer operators, 2 personnel officers, 4 secretaries, and 1 receptionist.(A) The secretaries work for the president and general manager, the vice president, the manager of sales, and the manager of personnel and office systems.(A) Ms. Pruitt, however, coordinates all secretarial assignments.

case material several times and study the organizational chart shown in Figure 22.3. Use the outlining procedure to list the issues raised in the Questions/Statements at the end of the case. List the issues as shown in Figure 22.5.

To complete Specific Objective No. 2 using the outlining procedure:

1. Draft an outline from the case material.
2. Revise the outline.
3. Produce the final outline.

Figure 22.5 Outlining procedure sample answer

I. Nepotism in organizations.
(Fields' brothers as managers of two departments)
II. Role of Tim Fields.
III. Appropriate placement of key personnel based on their education and technical expertise.
IV. Communication in organizations.
A. One-way
B. Two-way
C. Written form for all decisions

Based on critique of organizational chart, shown in Figure 22-3, the following are issues to be questioned.

I. Unrelated departments—Office Systems and Personnel—under one manager will lead to communication problems.
II. Inequities in numbers of employees for each manager.
III. Purchasing agents will communicate better with sales.
IV. Secretaries report to more than one manager.
V. Productivity and communication enhanced through developing an Information Processing Center.

Go-beyond-the-Question Procedure. To fulfill the remaining objectives requires in-depth analysis. You go beyond the question itself. This procedure requires that you use knowledge about business in general. Your responses are much stronger if you use an integrated approach drawing on the principles of different disciplines.

SPECIFIC OBJECTIVE NUMBER 3
Characterize the management of SP&P Company on the basis of the development of management thought.

Begin your analysis by studying three basic styles of management thought:

Autocratic. This style is based on rigid rules in which lines of authority are clearly delineated. The communication network supports the top-down approach. This approach employs a formal hierarchy in which each office by title is placed under the supervision and control of another. Promotion into higher position is based on demonstrated technical competence. All administrative decisions and policies are recorded in writing for permanent retention and referral.

Administrative. This style is similar to the autocratic but places a greater emphasis on the functions of planning, organizing, and controlling. Key personnel are obligated to communicate happenings within the organization to higher level managers. A person's position dictates authority which gives the right to command or advise others.

Participative. This style utilizes a more informal communication network for decision making. A major emphasis is placed on two-way communication whereby supervisors at the lower levels provide input to the higher levels. In this context, nonmanagers are not only invited but expected to communicate ideas and solutions to enhance productivity or planned change within the corporate environment.

From the case content you can see lots of evidence of how Davis's management style affects the company. In addition to the objective itself, think about the following questions before writing any responses:

1. Which style(s) of management does Mr. Davis advocate?
2. What specific characteristics relate to Mr. Davis's style of management?
3. How does Mr. Davis's style of management affect the communication process of SP&P?

These questions should provide additional insight for developing a response to Specific Objective No. 3. A sample answer is shown in Figure 22.6.

SPECIFIC OBJECTIVE NUMBER 4

Develop an alternative organizational chart for SP&P Company and address ways to alleviate some of the issues already identified.

The go-beyond-the-question procedure is applicable here. Before developing an alternative organizational chart, refer to the issues or problems for Specific Objective No. 2 shown in Figure 22.5. You want to respond to the following issues:

a. What will be the role of Tim Fields, and would the Fields brothers be retained as managers of two departments? Would this enhance open communication?

Figure 22.6 Go-beyond-the-question procedure (sample answer)

The main point of authority in SP&P Company is the president, Roger Davis. Mr. Davis uses management characteristics of the autocratic style. He believes that specific areas of competence are determined by the division of labor and are distinguished by titles, and promotion into administrative ranks should only be for those individuals who have proven technical ability. He also uses the principle of hierarchy, which is evident from the formal organizational chart for SP&P Company.

Mr. Davis practices the administrative style to a greater degree. In his memo Mr. Davis says that "responsibility for all major decisions . . . lies with the president and general manager." This coincides with the concept of authority in the administrative style which indicates that authority is derived from the position held in the hierarchy of the organization. Mr. Davis also feels that his work consists of planning, organizing, and controlling—especially controlling. For example, he states in his memo, "Please proceed through proper channels to obtain approval for all decisions and actions." He also maintains that levels of authority are created by a vertical division of the organization where communications flow from the top down. Support for this view of his management style is seen in two of his statements: "Please proceed through proper channels" and "because of the position I hold, your compliance with my request will be appreciated."

b. Are managers appropriately placed considering their background and training?

c. What about the communication process in the company?

d. How about the inequities in the number of people who are supervised by the different managers?

e. Should you separate personnel and office systems to promote effective communication?

f. What effect on communication is prevalent when employees report to more than one supervisor?

g. To promote productivity and communication, should SP&P consider installing an information processing center?

Again, you have managed to go beyond the question and develop other thought-provoking questions to guide your thinking. The issues listed above provide you with sufficient thoughts to aid in the design of a new organizational chart for SP&P Company. An alternative organizational structure that will increase productivity and a better system of communication is shown in Figure 22.7 with the supporting statement.

The process for completing Specific Objectives Nos. 3 and 4 using the go-beyond-the-question procedure required you to:

- ☐ Draw on previous academic courses.
- ☐ Use problem solving and logical reasoning.
- ☐ Develop additional thought-provoking questions or statements.
- ☐ Draft response to objectives.
- ☐ Revise/modify response to objectives.
- ☐ Write final response to objectives.

Figure 22.7 Alternative organization chart (sample answer)

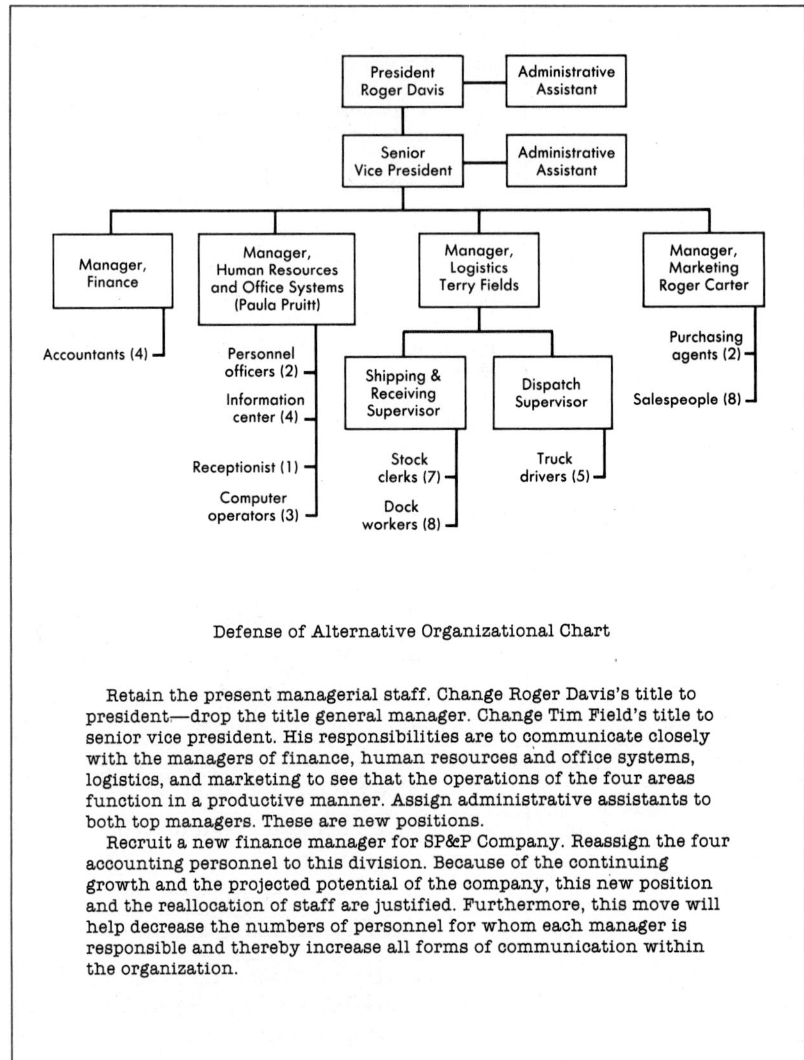

Defense of Alternative Organizational Chart

Retain the present managerial staff. Change Roger Davis's title to president—drop the title general manager. Change Tim Field's title to senior vice president. His responsibilities are to communicate closely with the managers of finance, human resources and office systems, logistics, and marketing to see that the operations of the four areas function in a productive manner. Assign administrative assistants to both top managers. These are new positions.

Recruit a new finance manager for SP&P Company. Reassign the four accounting personnel to this division. Because of the continuing growth and the projected potential of the company, this new position and the reallocation of staff are justified. Furthermore, this move will help decrease the numbers of personnel for whom each manager is responsible and thereby increase all forms of communication within the organization.

FORMAT

Up to this point, you have applied most of the strategy for communicating to the questions/statements-at-end-of-case method. Now you need to determine the appropriate Format for this communication. The case analysis lends itself more to the form of a business *report* than to any other type of written communication.

Figure 22.7 (*concluded*)

Include the following in the department of human resources and office systems: two personnel officers, one receptionist, three computer operators, and an information processing center consisting of four information specialists. Because of the relatively small size of the company, the personnel function and that of computer operations remain under the jurisdiction of Paula Pruitt, manager of human resources and office systems. The receptionist will continue to report to Ms. Pruitt. A new dimension of this area is the creation of an information processing center. Ms. Pruitt should designate one of the information specialists to coordinate the duties of this center (work assignments, priorities, etc.). These persons work primarily for the managers of finance, human resources and personnel, logistics, and marketing. SP&P Company should consider acquiring the newest automated equipment for the center. Under Paula Pruitt's supervision, the information specialists will no longer need to report to more than one person.

Terry Fields, head of the department of logistics, will manage the flow of goods to and from SP&P Company warehouses and premises. This department will include a shipping/receiving supervisor, seven stock clerks, eight dock workers, a dispatching supervisor, and five truck drivers. The supervisors will be recruited from inside the department or from outside the company at the discretion of the manager of human resources and office systems.

The department of marketing, headed by Roger Carter, will include eight sales people and two purchasing agents. More effective communication, as well as control of inventories, is achieved by having these departments closely related.

Four-Part Elements Method

An approach to case analysis used quite extensively is the four-part elements method. Here's a brief description of each element:

Makeup of the four-part elements method

1. *Description of content* presents a short synopsis or a general overview of the case. This element, as well as the other three elements, is presented either in outline or narrative form.

2. *Analysis* identifies problems and symptoms inherent in the case.
3. *Diagnosis* describes basic causes of the problems and symptoms.
4. *Recommended course of action* details what to do about the problem(s). How should the problem(s) be solved?

As a case analyst, you may develop alternative recommendations citing both pro and con. Use both qualitative and quantitative concepts (where applicable) to support and defend a recommended course of action.

You may use some of the concepts presented for use with the questions-at-end-of-case method to complete the four-part elements method (i.e., the underline procedure, the coding procedure, and the outlining procedure.)

Suggestions/Guidelines for Analyzing Four-Part Elements Method. The four-part elements method requires reflective thinking, making some assumptions, drawing on previous training, and maybe even some brainstorming with other classmates. When completing the *description of content* element, describe

Guidelines for completing the description of content component of the four-part elements method

a. Type of product or service.
b. Scope of operations.
c. Formal organizational communication structure.
d. Makeup of clientele.
e. Company's method of differentiating itself in the marketplace.
f. Leadership styles and communication of key personnel.
g. Other appropriate issues/statements.

Guidelines for completing the analysis and diagnosis components of the four-part elements method

Analysis deals with problems and symptoms of problems related to the case. *Diagnosis* treats the basic cause of the problem(s). Because these elements are not easy to assess, they require your best thinking—distinguishing facts from opinions. Some judgments and beliefs may be inaccurate or contradictory. Include in your analysis and diagnosis those areas that are relevant. For this section of the report, these types of questions may guide your thinking:

1. What are the critical issues facing the company?
2. What are the company's internal strengths? weaknesses?
3. Are the internal strengths and weaknesses applicable to special areas of the company's operations? For example, do problems seem to exist in accounting/finance, production, marketing, personnel, management, etc.?
4. Does the external environment seem to control or constrain the company? (Applicable factors are economic, social, political, technological, customers, suppliers, creditors, etc.)
5. What external threats to the company are prevalent? External opportunities?

Guidelines for completing the recommended course of action component of the four-part elements method

The recommended course of action is the last element. The action statement centers on what should be done. Recommendations should reflect your analysis and diagnosis sections. Present your recommendations directly and explicitly. State specifically and as clearly as possible what to do to correct problems and provide a supporting rationale. You may also suggest ways to implement your recommendations. To ensure that the report is effective, present your plan of action persuasively.

Some case analysts prefer to use a numbered list of recommendations followed by brief support for each. Others prefer to integrate the support and recommendations in narrative form. Actually, the person requesting the report may determine which style you use.

The four-part elements method is used in conjunction with longer cases—four or more pages. The application of this method usually requires the more complex case material. Because of space limitations in this chapter, we will not apply the four-part elements method. The guidelines presented, however, will prove beneficial to you when you use this method as an activity at the end of this chapter.

ADDITIONAL COMMENTS ON THE CASE METHOD

Adapting to various ways of completing case analyses

Once you have learned how to do a case write-up using the *questions-at-end-of-case* method or the *four-part elements* method, you will have mastered the *process* of case analysis. In the future, someone may request that you use some variation of one of these two methods; or you may have to write an analysis that is completely unstructured—"You're on your own." Several methods for completing case analysis assignments are available, all of which have some value in certain situations. When reporting your solution to a case problem, do so without fear. Each case analyst will probably have a unique approach to the problem. Remember, there is no one *best* answer to comprehensive case problems. Your report should provide evidence of the following accomplishments:

You understand the case situation.

You have searched for problem causes—and have not simply settled for symptoms.

You have considered different ways to solve the problem.

You have evaluated the alternatives by examining both advantages and disadvantages.

You have clearly selected one alternative.

You have thought about the most feasible way to implement that alternative.

A major point to keep in mind is that you are learning a process and that the form may vary. When you complete case analyses, the key is to be flexible and to adapt to the methods requested. The case approach is an effective way to learn, but it is a demanding way. The payoff is out there if you are willing to put forth the effort to acquire competence in this form of critical thinking.

SUMMARY

Writing case analyses is an effective way to develop further your conceptual or critical-thinking skills. Conceptual skills relate to imaginative ability—seeing the whole picture, recognizing how various functions of a reorganization fit together or depend on one another, or how changes on one level affect activities on another.

Your promotion potential within the corporate world is increased when you acquire competency in analyzing demanding case study material. Cases help you to see things from a systems approach; they aid in developing real-world problem solving; they develop logical thinking potential; and they develop divergent thinking in which you learn to look at alternative solutions to problems and justify your perceptions of what is most appropriate.

Cases are representative of actual situations where you recognize and deal with problems as they are. You formulate a plan of action to solve existing problems by addressing and defending alternative solutions. The case method is an experiential activity which simulates realistic business situations; it provides opportunity for you to discuss and support your analysis and plan of action. In this type of learning, your plan will be challenged by the opposing views of others.

As you assume the role of a consultant when analyzing cases, you may consider the use of such questions as *(a)* What internal problems are evident in the company? *(b)* What external environmental factors affect your proposed plan of action? *(c)* What short-range or long-range objectives are relevant to the case situation? *(d)* What action should the organization take? *(e)* What justification can you provide to defend your proposed action(s)?

Two types of methods for analyzing cases are the question-at-the-end-of-case method and the four-part elements method. The questions-at-end-of-case method is a popular one which includes use of the underline procedure, coding, outlining, and going beyond the question. These processes for case analyses are often used independently as well as collectively. The four-part-elements method incorporates a combination approach of the four elements of description of content, analysis, diagnosis and recommended course of action with appropriate justification. Mastery of these methods will assist your development of higher-order critical thinking skills.

END-OF-CHAPTER ACTIVITIES

DISCUSSION

1. Define and give examples of technical skills, human skills, and conceptual skills.
2. What are the advantages of using the case analysis method as a mode of learning? Disadvantages?

3. Discuss your interpretation of Figure 22.1 as it relates to the communication process.
4. Discuss the distinguishing characteristics of the questions-at-end-of-case method and the four types of procedures that make up this method.
5. Discuss the distinguishing characteristics and makeup of the four-part elements method for analyzing cases.
6. Interpret this statement as it relates to doing case analyses: "Develop divergent thinking where no one right answer exists."
7. Discuss what is meant by seeing things from a systems approach.
8. What do you perceive as the similarities to applying the strategy for communicating to a case analysis, a letter, an informational report, an analytical report?
9. Discuss the meaning of the concepts *flexibility* and *adaptability* with regard to analyzing cases.

ACTIVITIES

10-11. Use the questions-at-end-of-case method to analyze the following cases in the chapter appendix:
   a. The Fry Cook Who Was Late (Case Study 1).
   b. Competition in the Toothpaste Industry (Case Study 2).

12. Use the four-part elements method to analyze "A Simple Problem of Communication" (Case Study 3).

APPENDIX

CASE STUDY 1: THE FRY COOK WHO WAS LATE*

Rex Swenson was a fry cook for a local drive-in restaurant where he had been employed for three years while working his way through school. He was a dependable employee and well liked by the owner, Tim Wicks. However, something happened in late August that changed all that.

Rex was supposed to work the Sunday evening shift, but in the afternoon he went to visit his mother who was in a hospital in Dallas, some 20 miles away. On the way back, he got caught in a traffic jam after a Dallas Cowboys football game and got to work an hour late. Tim was not at the drive-in at the time, but other employees told him that the fry cook on duty had to wait over an hour until Rex got there. On Monday, Rex also had the evening shift, but his car broke down on the way to work, and again he was delayed an hour.

When he walked into the kitchen, Tim glared at him and said, "Late again, eh? Two times in a row. You know I can't put up with this. When you hired on here, you knew

* Reprinted by permission of the publisher from *Management Essentials,* Second Edition by Howard M. Carlisle. Copyright © 1987 by Science Research Associates.

how important it was to be on time. We can't expect everyone else to adjust their schedule to yours. I've had to pay overtime for the past two days 'cause you failed to get here. This is serious, Rex. What've you got to say for yourself?"

Rex was taken aback by Tim's abrupt approach, and he replied rather flippantly, "I had a few problems."

Before he could say another word, Tim shot back, "*You* had some problems! What do you think your lateness gives me? I'm trying to run this operation with employees who ignore work schedules and you tell me you've got problems. Things better shape up, Rex. What's wrong, anyway?"

By now Rex was obviously irritated and a little embarrassed. He answered sullenly, "I just had some problems."

"Is that all you're going to say? I'm going to have to start looking for another fry cook if you can't do better than that."

"Then why don't you?" Rex countered and turned to leave.

Questions

1. What communication breakdowns occurred in this situation?
2. Why did they occur?
3. How could the situation have been avoided?

CASE STUDY 2: COMPETITION IN THE TOOTHPASTE INDUSTRY*

Procter & Gamble has long been a leader in the consumer goods industries, especially those that rely heavily on marketing for success. P&G's three most profitable products are Crest toothpaste, Tide detergent, and Pampers diapers. Crest alone provides $300 million in annual revenues.

Since its introduction 25 years ago, Crest has dominated the dentifrice market. In 1978 Crest captured 40.5 percent of total sales, but by 1980 it had dropped to an alarming 36.2 percent. Hence the company is searching for new strategies to avoid any further deterioration.

When Crest was introduced in the mid-1950s, it immediately gained a major chunk of dentifrice sales through its emphasis on providing a product that prevented cavities. Prior to that, most toothpastes were sold for their ability to whiten teeth and for their taste. By including stannous fluoride as an ingredient and using an endorsement by the American Dental Association, P&G was able to demonstrate that cavities could be reduced. By 1960, Crest held one-third of the market and was the acknowledged leader. Recently, however, there have been signs that it may no longer be invincible.

Competition in the dentifrice market comes primarily from Lever Brothers. This company relies on two translucent gels, Close-Up and Aim. Close-Up was introduced in 1969 and Aim in 1975. These two products account for 17.3 percent of the market. The most recent newcomer to show significant success is Aqua-fresh, introduced by Beecham Products. Aqua-fresh is a striped combination of white paste and turquoise gel; and after being introduced nationally in 1979, it jumped to a commendable 13.5 percent of the market.

Procter & Gamble has not made any operational changes that would account for the decrease in sales. For instance, its advertising budget for Crest in the first 9 months of 1979 was $19.1 million and in the same period for 1980 it was $20.4 million.

Questions

1. What are the basic characteristics of the toothpaste marketplace?
2. How do economic, political, technological, and sociocultural variables influence it?
3. What are the various ways that firms compete in this industry?
4. What strategies would you recommend that Procter & Gamble employ?

CASE STUDY 3: A SIMPLE PROBLEM OF COMMUNICATION*

Chicago Chemicals is one of the three largest producers of chemicals in the United States. Because of the size of the organization and the nationwide scope of its activities, Chicago Chemicals relies on a regional system for recruiting future personnel. Each regional office is responsible for locating, screening, and hiring all persons to be employed in that area. Depending on the part of the country, this may include engineers, production staff, and marketing personnel, in addition to persons employed in other supporting departments. The North Central Regional Office is responsible for recruiting in Wisconsin, Illinois, Michigan, Indiana, Ohio, and Pennsylvania. In addition to the North Central main office, there are seven smaller district recruiting offices that in turn employ 67 full-time recruiters.

There are 35 persons currently working in the regional office under the management of Richard Thompkins. The office itself is composed of four departments: administration and personnel; scheduling; advertising and publicity; and recruiting operations (see Exhibit 1).

Exhibit 1 Organization chart: Chicago Chemicals, North Central Regional Office

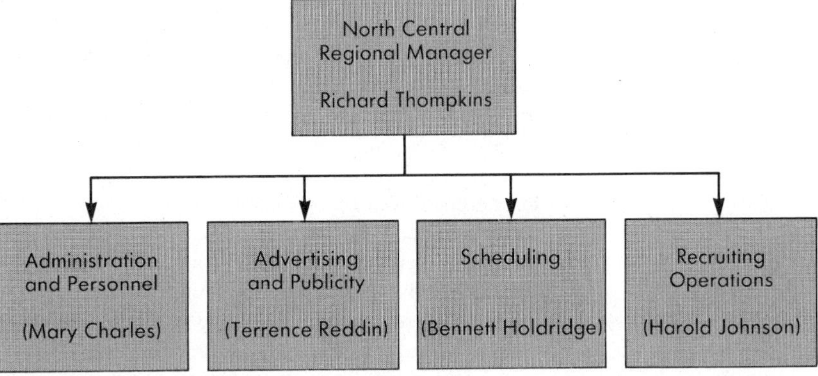

* Donald D. White and H. William Vroman, *Action in Organizations,* 2nd ed. (Boston: Allyn & Bacon, 1982), pp. 144-147. Used by permission.

Departmental Responsibilities

Director of the administration and personnel department is Mary Charles. The department is responsible for coordinating activities at the regional office, designing and printing all recruiting materials, and developing specific programs for all recruiting activities in the region. In addition, the department maintains a reporting and control system and initiates security checks on potential employees when necessary. The department is responsible also for selecting and training all recruiters and for assigning them to individual offices.

The advertising and publicity department, under Terrence Reddin, directs the advertising and publicity program for the regional office in support of its recruiting function. Members of the department provide guidance and assist recruiters on special projects. Mr. Reddin has initiated a high school education information program and a widely based public relations program in the region. These two programs are not directly related to activities of the individual recruitment offices. An internal information program for the region has been initiated by the department.

The scheduling department is a small but powerful unit under the direction of Ben Holdridge. Holdridge's department prepares, maintains, and monitors all contract agreements for office space, vehicle rental and maintenance, and other forms of transportation. The time frames for all recruitment trips must be cleared through the scheduling department. In addition, the scheduling department provides staff assistance to the regional director and to each recruitment office supervisor.

Work in the scheduling department is often exacting and requires a considerable amount of detailed paperwork. Staff members find it necessary to be thorough and deliberate when completing assigned tasks. An expansion at the Chicago office which took place one year ago drained off many of the "older hands" from the department. Therefore, existing members of the department average a little over two years' experience in their jobs (see Exhibit 2). The department received a rating of *excellent* in the last regional office evaluation. Some of the group norms are: strive for accuracy; pay attention to detail; do the job right the first time.

Recruiting operations, under Harold Johnson, is responsible for a wide range of activities. Principally, it directs the development of plans and programs pertaining directly to personnel selection. The department establishes policies and carries out plans from the Chicago office to achieve personnel procurement objectives. Johnson's staff formulates and initiates recruitment programs and policies for the region. Evaluation of the performance of individual recruiters is handled by the department, and certain personnel programs, such as a recent incentive awards program and a safety program, were initiated there. It is not unusual for Johnson or individual department members to recommend additions, changes, or new programs to other departments or to Mr. Thompkins himself.

No serious problems have ever arisen between recruiting operations and the other departments. However, some members of other departments have complained of interference from operations. For example, all divisions are required to make staff assistance visits into the field. Recruiting operations often exhausts its travel money prior to the end of the quarter. The department claimed that there were numerous unanticipated changes in requirements. On the other hand, many persons outside the department suggested the difficulty was the result of poor planning. Additional travel funds eventually were obtained from Chicago, and the matter was dropped.

A final function of the department is to analyze district operations and investigate "slow employment areas" or unduly large numbers of unsuccessful placements.

Exhibit 2 Department members (Recruiting operations and scheduling)

Position	Name	Age	Years' experience on the job
Recruiting operations department manager	Harold Johnson	52	18
Staff	Gerald Thomas	34	8
Staff	James Lawson	38	7
Staff	Betty Jennings	36	3
Staff	Richard Horn	44	14
Staff	Joe Sutton	46	11
Staff	Gene Maddox	46	14
Staff	Gordon Edwards	49	14
Staff	Tom Campbell	36	7
Scheduling department manager	Ben Holdridge	48	9
Staff	Gary Ford	22	New employee
Staff	John McGee	34	4
Staff	Robert Webb	35	3
Staff	Barbara Peterson	24	2
Staff	Jan Owens	21	New employee

Reports concerning these investigations are forwarded directly to the regional manager.

The members of the department averaged over eleven years' experience and each had served in the field for up to three years as a recruiter (see Exhibit 2). In fact, their appointment to the recruiting operations department was based on *outstanding performance* as a recruiter. Department members take pride in their appointments. They are a cohesive group and often socialize off the job. Norms of the operations group include: keep the recruiters in the field well informed; delays hamper accomplishment.

Personnel Problems at Home

In recent months, word of conflict between the recruiting operations and scheduling departments filtered up to Mr. Thompkins. Symptoms of conflict were numerous and varied. For example, he noted that members of each department seemed to avoid having conversations with one another whether on or off the job. On more than one occasion, he had observed a group of employees from one of the two departments quickly disperse when members of the other department entered into the discussion. Moreover, activities of the two departments have been marked by a noticeable lack of communication. On three separate occasions during the last six months, directives from the operations department to local recruiters in the field have instructed those recruiters to move out of old facilities and into new ones before the scheduling department had finished the paperwork on the move. On another occasion, field offices were instructed by the operations department to have additional telephone lines installed in their offices before approval had been received from scheduling. Scheduling had an extremely difficult time justifying them after the fact, since expenditures of this nature were closely scrutinized by the Chicago office.

Richard Thompkins decided that steps must be taken to discover the underlying cause of the interdepartmental difficulties. After talking with members of each of the two departments on an informal basis, he began to make some notes to himself about the conversations. His findings are summarized as follows:

1. No one really wants to talk about the other department; most do not complain readily.
2. Members of each department believe that they are doing their job, but they claim that the other department hinders their work.
3. Attitudes of scheduling and personnel about the operations department is best summed up in comments from the scheduling supervisor: "Those guys just seem to me to be pushy and self-centered. They're too much rah-rah and go-go-go. Who do they think they are, anyway?"
4. Operations department members describe the scheduling department as "slow as hell"; "They never want to cooperate with us"; "We really care about this recruiting operation, but those guys just don't seem to understand the importance of getting to these people (potential employees) the fastest with the most!"
5. A comment from Harold Johnson: "My people know the importance of their job and I think they have real company loyalty. To tell you the truth, I can't say the same for the fellows in some of the other departments."

After reading over the list a couple of times, Thompkins leaned back in his chair and smiled knowingly. Later that day he called into his office the two department heads. He began his discussion by saying, "Ben, Harold, I think we have a bit of a communication problem here. It's as simple as that."

APPENDIX A

ENGLISH MECHANICS

1 PUNCTUATION
2 FORMS OF ADDRESS
3 CAPITALIZATION
4 NUMBERS
5 SPELLING
6 WORDS FREQUENTLY MISUSED

PART ONE: PUNCTUATION

The overall purpose of punctuation is to clarify the meaning of written communication. In other words, use punctuation if it helps to clarify your thoughts and ideas. Don't use punctuation if it unnecessarily interrupts the flow of the message or prevents accurate interpretation. If in doubt as to correct usage, the following quick reference guide should prove helpful.

Apostrophe

1. Use an apostrophe in contractions where letters are omitted.
   Examples:
   a. won't
   b. I'll
   c. haven't
2. Use an apostrophe to show possession.
   Examples:
   a. Please evaluate Mark's progress. (Add 's; basic word does *not* end in s.)
   b. Gladys' application was incomplete. (Add ' only; basic word ends in s.)
   c. Elliott and Smith's book . . . (Book owned by Elliott and Smith.)
   d. Visit Brown's and Green's stores. (Each owns one or more stores.)
3. Use an apostrophe with words that are idiomatic in nature.
   Examples:
   a. ten dollars' worth
   b. five days' time
4. Use an apostrophe to show possession with indefinite pronouns.
   Example:
   a. one's values
   b. someone's overcoat
5. Use an apostrophe with Jr., Sr., to show possession.
   Examples:

   Harvey Alexander, Jr.'s car . . .
6. Use an apostrophe to form plurals or letters, words, symbols, and numbers.
   Examples:
   a. Dot your i's and cross your t's.
   b. He did not know his 5's.

   Note: Pronouns in the possessive case do *not* use the apostrophe to show ownership: hers, his, ours

   Avoid possessives with inanimate objects: house's roof; car's motor.

Colon

1. Use the colon to indicate that something will follow.
   Examples:
   a. The prizes to be given away are as follows: a TV set, a stereo console, a 35 mm camera, and a popcorn popper.
   b. These are the items found on the park bench: a set of car keys, a coin purse, a pocket knife, and a nail clipper.
   c. Call 839-4276 if you are interested in any of the following used equipment: an IBM Selectric typewriter, a 10-key adding machine, a secretary's desk, a secretary's chair.
2. Use the colon to introduce other material.
   Examples:
   a. You can vary the letter style according to preference.
   For example: Block
   Semiblock
   AMS
   b. Most of the tours cover more than one country.
   Example: Tour A—Britain, France, and Germany
   Tour B—Japan, Indonesia, and Philippines
   Tour C—Denmark, Norway, and Sweden
3. Use the colon to express time and proportions.
   Examples:
   a. She left at 2:15 p.m. (no space before or after colon.)
   b. The ratio of women to men in attendance at the conference was 2:1.
4. Use the colon after salutations.
   Examples:

   Dear Mrs. Fletcher:

   Gentlemen:

   Ladies and Gentlemen:

Comma

1. Use commas with coordinating conjunctions (and, but, or, for, nor, yet) when they join two complete thoughts.
   Examples:
   a. Management and labor are improving their working relationship, and this is a step in the right direction.
   b. The United States has taken steps to reduce the national debt, yet our indebtedness continues to climb.
   c. Martin left the office earlier today, but he plans to return for the committee meeting at 2:00 p.m.

   Note: Do not use a comma if one of the clauses does not express a complete thought.

Martin left the office earlier today but plans to return for the committee meeting at 2:00 p.m.

2. Use commas to separate items in a series.
   Examples:
   a. Our clients expect quality products, modest prices, and efficient service.
   b. All that is needed are a few spare parts, a small block of time, a little bit of ingenuity.
   c. Fishing, backpacking, hiking, swimming, and horseback riding are some of the activities planned at the Horseshoe Falls Camp.

3. Use commas between coordinate adjectives when they modify the same noun.
   Examples:
   a. A clear, modern look was given to the renovated office complex.
   b. Use the small, handy express card to charge all your purchases.
   c. This practical, do-it-yourself building guide illustrates each project in completed form.

4. Use commas to set off parenthetical expressions and words.
   Examples:
   a. Marvin's book, as a matter of fact, was four years in the making.
   b. To strengthen his case, however, Bob is using some impressive statistics.
   c. Margaret will, nevertheless, continue her graduate studies in spite of the rise in tuition rates.

5. Use commas with nonrestrictive clauses and appositives.
   Examples:
   a. The service sector, which has reached an all-time high, is responsible for this year's economic and employment growth.
   b. The department chairman, Mr. Leroy Evans, spoke to all employees about the new procedures for requisitioning supplies.
   c. Ann Fogg, who wrote "Myra's Answer," will speak to the journalism class next Monday.
   d. John Naisbitt's book, *Megatrends*, discusses 10 new directions which are transforming our lives.

6. Use commas to set off words in direct address.
   Examples:
   a. You were correct, Joan, in your predictions of consumer response to the new cola.

b. Thanks again, Bob, for all your efforts in the community fund drive.

c. When the letter is typed, Miss Carter, we will place it on your desk.

7. Use commas to set off introductory words, phrases, and clauses.
Examples:
a. So far, efforts to improve campus parking have failed.
b. Lastly, don't forget to include your ZIP code.
c. In the final analysis, everyone needs to experience self-worth.
d. During the past two years, the company has experienced unprecedented growth.
e. Because of the new tax laws implemented in 1987, conference attendance is down.
f. Acting on Carter's advice, Mary went to see the play.

8. Use commas to set off items in addresses and geographical locations.
Examples:
a. The Houks' home in Miami, Florida, is located one block from the beach.
b. Please send a copy of the report to my office at 409 Main Street, Hutchinson, KS 67501.

9. Use commas to indicate omitted words.
Examples:
a. Students registering for Biology 112 should report to Room 9B and those for Biology 113, Room 16A.
b. Graduate classes use the green-coded cards, undergraduate classes, the yellow ones.

10. Use commas to separate the day from the year.
Examples:
a. The article appeared in the May 13, 1987, issue of *Newsweek*.
b. On September 15, 1987, John will leave the country for service overseas.

11. Use commas with contrasting expressions.
Examples:
a. The Nelsons, not the Radkes, have listed their property with Century 21 Real Estate.
b. James will accept the car, but only if repaired to its original condition.

12. Use commas to supplement other punctuation and to prevent misunderstanding.
Examples:
a. Martin asked, "Who is responsible for this excellent report?"
b. To foreigners, Americans seem blunt.

Dash

1. Use the dash to set off a sudden break in thought, interruption in dialogue, an introductory series, and a parenthetical element for emphasis or clarity.

   Note: For emphasis, a dash is often used in place of a comma, semicolon, colon, or parenthesis.

   Examples:

   a. Most of the employees—especially those just hired—don't understand the examples in the procedures manual.

   b. Add sand to the mixture—about 1 part sand to 2 parts mulch.

Ellipsis

1. Use an ellipsis (a row of three dots) to show the omission of words, phrases, sentences, or passages.

   Examples:

   a. Joe reported . . . on the July meeting.

   b. I suggest that the authors . . . use their strategy throughout the entire book.

Exclamation Point

1. Use an exclamation point after words, expressions, or sentences to show strong feeling.

   Examples:

   a. Don't bother me!

   b. Hurrah! We won!

Hyphen

1. Use a hyphen at the end of a line to indicate that one or more syllables of a word are in the line following.

   Example: . . . ex-
   ample

2. Use a hyphen in compound words composed of two or more elements.

   Examples:

   a. self-denial

   b. brother-in-law

   c. full-fledged

3. Use a hyphen to separate figures and letters in telephone numbers.

   Example: 974-3340

4. Use a hyphen in one or more words joined together to indicate a single unit.

Examples:
a. better-housing campaign
b. time-honored benefit
c. up-to-date job description

Parentheses

1. Use parentheses to show that inserted information is independent from the main thought of the sentence.
   Examples:
   a. I paid cash when checking out of your hotel on November 15 (see attached receipt).
   b. Mrs. Martin called my attention to the error (this is the second incident in a week) and asked to have it corrected.
2. Use a parenthesis to set off information not intended to be part of the main statement.
   Example:
   a. Rental housing is up for the month of March (see Figure 3.1).
   b. The EPA (Environmental Protection Agency) is concerned about the pollution caused by Plant B.
3. Use parentheses to enclose figures or letters within a sentence.
   Examples:
   a. Each letter was critiqued on: (a) appearance, (b) content, and (c) style.
   b. Look for: (1) the parking area number, (2) the color-coded symbol, and (3) the direction arrows.
4. Use parentheses to identify an unfamiliar term.
   Example:
   The AMA (American Management Association) strives for excellence in management leadership.
5. Use parentheses in legal documents to confirm the amounts.
   a. In consideration of twenty-five dollars ($25.00), . . .

Period

1. Use a period after a declarative or imperative sentence.
   Examples:
   a. I understand the importance of business writing.
   b. Plan your career carefully.
2. Use a period after most abbreviations.
   Examples:
   a. Mr.
   b. Mrs.
   c. Dr.
   d. p.m.
   e. lb.
   f. oz.

Question Mark

1. Use a question mark at the end of a direct question.
   Examples:
   a. Why is English grammar important?
   b. What are your career plans?

2. Use a question mark in parentheses to indicate uncertainty.
   Example:
   The page was mailed September 10 (?).

Quotation Marks

1. Use quotation marks to indicate direct quotations, slogans, slang expressions, and words used in an unusual way.
   Examples:
   a. Patrick Henry said, "Give me liberty, or give me death."
   b. He cried, "Where's the beef?"
   c. She really did an "A-1" job.
   d. A "No" could be heard from the back of the room.
2. Use quotation marks to denote parts of published works.
   Examples: chapter letters, lessons, topics, book sections, themes, sermons, lectures, magazine and newspaper articles, and songs.
   Examples:
   a. Read the section, "How to Develop a Communication Strategy," before coming to class tomorrow.
   b. The article, "How to Get into Grad School," was very informative.

   Note: In quoted material,
   a. Commas and periods appear inside the quotation marks.
   b. Semicolons and colons appear outside quotation marks.
   c. Question marks, exclamation points, and dashes appear inside the quotation marks when they apply to the quoted matter; outside when they refer to the whole sentence.

Semicolon

1. Use a semicolon to separate two or more independent clauses when coordinating conjunctions are not used.
   Examples:
   a. Meet me at 202 Central Hall; we'll discuss the terms further.
   b. The on-campus students attended the rally; the off-campus students didn't bother.
2. Use a semicolon to separate items in a series when commas have already been used.

Examples:

a. The new officers for the coming year are Jerry Michells, president; Marsha Peterson, vice president; Robert McConnell, secretary; and Judy Kramer, treasurer.

b. The conventions for the past three years have been held in Las Vegas, Nevada; Hollywood, Florida; and Boston, Massachusetts.

3. Use a semicolon to set off conjunctive adverbs (Conjunctive adverbs are: however, although, therefore, nevertheless, etc.). These are normally used in the middle of the sentence.

   Examples:

   a. Harold's plane is being delayed for two hours; however, he still plans to arrive in time to attend the meeting.

   b. The house plans were not drawn exactly as Karen had specified; nevertheless, she was pleased.

   c. Heavy rains and high winds are predicted for the rest of the week; therefore, all outdoor sports functions have been canceled.

4. Use a semicolon when two clauses are linked with *for example* or *namely*.

   Examples:

   a. Every camper should take safety precautions in undeveloped areas; for example, drink only water that you know is pure.

   b. The invitation omitted one main item; namely, where the reception is being held.

PART TWO: FORMS OF ADDRESS

The following represents a selected list of address forms and salutations for people in various positions to use in business correspondence:

Inside Address	*Salutation*
Alderman:	
Alderman Herman Talbot	Dear Alderman Talbot:
Ambassador (U.S.):	
The American Ambassador to Germany	Dear Mr. Ambassador:
Ambassador (foreign):	
His Excellency	Sir: or Excellency: or Your Excellency:
Archbishop:	
Most Reverend Charles Jones	Your Excellency: or Your Grace:

Inside Address	*Salutation*
Cabinet Officer:	
The Honorable Secretary of State	Dear Mr. Secretary:
Chief Justice of the United States:	
The Honorable Warren Burger Chief Justice of the Supreme Court of the United States	Sir: or Mr. Chief Justice: or Dear Justice Burger:
Chief of Police:	
Mr. Lloyd Pace Chief of Police	Dear Chief Pace:
Congressman/Congresswoman:	
The Honorable Sam Nunn United States Senate	Sir:/Madam: or Dear Senator Nunn:
Governor:	
His Excellency the Governor of Missouri	Sir: or Dear Sir:
Judge:	
The Honorable Michael Fox United States District Judge	Dear Sir: or Dear Judge Fox:
Lawyer:	
Ms. Ann Sutton Attorney at Law	Dear Ms. Sutton:
Mayor:	
The Mayor of the City of St. Louis	Dear Sir:
or The Honorable James Stewart Mayor of the City of Concord	Dear Mayor Stewart:
President: (college/university)	
President Jonathan Motley The State University	My dear President Motley:
President (of the United States):	
The President of the United States	My dear Mr. President: or Dear Mr. President:
Professor:	
Professor Laura Twin	Dear Professor Twin:
Speaker of the House:	
The Honorable Joseph Stills Speaker of the House of Representatives	Dear Mr. Speaker:

PART THREE: CAPITALIZATION

Follow these generally accepted rules for capitalization in your writing.

1. Capitalize the first word of a sentence—including direct quotations.
   Examples:
   a. Please return the completed questionnaire in the enclosed envelope.
   b. She exclaimed, "You shouldn't go!"

2. Capitalize titles that precede names or words associated with other proper names; except for titles of high government officials, do not capitalize a title that follows a person's name.
   Examples:
   a. Professor Jones
   b. Ms. Walters
   c. The President (of the United States)
   d. State College
   e. Judge Warren
   f. Prime Minister Olsen
   g. . . . George Allen, our company president, . . .
   h. Queen Elizabeth

3. Capitalize the first word and succeeding words (except articles, prepositions, and conjunctions) in titles of books, magazines, plays, articles, essays, reports, etc.
   Examples:
   a. *Introduction to Basic Programming* (book)
   b. *Automation of America's Offices* (book)
   c. "The Transformation of Work in the Electronic Age" (article)

4. Capitalize the names of the days of the week, months, holidays, days designated as holy days, and historical events and periods.
   Examples:
   a. New Year's Day
   b. Monday, January 1
   c. Roaring 20s
   d. Thanksgiving
   e. Old Man Winter
   f. Yom Kippur
   g. The Great Depression

5. Capitalize the first word of each item displayed in a list or an outline.
   Examples:
   a. The chapter includes these types of letters:
   Invitation acceptance
   Recommendation

b. I. Introduction
  II. Discussion
    a. Part A
    b. Part B
  III. Summary

6. Capitalize the first word of a complimentary close in a business letter.
   Examples:
   a. Sincerely yours
   b. Very truly yours

7. Capitalize directional words used to designate specific geographic regions; do not capitalize when these words are used to indicate direction.
   Examples:
   a. The Southwest is growing rapidly.
   b. Their plant is located 75 miles northeast of Columbus.
   c. Investors from the Far East are arriving today.
   d. To get to the airport, go south on Aloca Highway.

8. Capitalize official names and nicknames of cities, states, countries, rivers, etc. (Capitalize the words *city* and *state* only when they follow the name of the city/state.)
   Examples:
   a. St. Louis, Missouri
   b. Old Man River (Mississippi River)
   c. The Windy City (Chicago)
   d. Canada
   e. Panama City, Florida
   f. city of Dallas; state of Wyoming

9. Capitalize words derived from proper names related to nationality, language, or religion.
   Examples:
   a. Canadian
   b. English
   c. Afro-American
   d. Protestant
   e. Moslem

10. Capitalize titles of specific academic courses and courses related to a country; do not capitalize reference to general school courses.
    Examples:
    a. She completed Principles of Management 101 last year.
    b. He plans to add a course in computers as an elective.
    c. How about taking Spanish or German?

11. Capitalize religious names referring to the deity, a religious book, and other references.
    Examples:
    a. Koran; Torah; Bible
    b. Allah; God

12. Capitalize proper names designating governmental references (national or international) such as department names, treaties, laws, acts, commissions, and documents.
    Examples:
    a. Warren Commission
    b. Salt II Treaty
    c. Department of Transportation
    d. United Nations
    e. Common Market
    f. Bill of Rights

PART FOUR: NUMBERS

In business communication, numbers can be expressed as figures or words. There isn't one set of rules to follow in expressing numbers; there are exceptions to most rules. However, here is a general set of rules most writers follow.

General

1. Isolated numbers 10 and under are spelled out in a sentence; numbers 11 and above, figures.
   Examples:
   a. She estimated that 45 people would attend the session.
   b. Only five items were included on the agenda.
   c. Enclosed are four sets of blueprints,
   d. The survey included 234 households.

2. Spell out the number if it is the first word in a sentence.
   Examples:
   a. Twenty-three brochures are being mailed to you, as you requested.
   b. Fifteen applicants applied for the manager's position announced in February.
   Note: Usually, these sentences can be revised to avoid using a number as the first word:
   a-1. As you requested, 23 brochures are being mailed to you. Or you will shortly receive the 23 brochures you requested.
   b-1. The February announcement for the manager's position resulted in 15 applicants.

3. Use figures for each number in a series in a sentence.
   Examples:
   a. Whether 4 or 25 people attend, we will conduct the seminar.
   b. The number of employees classified by employment group is: managers, 5; professional, 3; support personnel, 12.

4. Spell out the smaller number when two related numbers come together in a sentence; use figures for the larger number.
   Examples:
   a. The 15 three-bedroom condominiums will be completed by early June.
   b. The two 3-volume record sets are yours as a gift.
   Note: Separate unrelated groups of numbers that appear together with a comma:
   By 1990, 75 percent of U.S. workers will earn their income through information-related jobs.

5. Use a comma for each group of three numerals when a number contains more than four digits.
   Examples:
   a. We expect to get at least 4,500 signatures on the petition.
   b. More than 1,500,000 shares of stock exchanged hands today.

Addresses

1. Use figures for street, box, or route numbers except for the number *one.* Spell out *one.*
   Examples:
   a. Their new address is 403 Oak Drive.
   b. Please mail the package to me at 222 Broadway.
   c. Our new address is One Western Plaza.
   d. Please send the package to me at 400 North 800 West.

2. Use words for street names one through ten; figures for 11 and above.
   Examples:
   a. The letter was sent to you at 204 Ninth Avenue instead of 204 29th Avenue.
   b. Our new building at 28th Street and Lexington Avenue will be completed by January 1.

Age

1. Use figures to express exact age; words if approximate.
   Examples:
   a. In most states, you can obtain a driver's license at the age of 16.

b. On your application, you indicate 23 years and 6 months as your age.
c. I believe he is about sixty-five years old.

Dates

1. Spell out the month name.
   Examples:
   a. Please send your check by April 1, 19__.
   b. By December 31, 19__, we plan to complete our report.
   Note: The North American custom is to place the month first; however, in the military and in many countries throughout the world, the date precedes the month as: 31 December 19__.

2. Use st, nd, rd, or th with the day of the month when the date precedes the month or stands by itself.
   Examples:
   a. We will be closed on the 4th of July.
   b. Please vacate the building by the 30th.

Decimals and Fractions

1. Use words when a fraction stands alone.
   Examples:
   a. Please complete one-half of the report by June 10.
   b. Nearly three-fourths of the building was destroyed.

2. Use figures for mixed numbers.
   Examples:
   a. The new interest rate will be 8 3/4 percent.
   b. The beam measured 14 1/2 feet.

3. Precede the decimal fraction with a zero if the decimal fraction begins with a whole number; omit the zero if the decimal fraction begins with a zero.
   Examples:
   a. The new interest rate will be 0.1245.
   b. Is the current interest rate .0675?

Money

1. Use figures for amounts of money.
   Examples:
   a. Please send your check for $25.43 today. (Dollar sign precedes amount.)
   b. Enclosed is my $50 check. (Omit decimal point and two zeros if only dollars.)

c. The amounts for my last three bills were $45.00, $75.43, and $102.44. (Use decimal point and two zeros for consistency in series.)
d. My refund check was for 83 cents. Amounts less than a dollar can be expressed in these ways:
83 cents; 83¢; or $.83.
e. . . . for seventy-five dollars ($75.00) . . . (Use only in legal or financial documents.)

Miscellaneous

1. Use figures for the following:
   Examples:
   a. Distances—15 miles; 4 kilometers (except for distances less than a mile: one-fourth of a mile.)
   b. Dimensions—20 feet by 20 feet; 8 1/2 by 11 inches.
   c. Page numbers, chapter numbers, section numbers, figure numbers, table numbers, charge account numbers, serial numbers, telephone numbers—Page 24; Table 4.
   d. Percent—95 percent.
   e. Financial quotations—98 7/8.

Time of Day

1. Use figures with a.m. and p.m. (Omit :00 for the time with hour only indicated.)
   Examples:
   a. Please plan to start our seminar at 8:30 a.m.
   b. We must end our session by 5 p.m.

2. Spell out the hour when used with o'clock.
   Examples:
   a. We can stay no longer than ten o'clock.
   b. Your income tax return must be in the mail by twelve o'clock on April 15.

PART FIVE: SPELLING

College students frequently misspell the following 580 words:

academy
accept
accidentally
accommodate
accumulate
accustom
acquainted
acquire
acquit (acquitting)
across
addressed
advice
aerial
affect
aggravate
airplane
alley
allot (allotting)
all right
ally
almost
already
altogether
alumnus (alumni)

always
amateur
among
amusement
analysis
ancestor
annual
apparatus
apparently
appearance
appetizing
appreciate
appropriate
approximately
arctic
argument
arise
arithmetic
around
arrange
arrive
article
ascend
ascension
assistant
athlete
athletic
attacked
attendant
audience
authority
auxiliary
average
awkward
balance
bachelor
bar (barring)
based
bear
beautiful
because
become (becoming)
before
beggar
begin (beginning)
believe
benefit
bigger
bite (biting)
boundary
breath
breathe
brilliant
Britain
bulletins
bureau
business
busy
buy
calendar
candidate
capitalists
care (caring)
career
careful
carry (carried, carrying)
cemetery
certainly
changeable
characteristics
chauffeur
chemistry
chief
choose (choosing)
clothes
coarse
college
column
come (coming)
commercial
commission
commit (committing)
committee
common
community
company (companies)
comparative
compel
competition
complete
comrade
concede
conceive
confer (conferring)
conqueror
conscience
conscientious
conscious
consequently
consider
continuous
control (controlled)
convenience
course
courteous
courtesy
criticism
cry (cries)
curiosity
(deal) dealt
deceitful
decided
decision
defer (deferred)
definite
derived
descendant
descent
describe
description
despair
desperate
destroy
determined
device
devise
dictionary
differ (different)
difficulty
din (dinning)
dine (dining)
direction
disagree
disappear
disappoint
disapprove
disastrous
discipline

disease
disillusion
dissatisfied
dissipate
distinctive
divide
divine
doctor
don't
dormitory
drop (dropped)
during
duty (duties)
dying (die)
effect
efficient
eighth
eliminate
embarrass
empty
enable
encourage
endeavor
enemy
enforce
engineer
enjoy (enjoyable)
enterprise
entertain
enthusiastically
entirely
environment
equip (equipping)
equivalent
especially
etcetera (etc.)
evidently
exaggerate
exceed
excellent
except
exceptionally
excitement
exercise
exhaust
existence
expensive
experience
experimental
explanation
facility
familiar
family (families)
fascinate
fault
February
field
fiery
fifty
finally
financier
finish
first
forced
foreign
forfeit
formally
formerly
forth
forty
fourth
fraternity
freshman
friend
fulfill
fundamental
furniture
gamble
gardener
generally
goddess
government
governor
grammar
grievance
group
guard
guarantee
guidance
happened
happy (happiness)
haul
have (having)
hear
height
here
highest
hindrance
hobby
holly
holy
hoping (hope)
hopping (hop)
humor
hundredths
hungry
hurrying (hurry)
imagine
immediately
immense
immigration
incidentally
increase
independent
induce
industry
infinite
innocence
intellectual
intelligence
intentionally
intercede
interest
interrupted
introduced
involved
itself
kindergarten
knowledge
know (knew, known)
label
laboratory
lay (laying, laid)
later
laziness (lazy)
lead (led)
leisure
lenient

liable
library
license
lightning
listening
literally
literature
live
livelihood
lonely
loose
lose
loss
lying (lie)
maintain
maintenance
manual
manufacturer
marriage
material
mathematics
maybe
meant
mechanical
medicine
millionaire
miniature
minute
mirror
mischievous
misspelled
model
monkeys (monkey)
mosquitoes
muscle
mystery (mysterious)
naturally
necessary (necessarily)
Negroes
neither
nickel
night
nineteenth
ninety
ninth
no
noisy (noisily)
noticeable
noun
nowadays
obstacle
occasion (occasionally)
occupy (occupying, occupied)
occur (occurring, occurred, occurrence)
o'clock
off
offer (offering, offered)
omission
omit (omitting)
opening
opinion
opportunity
optimistic
ordinary (ordinarily)
organization
original
outrageous
parallel
participating
particularly
partner
passed
pastime
peaceable
peculiarity
penalty
perceive
perception
perform
perhaps
permit (permitted)
permission
permissible
personal
personnel
perspiration
persuade
pertain
phase
physically
piece
(plan) planning
pleasant
politician
positive
possess
possible
practically
prairie
precede
prefer (preferring)
prejudice
preparation
presence
primitive
principal
principle
prisoner
privilege
probable
proceed
profession
professor
prohibition
prominent
proud
prove
psychology
purchase
pursue
putting (put)
puzzle (puzzling)
quantity
quiet
quite
quitting (quit)
quizzes (quiz)
rapid
ready (readily)
realize
really
reasonably
receive
recognize
recollection
recommend
refer (referring)

regard
registration
relative
relieve
religious
remembrance
repetition
replies (reply)
representative
resource
responsibility
restaurant
rheumatism
rhythm
riding (ride)
ridiculous
rode
roommate
sacrifice
safety
sandwich
satisfactorily (satisfactory)
Saturday
schedule
scholastically
science
screech
seize
sense
sentence
separate
sergeant
severely
shepherd
shining (shine)
shone (shine)
shown (show)
siege
significant
significantly
similar
since
sincerity
site
smooth
solely
sophomore
source
southern
speak
specialize
speech
specimen
staring (stare)
stationary
stationery
stopped (stop)
stories (story)
strength
strenuously
stretches
strictly
studying (study)
succeed
success
summarize
superintendent
suppress
surely
surprise
swimming (swim)
syllable
temperament
temperature
tendency
than
their
there
therefore
they're
thorough
till
to
together
too
track
tragedy
transfer
transferring
transferred
travel
treacherous
tremendous
trial
trouble
true (truly)
try (tries)
Tuesday
two
tyranny
undoubtedly
unnecessary
until
upper
usefulness
using (use)
usually
vacancy
valleys (valley)
variety
vegetation
vengeance
very
view
vigorous
village
villain
weak
weather
Wednesday
week
whether
where
whole
wholly
who's
whose
winning (win)
without
witness
woman
worrying (worry)
writing (write)
written
your (poss.)
you're

PART SIX: WORDS FREQUENTLY MISUSED

Accede	to consent to or comply with
Exceed	to surpass or go beyond
Accept	to take; to receive
Except	to exclude; to omit
Access	admittance; make use of
Excess	overabundance; surplus
Adapt	accommodate; adjust
Adept	skillful at
Adopt	to choose
Advice	to receive counsel; recommendation (n)
Advise	to give counsel; to recommend (v)
Affect	to impress; to influence
Effect	consequence; outcome; result
Almost	approximately; nearly
All most	incorrect use of almost
Already	earlier; previously
All ready	all prepared
All right	all is correct
Alright	incorrect use of "all right"
Altogether	completely; entirely
All together	everyone in unison
Always	at all times
All ways	all the possible options or means
Amend	alter for the better
Emend	removal of errors
Anyone	anybody
Any one	any person in the group
Attendance	presence
Attendants	escorts; helpers
Beside	next to
Besides	in addition to
Capital	most important; primary
Capitol	building for legislature meetings
Cite	to quote
Sight	view; vision
Site	a place of location
Complement	supplements or completes
Compliment	commend; praise

Correspondence	written communication
Correspondents	persons who write
Corespondents	parties in divorce suit
Council	an assembly
Counsel	to advise; give recommendations
Consul	a foreign official
Credible	believable; authentic
Creditable	deserving of praise; honorable
Device	apparatus; invention
Devise	to design; to invent
Discreet	conservative; prudent
Discrete	distinct; unique
Disinterested	detached; neutral
Uninterested	bored; lacking interest
Elicit	evoke; bring out
Illicit	illegal; unlawful
Eligible	qualified; suitable
Illegible	not readable
Emerge	to appear; come into view
Immerge	to plunge into
Envelop	to cover; to surround
Envelope	container for a letter
Everyday	daily
Every day	each single day
Everyone	everybody
Every one	each person in the group
Farther	at a greater distance in time or space
Further	to a greater degree or extent; in addition to
Formally	according to the rules
Formerly	before; previous
Forward	ahead; advance; send
Foreword	preface
Hear	to perceive by ear; listen
Here	in this place
Insure	underwrite
Ensure	make certain
Assure	give confidence
Interstate	between states
Intrastate	within one state
Lead	a heavy metal; to guide

Led	guided; past tense of lead
Loose	unconfined; free
Lose	to part with
Maybe	perchance; perhaps (adverb)
May be	could be or might be (verb)
Miner	a mine worker
Minor	less important; underaged
Mood	disposition; state of feeling
Mode	condition; style; method
Nobody	no one
No body	no group
Ordinance	law; principle
Ordnance	ammunition; military weapons
Ought	should
Aught	nothing; not anything
Naught	zero
Overdo	overexert
Overdue	past due
Packed	crowded; full
Pact	an agreement
Peak	summit top; climax
Peek	a quick glance
Perpetrate	commit; guilty of
Perpetuate	immortalize; endless
Personal	private
Personnel	employees; staff
Practicable	feasible; possible
Practical	functional; useful
Precede	prior; forerun
Proceed	to advance; to go forward
Precedence	priority
Precedents	established rules; example
Principal	chief; main; boss; primary; capital sum of money
Principle	basic rule; law; fundamental belief
Quiet	subdued; motionless; silence
Quite	considerably; fullest extent
Quit	terminate; resign; relinquished
Receipt	a written acknowledgment
Recipe	formula
Recent	close to the present; lately

Resent	to feel strongly; to feel hurt
Residence	dwelling place
Residents	persons who reside in a place
Respectably	meriting respect
Respectfully	courteously
Resume	to take up again; continue
Résumé	a brief record of one's personal history
Set	to place
Sit	to be seated
Sight, site	(see cite)
Someone	somebody
Some one	some person in a group
Sometime	anytime; unspecified time
Some time	some period of time
Stationary	fixed; unmoveable
Stationery	writing paper
Statue	a carved or molded figure
Stature	height; level of superiority
Statute	a law
Straight	not crooked; direct
Strait	a narrow passage of water; narrow or constricted
Than	introduce comparisons
Then	next; at that time
Their	belonging to them (possessive)
There	in that place
They're	contraction for "they are"
Through	passing from one side to the other
Threw	past tense of "throw"
Thorough	completeness
To	(preposition) toward
Too	also; in addition
Two	the number *2*
Toward	preferred meaning for "in the direction of"
Towards	(nonpreferred)
Track	a trail; path
Tract	a piece of land; a religious paper
Undo	to open; to untie; disassemble
Undue	exceeding the normal
Weak	not strong
Week	a seven-day period

APPENDIX B

LETTER STYLES

1 MODIFIED BLOCK: MIXED PUNCTUATION
2 MODIFIED BLOCK: OPEN PUNCTUATION
3 BLOCK: MIXED PUNCTUATION
4 BLOCK: OPEN PUNCTUATION
5 SIMPLIFIED: SUBJECT LINE
6 TWO-PAGE MODIFIED: MIXED PUNCTUATION

987 MEMORIAL DRIVE
GREENVILLE, SOUTH CAROLINA 29600
PHONE (803) 716-4217

SUPPLIES
WHITESIDE
WHOLESALE

January 5, 19__

Ms. Christine Cooper
Oberal Office Supplies Company
237 Colorado Avenue
Lincoln, NE 68500

Dear Ms. Cooper:

Thank you for your first order of January 2 for the versatile Whiteside microcomputer supplies and your check for $1,920.50. The items are being shipped to you on January 15 via Roadway Xpress. With the additional advertising campaign now underway, you can look forward to increased sales because of the high demand for these quality office supplies.

To make ordering easier, why not apply for a credit account at Whiteside? Fill out, sign, and mail the enclosed background data form. As soon as the completed form is received, careful attention will be given to your request. Purchasing with a credit account will make your future ordering more convenient.

Take advantage of the exceptional savings offered in the enclosed mid-winter sales catalog. For instance, look on page 10 at the end-of-season offer for microcomputer floppy disks. You can enjoy savings from 10 to 40 percent by placing an order today.

You have made a wise choice in ordering from Whiteside Wholesale Supplies. At Whiteside, you can select from a wide assortment of dependable major brands. And you are guaranteed 100 percent satisfaction and prompt delivery! Welcome as a WHITESIDE customer.

Cordially yours,

Marcee Whiteside
Mail Order Manager

ct

Enclosures: Background Data Form
Mid-winter Sales Catalog

Modified style
Mixed punctuation
Indented paragraphs
Enclosure notation
(Source: Figure 8.5, p. 211)

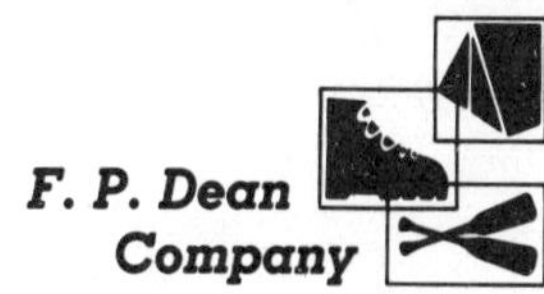

February 27, 19__

Mr. Jonathan Willard
203 Stockton Drive
Pueblo, CO 81001

Dear Mr. Willard

Thank you for your January 10 order. Just as soon as we receive your inseam size and cuff/no-cuff preference for the two pairs of 100% cotton hiking trousers, your order will be sent immediately by UPS. Merely indicate at the bottom of this letter the inseam size and cuff/no-cuff preference and mail in the enclosed envelope.

The freedom of the double-stitched front pleats will give you many comfortable miles of hiking pleasure; and the sturdy twill weave with its abrasion-resistant feature will be comfortable against your skin no matter how long you hike. You have certainly made a wise choice in selecting one of the most popular hiking trousers offered by F. P. Dean.

The hiking trousers will be shipped along with the navy, medium-sized lined parka the day we receive your response. The total $134 will be charged to your American Express credit card as you requested.

Thank you for letting F. P. Dean Company supply your outdoor sporting needs over the past three years. Be sure to take advantage of the specials in the Spring catalog that you will receive shortly. Remember, you are guaranteed 100 percent satisfaction. Quality counts at Dean's!

Sincerely

Mark Allen
Customer Service Representative

MA:ct

Inseam Size Preferred: __ inches
Style Preferred: __ cuff __ no cuff

1123 Kingsley Road • Minneapolis, MN 55400 • Phone (612) 703-9470

Modified style
Open punctuation
Blocked paragraphs
(Source: Figure 9.1, p. 238)

MS. CASSANDRA NOBLETT

3001 John B. Dennis Hwy.
Kingsport, TN 37660
Telephone (615) 644-7711

September 23, 19__

Dr. Adam Lerner, Executive Director
National Council of Private Schools and Colleges
111 North Boulevard
Kansas City, MO 64100

Dear Dr. Lerner:

I am pleased to accept your invitation to speak at the National Council of Private Schools and Colleges on Thursday, March 12, 19__, in Chicago, Illinois. The honorarium of $500 and expenses are quite acceptable. The topic, "Curriculum Implications of the Changing Work Force," is a very timely one. Since rapid changes are taking place in business offices, there is a great need for schools to keep up with the changes. You are definitely on target to consider modifying your curriculum to meet these expanding needs.

To help me prepare for the presentation, will you please answer the following questions:

1. How much time will be allocated for the speech? What is the scheduled time for my speech? Will there be a question-and-answer session afterward?
2. What arrangements will be made for ground transportation from the airport? to the airport?
3. Do you need a copy of the presentation for the proceedings? Date needed?

It is an honor to be asked to speak to such a distinguished group. If you need to discuss any details concerning the presentation, you may call me at 615/644-7711.

Cordially yours,

Ms. Cassandra Noblett

Block style
Mixed punctuation
Blocked paragraphs
(Source: Figure 8.1, p. 202)

Norris Companies, Inc.

October 5, 19__

Bartlett Supply Company
3810 Regal Street
Memphis, TN 38117

Attention: Credit Manager

Gentlemen

To improve our process of invoice payment, please follow the new procedures outlined below. You will receive your money in a shorter time by

1. Sending your invoices to me at Norris Companies, Inc., Box 1120, Long Beach, CA 90802 (instead of to our individual branch stores).

2. Indicating in the "Ship To" column of your invoice the store where the merchandise is shipped.

3. Using our purchase order number on your invoice to expedite payment.

4. Continuing to ship the merchandise to the branch stores.

Yours very truly

Alexander Bryne
Purchasing Manager

jm

Box 1120
Long Beach, California 90802
Telephone (213) 288-5604

Block style
Open punctuation
Blocked paragraphs
Attention line
(Source: Figure 10.2, p. 271)

January 10, 19__

Selection Committee
Distinguished Community Achievement Award
Houston Chamber of Commerce
102 West End Boulevard
Houston, TX 77001

SUBJECT: Recommendation of Amanda Lane

What a privilege it is to write a letter supporting Miss Amanda Lane as a candidate for the Distinguished Community Award sponsored by the Houston Chamber of Commerce.

Having worked with the Chamber for six years, I am fully aware of this most significant honor and the caliber of individuals competing for this award each year. Miss Lane certainly meets your high criteria. As a person who exemplifies community involvement and leadership, she would bring honor to the award.

Miss Lane recognizes the importance of community service. She has demonstrated her concern by serving as the local United Way leader for two years. During this time, the campaign reached unprecedented goals.

Miss Lane also acted as chairperson of the United Way program at Jones & Jones for three years. Each year, she worked diligently to achieve the goals established by Jones & Jones--and with great success!

For five consecutive years, Miss Lane involved herself with the community through her sponsorship of a Junior Achievement Group. This program assists youngsters to learn about the free enterprise system.

In other words, Miss Lane has won the admiration of everyone in the community because of her caring attitude and unselfish dedication to others. I know of no one more deserving of the Distinguished Community Award than Miss Amanda Lane.

Dean Varlan
Personnel Director

dv/sp

123 Mockingbird Lane • Houston, Texas 77121 • Phone (713) 288-7023

Simplified style
Subject line
(Source: Figure 8.2, p. 205)

The Gourmet Supplier
1200 Davis Avenue, San Francisco, California 94102, Telphone (818) 756-8145

May 12, 19___

Miss Sephena Nichol
The Unique Shop
P.O. Box 2112
Billings, MT 59101

Dear Miss Nichol:

The My Cafe Automatic Drip Coffee Maker returned to you by a customer and then sent to us for replacement arrived on May 10, 19___. Mr. Joe Terrence, our service technician, examined the unit at once to determine why it did not function properly. His examination revealed that residue had built up, clogging the tube through which the water passes from the reservoir to the brew basket. This resulted from the lack of monthly internal cleaning with the recommended vinegar-water solution. Some city water systems have higher mineral levels than others.

Mr. Terrence thoroughly cleaned the inside of the coffee maker so that it once again brews the freshest, most flavorful coffee which your customer expects from and appreciates in the My Cafe unit. The good-as-new Coffee Maker is being returned to you by UPS today.

Because you are one of our regular customers, there will be no charge for the special cleaning this time. Please be sure, however, to point out to your customers the cleaning instructions that appear on Page 3 of "Maintenance Tips," the booklet that comes with each My Cafe unit.

> "Once each month, clean the unit internally by pouring a solution of 2 parts vinegar and 2 parts water into the reservoir and operating the unit through a regular cycle. This regular maintenance will prevent residue from collecting on the internal portion of the unit. . . .
> CAUTION: Lack of periodic, internal cleaning can result in damage to the unit."

Two-page letter modified style
Mixed punctuation
Blocked paragraphs
(Source: Figure 9.4, pp. 251–252)

-2-

The My Cafe model has proved to be one of the best selling automatic drip coffee systems, as you have indicated through your repeat orders. Because the coffee mill is built right into the brew basket and because the 24-hour digital timer can be set for any time, the owner can wake up in the morning to the aroma of freshly ground and brewed coffee--a good way to start the morning! Because of these and other unique features, the My Cafe Automatic Coffee Maker will continue to be a BEST seller for THE UNIQUE SHOP.

Cordially yours,

Basil Lloyd

sp

APPENDIX C

TWO-LETTER STATE ABBREVIATIONS

TWO-LETTER STATE ABBREVIATIONS

The United States Post Office recommends the use of the following two-letter state abbreviations as a part of the ZIP code system.

Alaska	AK	Montana	MT
Alabama	AL	Nebraska	NE
Arizona	AZ	Nevada	NV
Arkansas	AR	New Hampshire	NH
California	CA	New Jersey	NJ
Colorado	CO	New Mexico	NM
Connecticut	CT	New York	NY
Delaware	DE	North Carolina	NC
Florida	FL	North Dakota	ND
Georgia	GA	Ohio	OH
Hawaii	HI	Oklahoma	OK
Idaho	ID	Oregon	OR
Illinois	IL	Pennsylvania	PA
Indiana	IN	Rhode Island	RI
Iowa	IA	South Carolina	SC
Kansas	KS	South Dakota	SD
Kentucky	KY	Tennessee	TN
Louisiana	LA	Texas	TX
Maine	ME	Utah	UT
Maryland	MD	Vermont	VT
Massachusetts	MA	Virginia	VA
Michigan	MI	Washington	WA
Minnesota	MN	West Virginia	WV
Mississippi	MS	Wisconsin	WI
Missouri	MO	Wyoming	WY

BIBLIOGRAPHY

Abelow, Daniel, and Edwin J. Hilpert. *Communications in the Modern Corporate Environment.* Englewood Cliffs, N.J.: Prentice-Hall, 1986, p. 202.

Allen, Steve. *How to Make a Speech.* New York: McGraw-Hill, 1986.

"AMS Officer Reaches out to Japan, Hong Kong." Quoted in *Management World* 13, no. 3 (March 1984), p. 42.

Andrews, J. Douglas, and Norman B. Sigband. "How Effectively Does the 'New' Accountant Communicate? Perception of Practitioners and Academics." *Journal of Business Communication* 21 (Spring 1984), p. 17.

Andrews, Kenneth R. *The Concepts of Corporate Strategy.* Homewood, Ill.: Dow Jones-Irwin, 1987, p. 23.

Angel, Juvenal L. *The Complete Résumé Book.* New York: Wallaby Books, 1980.

Baldrige, Letitia. *Letitia Baldrige's Complete Guide to Executive Manners.* New York: Rawson Associates, 1985, p. 160.

Basta, Nicholas. "Computer Update: Where We Are, Where We're Going." *Business Week Careers* 5(2) (March-April 1987), pp. 50, 51-52, 58.

Bennett, James C., and Robert J. Olney. "Executive Priorities for Effective Communication in an Information Society." *Journal of Business Communication* 23 (Spring 1986), p. 16.

Behrman, Jack N., and Richard I. Levin. "Are Business Schools Doing Their Job?" *Harvard Business Review* 62(1) (January-February 1984), p. 144.

Bixler, Susan. *The Professional Image.* New York: Putnam Publishing, 1984, p. 18.

Bolles, Richard N. *The 1986 What Color Is Your Parachute?* Berkeley, Calif.: Ten Speed Press, 1986.

Bostwick, Burdette E. *Résumé Writing.* New York: John Wiley & Sons, 1985.

Bound, William A. J. "Security—Protecting Information Resources and Media." *Information Management* (August 1984), pp. 18-19.

Brinkerhoff, David, and Abbott P. Smith. "Write a Résumé, Not an Obituary." *Training* 23(7).

Brusaw, Charles T., Alred, Gerald J., and Walter E. Oliu. *The Business Writer's Handbook.* New York: St. Martin's Press, 1987, p. 471.

Burke, James. *The Day the Universe Changed.* Boston: Little, Brown, p. 69.

Burstein, Daniel. "The Year of Software." *United Airlines Magazine* 19(10) (October 1984), p. 90.

Business Week, May 5, 1986, cover page.

Calhoun, Mary E. *How to Get the Hot Jobs in Business and Finance.* New York: Harper & Row, 1986.

Cameron, Alex B. "CPA Savvy." *Management World* 14(7) (July-August 1985), pp. 40-41.

Carlisle, Howard M. *Management: Concepts, Methods, and Applications.* Chicago: Science Research Associates, 1982, pp. 241, 443.

Connell, John J. "Return on Investment in Information Technology." *Information Center* 11(10) (October 1986), p. 51.

Conner, J. Robert et al., eds. *Business Week's Guide to Careers,* 4(3) (Spring-Summer 1986), p. 27.

CPCU Journal 39(3) (September 1986), pp. 174-79.

Detz, Joan. *How to Write and Give a Speech.* New York: St. Martin's Press, 1984.

Ellis, Leann K., Wallace V. Schmidt, and Virginia Eman Wheeless. "An Empirical Study of Sex-Characteristic Stereotypes Versus Sex-Role Stereotypes Affecting Women in Management." *Proceedings of the Association for Business Communication, Southwest Division* (1985), p. 83.

Flanagan, William G. Interview—Take One! *Forbes* 136 (November 18, 1985), pp. 244-246.

Foster, Timothy R. V., and Alfred Glossbrenner. *Word Processing for Executives and Professionals.* New York: Van Nostrand Reinhold, 1983, p. 1.

Gschwandtner, Gerhard. *Personal Selling Power.* Fredericksburg, Va.: Tabloid, 1985.

Gould, John W. "For Doing Business Abroad, How Much Foreign Language Proficiency Is Enough?" *Bulletin of the Association of Business Communication* 49, no. 3 (September 1986), p. 26.

Gray, Harry J. "The Changing Technological Times." *Business Week's Guide to Careers* 3, no. 2 (March-April 1985), p. 9.

Greenwood, Frank, and Mary M. Greenwood. *Office Technology: Principles of Automation.* Reston, Va.: Reston Publishing, 1985, p. 101.

Gump, Phillis Schaffer. "Identification and Evaluation of Concepts Pertinent to the Basic Business Communication Course at the Collegiate Level." Ed.D. dissertation, Indiana University, 1979.

Guptara, Prabhu. "Searching the Organization for the Cross-Cultural Operators." *International Management* 41, no. 8 (August 1986), p. 40.

Half, Robert. *The Robert Half Way to Get Hired in Today's Job Market.* New York: Bantam Books, 1981.

Half, Robert. "How to Really Check an Applicant's References." *Office* 102, no. 5 (1985).

Hall, Virginia M., and Joyce A. Wessel. "Communication Skills Are Basic to Good Results on the Job." *Atlanta Journal,* October 12, 1986, p. 7IL.

Harmon, Frederick, and Garry Jacobs. "Survey: Looking beyond Profitability: Where U.S. and European Cultures Meet." *International Management* 41, no. 7 (July 1986), pp. 54-56.

Hawes, Gene. *Speak for Success.* New York: Bantam Books, 1984.

Hegarty, Edward J. *How to Talk Your Way to the Top.* West Nyack, N.Y.: Parker Publishing, 1973.

Helitzer, Morrie et al., eds. "Popularity Poll Results." *New Accountant* 2, no. 1 (September 1986).

Hemingway, Patricia Drake. *The Well-Dressed Woman.* New York: First Signet, 1977.

Hodges, John C., and Mary E. Whitten. *Harbrace College Handbook.* 10th ed. New York: Harcourt Brace Jovanovich, 1986, p. 346.

Holtz, Herman. *The Business of Public Speaking.* New York: John Wiley & Sons, 1985.

Irwin-Dorsey Guidelines for Use of Nonsexist Language. Homewood, Ill.: Richard D. Irwin, 1981.

Jenson, Eric. *You Can Succeed, The Ultimate Study Guide for Students.* New York: Barron's Educational Series, 1979.

Kilpatrick, Retha H. "International Business Communication Practices." *Journal of Business Communication* 21, no. 4 (Fall 1984), pp. 33-34.

Kornbluh, Marvin. "The Electronic Office—How It Will Change the Way We Work" In *Career Tomorrow: The Outlook for Work in a Changing World.* Bethesda, Md.: World Future Society, 1983, p. 63.

Kravette, Steve. *Get a Job in 6 Seconds.* New York: Bantam Books, 1982.

Lapointe, Archie. "If We Demand More, We Can Expect to Get It." *USA Today,* December 9, 1986, p. 12A.

Lathrop, Richard. *Who's Hiring Who?* Berkeley, Calif.: Ten Speed Press, 1977.

Leech, Thomas. *How to Prepare, Stage, and Deliver Winning Presentations.* New York: American Management Association, AMACOM, 1982, p. 47.

Maher, Thomas M. "Job Search DataBase Set." *National Underwriters,* March 30, 1987, p. 65-69.

Managers Career Letter. Willow Grove, Pa.: Administrative Management Society, 1986.

McCaffrey, James A., and Craig R. Hafner. "When Two Cultures Collide: Doing Business Overseas." *Training and Development Journal* 39, no. 10 (October 1985), pp. 26, 27-29.

Meth, Clifford. "Write with Light!" *Administrative Management* 47, no. 3 (March 1986), pp. 39-43.

Molley, John T. *Dress for Success.* New York: Warner Books 1975.

Molley, John T. *The Woman's Dress for Success Book.* New York: Warner Books, 1977.

Naisbitt, John, and Patricia Aburdene. *Re-Inventing the Corporation.* New York: Warner Books, 1985, pp. 79-80.

"On-Line Jobs." *Training* 23, no. 5 (May 1986), p. 93.

Paxson, William C. *The Business Writing Handbook.* New York: Bantam Books, 1981, pp. 3-4.

Perlez, Jane. "U.S. Aide Quits, Charging Pressure over LILCO's Drill." *New York Times,* April 15, 1986, p. B5.

Pilla, Lou. "AMS Survey Report: Tips for Landing Your Next Job." In *Job Search Guide.* Willow Grove, Pa.: Administrative Management Society, 1986.

Posner, Barry Z., and Warren H. Schmidt. "Ethics in American Companies: A Managerial Perspective." *Journal of Business Ethics* 6, No. 5 (July 1987), pp. 385-88.

Quinn, John C. "Kids Need to Write if They're to Succeed." *USA Today,* December 9, 1986, p. 12A.

Renault/Jeep Guide to Starting Your Career. *Business Week's Guide to Careers,* 4 no. 3 (Spring-Summer 1986), p. 27.

Ricks, David A. *Big Business Blunders.* Homewood, Ill.: Dow Jones-Irwin, 1983, pp. 5, 8, 17, 32, 63, 66.

Rumberger, Russell W., and Henry M. Levin. "Forecasting the Impact of New Technologies on the Future of the Job Market." Project report #84-4A. Institute for Research on Educational Finance and Governance, School of Education, Stanford University.

Sarnoff, Dorothy. *Speech Can Change Your Life.* New York: Dell Publishing, 1970.

Selzer, Jack. "Some Differences between Journalism and Business Writing." *ABCA Bulletin* 46, no. 3 (September 1983), pp. 8-9.

Shames, Germaine. "Training for the Multicultural Workplace." *Cornell Quarterly* 26, no. 4 (February 1986), p. 26.

Simmons, S. H. *How to Be the Life of the Podium.* New York: Amacon Publishing, 1982.

Skapinker, Michael. "Why Speaking English Is No Longer Enough." *International Management* 41, no. 11 (November 1986), pp. 39, 40, 49.

Smith, Harold T. *The Office Revolution.* Willow Grove, Pa.: Administrative Management Society Foundation, 1983, p. 34.

Snelling and Snelling, Inc. *Jobs! What They Are . . . Where They Are . . . What They Pay!* New York: Simon & Schuster, 1985.

Stallard, John J., E. Ray Smith, and Donald Reese. *The Electronic Office.* Homewood, Ill.: Dow Jones-Irwin, 1983.

Stevens, Edward. *Business Ethics.* New York: Paulist Press, 1979, p. 127.

Stine, Donna, and Donald Skarzenski. "Priorities for the Business Communication Classroom: A Survey of Business and Academe." *Journal of Business Communication* 16, no. 3 (Spring 1979), pp. 16-26.

Strassmann, Paul A. *Information Payoff: The Transformation of Work in the Electronic Age.* New York: Free Press, 1985, p. 43.

Summerfield, Joanne. *Listening . . . It Can Change Your Life.* New York: McGraw-Hill, 1983.

Terpstra, Vern and Kenneth David. *The Cultural Environment of International Business.* 2nd ed. Cincinnati, Ohio: South-Western Publishing, 1985, pp. 18, 32.

Thompson, Arthur A., Jr., and A. J. Strickland III. *Strategic Management: Concepts and Cases.* Plano, Tex.: Business Publications, 1984, p. 17.

"Transputer Chips: Linchpins of a Mighty Supercomputer." *Business Week* 2942, April 21, 1986, p. 47.

"U.S. Business—Trends That Shape the Future." *U.S. News & World Report* 97, no. 9 (August 27, 1984), p. 54.

Vardaman, George T. *Making Successful Presentations.* New York: Amacon Publishing, 1981.

Webster's Third International Dictionary of the English Language. Springfield, Mass.: Merriam-Webster, 1981, p. 460.

Welter, Therese R. "Interviewing for a Job—by Satellite." *Industry Week* 223 (May 18, 1987), p. 94.

White, Donald D., and William H. Vroman. *Action in Organizations.* 2nd ed. Boston: Allyn & Bacon, 1982, pp. 144-47.

White, Virginia. *Grant Proposals That Succeeded.* New York: Plenum Press, 1984, p. 2.

INDEX

A
Abbott Smith Associates, 537
Abbreviations
  punctuation for, 667
  for states, 691
Abelow, Daniel, 27
Abstracts
  advantages of, 496
  book, 498-501
  defined, 496
  drafting of, 496-97
  indicative, 497-98
  informative, 498
  of journal articles, 501-8
  questions to cover in, 445
  of related research, 444-46
Aburdene, Patricia, 21
Acceptance letters, 199-201
Acknowledgments
  of an order, 205-8
  in reports, 437
Acronyms in writing, 105
Adjustments
  refusals of, 245
  positive responses to, 220-25
  requests for, 167-68
Agriculture Index, 345-46
AGRICOLA database, 346
Alfred, Gerald J., 68
American Psychological Association (APA)
  bibliographies for, 372-74
  style manual, 347
American University international training courses, 58
Analogies, 117-18
Analytical reports
  appendixes to, 453, 485
  bibliographies for, 371-74, 453, 485
  constraints discussed in, 443-44, 470
  content for, 435
  data analysis section, 447-48, 471-80
  defined, 315, 334, 435
  definition of terms for, 444-45, 470
  developing recommendations in, 450-51, 484-85
  documentation style for, 452-53
  endnotes to, 452-53
  format for, 473-73
  implications discussion, 451-52, 280, 485
  initial section of, 437-47, 466-70
  major findings discussion, 449-50, 480-83
  objectives delineated in, 439-41, 468-69
  organization of, 446-47, 471, 473
  preliminary parts of, 436-37
  problem definition in, 438, 464-66
Analytical reports—*Cont.*
  procedures delineation in, 469-70
  review of literature in, 444-46
  synthesis section of, 448, 480-81
  writing conclusions for, 450, 483-84
Anderson, R., 10-11
Andrews, Kenneth R., 66
Announcement reports, 317-20
Apostrophes, 660
Audience/reader
  analysis, 68-69
  anticipating reaction of, 73
  characteristics, 69-73
  primary versus secondary, 70-71

B
Baldridge, Letitia, 58-59
Bar charts
  horizontal, 396, 398
  multiple, 396, 399
  segmented, 397-98
  stacked, 397
  use of, 395
  vertical, 396-97
Basta, Nicholas, 28, 35
Bates, R. C., 604
Behrman, Jack N., 6-7, 435
Bennett, James C., 435
Bibliographies
  APA format for, 372-74
  traditional format for, 372-72, 453
Biological Abstracts, 346
BIOSEARCH database, 346
Bixler, Susan, 580
Body language
  in international communication, 56
  in oral presentations, 581
Booklets as a report format, 312
Bostwick, Burdette E., 540-41
Bound, William A., 504, 508
Brinkerhoff, Daved, 538
Brusaw, Charles T., 68
Burke, James, 6
Burstein, Daniel, 9
Business Council for International Understanding, 58
Business Periodicals Index, 345
Business trips, 59

C
Cameron, Alex B., 118
Capitalization rules, 668-71
Carlisle, Howard M., 653-54
Case analyses
  benefits of, 651
  four-part elements method for, 637, 649-51

Case analyses—*Cont.*
- pitfalls in, 635-36
- questions-at-the-end-of-case method for, 637-48
- relevant questions in, 636
- systems approach to, 636

Central tendency (statistics), 377-80
Chalkboards, 586-87
Clarity; *see also* Word choice
- and abstract words, 101-2
- importance of, 74, 139-40
- and jargon, 105
- and overused words, 103

Clothing, 582
Colons, 661
Commas, 661-63
Communication
- basic strategy for, 65, 86-88
- costs in, 86
- data arrangement in, 74-75
- defined, 9
- horizontal, 72
- formats for, 79-86
- importance of, 6-15
- informal, 73
- objectives of, 66-68
- order of, 74-75
- process model, 40
- and technology, 7, 20-42
- types of, 6, 16
- vertical, 72
- voice, 36

COMPENDEX database, 346
Computers; *see also* Word processing
- advantages of, 20-33
- cost effectiveness of, 25-26
- database searching with, 26-28, 31, 346
- forecasting with, 28
- glossary for, 41-42
- graphics capabilities of, 26, 29, 35, 400-402
- networks, 34
- portable, 33
- printers for, 28, 35, 146, 400
- and privacy invasion, 21
- and productivity, 25, 30-31
- voice communication with, 36
- writing style analysis with, 123-26

Conceptual skills, 634
Congratulations letters, 289-92
Connell, John H., 26
Connor, J. Robert, 582
Corporate Interviewing Network (CIN), 566
Correlation (statistics), 383-84
Correspondence; *see also* Letters *and* Memos
- international, 49-51
- planning of, 47-50

Courtesy titles, 83
Credit refusals, 253-56

D

Dashes, 664
Data
- business-related publications for, 369-71
- collection methods
  - through interviews, 356-59
  - nonprobability sampling in, 360
  - from observation, 348-49
  - probability sampling in, 359-60
  - through questionnaires, 349-56
- forms for reporting, 330-35
- versus information, 343-45
- interpretation of, 376, 447-48
- for mail merge, 22
- in office networks, 34
- personal, 21
- primary sources of, 347-60
- quantitative representation of, 376-402
- secondary sources of, 345-47, 369-71
- statistical measures for, 376-402

Databases
- defined, 41
- job search, 26, 528
- online, 26-28, 346-47
- search costs for, 346-47

Dates, 673
David, Kenneth, 53-54
Debt collection
- form letters for, 175
- legalities of, 141, 175
- request letters in, 174-85

Delphi technique, 457
Descriptive index, 123
Desktop publishing, 35
DIALOG database, 346
Dictation
- editing of, 38
- method for, 38-39
- organization of, 37
- punctuation of, 38-39
- types of, 36-37

Direct mail sales letters, 283-86
Dispersion (statistics), 380-83
Dot matrix printers, 146

E

Electronic mail
- defined, 41
- use of, 22, 30-31

Ellipsis points, 664
Ellis, Leann K., 106
Engineering Index, 346
English language
- capitalization in, 668-71
- number usage in, 671-74
- prevalence of, 52-53
- proficiency in, 55
- punctuation in, 82, 660-68
- words misused in, 679-82

ERIC database, 347
Ethics, 8, 51, 71
Exclamation points, 664
Executive summaries
  guidelines for, 509
  nature of, 85, 509
  strategy for, 509-10

F

Facsimile devices, 22, 41
Fair Debt Collection Practices Act of 1978, 141, 175
Flanagan, William G., 566
Flip charts, 587
Flowcharts, 620-24
Follow-up letters, 276-79
Forecasting, 28
Foreign languages
  study of, 47, 52-54
  translations into, 53-54
Formal reports, 316
Form letters
  individualizing, 22-23, 146
  mail merge of, 22-23
  as safeguards, 175
Forms
  control, 25
  design, 25
  procedure statements with, 625-28
Forms of address, 664-65
Foster, Timothy R. V., 138
Four-part elements method of case analysis
  advantages of, 651
  guidelines for, 650-51
  nature of, 649-50
Fractions in text, 673
Fuld, Leonard M., 369
Funk & Scott Index of Corporations of Industries, 345

G

Gillespie, Karen, 436
Glossbrenner, Alfred, 138
Gould, John W., 47
Graphics
  advantages of using, 384
  with computers, 26, 29, 35, 400-402
  defined, 41
  guidelines for, 384-85, 401
Gray, Harry J., 7
Greenwood, Frank, 138
Greenwood, Mary M., 138
Guptara, Prabhu, 46

H

Hafner, Craig R., 49, 51
Half, Robert, 535
Hall, Virginia M., 7
Handwritten notes
  of congratulations, 289-92
  in debt collection, 177
Handwritten notes—*Cont.*
  file copies of, 85
  as a form of response, 85-86
  of sympathy, 292-95
Harmon, Frederick, 58
Helitzer, Morris, 527
Hilpert, Edwin J., 27
Hodges, John C., 76
Huff, Darrell, 378
Hyphens, 665-66

I

Iacocca, Lee A., 13
Index of Government Publications, 345
Information
  brokers, 28
  and office networks, 34
  online access to, 26-28
  on optical disks, 35
  overload, 20
  processing costs of, 25
  sources
    for business data, 369-71
    on corporations, 528, 530-31
    secondary, 345-47
Informational reports
  announcements, 317-20
  characteristics of, 412
  data forms as, 328-34
  defined, 315
  guidelines for, 316-17
  proposals, 323-28
  quarterly, 421-22
  samples of, 419-22
  status reports, 320-23
  summary, 420
  types of, 412-22
Inquiry letters; *see also* Job seeking
  answering, 208-20
  for information, 162-66
International communications
  barriers to, 57-58
  cultural considerations in, 49-52, 54-57
  direct approach in, 49-50, 55
  formality in, 50-51, 55
  importance of, 46-47
  indirect approach to, 49
  and language problems, 50, 52-54
  message planning in, 47-50
  nonverbal elements in, 56
  personal preparations for, 59-60
  religious considerations in, 54
  success in, 58-60
  training courses for, 58
Interviews; *see also* Job interviews
  for data collections, 356-57
  guide sheets for, 453
  structured versus unstructured, 356
Invitations
  acceptances of, 199-201
  to speak, 168-71

J
Jacobs, Garry, 58
Jargon
  and acronyms, 105
  defined, 105
  index, 123
  in oral presentations, 584
Job interviews
  anticipating questions for, 559-62
  demeanor during, 563-65
  follow-ups to, 566-67
  goals of, 558
  interviewer's viewpoint in, 558, 560
  legal questions for, 563
  nature of, 558
  preparation for, 558-63
  reahersals for, 563
  via satellite, 566
  self-management procedure during, 563-65
  what to take to, 564
Job offers
  accepting, 567-68
  declining, 568-70
Job seeking
  attitude in, 528
  and career goals, 523, 526-27
  computers in, 26, 528
  and job preference, 525
  networking in, 528-29
  panic in, 522-23
  preparation for, 522
  researching companies, 528-31
  self-analysis for, 523-26

K
Keogh, Donald R., 14-15
Key Man Course, 58
Kienast, Kay Earlene, 457
Kilpatrick, Retha H., 50-51
Kornbluh, Marvin, 35

L
Lapointe, Archie, 8
Lead-in statements, 448-49
Leech, Thomas, 69
Letters; *see also by type*
  of acceptance, 567-68
  answering inquiries, 208-20
  appearance of, 146
  of application, 544-47
  block style for, 81
  about changes, 267-74
  effectiveness in, 139-47; *see also* Writing
  evaluation form for, 149
  follow-up, 276-79
  of introduction, 264-67
  versus memos, 80, 139
  modified style for, 81-82
  negative, 234, 256-58
  parts of, 81
Letters—*Cont.*
  personal, 83-84
  positive, 198-99
  of resignation, 570
  samples of, 683-89
  simplified style for, 83
  thank you, 567
Levin, Henry M., 498
Levin, Richard I., 6-7, 435
Likert-Scale tables, 393
Line charts
  guidelines for, 398-99
  interpretation of, 401
  use of, 395, 398
Listening
  active versus passive, 597
  defined, 596
  effective, 598
  importance of, 597
Long, Jeffrey E., 46

M
McCaffrey, James A., 49, 51
McQuillan, John M., 502
Maher, Thomas M., 27
Mail merge
  nature of, 22-25
  pitfalls in, 146
Management styles, 646
Manzer, Martin, 9
Mean, 379
Median, 379-80
Meetings
  conducting, 594-96
  effective size for, 594
  large-group, 593
  managing, 595
  one-on-one, 591-92
  preparing for, 594-95
  small-group, 592-93
  teleconferencing, 35
Memos; *see also* Letters *and* Reports
  appearance of, 146
  characteristics of, 79
  effectiveness in, 139-47; *see also* Writing
  evaluation form for, 149
  forms for, 80
  versus letters, 139
  with special subsections, 418
  transmittal, 274-76
Message
  arrangement of, 75, 142
  computer generation, 146
  strength, 123
  tone of, 98-99, 110-11, 143; *see also* Word choice
Meth, Clifford, 133
Micrographics equipment
  defined, 41
  integration of, 22, 34
Microphone usage, 593

Mills, Gordon H., 132
Mode, 380
Monterey Institute of International Studies, 58
Mynett, Jack W., 46

N
Naisbitt, John, 21
Networking, 22, 34, 41
The New York Times, 345
NEXIS database, 346
Null hypothesis, 440-41
Numbers
  in addresses, 672
  in dates, 673
  decimal, 673
  for fractions, 673
  usage rules for, 671-74

O
Oliu, Walter E., 68
Olney, Robert J., 435
Optical character readers, 22, 41
Optical disks, 35
Oral presentations; *see also* Meetings
  advantages of, 85, 575
  audience needs, 85, 576-77
  dramatic close for, 585
  extemporaneous, 579
  feedback from, 577-78, 581
  handouts with, 587-88
  humor in, 584
  media for, 85, 585-89
    effectiveness criteria, 588-89
    selection principles, 589
    types of, 85, 585-88
  memorized, 579
  message development in, 582-85
  nonverbal elements in, 580-82
  objectives of, 575-76
  openers for, 583-84
  personal manner during, 580-82
  PMM concept in, 579-89
  question-and-answer sessions, 577-78
  from a script, 578-79
  strategy for, 589-91
  stress in, 580-81
  visual aids to, 85, 585-89
  voice quality for, 581, 583
  word choice in, 584
Orders for merchandise
  acknowledgement of, 205-8
  incomplete, 235-37
  requests for, 279-83
  substitutions in, 237-43
Outlines
  nonstandard, 87-88
  rules for, 669

P
Paragraphs
  chronological order for, 120
Paragraphs—*Cont.*
  closing, 119
  continuity in, 122-23
  defined, 113-14
  development methods, 117-18
  effective, 76, 115
  geographical/spatial order for, 120
  logical order for, 120-21
  opening, 119
  psychological order for, 121
  sentence sequence in, 78
  topic sentence in, 78, 114-15
  unity in, 115-17
  visual impact of, 123
Parentheses, 666
Pearson Product-Moment Correlation, 383-85
Penrose, John M., 386
Periodic reports
  characteristics of, 412
  defined, 412
  types of, 412-15
Perlez, Jane, 436
Persuasive writing
  defined, 144
  in letters of application, 546
  repetition in, 122, 144
  in request letters, 168
  techniques of, 144-45
  for unsolicited sales letters, 283-86
Pie charts, 394-96
Plotters, 400
PMM concept, 579-89
Policy statements
  defined, 603
  strategy for, 604-6
  uses for, 603-4
Posner, Barry Z., 313
Printers/scanners
  integration of, 22
  types of, 28, 35, 146, 400
Privacy
  in job interviews, 563
  and personal data banks, 22
Problem identification, 65-66
Procedure statements
  to accompany forms, 625-28
  benefits of, 606
  defined, 606
  flowchart format for, 620-24
  guidelines for, 607
  informational, 615-20
  step-by-step, 611-15
  strategy for, 608-10
Production reports, 412-15
Progress reports
  characteristics of, 415-16
  defined, 415
  monthly, 416-19
Proposals
  bid, 324-28
  characteristics of, 324
  defined, 323

Punctuation
of dictation, 38-39
mixed, 82
open, 82
rules for, 660-68

Q

Question-and-answer sessions, 577-78
Questionnaires
in analytical reports, 453
closed-end questions on, 351-53
for data collection, 349-51
open-ended questions on, 354-55
rankings in, 352-53
wording guidelines, 355-36
Questions-at-the-end-of-case method of case analysis
advantages of, 638
coding procedure in, 641
go-beyond-the-question procedures in, 645
guidelines for, 641
outlining procedure in, 643
strategy for, 639
underline procedure in, 641
Quinn, John C., 7
Quotation marks, 667-68
Quotations in text, 668

R

Random samples
cluster, 360
simple, 359
stratified, 360
Rating scales
group comparisons, 392-94
in questionnaires, 352-53
of survey data, 391-94
Readability index, 123
Reader's Guide to Periodical Literature, 345
Reagan, Ronald, 582
Recommendation letters
strategy for writing, 201-5, 548-49
in support of a resume, 548-49
Recommendation reports, 420
Records management, 34
Redundancies versus repetitions, 112
Reese, Donald, 77, 502
Reimbursement request, 167-68
Repetition, 112, 117-18, 122
Reports
analytical, 315; *see also* Analytical reports
announcement, 317-20
basic strategies for, 316
characteristics of, 85-86, 313-14
data for, 343-45; *see also* Data
definition of, 314-15
direct versus indirect approach to, 312, 316
executive summary of, 85
formality in, 316-17
formats for, 84, 312
Reports—*Cont.*
informational, 315; *see also* Informational reports
intended audience for, 314-15
nature of, 312-14
Request letters
for action, 158-62
for an adjustment, 167-68
direct approach to, 171-72, 177, 182
to a guest speaker, 168-71
indirect approach to, 171, 177
for information, 162-66
versus memos, 158
for payment, 174-85
Request refusals
for an adjustment, 245-53
for a contribution, 244-45
for credit, 253-56
for item repair, 251-53
for item replacement, 245-51
Resale, 221
Resignation letters, 570
Resumes
appearance of, 548
basic, 536, 540-43
categories for, 533-35
characteristics of, 532
chronological, 536
courtesies with, 544
cover letters for, 544-47
creative, 540
effectiveness of, 529
falsifications on, 535
follow-ups to, 549, 566-67
functional, 537-38
guidelines for, 532
objectives of, 532
pitfalls in, 548
references for, 535, 548
style for, 535
word choice in, 536
worksheet for, 533
Ricks, David A., 54
RightWriter software, 123-26
Rumberger, Russell W., 498

S

Salutations
forms of, 664
versus subject lines, 82-83
for unknown persons, 83
Sampling
defined, 359
nonprobability, 360
probability, 359-60
random, 359-60
Schaeberle, R. M., 12
Schmidt, Wallace V., 106
Schmidt, Warren H., 313
Science Citation Index, 346
SCISEARCH database, 346
Search Helper, 347
Selzer, Jack, 69

Semicolons, 668
Sentences
  active versus passive, 109
  computer analysis of, 123
  construction, 78, 107-13, 123
  defined, 108
  guidelines for, 110-13
  sequence for, 78
  topic, 78, 114-15
  types of, 108-9
Shames, Germaine, 46
Skapinker, Michael, 52-53
Skarzenski, Donald, 74
Slang, 105, 123
Slides, 586
Smith, Abbott P., 538
Smith, E. Ray, 77, 502
Smith, Harold T., 35
Smits, Stanley J., 516
Software
  for calendars, 28
  database search, 347
  spelling checkers, 28, 30, 123
  for statistics, 28
  writing style analysis, 123-26
Speech compressors, 34-35
Spelling
  checkers, 28, 30, 123
  of troublesome words, 674-79
Stallard, John H., 77, 502
Standard deviation, 380-83
Statistical data measures
  central tendency, 377-80
  correlation, 383-84
  dispersion, 380-83
  frequency, 377
  mean, 378-79
  median, 379-80
  mode, 380
  percent, 377
  range, 380-81
  standard deviation, 381-83
Status reports
  defined, 320
  strategy for, 321-23
  variations of, 420
Steil, L. K., 598
Stevens, Edward, 526
Stine, Donna, 74
Strassman, Paul A., 25
Strength index, 123
Strickland, A. J., III, 65
Style manuals
  APA, 347
  Council of Biology Editors, 453
  MLA, 453
  Turabian, 347, 372-74
Sympathy messages, 292-95

T
Table of contents, 437
Tables
  interpretation of, 387-88, 392-94
  construction of, 384-87
  cross-referenced, 389-91
  list of, 436-37
  multipage, 453
  weighting in, 392-95
Tanner, John R., 516
Telecommuting, 34
Teleconferencing, 32, 35, 42
Terpstra, Vern, 53-54
Thank you letters, 567
Thompson, Arthur A., Jr., 65
Title page, 437
Tone, 98-99, 110-11, 143
Transmittal memos
  form letters as, 286-89
  strategy for, 274-75
Transparencies, 585-86

V
Video Placement Co., 566
Viewpoint
  nature of, 143
  you, 110-11
Voice communication, 36
Vroman, H. William, 655

W
The Wall Street Journal Index, 345
Walter, John A., 132
Weighted averages, 393
Welter, Therese R., 566
Wessel, Joyce A., 7
Wheeless, Virginia Eman, 106
White, Donald D., 655
Whiteboards, 586-87
Whitten, Mary E., 76
Word choice
  clarity through, 101-2
  ethical considerations in, 99
  legal considerations in, 99, 105-7
  and message tone, 98-99, 110-11, 143
  nonsexist, 105-7
  in oral presentations, 584
  for positive impressions, 102
  for questionnaires, 355-56
  for resumes, 536
  tools for, 98
Word processing
  accuracy checks for, 28
  defined, 42
  and desktop publishing, 35
  and message appearance, 146
  for routine tasks, 21
  writing style analysis in, 123-26

Words
abstract, 100-102
concrete, 100-102
connotations of, 98, 100
denotations of, 98
length of, 102-3
misused, 679-82
negative, 99-100
overused, 103
positive, 99-100
technical, 105
transitional, 122
unbiased, 105-7
Writing
accuracy in, 28, 99
clarity in, 139-40
completeness in, 140-141
Writing—*Cont.*
conciseness in, 140
emphasis aids, 123
forcefulness in, 141
formal, 51
goals of, 145-46
pitfalls in, 74-75, 99, 101
reader-oriented, 142-45
simplicity in, 103-5
Writing style, 51, 57; *see also* Style manuals
analysis of, 123-26
defined, 97
effective, 74-75, 97
paragraph development in, 113-23
pitfalls in, 112-13
sentence development in, 107-13
and word choice, 97-107